MW00770208

The New Deal

AMERICA IN THE WORLD

SERIES EDITORS
SVEN BECKERT AND JEREMI SURI

A list of titles in this series appears at the back of the book.

The New Deal

A GLOBAL HISTORY

Kiran Klaus Patel

PRINCETON UNIVERSITY PRESS

PRINCETON AND OXFORD

Copyright © 2016 by Princeton University Press
Published by Princeton University Press, 41 William Street,
Princeton, New Jersey 08540
In the United Kingdom: Princeton University Press,
6 Oxford Street, Woodstock, Oxfordshire OX20 1TW

press.princeton.edu

Jacket photograph: Franklin D. Roosevelt being presented a globe by the
United States Army at the White House, December 1942. Courtesy of
the Franklin D. Roosevelt Presidential Library & Museum.

All Rights Reserved

Library of Congress Cataloging-in-Publication Data

Patel, Kiran Klaus.
The New Deal : a global history / Kiran Klaus Patel.
  pages cm. — (America in the world)
Includes bibliographical references and index.
ISBN 978-0-691-14912-7 (hardcover : alk. paper)   1. New Deal, 1933–1939.
  2. Depressions—1929.   3. Economic policy—History—20th century.
    4. International relations—History—20th century.   I. Title.

E806.P3559 2015
973.917—dc23   2015010403

British Library Cataloging-in-Publication Data is available

This book has been composed in Sabon Next LT Pro

Printed on acid-free paper. ∞

Printed in the United States of America

1 3 5 7 9 10 8 6 4 2

CONTENTS

ACKNOWLEDGMENTS

THIS BOOK HAS ITS ORIGINS in Zurich, where on a cold December day several years ago, I had a couple of drinks with Harvard's Sven Beckert. Sven asked me if I was interested in writing a book for a series that he had recently set up with Jeremi Suri. Sven settled the bill. I felt that I had to pay him back and accepted his offer to do the book. Never in my life have I worked harder for a few beers, and never have I enjoyed it more.

Writing this book turned into a true intellectual journey. It would look different had I not started thinking about it on the hills overlooking Florence, where the dark as well as inspiring sides of the twentieth century seem remote, and had I not completed it in Maastricht, a charming place and increasingly a hub for young Europeans in search of a decent university education. Harvard's Charles Warren Center along with its Center for European Studies and Weatherhead Initiative in Global History all have been home for several stays while writing this book. The book's first sentences were penned at the Freiburg Institute for Advanced Studies, and I am indebted to its two directors, Ulrich Herbert and Jörn Leonhard, for their hospitality in hot, humid summer 2010. In 2011, a visiting professorship brought me to the École des hautes études en science sociales in Paris. *Merci beaucoup*, Michael Werner and Falk Bretschneider. The excellent collections of the Roosevelt Study Center in Middelburg in the Netherlands were twice my destination in 2012—*hartelijk bedankt*, Kees van Minnen and Giles Scott-Smith. In 2013, I enjoyed the hospitality of Oxford's Modern European History Research Centre, and my special thanks go to Patricia Clavin and Martin Conway—to Patricia also for putting me in the hands of Jesus (College). Freie Universität Berlin's Kennedy Institute was the destination of many short trips; *vielen Dank*, Tanja Börzel, Thomas Risse, and all the colleagues in the Kolleg-Forschergruppe Transformative Power of Europe. The book received its finishing touches during academic year 2014–15, which I spent in London as the Gerda Henkel Visiting Professor at the London School of Economics and German Historical Institute London. Particular thanks go to the Henkel Foundation, LSE, and the German Historical Institute as well as Andreas Gestrich and Sönke Neitzel. Finally, I would like to thank my colleagues at the Faculty of Arts and Social Sciences in Maastricht, particularly in the Politics and Culture of Europe research group, for creating such a collegial and inspiring academic environment.

Another dimension of this journey was the various occasions on which I had the privilege of presenting parts of this project. I have profited from feedback at conferences and seminars at Columbia, Harvard, Princeton, and

Yale universities, UC Santa Barbara, Boston College, the 2013 Society for Historians of American Foreign Relations conference in Arlington, VA, and the 2014 conference of the Organization of American Historians in Atlanta, GA. In Europe, I had the chance to discuss my work at the universities of Augsburg, Bologna, Cambridge, Galway, Konstanz, Leiden, Sheffield, and Utrecht as well as the Graduate Institute in Geneva, Royal Holloway in London, and Historisches Kolleg in Munich.

People were more important than these places. For their invitations, input, and feedback at different stages of this project, I would like to thank Gareth Austin, Thomas Bender, Volker Berghahn, Kenneth Bertrams, David Blackbourn, Alan Brinkley, Patricia Clavin, Patrick Cohrs, Sebastian Conrad, David Ekbladh, David Engerman, Angelika Epple, Gary Gerstle, Michael Göbel, Victoria de Grazia, Valeska Huber, Daniel Immerwahr, Akira Iriye, Harold James, Matthew Jones, Ira Katznelson, Alexander Keyssar, Michal Kopeček, Sandrine Kott, Nelson Lichtenstein, Stefan Link, Charles S. Maier, Christof Mauch, Mark Mazower, Andrew Moravcsik, Dirk Moses, Jan-Werner Müller, Paul Nolte, Jürgen Osterhammel, Margit Pernau, Andrew Preston, Jakub Rákosník, Martin Rempe, Daniel T. Rodgers, Davide Rodogno, Federico Romero, Ellie Shermer, Steve Smith, Matthew Sohm, Philipp Stelzel, Dan Stone, Adam Tooze, Cornelius Torp, Ian Tyrrell, Maurizio Vaudagna, Jens Wegener, Heike Wieters, Sean Wilentz, Mason Williams, David Woolner, Princeton's anonymous reviewers, and particularly Aurélie Gfeller, Vincent Lagendijk, Mario del Pero, and Kenneth Weisbrode. I also would like to thank Sven Beckert for all his support and enthusiasm.

Moreover, I am indebted to Pablo del Hierro for his help with some of the Spanish literature, and Flávio Limonic, Letícia Galluzzi Bizzo, and Antoine Acker for their help on Brazil. Mia Saugman and Anja Servais were key in helping me with administrative and logistical challenges. Edmund Gavaghan, Aaron Vinnik, and Ingrid Hampe provided invaluable help as research assistants, and Med Dale played an indispensable role in editing my book. At times, Med knew what I was trying to say better than I knew myself. When Med was traveling, Mel Marquis, Jane Rafferty, and Angela Davies were kind enough to step in. Later in the process, Cindy Milstein did a great job as copyeditor, and Jan Williams prepared the index. Finally, I would like to thank all the students who helped me think about this topic and inspired me.

"Digressions, incontestably, are the sunshine;—they are the life, the soul of reading," English eighteenth-century novelist Laurence Sterne once quipped. This does not hold true for academic writing. Several projects have kept me from completing this book quicker. I am grateful to Brigitta van Rheinberg for bearing with me despite my slow tempo. Brigitta's enthusiasm is infectious, and her professional support was unsurpassed. Quinn Fusting and Natalie Baan steered me wonderfully through the publication process, and I am grateful to the whole team at Princeton for its commitment and friendly professionalism.

Special thanks also go to librarians and archivists in a long list of places. While attempting to bring literatures into a dialogue that have long been segregated by the dominant principle of parceling out history along national and other territorial lines, this book also builds on research in roughly a dozen archives in the United States and Europe. Like in 1999, when I first worked in the National Archives in College Park, MD, on a different project, Eugene Morris was extremely helpful. In Geneva, Jacques Oberson was of great help, and so were dozens of others. Without them, this book would have been impossible.

Christina, my wife, supported this project in too many ways to summarize here. Nina, Emma, and Benjamin grew quicker and flourished faster than this book developed. The long arch spanning from Cambridge, MA, over London, on to Maastricht/Aachen and Berlin, with a dip down to Florence, did not just see most of the writing of this book; it also forms the itinerary of our children's young lives.

I dedicate this book to the memory of my late father, Mahendrakumar Rajeshwar Patel. Born in India the year before the New Deal commenced, he spent good parts of his childhood and youth in Uganda, from where he went to England to receive his university education. Together with my mother, Alice, he later raised a family in Ghana and Germany. He only visited the United States once. Still, his twentieth century also would have been markedly different had it not been for the New Deal.

ABBREVIATIONS

AAA	Agricultural Adjustment Administration
AALL	American Association for Labor Legislation
AFL	American Federation of Labor
CCC	Civilian Conservation Corps
CWA	Civil Works Administration
DH-FDRP	*Documentary History of the Franklin D. Roosevelt Presidency*
EFO	Economic and Financial Organization
FAO	Food and Agriculture Organization
FBI	Federal Bureau of Investigation
FERA	Federal Emergency Relief Administration
FRUS	*Foreign Relations of the United States*
GATT	General Agreement on Tariffs and Trade
GDP	gross national product
IHS	International Historical Statistics
ILO	International Labour Organization
IMF	International Monetary Fund
INGO	international nongovernmental organization
JHRP	James Harvey Rogers Papers at Yale University Library
LoN	League of Nations
LULAC	League of United Latin American Citizens
MARBL	Manuscript, Archives, and Rare Book Library of Emory University
NARA	National Archives and Records Administration
NATO	North Atlantic Treaty Organization
NIRA	National Industrial Recovery Act
NPB	National Planning Board
NRA	National Recovery Administration
NYT	*New York Times*
OCIAA	Office of the Coordinator of Inter-American Affairs
PRERA	Puerto Rico Emergency Relief Administration
PRRA	Puerto Rico Reconstruction Administration
PSF	President's Secretary's Files
PWA	Public Works Administration
RA	Resettlement Administration
REA	Rural Electrification Administration
RFC	Reconstruction Finance Corporation
RSC	Roosevelt Study Center
SSB	Social Security Board

SSN	Social Security number
TVA	Tennessee Valley Authority
UFCO	United Fruit Company
UMW	United Mine Workers of America
UNRRA	UN Relief and Rehabilitation Administration
USDA	US Department of Agriculture
USHA	US Housing Authority
WIB	War Industries Board
WILPF	Women's International League for Peace and Freedom
WPA	Works Progress Administration
WRA	War Relocation Authority

The New Deal

FRANKLIN DELANO ROOSEVELT HATED FLYING. Having traveled to Europe by ship frequently during his childhood, he spent almost all his prewar presidency either in Washington, DC, on his beloved family estate in Hyde Park, NY, or crisscrossing the United States by train, ship, and car. Rarely did he interrupt this routine for trips abroad, which took him exclusively to destinations in the Western Hemisphere: Canada, the British Bahamas, Panama, and Colombia, among other places. Almost all these trips were vacations, however. Roosevelt, an omnivorous saltwater angler, tended to add meetings with state leaders and other politicians to his itinerary only if they happened to coincide with his expeditions to catch tarpon, sailfish, sharks, and similar species.[1] A voyage down to Buenos Aires in late 1936 to attend the Inter-American Peace Conference was the only major prewar trip with a genuinely political agenda—yet even for this long tour, FDR preferred to travel by ship rather than by plane.[2] And most of the time he simply stayed in the United States.

Most accounts of the prewar Roosevelt and the New Deal are conceived in a similar way. They focus on events and processes in the United States only, as if the country was surrounded by uncrossable oceans. They describe a nation deeply shaken by the Great Depression—the longest, most extensive, and deepest economic disaster of the twentieth century. As a result, so the standard story goes, the United States struggled to find an answer to the double crisis of capitalism and democracy, and finally lifted itself up by its own bootstraps. Roosevelt himself argued in 1936 that "here in America we are waging a great and successful war. It is not alone a war against want and destitution and economic demoralization. It is more than that; it is a war for the survival of democracy."[3] Note the "here in America"—as if the rest of the world was concerned with fundamentally different issues. The New Deal, a period sandwiched between the two truly global events of the Great Depression and World War II, thus appears as a genuinely national story, contained and explained within the confines of US history.

This book takes a different approach. It argues that the territorial space of the nation is insufficient to understand US history, since every national history is but a part of global history. The Great Depression created one of the most intense global moments in contemporary history. It was a phase during which societies around the world simultaneously faced similar questions and threats, however different their longer trajectories, the precise ways in which problems intersected, and the answers eventually chosen. In such a view, the New Deal was but a distinct, national variation within a larger pattern, and its domestic and foreign dimensions were powerfully linked. This does not mean that the world was flat and the United States was identical to other nations. The United States differed—as did all the other nations. The point is that America's course was not exceptional; it was not the one digression from the "normal" path chosen by all others.[4] Instead, exceptionalizing differences often enabled contemporaries and later interpreters to produce "relations of hierarchy, discipline, dispossession, extraction, and exploitation."[5] But even an interpretation that simply ignores related processes in other parts of the world has serious shortcomings. It tends to overlook the fact that the 1930s was a defining moment in America's stance vis-à-vis the wider world from which important lessons can be drawn.

More precisely, a nation-centered interpretation of the New Deal is misleading for three reasons. First, the setback to globalization caused by the Depression was the main reason why the early New Deal in particular had an inward-looking tendency on many issues, and why the New Dealers (and many other Americans) conceived of the New Deal as an antidote to the wider "world" crisis. Maybe the best term to capture this attitude was coined by Republican senator Arthur Vandenberg long before he became a protagonist of American internationalism: the "insulationist" approach of the United States emerged less from genuine parochialism than from perceived vulnerabilities to global forces.[6] The threat was not only seen as economic; instead, the Great Depression has to be understood as a general crisis of (Western) modernity that affected the very fabric of societies and led to a critical repositioning of America in the world.

Second, the domestic focus that characterized the initial US response to the global crisis had parallels in many parts of the world, be they in Europe, Latin America, or Asia. Economic nationalism, welfare state building, and new styles of charismatic national leadership—to name just three examples—were trends shared with many other countries and drew on a rather narrow arsenal of alternatives. Nations around the globe reacted to the crisis with a massive mobilization of society and state, frequently sharing a "high-modernist" ideology that emphasized the interconnectedness of technological and societal progress, feasibility of societal change, and rational design of social order. Most of these ideas pivoted on state action, and less on a local or cosmopolitan focus. Building on this ideology, many countries forged stronger, more permanent links between state and society than ever before.[7]

Third, in their race for the best "national" solution to the crisis, national leaders and publics closely watched as well as learned from one another, however loath they were to admit it. Particularly since World War I, people had developed a stronger sense of the world's interconnectedness and paid more attention to developments elsewhere. They were surprisingly flexible in these exchanges, because the horizon of experience of the 1930s was fundamentally different from 1945 or today. World War I, the relatively new threat of Communism, the quite undefined scope of fascism, and probably most important, the Great Depression were the defining experiences, especially in the United States—and not yet the Holocaust and Cold War. This may sound banal, but it helps to explain why, for example, American trade unionists were so fascinated by the Soviet Union, why Fordism was discussed around the world, and why FDR personally ordered reports about Nazi welfare programs in order to learn from them—again, in order to find the best national answer to the global crisis.

Modernity, also in a broader sense than the high-modernist incarnation dominating the interwar years, was "a global and *conjunctural* phenomenon, not a virus that spreads from one place to another," as Sanjay Subrahmanyam has contended.[8] The search for the true origins of a phenomenon—in America or elsewhere—therefore is often a dead end. By the 1930s, the world was so interlinked that a truly national path was impossible, particularly for a large, industrialized nation like the United States. Decades—and on some issues, even centuries—of mutual observation, transnational conversation, and global awareness among actors from various parts of the world had turned most ideas into cultural hybrids by the 1930s, and inserted them into a transnational canon of options. Instead of focusing on *roots*, it is more interesting to investigate the *routes* on which knowledge traveled at the time, and look into the global conditions facilitating and driving such debates and exchanges.

Building on these three reasons why an Exceptionalist or even simply nation-centered interpretation is insufficient, this book advances three general arguments. First, even if the United States was just one of many countries opting for insulation in the wake of the Great Depression, its course made a huge difference. Due to its economic power, the fate of the global economy depended on decisions taken in the United States to a much larger extent than on those taken in any other society. Confronted with the Great Depression, American elites gave pride of place to short-term domestic needs, even if in the midterm this approach also proved harmful for the United States itself. Globalization did not come to a standstill in the course of the 1930s. In many respects, however, it slowed down dramatically, and America was the only power with the capabilities to forestall this fate. At the time, Americans failed to accept this form of global leadership.

Second, in comparison with other industrial countries, the economic and political answers given by the New Dealers usually straddled the middle. In terms of laissez-faire or state intervention, the United States did not stick out as an outlier in either direction. While it was often self-contradictory, its concrete policies frequently gravitated to a moderate form of intervention and mobilization. This mattered, though. Up to that point, dictatorships—

whether of the Far Right or Far Left—had typically appeared to be the more dynamic forces compared to more liberal regimes. They seemingly either reacted to the crisis more swiftly or managed to avoid it in the first place. Democracies, in contrast, seemed to lag behind. With the New Deal, the United States turned into the society that showed the world that democracy and capitalism could be reconciled despite the challenges of the Great Slump. In that sense, the New Deal turned into a global icon. The post-1945 triumph of democracy across the Western world cannot be explained merely by the results of World War II; one also needs to consider events that arose in connection with the New Deal, an undertaking central to saving the international prestige of democracy in that it demonstrated the ability of the United States to reform and reinvent itself.

The third and final contention concerns the New Deal's lasting impact. The nation-centered—but certainly not "isolationist"—answer that the New Deal provided to global challenges was not a repudiation of America's global role. Rather, it became the main prerequisite and institutional scaffolding for building global hegemony, which some critics have depicted as a new world empire. More precisely, war preparation and the war itself not only challenged the insulationist approach of the New Deal but also saved many of the strong federal structures that the Roosevelt administration had established. World War II thus helped to perpetuate many elements of the New Deal order. These then became the springboards to global leadership, thanks in part to the eclipsing of any real national competitors.

The new multilateralism did not simply result from Pearl Harbor; it had to do with the cumulative impact of the New Deal along with the way it reshaped American views of what a state should do domestically and internationally. An early awareness of this shift—and a revealing sign of the missionary zeal that went along with it—is captured in Roosevelt's aforementioned 1936 speech: after describing the challenges, he emphasized that America was fighting to preserve democracy "for ourselves and for the world." This incremental shift to a global direction is one of the greatest legacies of the New Deal, and also formed a lesson learned from the early 1930s, when Americans had not accepted such a role on the global stage.

These three arguments take a direction radically different from most existing studies. The long-standing debate about the rootedness of the New Deal in American history is a case in point. The early proponents of the classic interpretation of Roosevelt's policy—scholars such as Richard Hofstadter, James McGregor Burns, and Arthur Schlesinger Jr.—have all stressed the deep ties to an American reform tradition. Schlesinger even went back to the age of Andrew Jackson in order to prove the New Deal's anchoring in the nation's past.[9] Others have emphasized that the New Deal was a radical new departure—either subverting or revolutionizing existing patterns. Still, all these discussions remained within the confines of American history. Other important advances only superficially went in a completely different direction: for some two decades, Lizabeth Cohen and others have contended that New Deal historiography has been too centered on the national level.[10] As an alternative, they convincingly advocated taking research more to the local dimension and giving more voice to ordinary Americans. The time is now ripe for turning around and rethinking the national stories in a global perspective, too. Next to local and national factors, transnational patterns and processes had a deep impact on the agenda, course, and eventual results that the New Deal yielded. Its significance can only be fully understood by stepping back and seeing it in a wider, global context. Over the past ten to fifteen years, quite a few studies have contributed to that agenda, including the pioneering work of John A. Garraty along with books by Daniel T. Rodgers, Ian Tyrrell, Mary Nolan, and Ira Katznelson.[11] Each of them, however, has only dealt with a segment of such a global history. It is now time to pull these various strands together, and this book is the first attempt to do so.

What, then, was the New Deal? Neither Roosevelt, nor his brilliant brain trusters, nor research since the 1930s has been able to answer this question properly. Until the war broke out in Europe in 1939, the New Dealers were primarily concerned with issues of political economy: Could capitalism be saved? How much state interventionism was needed to overcome the crisis? At a very general level, the answers they found helped to save capitalism and reform democracy. In its details, though, the program associated with FDR was awash in contradictions and inconsistencies, and its effects were highly ambivalent. The New Deal spent and saved, alleviated and aggravated the economic crisis, and fought and facilitated racial discrimination. What it did quite consistently was to make the US government—and at a general level, the "state"—matter more.

This book is therefore about the new role of government in the everyday lives of Americans and the way community life was organized, while also drawing out parallels to developments in other parts of the globe and analyzing new transnational interconnections created at the time. In the existing literature on these questions, the term "New Deal" is generally only used for FDR's domestic agenda. Yet in a global perspective, a clear-cut distinction between domestic and international policies does not hold water. Some programs, such as the Silver Purchase Act of 1934, were mainly meant for domestic consumption, especially to please the "Silverites" in the western states. But it had massive implications internationally, too, chiefly for China. Conversely, diplomatic recognition of the Soviet Union in 1933 was driven largely by domestic economic concerns. Immigration policy is crucial to understanding the emergence of the New Deal welfare programs. Hence, this book also deals with the international links that the New Dealers forged, and discusses the interplay between domestic and foreign agendas. It considers issues that were deeply ingrained in the zeitgeist and global conversations of the 1930s, such as eugenics, even if Washington, DC, did not play a prominent role in them. In a global perspective, things not only done but also items left untouched (or left to others, such as the individual states and nonstate actors) are of relevance.

Revisiting the 1930s introduces us to an America and a world very different from today—yet the present age owes much to the dynamics of that era. Capitalism was in the deepest crisis that it had ever experienced in the United States and beyond. Long-distance travel and communication were cumbersome. Vast parts of Africa and Asia were still colonies, and democracy found itself in global retreat. There were far fewer sovereign states, and the web of international organizations and transnational nongovernmental organizations was much more loosely knit than today. The League of Nations, as the foremost international organization at the time, was founded in 1919 with forty-two sovereign states—mostly from Europe. At its greatest extent, in 1934–35, it had fifty-eight members, with only two—Liberia and Ethiopia—in Africa, as compared to the almost two hundred of the United Nations today. Certain decisive states—and most important, the United States itself—never joined the League. Modern statehood building on a clear-cut territorial base dominated the global political agenda at the time, as historian Charles S. Maier has demonstrated—be it as political practice on the ground, as in the United States, or an aspiration, as in good parts of the nascent decolonization movements. Moreover, statehood was increasingly associated with the ambition to regulate welfare—in marked difference to both the earlier laissez-faire approach and free market developments since the 1970s.[12]

This book sets out to achieve more than conventional political history. It is not just about the role of government; it is also about "governmentality," to use a term coined by Michel Foucault. Beyond describing the waxing and waning of political actors and institutions as well as the management of state affairs, it investigates the techniques and technologies of power by which a society is rendered "readable" and governable.[13] Population statistics, migration laws, and public housing schemes all contributed to this endeavor. While emphasizing political history, the book also features social, economic, and cultural history perspectives. Moving beyond a state-centered approach is necessary in order to understand the significance of the federal administration and state more broadly in advancing a global agenda. On many issues, nonstate actors had a pioneering role and became catalysts for the global New Deal—equal to and in many cases surpassing the expanding state. The role of nongovernmental organizations, big business, missionaries, and other actors thus needs to be factored in, and the same holds true for the flow of ideas, institutions, commodities, and other objects. For though the rhetoric of the New Deal was heavily statist—and crucially so—the reality of its execution was far more complex and varied, particularly when the global dimension is taken into account.

In addition, the book's chapters shed new light on the history of capitalism. With the notable exception of the Soviet Union, all societies analyzed here clung to a capitalist economic system in one form or another, even if debates and policies focused on refashioning the economic system. This—and not democracy or any other feature—was the true vector of continuity, and a key reason why exchange between these societies and all four corners of the globe was so intense.

The global, as understood here, is conceptually broken down into two distinct but compatible levels of investigation. For one, the book compares developments in the United States with parallel processes elsewhere and demonstrates that the New Deal can be seen as a national version of larger patterns. One obvious example is welfare state building, where the book challenges the existing interpretation that America was the laissez-faire "latecomer" among modern industrialized nations. In fact, Germany—normally seen as a pioneer in this field—introduced unemployment benefits only a few years prior to the American Social Security Act of 1935, and state involvement (taking the federal and state levels together) in the United States then became stronger than in Belgium or Denmark. The few published comparative studies, it has to be added, privilege the North Atlantic region. Considering the importance of Europe in the interwar period, many strong links connecting the New World to the Old World, and similarity between developments there and in the United States, the North Atlantic region plays a central role in this account, too. That said, the book places American history in a truly global framework—also paying attention to the Americas, Asia, and other world regions. Economic planning, for instance, was debated (and to some degree implemented) in places as diverse as Australia, Sweden, and Mexico. New forms of political leadership, and their representation in the media, were negotiated in Turkey as much as in the United States, the Soviet Union, and Japan. And the 1935 Social Security Act looks different when contextualized with similar efforts in Brazil, New Zealand, and Norway. While one must not, of course, neglect power imbalances and vast local differences, such a broader view can begin to redress the prevailing Eurocentrism of comparative work on the period.

For another, transnational connections, networks, and transfers were central to the history of the New Deal. This dimension is not just important in order to counterbalance the danger of comparisons parceling out history as national history and thus reconfirming the hitherto-dominant approach to the past. It also opens up room for going below the level of the nation, and looking at local and regional transnational links. Where in the world did the New Dealers turn for inspiration, and which other references did they ignore? Which new interconnections were built, and which existing ones were discontinued? And equally critical, how did things look when seen from a non-American perspective, be it from Rio, Rome, or Riyadh? How much were American practices adopted or even emulated? Here, too, a truly global approach is adopted. The New Deal for Puerto Rico, say, shared key features with the Tennessee Valley Authority (TVA), and both shed new light on the postwar occupation of Germany and Japan. US silver policies not only impacted China but from there also had repercussions in Mexico and Britain. Beyond the comparably well-known Atlantic crossings, many other links connected the New Deal to the wider world.

A transnational perspective also helps to find answers as to the motives and causes of developments: sometimes, similar developments resulted from independent, parallel processes in different parts of the world, and in other cases emerged from acts of selective appropriation. Usually both are true. For instance, charismatic leadership forging new links between the average follower or citizen and the political leader can be discovered in many different political systems around the globe. To some extent, they were all reacting to similar structural and functional needs, and were informed by developments elsewhere.

Deglobalization, divergence, difference, distrust, and disconnection are all integral parts of this story as well. During the "age of ideologies," delimitation often superseded dialogue and other forms of engagement with the wider world, but this need not mistake causes for effects, or rhetoric for social and political practices. The 1930s was a protean phase, in which the quest for modernity created a relative openness to experimenting with unorthodox political and economic solutions. Sometimes, policy impulses were received from foreign sources and then quietly incorporated into the bureaucratic process. Few politicians around the world boasted of having learned something elsewhere. Certain options were repeatedly ruled out as "alien" or "totalitarian" (sometimes correctly, and sometimes not), and quite generally, national trajectories were often reinvented, stabilized, and reified through their exposure to a global market of alternatives. Only a global perspective can reveal this aspect and move beyond a simplistic dichotomy of transnational influences on the one side and parochialism on the other.

These dimensions of the Roosevelt presidency have long been buried under the overtly global role that the United States came to play during World War II and the Cold War. To unearth them, chapter 1 sets the stage and interprets the Great Depression as a global event, as a time of testing for both democracy and capitalism. Chapter 2 zooms in on the early New Deal years and explores the Roosevelt administration's initiatives while putting them in global context. Among many other things, it analyzes the kind of "kinship" that many contemporary observers saw between the New Deal and political systems of completely different fabric, such as fascism. Chapter 3 then concentrates on the multiple global connections that the New Deal created, redirected, or discontinued—and how the meaning of "global" changed thanks to these encounters during the 1930s. Chapter 4 builds on the findings of chapter 2 and examines the New Deal's domestic initiatives in a global context during the second half of the 1930s. It stresses the radically different internal and global situation at the time. The United States and countries around the world were in search of greater security for their peoples, thereby stabilizing the development toward more statism. Chapter 5, finally, is an epilogue. It assesses the medium- and long-term effects of the New Deal through 1945 and beyond. As a result of the New Deal, so it argues, Americans showed growing willingness and capability to engage the world explicitly, with massive (and often-unintended) effects both for America and other parts of the world.

America thus incrementally turned into a superpower, and its interconnections with every last corner of the world became too obvious to ignore. However reluctantly, Roosevelt started to travel extensively during the last years of the war. He went on his first intercontinental trip in 1943. This 16,965-mile tour took him to Casablanca (including some detours), and forced him to board an aircraft—the first serving president to do so.[14] According to Harry Hopkins, one of his closest advisers, it was on this trip that the president finally came to enjoy flying.[15] Further visits to Brazil, France, Egypt, Iran, Britain, the Soviet Union, and other places soon followed, turning the last years of Roosevelt's presidency into a string of global encounters that ended a bare two months before his death in April 1945. This book revisits the prewar New Deal as a period that laid the groundwork for such developments.

Chapter 1

A GLOBAL CRISIS

A Fragile Boom

"In the large view, we have reached a higher degree of comfort and security than ever existed before in the history of the world."[1] Herbert Hoover's inaugural address very much summarizes the spirit in America in spring 1929. Also in 1929, journalist Charles Merz proclaimed that a "brand-new America" was coming about, boasting the "triumph of the urban culture" and "prowess of the giant mills." More fundamentally, he asserted, "the rules of thumb that once seemed everlasting principles" had been overturned.[2] Many Americans amassed unknown wealth during the course of the 1920s, leaving behind the want and shortcomings of the past, but also the traditional ways of life. The departure into a new age was fueled by the belief that everything was possible and that (social) technology was the key to success. The United States self-fashioned itself and was seen internationally as *a*, if not *the*, quintessentially modern nation. Hence, the Great Depression unfolded against the backdrop of not only an economic success story but wider changes in American society, too.

After a short decline during 1920–21, America experienced substantial economic gains. Between July 1921 and May 1923, industrial production rose by 63 percent. The intervening years until 1929 also saw significant growth—between 1921 and 1929, the gross domestic product (GDP) rose by almost 50 percent.[3] The car industry and its suppliers formed the backbone of the boom in America. Prior to World War I, railroads and waterways had been the largest and most prestigious infrastructure projects, whereas the road network was much less developed. Rural transportation posed a particular problem, since many important connections remained dirt roads made impassable by a few days of rain. During World War I, the transport systems could barely cope with the new demands of the war effort and national mobilization. Motor transportation was seen as the best solution to the challenge, and this latest revolution in American transport infrastructure drove the economic upsurge. The trend was further substantiated by the war in Europe, which turned into a major testing ground for the potentials of infrastructure and logistics built around the combustion engine. In this context, US federal and state governments intensified their efforts to get farmers out of the mud and improve driving conditions outside urban centers. Economic and social debates went hand in hand with the idea of building a new America: in 1916, President Woodrow Wilson trumpeted how new streets would not only connect the various parts of the country but also support the "nationalization of America."[4] His insouciant Republican successor, Warren G. Harding, then became the first American president to ride to his inauguration in a car rather than a carriage—thus heralding not just an important political change in US political history but also the breakthrough of the automobile age.[5]

Despite their instrumental role in initiating and building new roads and highways, state actors were not in the driving seat of the boom. Even before Americans had decent roads to drive on they had started to purchase cars, which both symbolized and stimulated this newfound prosperity. In 1926, Ford's Model T produced some 40 percent of all new cars sold in the United States; all in all, the company built fifteen million units of this model. The connection between the overall economic situation and Ford Motor Company's performance was especially close: a temporary recession in 1927 reflected Henry Ford's decision to stop production for six months in order to retool for the new Model A.[6] Alongside changes in individual transportation, bus services grew in importance during the 1920s. Starting as a one-man show in 1914, the Greyhound system was operating forty thousand miles of scheduled services by 1933.[7] Tractors and trucks also fueled the trend, reducing the isolation of rural America and speeding the shift away from rail and ship. Instead, gas stations, garages, and suburban sprawl became the hallmarks of the American landscape of the 1920s.

Other consumer industries also played a crucial role in the boom of the 1920s. Electrification, albeit far from complete, paved the way for domestic appliances like radios, refrigerators, vacuum cleaners, and most commonly in 1929, electric irons. All these products, hardly in use before World War I, had become widespread in the United States by the eve of the Great Depression; the electric iron, for example, had found its way into 60 percent of all American homes.[8] Rising incomes made these gadgets affordable, and the new economic instrument of installment credits facilitated their purchase.[9] Moreover, rising earnings and declining work hours revolutionized leisure activities. Tourism became a significant economic factor, with the number of visits to national parks rising from half a million in 1917 to 2.4 million in 1930. National Park Service director Stephen T. Mather stood at the forefront of innovative public relations strategies to raise these figures still further.[10] Professional sports became big business, and during the 1920s Hollywood became the film industry's world capital. To be sure, big business and finance were not alone in driving prosperity; state assistance and new consumption patterns also contributed substantially. And not all sectors of the economy profited to the same extent from these developments. Some,

especially mining and farming, stagnated, and the boom was neither inces-
sant nor ubiquitous, nor even expansive.[11]

Still, prosperity did a lot to knit Americans closer together. Roads and
radio stations began to lift rural isolation, and the changes affected more
than transport and communication. A 1929 sociological study listed no less
than 150 "social effects" of the radio—most important, that it increased the
"homogeneity of peoples ... because of like stimuli."[12] Admittedly, there
were clear limits to such convergence. The South remained less affected by
these changes, with Mississippi having the lowest number of radios per
household, and critics deploring such innovations as the latest invasion of
Yankee culture.[13] The rumble of vacuum cleaners was heard primarily in
the homes of the middle class, while refrigerators were even more exclusive.[14] Also, historiography has been too quick to assume that the new mass
culture embraced all workers and eradicated difference. Many of Chicago's
numerous foreign-born citizens, for instance, liked listening to the "Polish"
or "Italian" hour on their local networks, and did not simply aspire to an
all-American, middle-class lifestyle.[15] Despite these qualifications, the new
prosperity impacted the lives of all Americans in various respects. It was
perceived as a particularly *American* experience. And as such, it also changed
America's role in the world.

Exporting the American Dream

The strongest new global ties were economic, too. American exports more
than doubled between 1911–15 and 1921–25, and the United States was set
to overtake Great Britain as the world's largest trading nation and dominant industrial force. American industrial products now achieved international visibility—Hoover vacuum cleaners, Gilette razors, and Ford cars
became household names as well as objects of aspiration, epitomizing modernity not only in Poughkeepsie, NY, and Pasadena, CA, but also in Havana, Hamburg, and Hiroshima. The United States accrued a large export
surplus, particularly with Europe, which continued to be its most important trading partner. The annual trade surplus stood at $1.8 billion in the
decade after the war, a sevenfold increase compared to the prewar years.[16]

This new position did not result just from America's strength; it also
came from the weakness of others. The United States' two most important
competitors, Great Britain and Germany, were both diminished by the
Great War and relatively poor economic performance throughout much of
the 1920s. The Japanese economy did not participate in the boom, and its
rather loose economic connections beyond East Asia also reduced its global
impact.

The United States utilized its new commercial position to amplify its
global role. Only part of the trade surplus went into monetary reserves;

United States and British Foreign Lending (in Hundred Thousand Dollars)

	Europe	Asia and Oceania	Africa	Canada and Newfoundland	Latin America	Total
United States						
1924	527	100	–	151	191	969
1925	629	147	–	137	163	1,076
1926	484	38	–	226	377	1,125
1927	577	164	–	237	359	1,337
1928	598	137	–	185	331	1,251
1929	142	58	–	295	176	671
1930	233	62	–	281	199	905
1931	78	25	–	125	1	229
1932	–	–	–	29	–	29
Total	**3,268**	**731**	**–**	**1,666**	**1,797**	**7,592**
United Kingdom						
1924	159	314	66	20	31	590
1925	53	216	72	10	68	424
1926	120	226	32	29	129	546
1927	105	238	136	34	126	674
1928	164	232	80	98	96	698
1929	105	139	51	74	78	459
1930	53	195	129	17	101	529
1931	14	125	36	6	26	209
1932	–	40	45	9	–	102
Total	**773**	**1,724**	**647**	**297**	**655**	**4,231**

Source: League of Nations, *Balances of Payments, 1930*, 30; League of Nations, *Balances of Payments, 1931 and 1930*, 16.
Note: The totals include unspecified sums, so regional figures do not necessarily add up to the totals.

American bankers used the rest for large-scale, demand-driven foreign lending and investment. Between 1924 and 1929, the United States loaned some $6.4 million to foreign borrowers—almost twice the total of Great Britain, the other global lender (see table 1). Obviously, Americans did not shy away from deep economic entanglements with other parts of the world.

Moreover, the lending patterns differed from those of Great Britain. For the United States, Africa was nonexistent and Asia much less important than for Britain, due to its global empire. US lending until 1929 went largely to the Americas, but Europe was also a higher priority than for Britain.

Americans did not just lend money but also acquired lasting management and business interests abroad. US foreign investment was particularly strong in car production in the early 1920s, especially in Canada and Latin America, and subsequently in Europe, South Africa, India, Malaya, and Japan. Commercial interests often trumped political considerations: in 1929, the Ford Motor Company sold $40 million worth of automobiles and parts to the Soviet Union, also giving technical assistance to a manufacturing complex at Nizhniy Novgorod, the birthplace of writer Maxim Gorky and heart of the Volga-Vyatka economic region. By the late 1930s, the "Gorkovsky Avtomobilny Zavod" in the "Soviet Detroit" was producing some eighty to ninety thousand "Russian Fords" annually.[17] Henry Ford's anticommunism was conspicuously less orthodox than sometimes thought. Not only did he trade with Joseph Stalin, he actually became the dictator's largest foreign business partner between 1929 and 1936. Ford even developed an affectionate friendship with a Communist, Mexican intellectual Diego Rivera, building on a shared belief in technology, the feasibility of social change, and by and large, an illiberal vision of modernity.[18] Ford's competitors were not quite as aggressive, yet they were equally pragmatic; America's largest car producer, General Motors, for example, set up plants in places as far away as Osaka, Japan, and Anvers, France.[19]

Foreign lending, direct investment, and trade created strong commercial links with other parts of the world, especially Europe and the Americas. Britain and the United States were the powerhouses of economic globalization. The 1920s, normally characterized as a period in which globalization ebbed due to instability and nationalism after the war, would have been much more strongly deglobalized had it not been for America. This counterfactual argument is often not taken into account.

Still, the continental size of the United States and its huge domestic demand made it easy to overlook its new global role. US foreign trade amounted to only some 7 percent of overall production—whereas all other major economies, with the exception of the Soviet Union, depended much more heavily on exports.[20] It would be wrong to assume that America's international rise took place in a fit of absentmindedness; but still, for many Americans it seemed rather marginal. At first blush, the United States could do it alone, and if anything, others were much more dependent on America than vice versa—two suppositions that were to be proven wrong during the Depression.

At the political level, the United States was less willing to take the lead. America never joined the League of Nations, even though it had been enthusiastically promoted by President Wilson and formed the institutional centerpiece of his famous Fourteen Points program of 1918 for securing international peace in the postwar era. The United States also remained absent from other pillars of interwar internationalism, such as the World Court. Still, it did not withdraw completely from international politics. A closer look at the League is revealing. Many of its services would have collapsed without the financial help of US philanthropic organizations. The Rockefeller Foundation, for one, heavily funded the League of Nations' Health Organization, a predecessor of the World Health Organization, and by the early 1930s it was paying the salaries of one-third of the Health Organization's staff members.[21] Taking all its branches together, the League of Nations employed more than two hundred Americans.[22] Meanwhile, most of the trustees of the Carnegie Endowment for International Peace, which was engaged in similar activities, maintained close ties to Washington: one of its directors considered running for the presidency, another played an instrumental role in founding the International Labour Organization (ILO) in Geneva, and the Carnegie Endowment as a whole was crucial in the creation of the Kellogg-Briand Pact of 1928, outlawing war as a means of foreign policy.[23]

Alongside these indirect routes to internationalism, the US government played a visible and critical role, such as in the Washington Naval Conference of 1921–22 limiting fleet sizes and the Kellogg-Briand Pact. Salesmanship, philanthropy, and statesmanship were not mutually exclusive, however. Instead, American elites reveled in creating ever-closer synergies between them. The Carnegie Endowment, for instance, promoted international peace and free trade, championing a system built on the pillars of democracy and capitalism. More and more, America became identified with such a model, and in comparison to prewar diplomacy, its involvement in international affairs was unprecedented. It therefore would be wrong to call the 1920s an age of isolationism for America.[24]

But America did not just project economic and political power. It also became a major cultural force. Technical innovations were one side of the equation; jazz, Hollywood, and the new role of women were another. When, in 1901, British journalist William Thomas Stead announced the "Americanization of the world," this had still been rather prophetic; by the 1920s, it had turned into reality. It was "obvious" in 1923 to Stead's compatriot Bertrand Russell that "the next power to make a bid for world empire will be America," and its resources "are more adequate than those of any previous aspirant to universal hegemony."[25] Americanization or, for that matter, hegemony never meant that American cultural practices simply spread across the globe. Americanization stood for intense discussions, particularly in industrialized countries, in which America was seen as the quintessential materialization of modernity, as the desired or abhorred future of one's own society. Although, paradoxically, the debates about Americanization were predominantly nationally framed, they shared fundamental similarities. French and German intellectuals, for instance, invested great energy in underlining their differences—yet the two national discourses

Figure 1. Front cover of a Chinese magazine featuring
the "Modern Girl," 1932.

drew from an identical pool of stereotypes and interpretative patterns. Debating "America" brought communities closer together, even if they did not
realize it.[26]

Nonetheless, American ideas and practices did travel around the world.
As early as the 1920s, the United States started to build an "irresistible empire" of commercial commodities and mass consumption. Fordism, Taylorism, and business practices more generally, but also haircuts, manners,
and tastes, were promoted internationally, especially in Europe. The Old
World served, as Victoria de Grazia has shown, as America's prime theater to
stage "a great imperium with the outlook of a great emporium."[27]

As another example, American cosmetics advertising had a tremendous
impact on the image of the "modern girl," characterized by her fashionable
apparel, explicit eroticism, and independence. This applied not only to the
French *garçonne* or German *Neue Frau*; far beyond Europe, America's mores
also impacted China's *modeng xiaojie* or India's *kallege ladki*. Actresses like

Hollywood star Clara Bow became role models. Indian film star "Glorious" Gohar, for instance, referenced her bobbed hair, large eyes, and mascara-laden eyelashes, but combined this with Indian elements such as a sari and Indian-style jewelry. To be sure, America did not simply set the one and only path for the "modern girl." Instead of one-to-one copies, we find a whole host of appropriations, which in turn had an impact on America. The modern girl did have American roots, yet was ultimately a global hybrid.[28]

Against this backdrop, many Americans strove for stronger engagement with the wider world. During the 1920s, some forty thousand US citizens lived in France alone—among them Cole Porter and Ernest Hemingway, but also many who did not compose or write, such as businessmen or well-heeled American women with cash-strapped aristocratic European spouses.[29] In America, many groups began to embrace their ethnic heritage. From the mid-1920s onward, ethnic American identities gained traction, overcoming the "antihyphenism" of World War I. The village of New Glarus, WI, epitomizing an imagined Swiss homeland, is only one illustration of how images of the wider world were imported into the lifestyles of (white) Americans.[30] Building on their prewar work, African American intellectuals like W.E.B. Du Bois or the more radical Marcus Garvey continued to transcend the structures of the nation-state and constraints of ethnicity—for instance, by intensifying their links to the rising anticolonial movements in Europe as well as in African and other colonies. By and large, the 1920s were a golden age of Pan-Africanism, and powerful transcontinental links were established in 1930, when Haile Selassie became emperor of Ethiopia; Garvey's American and particularly Jamaican followers saw this as the realization of the biblical prophecy that kings would come out of Africa.[31] Even before this, Wilson's call for national self-determination at the end of World War I—primarily meant for American and European ears—had fired the imagination of anticolonial groups in Egypt, China, and India, thereby adding legitimacy to their quest.[32] Philanthropic organizations pushed for peace and social reform and started to globalize their activities beyond a US and European focus. The Rockefeller Foundation, for example, gave major financial support to several universities in China, mainly to introduce Western economic ideas, while also promoting Christianity. Such work bolstered the global network of American missionaries and organizations like the Young Men's Christian Association, which had already built a distinctly Protestant American moral empire with global pretensions prior to World War I.[33] At the same time, the fate of two Italian anarchists, Nicola Sacco and Bartolomeo Vanzetti, tried and executed in Massachusetts, reveals a paradox typical of the age: on the one hand, they were scapegoats for a growing fear of all ideas perceived as foreign; on the other hand, their execution stirred the solidarity of workers in places as far afield as Montevideo, Marseilles, Moscow, Milan, and Casablanca. America's new global role and

self-projected image as a beacon of freedom and democracy turned any flagrant violation of justice into an international issue.[34] In light of all these
activities, it does not come as a surprise that Nobel Peace Prize laureate Jane
Addams saw a "nascent world consciousness" developing during the 1920s.[35]
Addams had been a transnational actor of sorts herself since the 1880s, and
yet the new level of global interaction in the decade after 1918 impressed
her greatly. If these movements did not have a larger impact on the official
US position, it was mainly because internationalist organizations were
highly fragmented and fought for fundamentally diverging causes. Their
very pluralism and diversity thus reduced their political clout.[36]

Nevertheless, globalization continued throughout the 1920s, not least because of American actions. The decade was a truly transnational phase of
exchange, and debates more than ever before transgressed the confines of
the Western world. To date, the literature has stressed a one-sided approach
positing that economic globalization did not regain prewar levels during
this decade.[37] But if one also factors in the changes at the political, technological, and cultural levels, the picture begins to look different: the number
of international nongovernmental organizations (INGOs) more than doubled between 1910 and 1930, to reach 375. Whereas most INGOs had been
a North Atlantic phenomenon until the 1910s, they now drew more members from other parts of the world and dealt with an ever-increasing number of issues. The first nonstop flight spanning the North American continent, the first round-the-world flight, and Charles Augustus Lindbergh's
flight across the Atlantic to Europe all fell in the 1920s, as did the first transatlantic telephone call. Finally, the cinema provided a global vernacular,
both before and after the introduction of "talkies."[38]

A Cosmopolitan Age?

That said, many Americans abhorred the brave new world that their own
country helped to create. Cosmopolitanism was not the dominant mood in
America. When the Senate killed US participation in the League of Nations
in 1919–20, national sovereignty was a central argument. As Senator William Borah, the square-chinned "Lion of Idaho," leveled against Wilson's
plan: "It imperils what I conceive to be the underlying, the very first principles of this Republic. It is in conflict with the right of our people to gov-
ern themselves free from all restraint, legal or moral, of foreign powers."[39]
Borah had a point. His view echoed the predominant tenor of US diplomacy since the days of George Washington's farewell address and the Monroe Doctrine. In the early nineteenth century, however, the United States
had been a marginal power at the rim of what was at best a fragmented international system. By the 1920s, the international stage and America's role

in it had changed dramatically. The question now was whether the country could afford to abstain from genuinely global commitments and responsibilities.[40] Officially, the answer remained "yes," but there were many loopholes through which the United States did participate in international politics.

On some issues, this ambivalence vis-à-vis the wider world turned into a call for self-seclusion. Immigration is the most important example. In particular, the Quota Act of 1921 and the Immigration Act of 1924 aimed at curbing immigration. The effects were drastic. Total immigration plummeted from 360,000 in 1923–24 to 165,000 in 1924–25, and the quota system remained in place until the 1960s. The key motivations were anticommunism after the Russian Revolution along with fears that European-style radicalism might inundate and undermine American society. Moreover, the new laws had strong racist underpinnings. Policies predating World War I had already closed the door to Asians, who had begun immigrating in large numbers in the mid-nineteenth century. This time, nativism targeted migrants from eastern and southern Europe, with Jews and Gypsies being especially unwelcome. The new acts reduced their numbers in particular.[41]

Madison Grant and his 1916 book, *The Passing of the Great Race*, as well as similar quasi-scientific eugenics and racist works provided an important inspiration and legitimation for this new take on immigration. Grant was born into a well-to-do New York family and was a close friend of several US presidents, including Theodore Roosevelt, FDR, and Hoover. He feared that America's racial stock, with its strong "Nordic" element, was seriously deteriorating in the face of constant new waves of immigration. Grant detested Polish Jews, "whose dwarf stature, peculiar mentality and ruthless concentration on self-interest are being engrafted upon the stock of the nation," as he saw it, and his attitude toward people from Mediterranean and Slavic countries was hardly any better. Combining anti-Semitism, racism, so-called Nordic supremacy, and elitism, Grant's long and convoluted book urged stricter immigration control as well as a eugenic social policy; otherwise, America would face a "racial abyss."[42]

Nativist policies were not just driven by xenophobic and ideological arguments. Labor was also in favor of restrictions, which in its view served the interests of the existing workforce. Even the founder and president of the mighty American Federation of Labor (AFL), Samuel Gompers, wanted to curtail immigration—despite being a Jewish first-generation immigrant himself.[43]

Such schizophrenia notwithstanding, these ideas were not universally shared in the United States at the time. While Columbia anthropologist Franz Boas had already developed scientific arguments against racial determinism before World War I, publications like the *New York Times* and the

Nation upheld the ideal of "the brotherhood of all human beings," and contended that the country's "hopes lie rather in our fusion of many cultures."[44] In the end, though, cosmopolitanism succumbed to restrictionism.

Yet the new US immigration policy left a large loophole. The southern border remained wide open, allowing a growing influx of Mexicans to enter the country. Many of these immigrants replaced African Americans moving to the northern industrial districts. Both Mexican immigration and African American internal migration resulted directly from restrictionism, as both groups of people filled jobs that otherwise would have gone to European immigrants.[45] By the racial standards of the white Anglo-Saxon Protestant elite, the cheap and easy-to-dispose-of "wetbacks" from Mexico were at least as objectionable as southern or eastern Europeans, while African Americans were even worse; but grandees like Grant needed invisible hands to starch and iron their white shirts, while cotton plantations and steel mills would have gone out of business without this labor force. Therefore, the US Border Patrol, set up in 1924 with some forty men, was less interested in Mexicans or Canadians than in unwanted Europeans and Asians trying to cross the border.[46] Soon, the force was increased and professionalized, and America's borders hardened further. Between 1908 and 1920, an average of two to three thousand unwanted immigrants annually had been deported from the United States; by 1930, that figure stood at thirty-nine thousand.[47]

Immigration laws with their pseudoscientific, racist underpinnings were just the tip of the iceberg. The furnishings of middle-class American households also showed less international influence and less explicit exoticism than prior to World War I. Instead, colonial revival gained in importance. Seemingly innocent objects such as houses and furniture stood for ethnic purity and national self-assertion. Together with the arts and crafts movement and the mission style, colonial revival refuted cosmopolitanism. This was more than an abstract debate about style and taste. In the Country Club District of Kansas City, the largest master-planned community in the United States and crammed with this kind of architecture, real estate developer J. C. Nichols used restrictive covenants to bar African Americans, Jews, and other ethnic minorities from ownership or occupation. Others adopted a seemingly more welcoming policy. Particularly during the 1920s, colonial revival was used as an educational tool for recent immigrants. Living in colonial homes would, so supremacist hopes went, Americanize these immigrants, thus turning them into patriotic citizens.[48]

Beyond embellishment and embroidery, the 1920s saw the revival of the Ku Klux Klan, new Jim Crow laws in the South, regulations restricting Japanese landownership in the West, and discrimination against Jews and Catholics in Ivy League universities in the East. "Racial nationalism," to use a term coined by Gary Gerstle, also shaped Prohibition.[49] Effectuated in January 1920, Prohibition was designed as a deterrent against foreign ways.[50]

The term "mafia" was directly associated with such un-American behavior, ironically during a period in which mass immigration from Italy was long over.[51] Many in small-town America were suspicious of the new global possibilities and urban culture that gained the upper hand during this period. For them, Wall Street represented original sin, and the defense of traditional ways often had anti-Semitic overtones. Expatriates in Paris were perceived as rootless, hedonistic, and flamboyant. Small government, family values, immigration restrictionism, and individualism (the latter for white Anglo-Saxon Protestants only, to be sure) were the rallying cries of this camp. For every flapper, there were dozens of religious white Protestants bemoaning the modern ways. By and large, and despite the Wilsons, Addams, and Du Boises, post-1918 America was "a society that had moved to a restricted view of itself, of a culture that was beginning to think of itself as fixed rather than fluid, of a society tempted to prefer conformity over diversity," as Oscar Handlin once put it.[52]

Ironically, however, a hardening of national borders substantially increased state action, thus contradicting the creed of small government. Next to border patrol and immigration officers within the country, the US Department of State created a considerable overseas bureaucracy in order to execute the new immigration rules.[53] While hating standardization and the acceleration of life, proponents of regionalism thoroughly enjoyed driving their Fords and Chevrolets—and just as they were unable to separate the bright from the detested sides of modernity, their relationship to the wider world was similarly caught up in paradoxes.

Americans, as hard as they tried, could not escape the world. President Calvin Coolidge is a good example: born as the son of a village shopkeeper from Vermont, he visited Washington only once and had never been west of the Alleghenies, let alone abroad, until midcareer. Still, he had no problems cooperating with big business—for example, insisting on an open door in China.[54] Colonial revival had its roots in England, not in America, and a good pinch of Orientalism had been part of its original recipe. Grant's work built on that of race "scientists" like Arthur de Gobineau or Houston Stewart Chamberlain, and his footnotes sported a long list of European authors in several languages. Entanglements had already gone so far that the most national and inward-looking movement was part of the global condition and its idiosyncrasies.

Was America singular in its restrictiveness and ambivalence? National prohibition laws had been adopted in other areas of the Northern Hemisphere, particularly in Iceland, Norway, and Russia, before the United States took this step. Ideas of racial purity with immigration bans, border controls, and the need to procure passports and visas were part and parcel of the consolidation of the nation-state system during as well as after the Great War, with countries monopolizing their power to control transnational movements and migration flows.[55] Some impulses predated 1914 and reveal the global reach of this process: Australia introduced a "White Australia" policy with its Immigration Restriction Act of 1901, following up on the US Chinese Exclusion Act of 1882, and was soon admired by Americans as the next necessary step to a progressive society.[56] In both cases, the main target was immigration from Asia at a time when the "yellow fear" became a xenophobic trope shared by Australians and Americans, and indeed South Africans, Malays in colonial Indonesia, and to some degree, even Germans.[57]

After 1914, chauvinistic nationalism loomed even larger, with the conflict and later the postwar reorganization of states, empires, and international order providing ample room for states to mistreat minorities, expel unwanted populations, and close borders. Turkey's Armenian genocide of 1915 and the displacement of its 1.25 million Christian Greeks in 1923 were extreme cases but demonstrate the radical potential of states that fashioned themselves as modern.[58] In South America, where racism had long had less impact than in the United States, the white British dominions, or Europe, governments now stifled immigration on an ethnic basis. Brazil, for instance, had a long tradition of welcoming immigrants until its related policy hardened in the early 1930s.[59] Argentina had already started excluding *los rusos* (the Russians) the decade before, in a move that in fact mainly targeted eastern European Jews.[60] By the 1930s, eighteen of twenty-two independent states in the Americas excluded Asian immigrants, even if they actually had little or no experience with migrants from that part of the world.[61] Viewing the more homogeneous European societies as an ideal, ethnicization was the trend across the globe; it created an ideal to which the anticolonial liberation movements and even the Soviet Union aspired.[62] New Delhi's Indian Naturalization Act of 1926 was both an expression of these trends and a direct reaction to the new course in the United States, since it denied Indian citizenship to nationals from countries that did not naturalize Indians—such as America.[63] All in all, the timing, instruments, and consequences of policy patterns varied, but in the drive for modernity, immigration policies and nation-states' behavior vis-à-vis migrants converged all over the world.

Quite generally, the internationalism of the 1920s was not just advanced by a cosmopolitan creed. Some of its cutting-edge elements appear highly dubious from today's perspective, even if they were perceived as particularly modern at the time. Eugenicists cooperated across the globe and convened at various points, most notably at the International Congresses of Eugenics of 1921 and 1932, both hosted in New York City. In these exchanges, the United States served as an important link between European and Latin American debates, and with plans of Pan-American cooperation on eugenics failing, the United States oriented itself more toward the North Atlantic than the Western Hemisphere. In their struggle to "improve the breed," nativists, racists, and eugenicists could not help cooperating across national borders. Alongside cosmopolitanism, the language of race became a truly globalized vernacular.[64]

America's World

In 1918, Wilson became the first US president to pay an official visit beyond the Western Hemisphere. In mid-Atlantic, on his way to the Paris peace conference, he mused about the role that the United States played in the world. His close collaborator George Creel later recalled Wilson's thoughts:

> It is to America that the whole world turns to-day, not only with its wrongs, but with its hopes and grievances. . . . Yet you know, and I know, that these ancient wrongs, these present unhappinesses, are not to be remedied in a day or with a wave of the hand. What I seem to see—with all my heart I hope that I am wrong—is a tragedy of disappointment.[65]

Nobody knows if Wilson really uttered these prophetic and millenarian phrases, but it was true that the United States now wielded more power than ever before, even if its role remained somewhat veiled. America soon had the most dynamic economy, the largest lending resources, and a cultural model that was associated with modernity. It did not simply inherit the hegemonic role that Britain had played in the nineteenth century; instead, its capacity to exert global influence was unprecedented.[66] America was the main force refueling the sputtering motor of globalization after the rupture of the war. Its new role and global connections were about more than just GDP, trade flows, and foreign investments. They were also about hopes, aspirations, and models, or more precisely, about hairstyles and skyscrapers, suburbs and Hollywood divas. They were about finding a new way of life, about modernity with its gospel of progress and prosperity. "Scientific" racism, eugenics, and xenophobia were ingredients in this cauldron—the project of building confident, powerful, and rationally designed nation-states. On some of these issues, like "racial purity," the United States was on the bandwagon rather than spearheading developments, and in the 1920s it was still unclear whether the American version and vision of modernity would rule the day—a version that was in itself paradoxical and highly ambivalent, revealing a deep insecurity about the United States' position in the world.[67] Even the most parochial position had parallels in other corners of the globe, and was often informed by thinkers and practices elsewhere. In their quest for stability and authenticity, for ethnic purity and national strength, such views and practices are best characterized, ironically, as cultural hybrids.

The destination of the first official foreign trip by an American president, Europe, has to be seen as symptomatic. During the 1920s, the Old World remained the main external intellectual reference point for the United States, both in the connections it made and the ones it unmade. This holds true for its financial links as well as its market empire and the mutual exchange of ideas and people. America's doors had been closed to Asian immigrants for quite some time already, and the United States was now becoming more restrictive to some Europeans, but still most of the American discussion about the nation's place in the world revolved around the Old World. On the other side of the North Atlantic, Europeans began to abandon their presumptuous habit of seeing themselves as central. Instead, an increasing number closely watched the United States, and some acknowledged its new centrality. For people in many other parts of the world, the United States appeared as a fresh alternative to the European domination that they had come to know so well. As such, fascination about and proclivity toward America during the 1920s outweighed the disappointment that Wilson had dreaded. But this was soon to change.

The Crisis and Its Origins

Before the stock exchange opened on October 24, 1929, storm clouds had been gathering over Wall Street for several weeks. Markets had been unstable and nervous, and the Dow Jones Industrial Average had been trending down since its all-time peak some seven weeks before. The day started rather quietly, with firm prices but high trading volumes. By eleven, the atmosphere had changed dramatically. Shareholders suddenly panicked, with no obvious catalyst, no event or piece of information that had not been available the day before. "Black Thursday" then saw a landslide of sell orders, with almost thirteen million shares traded—four times more than on a normal day. Together with "Black Tuesday" the following week, this was the most devastating stock market crash in the history of the United States.[68]

Still, contemporary perceptions and economic processes remained ambivalent. In October 1929, people were not aware that they had entered a new phase in history. Wall Street bankers and Washington politicians were deeply worried, of course. Knowing how much psychology affects any crisis, they sought to calm the population. On October 25, 1929, President Hoover tried to reassure the public by emphasizing that the economy stood "on a very sound and prosperous basis."[69] Commentators like tycoon John D. Rockefeller or star economist Waddill Catchings made similar statements. The *New York Sun* concluded: "No Manhattan housewife took the kettle off the kitchen stove because Consolidated Gas went down to 109. Nobody put his car up for the winter because General Motors sold 40 points below the year's high."[70] And indeed, things did not look that bad. Contrary to the widely held belief, the crash did not involve a wave of suicides. While stock prices continued to slide in November, the index had recovered almost half its losses by April 1930.[71] As Peter Temin has shown, American business remained confident after the events of October 1929; journals such as *Business Week* were discussing a recovery by summer 1930.[72] To some, Black Thursday looked more like the healthy correction of a speculative fever than the herald of a crushing maelstrom.

Moreover, immediate global repercussions remained limited. Information did not travel as quickly as it does today. News about Black Thursday reached most Europeans, Asians, and Africans only the day after, which explains why even today non-Americans often associate the crash with a Friday. More important, Wall Street's meltdown did not spawn similar panics in Europe, Asia, or elsewhere. In London and Paris, experts even welcomed the news from New York. Between 1925 and 1929, the Dow Jones had risen by 250 percent, thus attracting many investors who otherwise would have placed their money in the Old World. Viscount Rothermere, the mighty British press baron, complained that "scores of thousands of American shares are bought everyday in London alone" and that Europeans quite generally were "pouring money into New York as fast as the cable can carry it."[73] Now that the bubble had burst, this crash seemed almost an act of poetic justice.

On the whole, the ramifications of the Wall Street crash were not properly understood at the time. The crash was largely an American phenomenon, yet its consequences even for the United States were ambiguous, and those for other parts of the world were still more so. Black Thursday epitomizes the irrationality of financial markets, but on a causal level it did not bring about "the end of an era."[74] It was neither the sole trigger of the global Great Depression nor its main cause. Both for the United States and the wider world, it was instead a symptom and symbol of a larger, much more complex process of economic contraction. The origins and causes as well as catalysts of the Great Depression were manifold, and traversed national and regional frontiers. That Black Thursday is still synonymous with the Great Slump mainly comes down to its emblematic power.

War Debts, Reparations, and Foreign Loans

If 1929 was more the symbol, what then was the real starting point or trigger of the Great Depression? Several of the true origins of the crisis hark back to World War I and hence to yet another global event, or had even deeper historical roots. In all of them, the United States was key, both for its actions and omissions.

International war debts and reparations represented a toxic legacy of the Great War, impacting heavily on the economy of the 1920s and 1930s. When the guns began to speak in August 1914, all sides had expected a rather brief conflict, ideally over by Christmas. Instead, the war dragged on for more than four years and was extremely expensive in financial as well as human terms. No nation had been prepared for such a burden, and the states involved responded by increasing taxes, issuing government bonds, taking out loans, and extracting foreign property in occupied areas. Germany, soon cut off from international money markets, amassed the largest domestic public debt of all the warring nations. But Britain and France also accumulated large international debts, particularly to the United States. By 1918, their liabilities amounted to some $8.5 billion, and America held foreign public obligations worth another $3.2 billion from other countries. This made the United States the largest international moneylender for the war effort. France owed another $3 billion to Britain, while both states lent large sums to their subsidiary allies, such as Russia, Italy, Serbia, and the British dominions, including Australia and Canada. Due to imperial connections, other large parts of the world also became dependent on American loans. This created a complex web of liabilities that spanned the globe, interlocking the fates of societies as never before. Furthermore, these dynamics put America in an unprecedented position as the world's banker.[75]

America's crucial role as the world's creditor was further strengthened during the 1920s by its trade policy. The United States was happy to export, but the Fordney-McCumber Act of 1922 drastically increased its tariffs, according to some calculations, from 26.8 percent to 38.2 percent to shield its domestic markets. This left debtor countries facing problems selling their products in America and consequently servicing their loans.[76]

German reparations came on top. At the time, it was normal practice for the defeated side in a war to compensate the victors through reparations. The unprecedented all-encompassing quality of the war coupled with the enormous suffering and costs it entailed raised astronomical expectations as to the level of reparations on both sides of the trenches. Had Germany won, the entente nations would have suffered severely. Nor were France and Britain conciliatory in this regard. In the United Kingdom's "khaki election" of December 1918—roughly a month after the end of the war—"Hang the Kaiser" and "Make Germany Pay" were popular slogans.[77] The Versailles treaty did not state a specific sum for reparations, and debates on how much Germany would have to pay under what conditions dragged on for more than a decade. This irksome uncertainty combined with the austerity imposed by the Weimar Republic in order to satisfy the demands fueled German nationalism and helped to pave the way for Nazism.[78]

Besides destabilizing Europe's postwar order, reparations also impacted negatively on the world economy. With its negative trade balance, Germany was unable to pay in full. It had to take out loans, mainly from the United States, to pay its former European enemies, and the Weimar Republic became the world's largest borrower over the course of the 1920s. The United

States provided Germany with the funds to pay its reparations; these payments, in turn, became the backbone of Allied debt repayments to America. New debts were made to pay old ones. This circular arrangement worked well for some years, but it was fragile. Farsighted observers had pointed out some of the intricacies of the situation early on. In 1919, for instance, British economist John Maynard Keynes warned that the oppressive financial burden on Germany threatened Europe's entire financial and economic equilibrium. Roughly a decade later, when the whole system ground to a halt, the global ramifications became crucial.[79]

The key to the debt and reparation problems did not lie in Paris, London, or Berlin but rather in New York and Washington. Washington long refused to acknowledge the link between German reparations and the Anglo-French war debts. Legally, this position was watertight: the US government had never asked for reparations, and since the Senate had refused to ratify the Versailles treaty, none of its stipulations were binding on the United States. The former allies simply had to pay their debts to America, no matter where they found the money. Thus, any American appeal to ease Germany's reparations went hand in hand with declarations that this could not imply any reduction of inter-Allied war debts. This position was not only consistent but also reflected domestic budgetary constraints, since the debt repayments represented a substantial part of the federal budget and affected important commercial interests.[80]

The intricacies of this international financial system became fully apparent in the late 1920s. In 1928, US monetary policy became more restrictive in response to the first signs of the doldrums. Foreign lending was reduced, with the trend accelerating in 1929. The effects on other nations whose economies relied heavily on American money were severe. A closer look at the structure and timing of capital movements around the world reveals that the drying up of US capital exports was usually not the cause, yet it only deepened a crisis that often had strong homegrown roots.[81] Still, by pulling the plug, America exported and exacerbated the global crisis. Due to the entanglement that war debts, reparations, and normal monetary relations had created, Europe was particularly affected, but repercussions also spread to other shores. Australia is a good illustration: on the eve of the Depression, it was heavily indebted to British banks, and through London, the New York crisis quickly reached the avenues of Sydney and farm roads in Tasmania.[82] In India, credit lines through the local *bania* or *sowcar* were so efficient that the crisis reached every last village.[83]

Whereas war loans and reparations mainly concerned Europe and its colonies, Canada along with Central and South America were also heavily indebted to the United States. Paradoxically, the strong direct US interest in these parts of the world lessened the effects of the crisis in Central America, whereas South America was hit hard, as the example of Argentina demonstrates. Between 1925 and 1929, foreign debt repayments amounted to 31 percent of the gross exports. After US lending dried up, the crisis was felt immediately, and was further aggravated by crop failures in 1929–30.[84]

Certainly there were no easy choices to be made. America's web of foreign debts and loans had contributed to the prosperity of the 1920s. The blanket cancellation of war debts or foreign loans would have meant political suicide at home. Having said that, the United States was not a hardhearted Shylock, blind to the grievances of others. For instance, it played an instrumental role in several rounds of renegotiating German reparations, leading to the Hoover Moratorium of 1931 and the Lausanne Conference the year after that ended German payments. But when it came to war debts and normal foreign loans, America refused to compromise: France defaulted in 1932, followed by Belgium, Greece, Hungary, and Poland. Britain chose the same path in mid-1934. Nevertheless, the United States continued to insist on every last cent. It did not break the deadlock by facilitating an overall solution for both war debts and negotiations.[85]

Overall, the responsibility placed on American shoulders was immense. Obviously, neither the war nor the debts, reparations, or other foreign loans had been primarily America's responsibility, but by withdrawing substantial funds from other parts of the world from the late 1920s on, the United States contributed substantially to spreading the crisis across the globe. Faced with these challenges, the American economic and political elite prioritized short-term domestic needs, even if in the medium term this approach would boomerang. On the eve of the Great Depression, America was not yet ready for bold leadership and cooperation in stabilizing the world economy.

The Mysticism of Gold

Another link to a globally shared past was closely connected to war debts and reparations: the gold standard system. During the last third of the nineteenth century, many of the world's leading currencies had adopted this form of monetary system, creating an international framework of fixed exchange rates and currencies convertible into gold. This scheme worked remarkably well prior to 1914, guaranteeing monetary stability and generating economic growth around the globe, but it became one of the much-deplored victims of World War I. After 1918, it took more than a decade to reinstitute the system—and then in a less effective form.

Charles Kindleberger famously described the difference. Prior to 1914, the Bank of England stabilized the global system through effective management, especially an anticyclic foreign-lending policy, and played the role of the lender of last resort. The interwar years, in contrast, saw Britain too weak to stabilize the system and the United States unwilling to take over the responsibility. While Kindleberger's interpretation is generally correct, others have added nuance. Barry Eichengreen has argued that the prewar gold standard was both decentralized and multipolar, with Paris and Berlin in particular challenging London's role. Indeed, the old gold standard was vulnerable; even prior to 1914, it did not function automatically. The Bank of England always remained the center of gravity and was looked on as such, but it could not have acted unilaterally as lender of last resort. In sum, it behaved more like a team captain than an absolute monarch.[86] After 1918, in contrast, this position remained unfilled.

It took quite some time to reinstitute the international gold standard. Not until 1929 had almost all the nations that left the system in 1914 returned to it, with the Soviet Union, China, and Turkey the most notable exceptions.[87] Members of the gold club attributed an almost mythical quality to the gold system as a factor of international stability and prosperity. During the Great Depression, the gold standard's absence was also held as the reason for the doldrums. This high esteem for the gold system also dominated in the United States, which had never been forced to abandon it in the first place.

The hope of returning to prewar stability soon proved to be illusory. After 1918, important players, most notably the United States, disregarded central factors of the old standard's success. If, in the prewar system, gold flowed into a country—for instance, as a consequence of high interest rates—this resulted in a pressure on the price level in that nation and allowed some of this gold to flow out again. America now simply stashed most of the gold away in its reserves and thus impeded its free flow—something that contemporaries called "gold sterilization." Certainly, the US Federal Reserve was not the only player to break the unwritten rules of gold orthodoxy. The Banque de France opted for a similar course, but since much less gold flowed into France, it was America's sterilization policy that mattered most. By the end of the decade, the United States had amassed nearly 40 percent of the global gold reserves.[88] This policy helped to insulate the nation's domestic economy from the consequences of the gold system and its politicians from making hard choices, such as raising interest rates in order to maintain the global gold standard system. Unlike their cosmopolitan counterparts on the other side of the North Atlantic who—especially until 1914—had run the show like an old-fashioned gentlemen's club, many American reserve city bankers came from the interior and had little time for international considerations. Instead, the local interests of a nation of farmers and manufacturers ruled the day, particularly after the death in 1928 of Benjamin Strong. Strong, the governor of the Federal Reserve Bank of New York, was an advocate of international cooperation, and he sometimes disappeared for several months to Europe, including extended vacations with his British counterpart, Montagu Norman. His successor,

George L. Harrison, a Yale graduate and Skull and Bones member, was affable and easygoing, but he never allowed himself such extravagances.[89]

To be sure, idealism did not rule the day internationally, and Harrison's colleagues in other countries also often prioritized their own national interests. Intriguingly, compared to autocracies, democracies seem to have been generally less responsive to international needs and more receptive to domestic pressures.[90] Even if America simply did the same as all the others, the effects were more adverse. Only the United States had the potential to play a leading role as the lender of last resort. As opposed to taking on this role, the Federal Reserve by and large acted restrictively. In 1929, the New York Federal Reserve, as the US central bank, launched some open market operations, but was soon put in its place by Washington, which insisted that the ultimate responsibility for monetary policy rested with the federal government. Haggling over competences aside, this step can best be explained by an economic doctrine that soon proved outdated and a rather inward-looking approach to monetary policy. Through its inaction, the United States therefore worsened the crisis. Beyond this aspect of American responsibility, the gold standard proved to be outmoded as an instrument of monetary affairs because it presupposed a level of international leadership and cooperation, credibility, and even largesse that was no longer available.[91]

This was to have drastic global consequences. In order to pay for war debts, reparations, and even normal imports, governments across the world were forced to pay with their gold reserves, which they actually needed in their central banks for currency management. In a situation of global crisis, the gold standard proved to be a straitjacket, prohibiting national governments from actively stimulating employment and consumption. Beyond certain expert circles, alternatives to the gold standard system were mostly identified with inflation—the specter of the early postwar years.[92] The deflationary pressure of the existing system was seen as the lesser evil, even if this strain grew tremendously when America started to repatriate its overseas funds. Without easily available dollars, the shortcomings of capitalist economies around the world became more visible, and this further accelerated the downward spiral. States, no matter if they were democracies like Britain under Ramsey MacDonald or authoritarian like the Shōwa in Japan, generally reacted by drastically curtailing domestic spending. While this was the only option consistent with maintaining the gold standard, it had devastating effects both for these countries themselves and for the world economy. As one of the last states to return to the gold standard in 1930, Japan felt the effects of this rigid framework. Finance Minister Inoue Junnosuke considered it a question of national pride to fully obey the rules of gold orthodoxy. A severe depression followed immediately, and in 1932, ultranationalists assassinated Inoue.[93] On the eve of the Great Slump, only a small group of experts criticized this "mysticism of gold," as Russian exile Wladimir Woytinsky put it in a letter to Keynes.[94] All in all, the gold standard and disorderly financial markets more generally acted as international transmission belts for monetary deflation.

The United States was not always the starting point of such domino effects, and some have even contended that the primary impulse that turned the doldrums into the *Great* Depression came from Europe.[95] In May 1931, mainly homegrown problems at Austria's largest bank, Credit-Anstalt, sparked a European banking crisis. From there, the malaise soon spread to Hungary, Czechoslovakia, Romania, Poland, and Germany. Panic swept from the continent to Great Britain, which was forced off the gold standard in September, and on to America, where speculators presumed that the dollar would be next. American depositors withdrew their savings, fearing a banking collapse, and gold was moved abroad by foreigners afraid that America would also leave the gold standard. The Fed, however, did not yield to this pressure; instead, it raised interest rates and accelerated the decline in the money supply. Consequently, interest rates rose markedly, with a detrimental effect on industrial production. The Fed's reaction to a crisis spreading from Europe and exacerbated by the gold standard was, in short, the main reason why the situation turned from bad to worse in America.[96]

The internationally shared belief in the gold standard ultimately did not cause the crisis but aggravated it. Without actively seeking the role, the United States stood at the center of global economic attention. There was a huge tension built into the epigonic postwar gold standard, which could not replicate the halcyon days of an earlier wave of globalization. America alone had the means to assume leadership and reduce this pressure, but it soft-pedaled its commitment to the wider world. Actors across the globe were trapped in believing in a system that no longer worked. The tendency to isolate and save one's own hide first was strong in all markets—and tragically, this intensified the crisis for everyone.

The Crisis of Agriculture

The third main dimension of the Great Depression besides the problems of debts and reparations along with the gold standard was the crisis of agriculture, which also had its origins in World War I. The global conflict destroyed large agricultural areas and cut off countries from their established supply chains. The average wartime output was one-third lower than prewar levels in France, Germany, and Austria, and some theaters such as the fields of Flanders ceased to produce beef or wheat, and instead specialized in crosses and poppies, as eternalized in the poem by Canadian lieutenant colonel John McCrae (1872–1918).[97]

Paradoxically, surplus and not want soon became the pressing problem: given the shortages, new suppliers quickly stepped in to fill the gaps. Comparing the periods from 1909 to 1914 and 1924 to 1929, wheat acreage more than doubled in Canada, and increased by nine million acres (roughly the area of farmland today in Alabama) in the United States.[98] Moreover, agricultural production in all industrialized countries surged due to progress in mechanization and the intense use of chemical fertilizers, even if the real breakthrough on this front was not to come until World War II. This combination of technological progress and war-induced demand as a global phenomenon reshaped landscapes all over the world. In the United States, for instance, it accelerated the shift from the small farms in the east to large-scale mechanized farming further west. Epitomizing the change, more than one million tractors tilled the American soil on the eve of the Depression; in 1910, by contrast, there had only been some one thousand.[99] Hence, it was not only the doughboys from Kansas fighting on the Marne and Meuse who symbolized new global entanglements but also their parents and siblings back home who expanded their harvests to compensate production falls in Europe.

These changes came at great cost, even if one leaves aside the ecological problems they entailed. American farm debt jumped from $3.3 billion in 1910 to $9.4 billion in 1925, mainly as farmers borrowed money to purchase additional land. These debts in turn led to foreclosures, with about every sixth American farm affected between 1921 and 1929. Several decades later, an interviewee recalled his childhood in Iowa, where at such a foreclosure the family members "were forced off, and all their household goods were sold. Even family pictures." Despite the passing of time, he recalled the scene with "morbid fascination."[100] Due to the decentralized setup of the American banking system, small rural banks were often sucked into the agricultural crisis, with their failures later exacerbating the banking panic of the early 1930s. During the 1920s, the situation worsened further as increasing global agricultural production failed to find customers, at least not in the Western part of the world, particularly once world output had returned to prewar levels by the mid-1920s.[101]

The crisis of agriculture also hit other countries, especially Argentina, Australia, Canada, India, New Zealand, and the Union of South Africa, as the other major agricultural exporters. The preceding lending boom and an element of speculation contributed to the deterioration in these regions, too. Even if the situation varied between countries and commodities, the perspectives for agriculture in most places were quite bleak by the late 1920s. For wheat, for instance, global stocks rose from 1925. An attempt at international coordination at the World Economic Conference in 1927 failed—as did a series of no less than twenty other international conferences between 1930 and 1933. Consequently, global prices slipped, accelerating into a steep fall from 1929 onward.[102]

The abrupt fall in prices did not just affect agricultural commodities but also raw materials such as rubber. The infamous Stevenson plan of 1922 in British Malaya and Ceylon created a system of price supports that guaranteed the existence of a highly profitable rubber industry for Britain, which at the time controlled some 75 percent of the rubber production. With the United States consuming almost the same proportion, the revenues of the rubber industry were important for Britain paying its war debts to America, but strong protections sparked overproduction. This process was intensified by American schemes to extract resources from other parts of the world—so as to break the British monopoly, safeguard American business interests, and guarantee free access to raw materials. As a result, rubber prices collapsed after 1929, and one finds similar trajectories for other commodities such as copper, nickel, and nitrates. So there were powerful links between rubber trees overlooking the Indian Ocean, London's need to pay for the Lee Enfield rifles deployed in 1917, the tires moving Ford's Model T, the 1926 opening of the world's biggest rubber plantation in Liberia by the American Firestone company, and the consequential plight of rubber tappers in Brazil, Liberia, Ceylon, and the Dutch East Indies.[103] Debt and low prices—and much less overproduction itself, as is often claimed—thus were highly detrimental to the world agricultural situation.[104] What is more, these factors added layers to the global financial and economic connections and dependencies, making the world even more vulnerable.

Agriculture also had its own weight: the United States was still a strongly agricultural country during the 1920s. In 1929, farming accounted for one-quarter of the active workforce, and exports for 28 percent of farm income. Agriculture was in fact more dependent on a functioning world market than most other sectors of the US economy. The same holds true for countries as diverse as Argentina and Algeria, India and Denmark, New Zealand and Uruguay. Overall, 40 percent of world trade was in agricultural products, and flows of cotton, wheat, veal, and coffee connected the world almost as much as the less visible financial streams.[105]

After the Wall Street crash, and even more so after mid-1931, American finance recalled its loans from the US farming sector and other parts of the world. Most farmers around the globe were indebted and now found themselves unable to make repayments. Indirectly, the crash also impacted international trade. Agricultural commerce was a market of confidence. Most commodities were shipped on consignment rather than paid in advance, and after the crash confidence that goods would find their customer collapsed.[106] Financial problems dovetailed with the instability of agriculture and other raw material markets long before 1929, but the liquidity problem and lack of confidence after 1929 fully short-circuited them. A card was removed from the bottom layer, and the entire house of cards collapsed.

The World Cut Off

How did the United States react to the international crisis? After a decade of ambivalence vis-à-vis the wider world, its position stiffened, and it now cut many of its wider global links. Explaining the main causes of the crisis to the American people in December 1930, Hoover insisted that "in the larger view the major forces of the depression now lie outside of the United States, and our recuperation has been retarded by the unwarranted degree of fear and apprehension created by these outside forces." To make sure that nobody misunderstood, he went on, adding, "Had there been no other malign forces in the world, the American depression to all appearances had run its course."[107] Hoover's statement, months before the 1931 banking crisis in Europe, totally misrepresented the course of events, but demonstrated a certain mind-set in Washington. In a similar vein Herbert Feis, economic adviser for international affairs to the Department of State under Hoover, asserted, "Never again should we lend or invest our money in foreign lands."[108] While most academic economists disliked Hoover's approach for its nationalist overtones and because it contradicted their neoclassical understanding, government officials were quick to find their scapegoat abroad, and such views resonated well with the way that Americans tended to perceive the wider world in the first place.[109]

The Smoot-Hawley Act of 1930 epitomized America's official response. Building on the Fordney-McCumber tariff of 1922, the act raised US tariffs on over twenty thousand imported goods to record levels, thereby protecting American production from foreign competition. Smoot-Hawley also introduced instruments such as quotas, which further restricted trade. To be fair, President Hoover was a determined opponent of the bill, but yielded to business leaders and his party under the impact of the recession. Pressure came primarily from the industrialized Northeast, where Samuel M. Vauclain, president of the Baldwin Locomotive Works of Philadelphia, declared that a "protective tariff is necessary if we are to have full dinner pails for our boys."[110] Such circles had been demanding more protection when business was still good, and with the advent of the Depression the pendulum swung in their direction. Still, the new course remained highly contested. Even though it was a Republican initiative, thirteen Republican senators opposed the bill after it passed the House of Representatives, and a petition signed by more than one thousand American economists asked President Hoover to veto it.[111] Harvard economist Sumner Slichter went so far as to call the tariff "an act of almost incredible economic folly" because it ignored the "interdependence of nations," and "we cannot add to the world's disaster without inflicting injury upon ourselves."[112] Still, Hoover did not falter. In 1932, Democrats and progressive Republicans drafted legislation to revise Smoot-Hawley in favor of international cooperation. Their bill passed both houses, but Hoover vetoed it, not least because he opposed the call for international negotiations. Even if he had disliked the tariff before, he now stressed that tariff matters were "solely a domestic question in protection of our own people."[113] In the end, the well-traveled Hoover, who had lived in Australia, China, and Britain, pursued a nation-centered approach and failed to take a stand against the rising tide of protectionism.

Smoot-Hawley was not a major cause of the Depression in the United States, at least not directly in the short term.[114] Economic historians have convincingly argued that the law's effect on American trade was rather marginal, with dutiable imports standing only at 1.4 percent of the GDP. Even the highest duty could not have had a great impact on the domestic market. For other countries dependent on exporting to the United States, however, the new tariff bore drastic consequences, and this is what many US historians overlook.[115] Cuba's colonial ties to the United States now became a noose. The country was highly dependent on sugarcane exports to the United States, but after Smoot-Hawley, these collapsed from 3.5 million tons in 1929 to less than 1 million in 1933.[116] Cuban *colonos* (cane growers) suffered severely, and the new tariff became one of the main reasons for the Cuban Revolution of 1933 that toppled the pro-American government. Some countries with more diversified economic structures were equally affected. In Canada, the tariff frustrated earlier hopes that its own low-tariff posture would inspire a similar course from the United States. Smoot-Hawley offended everybody, from the halibut fishermen of the eastern provinces to the potato growers of Ontario, the ranchers of the prairies and the western provinces, and the timber and fruit producers of British Columbia and Alberta. In the election of 1930, Canada swung from a liberal, pro-Washington policy to a protectionist, more pro-British course in response to Smoot-Hawley.[117] Protectionism thus immediately boomeranged on the United States, just as Slichter and others had predicted. The tariff decoupled the country from the wider world—including its direct neighbors—more than even its supporters had hoped.

Also beyond the Western Hemisphere, Smoot-Hawley poisoned the economic climate. America's trading partners denounced the measure even before it became law, and enacted retaliation and discrimination against American export interests. The day after Hoover signed the bill into law, the Spanish government published a communiqué announcing that due to "the gravity of the situation created by the new tariff law for Spanish exporters," it was considering taking similar steps in retaliation.[118] Less than a week later, Spain had its Wais Tariff, which was particularly harmful to the American automobile industry.[119]

Another factor amplified the impact of tariffs: they were fixed in monetary terms, independent of the volume of goods. With the level of trade faltering, the ratio of import duties collected to the value of imports rose steadily. Moreover, a growing number of countries abandoned the gold standard from 1931 onward, thus revaluing their currencies. Exchange rates—and hence prices—could fluctuate substantially, creating an incentive to trade only within one currency or currency bloc. When Britain left the gold standard in September 1931, India, Iraq, Portugal, and other countries immediately followed suit. Some did so voluntarily; in other cases, such as India, it reflected British control in the context of empire and occurred against the wishes of many Indians.[120] At the same time, these countries pegged their currencies to sterling in order to limit exchange rate uncertainty within the new group. Britain also established a protectionist tariff area with some of its Commonwealth partners at the Ottawa conference in summer 1932. Soon, the world saw another group of countries, mainly in central and southeastern Europe, with nonconvertible currencies tied to the German reichsmark, which had practically left the gold standard in mid-1931. Conversely, a group of gold standard countries chose to center around France. The creation of trade and currency blocs was a variation of economic nationalism in its pure form. Intrabloc trade somewhat reduced the impact of the Depression, and gave Britain and Germany preponderance vis-à-vis their respective partners. The incentives for interbloc trade, on the other hand, shrank, and this link between trade and currency further accelerated the downward spiral in global trade.[121] By 1932, the world was deeply divided into competing monetary and trading blocs; it had taken less than three years to break the global links created in the previous decade and the prewar wave of globalization. Taking 1929 as a baseline of one hundred, world trade fell to thirty-five in 1933, and twenty-eight two years later. Economically, the world had been torn apart.[122]

Was this all America's fault? The US tariff was high by international comparison, but not an outlier. Levels in most of Latin America as well as Spain or Czechoslovakia were far higher.[123] It also is quite difficult to compare the overall effect of protectionism because of the sophisticated alternatives and supplements to tariffs that countries developed. France, for instance, worked with restrictive lists from which its domestic importers had to buy; for some commodities, states insisted on mandatory blending with homegrown production, and for others, protectionism was disguised as hygiene standards. There were no limits to the inventiveness of lobbyists and experts, and in comparison America's trade policy was not exceptional.[124] Furthermore, the United States still clung to the gold standard in the early 1930s, and therefore avoided pursuing an outright policy of building currency or trade blocs like the two biggest European economies, Britain and Germany. The US decision at the time to stick to gold was seen as a sign of international commitment, and it was a choice that became increasingly costly as an ever-increasing number of countries abandoned the gold standard. In its reaction to the crisis, America's policy was far from extreme.

So Smoot-Hawley was not the only reason for the surge to protectionism during the early 1930s. In light of the economic crisis, mutual suspicion and mistrust penetrated the veneer of international cooperation established after the Great War. Instead of a harmonious vision of an integrated and prosperous world built on capitalism and cooperation, most governments and societies reverted to prioritizing narrowly defined national interests and protectionism—a philosophy in which conflict formed the natural law of interaction.

Yet despite this shared turn to self-seclusion, Smoot-Hawley stood out. Due to its centrality in global economics, America's self-centered policy accelerated the widespread tendency to solve economic problems by trade measures, and reinforced the world's descent into beggar-thy-neighbor protectionism, nationalism, and the creation of separate trade blocs. The drawn-out negotiations preceding the legislation already created great uncertainty about the future of trade policy at the international level. What is more, the protectionist discourse in America concentrated on short-term effects for the United States, as if the country's global connections did not exist. America was the only country with enough leverage to change the course of international trade policy, even if its position in this field was not quite as towering as at the financial level. Only in the long run did America learn its lesson. After World War II, the United States and other countries actively sought to prevent such a surge of trade protectionism. The Bretton Woods Agreement of 1944 and the General Agreement on Tariffs and Trade of 1947 lowered global tariffs as well as created platforms for international negotiations on these issues. Such a will for cooperation had been dearly missing in the early 1930s.[125]

In the interwar years, the Great Depression challenged the very fabric of economies and policies, putting capitalism to the test (as a model firmly associated with the United States). Bishops in Latin America castigated the greed of speculators, the unemployed in Europe turned to the Radical Right or Left, and farmers in India and other parts of Asia deplored the impact of a money-driven global economy.

There seemed to be a clear-cut alternative: while most economies were stagnating or faltering, the Soviet Union trumpeted rapid growth. This obviously does not mean that Moscow championed free trade; quite the contrary. As a planned socialist economy, the Soviet Union instituted a foreign trade monopoly as early as April 1918, in the midst of the revolution. This extreme form of state intervention, supported by radical violence within the country, shielded the Soviet economy from competition. Even if its expansion of trade at times made it vulnerable to global developments, it strove for a form of semiautarky that decoupled domestic from world market prices.[126] In light of the Great Slump, Moscow's propaganda underscoring the superiority of its system appeared to stand to reason, and its state monopoly system was soon adopted by Persia. A highly diverse group of countries including Belgium, Czechoslovakia, Estonia, Switzerland, Turkey, and Uruguay also created monopolies. State intervention and protectionism as opposed to small government and free trade were the fashion of the day. This trend brought societies around the world closer to the Soviet model than to the version of modernity that America had spearheaded during the 1920s.[127]

The story of Robert Robinson summarizes the trend: a blue-collar worker of Jamaican origin living in Detroit, Robinson was offered a job in Stalingrad, with almost double the pay, rent-free quarters, a maid, thirty days of paid annual vacation, a car, and free passage to and from Soviet Russia. While Ford laid off workers due to the Great Depression, twenty-three-year-old Robinson believed that he had made the right choice in migrating to the Soviet Union, where the only racism he encountered came from his white American coworkers and where he would soon find himself nominated to sit on the Moscow Soviet, the Communist council in the city. Particularly for minorities, the Soviet experiment seemed to offer an appealing alternative to the hardships of second-class citizenship at home.[128]

Also at a cultural level, America had lost much of its splendor: Egyptians, for instance, were disappointed that the United States failed to support their struggle for self-determination. Increasingly, this feeling mixed with resistance against American missionaries and archaeologists who were rewriting the country's history—a trend nourished by the discovery in the early 1920s of Tutankhamun's tomb, which had first triggered a brief Egyptian fad in US popular culture. Instead of a source of hope, national elites in Egypt now perceived of the United States as a threat.[129] For anticolonial movements, the Depression was just one more reason to challenge the idea of Western supremacy. Pan-Africanism increasingly came under the influence of communist and socialist ideas, and, after 1931, the world saw the revival of an aggressive version of pan-Asian rhetoric in Japan.[130] Meanwhile, European intellectuals, who had always viewed America with ambivalence, became ever more critical of the United States, and published books with titles such as *The Crisis of Capitalism in America*, *The American Cancer*, and even *America's Abomination*. America's time as a leader and role model seemed over before it had really begun.[131]

At the same time, it would be wrong to infer that international cooperation came to a complete standstill. Central banks and the newly created Bank of International Settlements supported Austria in May 1931, joined by the Bank of England one month later. Germany received international help the same month—in this case, including the Federal Reserve—and June brought the Hoover moratorium, which foreshadowed the end of German reparation payments. Beyond that, there were bilateral negotiations and global plans to deal with war reparations, debts, and international finance as well as trade issues.[132] The League of Nations held three major international economic conferences, in 1927, 1929, and 1930, which were all aimed at reducing nontariff trade barriers and preventing further increases in protectionism. While all three failed, the conferences were certainly an international attempt to avert the Depression.

The new institutions that had emerged from Versailles not only became the central forums for all attempts at international cooperation but also provided clearinghouses of global expertise. Their work intensified substantially in the wake of the Depression, increasing the level of international exchange. Studies and resolutions offered guidance and created statistical yardsticks. The World Economic Conference of 1927, for instance, concluded that "tariffs, though within the sovereign jurisdiction of the separate States, are not a matter of purely domestic interest but greatly influence the trade of the world."[133] With the implications of excessive protectionism fully spelled out, political elites obviously knew what consequences their actions would entail. It was particularly against this backdrop that the disregard for the wider world displayed by Hoover and many others appeared so obnoxious and selfish.

Long-term historical lessons were also learned from the failures of internationalism in the early 1930s. The Bank for International Settlements, for example, was an instrument of central bank cooperation. This approach failed in 1931, and any successful interventions did not come through the central banks but rather through the ministries of finance and their stabilization funds. Ideas antithetical to the central bank influenced the postwar order, in which the International Monetary Fund (IMF) was governed through the ministries of finance, and not the central banks.[134] Another long-term reverberation involved French foreign minister Aristide Briand's plan for European economic and political integration, which he presented to the League of Nations in fall 1929. His idea was not taken up, yet it was not forgotten. Today's European Union cites it as one of its blueprints, and beyond the level of rhetoric, important political lessons for European integration were learned through the failure of Briand's plan.[135] More successfully at the regional European level, the Oslo Convention of 1930 led to economic and political cooperation between the Netherlands, Denmark, Norway, Sweden, Belgium, and Luxembourg, and later on also Finland, with a smaller group intermittently even seeking mutual tariff reduction.[136]

Evidently, certain mechanisms were in place to avert a downward spiral. Besides international organizations and the expertise that they generated, the latest technologies also facilitated communication. Hoover described this in his recollection of the European banking crisis of June 1931:

> During this period and subsequent weeks, I was in hourly touch with our representatives in London, Paris, Berlin, and Vienna by transatlantic telephone, and they were in similar close touch with one another. It was the first time that such extensive use had been made of the telephone by our government officials.[137]

It is revealing that Hoover only mentioned contact between Americans; at the time, it was unthinkable for an US president to pick up the telephone to negotiate with the heads of governments of Great Britain, France, or any other country. All in all, political elites around the world used the new means primarily to shield their national interests instead of fostering international exchange. America, as the only power that might have changed the course of events, did not take the lead.

Middletown and Marienthal

The effects were corresponding. The Great Depression was not solely an American experience, even if the United States was one of its main origins and particularly hard-hit by its consequences. The slump had global repercussions, and it fundamentally changed the way that Americans and others were connected to and interacted with the wider world. While political reactions tended to separate and segregate, the suffering was shared across latitude and longitude. Moreover, we know more about the distress of the 1930s than of any earlier period, not only for the United States.

In that respect, Muncie, Indiana, in the United States and Marienthal in Austria, for instance, shared a great deal. Beyond poverty, want, and hunger, the Great Depression questioned the very fabric of society, and cast a dark shadow on the future both in Muncie (often considered so quintessentially American that even today reporters travel there to find out what the average American believes) and the small industrial municipality of Marienthal, near Vienna. Pessimism hung over both places. In Muncie, for example, "it does not get better, only worse," as one interviewee put it,[138] while a counterpart in Marienthal observed, "Maybe better times are coming. Personally, I doubt it."[139] While not everybody was affected in the same way, what was shared was a new sense of the fragility of economic growth along with the idea of living "in one of the eras of greatest rapidity of change in the history of human institutions," as a report on Muncie stated.[140]

Both towns stand out for the amount that we know about them. Some at the time still remembered the Long Depression after 1873 as the most severe economic crisis in the Western world up to that point. They even referred to it as the "Great Depression" until the experiences of the 1930s superposed themselves. But for the crisis of the late nineteenth century or any other crisis of capitalism before the 1920s, we do not have contemporary scholarly scrutiny of the quality we find for the Great Depression, especially in the Western world. The way that economic change affected the everyday lives of ordinary people had long remained outside the orbit of academic interest. New techniques refining the legibility of societies had been developed since the 1880s, and the 1920s and 1930s saw another leap to ever more sophisticated forms of expertise. This new knowledge unveiled shocking details and a horrifying picture of the breadth of the crisis, while also supplying ideas on how to overcome it.

Both Muncie and Marienthal were subject to close sociological analysis. Muncie came first. In 1924–25, a team of scholars led by sociologists Robert and Helen Lynd came to the city to study contemporary life in an American community. After publishing their findings in 1929 under the lightly disguised title *Middletown: A Study in Contemporary American Culture*, the Lynds returned in 1935 to see how the community was coping with the crisis. Later, in 1937, they published *Middletown in Transition: A Study in Cultural Conflicts*. Marienthal, on the other hand, was studied by a team around social scientists Paul Lazarsfeld, Marie Lazarsfeld-Jahoda, and Hans Zeisel, who conducted their field research in 1931–32, between the two *Middletown* books, focusing primarily on the social and psychological effects of long-term unemployment. Both teams produced landmark publications in the development of modern sociology.

Developments in the social sciences were both driven by and informed a new political agenda. They went hand in hand with an intensified debate about welfarism and the role of the state in tackling social problems through intervention.[141] Scientific analysis was increasingly seen as a precondition for targeted intervention, while at the same time professionals such as social workers and psychologists were needed to institute these measures. Accruing sociological knowledge became part of the gospel of modernity; many states perceived it as the precondition for efficient and rational government. The Great Depression thus sparked a global debate about the role, responsibility, and resources of state action, and in many societies this led to a quantum leap in interventionism.

If this was the general trend of the time, Muncie and Marienthal also demonstrate that the relationship between new forms of academic knowledge and political action remained complex. Interestingly, the Austrian study refrained from making political recommendations, even though its authors were committed socialists. The scholars reported that long-term unemployment led not to revolt but instead to passive resignation—an interpretation that was proven tragically wrong in Germany during the very months that the book came out, where many of the extremist street fighters in the late Weimar Republic were unemployed men.[142] And although the

Lynds had developed liberal and even leftist ideas by the mid-1930s, their second *Middletown* study stressed the robustness of the values and fabric of American society, confirming the finding of their first study. Neither report argued strongly for state interventionism. Generally, new sociological research did not always easily translate into political action; it coevolved with the new debate about state interventionism, but there was no simple causality at work.

Finally, *Middletown* and *Marienthal* are interesting because they show that experts at the time were part of a global dialogue about the effects of the crisis. They reflected and relied on a well-established network on welfare questions dating back to at least the Progressive era.[143] *Marienthal*, penned in German and published in Leipzig four years after the first *Middletown* study, referred explicitly to the Lynds' findings. The Austrian socialists acclaimed the Lynds' methodological sophistication, yet considered it a "setback" to conceal the name of the city, and lose potential political impact by focusing on the benign aspects of the "healthy upper class" while ignoring rising rates of disease, crime, and suicide.[144] Four years later, when the Lynds published their sequel, they quoted at length from the *Marienthal* study and transferred some of its findings to their own work. In the end, however, they primarily used it to demonstrate that "Middletown's plight in the depression did not begin to approach in seriousness that of Marienthal."[145] A shared transnational space of sociological expertise thus fostered a dialogue on scientific methods and political agendas. Its experts helped to understand the relative depth of the crisis in various parts of the world and situate their own discoveries in a broader realm of possibilities.

And dialogue between the two teams did not stop there. Austria soon became a dangerous place for the socialist authors of *Marienthal*—even more so because Lazarsfeld-Jahoda was Jewish, and Zeisel was married to a Jewish artist. Robert Lynd played a central role in helping Lazarsfeld emigrate to the United States. Lazarsfeld and his by then ex-wife fled the Austrofascist regime before Adolf Hitler's takeover, and Zeisel followed shortly thereafter. All three ended up as professors in the United States: Lazarsfeld at Columbia, after working for some time at the New Deal's figurehead National Youth Administration; Lazarsfeld-Jahoda at New York University, from where she went to Great Britain; and Zeisel at the University of Chicago. By the end of the 1930s, the transatlantic traffic of ideas and people had become very one-sided.[146]

The *Middletown* and *Marienthal* studies also stand as reminders that we do not have similar studies for India's Muradabad, Egypt's al-Mansura, or Argentina's Mendoza, even if there, the social sciences were massively on the rise.[147] The crisis also reached the shores of these societies, and changed their place in the world. Even if contemporary academic scrutiny did not go so deep there, these places also witnessed a renegotiation of the relationship between the individual, society, and state. The Great Depression did not just unmake and reestablish global links; it sometimes also synchronized debates, and even the political and societal answers given to them.

At the Helm of Disaster

"In 1931, men and women all over the world were seriously contemplating and frankly discussing the possibility that the Western system of Society might break down and cease to work."[148] Historian Arnold J. Toynbee's words, written at the end of that year, capture the gravity of the crisis. According to Charles S. Maier, the Great Depression was one of three systemic global crises of capitalism during the twentieth century.[149] The key reason why the doldrums turned into a *Great* Depression was a chain of linkages through the financial market that challenged the very premises on which the 1920s' prosperity had been built. Hence, the Great Depression was a time for testing the existing form of globalization, revealing the degree to which the world economy had integrated by the early 1930s. To a good extent, these links were the outcome of America's new global role. Even if cultural and political contacts as well as links persisted, economic globalization now decelerated at a dramatic speed.

By 1933, it was still unclear whether the crisis would destroy or fundamentally transform capitalism along with the fabric of capitalist societies. The Soviet Union, comparably unaffected by the slump, became more attractive. In the United States, the forces that mistrusted cosmopolitanism and an unreserved embrace of global exchanges were now gaining the upper hand. During the 1920s, many Americans had remained nervous and insecure about their nation's global status. With its large domestic market and vast rural population, the United States was an inward-looking country of farmers and manufacturers. The wider world was of rather little concern, except to a small, cosmopolitan elite. Most people were primarily focusing on with local matters, and global exchanges seemed more a threat than an asset. New York City, particularly Wall Street and Broadway, symbolized the cosmopolitan, globalized thread, whereas life in Muncie, other parts of the Midwest, and even Washington, DC, stood for a more nation-centered alternative. But even there, the forces of modernity and globalization fundamentally impacted on people's lives.

In the wake of the Depression, this ambivalence reverted to economic nationalism, protectionism, and a rather parochial attitude. More than at most other times in American history, the world was perceived as a dangerous place, and the United States seemed to have learned the lesson—better to withdraw and abstain than to risk entanglements that might lead to economic, political, and cultural concessions. Such a view obviously harked back to the age of the American Revolution and resonated well with a general tendency in US self-understanding.

It is easy to overestimate the dimensions of this swing, however. First, earlier forms of self-seclusion had mostly concerned Europe and visible political involvement only, whereas the United States had always sought close economic and cultural links with the Old World. For Asia, Oceania, and the Western Hemisphere, these ties remained blended with a higher degree of political contact and interference. Only toward Africa, largely trapped in European colonialism, were the connections less dense.[150] America had never really played alone. Financially, it now pulled the plug on all the continents—and hence one could argue that in an ironic and unintended manner the United States now lived up to the spirit of President Washington's farewell address more than at almost any other time in its history.

Second, the tendency to self-seclusion made the United States anything but original or unique. In fact, most other societies that were able to choose for themselves and were not subjected to colonial rule opted for a similar trajectory, and on a spectrum of possibilities concerning trade protectionism, state interventionism, or the ban on immigration, America often walked the middle ground. In that sense, the United States was simply a nation among nations, sometimes radicalized by a perception of lagging behind (for instance, when it came to "racial purity"), and sometimes spearheading new developments.

And finally, America stood out for its newly acquired economic and cultural power. It made a big difference if it followed others. Global connections were already tight. In the medium and long term, most ideas that seemed good for America but bad for others in fact proved to be detrimental to the United States, too. Still, America was not yet ready to accept the vacant position of global leadership.

Chapter 2

IN SEARCH OF NEW BEGINNINGS

Setting Stages

The Great Depression was not just a crisis of capitalism and laissez-faire more specifically but also of existing political orders. Liberal democracy in particular saw itself in retreat, and some already heard its knell. At the level of political ideas, British political theorist Michael Oakeshott noted at the time, much to his dismay, a "deep and natural dissatisfaction" with this political order, observing that many perceived democracy as "intellectually boring" vis-à-vis fascism and communism as its seemingly more innovative, imaginative alternatives.[1] Political realities hardly looked any better. In Latin America, the governments of six very different states—Argentina, Brazil, the Dominican Republic, Bolivia, Peru, and Guatemala—fell to military coups in 1930. By 1932, Ecuador, El Salvador, and Chile had followed suit. Democratic gains in Japan during the Taishō years (1912–26) came under increasing pressure from authoritarianism and fascism, again especially after 1930, and the fall of the Inukai cabinet in 1932 signaled the virtual end of Japanese parliamentary democracy. In Europe, where the collapse of the Russian, Austrian, and Ottoman empires had produced roughly a dozen new sovereign states after 1918, many countries, including Lithuania, Hungary, Bulgaria, and Poland, quickly drifted away from democratic and parliamentarian moorings during the 1920s. The Great Depression accelerated this trend, with Czechoslovakia a great exception. Austria slid further into crisis on March 4, 1933, the same day that Roosevelt was inaugurated as president, eventually leading to an authoritarian dictatorship. In Germany, Hitler had seized power five weeks earlier in what was obviously the most consequential political development for Europe in the first half of the twentieth century. After a military coup in 1926, Portugal instituted its fascist Estado Novo Constitution in 1933 as well. The economic situation was never the sole reason in any of these countries for the collapse of the existing political order. But it often was the last straw. Democracies were the main victims of these dynamics, and social scientists have calculated that the global extent of democracy almost halved from the late 1920s onward.[2]

Even where countries escaped fundamental political change, they almost without exception saw serious political realignment during the first half of the 1930s, with Italy, Turkey, Persia, and China, which had witnessed massive political change during the 1920s, as well as Venezuela, where the autocratic government of Juan Vicente Gómez remained in power from 1908 until the dictator's death in 1935, representing exceptions that confirm the rule. Ireland's general election of 1932 ended a decade of economic laissez-faire, and the year before had already witnessed the electoral victory of a new, more interventionist party in Australia. Another year earlier, Canada's liberal Prime Minister William Lyon Mackenzie King had been driven out of office for his slow response to the crisis, and the same fate befell the British Labour government in 1931. Starting with the Kanslergade Agreement in January 1933, Denmark saw a political realignment based on a historical compromise between the social democrats and the agrarian party, with Sweden and Norway soon finding similar solutions. This marked the beginning of decades of social democratic political hegemony in Scandinavia. France experienced more continuity, although the 1930s still saw a succession of short-lived governments in a volatile political climate. In contrast, colonial rule still proved stable and repressive enough to ensure that no dramatic political changes took place in most parts of Asia and in Africa, despite numerous riots and uprisings. Switzerland and the Netherlands were among the few sovereign states to experience no real political reorientation in the half decade from 1930 to 1935—two happy islands in a storm ravaging the world's political landscape, but they were small islands indeed.

The Great Depression thus undermined and overwhelmed the floodgates of the post–World War I political order. It vitalized the political extremes, with particularly rightist authoritarian or fascist regimes mushrooming. The world's political landscape became more polarized, yet also more complex. Many of the new political orders refused easy categorization. Instead, they were marked by a logic of "overcoming," as Harry Harootunian has put it in his work on Japan—aiming to re-create a lost national unity focused on cultural authenticity, originality, and a space free from commodification and anonymous market pressures.[3] Contemporaries often framed this as a search for a "third way" between existing solutions. Anticommunism kept most societies from following the Soviet Union's course. While many political systems developed more nationalist and authoritarian traits, they frequently refrained from following fascism too openly—if only because emulating another country contradicted nationalism's basic contention that solutions had to be homegrown.[4] At the more technical level of economic politics, the picture was hardly clearer. The Great Slump deeply discredited laissez-faire, even as the unorthodox and interventionist policies lacked academic economic legitimacy during the early 1930s. This only changed slowly. In the public and political sphere, classical and neoclassical economic approaches dominated, preaching austerity and worshipping the outstripped gold standard. Politicians and experts who toyed with greater interventionism therefore entered uncharted waters and often incurred fierce resistance.[5]

For all these reasons, countries shied away from the clear-cut categories into which later scholarship has tried to put them. Rexford G. Tugwell of the New Deal's innermost circle rejected both laissez-faire and communism, and spoke of a "third course," while economist Stuart Chase pointed to a "third road," and Assistant Attorney General John S. Dickinson extolled the need to "Hold Fast the Middle Way."[6] Driven by the will to experiment, they sought new political solutions. This new spirit was even embraced by the Roman Catholic Church as the world's oldest organization and a truly global actor, which also argued for such a third way. Pope Pius XI's encyclical *Quadragesimo anno* of 1931 stressed the dangers arising from both communism and unrestrained capitalism. Instead, he pled for a new social order built on solidarity, subsidiarity, and—most important for him—true belief.[7] Meanwhile, Indian nationalist leader Subhas Chandra Bose contended that the "next phase in world-history will produce a synthesis between Communism and Fascism," and it would not come as a surprise "if that synthesis is produced in India."[8] The battle cry of the French intellectual nonconformists "ni droite, ni gauche"—neither Right nor Left—summarized the spirit of the time much better than the neat differentiation between liberal democracy, socialism, and fascism that later research has highlighted.[9]

How does the United States fit into this picture? Roosevelt's landslide victory during the presidential election of November 1932 marked a turning point in American political history. FDR won forty-two states with 57 percent of the popular vote, demonstrating how much credibility the old order had lost in America. The Democrats became the new majority party, with critical minority blocs shifting into the New Deal coalition. It has typically been argued that 1932 thus gave the coup de grâce to the old, Republican-dominated "system of 1896," and that the realignment brought about a long-term shift and a new political system that would define American politics for the next half century. At the time, however, nobody knew if the new constellation would last.[10] Landslides sometimes have the habit of leading to the complete collapse of a (political) landscape, and this is exactly what many Americans feared. Hollywood's *Gabriel over the White House*, released in late March 1933, captured this mood by openly advocating dictatorship through the story of a president Hammond who gives up his business-as-usual attitude after a brain injury, turns into a dictator, and manages to bring economic security and peace to the country.[11] Despite its democratic system, the United States shared important elements with extremist regimes around the world. As Ira Katznelson has recently stressed, they "included racism as a robust ideology, imperial expansion, and the control of subject populations."[12] Contemporary developments abroad under-

lined the potentials of radicalization, with places as different as Austria and
Uruguay serving as examples. In each case, an elected head of government
resorted to a coup d'état after one or two years in government—Engelbert
Dollfuß in early March 1933, and Gabriel Terra at the same month's end.
While the United States was neither Austria nor Uruguay, such developments seemed to be harbingers of a global Ides of March during the very
days Roosevelt took office.[13]

But what did New Deal Democrats aim for, and what did FDR stand for?
As with leaders in so many other countries, Roosevelt's victory was less an
affirmation of his own approach than a refutation of his predecessor's crisis
management. Even the term "New Deal"—today identified with the reform
program implemented after 1933—was to some degree an accidental product. Roosevelt did not use the expression during the early stages of the campaign, but in his speech accepting the Democratic nomination in July 1932,
he pledged "a new deal for the American people." He did not attach special
significance to the phrase himself, and his advisers intended it principally as
political rhetoric, until the press picked it up and identified it as the Democratic contender's slogan.[14] The term encapsulated what so many political
currents around the world asserted: something had gone fundamentally
wrong with capitalism, and government should take more responsibility for
overcoming the prevailing adversity. Beyond that, the term was largely devoid of content, and while Roosevelt consistently pledged to adhere to democracy, key issues remained open. His stance on how to combat the crisis
remained utterly vague during the campaign. In January 1932, journalist
Walter Lippmann opined, "Roosevelt is a highly impressionable person,
without a firm grasp of public affairs and without very strong convictions."[15]
In fact, the Democratic contender often contradicted himself, trying to
please whichever audience he was addressing. Sometimes he came out for
"social planning," and in other speeches, he chastised Hoover for having
introduced too much federal control. His opinion was similarly equivocal
when it came to issues such as the League of Nations, agricultural policy, or
the level of government spending.[16] Banker Marriner Eccles mused that
"given later developments, the campaign speeches often read like a giant
misprint, in which Roosevelt and Hoover speak each other's lines."[17]

Some of the problems in defining Roosevelt's political approach also result from the fact that Hoover's presidency was more ambivalent than is
usually claimed. The years from 1928 to 1932 cannot simply be summarized
as unbridled capitalism and laissez-faire. While Hoover firmly believed in
balanced budgets and rejected direct federal relief payments to individuals
for fear that this would reduce their self-initiative, he nonetheless created an
antitrust division at the Department of Justice, urged railway and public
utilities executives to expand their construction and maintenance programs, and doubled the number of veterans' hospital facilities. The Smoot-

Hawley tariff, which he ultimately defended, was the antithesis of laissez-faire liberalism.[18] Many governments in other parts of the world drew even more strongly than Hoover on classical liberal remedies to guide their crisis response. Germany and the Netherlands, for instance, initially reacted to the 1929 *krach* by tightening budgets and sharply cutting public spending. American pressure pushed them further in that direction, and their move to austerity underpinned by economic liberalism was at least as radical as Hoover's.[19] For this reason, one should not exaggerate the divide between Hoover and Roosevelt, even if both—and for a long time also historians—emphasized and spotlighted the differences between their approaches. Ultimately, the dichotomy tells us almost as much about perceptions and the polarized political climate during this period as about diverging economic philosophies.

Not just America's economic policy, but also its very political system seemed challenged. Even if a firm majority continued to believe in the future of democracy, there were many voices speculating about dictatorship as America's future. At the time, this was a vague concept, however. The use of the term is best illustrated by a commercial stunt: in summer 1927, Studebaker released a new car named the Dictator. The title for its lowest-price model seemed well chosen to connote that it "dictated the standard" that others would have to follow. But some loved the car simply for its name—for instance, right-wing Estonian prime minister (and later dictator) Konstantin Päts, who turned it into the official state vehicle of his republic. In other countries, though, the name was much less popular, and Studebaker advertised it there under the less provocative name of Director. In the United States itself, there was no controversy about the Dictator; Studebaker sold more than forty thousand, and the name was in use until 1937. Most Americans at that point had only vague ideas about the term.[20] Some associated the word "dictator" with Benito Mussolini, who stood for vigor and audacity. Those who had read the classics knew that in ancient Rome, dictators were the key crisis managers in the republican system. Reference to antiquity was, for example, the reason why the Swiss newspaper *Neue Zürcher Zeitung*, one of the strongholds of European liberalism, praised Roosevelt's election, comparing it to the emergency application of dictatorship in ancient Rome.[21] We have to be careful lest we too quickly impose our associations of a concept on the past.

All in all, it was not so much Roosevelt who was elected as Hoover who was defeated. The first half of the 1930s was a time of changing values and an evolving set of institutions, operating in shifting political and economic circumstances. The combination of vagueness of content and flamboyant rhetoric made the New Deal quite typical of the first part of the 1930s. In the interregnum between the election and Roosevelt's inauguration, it was still unclear what 1933 would bring—whether strong continuities to the

Hoover years, an economic regeneration in tandem with a revitalization of democracy, or even a dictatorship of sorts.

Given that the crisis reached its peak during the same days that Roosevelt finally took over, America and the world did not have to wait long to see the New Deal taking vigorous action. Generally speaking, during its first years in office, the Roosevelt administration used two main tools to achieve one overarching goal: insulation and domestic intervention to create security.

Arthur H. Vandenberg, a Republican senator from Michigan, introduced the concept of "insulation," as already mentioned earlier, into the American political debate. Vandenberg was an affable man, best remembered for his move from anti–New Dealer in the 1930s to staunch internationalist in the 1940s—but unfortunately without recognition for his one hundred unpublished short stories and a handful of popular ballads with catchy titles such as "Bebe, Bebe, Bebe—Be Mine."[22] In February 1940, he confided to his diary:

> It is probably impossible that there should be such a thing as old fashioned isolation in this present foreshortened world when one can cross the Atlantic Ocean in 36 hours. . . . But probably the best we can hope for from now on is "insulation" rather than isolation. I should say that an "insulationist" is one who wants to preserve all the isolation which modern circumstances will permit.[23]

During the 1930s, similar deliberations on the world's contraction had already led to an inward turn. Such a move did not result from parochialism but instead was a reaction to perceived vulnerability to global forces. This approach characterized Hoover's crisis strategy, and many parts of the New Deal continued along similar lines. At the time, Americans often pointed to the economic nationalism of others to explain why they chose to insulate themselves. Still, the United States was the only country with the financial, economic, and political means to change the direction of the global economy. Although the United States did the same as most other countries, its protectionist policies had fundamentally different effects.

While the withdrawal of credits, trade protectionism, and new approaches to monetary and foreign policy were central tools for insulating the American economy from global turmoil, the New Deal added domestic intervention to the mix. Certain policies predated 1933, but during the Roosevelt era they played a much more pivotal role than ever before. The new degree of state intervention would change America forever and is what the New Deal is best remembered for today. Obviously Americans had known state action before, yet prior to the New Deal the average American was rarely directly affected by federal laws. For the early twentieth century, prohibition forms the main exception to this rule: between 1920 and 1933, the Eighteenth Amendment and Volstead Act represented the most direct contact between citizens all over the country and Washington, DC—besides the post office and the always-controversial issue of tariffs, which also impacted directly on people's lives.[24] Ironically, Prohibition was one of the few fields in which the New Deal reversed the trend of an expanding federal state by repealing the "noble experiment." Instead, domestic intervention would soon pervade a whole host of other issues that were at least as basic to American life as the fight between "dries" and "wets."[25]

Neither insulation nor domestic intervention was an end in itself. They aimed mainly at fighting the Great Depression and its consequences. Historians have frequently referred to the triad of relief, recovery, and reform as the key dimensions of the New Deal. Most of the new agencies combined several of these functions, and, equally important, the New Deal was not particularly successful when measured against that yardstick. A more encompassing concept to describe its core tenet and effects is security. Enlarging the role of the national state was mainly geared to making the lives of Americans from all walks of life more stable and secure—as a concept that could entail economic, social, and political measures.[26] "Freedom from fear" and "freedom from want," two of Roosevelt's most famous slogans, thus encapsulated the core idea of the New Deal. Crucially, this goal was not to be achieved through laissez-faire and individualism but rather by strong state action.

The precise mix of the two strategies of insulation and domestic intervention, and even the meaning of security, vary quite a bit between the assorted ingredients of the New Deal alphabet soup. Still, they characterize both its various individual programs and overall tendency, as will be shown by assessing the many agencies created under Roosevelt as well as more general phenomena such as the hype around planning or new forms of leadership. Equally crucial, the triangle between insulation, domestic intervention, and securitization of society also drove developments in many other states during the 1930s. The challenges to which the New Deal reacted and the general direction of its answer shared much with—and owed much to—the trajectories of other societies. Such parallel developments, which partly resulted from having to confront global challenges, therefore deserve as much attention as the transnational circulation of knowledge and practices.

Banking Reforms

The banking crisis of the 1930s was more caused by than a cause of the Great Depression. Some countries, like Great Britain or Canada, were hardly affected; others, such as France or Belgium, were hit rather late, while Japan had already experienced its crisis by 1927.[27] Because of its exposed international position and certain characteristics specific to the American banking sector, the banking crisis loomed larger in the United States than in other countries. The United States had a long record of bank failures that revealed some of the internal weaknesses of its economy, with its high number of small, undercapitalized rural banks willing to take high risks in making loans. The crisis of farming added to the problems of the US banking sector in the second half of the 1920s. A first global moment arose in summer 1931, when shock waves from Austria spread across Central Europe and eventually touched American shores. The problem then simmered in the United States at the local and regional levels. Compared to Europe, the number of bank failures remained high in 1932, but below the threshold of real panic. The roots of the US banking crisis were thus primarily home-grown, although America's global economic links helped to amplify it in the early 1930s.

As a countermeasure, the Reconstruction Finance Corporation (RFC) was set up in January 1932 to provide aid to state and local governments in order to bail out banks, railroads, mortgage associations and other large lending institutions. The RFC was anything but President Hoover's idea. While he was still pushing for voluntary action, bankers, businessmen, and Congress pressured him to change his mind, and ultimately prevailed. So the RFC is another illustration of state interventionism starting prior to the Roosevelt era. Moreover, it is characteristic of early 1930s state interventionism in that it was modeled after a World War I institution: the War Finance Corporation was set up in 1918 to support industries essential to the war effort along with the banks financing them, and it had only been discontinued in 1929. Revealingly, its long-standing director, Eugene Meyer, spearheaded the call for a revival of this instrument, and with the RFC, the Republican government picked up this Wilsonian thread.[28]

The RFC performed well in the beginning and reduced bank suspensions in the first half of 1932. But in July, Congress passed a law that required the RFC to publish the names of the banks it supported in order to prevent abuse of state subsidies. Transparency had an important flip side: the public interpreted RFC help as a sign that a bank was weak and increased the pressure on it. The effectiveness of the RFC was substantially reduced, and this led to a new wave of bank runs. Most of these remained local or regional affairs, and several states responded with bank holidays. This helped, yet it also increased the pressure elsewhere, with affected banks often withdrawing funds from correspondents in other parts of the country to strengthen their position. Battered by three years of depression, the governor of Michigan declared a statewide bank holiday on February 14, 1933. This was the straw, as it were, that broke the camel's back. From Michigan, the crisis quickly spread to adjacent states, which were also forced to declare bank holidays, and in less than three weeks the country was completely paralyzed, with banks closed in forty-eight states, and tremendous uncertainty as to how and when they would reopen.[29]

The banking crisis also had a significant international dimension. With confidence in the American banking system faltering, there was a wave of international speculation against the dollar. US monetary gold holdings fell drastically. Rumors that the incoming Roosevelt administration would devalue the dollar further reinforced this process.[30] Against this backdrop, the new president and Congress had to act swiftly. On Sunday, March 5, 1933, the day after his inauguration, Roosevelt called Congress into a special session for March 9. A second proclamation of the same day declared a bank holiday and placed controls on gold exports using long-forgotten provisions of the 1917 Trading with the Enemy Act. The state interventionism of the Great War had to be reinvoked, standing at the cradle of the New Deal.

March 9 left a mark on the history of Congress. In a legendary session Henry B. Steagall, as chairman of the Banking and Currency Committee, read out aloud the only available copy of the proposed banking legislation. The bill had been hammered out in just a few days by a group of experts under Ogden Mills, Hoover's Treasury secretary, and most other members of the group also came from the Hoover administration.[31] On March 9, the bill was still full of last-minute handwritten corrections. Debate was limited to forty minutes, before the House unanimously passed a bill granting sweeping powers to the president, which most of its members had never read. Less then three and a half hours later, the Senate passed the bill, and another hour later, Roosevelt signed it. The Emergency Banking Relief Act allowed the Treasury secretary to reopen sound banks and reorganize the rest, granting the president $2 million to facilitate these changes. It also confirmed Roosevelt's earlier decision to control gold movements. The president reassured the country in his first "fireside chat" of March 12, in which he told the American people that it was now safe to return their money to the banks. Branches across the country reopened the next day, and to everybody's relief, depositors did return their savings. The worst was over.[32]

This law was supplemented some three months later by the Glass-Steagall Act of June 16, 1933, which established the Federal Deposit Insurance Corporation and introduced bank reforms. The corporation instituted a federal guarantee for bank deposits and hence underpinned the new state-secured approach to the banking system. The law separated commercial and investment banking and placed greater capital requirements on national banks, but also made it easier for them to refinance themselves through the Federal Reserve.[33]

These measures to fortify the American banking system seemed to deal primarily with the domestic dimension, and this is what the bulk of the literature focuses on.[34] But the New Deal also initiated a policy of insulating America's economy from the wider world. The gold embargo of March 1933 shielded the domestic banking system from further runs on American gold reserves. Rigid foreign exchange controls impeded speculation against the dollar, as did the devaluation of the American currency by almost 60 percent between April and July 1933.[35] In explaining the Emergency Banking Relief Act to the public, Roosevelt stressed the "extensive speculative activity abroad in foreign exchange" as a key cause of the crisis that now needed to be remedied.[36]

It was this combination of domestic and international measures that calmed the US banking system, which now looked quite different than before. Between 1929 and 1933, ten thousand of America's roughly twenty-five thousand banks had failed. Through the New Deal, the federal government gained substantial competences, even if it stopped short of nationalizing the banking system. Consequently, the political Left was soon lamenting that Roosevelt had not used the crisis for more radical measures. This, however, had never been his intention, despite some powerful rhetoric with strong biblical overtones. A close reading of the president's statements is revealing. In his first inaugural speech, Roosevelt spoke not of chasing the "money changers . . . from their high seats in the temple of our civilization," but said that they had fled themselves, and that it was now time to "restore that temple to the ancient truths."[37] The New Deal kept the basic structure of the banking system intact. Capitalism was neither overthrown nor even fettered, yet it was reformed.

For Hoover, the New Deal's banking success was a bitter pill. His own collaborators had helped the man he despised, and together they had managed to restore confidence in a week, while Hoover's efforts to do so had failed for several years. Officially, the government stuck to the gold standard during its first five months in office, while its draconian foreign exchange controls actually contradicted the orthodoxy of the old system. As a final component, the New Deal started by insulating a central sector of the American economy from international exchange. Like his predecessor in office, Roosevelt saw the wider world more as threat than opportunity; economic nationalism not internationalism was the direction, at least initially.

Insulation and a drastic increase in state intervention were not specific to America. Germany, as the other large economy hit by a severe banking crisis in the early 1930s, had reacted in a similar way in 1931. When the tsunami unleashed by the collapse of the Austrian Credit-Anstalt struck Germany, the government declared a two-day national bank holiday in July 1931 and tightened its foreign exchange controls. While officially adhering to the gold standard, Germany started a slow departure from the orthodox system, somewhat similar to what the United States was to do two years later. The new "managed" currency was intended mainly to insulate the country and control international monetary flows more tightly.

Besides insulation, the government in Berlin gained tremendous powers in the wake of the banking crisis, even if state action was less far reaching than in America. Here too, a new financial institution, the Akzeptbank, was among the measures instituted to help the banks. The reform hampered the free, market-driven flow of capital, and the creation of the Reich Commissioner for the Banking Sector in 1931 epitomized the shift to government supervision. All this happened during the final phase of the Weimar democracy, and the new instruments were continued when the Nazis took power two years later; many even remained in place in the Federal Republic until the 1960s.[38]

Obviously, Roosevelt's banking reforms were bold and fundamental, but not without parallel. The German liberal newspaper *Frankfurter Zeitung* argued in March 1933 that the Roosevelt administration was fighting its banking crisis so successfully because it had learned from Germany's situation two years earlier.[39] Indeed, American decision makers were fully aware of the German experience of 1931–32. The Democratic National Committee sent Roosevelt photostatic copies of the German decrees on the day before his inauguration, and Alexander Sachs, a top banker at Lehman Brothers, strongly urged the "adaptation of the methods which proved practical in Germany for solving the banking problem."[40] While American experts profited from these and other international experiences, one should not overemphasize the links. Ultimately, each national system with its panoply of newly created state instruments was so complex that simple emulation or direct parallels remained rare.

At a more general level, though, the New Deal's banking policy was not unique but rather part of a global trend to reform banking systems that included state guarantees for depositors in France; preemptive measures in Denmark, particularly the 1930 banking legislation that alleviated the situation during the next years; and a shift of financial authority away from Wall Street to Washington, in Berlin from the financial center Unter den Linden to the political heart on Wilhelmstrasse, and in Brazil from Rio de Janeiro to São Paulo.[41] All these reforms represent a double move: insulating the national banking system from international connections while introducing the phenomenon that contemporary observers already called the "universality of state intervention in banking in this crisis."[42] In societies across the world, the three main alternatives to this course were quickly dismissed. It seemed unrealistic to return to the "real" prewar gold standard system, and a complete meltdown of financial capitalism could not be accepted. Likewise, the third alternative—a joint effort of all major states to overcome the crisis—was not in the cards. Economic nationalism had gained too much traction by early 1933, and the United States—the only state with the economic power to lead such an effort—had only just emerged from a political interregnum paired with forced political inaction. In a world increasingly driven by financial capitalism, securing the banking sector on

economic nationalist terms was thus seen as a central precondition for regaining social stability. Many other steps were soon to follow.

Many New Deals

Farmers and the Gardening State

The global parallels—and some significant differences—were even more
striking in another branch of the economy soon known as a hallmark of
New Deal action: agriculture. The sector had spiraled into global crisis since
the 1920s, with debt and low prices increasingly beleaguering farmers and
peasants. In response, states around the world saw growing government intervention from the early 1930s onward. A second wave of modern protectionism inundated the sector. The first round, unleashed as a reaction to the
world economic crisis of the 1870s, had mainly consisted of tariff barriers,
and the first political reactions to the interwar depression continued that
theme, often combined with nontariff measures such as import quotas. In
this field, the less industrialized countries frequently spearheaded the move
to protectionism. In the West, America's 1930 Smoot-Hawley Act was a harbinger of the trend to fence off the national market, even if the globally
most spectacular step was Great Britain's U-turn two years later: the country
that had dominated the world's economy up until 1914 and had trumpeted
free trade for four generations to an extent where it had become part of the
country's national identity, now inaugurated protectionism. This demonstrated that even the staunchest defenders of economic liberalism had dramatically lost ground.[43]

At a time when international markets collapsed, countries around the
world ignored the conclusion of the World Economic Conference of 1927
and similar international gatherings where speakers had warned against
raising tariffs. Instead of trying to overcome the crisis by way of cooperation
and exports, they resorted to economic nationalism. Equally problemati-
cally, this policy failed to resolve the domestic issues confronting the agricultural sector. Instead, prices for agricultural commodities continued to
fall.[44] Many states soon added another ingredient to the cauldron of protectionism, drastically increasing state action by organizing domestic agricultural markets. Often building on measures established during World War I,
governments now set up boards to fix prices for agricultural commodities
and assume responsibility for selling them, hand in hand with state monopolistic control over foreign trade in those goods. This became the most
innovative form of state interventionism during the 1930s, with forerunners
particularly in Japan, Brazil, and other Latin American countries. A contem-

porary expert called the "unchecked spread" of such market regulations "the fundamental change" in global agricultural policies.[45] The mechanisms of agricultural production, trade, and policies therefore explain this global conjuncture.

Rather than want and hunger, deteriorating prices for agricultural commodities were the driving force behind these changes. State intervention during the 1930s was largely about farmers—and to a much smaller extent about consumers and their interests. Market interventions were designed to increase producers' incomes for several reasons. Economically, this move demonstrated a growing appreciation that agriculture was not like other sectors, and that its fluctuations in supply and prices were especially volatile, exposing producers to threats that they could not master themselves. Moreover, increasing purchasing power was meant to bolster demand for domestic industrial products, and sometimes to offset trade imbalances and currency problems. Through such synergies, agricultural protectionism was conceived as an instrument to help overcome the economic crisis in general.

Politically, agricultural protectionism reflected a new understanding of the state, according to which the poverty of a large portion of the population was unacceptable. Securing societies against fundamental economic risks became one of the key pillars of government's functioning and self-image. Modern societies sought to protect themselves against famine, mass emigration, and political unrest that frequently resulted from a depressed agricultural sector. Pampering the farming sector also seemed critical from another perspective: military conflicts typically disrupted international trade, and for this reason, a thriving domestic agricultural sector also had national strategic significance.

There was a deep sense of appreciation of agriculture at a cultural level, too: industrialized countries around the world cherished the social and cultural values of the farming community as sources of stability, identity, and orientation. While fascist regimes are well-known for their cult of agriculture, underpinned by a long tradition of agrarian romanticism, farming was also singled out as an essential aspect of national identity in other countries. This concept was particularly strong in Switzerland, where the rural population of independent farmers was praised as the true defenders of democracy and a bulwark against radical tendencies. Obviously, farming organizations had an interest in pushing such views, oftentimes combining the agrarian myth with an emphasis on the tangible economic and social contributions that farmers made to the national well-being. Ernst Laur in Switzerland and J. J. Morrison in Canada were among the most vocal representatives of such ideas. But even beyond special interest groups, appreciation of agriculture was part of the political climate of the interwar years.

With remarkably little opposition, such concepts lubricated the shift to agricultural protectionism in industrialized countries in the wake of the Great Depression.[46]

Ironically, less industrialized—and hence more agrarian—countries generally chose another path. In some, like Mexico, state interventionism took a rather different form and mainly concentrated on land redistribution, as enshrined in the 1917 constitution. The process of land transfer stretched from 1920 until the early 1960s, and the second half of the 1930s, during the Lázaro Cárdenas presidency, saw the peak of this trend.[47] In many other agrarian countries, however, state activism remained low, due to their comparably small state capacity, or because of exogenous forces such as war or colonial domination. Examples of such a trajectory in sovereign states include Turkey, Egypt, and China. India, a British colony at the time, is another interesting case, where the government did little to help the peasants. Its 1931 wheat tariff primarily supported a small segment of farmers in the Punjab region that were particularly crucial for British colonial rule. On the subcontinent as a whole, in contrast, a lack of state aid fueled peasant unrest, and turned many into ardent followers of Mahatma Gandhi and the National Congress. Antiprotectionist colonial crisis management thus paved the way for decolonization. China, as another huge country that saw no substantial increase in interventionism, was suffering from civil war, whereas in almost all industrialized states, different blends of economic, political, and cultural motives underpinned the surge of agricultural protectionism.[48]

Roosevelt's agricultural policy has to be seen against this backdrop. The Smoot-Hawley tariff, the centerpiece of the Hoover administration's reaction to the crisis, was already geared toward insulating American agriculture from a world in turmoil. By 1932, this form of trade protectionism was seen as insufficient, since prices and farmers' incomes continued to decline. The New Dealers did not strike out in a completely new direction. They basically kept the existing trade protectionism intact and added a layer of domestic intervention. The New Deal's green heart, the Agricultural Adjustment Act of May 12, 1933, was therefore handled separately from trade legislation. Focusing on domestic market intervention, it was in line with the latest global fashion of agricultural protectionism. Still, it did not break completely new ground but instead resulted from a longer learning process. Hoover had set up the Federal Farm Board based on voluntarism in 1929, raising prices through state aid without curtailing production. The Federal Farm Board lent $500 million to agricultural cooperatives, yet the situation of farmers hardly improved. As a consequence, most experts at the time thought that even more government intervention was needed—even if only a minority aimed at redistribution and far-reaching land reform.[49]

For this reason, the New Deal concentrated on market intervention, mainly aiming to increase producers' incomes. It authorized the secretary of agriculture to fix marketing quotas for seven basic commodities, including wheat, corn, rice, hogs, and milk. The main idea was to reduce and control the supply of these basics. Through the Agricultural Adjustment Administration (AAA), the government curbed production of agricultural commodities by offering farmers payments in return for voluntarily reducing their output. The allotment plan paid subsidies to farmers to cease land cultivation or kill off excess livestock. The money for these subsidies was raised through a tax on companies processing farm products. This "set-aside" policy was complemented by the Commodity Credit Corporation set up in October 1933, which guaranteed farmers a minimum price for their products. It basically reinstated Hoover's Federal Farm Board, now as part of the wider framework created by the AAA's system of production controls.[50]

The New Deal's green pillar was part of the flurry of the first hundred days. As with so many of the New Deal's other components, Roosevelt himself can hardly claim intellectual authorship. The 1932 Democratic platform had been vague on agriculture, and Roosevelt's campaign speeches did not establish much firmer ground.[51] He certainly felt that something had to be done, but was not interested in opting for any of the various proposals that were discussed at the time.[52] In a characteristic move, FDR left it to farmers' representatives and a small group of experts to decide on the new scheme. In the end, he settled on an omnibus bill melding together several competing interventionist approaches—generously ignoring that some of them were quite impossible to harmonize. It was only in the months after the passage of the Agricultural Adjustment Act that the New Deal's eventual course became clear. For instance, the law included provisions for sending farm surpluses abroad, thereby harking back to the discussions of the 1920s. This alternative to the production control that the AAA became famous for was soon sidelined by a group of closely networked agricultural experts sorting out the contradictory programmatic emphases. Men such as John D. Black, M. L. Wilson, Mordecai "Zeke" Ezekiel, and Beardsley Ruml, many of whom had trained in land grant colleges and were now on the payroll of the US Department of Agriculture (USDA), focused on production control, and shared this preference with Roosevelt's secretary of agriculture, Henry A. Wallace, and his assistant secretary, Tugwell.[53]

As a result of this, and despite some continuity, Roosevelt was right when he claimed that the Agricultural Adjustment Act represented "a new and untrod path."[54] In going beyond voluntarism, the act was much more proactive than Hoover's approach, and saw farmers as contested voters who had to be won through policy appeals.[55] Moreover, the act generated a new sense of state action in summer 1933. During the banking crisis, Washington's visibility had remained limited. The New Deal brought about structural change for banks, but its very success kept it from playing a more discernible role. It also went beyond the role of tariffs that mainly affected those producing for export markets. The Agricultural Adjustment Act, in contrast, impacted directly on the lives of millions of farmers, tenants, and sharecroppers. Instead of the market, prices were now set through political intervention. Farmers had to consider federal funding schemes when deciding which fields they would till, and the seal of the mighty USDA with its golden haystack overshadowed the emergency surplus-reducing programs of 1933–34, where farmers slaughtered six million hogs and plowed under ten million acres of cotton. The federal state in this way became a key player in agricultural matters, and its two pillars of intervention—the set-aside payments and the work of the Commodity Credit Corporation—turned into the foundation of all the farm programs of the next decades.[56]

To forge such direct links between Washington and farms all over the country, the Triple-A created a huge bureaucracy and employed thousands of new government agents. In 1933, some 1.2 million American farmers grew wheat. For the first year of the new adjustment campaign, the state employed some 6,000 agricultural extension workers and 30,000 volunteer helpers to convince producers of the new wheat plan and to work with them on realizing it. Similar groups were active for other commodities, and by 1934 more than 4,200 separate county-level production control committees had to be set up.[57] Hiring tens of thousands of qualified administrators in such a short period of time was only possible because America possessed a wealth of experts in this field. At the time, journalist John Franklin Carter observed, "Through the agricultural colleges of the States and the Federal Government, we have been developing men who think about agriculture in national terms. To-day, where industry has few men with a national social viewpoint, agriculture has hundreds of them."[58] These well-trained and state-paid technocrats based their decisions on a rational analysis of the situation, and to do so, they had to generate a great deal of information about the sector's situation in the country. Computing field sizes, setting prices, providing acreage allotments for each farmer, and monitoring compliance were just a few of their many jobs.[59]

The New Deal's green pillar had elements of a kind of "gardening state," as described by sociologist Zygmunt Bauman: a state rationally planned and managed, like a garden, by a massive bureaucracy that impacted enormously on society and separated wanted from unwanted elements. Legions of experts swarmed all over the country to scrutinize every aspect of production and trade. Libraries were filled with lengthy AAA reports on issues such as "crop insurance features of agricultural adjustment programs" or the development of the chick hatchery industry. Political decisions not only pertained to macroeconomic conditions but also regulated production output and prices, and all of this epitomized the new understanding of the state.[60] Based on the latest scientific knowledge, the New Deal's "gardeners" wanted to create perfect conditions for their seed so as to optimize their yields. It was also they who decided which "plant" was useful and which others had to be weeded out.[61] Secretary of Agriculture Wallace, for instance, contended that the "great cotton plow-up campaign" of 1933 was an "effort that in its sweep and boldness went beyond anything known to history." It seemed to go "against the soundest instincts of human nature," but was a necessary correction to the "unreasoning hopes" by which "our people had been lured."[62] The state claimed to have superior knowledge and means compared to farmers themselves. Underpinned by educational rhetoric and a paternalistic self-understanding, it created a large bureaucracy that would change US agriculture and rural life forever.

Next to the new sense of state that the AAA conveyed, it is remarkable for both its similarities and differences to developments elsewhere. To start with, the New Deal's green pillar was fully informed by developments in other parts of the world. A trip to Europe convinced "Zeke" Ezekiel, assistant chief economist with Hoover's Federal Farm Board and soon a key figure in the New Deal's USDA, that foreign markets would remain closed to the United States, and this motivated him to argue for a domestic allotment plan.[63] Along similar lines, as Secretary of Agriculture Wallace contended in 1934, "Today it is clearly apparent that there is no effective foreign purchasing power for our customary exportable surplus of cotton, wheat, lard and tobacco."[64] His assistant secretary, Tugwell, had spent some time in France in the late 1920s and published extensively on its agricultural policy. At the time, Tugwell did not find much to inspire him, but that changed a few years later, when a 1934 study tour to Europe left a more positive impression.[65] Forester Arthur C. Ringland was fascinated by European land utilization policies, particularly in Italy, and proposed a more detailed investigation.[66] Overall, the AAA's focus on insulation and domestic politics therefore resulted from a close assessment of the wider world.

Some aspects of the AAA's domestic allotment plan were inspired by European schemes as well, with Rockefeller Foundation manager Beardsley Ruml, as one of its backers, especially responsible for introducing such ideas to the American debate.[67] Even more important than tracing the specific, "non-American" roots of the AAA, it is crucial to acknowledge that expertise was transnationally shared at the time. Decades of exchange meant that any concept was a cultural hybrid to be appropriated to specific national or local needs. Nothing was either genuinely American or homegrown in any other sense. In this light, it also comes as no surprise that societies around the world paid a lot of attention to the AAA. Spain's fragile Second Republic, for instance, saw a detailed debate about the AAA, including technicalities such as its cotton policy, processing tax, and environmental effects, often comparing it to the Spanish agricultural law of September 1932. For some, the AAA was a "legislación heroica," while others considered it "bolchevique."[68] American soil conservation programs, under the banner of the AAA and other New Deal programs, served as a major reference point for similar efforts by British colonies in southern and eastern Africa, helping to justify massive state intervention in agriculture during the 1930s and 1940s.[69] As much as global discussions informed policy decisions in the United States, so did American models energize debates and policies elsewhere.

There is nothing more local than farming, and hardly anything more global than trade in agricultural commodities. During the 1930s, no other policy domain became as nationalized as agriculture. In this sense, the United States was only one of many players in the global search for more interventionist solutions for agriculture in order to secure the future of domestic farming despite the collapse of international trade in agricultural commodities. Still, its specific trajectory is conspicuous in a significant respect, at least at first glance: whereas it fully shared the aims of domestic intervention and insulating the national farming sector from global turbulence with most other societies, it stood out in advocating a decrease in output. Dictatorships of the fascist brand and the Soviet Union, for instance, were vocal in stressing the need for agricultural autarky, and for this reason incentivized producers to achieve higher yields.[70] But dictatorships were not alone in this. In 1930, Australia came out with a "Grow More Wheat" campaign. Based on a price guaranteed by the state, the land under wheat was expanded by three million acres to a total of eighteen million, leading to an enormous spurt in wheat production. Other countries also tried to fight the crisis by maintaining or increasing their output.[71]

That said, the American concept of reducing yields was not wholly without parallel in other parts of the world. At the time, British economist Lionel Robbins even declared an "Age of Restrictionism."[72] For certain commodities, the Great Depression saw ideas of regulating the whole world market through voluntary or state-backed agreements. Tea is a good illustration, since India, Ceylon, and the Dutch East Indies, as the three countries dominating the world tea trade, signed several agreements to reduce output between 1929 and 1933. These accords did not go as far as the Agricultural Adjustment Act in actively reducing acreage, but they stipulated that virtually no new areas were to be planted with tea. Even if compliance varied, the efforts were quite successful, since output fell and a steep decline in tea prices was reversed.[73] Several other experiments in reducing the production of and international trade in specific commodities such as sugar failed, however.[74] So the tea deal did not establish a path to an alternative system. Furthermore, there were two fundamental differences between such efforts and the New Deal's agricultural policy: the tea experiment was about the cartelization of an international market, not a domestic allotment plan, and

India, Ceylon, and the Dutch East Indies were all colonies rather than sovereign nation-states. The International Tea Agreement of 1933 was signed in London, not in Jakarta or New Delhi, whereas in the case of the Agricultural Adjustment Act, the US government based its policy on democratic decisions that affected its own citizens and not remote colonial subalterns.

Brazil offers another interesting comparison where action also took place in a sovereign state. In 1930, President Getúlio Dornelles Vargas empowered the Conselho Nacional do Café to ban new coffee planting. The Conselho also destroyed seventy-seven million sacks of surplus stocks between 1931 and 1943, and in this way served Robbins as an example of the age of restrictionism.[75] Yet the Vargas regime did not turn production control into a consistent policy; cotton and manioc, two other important agricultural staples, saw no restrictive policy. And Vargas ruled as a dictator and did not legitimize his decisions democratically.[76] Among economists, though, restrictionism was intensively discussed, and Britain destroyed surplus potatoes, while in Bengal the jute output was reduced. So the aim of curbing output was shared in several parts of the world—just as Robbins argued.

Still, political ambitions and programs are not identical with economic performance. The economic effects of the Agricultural Adjustment Act brought New Deal state action in line with the prevailing global trends of increasing production. In America, the impressive amount of 35 million acres was taken out of production—but this was just a drop in the ocean given that the total acreage in the nation stood at 1,906 million. As part of the allotment system, many farmers set aside their worst land and increased yields on the rest, for instance by using more fertilizers. Production for the targeted commodities fell in 1934 but quickly recovered for wheat and other important crops. All things considered, the act succeeded in its primary aim of helping farmers. In its more radical goal of reducing output, its balance was more mixed.[77] By 1940, the Commodity Credit Corporation was stockpiling huge surpluses; its warehouses and elevators held unmarketable cotton worth one-third of a billion dollars alone as well as other commodities.[78]

Basically, the economic effects of the Agricultural Adjustment Act were not fundamentally different from those of the agricultural policies of many other industrial societies. Some nations like France and Great Britain—neighbors with agroeconomic constellations oceans apart—used interventionism mainly to try to keep production from growing. Yet both saw an upward tendency. Although restrictionism, then, was a widely debated policy concept at the time, it did not bring the expected effects. In countries that touted new interventionist schemes as levers of substantial growth, output did increase. But both Italy and Nazi Germany remained far from achieving autarky and instead unleashed wars of imperial expansion. Nor did Australia's wheat campaign lead to a substantial increase, but only to an upward tendency. Hence, the AAA's economic effects were not fundamentally different from schemes in other parts of the world.[79] It reveals that the impact of political intervention remained limited across societies. For all its sophisticated experts and elaborate schemes, farmers' *eigensinn*, ecological constraints, and productivity gains through technological innovation reduced the effects of the gardening state. The state's impact on rural society increased massively, but there were other forces that continued to play important roles, too.

All this makes a second difference, most pronouncedly to dictatorships of the radical Right and Left, all the more fundamental. Both Bolshevism and fascism used their agricultural policies as vehicles to build a new man and a new society. While Franco in Spain unleashed civil war in order to create the agrarian order he cherished, Fascist Italy's "battle for grain" was to a good extent about staging national grandeur, encapsulated by a bare-chested Mussolini inaugurating the annual campaigns. The Nazi *Reichsnährstand* saw itself seeding a blond and blue-eyed new aristocracy for the Reich, and in the Soviet Union the kolkhozniks and their tractors epitomized the dawning of a new age. In comparison, the New Deal's rhetoric and political action aimed at enlightening farmers in order to lead them in a more rational direction. While this element was typical of high modernity along with its belief in progress and change, the New Deal's aspirations in agriculture remained limited when compared to the radical utopias in other parts of the world.[80]

Moreover, US farmers themselves were involved in the whole host of new committees, so it was not just technocratic experts who decided their fate. Indeed, the whole approach was based on the idea of incorporating farm groups into government intervention. The AAA had a corporatist streak, particularly during its first years, when bureaucrats gained critical assistance from farm organizations in defining and implementing their programs. Even if the United States did not develop a stable medium- or long-term alliance between bureaucrats and farm organizations, as happened in France or Japan, the producers themselves had some influence on the creation of policies that would affect them.[81] The New Dealers themselves contended that "it is extremely important as a means of retaining public confidence . . . that particular actions are taken in accordance with the recommendations of farmers and their accredited leaders."[82]

Beyond cooperation, many elements of the AAA remained voluntary, and unlike in Bauman's concept, the American way of gardening remained mostly restricted to acreage allotments, prices, and credits. In other words, the United States focused on the regime of agricultural production, but it did not use its massive apparatus to control the lives of individuals. In Germany or the Soviet Union, noncompliance with agricultural policy triggered terror and suppression, and both regimes aimed at maximal surveillance. In America, by contrast, opposition to the AAA always remained legitimate and vocal, from Minnesota farmers complaining about the "modern" scientific method that "seems to be solely employed by too many of our supposed saviors at Washington," to the well-organized resistance against the New Dealers by farm groups and other organizations all around the country.[83] While the state intervened massively in agricultural production and trade, while "superfluous" hogs were killed, cotton fields plowed under, and the environment degraded through intensive forms of farming, such opposition was always possible. The New Dealers respected the difference between flock and folk, at least most of the time.

The 1930s, in essence, saw the dawning of a new era of direct big government involvement in agriculture in most sovereign states of the industrialized world. Even if the rhetoric, concrete policy instruments, and social policies accompanying farm intervention varied, there was a widely shared trend toward significant state action and national planning. In its intentions of reducing output, the New Deal's system of production control was more extreme than most other programs, and much more interventionist than the agricultural policies of most democracies around the world. Finally, a global perspective fully reveals the irony that the United States, the country identified as the quintessentially capitalist society, went much further than other states in curbing entrepreneurial initiative and the "gospel of more."

Rise, Eagle, Rise

As went agriculture, so did industry. The economic blizzard also led to a reassessment of political strategies for this part of the economy, and traditional options were dismissed in most countries. Insulation through higher tariffs often initiated a broader shift of direction, just as with agriculture. Compared to farming, new domestic policies varied more between industrialized states, not least because national traditions were already quite distinct before the crisis. Not all nations ushered in an era of increased state interventionism, and political action came in different shapes and sizes. Whereas the United States opted for state-led cartelization, Great Britain had a more ad hoc approach that impacted only some sectors of industry. In France, the state encouraged cartelization, but was much less active when compared to other periods of French economic history or other states. Japan and Germany, in contrast, resorted to more heavy-handed forms of intervention, even if Japan, despite its attempt to emulate Germany's command economy, never went as far as Nazism. Across the republics of Latin America, finally, forced industrialization remained primarily in control of the private sector for most of the decade. Hand in hand with this, the rights of labor developed in very different directions.

Against this backdrop, the early New Deal's industrial policy featured a sharp but short-lived digression from the traditional American government-business relations, on the one hand, and a certain convergence with practices in other parts of the world, most notably with Europe, on the other. Contemporaries wondered in particular how much Italy and the Soviet Union served as vanishing points for American developments; industrial policy stood at the center of the discussion about the New Deal's alleged fascist or Bolshevist tendencies.

America's industrial policy had long revolved around antitrust legislation and reinforcing market competition. The 1890 Sherman Antitrust Act was a cornerstone of this approach, and the legal reasoning identified with Supreme Court justice Louis Brandeis in the early twentieth century added further sophistication to the policy. Prior to the Depression, antimonopolism was widely shared in American politics, and the Democratic Party especially had a strong antitrust tradition, open to circumscribing the power of big business. The New Deal's focus, however, was different. In light of a fall of almost 50 percent in manufacturing output from 1929 to 1932, its National Industrial Recovery Act (NIRA) of June 16, 1933, led to the first government-sponsored business planning effort. As with agriculture, the policy was premised on the domestic dimension; expansion into foreign markets seemed unattainable in an age of economic nationalism.[84] The crisis of industrial capitalism and the consequent political destabilization in so many societies ushered in the search for a new social contract under the auspices of the state. Government-sponsored business planning seemed to offer the much-desired economic security.

Under the newly minted National Recovery Administration (NRA), the New Deal jump-started a process of government-sanctioned cartelization of epic dimensions. Existing antitrust laws were largely suspended. Instead, stakeholders and government together were meant to create "codes of fair competition," and agree on minimum wages, maximum work hours, and price levels for products. The NRA's symbol, the Blue Eagle, summarized the new approach: in one talon, the eagle held a wheel, standing for industry, and in the other bolts of lightning, indicating power. As for agriculture, Roosevelt stressed that this policy was intended to remedy the surplus crisis battering the American economy, and NRA director Hugh S. Johnson contended that it posed an alternative "to the murderous doctrine of savage and wolfish competition and rugged individualism."[85] In less than two years, some 550 codes ordered many industries, affecting the job conditions of 22 million workers, while a long list of separate agreements covered another 16 million skilled, semiskilled, and unskilled workers. Johnson did not just drink harder, smoke more, and shout louder than anyone else in Washington; he also deserved his reputation for working longer hours.[86]

More than any other New Deal agency, the NRA ignited a debate about the "kinship" of the New Deal to political systems in very different quarters—namely, to fascism and Bolshevism. Did the ends of the political parabola really meet? Progressive writer Roger Shaw opined in 1934 that the

"NRA ... was plainly an American adaptation of the Italian corporate state in its mechanics," while orthodox Republican senator Simon Fess of Ohio scolded the NRA as having gone "too far in the Russian direction."[87] While obvious opponents of the NRA were particularly quick to see such parallels, many others joined the chorus. Gilbert H. Montague, an expert in antitrust law who had been one of Roosevelt's teachers at Harvard and part of the NIRA drafting team, concurred in 1935 that the "NRA snatched at a form of executive law-making that was unconsciously but nevertheless essentially fascistic."[88]

Many such comparisons were also made at the international level, most notably to Fascist Italy. Il Duce himself was particularly quick to detect such kinship. Mussolini stressed that the "atmosphere in which the doctrine and practice of the American system evolved is doubtless close to Fascism." Another Fascist official, Giovanni Selvi, seconded him by characterizing the NRA as "bearing a Fascist signature." Such statements were mainly meant to legitimize their own system and boost its international prestige. Both generously glossed over the fact that the New Deal did not seek to dismantle democracy.[89] But less suspect commentators also saw such parallels. While Spanish socialists put Roosevelt and Mussolini in the same box for offering no real solution to the crisis, British member of Parliament Fenner Brockway published a full book on "fascist tendencies in America."[90] In terms of the NRA specifically, Brockway was surprised that men who "were regarded as dangerous 'Radicals' a year ago [are] now working enthusiastically for the Government." For him, this was not yet fascism, but he wondered, "Can the scheme remain as it is?"[91] Conservative Dutch diplomats, in contrast, scolded Roosevelt for his "marxistische stijl" that could lead the United States into "staatssocialisme."[92] French intellectuals, who saw the New Deal as a uniquely American phenomenon, were outliers in a debate framed by global references.[93]

Such conjectures were not completely far-fetched. The NIRA law had given the president only vaguely defined competences, and in summer 1933 it was still unclear how sharp the Blue Eagle's claws would be. Ex-general Johnson's speeches recalled the thunderbolts of frontier Oklahoma, where he had been raised. He scolded the "chiselers" and greeted businessmen with sentences such as "Those who are not with us are against us.... We all know the possibility of an Iscariot in every Twelve. Even Judas survived for a season—and then hanged himself for shame. As soon as this great modern legion is marshaled, it will be time enough to look about us for Judas."[94] FDR himself portrayed the push for state action as "a great spontaneous cooperation" and added as a hidden threat, "But if all employers in each trade now band themselves faithfully in these modern guilds—without exception—and agree to act together and at once, none will be hurt."[95] Such ideas, according to which economic problems would be settled through negotiation and joint agreement as opposed to competition, echoed the corporative slogans that featured prominently in fascism's propaganda. And at second glance, Johnson's and Roosevelt's speeches invited darker thoughts: What would the New Deal ultimately do with chiselers and Judas? Who would "hurt" whom in case of noncompliance? There were no definitive answers to these questions in mid-1933.

The whole hoopla surrounding the NRA also nourished the debate about fascism in America. In July 1933, Johnson launched a gigantic public relations campaign. Businesses supporting the NRA were asked to put the Blue Eagle symbol in their shop windows and on their packages. While NRA membership was formally voluntary, noncomplying businesses found themselves under great public pressure and were even boycotted. At the same time, consumers were asked to sign "pledge cards" demonstrating their commitment to the common cause. Mass meetings, parades, brass bands, and resounding speeches full of biblical innuendo inundated American political life, culminating in the largest parade that New York City had ever seen, with 250,000 marching and another 1.5 million watching in early September 1933. Civilian Conservation Corps (CCC) boys in olive drab, industrial workers, and stockbrokers all strode the streets together led by "Miss NRA," while bands played "Happy Days Are Here Again."[96] Besides its economic goals, the NRA thus aimed at strengthening the bonds of American nationhood.

Such state-decreed forms of gaiety and celebration bore resemblance to similar rallies in the dictatorships of the radical Left and Right, with their modern tools of mass manipulation, corporatist rhetoric, and boycotts. And at a microlevel, certain visual representations in America made bizarre links. A Californian NRA advertisement, naming the list of conforming businesses under a huge picture of FDR, was embroidered with little swastikas. While in retrospect this was but a stylistic aberration, it showed how easy it was to associate the American Blue Eagle with its perched Italian or stark Nazi conspecifics.[97]

More important, some New Dealers displayed an irritating fascination with fascism. The Roosevelt administration officially distanced itself from the Italian regime, and Johnson clarified his wish to "avoid any Mussolini appearance."[98] Still, such delimitation was only half the truth. Many New Dealers, including FDR himself, secretly admired the scope of political action in Italy. Until the mid-1930s, Roosevelt mainly felt "sympathy and confidence" with Mussolini, that "admirable Italian gentleman."[99] Others held similar views. Tugwell, on his 1934 trip to Italy, entrusted his views on Fascism's economic and social policy to his diary in laconic though revelatory words: "It makes me envious."[100] None of this admiration was unreserved. Roosevelt, Tugwell, and others were quick to distance themselves from the political system behind the industrial policies in the Soviet Union or Italy, and stressed the merits of democracy. FDR argued that the United States' culture was inherently democratic, and that the NRA followed "the democratic procedure of our Government itself."[101] Yet Italy or the Soviet Union seemed to be leading the way, for their state interventionist policies had set in much earlier—for instance, with Mussolini's 1927 *carta del lavoro* and its *stato corporativo* that was in full operation by the early 1930s as the fascist reference point for the NRA. Moreover, Germany was often referred to. Representative David J. Lewis, economist Willard L. Thorp, and others recommended studying German industrial policies as a model for the NRA.[102] America did not appear as a pioneer of political innovation but rather as a country in desperate need of catching up.

What were the sources of the appeal of the dictatorships? The Italian hype is easier to understand if one considers that the country had fought alongside the United States during World War I, less than two decades earlier. The New Dealers also inherited good relations with Fascist Italy from the Republicans. By 1933, the regime's most violent revolutionary phase seemed over, and Western democracies accepted Italy as a member of the international community, not least because of its staunch anticommunism. Its corporatism had the charm of leaving private property and other core tenets of capitalism intact, while still offering an alternative to laissez-faire. Compared to Italy, the New Dealer's views of the Soviet Union and the Third Reich were not quite as positive, although even there one finds a blend of disgust and admiration. Since the 1920s, many American experts had found Soviet modernity worthwhile, despite its costs. Its strong planning dimension gained additional appeal with the advent of the Great Depression. The Soviet experiment fascinated Americans from diverse points on the political spectrum; its strong anticapitalism was the main obstacle to an even broader impact. Images of Germany had their own ambivalence. On the one hand, Americans saw many similarities to another "young," dynamic, industrial nation, and particularly those on the Left admired its social policies. On the other hand, perceptions of Germany were always underpinned by the fierce hostility of World War I. Where for many, Italy seemed chic but also a little ludicrous in its bombast and the Soviet Union appeared too radical, Nazi Germany was perceived as more violent and vile. In spite of such qualifications, all these dictatorships appeared fascinating because they seemed to offer answers to America's most pressing issue: how to create stability and security in a chaotic world. While the vast majority of Americans did not want to adopt any of these political systems, many felt that important lessons could be learned from them.[103]

The American discussion of dictatorship always focused on Europe—despite the fact that many other states, particularly Japan and good parts of Latin America, also moved in this direction. US views remained Eurocentric, though, not only since the Old World had always been the main external reference of American elites but also because all variations of dictatorship that were perceived as modern—from the rule of Robespierre in the wake of the French Revolution to communism, fascism, and Nazism—had their roots in Europe. Japan, Brazil, or Turkey, for that matter, were simply seen as the utterly Other, devoid of any kinship.

Taken together, the situation was quite unclear in mid-1933. On the one hand, the meaning of a term like fascism remained notoriously vague in America at the time, and for some, it was synonymous with state control in a mixed economy model. Since such concepts were still new and had not yet developed their own vocabulary, some resorted to terms as fascism for lack of better alternatives. Others, including some of the more radical New Dealers, genuinely admired certain components of Europe's dictatorships and found it inspiring to analyze their practices, if not more. But how far did this interest really go? And how similar was the NRA to the political course of Fascist Italy? As always, the proof of the pudding would be in the eating.

The most important point of reference for the creation of the NRA had a thoroughly transnational dimension. Yet neither fascism nor communism played that role; instead, World War I interventionism was the godfather of the NRA. The 1917 War Industries Board (WIB) had encouraged industry to use mass-production techniques to increase efficiency and output. In the wake of the Great Depression, resuscitating the WIB's industrial mobilization seemed even more interesting, and early on during the crisis, several of its veterans, including its former director, Bernard Baruch, and General Electric's president, Gerard Swope, called for a revival of the agency. Their ideas clearly impacted on the eventual NRA, and another continuity from World War I is seen in the WIB past of NRA director Johnson.[104]

Notwithstanding such continuities, the NRA's eventual trajectory was far from predestined. In March 1933, Roosevelt did not give high priority to ideas of promoting industrial recovery, despite the agony that had befallen this economic sector. This is all the more surprising if one considers that New Deal policies on banks and agriculture would only indirectly help to improve industrial production and employment. One month later, Roosevelt was still undecided as to what to do, since his advisers were split over how to deal with industry. On April 4, he shelved the question. Two days later, however, FDR rashly reversed his decision after learning that the Senate had passed the so-called Black Bill.[105] Proposed by Alabama senator Hugo Black, and supported by organized labor and the American Legion, the bill aimed at prohibiting interstate commerce in goods produced by employees who worked more than a thirty-hour week. Roosevelt thought that the Black Bill was unconstitutional and that instead of improving the economic situation, it would make matters worse. Something had to be done quickly. As in so many other cases, Roosevelt asked several groups to draft proposals, among them the WIB worshippers. At the month's end, he brought the various teams together and told them to reach a detailed agreement among themselves. So they did, but the tumultuous and rushed process explains why the NIRA had several dimensions, of which industrial policies were just one. Moreover, the law was rather vague on how the codes of fair competition should be achieved. Some like Tugwell wanted rather heavy-handed state intervention and planning, while others, including Secretary of Labor Frances Perkins as the first woman to be appointed to the Cabinet, simply aimed to improve wage-and-hour standards. Hence, the NRA's direction would primarily be decided once set into practice.[106]

With businessmen such as Swope and Baruch standing at its cradle, the NRA unsurprisingly followed neither Tugwell's nor Perkins's train of thought. Instead, it had a business spin right from the beginning. This tendency was reinforced by a lack of counterweights: the state did not have a lot of independent expertise and manpower in industrial affairs, unlike the situation in agriculture with its stronger tradition of state action and synergies with academic expertise. Of all the NRA officials working on the codes of fair competition, 89 percent had pursued a career in business prior to joining the agency. Its towering director, Johnson, who combined "the qualities of a top sergeant, a frontier editor, and a proconsul," could not compensate for this void, particularly since he and his second in command, Donald Richberg, interpreted the NRA in favor of industrial manufacturing corporations, too.[107] This reflected not just their backgrounds but also the fear that any tough policy on business would run the risk of being ruled unconstitutional. Other potential counterweights to business were even weaker than the state: unions and consumers lacked strong representation. Less then 7 percent of all code authorities included labor representatives, and only 1 percent included consumers' interests. In the end, the business community reached most of its goals from its crusade for antitrust liberalization during the Depression years, and the NRA's practice was quite close to these business ideals.[108]

Ultimately, such a stark reversal of traditional federal policies was only possible because of the emergency—and especially because the business-friendly policy revealed its true face only incrementally after its unplanned birth. The NRA is typical of the New Deal in that it did not build on a specific economic philosophy. Its approach remained contradictory and vague, and it had to work within the framework of existing state capacities. More distinctive than anything else were its experimental character and its proclivity for state intervention, but also its pinch of pragmatism. The early New Deal's quest for more economic security translated into a credo of size and reduced competition, since large units were perceived as more stable than an open market situation. The NRA epitomized the tendency of the New Deal to approach macroeconomic problems with microeconomic tools; while aiming at massive microeconomic management, it lacked the instruments to fully implant such a policy. Central planning was simply not on the cards, given the lack of state capacity. In general, New Deal experimentalism was mostly limited to means and only rarely extended to ends, as Barton Bernstein has argued.[109] On paper, the National Recovery Administration sounded like strong state action, like a gardening state for industry. In practice, control was largely left to the business corporations that the NRA was created to regulate. It was worlds apart from Roosevelt's rhetoric invoking "modern guilds" as a corporatist pattern in which the labor force and management would work in perfect harmony. References to instruments invented or implemented by dictatorships remained rather superficial; the New Dealers were acutely aware of these models, toyed with some of their rhetoric and symbolism, but ultimately opted for a different course. In the end, the NRA combined a corporative surface with a business-driven core. Or in philanthropist Edward A. Filene's words, "The Roosevelt Administration" was "the special champion of private enterprise."[110]

The reality on the ground therefore looked different than the original hopes or some of the government's assertions. The NRA's complex mechanism produced more red tape than prosperity, and like any highly interventionist policy, it turned into an avalanche of ever more codes and rules. In less than two years, it amassed some three thousand administrative orders filling over ten thousand pages.[111] A company like Armstrong Cork, the nation's largest producer of bottle corks, had good reason to complain, since it had to operate under no less than thirty-four different codes. The system disadvantaged small businesses in comparison to the large enterprises that also happened to man the NRA. And despite its antitrust agenda, Johnson's course was not particularly attractive for America's largest corporations either. Some of them—for example, in the steel and automobile industries—had already held quasi-monopolistic positions. Businessmen all over the country soon started to fear that the NRA could turn into a stepping-stone to a more pervasive form of state intervention. Fascism and European developments again became an important point of reference—in this case, not fired by fascination but instead as ammunition for those who disliked any kind of infringement of business freedom. Even those parts of business that had supported a corporatist approach and flirted with aspects of fascism changed their minds as soon as they gained firsthand experience with the NRA. In their eyes, it brought state involvement in business, but not the desired self-government by wealth. The Du Ponts, for instance, as one of the richest families in the nation, moved away from their initial tacit support of FDR, and by mid-1934 were complaining that the New Deal was "nothing more or less than the Socialistic doctrine called by another name."[112] Conversely, the Du Ponts and other industrialists increasingly tried to use the Republican party as a vehicle for anti–New Deal policies.[113] The roots of conservative politics, which were to come to full fruition during the Reagan era, lay in such forms of discontent with the rising New Deal order.

Overcoming Rugged Individualism

Business dissatisfaction with the NRA was further increased by the NRA's policies toward labor, particularly because of the NIRA's famous section 7(a), which granted workers the right to organize and bargain collectively through representatives of their own choosing and provided federal regulation for maximum work hours and minimum wages. As such, it buried the Black Bill that Roosevelt disliked so much; more important, it challenged the American tradition of company unions and nonorganization as well as the rights of employers to fire workers for union activity or even just membership. Trade unions in the United States traditionally had been much weaker than in almost any other industrial nation, and section 7(a)—building on World War I experiences along with tendencies throughout the 1920s—challenged this trajectory at least as profoundly as the other elements of the NRA queried existing industry relations.[114]

As with so many other parts of the NIRA, however, it remained to be seen what the law's intent might mean in practice. In some sectors, trade unions quickly grasped the new opportunity and won influence. This holds especially true for the United Mine Workers of America (UMW), whose charismatic president, John L. Lewis, grabbed the chance and drummed in support of the NRA. From a Republican who had officially backed Hoover in 1932, he converted into a staunch supporter of the New Deal agenda who soon eulogized the NRA as the most significant law "from the standpoint of human welfare and economic freedom ... since President Lincoln's Emancipation Proclamation." Encouraged by such rhetoric, UMW membership swelled during the course of 1933. Miners went on strike when employers rejected the UMW, often through militant family marches organized by the Communist-led National Miners Union. Through such pressure, the UMW left a deep mark on the code for the coal industry and won a historic collective bargaining agreement in September 1933.[115]

Coal, however, was far from representative. In the automobile and steel industries, for instance, employers insisted on company unions, and unions were too weak or passive to fight for a more independent position—in the latter case, a deep mistrust of the government kept them from seizing the opportunity. Textile workers borrowed some of the UMW's militant tactics, but against the resistance of armed company guards, strikebreakers, and National Guard troops called in by several governors in the South, they had to give in. What at its climax was the largest strike in US history with four hundred thousand workers participating, ended without the employers making any concrete promises. Many managers ultimately resorted to setting up company unions. Typically such unions only covered a single plant, and the bargaining position of workers remained weak since the employees directly depended on the employer across the table. The NRA also accepted this kind of representation, even if it had originally set out to foster trade unions.[116]

The role of the NRA and of the National Labor Board as an agency set up in August 1933 to handle management-labor clashes remained by and large ambivalent. In December 1934, Princeton law professor Alpheus T. Mason pointedly contended, "The Administration has had no firm or definite labor policy. It has vacillated and disagreed with itself so as alternately to give support to the employer and then to organized labor."[117] Indeed, the NRA raised huge expectations for labor that it could not meet in the end. Agricultural, public, and domestic workers were not covered at all under the NRA, and for this reason as well as due to some of the details of the concluded codes, the New Deal's industrial policy brought fewer gains for women and minority groups, particularly African Americans, than for white men in the industrial sector. Southern politicians, so crucial for the New Deal coalition and decisive in defining the limits of reform, made sure that Jim Crow prevailed. Inequality persisted, and in general employers continued to have the upper hand. But while remaining below the expectations it created, the NRA still improved labor's situation. On the whole, workers won more rights, their living standards rose, and there was a new sense of dignity for their work. While unions had been especially weak in the United States prior to the New Deal, the percentage of organized workers rose from 5 percent of the workforce in 1933 to 16 percent by 1940, and then to 22 percent by 1945.[118]

Simultaneously, these developments poisoned the climate on the shop floor. With the two visions of trade and company unions clashing across the country, the number of strikers rose from 320,000 in 1932 to 1,170,000 in 1933, and to 1,470,000 the year after.[119] Communists remained a small but efficient minority among the organizers of such protests, funneling parts of labor's discontent. Such action at the same time stoked the fears of the business community about the radical inclinations of its employees. During the 1934 West Coast waterfront strike, picketers were cursed as "red sons of bitches," several persons were killed, and hundreds were wounded.[120] The NRA remained far from introducing a less conflictual way of resolving management-labor relations. Even if the worst of the crisis was over, political divides hardened further.

Finally, the NRA ballyhoo did not render the desired effects economically. There was economic improvement in 1934 and 1935, but not a full recovery. Accepting the potential hazards of ever more governmental intervention in return for marginal improvements in economic stability was not ultimately attractive, and this further increased business and labor opposition to the NRA. Complaints about noncompliance and other forms of code violation flooded into Washington, and Johnson would have needed a whole army to investigate and resolve all such cases. This was not just impossible; another reason also called to caution: full enforcement ran the risk of triggering even broader resistance against the NRA and increasing questions as to the agency's constitutionality. But toleration was not unproblematic either, since it undermined the whole endeavor.

It was not these inner contradictions that finally brought down the hefty federal Blue Eagle. A few sick chickens from New York played that role. In May 1935, the Supreme Court ruled in *Schechter Poultry Corporation v. United States* that the case of the Schechter brothers' Brooklyn kosher poultry business, accused of selling "unfit" and uninspected poultry, had only an *intra*state character, and therefore the NRA's *inter*state commerce regulations did not apply. Beyond the sick chickens, the court used this case to render the whole NRA unconstitutional, ruling that Congress had impermissibly delegated its lawmaking authority to the agency.[121]

The NRA thus had a problematic long-term legacy. On the one hand, it antagonized an influential part of American society against the Roosevelt administration. The NRA's economic record remained far from impressive, and it poisoned the political climate, making it the most contentious piece of the New Deal. Moreover, it taught some businessmen to seize state power and use it for their own interests. Instead of free competition, businessmen took shelter in protectionism; instead of innovation, they preferred coordination. Some started to perceive big government as a tool for big business, for example by accepting government contracts. This did not keep them from fighting for deregulation and a more laissez-faire stance—another legacy of the New Deal with long-term consequences. Even small businessmen copied them—for instance, in Muncie, where the school board received offers from nine local coal merchants, all with the same high price. Attached to the bids was the usual affidavit stating that there had been no collusion, but adding "except as required by the compliance agreement of the retail solid-fuel industry."[122] During the 1930s, this process of tempering competition was not initiated by industrial corporations themselves but instead by well-meaning state authorities seconded by experts and philanthropists.[123] As so often happens, intentions were not identical with effects. It would be wrong to assume a direct relationship between the degree of state intervention and the level of opposition. Federal action went much further in agriculture yet met less resistance; business opposition to the NRA also cannot simply be identified with a free market position. The NRA stood for a rather light form of state intervention. Certain public relations stunts aside, it remained far from the idea of a gardening state.

All in all, then, the convergence with Europe's extremes did not go terribly far. The NRA resorted to propaganda and puff, because Johnson and

Roosevelt knew that full enforcement of the NRA codes could easily meet insurmountable resistance. Flapping the Blue Eagle's wings was primarily meant to compensate for the lack of legal and political authority. In 1933 and 1934, however, many thought that propaganda and political action were in lockstep, as in some other states.

While there were no parallels specifically with fascism, there *were* some with general global trends. The political economy of many states around the world turned to interventionism in the first half of the 1930s, and created a sheltered and rather uncompetitive environment for industry. As in America, the experience of World War I frequently featured prominently in defining new industrial policies. Trade barriers at the decade's beginning had often fended off foreign competitors; now, state-sponsored cartels were on the rise. Japan, for instance, saw the shift from the self-regulated market and private ordering by the zaibatsu conglomerates to mandatory cartels and compulsory trade associations during the first half of the 1930s. Here, too, minimum prices were now set. In doing so, Japan followed the German example, where a procartel approach loomed even larger. The main difference between the two dictatorships and the United States was the compulsory element that the New Deal always avoided, and yet coercion remained selective in Germany and Japan, too. The same basically holds true for Brazil under Vargas, where intervention went less far than in the United States. As in the United States, the active collaboration of business defined the eventual course in all three dictatorships, and governments left considerable leeway to the private sector. As in America—and unlike, for instance, in Sweden or Switzerland—these three nations lacked the institutions for a fully corporatist solution. Hence, the day-to-day differences in business-government relations were only gradual and not fundamental.[124]

Great Britain also held an interesting place on this spectrum. In industry, as in agriculture, it shied away from the level of across-the-board state interference that the New Deal, Japan, or Germany introduced. Certainly, one also finds protectionism and a lax antitrust regime there, facilitating the creation of large monopolistic firms. Still, the approach was ad hoc. Cartel-like arrangements were only organized in specific cases, and for these, state intervention reached a higher level than in the United States.[125] While practice thus remained much patchier than in the United States, there are also remarkable connections, particularly for the soft coal industry. The 1930 British Coal Mines Act, which an expert report for the US Congress called "a measure of compulsory cartelization," was the direct inspiration for a 1932 initiative by Representative David Lewis of Maryland.[126] And the American Guffey-Snyder Act of 1935, replacing the NRA code of fair conduct after the Supreme Court's ruling of the same year, followed the same British model.[127]

In a completely different political environment, the Portuguese dictatorship also cartelized only some industries, amounting to 10 percent of its overall industrial output.[128] France, by tendency, even reduced its industrial tutelage and saw little state action, particularly when compared to other phases of its history. Instead, industry adopted self-regulation. One contemporary French author noted the "delay" with which France moved in the direction of other countries, and the "liberal and individualistic ideas" that shaped its industrial relations. While recent research has stressed the strong inroads of corporatism in France, action remained more limited than in the United States or Germany during the first half of the 1930s.[129] The Netherlands was even more reluctant to interfere in domestic industrial production, leaving aside certain provincial initiatives. As such, state action mainly pertained to protectionist trade measures.[130]

Some Latin American countries chose a similar path. They experienced forced industrialization, not least to compensate for the decline of export-led growth. Business interests dominated the domestic industrial policies in some countries, like Brazil, whereas in others, such as Argentina, the state itself acquired a more prominent role. In most places, action remained more fragmented and did not go as far as the NRA or the European brand of cartelism. Taken together, however, US state intervention in industrial relations stood somewhere in the middle of the rather broad spectrum of industrialized and industrializing countries.[131]

The New Deal was not alone in its rhetoric of supporting labor, either. Roosevelt's warm words for the plight of industrial workers had echoes in many other countries, where governments showed more appreciation for the industrial shop floor as a central element of corporatism. Moreover, the New Deal not only increased state support of labor but also facilitated a more independent role for it. Contemporaneously, union membership rose substantially in the Netherlands, Belgium, Denmark, and Great Britain, and dramatically in Sweden, Norway, and France during the 1930s, while basically stagnating in Australia and Canada. Fascist and authoritarian dictatorships in Europe, at the same time, often suppressed and dismantled independent labor organizations, or used them as an instrument of state policy.[132] The rather weak trade unions in Brazil also became in instrument of the Vargas regime during the period, while membership fell in Argentina in the first half of the 1930s, but rose in Mexico and Chile. The same holds true for Colombia, which also saw a massive expansion of labor rights under the presidency of Alfonso López Pumarejo.[133] In this respect, too, the 1930s saw a drastic divergence between states; the only general tendency was the higher symbolic esteem granted to workers—whatever concrete policy this entailed.

Given America's briefer and more attenuated experience with unionization, many felt that the United States was simply catching up with developments in Europe and elsewhere. Ironically, the powerhouse of industrial production seemed to be a latecomer in these developments, needing to learn from foreign practices. While the analogy to fascism was soon banished to the political margins, some contemporary observers argued that Yugoslavian coal miners, Indian textile workers, and French trade unionists had inspired sit-down strikes and other protest techniques in America. While there were admittedly some direct transfers, as in the case of soft coal regulations, many forms of activism and regulation in America had important homegrown roots, too. In most cases, practices had become transnationally shared by the 1930s, so that it was impossible to identify clear roots. The whole discussion thus primarily reflects the feeling that the United States was "lagging behind."[134]

Overall, industrial and labor policies around the world varied considerably during the 1930s. Leaving the Soviet Union aside, the first half of the decade did not see straight-out government direction of the economy—neither in the United States nor in other nations. While the New Deal always remained distinct from fascism and even more so from communism, it was but one of many national variations stressing selective state intervention, business-led cartelization, and a new role for labor and consumption in industrial relations. Whatever the precise mix, societies around the world were struggling with faltering international trade, and they all tried to create new stability through economic nationalism for their industrial sectors. It is true that the United States remained distinct; for instance, it still did not have a labor party, unlike all other advanced capitalist countries (including Australia, which shared many New World characteristics with America).[135] But it certainly was not unique.

There was no single global, European, or other model from which the United States significantly digressed; instead, its course stood somewhere in the middle of the broad range of options.[136] Interestingly, though, it moved further away from the free market logic than some other societies. Maybe even more significant than the changes at the economic and political levels, which always remained contradictory and incomplete, was the New Dealers' attempt at ideational reorientation. Johnson and others in the Roosevelt administration rejected the "rugged individualism" that Hoover frequently cited in his speeches and today appears as a core tenet of American self-definition; rather, they prioritized "balance" over individualism and "cooperation" over competition.[137] Although workers were quite open to this alternative set of values, this did not hold true for Americans as a whole.[138] The NRA remained a short episode in American history. In labor relations, its push for unionization made the United States seemingly catch up to what was perceived by many as a "normal" level of workers' representation at the time, but the foundations of unionism always remained shaky when compared to other countries. It also fired the resistance of those who argued

IN SEARCH OF NEW BEGINNINGS

for more of a free market approach, leading since the mid-1950s to an erosion and later a sharp decrease in trade union membership.

From Crisis Creation to Work Creation

The New Deal's help for banks, agriculture, and industry did not offer immediate relief for the thirteen million unemployed in 1933. By then, the
Depression was in its fourth year, and the groups hit hardest by the crisis—
children and young employees, the elderly, the unskilled, rural inhabitants,
immigrants, and African and Mexican Americans—could not yet see light
at the end of the tunnel. Relief for the unemployed then came in various
ways and a makeshift manner. Besides breeding the NRA's Blue Eagle, the
NIRA also gave birth to the Public Works Administration (PWA), designed
to jump-start American industry by instituting a large public construction
program. The staggering amount of $3.3 billion was released for this pur-
pose—a sum even surpassing the $3 billion that all of private business in-
vested during 1933. To spend so much money, the PWA had several kinds of
authority: it could start its own projects, make allotments so that other federal agencies could engage in construction work, or offer a combination of
loans and grants to states or other public bodies to stimulate nonfederal
work. It thus mainly worked through private contractors, and similar to the
NRA, this reflected both the absence of strong state agencies to do the job
themselves and the idea of cooperating closely with business.[139]

When the PWA was created, Johnson hoped to use it to stimulate heavy
industry. In addition, he saw himself as the ideal administrator of the agency,
which he considered conjoined twin of the NRA. Yet much to Johnson's
anger, Roosevelt decided to separate the two brainchildren directly after
birth. Moreover, the president appointed Secretary of the Interior Harold L.
Ickes as head of the PWA. Johnson and Ickes could not have been more different, with Ickes just as cautious and pedantic as Johnson was hot tem-
pered and bold. Any project applying for money was checked scrupulously,
and given that the PWA undertook many large and complex projects such
as building bridges and dams, the agency was slow in spending its budget.
This kept paychecks from reaching the hands of workers and contradicted
the very idea of a public works scheme.

Ickes had good reasons for being so frugal. By carefully screening all ap-
plications, the PWA managed to steer free of large scandals, which so often
go hand in hand with big public expenditure. Furthermore, Roosevelt himself was distrustful of quick spending; choosing Ickes was his way of keeping the government's dollars together. The paradox of having a program
that was meant to spend money but was reluctant to do so resulted from the
eventful birth of the NIRA, in which contradictory approaches had been
put together in one law, with the administration only later deciding how to

use the various provisions. At a more fundamental level, the PWA's course reveals a central ambivalence of the New Deal. For Roosevelt, budgetary prudence had a high priority. During a campaign speech in Pittsburgh in October 1932, he stressed the virtues of a balanced budget and accused Hoover of overspending. Such a policy, Roosevelt argued, would end "on the road to bankruptcy."[140] Deficits had to be financed, and this either entailed hurtful cuts in other sectors or inflation. Many experts and politicians at the time felt that in any scenario, deficits would make economic matters worse instead of improving them. Moreover, being "on the dole" was considered bad for the work ethos. It could keep the unemployed from searching for a proper job and lead them to expect the government to take care of them. For these reasons, Roosevelt promised during the campaign to cut back costs, and after he became president, people like Lewis Douglas, the director of the budget, constantly reminded him of his Pittsburgh pledge. Douglas did not just send Roosevelt a steady flow of gentle notes to that end until his resignation in August 1934; he also left his imprint on the work of the PWA by canceling some of its projects due to budgetary concerns.[141]

The New Deal, then, always fluctuated between fiscal conservatism and pump priming. While the first option still enjoyed the backing of many economists and staunch support from the American public, the second was more popular among the recipients of aid and, in the political elite, among the more unorthodox New Dealers, such as Tugwell or Adolf Berle, who believed that massive public spending was necessary in order to overcome the crisis. Not only would it bring direct relief to the poorest of the nation. Workers also needed more dollars in their pockets, Tugwell and others contended, in order to boost the economy through their spending. For them, "underconsumption" was the main reason for the Depression. Roosevelt did not fully share this view, and in 1933, conceived of public works as mainly charitable and remained deeply worried about the unwelcome debt that these programs forced on him. Additionally, he doubted that there were enough useful projects around the country to engage millions of people. Hence, the New Deal was far from Keynesian, even if the British economist publicly praised the American president for his "reasoned experiment within the framework of the existing social system."[142] As in so many other policy fields, the New Deal's policy on public works was characterized by inner tensions and contradictions.[143]

While Ickes tightfistedly controlled his immense budget, others looked for ways of circumventing him. In November 1933, PWA money allowed for the creation of the Civil Works Administration (CWA), which by January 1934 put 4.2 million Americans to work. Typical of the labyrinthine structure of the New Deal, the CWA was not a subagency of the PWA but instead belonged to the empire of Harry Hopkins, the mighty director of the Federal Emergency Relief Administration (FERA). This agency had been set up as another relief program in May 1933, building on a similar program that Hoover had instituted in the wake of the 1929 crash. Hopkins, as a key architect of the New Deal, was particularly qualified to run FERA since he had directed the New York State's relief program during Roosevelt's time as governor. FERA gave out loans to states to operate relief programs, which the states had to match on the basis of three state dollars for every federal one. The agency primarily created unskilled jobs in local and state governments. In contrast to Ickes, Hopkins spent the $500 million given to him for FERA quickly and, faced with continued high unemployment during winter 1933–34, got Roosevelt's blessing to set up the CWA as a short-term measure. For fear that the unemployed would rely too much on government aid, the CWA was terminated in spring 1934. FERA provided jobs for over twenty million people before it closed in December 1935.[144]

On top of these came other relief schemes, such as the CCC, which like FERA was set up during Roosevelt's first hundred days. Taken together, these agencies were a first step in direct federal relief and modern welfare state building. The dimensions of this surge were noteworthy: the $3.3 billion for the PWA equaled some 165 percent of federal government revenues for 1933 or 6 percent of the 1933 GDP. As such, the PWA was the biggest construction effort that the nation had ever seen.[145] Even before FERA ended in late 1935, the Works Progress Administration (WPA) took off— the largest of all New Deal agencies, with an annual budget of $1.4 billion, representing some 6.7 percent of the 1935 GDP and 135 percent of the federal government's revenues of that year. Directed by the brash and free-wheeling Hopkins, the WPA provided more than eight million jobs between 1935 and 1943, and at its peak in 1938 employed more than three million.[146]

FERA, the PWA, the CWA, the CCC, and the WPA may have confused contemporaries with their acronyms, but had many virtues. They helped many of America's poorest at a time when poverty meant a lack of food, clothes, housing, and other fundamentals. Lorena Hickok, the garrulous and sharp reporter traveling the country on a federal government ticket, started a letter to Hopkins with "Three loud cheers for CWA!"[147] Obviously, Hickok was far from impartial, yet her praise was not without basis. While the various relief agencies did not spare their enrollees the humiliating experience of having to present themselves during the intake, they paid wages for work instead of handing out charity, helping Americans to keep up their work ethic and self-respect. Many of their projects also improved America's infrastructure, with the CWA alone building and improving some five hundred thousand miles of roads, forty thousand schools, over thirty-five hundred parks, playgrounds, and athletic fields, and nearly a thousand airfields.[148] The WPA in particular added many more roads and roofs, but in comparison to the other programs, its focus was even broader, encompassing artistic projects as well as vocational training and college education.

But not everything was perfect. The CWA, mobilized in great haste, was far from efficient. In the early days, many of its projects began without the tools to execute them. Two CWA enrollees sometimes spent their time watching a third man using the only available shovel.[149] Such problems were not specific to the short-lived CWA. In 1935, the *New York Times* popularized the term "boondoggling," which entered the American political language to describe a public scheme wasting time and money. The article targeted the $3 million spent on recreational activities for the jobless, especially on the crafts classes teaching people how to produce "boon doggles."[150] Against this background, it was not helpful if, for instance, Hopkins argued that he would love to provide orchestras for beer gardens so that people would have an even better time since it "would be a great unemployment relief measure."[151]

Some forms of racial discrimination came on top. The CWA cut contractors out of competition, because, unlike the PWA, it did its own contracting. In the South, relief program wages were sometimes higher than those for regularly paid workers. Competition was jeopardized, and many white southerners hated the New Deal for "spoiling" African Americans. While thus challenging Jim Crowism, the New Deal's public works programs did not systematically fight to overcome discrimination since a lot of their administration lay in local hands.[152] Quite generally, the social effects of the program remained mixed. By focusing its help on the construction industry and building trades, the early New Deal in particular supported a part of the economy infamous for its discrimination against African Americans and women. It thus reinforced the model of the male (white) breadwinner and bypassed the more maternalist legacies of public policy from the Progressive era.[153] The WPA had a better balance sheet in that respect, but could not escape the accusation of bias either. Complaints also came from the millions of applicants who were not accepted, and some projects were accused of political favoritism. And indeed, statisticians have demonstrated that relief appropriations paid direct political dividends and federal spending was not free from the hope of maximizing electoral returns. The PWA remained less controversial than the WPA, where federal state action was more visible, and the hiring body was the state itself and not, as in the PWA, private firms. Hopkins's spendthrift approach had a price compared to Ickes's more cautious course.[154]

Launching public works projects to fight unemployment was neither new during the 1930s nor specific to the United States. At the municipal level, for instance, they had been used as a means of relief during the depression of 1857, when the mayor of New York suggested giving the unem-

FIGURE 2. President Roosevelt planting a tree in Hilo,
Hawaii, 1934. Photo: Fritz Kraft, Honolulu, Hawaii.

ployed work such as street cleaning or stone quarrying.[155] Considerable
pressure had built up by 1933 to take federal action. As in so many other
fields, there was some continuity between the Hoover and Roosevelt administrations. What was new now was the strong emphasis on Washington
along with the sheer size of the projects and their longevity. Also internationally, public works projects were far from unique to America. Many
other countries had used public works long before the 1930s as well, but
often only at a municipal level or on a rather small scale. No government, as
American economist Arthur D. Gayer noted in 1935, had considered a public works scheme as a major national program, and "none attempted to
apply it on a comprehensive scale" before the Great Depression.[156]

Now governments around the globe felt forced to do so, driven by the
depth of the crisis, increased expectations concerning state action in the
wake of World War I mobilizations, and intense transnational interaction.
Since 1931, the League of Nations' Committee for Communications and

Transit turned into a clearinghouse for expertise on public works, working in close collaboration with the ILO, as the committee's secretary general, the Frenchman Robert Haas, stressed. As well as joint projects in Europe, the committee collated information about programs in states as diverse as El Salvador, South Africa, New Zealand, China, and Iraq.[157] International public works projects, promoted by the League of Nations and the ILO, were launched in 1931, and concentrated on transborder cooperation in Europe—for instance, in the Danubian Basin. After two years of discussions and negotiations, these plans collapsed in 1933, and instead the nation-states stood at the center of attention.[158]

In the United States as elsewhere, the national administration now gained in importance, even if this dimension is often overstressed. Certainly, the public works programs turned into the New Deal's centerpiece for fighting the crisis, despite the somewhat haphazard history of their creation. Still, all New Deal relief programs, except the CCC, were jointly financed by federal, state, and local governments, and the role of Washington at the bureaucratic level remained small, leaving public relations campaigns and other forms of ballyhoo aside.[159] Many other states likewise saw huge regional public works schemes next to the well-advertised national ones. Nazi Germany, for example, not only had its *Notstandsarbeiter* (emergency workers)—engaged in building the autobahns, among other things—but also smaller regional programs such as the Tapolski Plan for the Rhineland.[160] Still, in many states the biggest hoopla was concentrated at the national level, stylizing the state as a powerful actor providing relief and fighting the slump. Just as in the United States, public works schemes elsewhere remained hamstrung by scruples about keeping budgets balanced and stabilizing the currency. Even if Roosevelt was notorious for building new agencies, slashing their budgets, and then increasing them again, similar developments can be seen in other places, too.[161]

Despite these transfers and parallels, the extent to which states promoted public works in the wake of the Depression varied. If the United States during the early New Deal tended to be a country with an enormous emergency employment relief policy but little long-term social policy, in Great Britain the situation tended to be the reverse: British public works programs remained marginal in comparison to the United States. Simultaneously, a large proportion of the unemployed in Britain and Belgium were supported by unemployment insurance.[162] Latin America also saw many projects of a similar kind during the decade, leading to a dramatic expansion of the road system. In some states like Guatemala under Jorge Ubico y Castañeda, a dictatorship relied on coercion to obtain the labor needed to build roads, and also in Nazi Germany there was a large gray area between a free choice to enroll in relief programs and forced labor.[163]

All quantitative differences aside, work creation in sovereign states around the world was more than an administrative solution for a clearly defined group. In each society, these projects were also meant to epitomize a new sense of individual dignity and national community, created around a work-centered social contract. The state provided support and security through mass mobilization to a degree that the world had never seen before. To be sure, in practice these efforts always remained limited, and inclusion of some groups often went hand in hand with the exclusion of others, whether due to race, gender, class, age, or other criteria. Yet in many countries around the world, the use of such programs created new strong links between the state and society.

Finally, public works projects frequently endured longer than planned. In the United States, they were always understood as a temporary recovery measure, designed to relieve the short-term effects of the unemployment crisis. The public works scheme that Hopkins had run in New York during Roosevelt's time as governor was, revealingly, called the Temporary Emergency Relief Administration—with not just one but instead two words in its name referring to its short life span. Even if the CWA was quickly dismantled in 1934 and FERA came to an end one year later, the PWA under Ickes remained until 1943, as did the WPA under Hopkins. Obviously the New Deal did not resolve its inner conflicts, and state intervention was here to stay until the war boom made public works programs superfluous.

Facing Fascism? The CCC

Among the early New Deal's relief programs, the Civilian Conservation Corps was particularly intriguing both for what it did and what it avoided. Its taboos were thoroughly defined by global perceptions and exchanges.

On March 21, less than three weeks after his inauguration, Roosevelt formally asked Congress to select and organize 250,000 young, unemployed men and to put them to work within three months as a means of relief against unemployment. The CCC was to help underprivileged Americans between the age of eighteen and twenty-five. A combination of hard physical work outdoors, vocational training, a broad educational program, and a disciplined way of life in camps far from urban centers was meant to improve these men's self-confidence, physical shape, and employability. Ultimately, the enrollees were to become "law-abiding, respectable, and useful citizens."[164] Vis-à-vis public works schemes, the CCC stood out for its age- and gender-specific target group as well as the strong conservationist flavor of the projects it undertook. More important, it combined a work dimension with an explicit educational zeal, and as such, is best characterized as a labor service.

No other program of the first hundred days is as closely linked to Roosevelt's name as the New Deal's labor service, which was largely the product of his initiative and ideas. Building on measures that he had come out with during his time as governor of New York, Roosevelt set up an interdepart-

mental committee to design such a program only ten days after his inauguration. Besides being the president's personal interest, the CCC looked like
the perfect embodiment of the New Deal. It stood for bold state action, mass
mobilization, and an expanded welfare state. The corps had to organize hundreds of thousands in little time, and through this task, the federal government won new competences for relief and education. Even if many Americans disliked such interventionism in general, this did not hold true for the
CCC. Surveys show that it figured among the most popular New Deal institutions during the 1930s. The CCC was not just Roosevelt's pet agency but
also the darling of the nation. In 1936, for instance, Republican presidential
candidate Alfred M. Landon, then governor of Kansas, specifically endorsed
the CCC and thus removed it from the arena of campaign criticism. Against
this backdrop, the CCC became one of the most successful New Deal agencies. Hundreds of thousands of young Americans in need passed through its
camps, and by 1942, the total number stood at nearly three million men.[165]
The enrollees were given shelter, food, work, and an educational program to
improve their chances of future employment. Vocational classes included
cooking, clerical work, stone masonry, forestry, and road building. On a
more fundamental level, a literacy campaign was run. By 1936, after three
years of operation, the corps had taught more than thirty-five thousand men
to read and write. Enrollees with a higher standard of education had the
chance to complete high school or continue with college work in evening
classes. The CCC also offered courses such as arts and crafts, dramatics, and
music. Besides this educational dimension, the practical work of the corps
helped restore America's depleted natural resources. "Roosevelt's Tree Army"
became a popular nickname for the program, since planting trees was often
regarded as the CCC's primary field of work, and is now its best-remembered
task. In fact, the CCC was responsible for more than half of all the forest
planting ever done in the United States up to the 1940s. Even more camps
were engaged in other types of projects, however, such as firefighting, flood
control, wildlife conservation, and road construction.[166]

In the light of its accomplishments, it is not surprising that the corps was
highly regarded by the American people. Even after its discontinuation in
1942 due to the changed war context, it garnered a reputation. There is a
whole host of post-1945 programs that explicitly referred to the wording
and spirit of the CCC, most obviously in the case of the California Conservation Corps created in 1976. But John F. Kennedy's Peace Corps and Lyndon B. Johnson's National Job Corps also paid homage to the New Deal
labor service. The CCC still lives on today, too—for example, through the
CCC camp museums in various parts of the country.[167]

And yet this seemingly quintessential American institution was clearly
influenced by factors outside US history. The CCC had siblings in a long list
of nations; this kinship and its consequences partly explain the agency's

trajectory. When the CCC bill was presented to Congress back in March 1933, it met rather little resistance, even if it granted broad and only vaguely defined powers to the president. Among its critics, though, was the influential president of the AFL, William Green, according to whom the bill "smacks, as I see it, of fascism, of Hitlerism, of a form of sovietism."[168] Green's remarks were as opaque as they were polemic, and at the time "Hitlerism" had not yet shown its full face. Nevertheless, his anxieties were symptomatic of those Americans who feared the United States might take a turn to authoritarian leadership or even dictatorship.

This criticism acquired substance when it became clear that US Army officers would run the CCC camps and that the military in general would play a major role in the corps. From one point of view, this involvement made perfect sense, since Washington simply did not have other institutional capacities—the logistics, experts, housing, equipment, and the like—to set up such a large institution in such little time. In the early 1930s, the federal government was small. The task seemed almost impossible, and hence could only be managed by drawing on preexisting organizations.

On the other hand, this proved to be crucial for the public debate over the CCC, as an institution based on a paramilitary structure. Even if Green's worries remained rather vague, he and other critics could point to an immediate example of their worst-case scenario: developments in Germany. A few years before Americans discussed setting up the CCC, the unstable Weimar democracy had created a voluntary labor service in 1931, primarily to fight mass unemployment. In the Freiwillige Arbeitsdienst, young men were organized in camps and put to practical work, and as in America, the German institution had an educational zeal. The enrollees, some of whom had never worked at all, were to be reintegrated into society. Some voices in the German debate had much more far-reaching goals than their American counterparts. Beyond employability as an aim, they saw this organization as a mediator between social, religious, and particularly political tensions in Germany. Through joint work, the labor service intended to turn into the cradle of a new national identity. When the Nazis came to power in January 1933, they did not dissolve the voluntary labor service but instead reshaped it according to their ideology. The Arbeitsdienst from then on was called the "school of the nation" and glorified as a prototype of the National Socialist *Volksgemeinschaft*.[169] Alongside the Arbeitsdienst becoming a much-hailed cornerstone of the new regime, the Third Reich introduced premilitary training and tried to turn the labor service into a paramilitary institution.[170]

Leading American newspapers reported on all these changes in Germany. For instance, the *New York Times* wrote about the various steps that the regime undertook to force the labor service into line—a process that commenced during the very weeks that America was considering setting up a labor service, too.[171] Given the developments in Germany and the role of the army in the CCC's organization, some Americans feared that the corps could also be turned into a paramilitary institution with hundreds of thousands young men as an unconstitutional army for a potential dictator. Not only did organized labor hold these views with respect to the corps but also liberal journals such as the *Nation* or the *New Republic*. After 1933, they argued as well that the involvement of the army could lead the corps and country toward fascism. American Socialists and Communists were of the same opinion. At the other end of the political spectrum, conservative members of Congress, who opposed the quasi-dictatorial powers that Roosevelt asked for in order to establish the corps, voiced similar criticism.[172] Consequently, the German labor service became the embodiment of American anxieties about the CCC's future.

Roosevelt took great pains to allay such fears. He reiterated that major differences separated the American labor service from its German counterpart. It was for this reason that the president appointed Robert Fechner as director of the CCC. Fechner was a widely respected labor leader, vice president of the AFL, and anything but radical. A "down-the-line" Gompers's man on labor questions, the rawboned and patient machinist was far from embodying militaristic or protofascist qualities. This made him the perfect choice for Roosevelt. The CCC bill passed smoothly through Congress in the last days of March 1933 once the public's anxieties had been calmed.[173]

After the CCC had been set up, Fechner and his staff continuously emphasized that there was no military preparation as well as no kind of drill in the corps. In line with this stance, Roosevelt rejected all political attempts to introduce such training. When, for example, Assistant Secretary of War Harry H. Woodring suggested in January 1934 that the CCC should develop a more military character, the American public was outraged. The White House dissociated itself from Woodring's statement and forced him to apologize publicly.[174] Several similar initiatives, mostly expressed by high army officers, met the same fate. The American public and especially the press kept a close watch on developments within the corps. Every hint of military drill was harshly criticized as "fascist" or a form of "Hitlerism."[175]

Thus, the US perception of the Nazi labor service had a major impact on the CCC. It was the polar opposite from which the corps distanced itself. Furthermore, the perception of the Nazi labor service narrowed the American scope of action. Some options, such as the militarization of the CCC, were taboo because they allegedly resembled developments in Germany— even though a militarized corps would not necessarily have had a fascist or totalitarian character. Yet the political atmosphere of early New Deal society, fundamentally uprooted by the crisis of capitalism and democracy, made it impossible even to discuss the options of military drill or training publicly, and the vocabulary to denounce such options referred to existing programs beyond American shores.

Such transnational turbulences also characterized labor services introduced at the same time in other democracies, such as Sweden. The Frivillig Arbetstjänst, instituted in 1933, in many ways resembled the CCC as a voluntary, state-funded institution addressing the unemployed, giving them both work and education. At its inception, it was largely inspired by the labor service created in democratic Germany before Hitler's rise to power. After Nazism took over in Germany, the Swedish Arbetstjänst did much to distance itself from its southern sibling. With the military not involved, it was even easier than in America for the government to stress the civilian character of the labor service.[176]

At the same time, developments in both Germany and Sweden suggest that the CCC was less unique and specific to America than typically thought. During the early 1930s, in fact, more than a dozen nations experimented with this form of relief. After Bulgaria spearheaded the whole movement in 1920, going so far as to introduce a compulsory labor service for men and women, state institutions or civil society groups in Switzerland, the Netherlands, and Great Britain also set up such schemes. Beyond Europe, which was the center of labor service developments, the United States was joined by Peru and Japan. In 1934 and 1937, two international conferences were held to exchange views, with CCC officials contributing to both subsequent publications. Contemporary experts thus compared organizational patterns, educational goals, and work methods as well as positioning themselves in a wider international debate.[177]

At this international level, the CCC and the Nazi Arbeitsdienst were by far the largest as well as most important organizations, and also the two main points of reference. Despite the fundamental difference between democracy and dictatorship, they shared several characteristics with each other and their siblings elsewhere. All labor services were conceived as remedies for the Great Depression. They were designed to kill several birds with one stone by overcoming the slump through work creation and vocational training, strengthening the weakened and depleted through regular meals and physical exercise, disciplining the young through strictly organized camps to counter all sorts of deviance (particularly criminality and political extremism), and shoring up heterosexual masculinity through work in forests and swamps, or in the rarer cases of separate organizations for women, fortifying femininity through caregiving and housekeeping. Concurrently, they all epitomized a heightened level of state action—the idea of a new responsibility of the state to care for its citizens, but also a new level of mobilization along with deeper penetration of society through techniques of social engineering, disciplining, and ordering. They also had an implicit insulationist tendency, attempting to fight this multiplicity of crises primarily at the national level and through the nation-state—whereas previously, regional, transnational, and civil society actors had often played a larger role. Such ideas of interventionism had gained momentum since the late eighteenth century with the onset of a new age of political action and participatory as well as distributive ideas. It took World War I to give these aims full international visibility and finally the Great Depression to put them into peacetime practice in a host of societies.

If at this level the CCC shared astonishing similarities with labor services elsewhere, including the Nazi Arbeitsdienst, there were certainly basic differences.[178] While democracies were content to experiment with labor services, at most introducing voluntary institutions like the American Corps, authoritarian regimes and dictatorships tended to create compulsory institutions. Nazi Germany used its Arbeitsdienst to identify and discriminate against Jews and other minorities, whereas in New Deal America, African Americans or Native Americans remained strongly underrepresented in the CCC, but they were allowed to participate.[179] Moreover, and much like in Sweden's democracy, the CCC was more geared toward benefiting the individual, whereas in Germany, fostering nationalism and bonds between the *Volksgenossen* gained the upper hand. Finally, disciplining never became as harsh in America as it was in Germany, and the military dimensions of the Arbeitsdienst never made it across the Atlantic—not least because of the abhorrent German example.

Even more than for the NRA, European developments thus impacted on the trajectory of this New Deal agency. This process culminated in 1938, when the president of the United States personally ordered a report on the Nazi Arbeitsdienst from the US embassy in Berlin—notably not to gain propaganda material against the Third Reich but instead as a source of inspiration. Explaining his motives, Roosevelt himself pointed out in an internal letter, "All of this helps us in planning, even though our methods are of the democratic variety!"[180] Soon afterward, the CCC even adopted certain technical and apolitical elements of the Nazi agency. Developments had come full circle by then: whereas most of the time, the Arbeitsdienst had been the CCC's example to avoid, it now even served as a model. Altogether, the CCC became what it was because it was exposed to and part of a global marketplace of alternatives and contacts.

PLANNING AND MOBILIZATION

"We Are All Planners Now"

"It suffices to consider countries as different as the United States of America, Soviet Russia, Italy or Germany," the Belgian socialist Hendrik de Man (1885–1953) argued in October 1933, "to understand the irresistible force of this push towards a planned national economy."[181] Five months later, the

American ambassador to Greece, Lincoln MacVeagh, reported back to Washington: "We have had in Greece for the past year an example of a country operating almost completely under the principles of a planned economy," adding that this had led to "increased prosperity and national satisfaction."[182] In Britain, the left-wing politician and economist Evan Durbin had already proclaimed in 1930 that "we are all Planners now."[183] And the League of Nations praised Australia particularly for its economic planning efforts.[184]

Countries big and small, democracies as well as dictatorships of the Left and Right, all seemed to be heading in the same direction. While prior to the Great Depression many industrialized societies had first discussed Taylorism, and then a "rationalization" of economic relationships through much less intense and permanent state intervention, state-led planning now took over this role.[185] Planning meant more than specific schemes for banks, agriculture, industry, or other branches. It also was no longer confined to times of war. Indeed, societies around the world were wondering whether it should become a fundamental aspect of economic life.

The whole debate was not just driven by the Great Slump and the failure of laissez-faire but by the perceived successes of the Soviet Union, too. The planning hype basically resulted from a mixture of necessity, fascination, and fear. With the breakdown of America's 1920s prosperity, global eyes wandered east, and what they saw in the Soviet Union was planning writ large and yielding remarkable results: the first five-year plan from 1928 to 1932 extended centralized planning to every sector of the economy. While capitalist societies and their colonies were mired in depression, the Soviet Union had eliminated unemployment. Pig iron and coal production fell short of the unrealistic targets of the plan, but both almost doubled during this short interval. Magnitogorsk, inspired by steel mills in Indiana and Pennsylvania, and built with American help, developed from nothing into the world's largest steel mill. All in all, the country's scale and pace of change were breathtaking. Planning seemed the recipe to transform the USSR from an agrarian peasant society to an industrial power in the course of a decade.[186]

Soviet planning also had its dark sides. As part of the surge of industrialization, Stalinism unleashed shock waves of repression and violence. The five-year plan did more to cause than prevent the famine of 1932–33 with its millions of victims. Additionally, the planning machinery worked far from smoothly, and as recent research has demonstrated, the Soviet drive for autarky was more a defensive reaction to world economic developments than a deliberate decision on the part of the Soviet government.[187] But these aspects remained peripheral to the global conversation at the time. The regime was effective in suppressing any kind of information that would have impacted negatively on its international image. The apparent death throes of capitalism made some observers rather uncritical about developments in Stalin's planned economy.

International interest in the Soviet Union was enormous. This holds especially true for countries in central and eastern Europe, where traditional political elites feared Soviet economic and political pressure along with homegrown Communist groups—and often a combination of both. But experts and politicians in other parts of the world were also astutely aware of the Soviet experiment. In comparison to the Russian five-year plan of 1928–32, capitalist efforts seemed "hesitant and colourless" to Australian economist F.R.E. Mauldon in 1931. Capitalist societies should respond with "*super*-national planning," he insisted.[188] In Britain, the five-year plan was central to the change in public opinion in favor of state intervention.[189] In 1932, American historian Charles A. Beard published a volume surveying various suggestions on planning. His own chapter argued for a five-year plan for America and stressed that planning had more American than Russian roots.[190] American economist Stuart Chase simply asked, "Why should Russians have all the fun of remaking a world?"[191]

How exactly a capitalist planning model should look was much less clear, however. As early as 1931, Australian economist Colin Clark warned that the term "bids fair to become a cliché."[192] During most of the decade, the meaning of the word "planning" remained unstable; while at the beginning of the 1930s it primarily designated cartel planning with a state imprimatur, it later came to connote more invasive forms of collectivism. The whole debate was underpinned by appeals to science and modernity, and the new role that experts could play in molding the world.

Among fascist dictatorships, Italy spearheaded the move to economic planning well before the onset of the Great Slump, and contemporaries around the world largely identified the term "fascism" with such planning. A large public sector was created under the fascist banner, but while in theory the state gained control over the economy, in reality many industrial managers continued much as before, and there was no grand design for state intervention.[193] State control also increased substantially in Nazi Germany beginning in 1933, featuring plans named after secondary leaders— the Koch Plan to reduce unemployment in East Prussia, or the particularly radical Hellmuth Plan to reorganize Lower Franconia economically and along racial lines. More important were the two four-year plans of the mid-1930s, whose name referred to the abhorred Soviet example, while stressing that the Nazi regime would require even less time to bring about change. Still, the reality of the planned economy was as ambiguous in Germany as in Italy. Even in the aircraft industry, the Nazis' model of successful state-directed expansion, there was a scope for entrepreneurial initiative. Big business remained an active and independent partner of the regime. Despite the hopes of the party's statist fringe, intervention never became all encompassing. Central coordination was never established, much less control.[194] Japan followed a similar course, often emulating German ideas and policies, but also fascinated by Italy's trajectory.[195] Its 1931 Important Industry Control Law introduced a system of negotiated self-regulation, and direct state control and planning remained patchy throughout the 1930s here, too.[196]

With dictatorships of the radical Left and Right taking the lead, the world's democracies were seen as stragglers in the surge for planning. Among the countries that were soon identified with a strong planning dimension, Sweden is particularly interesting. The Social Democrats who ruled from 1932 onward rejected Marxist ideology and the Soviet example of socializing industry. Their centralized planning focused on certain economic dimensions, especially fiscal and housing policy and public works, while their approach to industry and agriculture remained much more cautious. As for all societies of the interwar years, political self-fashioning was as crucial as the measurable economic and social effects of a program, and Sweden proved successful in couching itself as a rational, modern society.[197]

Elsewhere too, a generation of young social democrats showed a proclivity to planning. By comparison, Belgium's de Man was already rather old when he returned from Germany in 1933 to formulate the *Plan van den Arbeid* for industrial Belgium. De Man advocated a socialist plan within a capitalist framework with a central planning body, the National Office for Economic Recovery. While de Man's *planisme*—itself inspired by the ideas of unorthodox social democrats in Germany's ill-fated Weimar democracy—was widely received in western Europe at the time, only parts of this approach were realized. Disillusioned, de Man drifted rightward and became a collaborator of the Nazis during World War II. In quite a few other countries, including Austria and Australia, unorthodox social democrats arguing for planning also failed to win political power in the course of the 1930s. Sometimes, as in Australia, they were defeated in elections and suffered from internal divisions; sometimes, as in Austria, they were crushed by right-wing regimes.[198] Austria is also significant because two of the most powerful free market critics of the emerging planning tradition, Friedrich August Hayek and Ludwig von Mises, were émigré Austrian economists. Asserting that planning was inherently authoritarian, their neoliberal ideas remained marginal at the time, but would rise to prominence decades later, scaffolding the policies of leaders like Ronald Reagan or Margaret Thatcher.[199] During the 1930s, politicians such as Dutch prime minister Hendrikus Colijn frequently ruled the day who was identified with the motto "geen 'planwirtschaft'" (no planned economy).[200]

In Latin America, national planning was "extensive and varied," as American economist Louis Lorwin noted in a report surveying global developments in 1941. Mexico launched its first six-year plan in 1934, Cuba kicked off its three-year plan in 1937, and Chile and Venezuela initiated their respective plans one year later. These and other states also instituted special agencies to take charge of national planning. Mexico went the furthest in projecting "a general outline of a new social system" that "indicated a series of legislative measures by which that system was to be established," as Lorwin maintained. Besides a land reform that included expropriation in favor of communal use under cooperative ownership and management (the *ejido*), the Mexican Plan argued for legislation strengthening the rights of organized labor and nationalizing natural resources. Brazil's 1937 constitution established the National Economic Council promoting a corporative organization of the economy, but during the 1930s partial planning also dominated here. All things considered, planning was by no means restricted to the global North, and land reform in parts of the global South and the Soviet Union went much further than in New Deal America.[201]

The US New Deal established an independent national planning agency, as in so many other countries; it was the first in the nation's history. The National Planning Board (NPB) was set up in July 1933 as an adjunct to the PWA under Title II of the NIRA, and complemented the sectoral or partial planning of the AAA and NRA. Originally instituted with the rather limited goal of offsetting economic downturns through public construction, the planners of the NPB were soon reviewing planning efforts around the nation and preparing a "plan for planning." The draft version of this report, presented to FDR in June 1934, dealt with planning in all its components. It included a section on the experience of other countries, yet in the end stressed the Americanness of the concept, listing a long line of planning efforts including the constitutional convention and Alexander Hamilton's 1791 *Report on Manufactures*. The NPB report did not come out in favor of complete government control but instead underscored the need for more action on a voluntary basis. Building on a firm belief in progress, science, and rationality, its authors contended that experts should take the lead in a newly created "coordinating secretariat," and work in concert with elected leaders and stakeholders.[202] The experts that the board members envisioned playing this role were none other than themselves. Roosevelt, while in general liking the idea of planning, was thinking much more short term. Instead of a grand design, he wanted concrete recommendations on specific issues, and the far reaching plans of the board did not fly. The NPB lingered on under different names as an advisory body until 1943, mainly producing research papers amounting to more than forty thousand pages of printed material, yet it did not turn into a central coordination or planning agency.[203]

Ideas of more central and coordinated planning were not realized during the early New Deal. Key members of the NPB were anything but radicals. All of them were old hands from the Hoover administration, including the agency's chairman, FDR's uncle Frederic A. Delano. In planning, often singled out as a key innovation of the New Deal, continuities prevailed at least for this body, the only national planning agency that America ever had. Admittedly, some early New Dealers argued for a more sweeping and centralized approach. Tugwell, for instance, had advocated the need for a central planning body in 1932. President Roosevelt rejected these more drastic ideas, however, and kept Tugwell and others busy working out sector-specific schemes.[204]

Roosevelt was not alone in his skepticism vis-à-vis the more radical plans. During the 1930s, planners remained a well-educated minority, in America as elsewhere. In the United States, congressional and public resistance against any all-encompassing planning was insurmountable. Opposition in other countries was also considerable. While economists like the émigrés Hayek in London and Mises in New York spearheaded new rationales against any kind of planning, the mainstream remained rooted in traditional liberal ideas that saw planning as an undue state intervention in the market and infringement of individual rights.

Under these circumstances, "partial" planning with a heavy associational dimension was the fashion of the day. Although some have claimed that this characteristic makes the American brand of planning unique, a wider historical perspective tells a different story.[205] First, it is difficult to condense the New Deal's take on planning, given that it played out differently in the AAA, NRA, NPB, and other agencies. Second, NPB discussions were fundamentally shaped by planning debates in other parts of the world, particularly in Europe, and actors around the globe were keenly aware of developments in the United States.[206] Third, planning remained eclectic and versatile in Europe, Latin America, and Australia as well. This was clearly the case in countries with a conservative government such as Greece under Panagis Tsaldaris or in Great Britain with its National Government, which officially refrained from planning even though its industrial reorganization policy contained some aspects of planning and it saw a remarkably complex variety of planning ideas.[207] Even social democrats wanted to avoid antagonizing big business. In Sweden, Australia, and Belgium, selective approaches with a strong voluntaristic element predominated. Latin American countries were no exception to this rule. In his aforementioned report, Lorwin concluded that despite many comprehensive plans, partial planning dominated in this part of the globe, too. Hence, the New Deal was not alone in going for partial planning and stumbling from program to program, trying to fix problems as they arose. The same holds true for most other capitalist societies. Those democracies that did survive the 1930s were often more reticent than the New Deal, while even authoritarian and fascist dictatorships were far from full-blown state control and coercion. The 1930s were not about a simple bipolar choice between laissez-faire and all-encompassing statism, nor was planning democracy's answer to the challenges of the time. Rather, partial planning, whatever its ideational sources, concrete programs, and degree of cohesion, was mainly about saving and changing capitalism. Most societies, regardless of their political system, were unwilling to touch the core tenets of the existing economic system, such as property rights and a certain level of profit orientation. In that sense, capitalism proved much more resilient than democracy.

The New Deal thus was part of a wide continuum of options, and it even went further toward a mixed economy model than most other democracies.[208] The only countries that were really unique when it came to the level of state intervention and planning were the Soviet Union in a general sense as well as Mexico as a state that basically retained a capitalist system, but a highly restricted one.

For the nonwhite elites of Africa and Asia, the global hour of economic planning would only strike in the decades after World War II. Certainly, the Kuomintang in China tried to enact planning, taking its cue from Sun Yat-sen's 1922 Industrial Plan (Shiye jihua). In 1933, the Chinese National Economic Council was invested with greater executive powers and was made responsible for the rehabilitation of the cotton and silk industries. For many reasons, such plans did not come to fruition.[209] Things were similar in India: the Congress Party, as a pivotal part of the independence movement, installed a planning committee that acted as a kind of shadow government. Planners such as engineer Mokshagundam Visvesvaraya drew lessons from the Soviet experience. But due to colonial rule, serious planned development only commenced after independence in 1947.[210] During the interwar years, planning was mainly a practice of the elites in Moscow, Rome, and Berlin as well as Mexico City, Santiago, Stockholm, Brussels, and Washington.[211]

European, Australian, American, and in this case even Soviet approaches all prioritized planning at the national level. During the 1930s, the League of Nations also adopted the rhetoric of planning, and as early as 1931, Alfred E. Zimmern, a British member of one of the League's many committees, contended that "the devotees of 'planning' must learn to think internationally."[212] The League's efforts were of little avail, however. Most planners at the time felt that "planning begins at home."[213] While the history of this phenomenon is replete with international exchange and the transfer of ideas, most societies invented long national planning traditions during the 1930s. The United States refashioned Hamilton as an ancestor of planning, and the British ennobled their post office to the same role. The only transnational dimension for which planning held some relevance was colonial possessions; at the time, interested circles in London discussed "imperial planning."[214] Here again, planning did not focus on international cooperation.

The 1930s also supplied fertile ground for economists like Britain's Keynes, Poland's Michał Kalecki, and America's Lorwin to rationalize as well as systematize the political practices that they witnessed all around them. In the West, the decade turned into a laboratory for the kind of mixed economy that would dominate the post-1945 order, while also serving as a breeding ground for its most radical critics, such as Hayek or Mises. In the East, the 1930s assured Stalin that large-scale planning worked and that others should be forced to follow socialism. The New Deal and similar approaches in other capitalist countries remained, for them, insufficient and incomplete copies of the real thing.

Reform River

If partial planning was the dominant mode in the United States at the time, there was also an exception that proved the rule. In one area, the government itself was the chief planning agent, acquiring a much more active role than with the NRA or AAA, or under the auspices of the NPB. In May 1933, the New Dealers launched the Tennessee Valley Authority to provide navigation, land reclamation, flood control, electricity generation, fertilizer manufacturing, and agricultural development in the Tennessee valley. The region covered no less than seven states and some forty-one thousand square miles, and was deeply mired in economic depression. Bold planning set out to change that, and indeed the TVA modified life in the valley forever.[215]

The new deal for the Tennessee River had its roots in a political controversy of World War I and the 1920s. The 1916 National Defense Act stipulated that facilities to produce nitrates for ammunition and fertilizers were to be set up at Muscle Shoals on the Tennessee River in Alabama. The first plant went into production shortly after the guns around the world were silenced, but the hydroelectric dam, included to supply the enormous amount of energy required for synthetic nitrogen production, was never completed. After the war, the debate shifted from fertilizers to hydropower. Republican Progressives lobbied to finish the project to generate cheap electricity, but opposition from utility companies, fearing public intervention in their business, proved too strong. This, in turn, was grist for the Progressives' mill: public power advocates led by Republican senator George W. Norris from Nebraska felt that corporations were doing too little to electrify rural America and to alleviate the plight of the rural South. Norris, who towered over the debate just as he wanted the Muscle Shoals dam to dominate the Tennessee River, steadfastly argued for government operation of the facility. Having introduced several bills to that end over the course of the 1920s, in 1930 he won the support of both branches of Congress. In the end, however, Herbert Hoover used his presidential veto to sink the bill. Private enterprise advocates and adherents of small government ruled the day.[216]

Against this backdrop, the TVA bill represented the confluence of several strands. It reacted to a long-standing concern of Republican Progressives, yet the TVA idea was also attractive to traditional southern Democrats, who hoped it would turn into a bonanza for a region that was mostly in their party's hands. The TVA thus helped to seal one of the most unlikely political alliances in American political history, which soon turned into a mainstay of the New Deal coalition. Washington also attempted to salvage its wartime investment through this bill. More important, the project allowed the government to showcase how the Roosevelt administration differed from Hoover and the Republican era of the 1920s. Given that the Tennessee region had long become a symbol of the depleted state of the nation, the new administration simply grasped an obvious opportunity for activism.[217]

And action there was aplenty. Roosevelt called the TVA a "cooperation clothed with the power of Government but possessed of the flexibility and initiative of a private enterprise"—a formulation as grandiloquent as it was gauzy.[218] The TVA Act of May 18, 1933, established a federal agency answerable directly to the president. It was subject to only limited congressional oversight, and quite autonomous in its finances and operations. Nor did the TVA have any formal connection to the governments of the seven riparian states; a three-man board of directors ran it. For the first time, a major American region was given an agency to address its total resource development needs in an attempt to achieve rapid modernization. Under this plan, the Tennessee River and its tributaries figured as a primary resource and so-called multipurpose dams—for flood control, navigation, electricity generation, and other goals all at the same time—as the key tool of economic development.[219]

On top of this, the TVA carried a great deal of political meaning. For the New Dealers, the TVA was to be a marker of national strength, coherence, and the controllability of nature at the hands of seemingly apolitical, technical experts. It was to demonstrate what vigorous federal intervention could achieve. They saw the Tennessee River as a gigantic metaphor for the need for unbridled capitalism to be contained, channeled, and put to use for the public good. The TVA therefore soon became a particularly potent—if not the most important—symbol of the New Deal.[220]

At the ideational level, finally, it stood at the convergence of two different planning tracks: the dominant strand during most of the century, focused on the nation's physical landscape and its relationship to its national resources; and its junior sibling, centered around comprehensive planning for social and economic ends.[221] Practically speaking, the former soon dominated, and reformist ideas of social engineering were cloaked in the guise of a technical infrastructure project. The TVA leadership played a crucial role in ensuring that the federal government juggernaut remained acceptable for most Americans—even if at the beginning, the TVA seemed to be floating in a different direction. Arthur E. Morgan, chairman of the board and a "social thinker touched with utopianism," had far-reaching ambitions to change the fabric of southern society. The president felt similarly, asserting, "Power is really a secondary matter.... [W]e are trying to make a different type of citizen."[222] With such backing, Morgan wanted to use the TVA as a laboratory for alternatives to the destructive aspects of liberal capitalism. He planned to turn the TVA into a vehicle for building community life with lively local participation. His ideas were driven by a missionary zeal undergirded by puritanism, a strong interest in eugenics, and benevolent paternalism. Arthur Morgan envisioned ambitious educational projects, considered introducing a local currency, wanted his valley dwellers to abstain from alcohol and tobacco, and intended to dispossess farmers who failed to apply sound agricultural practices.

Codirector Harcourt A. Morgan, in contrast, was mainly interested in fertilizer production and agricultural policy. David E. Lilienthal, whom Arthur Morgan characterized in an internal letter as "brilliant thorough accurate aggressive fair loyal [sic] and committed to public interests. Racial characteristics not obtrusive," had a strong record on utilities policy.[223] Together, the latter two thwarted their chairman's more exalted ambitions and shaped the TVA as an enterprise with a strong bottom-up dimension. While not formally accountable to local citizens, the authority did involve the valley's inhabitants, and strove to work with and through existing institutions. Only due to the direction taken by the technical intelligentsia that managed it— and not because of its original design—did the TVA become tied to influential local constituencies. Its agricultural program, for instance, worked with land grant colleges and county agents to test experimental fertilizers.[224] Lilienthal, who was gifted in dramatizing and selling the TVA approach, extolled its "definite rôle ... as a stimulating and coördinating force."[225]

And certainly the TVA achieved much. It improved navigation on the Tennessee River and its tributaries. It provided electricity for the first time to thousands of households. Floods became less frequent, and the standard of living of many in the valley improved. The TVA management succeeded in toning down the aura of vast and intrusive federal action. The luster of the monumental dams was nonetheless symbolic of New Deal activism, of the will to confront the challenges of the Great Depression head-on and instill hope in Americans.[226]

The TVA was by no means the only river basin planning project in America at the time. The Bureau of Reclamation, for example, constructed the gargantuan Hoover Dam on the Colorado River and had worked on projects in China during the 1920s. The PWA was responsible for the Fort Peck Dam in northeast Montana, and the Army Corps of Engineers was another major player engaged in this field long before the TVA. Still, the Tennessee valley and its colossal, centrally designed regional landscape stole the thunder from its rivals, with the exception of the Hoover Dam, authorized by

Coolidge and dedicated by Roosevelt in 1935. Sadly for Norris, the Hoover Dam was higher than the one carrying his name, but he could find solace in the fact that Hoover was a single, stand-alone dam, whereas "his" dam formed part of a much larger endeavor.[227]

Not all the TVA's hopes were realized, however. The authority did not turn into a template for grand projects on the Columbia or Mississippi rivers, as Roosevelt, Lilienthal, and others had planned.[228] Resistance from other parts of the administration, conservatives, and public utility companies always remained fierce. The TVA's monopolistic position as energy provider coupled with Washington's vast role in the Tennessee valley led to accusations that it was antibusiness and undemocratic. Republican representative Joseph William Martin of Massachusetts, for instance, contended that the TVA was "patterned closely after one of the soviet dreams."[229] The *Chicago Daily Tribune* ranted that the TVA "has invaded the state of Tennessee and in socializing the people is destroying private property."[230] The TVA achieved many things, but it parted rather than bridged America's divided political landscape.

There were other problems, too. Not everybody in the valley liked the TVA. A farmer on Big Barren Creek warned, "I'll take my hog rifle, and the first one of them TVA fellers come onto my land, I'll shoot him before he can show his hind quarters."[231] Despite such fulminations, some 125,000 persons were resettled to make room for dams and water. Many of them belonged to the most vulnerable ranks of American society and had little choice. For all the attempts to involve local citizens, the TVA did not dare challenge existing inequalities or the South's segregationist regime. The settlers of Norris, the model city planned as part of the TVA, were as white as the spray of a waterfall. The huge population of African Americans found little support, along with poor whites. In effect, the federal government cemented and implicitly sanctioned racial discrimination. Representatives of the South and hence the most illiberal part of the political order imposed clear limits to New Deal policy making.[232] Moreover, work was slowed by the tug-of-war between the three board members, leading to disagreements and changes of direction. Economic growth in non-TVA areas was also substantial, so that the authority's economic successes are less impressive at second glance. The TVA's underlying New Conservationist agenda, finally, with its focus on efficiency and raising living standards, had detrimental ecological implications in the midterm. In sum, the TVA revealed all the ambivalences of a high modern, technology-driven response to the challenges of the time.[233]

And indeed, many features of the TVA were far from unique internationally. The sense of awe produced by modern technology was by no means specific to America, even if some historians have argued so.[234] Long before 1933, other countries had pursued similar projects revolving around dams and electric power plants. Even the multipurpose character of the TVA dams was not without parallel. In France, for example, the Rhône River became subject to the integrated planning of electricity generation and navigation along with the promotion of agriculture soon after World War I. In 1921, an authority was set up to develop a three-hundred-mile stretch of the river in a law about as vague as America's 1933 TVA Act. On the Rhône River, progress remained slow during the interwar years, and the project only gained momentum after 1945. Still, the same technological ideas of multipurpose development, an even stronger contribution from private stakeholders, and comparable hopes of restoring national pride through a vast infrastructure project informed this plan.[235] The same holds true for the scalar transformation of the hydrologic structure of Spain under dictator Franco, leading to the construction of several hundred dams. Their magnitude and performance were smaller than the TVA's, but their aspirations were similar.[236]

An implemented project somewhat similar to the TVA was damming the Dnieper River in today's Ukraine, which was a central pillar of Stalin's first five-year plan in the late 1920s. American and German engineers played a key role in designing and building the Dneprostroi Dam, which initiated "a revolution in architectural design and construction," as one Russian historian put it. In fact, the dam won American engineer Hugh Cooper and five of his associates the prestigious Order of the Red Banner of Labor.[237] On the Dneprostroi Dam's completion in fall 1932, the *New York Times* commented that it was "an inspiring object-lesson in engineering method." Americans had no problems finding Soviet dams fascinating.[238]

And Europe was not the only competitor during the 1930s. In Manchukuo, Japan's puppet state in northeast China, dams were planned from 1933 onward, first building on proposals that an elderly Russian engineer made to the Japanese bureaucracy. Starting in 1937, the Japanese built several dams in Manchukuo and Korea, including the multipurpose Fengman Dam and the Sup'ung Dam; the latter one was part of a project to string together seven dams along the Yalu River to modernize the region. Both these dams were much higher than the Dneprostroi Dam, even if they shared its dependency on American and German expertise. Still, Japanese engineers and bureaucrats also sold their projects as symbols of Japanese civilization and the benefits it brought to its colonial subjects, or in the words of General Affairs Agency head Hoshino Naoki, speaking of the Fengman Dam, as "a great monument to Manchukuo."[239]

Decades earlier, harnessing rivers had already been seen as a harbinger of modernity. Imperial Germany entered the era of multipurpose dams in the years before World War I. The period formed a heroic phase for hydraulic engineers and other experts, fully supported by the Kaiser, who invited their brightest star, Aachen Polytechnic's Otto Intze, to deliver private lectures to him.[240] Similar prestige was attributed to dams in the colonies, which frequently served as laboratories for technologies that were then exported back to the metropoles. The Egyptian Aswan Dam, completed in 1902 under British control and a giant in comparison to Germany's dams, cannot be classified as a multipurpose dam. It nonetheless was a showcase of hydraulic science, dam building, and (colonial) grandeur, unsurpassed until the Russian, American, and then later Japanese dams of the 1930s onward. Some of the ideas underlying Aswan and other colonial projects—of which British and French planners built less in the interwar years than prior to 1914—also drove the TVA: the rhetoric of modernizing the underdeveloped South as well as ending its dependence on industrial and metropolitan centers reveals colonial tropes that propelled the work in Egypt and South Africa, and even discussions in Germany, too.[241]

For all their attempts to celebrate the grandeur of specific nations and empires, most of these projects built on extensive transnational experience. Years before going to Egypt, Aswan's main protagonist, Sir William Willcocks, had already won his spurs in India and received a knighthood for a report on irrigation potential in South Africa. Poor Intze, in comparison, had to make do with a medal from the Kaiser that fell short of being raised to the nobility. Together with the Soviet medals for Cooper (who also worked in the United States, Brazil, Mexico, and Canada), these accolades demonstrate the fundamentally transnational nature and global reach of large dam construction.[242]

There were more specific transnational interconnections as well. The TVA owed a good part of its appeal to its stylish modern architecture, for which Hungarian-born chief architect Roland A. Wank deserves credit. Before emigrating to the United States in 1924, Wank had studied in Budapest and, more formatively, Brno. Located in the newly established Czechoslovak Republic, Brno at that time was a hotbed of debates on how modern architecture could express democratic society by breaking with historicism and instead using industrial designs. On the TVA's payroll, Wank constantly compared his work to projects in Europe. This held true for his dams, but also for the houses of Norris, for which the 1920s garden cities of Vienna, Rotterdam, and Brussels served as reference points.[243] The layout and aspirations of the TVA's model city shared much with the new cities of the 1930s, such as Italy's Torviscosa and Germany's Salzgitter, as Robert H. Kargon and Arthur P. Molella have shown. All these places exuded a belief in the transformative power of technology, a penchant for planning, and the state-led pursuit of a new and superior community.[244]

At a more abstract level, the TVA also resembled other types of monumental infrastructure projects. In Fascist Italy, dams were less central than the land reclamation project of the Pontine Marches to the southeast of Rome. As was the case with the TVA, work there combined integrated development and monumental, state-of-the-art technology with the idea of symbolizing national unity and progress, as Wolfgang Schivelbusch has convincingly argued. For the Nazis, the autobahns came to play a similar role, whereas in the Soviet Union industrial sites such as the Stalingrad tractor plant, Magnitogorsk iron- and steelworks, and Nizhniy Novgorod automobile factory were central.[245] All these projects, like the TVA, combined economic change with social and cultural elements, and celebrated a nation overcoming the Great Depression. In other parts of the world, political elites were busy launching their own infrastructure projects—with Cárdenas in Mexico, for instance, pursuing land redistribution, and Persia building new rail connections and roads. In the high modernist mind-set of the 1930s, though, such projects counted for less since they referred to an earlier stage of modernity, whereas multipurpose dams, highways, and to a lesser extent industrialization were the main currency of "measuring" civilizational achievements.

These parallels between the United States and some of the world's most brutal regimes should not obscure the differences: communist, fascist, and authoritarian dictatorships used violence to achieve their ends, for which there was no equivalent in the United States. The Russians, as Arthur E. Morgan once dryly remarked, murdered those who disagreed with them while "Mr. Roosevelt, on the other hand, apparently gets his opponents to take a job with the government."[246] Also, social engineering there went much further than in the American South, where the TVA's planning ultimately concentrated on the country's physical landscape and natural resources. For all shortcomings of the New Deal, its adherents demonstrated that they were able to put big technology to political use in a democratic political environment. More than any other democracy in the world, the United States thus embraced the symbolic competition for national prestige through monumental "projects."

Having said all this, distancing from the international political alternatives to the radical Left and Right was less critical during the first few years of the New Deal than fixing the problems of a depleted region. The focus, hence, was less on the merits of democracy than on those of economic recovery and planning. In the language of high modernity, some Americans felt that they were lagging behind. Arthur Morgan, for instance, reflected in 1934, "I think we have ceased to make sport of Russia. We have come to realize that something important is happening there." Morgan did not want to "duplicate" any Russian programs due to their tendency to "destroy initiative and freedom of personality"; still, the role model was clear.[247]

Differentiation from America's "totalitarian" alternatives only emerged toward the decade's end. Only after the Norris, Hoover, and other dams had been completed did Americans become self-confident enough to advertise their underlying political system so actively.[248]

Charisma and the Radio

The New Deal was more than the various ingredients of its alphabet soup. It also developed a specific appeal to the American people, and in this, Roosevelt himself was an actor as well as a projection screen of people's hopes and fears. FDR stood for a new style of leadership and sophisticated techniques of mass communication. The latest technologies were swiftly employed; Roosevelt was the radio, and the radio was Roosevelt. The New Deal would have been quite different without its stylizing the president as a charismatic leader, standing above party politics and leading the country out of the Depression. He especially used his speeches in and outside Washington as well as on the radio as channels to the American people, bypassing Congress, other parts of the political apparatus, and the printed press. Through the radio, FDR gained access to the most intimate environment and social setting—the home and the family. He managed to forge a direct connection with the people, addressing his audience as appreciated individuals. Political leadership was real, immediate, and personal. Particularly during his famous fireside chats, Roosevelt appeared as a healer, taking the role of the family doctor treating the ills of a nation shaken by the Great Depression.[249]

Listeners praised Roosevelt for his distinctive and pleasant voice. He combined innate talent for public speaking with hard work, polishing and rehearsing his manuscripts carefully before delivery. Moreover, his way of speaking with confidence and pep was in line with the latest ideas of oratory. Unlike most political addresses broadcast at the time, Roosevelt's speeches were tailored to the needs of the medium, which gave them a ring of authenticity. They were highly accessible; Roosevelt made sure his fireside chats only employed the most commonly used words in American English. The audience liked the combination of a Groton accent and Roosevelt's informal, chatty tone; he epitomized the privileged patrician caring for the people. Already during the 1932 campaign, FDR started to call his audience "my friends."[250] Shortly after Roosevelt's death, author Carl Carmer recalled, "I never saw him—but I knew him. Can you have forgotten how, with his voice, he came into our house, the President of these United States, calling us friends...."[251]

Was all this new? To a good extent it was. Until the early twentieth century, most politicians cultivated a more aloof and distanced political style. "The Great Engineer" Hoover was a technocrat, hiding humor, sociability, and compassion under a thick layer of public shyness. As secretary of commerce, he had played an important role in regulating radio broadcasting and consequently also used it to disseminate his political message. Still, he never managed to turn it into the efficient instrument of power it was to become under Roosevelt. Politically, he believed in voluntary partnerships between government and business, rather than strong direct links between the federal executive and citizens. Following his laissez-faire credo, Hoover's predecessor, Coolidge, had even turned federal inaction into a public virtue. Coolidge sometimes disappeared for weeks from public view, and his rare radio appearances consisted of laconic statements instead of barnstorming speeches. Roosevelt's personal and intimate touch was foreign to the traditional ways of bourgeois and political culture in America as well as other parts of the world. The symbiosis between Roosevelt and the radio was only possible because this technology reached its breakthrough just in time for his presidency. While in 1924, radio sets were owned by less then 5 percent of American households, that figure skyrocketed to 61 percent in 1932 and 88 percent by 1945. As many other politicians, Roosevelt had already used the radio during the 1920s, well before the campaign period. But personality, public expectations, and technological means fully amalgamated during his presidency. The final component of his success was that radio networks supported the New Deal, giving the president ample airtime, since they depended on the government's favor.[252]

While Roosevelt is well known for his radio addresses, they were not his only means to forge strong emotional links with the American people. On average, Roosevelt spoke to the public more than once a week, and gave more speeches outside the national capital than any of the eight presidents who followed him.[253] The backbone of his communication efforts, however, remained the print media, given that the United States was still a newspaper-reading public at the time. During his twelve years in office, he interacted with the Washington correspondents 1.3 times per week on average.[254] Even if his disembodied radio voice was the innovation of political communication in New Deal America, Roosevelt displayed a physical presence in the country that no other American president had before him, and that few others developed in the remainder of the twentieth century. Finally, he gave the most press conferences of any US president to date.

For this, many Americans loved him. The White House was flooded with letters from Americans of all walks of life reacting to Roosevelt's public interventions. Hoover received some six hundred letters on a normal day; during his presidency, in contrast, Roosevelt heard from an unprecedented daily average of more than six thousand people, many of them reacting to his radio speeches.[255] And while in Hoover's days, one clerk had sufficed to open the president's mail, in Roosevelt's, as many as fifty people were required to open and process the White House mail. On March 13, 1933, after his first fireside chat, for instance, Louise Hill from Chicago wrote, "While listening to your broadcast Sunday night, our little home seemed a church, our radio the pulpit—and you the preacher. Thank you for the courage and faith you have given us."[256] The president certainly was not alone in using this new technology of mass communication. Huey P. Long and Father

Coughlin, as two of his most successful opponents, owed much of their success to the new medium, too. Moreover, others hated Roosevelt exactly because of his charismatic style and elaborate communication technology, which they perceived as inappropriate, intrusive, and demagogic. Challenging traditional political ways and antagonizing a good section of the establishment, though, made Roosevelt even more popular in other parts of American society.[257]

The "radio moment" in the world's history of communication was probably the last instance in which Roosevelt could have become president during the twentieth century. Since 1921, Roosevelt had suffered paralysis, diagnosed as poliomyelitis. Roosevelt could never walk again without help. With the aid of heavy steel braces, and more important, through effort and iron discipline, he learned to "walk" a few steps by swiveling his torso as he supported himself with a cane or leaned on a strong arm. Roosevelt used a wheelchair in private, but never in public; he even had a car adapted to his disability by installing hand controls so that he could drive himself. All his public appearances were carefully choreographed. For major speeches, an especially solid lectern was placed onstage so that he could support himself on it. Gripping the lectern, Roosevelt mainly used his head to make gestures. During his speeches throughout the country, he often spoke from the sheltered stage of the rear platform of his train. The White House controlled all visual images of him, monitoring the media, and keeping erring photojournalists away or at a greater distance. Ironically, the man stylizing himself as the "doctor" of a nation in distress suffered more physical pain than almost any other American.[258]

Although his disability was no secret, it clearly imperiled his political career. Rumors about his health flared up repeatedly, and Roosevelt and his entourage took the utmost care to downplay the challenges that he faced. Physical fitness played a key role in the political culture of Western societies at the time, with masculinity as a crucial corollary. Most Americans would not have accepted a person as president perceived as a sedentary cripple, and given this, Roosevelt became a master concealer of his own condition.[259]

During Roosevelt's presidency, there were only a few moments when his public performance was seriously jeopardized. The 1936 acceptance speech at the Democratic National Convention turned into an ordeal. It had been raining in Philadelphia, and the ground was muddy. On his way to the podium, Roosevelt fell and the steel brace holding his right leg snapped out of position. The pages of his speech floated into the crowd. FDR's aides clustered around him to hide the scene. Bodyguard August "Gus" Gennerich snapped the brace back into place. Roosevelt's son James helped him up and brushed the dirt off his suit. Others collected the scattered manuscript. Seconds later the president was at the podium; his expression calm and collected. "It was the most frightful five minutes of my life," he admitted later.[260]

FIGURE 3. President Roosevelt greets war wounded at the White House, 1935.

Overall, Roosevelt created a charismatic style of representing his leadership that relied heavily on a diligently managed public image and the use of the latest media of his day. The radio became his tool to forge the emotional and direct links that the electorate craved. Simultaneously, the media of the 1930s and 1940s respected a certain level of privacy that would erode during the second half of the twentieth century. Self-censorship by the press along with careful staging by Roosevelt and his spin doctors went hand in hand. Like Roosevelt's disease, his extramarital relations never turned into political dynamite.[261] The radio thus insinuated closeness, but also allowed for a certain distance. It is central to understanding how Roosevelt managed to become president despite being unable to walk on his own—the only such example in modern history.[262]

At a global level, charismatic representations of leadership were anything but original. Roosevelt was merely a particularly gifted child of his age. Mass politics and magnetic leadership that used state-of-the-art technology had started to gain traction in politics since the late nineteenth century, with World War I and the Great Depression adding further momentum. Since the 1890s, industrial countries had seen a debate about new forms of leadership, be they *rukovodstvo* (руково̀дство) in Russia, *Führung* in Germany, *commandement* in France, or leadership in the United States, as Yves Cohen has recently demonstrated. In an ever more complex world in which the state kept on demanding *and* promising, leaders had to create more direct links to their people. This held keenly true for times of crisis, in which the usual political systems no longer yielded results. In this sense, the Great Depression deepened a crisis of political representation. New styles of leadership were meant to overcome these problems.[263]

Charisma should not be confused with consensus, however. Some 40 percent of Americans rejected the New Deal and its promises, and it is quite appropriate to call Roosevelt "the great divider."[264] Most legislative innovations of the 1930s were born against the fierce opposition of an entrenched minority, and in this respect the 1933 Emergency Banking Act, which passed the House of Representatives unanimously, is one of the rare exceptions. Normally, FDR did not seek bipartisan support for his policies. The New Deal entailed a political realignment that in the end would lead to decades of Democratic leadership, but also deepened the rift in America's political climate. During the interregnum, Roosevelt coldly ignored any piece of advice that Hoover offered and did all he could to distance himself from his predecessor.[265] The New Dealers wished to cooperate with business, but they distrusted Wall Street, as Roosevelt's first inauguration speech already showed. Underpinned by Manichaean distinctions between friend and foe, Roosevelt lured his audience with the love of the New Testament and reproached his political enemies with anger more typical of the Old when chiding the "money changers."[266] Louisiana senator Huey Long, an important supporter during the campaign, fell into disgrace when he started criticizing the NRA and other parts of the New Deal. In summer 1933, Roosevelt cut Long out of federal patronage in Louisiana, and the year after, the Internal Revenue Service investigated him. Already in August 1932, Roosevelt had called Long one of the most dangerous men in America, and he was now ready to stop him.[267]

Obviously, not only the New Dealers polarized the debate; Long, Coughlin as another former ally, Republicans, and members of business groups all did their fair share in making conflict endemic in the 1930s. Personal hatred went so far that some anti–New Dealers despised the president so much that they only referred to him as "That Man." Hanna Coal executive George M. Humphrey always spelled Roosevelt with a lowercase *r*, and dinner guests of banker J. P. Morgan were not even allowed to mention the president's name at all.[268] Even if the political climate in other parts of the world was much more poisoned, and political foes characterized as "vermin" or "rats," Roosevelt's antagonistic style was quite in line with the political zeitgeist: joviality and friendliness were only meant for those who accepted charismatic leadership.

The New Deal stood out in a different respect: at a global level, dictatorships and authoritarian regimes were much more successful than democracies in forging charismatic links during the 1930s, at least if one looks for top politicians in office who transcended and fundamentally changed existing political alignments and coalitions. France's Third Republic, for instance, exhausted some twenty governments between 1930 and 1940, each of which was too short lived to have a broader appeal.[269] King, Canada's pedantic prime minister from 1935 to 1948, did not shine on radio; instead, he preferred matters of public business to create as little attention as possible. "King" was not synonymous with "charisma" but rather with "caution."[270] Similar things can be said about Greek prime minister Tsaldaris, who served from 1932 to 1933 and from 1933 to 1935.[271] Dutch prime minister Colijn, in office from 1925 to 1926, and 1933 to 1939, was stylized as a manly steersman, but mainly appealed to his own political camp and the elites.[272] Britain's Prime Minister Stanley Baldwin, holding power from 1923 to 1929, and again from 1935 to 1937, whose historical memory has been eclipsed by the towering shadow of Winston Churchill, used the radio as a medium of communication as early as 1924. Praising the beauty of the English countryside on the BBC, he won the support of a newly forged conservative electorate. Still, the so-called National Government lacked the drive and drama of the New Deal, and instead stressed traditional values such as stability and authority. Baldwin's attitude is best captured by his remark about the most charismatic British politician of the period, David Lloyd George: "A dynamic force is a very terrible thing." Lloyd George remained relegated to the political margins, and many Britons longed for a magnetic leader like Roosevelt.[273]

Compared to these democracies, some of the 1930s' dictatorships were quite successful in making a direct appeal to the people. Destroying the existing political system, they forged strong bonds between ruler and ruled. Mussolini, following a path spearheaded by Gabriele D'Annunzio and Giuseppe Garibaldi, epitomized this new form of political leader. His virile body, displayed bare chested or in fancy uniforms, and distributed on millions of postcards, symbolized that bourgeois aloofness had been replaced by immediate physical presence, mobility, and the will to take action. In this respect, he was much more radical than Roosevelt. His "oratoria di piazza"—speeches in front of huge gatherings—had a completely different style than Roosevelt's: they were loud and bombastic, and accompanied by heavy gesticulation. Stereotypes about Mediterranean politics do not suffice as an explanation; in fact, Mussolini found an efficient way of reaching out to large live audiences. While also making ample use of the radio, Mussolini's vernacular had a stronger pictorial and visual accent, be it through gestures and clothing, or the postcards, sculptures, or films transmitting the fascist message.[274]

The same basically holds true for Hitler, a disciple of Mussolini's public appearances. His speeches consisted of much more than the staccato-fortissimo for which they are best remembered today. In his own way, Hitler was also able to forge an emotional link of trust with his audience. Like Mussolini, Hitler spoke on the radio, but the Third Reich's preferred way of connecting the führer and his followers was the big party rally, as another new technique of reaching out to the masses.[275] The same holds true for Stalinism, but unlike Roosevelt, Churchill, or Hitler, Stalin was anything but a gifted public speaker. Instead, his Georgian accent was the cause of many jokes among Russians and even Georgians.[276] Leaders like Franco in Spain, Antonio de Oliveira Salazar in Portugal, and Vidkun Quisling in Norway also lacked relevant abilities, such as great oratory skills, a magnetic personal presence, or a compelling vision, and yet also developed a cult of the exemplary, missionary leader.[277]

Obviously, not all political systems followed this trend of combining charismatic leadership with modern technology. Some countries continued to follow traditional ways, such as in Switzerland with its collective seven-member executive council, leaving little room for the "stand-alone" leadership of one individual.[278] Others, like Mexico's future president Cárdenas, wanted to reach out to the people. But in Cárdenas's case, he found himself in a country where large regions were not accessible by train. In his 1934 campaign, he mainly traveled by plane, train, and car, yet also covered some five hundred kilometers on horseback. Mexico did have more than two hundred thousand radios at the time, but the majority of them were located in urban areas. For Cárdenas, charismatic politics had to do without the latest innovations, although his low-tech approach to mingling with the people also made a huge impression. Instead of giving lengthy speeches, he listened to villagers, attended their local fiestas, and never missed a dance with them.[279] Turkish leader Mustafa Kemal, or Atatürk (meaning "Father of the Turks," as he was called from 1934 on), is noteworthy as the creator of a powerfully independent Muslim nation in a world dominated by Christian states. Like Mexico, Turkey lacked the infrastructure and technology for state-of-the-art mass communication. The country saw an intense cult around its president, though, mainly centering on visual means. In the case of Turkey, the images and sculptures of Atatürk were a clear breach with the traditional Islamic aniconism. At the same time, Turkish iconography never showed Atatürk immersed in the masses but rather alone or among his advisers. There were no fine-tuned radio addresses and no big rallies; instead, Kemalism pursued an elitist and technocratic dimension, and a form of political mass communication targeting predominantly the country's political elite.[280] While Mussolini virtually merged with the masses and Atatürk remained the distant teacher, Roosevelt stood somewhere in between.

Some leaders stayed fully aloof. After a phase of greater public contact, Japan's emperors became practically invisible to the public from the late 1880s onward, hidden behind the walls of Tokyo's imperial palace. Shōwa emperor Hirohito was well known for remaining motionless for hours, and in speech, reticence or total silence suited royal dignity. Such behavior was not perceived as a sign of weakness; instead, his invisibility was seen as the very source of effectiveness and omnipresence of power.[281] It would be wrong to characterize this as strange Oriental manners: Japan was an industrialized and modern country. Moreover, the pope in Rome led a similarly secluded life until the early 1920s; it was only Pius XI (in power from 1922–39) who started to make use of the radio in 1931 to disseminate the Holy See's views, inaugurated by the pope himself with a message about "the secrets of an omnipotent and Divine Providence," which he delivered in Latin and was then repeated in other languages. Simultaneously, he disliked using the telephone, gave audiences only to hand-selected groups, and spent all of his papal life either behind the walls of the Vatican or at his remote summer seat of Castel Gandolfo. Pius XI thus remained at a distance from his followers, and in this respect his conduct was quite similar to that of the Japanese emperor (who served as a role model for Ethiopia's emperor Haile Selassie and who first spoke on the radio in August 1945, accepting Japan's defeat, where the sheer sensation of hearing their emperor's voice was a shock no Japanese ever forgot).[282]

On a global scale, the charismatic radio President Roosevelt stood for only one variety of a wider trend. Stalin (born 1878), Atatürk (born 1881), Roosevelt (born 1882), Mussolini (born 1883), Hitler (born 1889), and Cárdenas (born 1895) all represented as well as led a generation that shared the hope of overcoming nineteenth-century styles of political communication, even if they then opted for different alternatives to the status quo. Ironically, Roosevelt was the only old-stock patrician among this group, whereas all the others rose from rather humble backgrounds and often came from the margins of their societies. Roosevelt did not stand out as the only leader merging with the masses. Rather, he demonstrated that this form of leadership could be harmonized with liberal democracy at a time when around the world, it was largely the preserve of authoritarian and fascist leaders, as illustrated by developments in places as diverse as Argentina, Brazil, Italy, and Germany, but also Poland and Spain.

What were the limits of this new political style? In America, dissent could be voiced and always remained vocal. Charismatic leadership and freedom of expression were no contradiction. Roosevelt did not combine the carrot of his beguiling style with the stick so easily wielded in many other societies around the world, where regimes resorted to exclusion, terror, or even mass murder. He never went without opposition and had to defend his hard-won magnetism continuously.

Certainly there were also other democrats with charismatic qualities, such as Gandhi or Churchill, but political circumstances kept them away from power during the 1930s. There were not many FDRs at the time. It is in this context that British-Russian philosopher Isaiah Berlin wrote in the

1950s, looking back at the 1930s, "The only light in the darkness was the administration of Mr. Roosevelt and the New Deal in the United States. At a time of weakness and mounting despair in the democratic world, Mr. Roosevelt radiated confidence and strength."[283] On a more critical note, the Canadian minister to Washington, William Duncan Herridge, argued that Roosevelt had "charmed the people into a new state of mind." He had become friends with many of those close to FDR, including Henry Wallace and Raymond Moley. Herridge advised his brother-in-law, Prime Minister Richard Bedford Bennett, that Canadians needed "some means by which they could be persuaded that they also had a New Deal and that that New Deal would do everything for them *in fact* which the American New Deal had done in fancy."[284] Put more bluntly, he felt that the main difference between Bennett, a short, meticulously groomed man with a generous belly who looked like a stereotypical capitalist, and Roosevelt, with his charisma, made all the difference. Obviously, not only the supporters, but also some of the opponents of the Roosevelt administration had to acknowledge the symbolic dimension of its success.

A Sense of State

Two years into the New Deal, the political and economic situation was much less fluid than in 1933. To be sure, unemployment figures remained high, decreasing only from a staggering 25 percent in the year that Roosevelt took office to 20 percent in 1935.[285] Yet the extreme sense of emergency was over. On January 1, 1935, for instance, the *New York Times* front-page headline observed that the city was greeting "the New Year in one of gayest moods" and "champagne flows freely as [the] city goes on [a] record spending spree." This would have been quite unthinkable two years earlier.[286]

For the New Dealers, this changed environment did not necessarily make things easier; their attempt to rewrite America's social contract had deepened political divides. In 1935, Congress would never have accepted a federal bill as easily as it had the far-reaching Emergency Banking Act of 1933. Roosevelt had to continue his policy of "bold, persistent experimentation," not least because of the increasing resistance he was facing. Most famously, the Supreme Court struck down the two central pillars of the New Deal, the NIRA and AAA, in May 1935 and January 1936, respectively; new solutions had to be found for both sectors of the economy. While the level of contention thus remained high, the United States had gone through an important learning process since 1933. After Hoover's failed attempt to overcome the Great Depression and following the first months of the New Deal, when the streets of Washington had been awash with the blood of sacred cows, it was now more apparent in which direction America was heading. Even if the crisis of capitalism had not been fully resolved, the system was no longer on the verge of collapse.

Did US democracy remain unchallenged during the Great Depression? With the benefit of hindsight, the answer seems evident. Had economic developments been different, however, the political system would have come under even greater stress. There were in fact some forays into unconstitutional behavior—less so among the New Dealers than in other parts of the political elite. In July 1932, for example, General Douglas MacArthur, long before his spectacular victories during World War II, violently attacked thousands of protesters and removed them from their campsite in Washington, DC. These so-called Bonus Marchers were World War I veterans and their families demanding immediate help. Ordered by President Hoover to remove them, MacArthur's troops drove the protesters over the Anacostia River. After MacArthur ignored Hoover's order to stop the assault, two babies were killed by tear gas. Having behaved with flagrant insubordination, MacArthur outmaneuvered Hoover by holding a press conference praising the president for having taken action. Roosevelt, deeply worried about these events, called MacArthur one of the two most dangerous men in America— next to Father Coughlin, the populist opponent to the New Deal.[287]

While Roosevelt and the New Dealers themselves never strove to change the political system in any fundamental way, they were ready to do whatever it took to overcome the crisis. The partial success of some of their measures saved them from having to reveal how far they would actually go. A draft of his speech on March 5, 1933, suggests that FDR was ready to call up an army of veterans from World War I. The president never used that text and the extraconstitutional powers it implied; he never displayed the desire to assume absolute control over the nation.[288] By the mid-1930s, accusations that the New Deal was totalitarian still loomed large, and the overtones had become shriller than in 1933. Even if the political and economic situation had somewhat stabilized, the nation had become polarized, and the opposing political camps were more entrenched. The political environment remained filled with fear and was utterly fragile.[289] Nevertheless, any serious critic had to acknowledge that the New Dealers had not abused their power to dismantle democracy or capitalism in any fundamental way, however self-contradictory, incomplete, and fruitless many of their programs were. Roosevelt was a "master of inconsistency," but he was not a dictator.[290] Despite all these shortcomings, it was again easier to discern democracy from its alternatives—as indicated by the global rise of the term "totalitarianism" during the 1930s.

This clearer perception of differences between liberal democracy and its challengers on the Left and Right was not simply an effect of America's (or any other country's) national history and tradition. It was also informed and driven by intense transnational exchange as international fascination for the political extremes receded. Italian Fascism showed its ugly face in October 1935 by unleashing war against Ethiopia, recklessly ignoring international law and killing civilians with poison gas. Compared to Italy, the Soviet Union and Nazism had only appealed to intellectual minorities in the first place. The murder of Sergey Mironovich Kirov in late 1934 opened the doors to the Soviet Union's "Great Purge," and the expansionist course that Nazism embarked on with the reintroduction of the draft in 1935 and the remilitarization of the Rhineland in 1936 sparked more worry than admiration internationally.

In trying to reduce uncertainties and stabilize American society, the range of policy directions from which the New Dealers could choose was impressively broad. Given the reduced role that the federal government had played so far, no fixed repertoire existed. And the goal of creating security could be achieved through various routes. In making their choices, the New Dealers capitalized on the European experience from day one, building on the firm contacts that two generations of progressives from both sides of the North Atlantic had already established. In summer 1931, as governor of New York, Roosevelt sent his state industrial commissioner, Frances Perkins, to Europe for several months to prepare recommendations on unemployment insurance.[291] At FDR's request, Harry Hopkins, another key architect of the New Deal and particularly of its relief programs, visited Great Britain, Germany, Austria, and Italy on a similar mission in July 1934, and during that same year, Rexford Tugwell sailed to Europe to investigate agricultural policies.[292] New Dealers traveled to Europe to study policies as diverse as street cleaning and forestry, leisure organizations and labor services. While some of this work focused on how European problems affected the United States, most of the information and reports were collated in order to learn from the Old World.[293] The New Dealers were eager to listen to experts from abroad—for instance, William Beveridge, or Keynes, who met with the president himself. Transatlantic exchange thus appears as a permanent feature in the New Deal's reform efforts.[294]

Ironically, though, transnational learning and linking mainly served as a means to find a better *national* solution to the double crisis of democracy and capitalism. Ideas and programs revolving around international cooperation fell on deaf ears in New Deal Washington. While immersing itself in global conversations on role models and abhorrent examples, on "pioneers" and "laggards," the United States ultimately contributed to a loosening of the links between societies, and reduced economic globalization and political cooperation.

As much as the New Dealers' transnational exchanges built on decades of Atlantic crossings, there were four new elements to them, when seen from the American side. First, a new, much less cosmopolitan and more male-dominated generation of experts was now in the driver's seat. Admittedly, important representatives of an older generation with a lot of transnational credentials (and often also foreign university degrees) were still active when the New Deal commenced, including Frederic C. Howe and Jane Addams. But many of the protagonists of the New Deal, including Perkins, Hopkins, and Tugwell, were of a younger generation. Although schooled in the progressive social movement, their academic and early professional experience was much more US-centered than that of their predecessors. Even if the New Deal opened new career perspectives for women, transatlantic networking during the 1930s was more male dominated than it had been before World War I.

Second, the global economic and political environment was markedly different from the Gilded Age. Economically, capitalism underwent its hitherto toughest endurance test, and with the rise of communism and fascism, the global political landscape became much more polarized. Having said this, there were more established channels than ever before, including the League of Nations with its suborganizations and the expanding role of American philanthropic organizations. Globalization had not come to a grinding halt. If one moves beyond a narrow economic definition of the concept and includes political, cultural, and social links and flows, the picture looks more mixed. The global context, for sure, was much less propitious for transnational exchange than before World War I. The stakes were higher and the channels of exchange thicker, but not necessarily more resilient.

Third, the tiers of cooperation changed markedly. Prior to World War I, transnational cooperation—especially from the American side—had mainly been characterized by municipal and nonstate actors; with the New Deal, in contrast, many of them moved onto Washington's payroll and hence had more leverage over national policy choices. This corresponded with the greater role assigned to the federal state. World War I, a global watershed in the history of state action, had demonstrated to Americans as much as anyone else that the nation-state was capable of acquiring a greater role, and many transnationally networked experts aspired to fill this with life.

And finally, there were changes at the level of content. Whereas prewar cooperation had included a group of ardent international interventionists, this position had become marginal since the 1920s. Correspondingly, the New Dealers tended to avoid the moral aspects of progressive reform that touched explicitly on questions such as race, ethnicity, gender, and personal behavior, while—ironically—US nonstate actors and new institutions such as the League of Nations became more active as well as more universalistic in their aspirations in this domain. The transnational agenda basically shrank on a few issues, while many new registers and actors were added—

for instance, when it came to highway planning. And despite the new polarization of the global political landscape, the New Dealers chose to learn from liberal democracies and illiberal dictatorships in Europe alike.[295]

Yet certain societies remained completely off the radar. Uruguay introduced broad welfare provisions shortly before and during World War I.[296] Brazil and Japan pioneered new forms of protection for their farmers, and a remote country in the backwater of southeastern Europe, Bulgaria, was the first to install a labor service. Still, American pundits such as Tugwell or Ezekiel only looked to western and central Europe for inspiration—or directly traveled on to the Soviet Union, as in Tugwell's case.[297] The United States remained firmly Eurocentric in its search for global benchmarks, best practices, and abhorrent precedents, while in reality, many other societies also contributed to the global search for new political and economic answers.

The common pursuit of a new beginning along with the partial convergence of economic and political ideas in societies of different brands during the early 1930s has to be viewed against the backdrop of similar economic and social challenges, and their common point of reference: World War I. In all industrial states, the war had led to a new level of state interventionism and mobilization of society. It fundamentally changed both the setup of the economy and the relationship between state and citizen. This holds true for countries devastated by the war, such as Belgium or France; for states where it had a much smaller impact, like Japan, Australia, or the United States (all three brothers in arms until 1918); and for winners like Great Britain as well as losers like Germany and Austria. To sustain the war effort, all states extended their obligations to their people. One of the most important legacies of the war was therefore in the realm of ideas, particularly about the role of government in harnessing the economy for the greater benefit of society.[298] In exchange for heavier national duties, including the willingness to sacrifice one's own life, citizens now expected more from the state in return. Henceforth, public support of states and governments hinged on the prospects of their supplying economic stability, growth, and national prestige. Mass politics and mobilization was, in that sense, a central component of the interwar conjuncture that impacted on all industrialized societies at the time. If not before, such societal expectations were dashed by the advent of the Depression, leading to a fundamental crisis of state legitimacy. By the mid-1930s, most states had found new answers to this challenge in World War I's state interventionism and partial economic planning. Building on the political instruments created during this period, nations now tried to shield their citizens (and to a much lesser degree their colonial subjects, where applicable) from the buffeting of an increasingly globalized economy. Domestic intervention and insulation were the means proposed to bring the long-desired security from all kinds of threats. Such policies were often undergirded by bellicose rhetoric, even in the New Deal, where interventionism was legitimized using the analogy of war, again revealing the links to World War I.[299]

With regard to welfare statism, the United States seemed to do little more than catch up with other industrialized countries. Roosevelt himself told Ickes in October 1933 that "what we were doing in this country were some of the things that were being done in Russia and even some things that were being done under Hitler in Germany. But we were doing them in an orderly way."[300] He might have exaggerated the parallels, but the statement is revealing of Roosevelt's mind-set. On quite a few issues, European and other states had spearheaded the shift to state-run, national forms of welfare statism and economic intervention; America now adopted similar policies in such fields as agriculture, industry, and public works. Experts around the country associated the whole concept of "social experiment" with the Soviet Union, resulting from the experience of several hundred Americans who had traveled East in the years prior to the New Deal.[301] And this was only the most radical option—a myriad of other references created a densely knit web across the world and, in particular, the North Atlantic. The New Deal's bold and swift move into state interventionism was only possible because decades of debates had filled the coffers of ideas—both in the United States and at a transnational level. The problems of capitalism had haunted the world since the late nineteenth century, and since then interventionists had started to compare notes when implementing their policies.[302]

The New Dealers' attempt to beef up the American welfare state was of global significance. While many societies had a long-standing tradition of welfare provisions, authoritarian regimes and dictatorships were frequently at the forefront of the surge to install social policies at a national level. The tendency to associate welfare statism with democracy or European-style so-cialism is ahistorical. Bismarck's social insurance programs in the German Kaiserreich of the 1880s with their reactionary motive exemplify the prob-lematic roots of national social policies since the nineteenth century, as do the provisions of the Soviet Union and Italian Fascism for the interwar years. Some democracies certainly had also pursued welfare statism, but in general, they were slower to recognize the nexus between welfare and politi-cal legitimacy than authoritarian and outright dictatorial regimes. Now America was demonstrating that democracies, too, were willing and able to take care of their citizens.[303]

As a consequence, the United States moved in a new direction. There was no consistent philosophy or approach underpinning America's form of state interventionism and political action, so the result varied from sector to sec-tor and issue to issue. In many policy domains, the federal administration's approach was mainly characterized by the determination to act—and much less by any content-related agenda. Experts and pressure groups from that point on often determined the course of action. Ironically, the crudest version of the New Deal's anticompetitive approach, the AAA and its almost-identical successor, survived longest in the end, and the same holds true for its most ambitious project of regional economic planning, the TVA.[304]

If one assesses the various programs together, America stood somewhere in the middle of the spectrum of political options for economic intervention available at the time. The New Deal—whether for the banks, agriculture, or industry—was neither especially interventionist nor particularly liberal when compared to the policies of other countries. It was but one of many varieties of the mid-twentieth-century state, and showed that even liberal democracy could incorporate social policy by developing the kind of mixed economy approach that rose to predominance in the Western world during the second half of the twentieth century. For this reason, the rhetoric of "catching up" is misleading since it insinuates that there was only one road to modernity and only one form of state action. While such notions capture the mood of the day, we can discern a whole host of varieties of modern society.[305]

The extent to which the New Deal sought to impact on individual behavior and morality is intriguing. In comparison to the dictatorships, its activities in this field remained limited during the early New Deal. The TVA was an exception in that respect, and it is revealing that despite the president's endorsement, its approach did not manage to climb beyond the slopes of the Tennessee valley. In effect, and unlike elites in Moscow, Munich, and Tokyo, the New Dealers did rather little to create a "new man" through state action. This also holds true in comparison to the social engineers who set the agenda in Sweden: being a model democracy did not keep the Swedes from introducing a eugenics law in 1934, targeting the deviant and mentally ill. More than ten thousand Swedes were sterilized in the remainder of the decade, undergirded by a eugenics discourse that the country shared with other nations, including Nazi Germany.[306]

Americans' love of liberty and individualism cannot fully explain the choice generally to steer away from regulating morality and normality, however. Prohibition in the 1920s was a highly intrusive exercise, proving that during certain phases of their history, Americans put their faith in the state's capacity to instigate moral improvement. Yet Prohibition failed utterly, turning the "noble experiment" into a sobering lesson drawn at exactly the time when the New Deal commenced. This experience of the 1920s deepened certain antistatist sensibilities, but more important, it recalibrated the parameters of state regulation and explains why the national state recoiled from regulating public "moral" behavior.[307] The history of eugenics in America is even more complex. Many states had eugenics laws during the 1930s, with sunny California in the cockpit when it came to the number of sterilizations. Although legal sterilization in America peaked in this period, eugenics never became an explicit part of the federal political agenda.[308]

The New Deal, in sum, sought to relativize the culture of individualism; social control and the regulation of previously private matters were not foreign to it. Thus, eugenics were broadly compatible with New Deal ideals, and the increased New Deal funding to state agencies is a critical reason why sterilization figures went up in many states during the 1930s.[309] Even if it was the states that mainly took action, and even if eugenics never properly entered the national discussion, the New Dealers owed much to the general zeitgeist. While eugenics characterized the United States of the 1930s (thereby embedding it in global conversation and whole register of eugenic practices that reached far beyond industrialized countries and also impacted massively on Brazil, Argentina, and other parts of Latin America as well as Romania, as an example in eastern Europe, and on debates in India), it was not a formative element of the New Deal.[310] Roosevelt's agenda instead stood out for its focus on economic regulation. The New Deal aimed at improving individual morality and social behavior, but it did so mainly through the economic lens, whereas many other states also introduced programs directly aimed in this direction. Paradoxically, the failure of Prohibition during the 1920s and resistance even within the administration against the TVA's social engineering projects helped to safeguard America from more intrusive forms of intervention during the early New Deal. US history, though, has been less determined by "a deep and abiding individualism" than some accounts would have it.[311]

That said, there is one field in which the New Deal did not do anything but catch up. By the 1930s, in most other industrialized states, national politics had already turned into a year-round affair. This only occurred in the United States through the New Deal, bringing an end to what Daniel Boorstin once called the "periodicity of American political life."[312] Previously, national politics had remained distant to most people, leaving aside short moments, particularly around elections. From now on, there was no escape from Washington. The after-work beer certainly would see discussions about local issues, the newly introduced All-Star Game in baseball, or the rise of American football to national popularity. But conversations could hardly avoid touching on FDR or one of the newly created agencies. The old rule that citizens are best informed about local matters and less so about issues of the state or nation was reversed through the burgeoning of new agencies, Blue Eagles in shop windows in the remotest towns, and radio addresses by the president. Nobody could escape experiencing the American nation-state as a bounded geographic space providing the basis for material resources, political power, and common allegiance.

To create this new sense of nation-state, the New Deal vested additional powers in the executive, paving the way for what later came to be known as the "imperial presidency."[313] While the details of this power shift are specific to US history, global parallels loom large. Many other states likewise strengthened their own executive powers in the wake of the Depression, whether through new laws and institutions, by changing the constitution, or through more drastic means. This was most clearly the case in the dictatorships, be it Hitler's Germany or Stalin's Soviet Union, yet also in less extreme versions, like the Brazil of Vargas, the Persia of Reza Shah Pahlavi, and the Estonia of Konstantin Päts. Change in the United States came without a new constitution, whereas Brazil and Estonia introduced new constitutions in 1934, and Brazil did so again only three years later. Besides the United States, other democracies such as Czechoslovakia, Finland, and Ireland strengthened their executive branch. Writing in 1938, the German exile Karl Loewenstein, at the time based at Amherst College, discovered a "recent recrudescence of strong executive powers," regardless of the respective political system.[314]

Domestic politics in the United States shared trends seen throughout the world, but as during most other periods of American history, explicit references to parallel developments elsewhere or even foreign sources of inspiration remained rare. Despite thick layers of transnational exchange, Roosevelt and the New Dealers had an interest in presenting their political actions, especially the more unorthodox ones, as being deeply rooted in the tradition of American government as well. While not particularly helpful in explaining political action in the New Deal, Exceptionalism thus remained powerful political rhetoric. Insulation, obviously, also impacted on the way Americans thought during the 1930s.

Chapter 3

INTO THE VAST EXTERNAL REALM

GOLD, SILVER, AND OTHER BOMBS

Early New Deal action largely concentrated on domestic intervention. While Hoover had mainly blamed the outside world for the Depression, his successor was acutely aware of the structural difficulties and institutional inadequacies within the United States that had deepened and, to some extent, even caused the Great Slump. Exactly for this reason, solving the world's problems at the international level was not the main concern for the New Dealers, whereas Hoover had firmly believed that international cooperation was the only answer. Roosevelt's inaugural address clearly spelled out his priorities: "the establishment of a sound national economy" had to come first, while "our international trade relations, though vastly important, are in point of time and necessity secondary."[1]

Yet external relations mattered more than is often thought. Admittedly, the new administration was less concerned with foreign affairs, and for this reason the term "New Deal" is frequently only used for its domestic economic agenda. From a global perspective, such a narrow focus makes little sense, mainly for two reasons. For one, the New Dealers' dealings with the wider world and their domestic agenda interacted closely with one another. Monetary policy offers ample illustrations of where policy choices intended primarily for domestic consumption impacted massively on the wider world. For another, inactivity is a form of politics, too. The Roosevelt administration did nothing to revise the restrictive immigration laws of the 1920s, on the contrary. While it sought to replace the notorious Smoot-Hawley Tariff of 1930, the issue did not have high priority, particularly not for Roosevelt himself. By and large, the Roosevelt administration preserved the status quo on some issues, deepened the course of insulation it inherited from the Republican era on others, and in a third group, aimed to create new links around the globe. Still, insulation is a much more useful analytical category for explaining US foreign relations during the first years of the Roosevelt presidency than traditional categories such as isolationism or internationalism, which mainly describe American self-perceptions. Finally, the road to greater multilateral commitment, characterized by a fierce debate about neutrality, was long and winding, and it ultimately took a war to swing the pendulum of US foreign policy completely in that direction.[2]

The president himself had considerable influence on many issues, not least due to the wide powers granted to him by the Constitution. In fact, his scope was more far reaching in the sphere of foreign relations than on domestic issues, not only due to the Constitution, but also because of historic custom. For all these reasons, personality mattered, and here a comparison with FDR's predecessor is revealing. Hoover was a globally experienced engineer when he became president. He had lived and worked in western Australia, China, and London, among other places. In the White House, Hoover sometimes conversed in Chinese with his wife to evade eavesdroppers. Roosevelt, in contrast, was as well traveled as one would expect of a man of his aristocratic background. In fact, his first memories were of a jumping jack swept away by the sea on a return voyage from England when he was three. He knew Europe and its upper crust probably better than any of his predecessors since John Quincy Adams entered the White House in 1825. FDR had developed an internationalist approach during the early stages of his career, contending that America should resume its proper role in the world to promote peace and prosperity. In a programmatic *Foreign Affairs* article from 1928, he even argued for joining the League of Nations. The Roosevelt of the early New Deal, however, was quite different, and also quite different from the man who played a central role in restructuring the international order a decade later. "Doctor New Deal" and "Doctor Win-the-War," to use Roosevelt's own expressions, were miles apart. During his early years, Roosevelt was much less committed to the internationalist card.[3]

After FDR declared his candidacy in January 1932, domestic pressure made him revise many of his earlier views and align himself with the current nationalistic mood. He sought pragmatic solutions to protect America's interests in an increasingly unstable world. In pursuit of this goal, he could be charming, warm, and friendly, but also manipulative, devious, and stubborn. Particularly during his first years in office, foreign policy lacked presidential attention—and where Roosevelt did display clear leadership, the results were often quite mixed.[4]

London Bombshell

Not least due to the president himself, the first high-level international appearance of the New Deal dropped a real bombshell, with detrimental effects on the global economy and the international political system. In June 1933, representatives of sixty-five nations gathered in London for the World Economic Conference to coordinate the fight against the global depression. Special attention was paid to the questions of stabilizing exchange rates and reviving international trade.

Originally initiated by Hoover in 1931, the conference elevated hopes that the United States would vigorously take the lead in the negotiations.

Expectations rose even further when Roosevelt invited fifty-three governments for preliminary discussions in Washington in early April 1933. FDR
obviously felt bound by the outgoing administration, and reemphasized his
commitment in a lavishly publicized appeal to the world's heads of state in
May, advocating a "stabilization of currencies."[5] Writing in April 1933, British economist Sir Walter Layton contended that no international meeting
since the Peace Conference of 1919 had "been charged with more vital importance or anticipated with more hopefulness" than the gathering in London.[6] In a letter to Roosevelt in May, Nicaragua's President Juan B. Sacasa
stressed that "the greatest aspiration of the people of Nicaragua is to see the
success of your noble efforts looking to the stability of world peace and to
the general welfare of all the nations."[7] During the preparatory phase for the
London meeting, FDR held lengthy conversations with the Chinese minister of finance, Soong Tse-ven, or T. V. Soong, as he was called in English.
Both agreed on "the practical measures which had to be taken for a solution
of the major problems which today confront the world."[8] On the whole, the
conversations in Washington sparked genuine optimism that under American leadership, the international community would achieve a meaningful
result. While politicians from every corner of the world traveled to the
venue, the Geological Museum in central London, all eyes were set on
Washington.

The omens for the conference nevertheless were not particularly good. As
the first key participant in the preparatory talks, Britain's Prime Minister
Ramsay MacDonald, was about to land in New York, Roosevelt depreciated
the dollar—fueling speculation that he would take the currency completely
off the gold standard. Domestic concerns were behind this bold step, which
specifically antagonized the French and British. Roosevelt's move created
room for national economic programs that bucked budgetary orthodoxy
and economic shibboleths, whereas the gold standard would have obliged
the government to maintain strict budget control. Moreover, devaluation
was meant to help domestic prices recover and provide the country with a
trading advantage.[9] But there was a huge international flip side: even if the
gold standard was no longer sustainable, most politicians around the world
still saw it as the indispensable scaffolding of the international economy.
Roosevelt's step challenged the core tenets of 1920s economic diplomacy.
He also acted without prior discussion with his major international partners, thus disregarding the informal networks that had lubricated the transatlantic monetary and economic system. Altogether, the president sent a
mixed message to the world in spring 1933.

The London conference ended American ambivalence. Monetary negotiations centered on currency stabilization. Roosevelt now saw himself confronted with the choice of either pursuing an insulationist course that
would allow him to inflate his currency with the hope of a domestic recov-

ery, or following an internationalist alternative harking back to the monetary ideas of the 1920s and heavily committed to the global community.
With little hesitation, FDR chose the former. On July 2, 1933, while vaca-
tioning on his yacht, Roosevelt penned a message to be cabled from the
nearby cruiser *USS Indianapolis* to the London conference. He slated the
direction of the London debate as "a purely artificial and temporary experiment," and emphasized that "the sound internal economic system of a nation is a greater factor in its well being than the price of its currency in
changing terms of the currencies of other nations."[10] His words had a particular impact since he shunned the polite language of diplomacy, deriding
efforts to stabilize exchange rates in the kind of plain language that had
generated his success in domestic politics. In an international forum, this
made his message even more toxic. Twelve years before the cruiser would
carry the world's first atomic bomb to be used in war, and before Japanese
torpedoes sank it in twelve minutes a few days thereafter, the *Indianapolis*
thus launched a shot heard all around the world.

Historians have speculated for decades about Roosevelt's role. To some
degree, he was disappointed about the pace of progress in London. His own
course in this had been rather unfortunate, however, since he had himself
raised expectations and encouraged conversations about the kind of currency stabilization that he ultimately rejected. Another reason for the
bombshell message was his narrow domestic room for maneuver along
with the role of advisers such as Moley and Tugwell who clearly prioritized
domestic concerns. And indeed, American negotiators constantly cross-
referenced the potential effects of internationalist monetary decisions on
the emerging alphabet soup at home, especially the NRA and AAA, and
vice versa. They therefore were fully aware of the conflict of goals and faced
strong inflationist pressure, particularly from the agricultural bloc.[11] On top
of that, there was the president's antipathy toward the Federal Reserve,
which represented the monetary orthodoxy. He ultimately preferred a less
binding agreement and thought that other governments would also be
happy with a nation-centered approach disguised under some superficial
internationalist coating.[12]

Roosevelt's message shocked the representatives of most other nations.
They had genuinely hoped that he was committed to currency stabilization.
Especially those nations that still clung to the gold standard felt utterly betrayed. Roosevelt's noncooperative stance on the gold standard also brought
negotiations over other issues, such as central bank cooperation or tariffs, to
a halt. Thus far, Secretary of State Cordell Hull, the head of the US delegation, had fought for a liberalization of world trade by tariff reductions
through reciprocal trade agreements. At the domestic level, Roosevelt had
already shelved such ideas before the London conference, lest they increase
resistance against his federal projects. The president's blunt message in Lon-

don torpedoed Hull's hopes of international coordination.[13] Thereafter, the soft-spoken southern gentleman with a slight lisp could only collect the debris left by his boss. Economic nationalism ruled the day and fragmented the international monetary system into currency blocs. International trade remained low, and the problems of intergovernmental and commercial debts impeded the recovery of international capital markets. H. G. Wells was right when he concluded shortly after the conference, "Never did so valiant a beginning peter out so completely."[14]

The shock waves traveled even further. From Britain's bustling capital, they crossed the channel and converged on picturesque Geneva in Switzerland, where an international disarmament conference was being held in parallel to the World Economic Conference. These negotiations had already been deadlocked for some time, and aggressive dictatorships like Germany and Japan now read Roosevelt's message as a sign of noncommitment, and an indication that they would not have to fear palpable American intervention in their nationalistic economic policies and expansionist agendas. The Nazi regime, in particular, rejoiced as the bombshell message distracted the world's attention from Berlin's drive for autarchy and remilitarization. Under the headline "No More Twaddle," Reichsbank president Hjalmar Schacht ranted against the conference in an interview in the Nazi daily *Völkischer Beobachter*, equating its failure with the supposed inefficiency of parliamentarianism. Roosevelt could hardly have done Hitler a bigger favor.[15]

Still, it would be wrong to blame only Roosevelt or the United States for the failures in London and Geneva. All the other sides, especially the leading European powers, also lacked the will to cooperate.[16] But since the United States was the only nation with the potential to change the direction of negotiations, its obstructive course at the World Economic Conference was the last straw. Washington did nothing to counterbalance the increasingly nationalist bent of economic policies around the world, and London failed to check the insulationist and nationalist policies pursued in Washington.

The London conference therefore left a poisonous legacy. The last significant interwar effort at global economic cooperation branded Roosevelt an unreliable negotiating partner. Paradoxically, Hoover had much more strongly blamed the wider world, but he had considered international monetary cooperation to be a prerequisite of domestic recovery. Anglo-American cooperation had been more intense under Hoover. Roosevelt's unilateralist policy, in contrast, sparked mutual distrust and drove a wedge between the former World War I allies. Prime Minister MacDonald, whom Roosevelt had treated so courteously in April but dropped like a hot potato six weeks later, left the negotiations with "the most bitter resentment."[17] And Britain was not just any country at the time. It was one of America's closest allies and much more than a junior partner. While America already possessed more potential economic power, many politicians around the world still saw Britain as the fulcrum of the global order. Disharmony between these two states, then, was a central factor driving the world apart.[18]

The London conference is also important because it ushered in a new mode of diplomacy. Shortly before the showdown, Roosevelt dispatched Moley, a close adviser, to join the American delegation in London. The international press nervously followed Moley's progress by boat and plane across the Atlantic. Even if the term "airplane diplomacy" had been in use since the end of World War I, this was one of the first real examples of it, adding a new twist to the rhythm, public visibility, and face-to-face dimension of diplomacy.[19] Moley's trip was a complete failure. Roosevelt did not furnish him with precise firsthand instructions, and the media attributed a meaning to his mission that it did not actually have. Instead of carefully prepared policies, FDR preferred personal diplomacy, and London offered a perfect demonstration that the one could not fully replace the other. Tied to his wheelchair, Roosevelt either had action come to him or used personal emissaries who obviously could not replace his own presence. Air transport came to revolutionize international relations in the long run, but it did not always pull the world closer together.[20]

Ultimately, the 1933 World Economic Conference did have an important legacy. In the course of the decade, it became the poster child for how things can go wrong. In 1940, for instance, a British Cabinet committee discussed the London conference as a spectacular flop and an example of how not to effect cooperation. It thus became one starting point of a long genealogy of international economic crisis mechanisms. It was not so much the details of monetary agreements that made the reforms in international relations after 1945 so significant but rather the sheer fact that they regularized international cooperation.[21]

A Silver Bullet for China

The only issue where the London conference achieved a real result was its commodity agreement on silver, which limited the amount of silver in circulation on the world market and stabilized its price. Compared to the discussion on gold, this accord was restricted to a comparatively small group of countries.[22] It involved a double irony. First, for silver, America pushed hard for the kind of internationalist solution that it scuttled for gold. Second, the negotiator who fought hardest for this deal was an unlikely protagonist who earned himself a dreadful reputation in London. Senator Key Pittman not only talked endlessly about silver and gained notoriety for his drunken sprees; he also enjoyed putting out London streetlights with a six-shooter. Worst of all, when presented to King George V and

Queen Mary, he greeted them with the salutation, "King, I'm glad to meet you. And you too Queen." All this, however, did not reflect negatively on his negotiating skills.[23]

The agreement served as a silver bullet for quite different interests. In the case of "Silver Key," as his friends called him affectionately, this meant the silver miners of his home state, Nevada, and the hope that US exports would profit from a higher price. Other Silverites in America came out more openly for bimetallism, a currency based on both gold and silver, as the most appropriate tool to fight the Great Depression. Particularly popular in the agricultural sector and the West, the silver supporters were at the forefront of inflationary sentiment, with a strong representation in Congress.[24]

Of the other seven countries involved in the agreement, which was to run for four years starting from January 1, 1934, Mexico, Canada, Peru, and Australia were also silver producers, just like the United States, and hoped to stabilize demand. India, China, and Spain, as significant holders and consumers of silver, were interested in a stable price as well, even if a real rise would have been detrimental to their economies. During his May 1933 visit to Washington, Chinese minister of finance Soong stressed this point in his conversation with Roosevelt. India's case was different, since its currency policy was under tight control from London. British officials supported the accord chiefly because the Americans wanted it. They largely ignored the interests of Indian holders of silver and treated the issue as a bargaining chip for the World Economic Conference. While this larger desire proved unrealistic, India still had to foot the bill. In the end, special economic interests along with the American and British wish to conclude the London conference with a concrete result explain the silver deal.[25]

Within the American context, Pittman's success in London formed one of several decisions on silver that had global repercussions. The small but politically potent group of Silverites had already wooed Roosevelt successfully before the election. In a campaign speech in Butte, Montana, in September 1932, Roosevelt declared that "silver must be restored as a monetary metal."[26] FDR, normally no fan of bimetallism, obviously knew what an electorate of noble-metal miners—of which there were just a few more in Butte than saloons and brothels—wanted to hear. The Thomas amendment to the Agricultural Adjustment Act of May 1933 gave Roosevelt sweeping powers on monetary issues, including the right to remonetize silver through the free and unlimited coinage of silver dollars. He had not pushed for the amendment, but neither did he oppose it, since it preempted the even more radical suggestions of the inflationist camp. As in so many other difficult moments of decision making, Roosevelt also liked the amendment because it gave him a wide range of powers without the obligation to use them. The stipulation's nonbinding character further explains what the president did over the next months regarding silver—basically nothing. In December

1933, though, he directed the US mints to buy all newly produced domestic silver offered to them at a high price, and half a year later, the Silver Purchase Act stipulated that the secretary of the Treasury should acquire substantial amounts of silver at home and abroad. As before, these steps were mainly concessions to the Silverites and thus driven by domestic concerns.[27] In the United States, the provision basically translated into a major subsidy at the taxpayer's expense to domestic producers of silver, with doubtful effects for the national economy.[28] Even the *Chicago Daily Tribune*, normally the first to attack the New Dealers, felt compelled to defend the administration against a "small group of silver mine owners and a coterie of Rocky mountain [*sic*] senators who have built the silver molehill into a political mountain."[29]

Internationally, the New Deal's silver policy was a catastrophe for one country: China. While many currencies had been pegged to silver until the nineteenth century, the Republic of China was the only major nation still on a silver standard by the 1930s. What might have looked outmoded by the monetary fashion of the 1920s served the country well during the early stages of the Great Depression: until 1933, the Chinese economy was not hit particularly hard; the nation's silver-based currency sheltered it from the worst. Another source of prosperity was external. During the crisis, many Chinese emigrants who had grown affluent in gold standard countries bought silver and transferred it to China. With a world stuck in depression and deflation, China experienced a brief boom based on mild inflation.[30] The economic situation started to deteriorate in 1931, and the New Deal's silver policy ultimately accelerated the massive downward spiral. In 1934 alone, silver worth some 280 million yuan was exported from China because of the new American policy. Normally, such a volume of exports and the concomitant rise in the price of the commodity would have been a source of wealth, but since silver was China's currency, America's policy led to a major deflation. The yuan appreciated substantially with respect to other currencies, rising approximately 40 percent against the US dollar in 1933–35. Chinese agricultural prices and incomes fell violently. Exports plummeted. The Kuomintang government ultimately was forced off the silver standard in fall 1935. While other countries slowly recovered from the Great Slump, America drove a country on the other side of the world into a deep recession.[31] This destroyed China's monetary reserves and currency system, thereby delegitimizing Chiang Kai-shek and his government. The US consulate general in Canton reported "a certain feeling of resentment" in China.[32] Even if the federal administration helped China to stabilize its new currency, the damage remained substantial—so great that according to economist Milton Friedman, US silver purchases contributed (if only modestly) to the success of the Communist revolution in China.[33] This was how America began to lose China.

The US silver purchase program was not launched with complete disregard for the wider world, however. The silver bloc even argued in 1933–34 that China in particular would benefit from such an American initiative. In March 1933, Pittman insisted that a silver agreement "decreases the cost of foreign merchandise in China as compared to local merchandise, and must inevitably stimulate purchases from abroad."[34] In January 1934, he predicted that Roosevelt's plan to buy domestic silver would increase China's purchasing power by 50 percent, and in October, he came out with the bogus assertion that nothing would make the ordinary Chinese sell their silver and therefore there was no problem.[35] Pittman presented his ideas as a silver bullet not just for America but also for the wider world, and when problems arose, he chose to ignore them.

The US government also proved rather sensitive to the issue. In the run-up to the Silver Purchase Act of 1934, the president and the Treasury blocked a proposal by the Silverites, citing its potentially detrimental effects on China.[36] Soon afterward, Secretary of the Treasury Henry Morgenthau dispatched economist James Harvey Rogers of Yale University to China and India to find out what the effects of the planned silver policy would be. While the rather liberal Japanese newspaper *Asahi Shimbun* suspected that a US strategy to increase its foreign investment in China was behind the trip, the American silver bloc saw this merely as a delaying tactic and called Rogers's mission "the height of asininity"—since a professor prejudiced against silver could never learn anything by interviewing a few Chinese.[37] In fact, Rogers met with a long list of Chinese politicians and experts, including Chiang Kai-shek himself, and was quite sympathetic to the Chinese cause. In September 1934, Morgenthau publicly announced that he had received Rogers's report, but was uncertain whether it would be published.[38] The silver bloc thus managed to overrule and drown out domestic dissenters. Moreover, it managed to keep the implications for India completely out of public debate, even if a separate Treasury report demonstrated that these were highly problematic, too.[39]

Chinese officials and international observers attentively followed Washington's silver policy, and the Kuomintang government warned of the potential threats early on. In a conversation with Secretary of State Hull in April 1935, the Chinese minister Sze Alfred Sao-ke expressed the "concern of his government."[40] American businessmen on the ground reported that "anti-American feeling" was growing in China, and the US consul general in Shanghai urged Hull to take action in light of deteriorating American prestige. Several other messages followed, including a pressing cablegram in December from Chinese finance minister Kung Hsiang-hsi (known in English as H. H. Kung), which was brought to the president's direct attention.[41] Meanwhile, the *New York Times* reported extensively on China's plight, and the British politician and academic Sir Arthur Salter returned from a three-month trip depressed about the "farms denuded of their animals; cultivating owners forced down to the status of tenants through distress sales; [and] an increased burden of indebtedness both private and public."[42] In the end, China received kind words from Washington, but little real help. Nevada remained closer to the New Dealer's heart than Nanjing or Yunnan.

Why was Roosevelt not more forthcoming? The domestic pressure of the silver bloc and his prioritization of special interests in domestic politics go a long way in providing an answer. Racism and stereotypes were factors, too. As Roosevelt maintained in his reply to a July 1935 letter from the director of New York's Federal Reserve Bank, Fred I. Kent, who stressed the chaotic effects of the American silver purchases for China,

> Silver is not the problem of the Chinese past, nor the Chinese present, nor the Chinese future. There are forces there which neither you nor I understand but at least I know that they are almost incomprehensible to us Westerners. Do not let so-called figures or facts lead you to believe that any Western civilization's action can ever affect the people of China very deeply.[43]

The New Deal was a period in American history in which overt racism was legitimate in speech and action. Still, Roosevelt would not have made such a statement in public. While anti-Chinese animosity had been a strong feature of US politics since the nineteenth century, perceptions started to be slightly more positive by the early 1930s, not least under the impression of Pearl Buck's 1931 Pulitzer-Prize-winning novel *The Good Earth* and its Hollywood adaptation.[44] More important, FDR was more sensitive on this issue than many of his contemporaries, and there were other occasions where he came out quite strongly in favor of the Chinese, partly based on an old family involvement with the China trade.[45] Yet racist categories were not completely foreign to him either.

The China silver saga also reveals that economic nationalism and globalization are not polar opposites, but that their relationship is much more complex. America's economic nationalism translated into negative global shock waves for China. It affected China's internal situation and global links. America's silver policy was particularly detrimental to China's vast rural regions, while some of its financial centers and its small industrial sector in fact profited from the new situation.[46] It was one of many signals that proclaimed the demise of Britain's global leadership and the rise of America. Until the mid-1930s, Britain had exerted quasi-colonial rule over China, including the control of its ports and substantial influence over the nation's monetary policy. Given this, America's silver policy not only impacted on China itself but also showed that Britain no longer had the means to protect its interests in this part of the world.[47] Other centuries-old global ties were similarly challenged by the American silver deal. The policy was, for instance, one of the last nails in the coffin of the long-standing Chinese-Mexican relationship. Since the sixteenth century, silver had forged a bond between Mexican miners and Chinese consumers of the commodity; one scholar even argues that during the nineteenth century, this link developed into a "Sino-Mexican symbiosis."[48] China's massive silver exports after 1933 ended this relationship, while Japanese experts pondered the effects of the situation in China in light of their country's imperial appetite.[49] Roosevelt's silver policy thus triggered a great deal of global causation, and on top of unilateral and bilateral effects, it reoriented existing connections between third countries.

Debts and Dollars

On the question of international debts, it all seemed to start so well—at least from a British perspective. In late January 1933, a private emissary from Roosevelt met with Prime Minister MacDonald and told him that the future president wished for "closest co-operation."[50] The press soon leaked rumors that Roosevelt had promised Britain an 80 percent reduction in its war debts, and even if these rumors proved to be unfounded, they reveal some of the hopes—and fears—associated with the future president.[51] In spring 1933, Washington proposed an ambitious schedule consisting of a long-term settlement and a solution for the upcoming June 15 payment. Once the United States had raised such high expectations, concrete transatlantic discussions were anything but easy. During their meeting in April, Roosevelt and MacDonald reaffirmed their shared interests, but largely concentrated on "we-must-work-shoulder-to-shoulder-to-save-the-world talk," as Moley critically noted.[52] Few concrete results were achieved and, as during the 1920s, the contested question of whether to link inter-Allied war debts to the reparation payments of the defeated powers complicated the matter. On some issues, Washington now took a tougher stance. British hopes of full cancellation combined with a good dose of arrogance did not increase the chances of a compromise either. London made a token payment in June, without a more structural solution being found. Problems also arose elsewhere. On June 15, France simply suspended the payment. With the exception of Finland, which paid the full sum, all other European debtor nations either stalled or resorted to token payments.[53] Having raised expectations of a full resolution, the disappointment regarding Roosevelt's behavior was substantial. British chancellor of the exchequer Neville Chamberlain observed in September 1933 that "we are all in the dark as to what is in [Roosevelt's] mind, if there is anything in his mind."[54]

While negotiations lingered on, Roosevelt took another step that infuriated his western European partners. Building on his bombshell message, he started a policy of systematic currency inflation in October 1933. As with his earlier monetary decisions, Roosevelt's motivations were primarily domestic. The US economy had started to stall once more after some improvement since spring, and by fall unrest among farmers in particular was rising. Roosevelt hoped that currency inflation would boost commodity prices and therefore enable agriculture and industry to increase employment along with the standard of living. To this end, the Reconstruction Finance Corporation began buying newly mined domestic gold and the Federal Reserve banks purchased gold abroad. This policy was designed to raise the price of gold, reduce the value of the dollar, and ultimately help increase commodity prices. Explaining the policy in a fireside chat on October 22, 1933, Roosevelt stressed that in the existing system, the dollar was "too greatly influenced by the accidents of international trade, by the internal policies of other Nations and by political disturbance in other continents." The eventual goal was "to establish and maintain continuous control."[55] State intervention would insulate the dollar and the American economy from global turbulence.[56] The accusations against the wider world were not well founded and were meant mainly for domestic consumption. Again, a decision that was poorly communicated internationally prioritized national interests over global cooperation.

Roosevelt managed the world's gold price in a haphazard manner, too. Every morning at nine o'clock over breakfast, he met with Acting Secretary of the Treasury Morgenthau, Jesse H. Jones, the head of the Reconstruction Finance Corporation, and economist George Warren. While the president sat comfortably in his bed and ate his soft-boiled eggs, these four men set the gold price of the day. Warren, the intellectual father of the currency inflation program, and the representatives of the agencies supplied the economic expertise, with the main idea being to steadily increase the gold price. Still, the concrete figures were sometimes chosen rather randomly. One day, for instance, Roosevelt selected an increase of twenty-one cents, since he thought it was a lucky number.[57]

Parallel to the effects of Roosevelt's silver policy on China, this gold program had a massive impact on the reserves of gold standard countries, either forcing them off gold or increasing deflationary pressure.[58] Trade losses came on top of that: Montagu Norman from the Bank of England, whom Roosevelt nicknamed "old pink whiskers," called the American policy "the most terrible thing that has happened. The whole world will be put into bankruptcy."[59] France, as leader of the remaining gold standard countries, also felt betrayed. According to New York Fed governor George L. Harrison, French government representatives "nearly jumped out of their skins," and even a balanced and well-argued commentary in the influential *Journal de débats* scolded the president for overemphasizing the global rationale of his decision.[60] Roosevelt concluded his gold-purchasing program in January 1934, after it had achieved some of its domestic aims, and the dollar returned to the gold standard. With this swing back from monetary heresy to a more orthodox position, Roosevelt ended the experiment of a fully managed currency. Domestic prices had moved up, while internationally, respect for the president had suffered serious harm.

Roosevelt's currency experiment also became the context for the subsequent round of transatlantic debt negotiations, since the next installment had to be paid at the end of 1934. Despite the urgency, preparations remained lackadaisical on the American side. The president urged Britain to make a proposal, which he then found too low. FDR also sank all other ideas that the State Department, Treasury, and British negotiating partners aired, and on November 7, he stated publicly that no agreement had been reached, adjourning the negotiations "until certain factors in the world situation—commercial and monetary—become more clarified."[61] Of their December installment, Britain, Italy, Czechoslovakia, Lithuania, and Latvia paid token sums, while France, Belgium, and others defaulted. Once again, only Finland—with an installment amounting to a mere $230,000—fully lived up to its commitments.[62] A couple of months later, Roosevelt summarized his views on this experience in a confidential letter to a New York banker, complaining about "our European friends" proposing "such ridiculous sums that no self-respecting Congress and, for that matter, no self-respecting President, could go on with the discussion."[63]

These mixed results sparked congressional resistance against any debt concessions. In early 1932, Senator Hiram W. Johnson of California had already proposed a bill banning the trading of bonds or securities from states that were in default on their war debts. Support for this position increased as the debt saga unfolded over the course of the following year. Negotiations fine-tuning the bill made sure that Latin America was exempted so that the legislation specifically targeted Europe. To the shock of the British and many other Europeans, Congress passed the bill and Roosevelt signed the Johnson Act on April 13, 1934. The president had avoided public support to escape international criticism, but his signature was an unequivocal confirmation that he now opted for a tough stance vis-à-vis the debtor nations, fully reversing the dulcet tones of the previous year. He now also abandoned the promise of a debt revision that he had made to the scrupulous Finnish government as late as mid-November 1933. While domestically many welcomed the president's tough course, the Johnson Act met with varied responses at the international level. It did not induce a single debtor nation to pay; instead, those that had been making token payments now defaulted. Both in what it did and what it did not achieve, the Johnson Act thus undermined FDR's international credentials.

There was no easy solution to the debt conundrum. On the European side, the Great Depression had substantially reduced nations' abilities to repay debts that were so large that they should not have been agreed on in the first place. On the American side, strong domestic forces insisted on the formal and moral obligation of repayment, reducing the options of any president who thought differently. The problem with Roosevelt was that he came out with announcements that raised hopes for a final and relatively mild settlement. He immersed himself in the details of decision making without a proper understanding of complex economic processes. Negotiations were a roller coaster, ending with a rather harsh result that was poorly communicated to the European partners. The token installments (and petty sums from Finland) were economically marginal for America, while the political cost of its hard stance was high. Roosevelt, the grand communicator at home, failed to play the same role consistently at the international level. Instead, he came across as an unreliable and erratic partner, and the plaything of special interests in Congress. In November 1932, after his first White House meeting with Hoover, president-elect Roosevelt quipped to reporters that the war debts were "not his baby."[64] Obviously, this did not change after he assumed the presidency.

Disarming the World

Roosevelt's entry into international politics was rounded off by his treatment of the thorny questions of arms limitation and America's relationship to the League of Nations. The World Disarmament Conference had been meeting in Geneva since 1932. Rising German-French tensions and other problems had beset the negotiations from the beginning. Dictators around the world had understood Roosevelt's bombshell message of July 1933 as a signal that the United States was not terribly committed to international cooperation. The next month, though, Roosevelt launched an initiative to overcome the deadlock in Geneva. He sent Norman H. Davis—an experienced diplomat who had served as a delegate to the conference since the Hoover days—to Europe with letters for the British and French prime ministers, Ramsay MacDonald and Edouard Daladier. Roosevelt suggested that they should get together with Hitler and Mussolini, since he reckoned that "the perplexing problems could be solved" by such a meeting.[65] Europe should take the lead on disarmament, because the main bones of contention lay on that side of the North Atlantic. While arguing that "England and the United States think along parallel lines" on these issues, Roosevelt underscored in his letter to MacDonald that "You and Great Britain, however, have an even greater influence in the European situation than we have," and asked him to "do all you can."[66]

When, despite such efforts, the negotiations reached a complete stalemate by October 1933, Roosevelt agreed with Davis that the United States should not form a "united front" with France and the United Kingdom against

Germany and other dictatorships but rather stay in the background and leave it to the Europeans to sort out their problems. As the prospect of failure increased, the president seemed more worried about the public image of the United States than about the eventual result of the negotiations; to Davis, he stressed that "we do not want to have them blame it on us."[67]

Roosevelt had never raised false expectations on disarmament. And as on other issues, a strong internationalist commitment would have been difficult in light of domestic pressures. Any binding international agreement had to be approved by the Senate, and this seriously restricted Roosevelt's room for maneuver. Furthermore, Europe's dictatorships were not at all impressed by international pressure, and on October 14, 1933, Nazi Germany withdrew from the Geneva conference and League of Nations altogether.[68] Six days earlier, the head of the German delegation in Geneva, Rudolf Nadolny, had urged Davis to exert more pressure on his own country since "You are in a unique position. We can accept things that you propose that we cannot accept from anybody else."[69] Yet even this call for action by one of Germany's few remaining conciliatory diplomats did not change Roosevelt's passive attitude. After the Geneva collapse, Roosevelt moved to limit America's involvement in European matters even further. Secretary of State Hull informed Davis just days after the German withdrawal that "a distinctly passive role for some time to come" should define American policies on the matter.[70]

If a passive stance characterized Roosevelt's role in the disarmament talks in Europe, his approach to the Far East was not altogether different, even if it might look so at first glance. From 1933 on, FDR systematically worked to expand the US Navy, thereby contradicting the thrust of the Geneva disarmament talks. While his past experience as assistant secretary of the navy might partially explain his course of action, the naval buildup was mainly motivated by two concerns. First, Roosevelt was deeply worried about the expansionist policy of Japan, particularly after its invasion of Manchuria in 1931. The leadership of the Japanese navy and the militarist faction more generally also wanted to nullify the international agreements from the early 1920s that limited the size of its forces. In 1933–34, the more moderate group in the navy's leadership—adherents of the legacy of Prime Minister Katō Tomosaburō—was marginalized by Navy Minister Ōsumi Mineo, a supporter of the more radical group. American and Japanese fears as to the other side's will to build new ships fed a spiral of radicalization, too.[71] Second, Roosevelt saw the naval program as a means of national economic recovery: each battleship created thousands of jobs in a whole host of trades and professions, in all parts of the country. In June 1933, the US government launched a program to build thirty-two new ships worth $238 million. This military buildup met clear resistance from a public wary of high costs, foreign entanglements, and a militarized foreign policy. On this issue,

however, Roosevelt spared no effort to allay concerns, publicly downplay-
ing his efforts as well as the international threats that worried him so
much.[72] Roosevelt's naval policy as president implied yet another change of
views. In his 1928 *Foreign Affairs* article, he had advocated a "wholly new
approach" to naval affairs and a substantial reduction of American forces,
since "there is, in the last analysis, no real need for much more than a police
force on the seas of the civilized world today."[73]

Naval expansion was thus motivated by international security and domestic economic concerns and was fully in line with the insulationist approach of the New Deal. While preparing America for future conflicts, Roosevelt did not push for international cooperation on the issue. He also
backed the State Department's Far Eastern policy of inaction and non-
provocation vis-à-vis Japan. Most tellingly, America did nothing to stop or
publicly criticize Japanese aggression against China. In April 1934, Japanese
Foreign Ministry spokesman Amau Eiji stated in a convoluted document
that Japan assumed total responsibility for peace in Asia. His country
strongly opposed "any attempt on the part of China to avail herself of the
influence of any other country in order to resist Japan." He also warned
third countries against assisting China with military equipment and expertise.[74] The "Amau Doctrine," which the British press quickly called "a Monroe Doctrine for the East," was mainly aimed at the United States and Germany, since (for totally different reasons) both maintained intense military
and commercial links to China.[75] Stanley K. Hornbeck, chief of the State
Department's Division of Far Eastern Affairs, clearly recognized the threat
to America's traditional open-door policy toward China, but did not feel
that the United States had enough military capacity in the region to act assertively. He therefore advised both to build up America's naval forces and
to avoid anything that would irritate the Japanese government. Fully in line
with this approach, Hull decided not to comment publicly on the Amau
Doctrine. Business and military relations with China were in the meantime
to continue as before. Despite intensive correspondence on the matter, particularly with the British, and notwithstanding Chinese initiatives for con-
certed action with Washington and London against the Amau Doctrine,
Hull and the Roosevelt administration did not push for the option of international cooperation.[76]

In spring 1933, even before the discussion about the Amau Doctrine, the
League of Nations had pressed for an arms embargo against Japan in light
of its aggression against China. The American representative stressed that
"the attitude of the American government will be in a large measure the
determining factor" in the decision-making process, and the Chinese exerted direct pressure on Washington to support the proposal.[77] But Hull
insisted on his intention

to avoid being drawn into any discussion of this Government's attitude with regard to any proposed embargo on export of arms. . . . I do not intend that this Government shall assume the rôle of mentor to the League or accept a responsibility which initially lies with and belongs to the League under the League's Covenant.[78]

America was neither willing to take the lead nor mediate the Sino-Japanese conflict. It rejected the League of Nations as a forum and decided to bowl alone.

Beyond Japan and the navy issue, the relationship between the United States and the League remained highly ambivalent during the early New Deal years. For the first time, in June 1933, an American delegation attended the annual meeting of the International Labour Organization as an observer—which according to the Versailles treaty of 1919 was "part of the organisation of the League." Bearing the deep imprint of its long-standing director-general, the French socialist Albert Thomas, the ILO had developed into a powerful agency for the protection of workers' rights and was concerned with collecting and disseminating information about labor in all parts of the world. In 1934, America even joined the ILO as its fifty-ninth member. This required much legal tinkering to create a form of ILO membership that did not imply membership in the League; one pundit at the time contended that American ILO accession was an act "*sui generis* in the annals of the League" since it did not imply any encroachments on America's sovereignty. He went on to assert that "never in the history" of the ILO had "American industrial philosophy and attitude been more akin to that of the Organization," and indeed, Roosevelt and Secretary of Labor Perkins sought closer collaboration with this international organization because of the New Deal's affinity with its agenda.[79] On a technical level, Washington and the ILO now intensified their cooperation on a range of issues.[80] But Roosevelt publicly emphasized the limits of American commitment: "We are not members and we do not contemplate membership."[81]

The Permanent Court of International Justice, normally referred to as the World Court, suffered a similar fate. In his 1928 *Foreign Affairs* article, and again in March 1933, Roosevelt had come out strongly in favor of American participation in this institution, which was independent of the League though often associated with it. As president, he soon shelved the issue. Roosevelt opted against World Court membership because he believed that the international situation in Europe was so bleak that there was little prospect of meaningful cooperation. On top of that, there was domestic resistance. Senator Hiram Johnson feared that World Court membership would entail a loss of sovereignty: "Once we get in we are gone." Proudly provincial and revealingly racist, Huey Long of Louisiana added,

I do not intend to have these gentlemen whose names I cannot even pronounce, let alone spell, passing upon the rights of the American people. I do not intend to have the affairs of this country meddled in by various and sundry men from the four corners of the Orient, telling us what is and what is not an American policy.[82]

More important than his fears about the global situation, Roosevelt was afraid of the poisonous domestic political debate that raising the issue of membership publicly could entail. Concretely, he was worried that this could "delay some necessary legislation for the recovery program." Even at the height of his popularity, Roosevelt was not willing to take the slightest risk.[83] The New Dealers and particularly Roosevelt himself thus saw a strong link between the international and domestic agendas, giving full preference to the latter. They carefully avoided antagonizing progressive Republicans like William Borah of Idaho, Hiram Johnson of California, Gerald P. Nye of North Dakota, and Robert La Follette Jr. of Wisconsin. All these men supported the state interventionism of the New Deal. Internationally, Borah and Johnson had already spearheaded resistance against League membership in 1919. Nye and La Follette belonged to a younger generation that had become politicians of national standing only during the mid-1920s, but they were just as vocal in their resistance against binding international commitments or anything else they perceived as foreign interference. Roosevelt never jeopardized these strategic friendships, which he perceived as central to the overall success of his policy.

The president's choice, on the other hand, was not without alternatives. In January 1934, the supporters of World Court membership sent Roosevelt a Senate poll according to which sixty-five senators agreed to join, while sixteen were opposed, and fifteen were doubtful.[84] Hence, the shorthand "domestic interests" does not provide a full reason for Roosevelt's preferences. While on other issues Roosevelt was ready to fight for his agenda against strong resistance, here he fully prioritized specific domestic concerns—spearheaded by men like Key Pittman and Hiram Johnson—over a more internationalist agenda. Quite generally, domestic intervention came before internationalism, and on the international stage, insulation overruled cooperation. Important parts of Roosevelt's domestic agenda ironically were in line with the work of existing international organizations, such as the ILO, which very much reflected the influence of European countries. The same holds true for the International Institute of Agriculture, an international organization that served as a clearinghouse for statistical information and a policy coordination forum. Only in the case of this minor organization did Roosevelt openly support participation, and the United States did in fact join in late 1933. The institute was the exception that proved the rule.[85] While the North Atlantic thus became narrower intellectually, the New Dealers widened it diplomatically by loosening their links to partners in Europe and keeping at a distance from the League framework.

GOOD NEIGHBORS

Recognizing Russia

Geographically, Russia is one of the United States' closest neighbors. Some fifty miles separate Alaska from Siberia, and the two Diomede Islands, sitting in the middle of the Bering Strait, are less than three miles apart—one belonging to the each of the two nations. Politically, the distance between the two countries was smaller in the early 1930s than during most parts of the twentieth century, but still substantial. The United States had intervened militarily in the civil war following the Russian Revolution. Two key factors fueled US distaste for the Bolsheviks: the Communist revolutionaries did not feel bound to repay the debts of the czarist and provisional governments, thereby clearly breaking with the accepted rules of international economic affairs; and the Bolsheviks dreamed of world revolution to overthrow capitalism and the established system of political order. In 1920, Secretary of State Bainbridge Colby therefore argued that the United States could not diplomatically recognize a state "whose conceptions of international relations are so entirely alien" to the American, and "which is determined and bound to conspire against our institutions."[86]

A long decade of nonrecognition followed, with the State Department becoming *the* standard-bearer of an uncompromising stance.[87] American businesses, in contrast, gradually entered the Soviet market. As such, economic reasoning played a crucial role in the American discussion about recognition, and its weight increased substantially with the advent of the Great Depression, when any means to overcome the slump were considered. The most vocal business advocate of recognition was James D. Mooney, vice president of General Motors. In 1930, for instance, he publicly promoted recognition in order to achieve the "same goal of welfare for all our people." Mooney clearly saw politics as a means of economic improvement through foreign trade and treated the diplomatic ramifications of recognition as secondary.[88] His approach resembled that of Henry Ford, who had built up close business connections with the Soviets long before recognition. Fascination with how well the Soviet Union seemed to weather the slump contributed to this mind-set. Efficiency, Fordism, and high modernist ideas in general served as a bridge between American intellectuals and experts and the Soviet model of modernity. Liberal periodicals such as the *Nation* and *New Republic* praised the country's economic stability and demanded a resumption of trade and diplomatic relations. In January 1933, eight hundred college professors sent a petition for recognition to Roosevelt. Anticommunism was apparently not the overriding sentiment in this complex relationship.[89]

While the State Department's rank and file, particularly its Division of Eastern European Affairs, remained highly critical of any serious form of détente, and Hoover stuck to the policy of his predecessors, Roosevelt had already considered a change of direction in 1932. Roosevelt viewed the creation of a working relationship as rational, since all other major nations, including the United Kingdom, had already recognized the Soviet Union some years earlier. The Soviet regime had come a long way from the chaos of the revolution, stabilizing over the course of the 1920s. Moscow's reluctance to pay its past debts remained an annoyance, but since 1929 many other nations had done the same. Finally, the globe was now densely populated with dictators, and the United States maintained diplomatic relationships with most of them besides Stalin. Commencing diplomatic relations, then, appeared as a tardy acknowledgment of irreversible facts.

Besides these political assertions, Roosevelt saw the advantage of satisfying the interests of important branches of American business. Soviet trade was too small to have a substantial impact on the American economy. Due to the Depression, US exports to the Soviet Union had plummeted from some $111 million in 1930 to a mere $9 million in 1933. In comparison to the overall total of US exports, worth $1.6 billion, the Soviet market was almost negligible.[90] Still, some experts saw it as an appealing growth market, especially given its breathtaking industrialization, and FDR was ready to clutch at any straw that might alleviate the domestic situation.[91] In this sense, international recognition was in line with the domestic priorities of the New Deal: recovery at home came first, even if there was a price to pay at the level of international relations.

The third and final reason for establishing diplomatic contacts had to do with Japan and to a lesser extent Germany. Recognition of the USSR was intended to contain rightist dictatorships, and this motive was even more significant for the Soviets than for the Americans. After the Japanese occupation of Manchuria in 1931, the Soviet Union saw its eastern border threatened by a nation with an expansionist appetite. Vyacheslav Mikhaylovich Molotov, who as chairman of the Council of People's Commissars held a position similar to that of a prime minister, maintained that the Manchurian situation posed "the most important problem of our foreign policy."[92] Henceforth, the Soviet Union saw the United States as a powerful potential ally to check Japanese ambitions and had already started to woo Washington before 1933. On the other side of the Pacific, Roosevelt shared some of these concerns, and next to building up the US Navy, he saw a rapprochement with the Soviet Union as a means to keep Japanese ambitions in check. In May 1933, he sent the first positive signals to Moscow. One of the addressees of his lavishly publicized appeal to the world's heads of state in the run-up to the London economic conference was the Kremlin. In the small world of diplomacy, this was a big sign, because Roosevelt's letter was the first direct US government communication with the Kremlin since the Revolution. In this way, Roosevelt showed real commitment to ending the Soviet Union's pariah status.[93]

Not everybody liked the idea of rapprochement. The Russians were much more receptive to this change of approach than the State Department's establishment in Washington. Given this, Roosevelt circumvented normal diplomatic procedure and put the negotiations with Moscow in the hands of a team led by Acting Secretary of the Treasury Morgenthau—a neighbor of Roosevelt in Dutchess County and one of his close friends—and Special Assistant to the Secretary of State William C. Bullitt. Meanwhile, the Division of Eastern European Affairs maintained its reserved attitude and insisted that the settlement of debts, prohibition of Communist propaganda in America, clarification of the rights of US citizens in the Soviet Union, and other issues should precede recognition.[94] Although Roosevelt harbored distaste for the "striped pants boys" of the State Department and their lack of trust in the Soviets, he promised to endorse this agenda. On November 15, 1933, FDR and Soviet Foreign Minister Maxim Litvinov met in Washington and agreed on a memorandum outlining the terms of recognition. For the long-standing debt issue, they settled on a gentlemen's agreement under which the Soviet Union was to pay a sum "no less than $75,000,000"—a loose formulation for a debt that the State Department calculated to be over $600 million.[95] On this basis, Roosevelt informed Litvinov the following day that the United States had decided to establish normal diplomatic relations with the Soviet Union. He further expressed the hope that this new relationship "between our peoples may forever remain normal and friendly, and that our nations henceforth may cooperate for their mutual benefit and for the preservation of the peace of the world."[96] From Moscow, Stalin soon let Roosevelt know that FDR was "today, in spite of being the leader of a capitalist nation, one of the most popular men in the Soviet Union."[97] Congeniality and cooperation seemed to have replaced conflict and competition between the two nations.

The American public was rather indifferent about this change of policy. Fearful of resistance, Roosevelt conducted a systematic analysis of public opinion prior to starting the negotiations. Opinion leaders were mildly positive, but the White House received many letters critical of any change to the status quo. Catholics seemed particularly worried about religious persecution, and FDR made sure to meet with the leader of the Catholic antirecognition camp, Father Edmund A. Walsh, to allay such fears. Over the summer, the views in letters from Americans from all walks of life started to change, and when the November accords were struck, the majority of newspapers and magazines applauded Roosevelt's decision. Soviet recognition was one of Roosevelt's first foreign policy successes in the aftermath of the debacle in London.[98]

The Soviet-American honeymoon did not last long, however. Misunderstandings resulting from the swift November 1933 negotiations soon led to frustration and charges of bad faith on both sides. After some encouraging signs from Roosevelt during the meeting with Litvinov, the Soviets soon sought to build even stronger commitments into the new relationship, specifically to contain Japan. This is exactly what *Izvestia*, the Soviet's official newspaper, was driving at when it argued that recognition had turned the United States and the USSR into partners "in all Asiatic questions."[99] Traveling to Moscow in mid-December 1933, newly appointed ambassador William C. Bullitt was impressed by the level and sincerity of the Soviet fear of an imminent Japanese attack in the Far East. Litvinov urged Washington to set up a series of bilateral nonaggression pacts between the United States, the Soviet Union, China, and Japan. The hopes placed in the United States became fully apparent when the Soviet Foreign minister admitted to Bullitt that "anything that could be done to make the Japanese believe that the United States was ready to cooperate with Russia, even though there might be no basis for the belief, would be valuable." Although Moscow pushed over the course of several months, Washington rejected these proposals, stressing that the multilateral Kellogg-Briand Pact of 1928 served that purpose sufficiently. Washington was not ready to do anything that would antagonize Japan. There was a clear limit to the rapprochement with Russia as well as how far the United States would commit itself to international cooperation.[100]

Washington, on the other hand, was soon upset about the way that the Soviets dealt with the debt issue. On the basis of the gentlemen's agreement of November 1933, in February 1934 Washington asked for $150 million. Litvinov offered $100 million. Although both sums were substantially higher than the agreed-on minimum of $75 million, Roosevelt was dismayed. Moreover, the Russians became much less committed to making repayments after spring 1934, when ebbing Russo-Japanese tensions—as well as American reluctance to deepen the partnership—led to second thoughts in the Kremlin. Negotiations lingered on for several months until they broke down in summer 1934, to be resumed only in 1938.[101]

Russia also backed away from another commitment. In November 1933, Litvinov had promised no Soviet support of subversive or revolutionary activities in America, but in early 1934, rumors to the contrary emerged. While many of these rumors were unsubstantiated, the State Department held some proof of Soviet interference. Conflict on this issue simmered throughout the period. Bullitt got frustrated with the whole affair and contended that the situation merited a "break of relations."[102] Roosevelt disagreed and clung to the new status quo. Still, the honeymoon period between Washington and Moscow was brief, and followed by a long period of estrangement.

In hindsight, Roosevelt had not taken the State Department's warnings seriously enough, and his reluctance to work closely with the traditional diplomats on these technical issues weakened the settlement. By accepting a vague gentleman's agreement, he had given away an important bargaining chip in the negotiations with the Soviet Union—a gamble that would backfire in the medium term. Additionally, Roosevelt and his team completely ignored the human catastrophe unfolding in parts of the Soviet Union at the time. In 1932–33, several million people died of starvation in Ukraine, partly because of Stalin's repressive policies. Roosevelt did not mention it once in his exchanges with Litvinov. No aid was offered, and no cooperation to rescue the victims was proposed. Recognition came cheap for the Soviet Union.[103]

Domestically, these hiccups did little to harm the New Dealers' prestige, which was not the case internationally. The debt settlements with Litvinov especially antagonized Washington's western European partners, to whom Roosevelt offered no comparable token payment option. They found it difficult to comprehend why the president was so forthcoming to the world's only Communist country, and so tough on them. Once again, leaders in Paris, Prague, or London were reminded that "Roosevelt" did not rhyme with "reliability."[104]

The consequences of the Russo-American rapprochement on Japan were also mixed. In the short run, recognition did have a restraining effect on Tokyo, or at least that is what both the US ambassador to Japan and the Soviet elite believed.[105] Since Roosevelt refused to do anything that would have contained Japan, though, the effects were not sustained. Over the course of the 1930s, there were more than a hundred minor military incidents between Soviet and Japanese troops, culminating in the undeclared border war of 1939. Japanese containment, as a key ingredient of the glue between Washington and Moscow, had no lasting effects, and soon turned into a bone of contention between the two powers.[106]

The economic side of the balance sheet hardly looked any better. The protracted negotiations over the debt issue slowed down the development of stronger commercial links. Even if some additional measures were taken to expand US-Soviet trade—such as the elimination of certain trade restrictions, the establishment of the Export-Import Bank of the United States in 1934, and a new commercial agreement in 1935—the economic windfall should not be overestimated. Some sectors profited, such as farm equipment and electric manufacturers. By 1936, US exports to the Soviet Union had risen, although they remained below pre-Depression levels. Any hopes that recognition would create a Bolshevik bonanza soon proved unfounded.[107]

Personnel policy did little to enhance the situation either. Roosevelt's choice of Bullitt as ambassador to Moscow antagonized the State Department establishment, which was skeptical of recognition. On top of this, Bullitt was a difficult personality: sophisticated and witty, but also self-righteous and fickle. During the first phase of his ambassadorship, he developed a great capacity to ignore the darker sides of the Soviet Union. In 1933, Stalin's entourage, and even the dictator himself, beguiled him with Russian hospitality, and Bullitt was enthralled about the rapprochement. The saga of his plans for a new embassy building in Moscow was symptomatic of his original high expectations and the sorry course of events. Yale graduate Bullitt had a fine eye for landscapes and in a letter to Roosevelt raved of an American representation modeled on Monticello built on a hill overlooking Moscow. Stalin, to whom he mentioned his plans, offered full support. In the end, negotiations as to the terms and conditions of this project were fruitless, and the embassy moved into quarters near Red Square. The Monticello overlooking Moscow was never constructed.[108]

Other events affected the relationship as well. During his first trip to Moscow, Bullitt was greeted with utmost courtesy, but the orchestra that was playing when he arrived the second time was there to welcome other dignitaries. Bullitt was a man to take such things personally. When he realized that the Soviet rulers were no longer reading his every wish from his lips, Bullitt changed his views on US-Soviet relations. He now signed up to the critical mainstream position in the State Department, stressing the limits of cooperation and the Bolsheviks' goal of world revolution. Roosevelt, prioritizing good relations with the Soviet Union, was quite unhappy about Bullitt's increasingly anti-Soviet views and in 1936 found him a new post in Paris.[109]

Yet Roosevelt did not display a particularly good hand in choosing Bullitt's successor. Joseph E. Davies was an old friend who had risen from a humble background to become a wealthy lawyer. Career diplomats like George F. Kennan disliked his love of luxury—which included yachting excursions on his wife's classy *Sea Cloud*, moored in Leningrad, with a crew of fifty men. Kennan and other diplomats in Moscow were also shocked by Davies's rosy views of Stalin and the Soviet Union. While not fully uncritical, Davies even found some justification for the purge trials. And in 1938, he noted the "common ground between the United States and the U.S.S.R. . . . that both are sincere advocates of World Peace."[110] When Davies dispatched such reports to Washington, his subordinates at the embassy usually made sure to send their own accounts to balance the picture.[111]

With these views, Davies was out of touch with general developments in America. Public ideas about Soviet policies had become more critical since 1934–35, particularly in light of Stalinism's increasing violence. The repression unleashed after the Kirov murder in December 1934, and later Stalin's purges and show trials, harmed the regime's international image. The more skeptical overtones also reflected changes in access to information. In summer 1934, for instance, the Institute of International Education established the Anglo-American Institute of the First Moscow University. Two hundred American students attended, taught by Soviet professors. Most of the students initially held pro-Soviet views, but the purge changed many minds. By 1937, students began to return home, and simultaneously, Moscow started to drive out many of the US citizens who had immigrated to the Soviet Union in the wake of the Depression. In the early 1930s, the regime had invested quite some energy in impressing tourists. A decade later, however, it took a more xenophobic stance—and this clearly backfired on its international image.[112]

Roosevelt, in contrast, disposed of an enormous quantum of optimism when it came to Stalin. For him, peaceful coexistence came first, and he hoped that cooperation between the two great powers would secure peace. Given his domestic priorities, Roosevelt was not fully committed to bringing this relationship to fruition, and given the immense ideological rift between the two nations, there was a clear limit to cooperation. Both sides bore responsibility for recognition not leading to strong bonds. Although the more far-reaching aspirations associated with recognition were not achieved during the 1930s, the relationship was stable enough to serve as a basis for further rapprochement on the advent of World War II. Ironically, insulationist motives for establishing relations with the Soviet Union led to some new links, and thus US policies vis-à-vis the world's only Communist state were less unilateral than toward most other nation-states. Being good neighbors across the Bering Strait was obviously not easy.

Modifying Monroe

In 1933, relations with Latin America were colored by a long history of US intervention in many of the hemisphere's nations, nourishing a culture of distrust. While the original Monroe Doctrine of 1823 was mainly aimed at preventing European efforts to colonize or interfere with states in the Americas, the United States had gradually expanded its role south of the Rio Grande. The 1904 Roosevelt Corollary to the Monroe Doctrine— named after FDR's cousin Theodore—epitomized this approach. In it, the United States asserted its right to preemptive military intervention not only to enforce the claims of its own citizens but also in anticipation of European action in the region to secure the claims of Europeans. On the basis of the Roosevelt Corollary, Washington had intervened militarily roughly a dozen times during the first quarter of the twentieth century—in Cuba, Nicaragua, Haiti, and elsewhere—causing great resentment. President Coolidge, and Hoover as his successor, then took steps to overcome the aggressive big stick approach: at least in the Caribbean and Central American region, US economic and military domination was utterly unchallenged, and as such, tough intervention was rather unnecessary and counterproductive. Furthermore, public opinion at home and abroad increasingly viewed military intervention as a failure. The Clark Memorandum, drafted in 1928 and published in 1930, critiqued the Roosevelt Corollary for diverging from the true intentions of the Monroe Doctrine and stood for the search for a less aggressive form of interaction.[113] In 1930, the State Department carried out a survey of its diplomatic representations across Latin America on how relations could be improved, and specifically invited "the fullest and frankest criticism of its present policies."[114]

Roosevelt's general thrust was quite in line with his Republican predecessors when, in his first inaugural address, he called for a "policy of the good neighbor" in global diplomacy and particularly in relation to Latin America. He stressed "our interdependence on each other; that we cannot merely take, but must give as well," thereby publicly renouncing the heavy-handed approach of his cousin Theodore. For FDR, this was quite a reversal: as assistant secretary of the navy he had supported US military interventions, and in 1920 had boasted about having written the new constitution of Haiti. That was not only factually incorrect but also revealed an imperial and arrogant mind-set.[115] It was quite unclear in 1933, then, whether FDR would match his carefully vague declarations of "fraternal cooperation" with action.[116]

Events in Cuba in summer and fall 1933 provided the first litmus test of the new approach. The country had seen a long history of US interference. Dissatisfaction with Gerardo Machado, who had taken office in 1925 as a US favorite and soon ruled as a ruthless dictator, had been growing for quite some time. In 1927, for instance, opposition politician Fernando Ortiz appealed to the US State Department for "moral intervention." Even before the unilateral Roosevelt Corollary, the Platt Amendment to the Cuban-American Treaty of 1901 granted the United States the right to intervene in Cuba. Despite the growing discontent with Machado's iron rule, Hoover and his secretary of state, Henry L. Stimson, refused to take action. They had learned from the debacle in Nicaragua in the 1920s, where US prestige had suffered severely from the application of blunt political pressure to install a new, pro-US president, and from the subsequent landing of Marines when the Nicaraguans failed to comply as expected.[117] That Machado's violence was mainly directed against Cubans rather than US citizens or other foreigners added to Washington's reluctance to intervene.[118] So did the traditional, disdainful, and often also hypocritical views on Latin America, and Cuba specifically. Stimson, for example, admitted in a letter to Senator Borah that the Machado regime "was not the government we should care for in America, but that it seemed to be in full control of Cuba; that it was popular with the Army, and that was the main thing in Latin-American countries." Renunciation of traditional imperialist ways and pragmatism along with paternalism and supercilious disregard—together these characterized US policies in the years immediately before the New Deal.[119]

The Roosevelt administration took matters more assertively in hand, but when push came to shove, it eschewed forceful action. Washington now mediated between the Cuban regime and opposition groups and ultimately played a crucial role in engineering Machado's resignation on August 12, 1933. Roosevelt's special envoy to Cuba, Sumner Welles, was enthusiastic about the new government under Carlos Manuel de Céspedes, stressing that it was "unquestionably constitutional in its formation and that the Cabinet is of a high class representative character."[120] Welles's words were self-congratulatory, since he had played a huge role in putting the cabinet together. Yet unrest soon flared up again, and after less than a month, a military junta overthrew the Céspedes government. Welles immediately urged Washington to send troops. The United States dispatched warships, but both Roosevelt and Hull counseled caution. The secretary of state informed Welles that Marines should not be landed "before we are absolutely compelled to do so," "because if we have to go in there again, we will never be able to come out."[121] In a similar vein, Roosevelt urged journalists to "lay off on this intervention stuff. As you know, that is absolutely the last thing we have in mind. We don't want to do it."[122] On September 10, the junta appointed Ramón Grau San Martin, a physician and former protester against the Machado regime, as provisional president. While Grau started to form the republic's first-ever government without the blessing of the United States, Welles continued to urge outright interference, highlighting the radical and Communist support of the revolutionary movement. The United States did not recognize the Grau government, but neither did Roosevelt encourage attempts to incite a counterrevolution by the deposed, pro-American Céspedes. Despite some behind-the-scenes maneuvering, Washington stopped short of any visible and vigorous action to change the course of the Cuban Revolution.[123]

So US policy toward Cuba was far from noninterventionist. The brutal Machado regime had been first backed and then tolerated by Washington, and the Smoot-Hawley tariff had massively contributed to the unrest on the island. Washington's role in ending Machado's rule was a case of clear interference, undergirded by a paternalistic understanding of US-Cuban relations. In a threatening move, the United States sent some thirty ships into the region, including the battleship *Mississippi* along with the cruisers *Richmond* and *Indianapolis*. Even if in domestic discussions Roosevelt played down this substantial naval force patrolling the Caribbean as "little bits of things," Washington remained ready to revert to the big stick.[124]

Yet FDR's approach differed from the kind of policies pursued by his cousin Theodore in two major respects. First, he argued strongly against military intervention during the whole discussion of summer and fall 1933, reserving this option only as a last resort. Notwithstanding Welles's urgent requests to land Marines in Havana, Roosevelt refrained from following the advice of his ambassador and old friend. In this respect, he drew the same lesson from the Nicaragua fiasco as Stimson and Hoover, adhering to the position that he had already outlined in his 1928 *Foreign Affairs* article, even if his views had been tainted with imperialist undertones.[125] Second, the president created a new mechanism in US-Latin American relations by personally consulting with the representatives of several other countries in the Western Hemisphere—another idea that he had already elaborated in *Foreign Affairs*. The State Department's division chief of Latin American affairs, Edwin C. Wilson, and the US ambassador to Mexico, Josephus Daniels, strongly supported this approach.[126] Even if it did not result in a radical policy change, the Good Neighbor concept proved to be more than mere talk. Intervention was now supposed to remain limited and nonmilitary. While the basic tenets of the Monroe Doctrine remained sacrosanct, events in Cuba boiled down to a major revision of its interpretation.

The Seventh Pan-American Conference, scheduled to take place in Montevideo in December 1933, presented another practical test for the new approach to US-Latin American relations. Having learned from the debacles in London and Geneva, the New Dealers did everything to lower expectations. In November, the US delegation was officially instructed not to "assume a role of leadership" and to work to limit the meeting's agenda to a short list of uncontroversial issues. Roosevelt paid little attention to the conference's preparations until October 1933 and then prioritized good atmosphere over concrete results.[127] Hull, who led the delegation, was more ambitious and determined to fight for his long-standing agenda of lowering tariffs and trade barriers. At the end of October 1933, Roosevelt cautioned that the "domestic program both in the field of industry and agriculture" made it "impossible for the time being to make a proposal at Montevideo for the retention of the tariff truce or to commit this Government at the present moment to any multilateral commercial agreement."[128] But when Hull insisted on a resolution aiming at the long-term liberalization of trade policies, Roosevelt agreed under the condition that this would not impact on the NRA and the AAA. The president strongly emphasized this condition; only "with this safeguard" did he "gladly approve" trade liberalization.[129]

Such good intentions could not undo the longer history of US imperialism vis-à-vis Latin America. When the *American Legion* with Hull on board anchored in Montevideo, protesters greeted it by flying a red flag with the words "Out with Hull."[130] The secretary of state worked hard to convince each of the twenty delegations of Washington's good intentions, particularly pressing Argentina's skeptical foreign minister. This time, Roosevelt left Hull room to maneuver and did not interfere at the last moment, as he had done in London. The six-person-strong US delegation operated highly professionally and for the first time included a woman representing the United States at a high-level conference—the social reformer Sophonisba P. Breckinridge. Led by Hull, the US delegation carefully avoided clashes over America's past military interventions and inter-American debts. On December 19, a subcommittee on the rights and duties of states came up with a proposal to restrict the right to interfere in the domestic affairs of another state, returning to a draft formulated at the Sixth Pan-American Conference of 1928. This stipulation was targeted, as before, mainly at the behemoth to the north. In the plenary debate, many Latin American countries argued for a unanimous vote, voicing their bitterness toward the United States. While Washington had fought against the resolution in 1928, it agreed to the 1933 version with only minor reservations. As Hull declared,

> Every observing person must by this time thoroughly understand that under the Roosevelt administration the United States Government is as much opposed as any other government to interference with the freedom, sovereignty, or other internal affairs or processes of the governments of other nations.[131]

This position reflected not only a new mind-set in Washington; it also involved the pressure of several Latin American countries. Mexico in particular had contemplated putting the whole issue of the Monroe Doctrine on the conference's agenda, proposing to exclude not only European but also US interference in the affairs of other American countries.[132] Hull, who noted these plans with "some anxiety," tried to preempt such discussions by being forthcoming.[133] The US ambassador to Mexico, Daniels, who had been secretary of the navy (and hence FDR's direct boss) during World War I, pushed even harder for such a conciliatory agenda. Together, they played an important role in changing the US position.[134] Nonetheless, Latin Americans with their tradition of liberal internationalism also influenced FDR's Good Neighbor policy, even if this policy source is often overlooked in favor of homegrown developments.[135]

Most Latin American leaders liked the direction and intent of Hull's announcements, but were not fully satisfied. In light of continuing tensions, Roosevelt soon followed up. Nine days after Hull, he stressed his commitment to peace and disarmament. Roosevelt noted with regard to Latin America specifically that "material interests must never be made superior to human liberty." Only in cases in which the "failure of orderly processes af-

fects the other Nations of the continent" should others have the right to
intervene. Even then, Roosevelt argued for the "joint concern of a whole
continent."[136] This represented a clear shift from unilateral and preemptive
military intervention to cooperative and collective action, and the events in
Cuba lent credibility to this new course, particularly since it was backed up
with smaller steps in the context of the Montevideo conference. A few days
before the meeting, Roosevelt announced that Ambassador Welles would
soon return to his Washington desk. Removing the person who had proposed a tougher stance on Cuba was another concession to Latin American
views. On top of this, the president announced that his government "wished
to commence negotiations for a revision of the commercial convention between the two countries and for a modification of the permanent treaty
between the United States and Cuba."[137] He thus called into question the
Platt Amendment, which had been unraveling for some time already. Indeed, in late May 1934, Washington rescinded the amendment. Washington
retained close military and economic links, including the use of Guanta-
namo as a naval base, but reduced its domination and right to intervene—at
least at the legal level.[138]

Montevideo also achieved successes on issues where London had been an
utter failure. The conference bore the hallmark of Hullianism, since the
secretary of state succeeded in negotiating several declarations on reducing
trade barriers. The president left Latin America—as a foreign policy field
that many Americans considered secondary—to his secretary of state. After
his awkward role in London, Hull now found a stage on which he could
achieve meaningful results. On a completely different note, the rights of
women were strengthened: the conference adopted a recommendation for
suffrage that stopped short of the hopes of the transnationally organized
women's movement, but turned into a significant medium-term stepping-
stone.[139] Parallel to negotiations with Moscow, Montevideo saw some tenta-
tive beginnings of a more internationalist and multilateral policy. For this,
Hull bore greater responsibility than the president himself.

Like in the negotiations with the Soviet Union, as the other foreign policy achievement of the early New Deal, all these decisions had loopholes.
The key question was whether they would be backed up with concrete political steps. Still, George Howland Cox, a close US observer of Pan-
Americanism, was quite right when he called the conference a true success,
especially since "a feeling of good-will was re-born, and that, after all, is essential to the future amicable adjustment of Pan American problems."[140] On
the same subject, after the war, Bolivian diplomat Victor Andrade wrote
that Roosevelt had "swept aside a century of fear and distrust which has divided Latin America and the United States," and Mexican economist Eduardo Villaseñor added that Good Neighborism lacked "that sense of superiority which has always characterized prior [US] international policies."[141]

Hemispheric Politics

Montevideo instigated a new era for trade policy. The 1934 Reciprocal Trade Agreements Act granted the administration the power to reduce tariffs by up to 50 percent on a reciprocal basis. Ironically, the act was an amendment to Smoot-Hawley, despite being intended to counterbalance or even overcome the economic nationalism of the 1930 act. Several trade agreements were struck with Latin American nations on this new legal basis before the end of the decade. Their technicalities differed considerably, and not all of them adhered to an unconditional most-favored-nation clause. A group including Argentina, Peru, and Paraguay also stood aside. Nevertheless, these treaties strengthened trade links in the Western Hemisphere and were soon complemented by a new Export-Import Bank, which, like its homologue in commerce with the Soviet Union, extended credit for trade. In this way, Good Neighborism no longer stood out only for its commitment to abandon unilateral military action in the Western Hemisphere and hence for what it did *not* do. Instead, it yielded concrete and constructive steps to help overcome the economic crisis in the Americas. Due to such agreements, US trade with Latin America tripled in dollar value between 1934 and 1941.[142]

In a hemispheric context, internationalism slowly gained momentum, but primarily indirectly. Hull had clearly been driving this new policy approach. While Roosevelt supported internationalism in principle, with free trade as one of its attributes, the domestic agenda ultimately came first. Hull's assurance that trade agreements would not impede the work of the NRA and the AAA made a difference. Again, domestic priorities dominated. Moreover, increasing domestic resistance against these two key ingredients of the New Deal's alphabet soup prompted Roosevelt to look for new political relationships and venues. Easing the economic situation through trade expansion was also meant to secure support for the New Deal's welfare institutions. Hullianism thus appears as a vehicle of domestic reform.[143]

Two disputes, settled in 1933 and 1935, respectively, reveal how US–Latin American relations became more multilateral on questions of war and peace, too. In the Leticia conflict between Peru and Colombia over a piece of rain forest, the League of Nations stepped in and formulated a plan of settlement. Washington fully supported this proposal, and one of the three administrators authorized by the League was a US citizen. After an agreement had been reached, Washington congratulated the League, calling the settlement a "definite contribution toward world peace."[144] This was a remarkable involvement considering that the United States was not a League member. In the war between Bolivia and Paraguay over the northern part of the Gran Chaco region, Washington first argued for joint action by neutral American states. When such plans failed to produce results, the League again took action. This time, the United States declined to become part of a consultative committee, but supported the League's efforts to impose an arms embargo. Even if Washington did not cooperate with the League on all issues in the Chaco negotiations—the Roosevelt administration, for instance, disagreed on the League's assignment of blame and was not represented in the League's committee dealing with the conflict—it showed a clear commitment to multilateral solutions and involvement with the League.[145]

Against this backdrop, Roosevelt's 1936 trip to the Inter-American Peace Conference in Buenos Aires was a triumph. Traveling on the *Indianapolis*, he became the first US President to pay a visit to Argentina. More than a million people greeted him when he arrived in the nation's capital in late November, and Argentine president Agustín Pedro Justo smothered Roosevelt's attempt to greet him in Spanish in a huge fraternal hug. The *New York Times* proudly noted that his reception was "in every way the largest and most jubilant this country has ever extended to anyone."[146] The old rivalry for leadership in the Western Hemisphere seemed forgotten, blown away by Roosevelt's commitment to cooperation and solidarity. Building on the results of the Montevideo gathering three years earlier, delegates in Buenos Aires agreed on an even stricter declaration prohibiting intervention—celebrated by Argentine foreign minister Carlos Saavedra Lamas, the president of the conference, as "a definite triumph of international neighborliness."[147]

As the *Indianapolis* sailed north again, Roosevelt penned an exuberant letter to his old political mentor James M. Cox:

> On the whole I think the trip has been worth while [*sic*] and there is no question of the excellent reaction in South America. That, after all, was the primary objective because three years ago Latin-American public opinion was almost violently against us and the complete change is, I hope, a permanent fact.[148]

The very same cruiser from which Roosevelt had fired his bombshell message three years earlier now became a vessel of international cooperation, symbolizing the move from insulation to greater international commitment.

Some, however, were less convinced of the economic and political benefits of the Good Neighbor policy, and its balance sheet did indeed remain mixed. Saavedra Lamas scuttled several of Roosevelt's more far-reaching ambitions. He clearly opposed US proposals for a common neutrality policy, seeing them as a means to increase Washington's power in Latin America, but was committed to a larger role for the League of Nations and Argentine supremacy in South America. In light of these rows, Hull was not even received by his Argentine colleague—in marked contrast to the way that Justo had greeted Roosevelt a few days earlier.[149] And revealingly, the Bolivian diplomat Andrade qualified his glowing remarks on the results of the Good Neighbor policy—referred to above—by adding that it had "magnificent and immeasurably favorable results—for the United States."[150]

Cuba is another interesting case. In 1934, the United States lowered its protectionist tariffs on sugar imports, but simultaneously introduced a quota system. Liberalization did not go far. Cuban participation in the US market nonetheless increased, expanding from 25 percent in 1933 to 31 percent by 1937, while Cuban sugar output rose from 2.2 to 2.9 million tons during the same period. Besides its beneficial effects for the Cuban sugarcane business, this expansion of production and trade hampered economic diversification and industrialization efforts on the island. The policy exacerbated the ecological degradation of the island, and helped keep Cuba largely dependent on a single crop and its huge neighbor to the north. Both economically and politically, the country became more vulnerable; in fact, the Good Neighbor policy led to a new phase of North American primacy in the Cuban economy, after years of increasing independence since the early 1920s.[151]

The new growth in trade did little to alleviate the situation of most Cubans. Sugarcane was in the hands of just a few owners, many of whom were *norteamericanos*. The State Department was by no means blind to these ambivalent effects. In 1935, vice consul Hernan C. Vogenitz stressed that most of the benefits of the trade agreements landed in the pockets of American sugar interests: while "a few American corporations might gain larger profits ... the policy will most certainly lead to internal disorder in Cuba."[152]

The Cuban case cannot be generalized, as the Good Neighbor policy had diverse effects across the various Latin American countries. In some, like Brazil, its economic aspect was soon seen as forestalling links to European countries like France or Britain. Nazi Germany was perceived as an even bigger threat, given that in 1933 alone, Brazilian imports from Germany increased by 93 percent—compared to a mere 4 percent increase in US-Brazilian trade.[153] The New Dealers were acutely aware of the Nazi challenge. Indeed, Roosevelt concluded his letter to Cox from aboard the *Indianapolis* with a gloomy remark on developments in Europe, and the *New York Times* complemented its report on Roosevelt's speech in Buenos Aires with a lengthy piece on Nazi Germany's reactions.[154]

From 1936 onward, rivalry with fascism became an increasingly important dimension of the Good Neighbor policy, such as vis-à-vis Brazil. In 1937, the US embassy in Brazil alerted Hull that the Brazilian-German trade arrangement "has in fact been harmful to our trade and has practically nullified any benefits which we might have received from the Brazilian-American trade agreement."[155] In Europe, meanwhile, the US ambassador to Berlin, William E. Dodd, was deeply worried about the fascist influence in

Brazil undermining the Good Neighbor policy.[156] The United States struck a wide-ranging economic agreement in March 1939 with Brazil. By promising extensive capital investment, Washington was able to marginalize Nazi economic influence there.[157] Vargas personally disapproved of the intensifying alignment with the United States but could not help accepting it.[158] In this light, Latin America became the first testing ground of US cultural diplomacy as an explicit and state-led attempt to win hearts and minds in other parts of the world.[159]

Rivalry with Nazi Germany and other European powers also became a major issue in relations with Argentina. Guatemalan dictator Jorge Ubico held his reciprocal treaty with Washington in particularly high esteem since it implied political approval of his regime. The situation was similar in the Dominican Republic, where the Good Neighbor policy stabilized the reign of terror of General Rafael "El Jefe" Trujillo. Five hundred US flags flew in 1936 when the coastal road in Ciudad Trujillo was renamed Avenida George Washington—featuring a scaled-down replica of the Washington Memorial. By and large, Trujillo's style was to piggyback on Roosevelt's Pan-American rhetoric, going as far as calling his agricultural policy the "Dominican New Deal."[160] Obviously, there were many different ways of interpreting "la política del Buen Vecino."

While tolerating dictatorships politically as long as they did not flirt too enthusiastically with fascism or communism, the United States made few concessions at the economic level. Its bargaining position vis-à-vis its southern neighbors was so strong that trade agreements were mostly tailored to open new perspectives for US business without creating any major challenge to domestic industries. For instance, Washington did not push hard for a trade agreement with Argentina, since Argentine agriculture would have represented a real threat to US farmers.[161] The United States avoided making any significant sacrifices itself, and reciprocal trade agreements mainly served American rather than world economic interests. In some cases, asymmetries also arose from the weakness of its southern neighbors. The unbalanced agreement with Honduras, for example, came about because the dictator Tiburcio Carías was more interested in its political value than in its economic consequences.[162]

Another factor complicating US policy in Latin America was Japan. As well as playing the Nazi card, some Latin American governments stressed their commercial ties with Japan. Unlike the political elites in Europe and the United States, Japan started using trade expansion as a means of domestic recovery early on during the Depression. In parallel to its aggressive expansion in the Far East, it turned to Latin American markets during the early 1930s and to a lesser extent also to Africa. Exports to Latin America more than tripled in value in the short period from 1931 to 1933.[163] For Latin American countries, trade with Japan had political as well as eco-

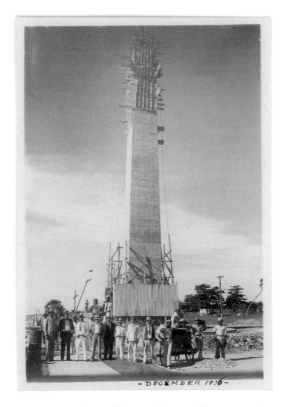

FIGURE 4. Replica of the Washington Monument in
the Dominican Republic, 1936.

nomic motives. In January 1939, for instance, the Bolivian government informed the State Department of Japanese plans to buy large amounts of ore
and other minerals. The United States did not have any trade agreement on
these commodities with Bolivia, and in discussions with Undersecretary of
State Sumner Welles, the Bolivian foreign minister argued that "in the absence of such basis," his government "would be 'obliged' to make some such
arrangement with Japan."[164] In comparison to the Nazi challenge, the total
volume of Japanese–Latin American trade remained low. Nonetheless, Japan's new role provoked alarmist reactions in the United States.[165]

   With the benefit of hindsight, trade policy reveals the global connections
in which the Good Neighbor policy was embedded, and the New Dealers'
acute awareness of worldwide competition for commercial and neighborly
links. The United States in this context was not a trailblazer of new links but
rather a reactive latecomer. The New Deal's more internationalist aspects

were thrust on it as opposed to consistently sought for. In the medium run, however, the US trade program shifted from economic and domestic self-interest to promotion of the war effort, especially from 1941 on. The fact that the majority of Latin American nations took sides with the United States during World War II is often quoted as the foremost achievement of the Good Neighbor policy.[166]

At the economic level, American corporations profited massively from new arrangements under the Reciprocal Trade Agreements Act, expanding their market share in Latin American trade by some 10 percent between 1932 and the decade's end. The United Fruit Company (UFCO) is a case in point. In Guatemala, for instance, the production of bananas almost doubled between 1934 and 1939. The UFCO not only held a monopoly on trade in this fruit; it also was the largest landowner in the country, ran its telephone and telegraph facilities, and owned roughly three-quarters of its railway tracks. People in Central America and the Caribbean nicknamed the UFCO, the largest employer in Central America, "El Pulpo" (octopus), because its tentacles reached into almost every aspect of the economic and social fabric of Guatemala, Nicaragua, and other countries. Although the UFCO experienced losses over the decade, its overall position grew stronger, also due to its diversification strategy.[167] Fruit and other agricultural products were not the only businesses with heavy US American involvement. Banks such as the National City Bank, utility companies like General Electric, mining firms such as Daniel Guggenheim's American Smelting and Refining Company, and meatpacking firms such as Armor were also active and quite successful south of the Rio Grande.[168]

For some companies, though, the balance sheet was more mixed. This is particularly true of the oil industry, including giants such as Standard Oil of New Jersey. In 1938, the Mexican government under President Cárdenas nationalized and expropriated American- and British-owned oil companies. Even before this, Mexican land worth some $10 million owned by US citizens had been nationalized as part of the land reform program to alleviate the situation of the poor. US oil companies lobbied hard for action and instantly provided lengthy legal documents demonstrating the unconstitutionality of Cárdenas's policy.[169] While demanding compensation, Secretary of State Hull still upheld the New Dealers' commitment to nonintervention. Welles urged the Mexican ambassador to the United States to make proposals for compensation, but added that his own government "is not proposing to act finally on behalf of these companies."[170]

Washington thus refused to turn the conflict into an issue of state. Instead of retaliating, it cited the principles of the Good Neighbor policy to put Mexico under pressure; nonintervention had become an ethos in itself. Fascination among US intellectuals with the experimental policies in Mexico supported this approach further. In return, Mexican diplomats sought an elegant way to beat their northern rivals with their own weapons: Mexican foreign minister Eduardo Hay justified the expropriation by reference to the "social reforms recently carried out in the United States of North America," which to him proved that "the present hour demands a fundamental readjustment in the methods of government."[171] Alongside the Good Neighbor policy, the domestic dimensions of the New Deal turned into a discursive device of international politics. Although the oil imbroglio kept US-Mexican relations tense and bilateral trade plummeted, Washington did not resort to draconian measures. Daniels, who was still serving as ambassador to Mexico, encouraged Hull to consider the plight of the Mexicans and responsibility of US oil companies themselves. Washington should adhere to the Good Neighbor policy and not emulate the imperial policies of Germany or Italy, he said. The Good Neighbor rhetoric, with its philanthropic overtones, in this way developed a certain self-binding quality, and this tendency increased rapidly in fall 1939 with the advent of World War II: Mexico and the United States moved more closely together, and Washington's forthcoming policy was designed mainly to prevent Mexican oil from being shipped to Germany.[172] British reactions to the expropriation were harsher. While originally hoping that Washington would take the lead in dealing with Mexico, Whitehall implemented a boycott of Mexican oil. But Britain had to learn that without US support, its policies remained rather ineffective.[173]

Global Reconfigurations

The Good Neighbor policy, then, incrementally moved beyond the New Deal's initial focus on insulation. Especially thanks to Hull's credo of trade expansion, US–Latin American relations acquired an internationalist dimension that was less visible in the transatlantic relationship. Through trade, the New Deal reoriented its global economic links: Brazil became more important than France, and Cuba became more significant than the Netherlands. Good Neighborism also ended a long tradition of aggressive intervention in the Western Hemisphere, building on first moves during the late Republican era of the 1920s. While the US federal government gained new powers and visibility domestically, it withdrew good parts of its military presence from Latin America. In 1927, the US Marine Aviation Force in Nicaragua had prided itself on being the first in military history to use air power systematically against ground troops through innovative tactics like dive-bombing. Its planes were soon replaced by those of Pan Am, established the same year, which now transported businessmen and politicians from one American country to the other. Gunboats and Marines, two central instruments of America's imperial policies in the region, were not to reappear until the 1950s and 1960s.[174]

The Good Neighbor policy was not simply internationalist, however. It also bore the imprint of insulation, since it resulted from Roosevelt's priori-

tization of domestic affairs. In 1928, for example, Washington had sent five
thousand Marines to Nicaragua to supervise the election.[175] Refraining
from military intervention simply saved money in times of economic depression. A less interventionist approach also reflected Latin American resistance along with the insight that military interventions hardly ever produced the expected results and were detrimental to the United States'
international prestige. In addition, a robust presence to fend off European
claims in the Western Hemisphere—as a main driver of the Monroe Doctrine—was hardly needed anymore in 1933. And when the Nazi (and to a
lesser extent, Japanese) threat became more visible in the second half of the
decade, a soft approach of strengthening economic links proved superior to
any kind of gunboat diplomacy.

The Good Neighbor policy, moreover, was not completely noninterventionist. In Cuba, the United States tried to act as kingmaker in 1933, with
mixed results. After that lesson, the New Dealers refrained from that kind of
interference. By accepting the principle of legal equality among nations,
they moved closer to the conciliatory course that Hoover had already pursued before them. Prioritizing the principles of national sovereignty and
self-determination implied accepting, as gracefully as possible, the existence
of military dictatorships that openly flouted democratic principles. Simultaneously, new trade agreements amplified the US economic presence across
Latin American countries and increased their dependence on the behemoth
to the north. This development stood in sharp contrast to Hoover's policy
and to the Smoot-Hawley tariff. No master plan of hemispheric or global
dominance drove these efforts, but rather an idealist and at times naive belief in the power of trade. As a result, though, Pan-American connections
became closer, with the United States clearly in the driver's seat.

For the countries concerned, the economic effects remained mixed. The
new dynamism mainly stimulated plantation agriculture. Wealth south of
the Rio Grande concentrated in comparably few hands, and the classes were
polarized. There was no direct line from growth and regional economic
integration to democratization and widespread prosperity; quite the opposite.[176] Still, criticism that the Good Neighbor policy inadvertently facilitated or stabilized the rule of repressive Caribbean dictators is debatable.
The alternatives would have been even more problematic; both continuous
military intervention and political nonrecognition had utterly failed—in
the latter case, particularly with the Soviet Union and Mexico. These experiences led the New Dealers to opt for a lower level of commitment, which
reflected their insulationist agenda as well as a certain commitment to
multilateralism.

The Good Neighbor policy increased the level of state economic intervention, too. Admittedly, men like Calvin B. Matthews, who had combined
his post as general of the US Marine Corps with being *jefe director* of the

Nicaraguan National Guard before the Marines withdrew in January 1933, now had to look for new tasks.[177] Bayonets and boots no longer marked the US presence in Latin America. Instead, the region was now populated by people like Russian-born US businessman Samuel Zemurray, nicknamed "Sam the Banana Man," of the almighty UFCO—a handsomely dressed gentleman who hid his ruthless business practices behind a refined interest in the arts and hunting.[178] But on closer inspection, a host of planners also came to the fore. The new trade agreements needed experts dealing with the intricacies of quota agreements, loans, grants, and tariff rebates.[179] Soft-spoken statisticians and discreet diplomats, as opposed to dashing career officers and heavily armed jarheads, hailed the advent of the new era of commercial policy. While businessmen and bankers filled this policy with life, state officials from the north and south meticulously set the parameters. In Washington, new forums bearing unassuming and technical names such as the Interdepartmental Advisory Board on Reciprocity Treaties or Executive Committee on Commercial Policy were set up in 1933.[180] The creation of the Export-Import Bank soon followed. Instead of the reckless and incautious lending that had characterized the business-driven US practices prior to the Depression, the federal state now assumed a larger role in organizing and protecting US foreign investments. Eleanor Lansing Dulles, principal economic analyst at the State Department and member of the Dulles diplomatic dynasty, lauded the bank as the embodiment of "constructive commercial and financial statesmanship."[181] Hence, in the economic realm, executive responsibility and planning efforts expanded substantially; this was replicated in matters of foreign affairs, and the trend accelerated further after 1939 when the prospect of war led the US armed forces to push for new institutions in charge of international stockpiling.[182] The rise of an economically driven, global foreign policy thus had deep roots in the Good Neighbor policy.

Finally, Good Neighborism also led to unexpected discussions during the 1930s. In 1934, Charles Cheney Hyde, a professor at Columbia University and acknowledged authority on international law, wrote an article on the aforementioned Amau Doctrine, which in retrospect appears a harbinger of Japanese aggression. Hyde's view was different. While worried about the consequences of the new Japanese doctrine for the United States, he compared the Japanese policy to the Monroe Doctrine, stressing that its main principle "finds obvious precedent in the conduct of the United States in pursuance of the Monroe Doctrine." On this basis, Hyde went so far as to contend that one "cannot reasonably claim that Japan has put herself beyond the pale of the law."[183]

Although the law professor was obviously soon proved wrong, two processes make his remarks noteworthy. First, by the mid-1930s, economic nationalism was usually complemented by political and economic forms of regional cooperation. While the United States rethought its Monroe Doctrine under the auspices of Good Neighborism, Japan resorted to the Amau Doctrine, the Nazis increasingly penetrated central and eastern Europe under the banner of *Großraumwirtschaft*, and countries intensified their cooperation within the British Sterling area and remaining gold bloc around France.[184] Nations knew well how dependent they were on each other—as well as on their colonies—and particularly during the second half of the 1930s, competition between the blocs ramped up, not just in Latin America. Good Neighborism was partly driven by genuine internationalism, but partly it simply represented one variety of the regional economic cooperation and integration characteristic of the 1930s.

Second, Good Neighborism was also a means of distinguishing the American way from its nondemocratic alternatives. After Japan spearheaded aggression and war as a means of foreign policy in the early 1930s, first Italy and then Germany followed suit. During the same period, the United States renounced military forms of intervention in Latin America. There was a degree of global causality between these trends, too. In March 1931, Secretary of State Stimson met with a National City Bank representative, who pressured him to land forces in Chile to protect US banking interests. According to his diary, Stimson replied,

> I told him not on your life; that if we landed a single soldier among those South Americans now, it would undo all the labor of three years, and it would put me in absolutely wrong in China, where Japan has done all this monstrous work under the guise of protecting her nationals with a landing force.[185]

A few years later, the New Dealers drew similar lines. The Good Neighbor rhetoric, increasingly invoked by the various sides, gained international meaning and credibility, against the backdrop of the imperialism of fascist powers.

Time-Warping Puerto Rico

If self-restriction was the main theme in relations with territories south of the Rio Grande, there were also notable exceptions. In Puerto Rico, legally an unincorporated territory of the United States and as such a legacy of US imperialism following the Spanish-American War of 1898, Washington now for the first time assumed a prominent role in providing welfare and job creation measures. Earlier programs, such as public schools and a road system, had established a certain level of state action, but thus far, state intervention in the economy had remained low.[186] The Roosevelt administration expanded provisions in Puerto Rico in similar directions to the mainland United States. The New Deal for the tropics was meant to give the US presence on the island a more benevolent ring, fulfill the promises of modernity, and end what one scholar has called the "imperialism of neglect."[187] While resorting to different means than the Good Neighbor policy, the overall goal remained similar, particularly from 1934 onward when Puerto Rican affairs were transferred from the US Department of War to the Department of the Interior as part of an administrative reorganization. There, it became part of the newly created Division of Territories and Island Possessions led by Ernest H. Gruening, a distinguished opponent of military interventionism in the Caribbean since the 1920s. Gruening and others wanted to bring to Puerto Rico, as the United States' major Latin American colony, the blessings of the New Deal state. Concomitantly, Puerto Rico and other American colonies soon turned into testing grounds for some of these strategists' more radical ideas.[188]

The situation on the island was bad enough to interpret it as a call for action. Puerto Rico had long been mired in crisis, with a 36 percent unemployment rate in December 1929, and a rate of 65 percent four years later.[189] The situation was further aggravated by the advent of the New Deal: its policy of economic insulation focused on a nation with its imperial wings clipped. Specifically, the AAA drove up consumer prices for agricultural commodities while simultaneously reducing the production quota for Puerto Rican sugar, the aching backbone of the island's economy. The protest of Puerto Rican sugar producers in Washington was of little avail. Acreage reduction cost thousands of jobs, leading to unrest, strikes, and political instability. The implementation of the NRA was also chaotic and poisoned local politics, since it met clear opposition from the business community. The Puerto Rican Chamber of Commerce estimated that the NRA and the AAA increased the cost of living by $12 million per annum. The colony found itself stuck both in and out of New Deal provisions, leading to a thoroughly negative economic balance sheet.[190]

The Puerto Rico Emergency Relief Administration (PRERA) was established in August 1933, before all these problematic effects of the emerging alphabet soup became fully visible. Technically, it was an operative extension of FERA, but in contrast to FERA, it was designed from the outset as a tool of structural improvement and modernization, and not just a means of temporary relief. PRERA administrator James R. Bourne was a onetime neighbor of FDR's and had worked as an administrator at a canning company on the island before Harry Hopkins appointed him to the new job. Bourne quickly proposed a sweeping plan for the island's rehabilitation. Presented in December 1933, the plan combined work creation, infrastructure improvements, slum clearance, malaria eradication, and other projects. The whole package was intended to fulfill the promise of modernity through state intervention. Based on rational methods and scientific planning, it aimed at demonstrating the superiority of US colonial policies compared to those of other nations.[191]

Bourne built up a massive state apparatus. In 1930, the island's total labor force was some 500,000, including 11,500 local government employees. By August 1934, PRERA alone had hired some 5,000 additional people in white-collar positions. Most of these hires were Puerto Ricans, since Bourne sought greater local involvement in state affairs. People on the island thus were heavily involved in this attempt to reform society. At the same time, PRERA created employment opportunities and upward mobility.[192]

Driven by this rationale and with Gruening's support in Washington, PRERA introduced new local sanitation systems, built houses, and opened hospitals. It supported artists and showcased new agricultural techniques to overcome the monoculture economy, itself largely an effect of US colonialism over the previous thirty years. PRERA organized baseball teams and nursery homes, cooking courses and literacy campaigns.[193] It is estimated that as much as 35 percent of the island's population profited directly or indirectly from PRERA relief, thereby creating a welfare system unequaled by any region within the United States, possibly with the exception of the Tennessee valley.[194]

The president and his wife fully supported this attempt to remodel a whole society. In an uncoordinated move, Eleanor Roosevelt and Rexford Tugwell both visited the island in early March 1934. The First Lady was so shocked by the dilapidated housing in some of the districts of San Juan, the island's capital, that she called for a "plan . . . to end the slum conditions that are a menace to the general health."[195] Visiting the island in July, the president himself stressed that the challenges "on the island are very much the same kind of problems that we have in many other parts of the United States." Consequently, the "same methods that we use to solve them in other parts of the country will be applied here in Puerto Rico."[196]

Given this situation, even grander plans were developed. During his 1934 trip, Tugwell asked the chancellor of the University of Puerto Rico, Carlos E. Chardón, and two other distinguished Puerto Ricans to draw up a modernization scheme for the island's economy and society. Presented some three months later, the "Chardón plan" included sweeping ideas for industrialization, emigration, and land redistribution.[197] Politically, Luis Muñoz Marín, a Liberal Party senator in the island's legislature and friend of Bourne, and many other New Dealers, backed Chardón and other planners. Typically for late colonial societies, all these men were part of the local elites that both profited from and contributed to the reform agenda of the metropole. Some, such as Muñoz, had been educated in the United States, and their hybrid cultural background helped them to serve as interlocutors between mainland reformers and insular concerns.[198]

Meanwhile, planners in Washington picked up the thread, forming an interdepartmental committee for the economic rehabilitation of Puerto Rico that included Tugwell and other representatives of the New Deal's more radical camp. In the debates, some went as far as to propose a powerful corporation, modeled after the TVA, and the federal government sent various experts down to Puerto Rico to study the situation. "The supplementing and possible supplanting of the private agencies of American economic expansion by the Government" was at the core of all these plans, as Tugwell put it in a report to Roosevelt.[199] The Puerto Rico Reconstruction Administration (PRRA) was established in May 1935. In an internal memorandum, FDR summarized it as the expression of Washington's will to give the island more than "merely a relief barbecue lasting a year or two."[200] As to the content, the PRRA picked up many of PRERA's threads while focusing more on the problems of the island's monocultural sugar production. It shared PRERA's social engineering agenda yet took the reform effort even further. Attention turned to rural resettlement, agricultural diversification, low-cost housing schemes, and rural electrification. The PRRA also aimed at creating "workers' concentration camps" to improve efficiency and morals. At its peak, the PRRA employed no less than 59,100 persons, elevating state action to a level hitherto unknown.[201]

All this was done with a clear view of global contexts: the New Deal for Puerto Rico was meant to demonstrate US superiority over Europe in the handling of its empire and to complement Good Neighborism in the Western Hemisphere. In a speech on Puerto Rico in 1935, Gruening insisted that he wanted Puerto Rico to become a counterweight to the dictatorships of the Caribbean and emphasized the "American tradition of freedom."[202]

Not all islanders liked the New Deal for the tropics, despite the attempts to create a new discourse of consent. The ruling coalition of Union Republicans and Socialists was more critical than Muñoz and Chardón. They accused the island's Liberals and the new agencies of corruption and nepotism. Initially, the New Dealers saw criticism and opposition as a call for even more intervention. In the end, however, PRERA fell victim to Puerto Rican political infighting. The political resistance became fierce in late 1934, and Bourne was accused of mismanagement and partisanship. Although a FERA investigation declared him innocent, Bourne quickly resigned. Many of PRERA's operations were canceled in 1935, and the whole organization was wound up the next year. The PRRA soon became dysfunctional for similar reasons, even if it continued to exist until 1955.[203] Three personnel decisions from the end of the decade illustrate how the New Dealers ultimately admitted the failure of their vast ambitions in Puerto Rico. In 1939, Gruening was palmed off with the job of territorial governor of Alaska. In May of that year, Roosevelt appointed former Chief of Naval Operations William D. Leahy as the new governor of the island, showing that security considerations now dominated Washington's strategy. When, two years later and after three intervening replacements, Tugwell succeeded Leahy, this was not a promotion but instead the next step in his fall from grace. As governor, Tugwell was not particularly successful and complained to Roosevelt about a lack of support both on the island and in Washington, while in the capital of the United States the political elite continued to talk about the "Puerto Rican problem."[204]

The most ambitious plans were therefore never realized. These included radical fantasies concerning eugenics and sterilization. Given that the island's strong population growth was seen as a major source of economic problems, debates about overpopulation, birth control, and eugenics gained momentum as early as the 1910s. In private, Roosevelt himself talked of dealing with the high Puerto Rican birthrate via "the methods which Hitler used effectively," adding that "it is all very simple and painless—you have people pass through a narrow passage and then there is a brrrrr of an electrical apparatus. They stay there for twenty seconds and from then on they are sterile."[205] While such violent, racist ideas were never enforced, with the New Deal, "eugenics became a dominant paradigm in public health on the island," as one scholar argues, with birth control at the center. A eugenics sterilization law that included poverty as a legitimate reason for sterilization was introduced in 1939. In Puerto Rico's complex political and cultural environment, the New Deal state thus acquired a new role in social engineering. This whole agenda enjoyed strong support among the island's modernizing middle classes and was shaped by mainland Americans who felt that they had to educate the islanders on how to avoid "un-Puerto Rican" practices. Yet the state's role should not be overstated. After 1936, nonstate actors mainly propagated the notion of eugenics. Resistance by the Catholic Church was the main reason why the New Dealers did not pursue this policy more actively. All in all, Puerto Rico became a key arena for probing and redrawing the limits of paternalistic state action.[206]

In the economic realm, too, action fell short of the declared modernization objectives. Unemployment, poverty, and labor conflicts continued to shape the everyday lives of most Puerto Ricans. Federal spending on the island remained modest, at least at a comparative level. In relation to its population, Puerto Rico received much less financial support than the mainland United States, as Bourne, Gruening, and others never tired of pointing out. By November 1934, for instance, the island had only received some $2.3 million instead of $32.2 million, and given the severity of the crisis in Puerto Rico, population size was a dubious indicator in the first place. Mismanagement was also a factor, partly due to incompetence, and partly because of the multiplicity of and tug-of-war between the various New Deal agencies involved on the island. Governor Blanton C. Winship complained in May 1935 that the "actual accomplishments have been comparatively small" and that "Puerto Rico stands in practically the same situation that she was a year ago."[207] The Roosevelt administration brought benevolent words and more bureaucracy, but most people saw no sustained economic effect.

Reality raged like a tropical hurricane through the New Deal's far-flung ambitions for another reason as well: the 1930s saw a massive upsurge of Puerto Rican nationalism, which the Roosevelt administration's paternalistic initiatives did nothing to de-escalate. Nationalists saw agencies like PRERA not as innocent reconstruction programs but rather as tools of colonial domination. Led by Harvard Law School alumnus Pedro Albizu Campos, the Nationalist Party increasingly radicalized. Violence that had long tinged local politics escalated in July 1935, when the Nationalists started a bombing campaign. Colonel E. Francis Riggs, the chief of the Insular Police who previously made a career by organizing the police and paramilitary apparatus of Nicaraguan despot Anastasio Somoza DeBayle, was killed seven months later. Soon after his murder, his two assassins experienced the same fate under dubious circumstances in the police headquarters. The mid-1930s saw a swing from welfare statism to draconian repression of the independence movement. This culminated in a police massacre in Ponce in spring 1937, when the island police attacked a peaceful Nationalist parade; nineteen Puerto Ricans were killed, and over two hundred wounded. The anti-imperial image of the United States was seriously damaged on the island as well as internationally.[208]

Debates about Puerto Rican independence complicated things further. Two months after the assassination of Riggs, Senator Millard E. Tydings introduced a Senate bill to set Puerto Rico on the road to independence. The Maryland Democrat wanted independence as a means to limit Puerto Rican immigration to the United States; hence, even the offer of independence was a form of "rule of colonial difference"—to borrow Partha Chatterjee's term—meant to represent the colonized as incorrigibly inferior.[209] Washington should discontinue its massive reconstruction programs and let the island go, he believed. His bill was clearly punitive in nature and built on a highly racist worldview. It foresaw a steep increase in tariffs as the iron thorn, so to speak, attached to the olive branch of independence. Not least for this reason, a referendum in November 1937 resulted in a sweeping victory for the camp advocating the status quo. Tensions on the island remained high, and only subsided in late 1938 when the island administration managed to incarcerate and silence the militant nationalists.[210]

In sum, the New Dealers did not achieve much in Puerto Rico. As in the Tennessee valley, economic intervention was paired with ideas of remaking a whole society. When it came to social engineering, James Bourne was as unsuccessful as the TVA's Arthur E. Morgan, even if for different reasons. While the New Dealers' balance sheet was already mixed in mainland America, in Puerto Rico they had to learn that their hope of exporting projects unchanged to a fundamentally different society was doomed. Some, among them Tugwell, counseled caution early on. In 1934, Tugwell warned that "the attempt to apply the criteria to the tropics" would not work. Whereas the radical New Dealer normally found himself drowned out by less interventionist voices, his oxymoronic advice to "make haste slowly" was overruled by a more straightforward approach: trying to shuttle Puerto Rico into high modernity by applying the tools invented for the American mainland.[211] In the medium term, the failure of the New Deal's attempt to revamp a whole society led to a reversal of course both in the Tennessee valley and on Puerto Rico: the TVA resorted to a more technological and economic agenda as an alternative to social engineering. In its Puerto Rican sibling, in contrast, welfare state building simply ebbed away, thereby reaffirming the distinction between metropolis and colony that early New Deal action had challenged. The *New Republic*, which had long become a supporter of the New Deal, concluded in 1937 that "there is no point in going on with the expenditure of enormous sums for relief while we also continue the economic policies that make Puerto Rico's poverty even deeper."[212]

In the long run, however, San Juan held a different lesson. PRERA and similar agencies were forerunners of overseas development projects during the Cold War, as Manuel R. Rodríguez has argued.[213] After 1945, economic intervention, reeducation, and other expressions of social engineering and planning became central to projecting American power. In contrast to the 1930s, the United States now showed more willingness to invest major sums and build up the administrative capacities necessary to implement vast programs.

Finally, beyond the comparison with the TVA, Puerto Rico was no exceptional case. Social engineering had already played a major role in the Philippines, another US colony, in the decades prior to World War I. After losing importance after 1913, it was kick-started again during the New Deal years. The Philippines, in contrast to Puerto Rico, were offered independence on more acceptable terms in the mid-1930s, fulfilling earlier promises and resulting in the decision to grant liberty after a ten-year period. The Philippines in this way spearheaded the global age of decolonization after 1945. In both colonies, local elites were built up, but structural reforms ultimately remained limited. Most crucial, given the setup of American colonies, no serious land reform was attempted, leaving these territories with a heavy burden regardless of whether they gained independence.[214] Land reform only became a core component of US overseas policies after 1945—for instance in Korea. Such massive intrusion into property rights only seemed acceptable where US possession was not significantly concerned.[215]

There were further important parallels at the global level. Other overseas empires also focused on consolidating rather than expanding their colonial

possessions during the 1930s. Colonial reformism, trying to make administration more professional and scientific as well as give it a more humane
touch, also came to characterize developments in the British, French, and
other overseas empires from the mid-1930s on, even if each empire operated
within its own specific configuration of power. In general, the district administrator who "knew his natives" was supplemented or even replaced by
technical officers and scientific advisers.[216] Colonial rule nonetheless remained largely a matter of repressive mechanisms. In few colonies anywhere in the world did the rhetoric of welfare state building go as far as it
did in Puerto Rico, where it was embedded in a wider modernization discourse anchored by what one scholar has called a "paternalist consensus."
Accordingly, more subtle justifications had to be found for raising the standard of living and bringing "civilization" to Asians and Africans, whom
many whites deemed to be languishing on the lower rungs of the civilizational ladder.[217] Nazi imperialism, with its focus on ruthless exploitation of
other peoples, was the outlier in this trend, and Japan was the most extreme
combination of rational planning and modernization *combined* with violence of immense dimensions.[218] On balance, however, Puerto Rico represents an often-neglected testing ground of New Deal activism and corrects
an exclusive concentration on Good Neighborism with regard to the United
States' relationship to regions south of the Rio Grande. It also reveals the
tensions that the New Deal had to face when straddling the divide between
domestic insulation and imperialism.

Prometheus Bound

The self-restricting elements of the Good Neighbor policy—to which
Puerto Rico represented an exception—resonated well with developments
in other fields of international affairs. The mid-1930s saw an intense discussion on neutrality as a fundamental foreign policy orientation. At the level
of security, insulation mostly translated into such a neutralist position. Due
to congressional and other influences, policy restraint in this area in the end
went much further than Roosevelt and other New Dealers wished.

Some fifteen years after World War I, it was quite unclear to most Americans what their country had gained from participating in the global conflict. Sacrificing more than a hundred thousand doughboys and material
resources worth billions of dollars had neither prevented the mushrooming
of dictatorships in many European countries nor forestalled the Great Depression. With international tensions on the rise along with turmoil in Europe and Asia, the dominant mood in the United States reflected a pacifist
sentiment, and the debate was tinged by a critique of capitalism. Publications such as George Seldes's *Iron, Blood, and Profits* of 1934 argued that war

profiteers had largely orchestrated entry into the Great War. Soldiers giving aid to the enemy, Seldes wrote, faced capital punishment, even as arms manufacturers and other merchants of death "received baronetcies and the ribbons of the Legion of Honour while making a profit of millions of dollars." Playing on a Latin saying, *si vis pacem, para bellum* (he who wants peace, should prepare for war), Seldes ends his book with the words *si vis pacem para pacem* (if you want peace, prepare for peace).[219]

Such publications were grist to the mill of groups like the Women's International League for Peace and Freedom (WILPF), which had already petitioned for an investigation into the warmongering role of the American armament industry. Dorothy Detzer, head of WILPF's US section, played a key role in convincing Senator Nye to take up the issue in Congress in spring 1934. Motivated by a public debate on how to stay clear of both international conflicts and the interests of greedy bankers and arms producers, the Senate set up a Committee Investigating the Munitions Industry. Nye, who had made a name for himself as an isolationist Republican from North Dakota, was appointed as committee chair. Supported by WILPF and other groups, the committee soon uncovered inappropriate behavior by US companies. What is more, it also became a platform for a general reckoning with the internationalist credo.[220]

Seldes, Nye, and others meant to prevent a second 1917. Nye reasoned

> that our American welfare requires that great importance be given to the subject of our neutrality when others are at war.... Let us know that it is sales and shipments of munitions and contraband, and the lure of profits in them, that will get us into another war.[221]

Nye did not simply resort to the old argument that foreign entanglement burdened the United States with problems created in other parts of the world. A neutralist foreign policy was also meant to rein in American capitalism, and was driven by the same kind of hostility toward big business and finance from which the New Dealers profited.

International fears strengthened such views, and they were by no means unwarranted. In October 1935, after a period of great tension stemming from a skirmish the December before, Mussolini's forces invaded Ethiopia. In March 1936, Hitler's Wehrmacht entered the Rhineland, violating the terms of the Versailles treaty that permanently demilitarized the region. In summer 1936, civil war broke out in Spain, and exactly one year later, Japanese aggression against China escalated into full-scale war. Equally threatening was the global alliance concluded by extremist dictatorships at that time. In November 1936, Germany and Japan signed a pact directed against international communism, which Fascist Italy joined one year later. Their extreme nationalisms and potentially conflicting notions of racism did not keep these three regimes from uniting forces to openly oppose the global status quo.

In this intellectual and international climate, Congress passed a first neutrality act in summer 1935, which imposed an embargo on any belligerent nation, without distinguishing between aggressor and victim. These provisions were renewed in 1936, augmented by a ban on loans to all parties at war. The year thereafter, another loophole was closed, with all parties in civil wars now covered by the legislation, thus drying out the business that Ford, Texaco, and others had started in Spain, despite—or rather in light of—the civil war. The neutrality act of 1937 continued many of these provisions. And beyond enacted legislation, Americans continuously discussed the so-called Ludlow Amendment, which called for a national referendum on any declaration of war by Congress. The amendment would have changed diplomacy radically, and even if it did not win the necessary majority, it drove the debate on the various neutrality acts. Insulation had reached a new pinnacle.[222]

Roosevelt and Hull always remained critical of this form of self-restriction but failed to take decisive action. As on so many other issues, FDR wanted to keep his discretionary power, yet soon learned that Nye was able to outmaneuver him. Nye pushed for a mandatory form of neutrality, whereas Roosevelt tried to use Key Pittman, chair of the Senate Foreign Relations Committee, to prevent such an extreme move. In the negotiations, Silver Key experienced several defeats, and FDR refrained from using his means of last resort, the presidential veto. Yet again, he showed himself reluctant to pick a fight, particularly since many of the neutralists were ready to support his domestic agenda. In 1935, for instance, the neutralist camp threatened to filibuster the Guffey-Snyder Coal Bill, and the president accepted the neutrality act in order to save this NRA ersatz. Ironically, neutrality was the price for an act that was strongly influenced by British legislation.[223]

In fact, Roosevelt contented himself with drilling a few loopholes into the neutrality acts. In 1935, he insisted that the act would expire after six months—in the hope that the neutralist camp would lose influence by then. He decided in 1937 to allow arms shipments to support the Chinese government in its struggle against Japan, since war had not been officially declared between the two countries. The 1937 act also included a "cash-and-carry" clause that gave the president the right to permit sales to countries at war as long as they paid in cash and carried out the transport of the goods themselves. Still, these exceptions remained marginal. While Roosevelt's famous "Quarantine Speech" on October 5, 1937, asserted that "there is no escape through mere isolation or neutrality," and called for an international "quarantine" of the aggressor nations, he did not openly oppose neutrality legislation.[224] Almost two years would elapse before the president publicly declared in Congress, three weeks after the outbreak of World War II, "I regret that the Congress passed that act, I regret equally that I signed that act."[225]

With the benefit of hindsight, it is easy to criticize the views of Nye and others as a naive head-in-the-sand policy. They reacted to the rise of fascism even more myopically than Roosevelt, hoping that the Atlantic and Pacific were wide enough to keep the United States out of future conflicts. The global role that the United States had assumed and worldwide contraction that allowed Japanese warplanes to attack Hawaii some four thousand miles from their own shores soon proved them wrong. At the time, though, many still saw the armed intervention in World War I as the true mistake. The prominent Yale law professor Edwin M. Borchard, for example, argued in 1938 that for the United States, the "entire history is associated with the growth of neutrality and advantage from its practice."[226]

Americans were not alone in pondering political neutrality during the 1930s. Not even the moral overtones of the debate were specific to the United States. After a first spike during World War I, the international debate about neutrality saw a second peak during the second half of the 1930s. Prior to 1914, Belgium and Switzerland had been the main permanently neutral states, but after 1918, the Netherlands, Norway, Denmark, Austria, Portugal, and other countries also moved in this direction. Most of these were small, European nation-states, presenting their foreign policy choice as a form of moral rectitude. Meanwhile, countries like Great Britain prioritized appeasement over a robust response to fascism's expansion. At the end of the decade, many of these nations had to learn the bitter lesson that neutrality and appeasement did not work with warmongering nations like Nazi Germany, and that a policy of de-escalation ultimately played into the hands of dictators. With this history, neutrality came to play a quite different role in the era after World War II. The United States now embraced the lesson that the costs of abstention and self-restraint were higher than those of active commitment to international affairs.[227]

A long and bitter learning process running throughout the 1930s was needed to arrive at this conclusion. After the end of the decade, the United States revised its neutralist position, which was eventually repealed in 1941. Until then, the United States was limited in its ability to aid its European allies against fascist aggression. American insulation also encouraged dictators throughout Europe and Asia to take ever more expansionist steps. On questions of international security, the United States thus retreated from the scene when the world needed it the most. By muddling through on this issue during the 1930s, Roosevelt again prioritized domestic concerns over international considerations.

This inward turn on questions of security nevertheless reflected an acute awareness of the wider world. It was during the hottest phase of the neutrality discussion in 1935 that Roosevelt erected several cornerstones of his New Deal agenda, including the National Labor Relations and Social Security acts. Although these policies were highly divisive at the time (and ever since), the president pushed for initiatives aimed at strengthening the domestic political order. Insulation was intended to display the vitality and assertiveness of US democracy. By the second half of the 1930s, self-assurance had overcome the doubts that many Americans had entertained about democracy a few years earlier. In June 1936, for instance, Roosevelt summarized this new self-confidence and global sense of mission in a speech at the Democratic National Convention, stressing that "in other lands, there are some people, who, in times past, have lived and fought for freedom, and seem to have grown too weary to carry on the fight." He continued:

> I believe in my heart that only our success can stir their ancient hope. They begin to know that here in America we are waging a great and successful war.... We are fighting to save a great and precious form of government for ourselves and for the world.[228]

Making democracy work in the United States came first. A partial commitment to multilateralism on trade issues was complemented by insulation regarding questions of security. For the time being, it sufficed to demonstrate America's role as a beacon, as a clear alternative to fascism and dictatorship.

Borders, Hard and Soft

Barring the Huddled Masses

The United States' links to the wider world changed not only through the New Dealers' actions but also due to the issues they left untouched. Immigration is a case in point. Roosevelt left the field to others, which also explains why it does not figure at all in many accounts of the New Deal, even though the consequences of immigration policy were inextricably tied to domestic developments. By cutting migratory connections, the United States became more inward looking during the New Deal years, thereby reinforcing the insulationist agenda.

By the early 1930s, the restrictive legislation implemented in the previous decade was impacting on population trends. Hoover had even stiffened the regime in 1930 by reinterpreting an old provision precluding people "likely to become a public charge" from entering the United States. So far, the clause had only barred those who lacked the physical or mental skills needed for a job. Now, they also had to have financial means to support themselves. As American consular officers began applying this restrictive

TABLE 2
Immigration into the United States, by Continent

Year	Overall	Europe	Asia	Americas	Africa	Australasia
1927	335,175	168,368	3,669	161,872	520	746
1930	241,700	147,438	4,535	88,104	572	1,051
1933	23,068	12,383	552	9,925	71	137
1935	34,956	22,778	682	11,174	118	141
1937	50,244	31,863	1,149	16,903	155	174
1940	70,756	50,454	2,050	17,822	202	228

Source: Bogue, Population of the United States, 349–53.
Note: Australasia includes Australia, New Zealand, and the Pacific Islands. In most years, the statistics register a small number of immigrants from "all other countries."

interpretation, even the low quotas set for each country during the 1920s often remained unfilled.[229] The United States, the nation that had prided itself on accepting the "huddled masses yearning to breathe free," to cite Emma Lazarus's famous 1883 sonnet "The New Colossus," was now taking an intransigent stance.

In 1933, the same year that the New Deal commenced, immigration hit an all-time low since the mid-nineteenth century, and, under the strong influence of nativism, showed a clear bias toward northern and western Europeans. It would take until the mid-1950s to return to the levels of the late 1920s. While the New Dealers bore no responsibility for the immigration laws of the Republican era, they did not do anything to revise them.

Times were hard, of course. After 1929, some pressed for an even tougher stance. In 1934, for instance, Democratic representative Martin Dies scolded the "industrial greed and legislative stupidity" that had led to "unrestricted immigration" in the past. He claimed that "the unemployment would never have assumed such serious and unprecedented proportions in this country" without the "millions of impoverished aliens" who "invade our shores in hungry quest of jobs and fortunes." For the Texas politician, the implications were obvious: "We must ignore the tears of the sobbing sentimentalists and internationalists, and we must permanently close, lock and bar the gates of our country."[230]

This sentiment was widespread in America. Xenophobia, nativism, and bigotry heavily colored the general atmosphere. While Japan started to campaign for solidarity among the "darker races," the international communist movement used the trial of the Scottsboro boys and similar racist miscarriages of justice to accuse the United States of double standards. With activists rallying for interracial solidarity in places as diverse as Moscow, Sidney, Liverpool, Shanghai, and Buenos Aires in the early 1930s, America's international reputation on this issue was extremely mixed.[231]

Domestically, the early 1930s saw persistent congressional moves to reduce immigration, and eugenics gave the restrictionist camp a pseudoscientific attire. In a 1934 report on immigration control, for instance, leading eugenicist Harry H. Laughlin argued against exceptional admission of Jewish refugees from Nazi Germany. Described in the *New York Times* as the "foremost authority in the United States today on the subject," Laughlin maintained that the nation should abide by its "white standard in the selection of immigration."[232]

Against this backdrop, some of the last loopholes were closed during the New Deal years. Imperialism and migration, racism and decolonization, were inextricably connected in the case of the Philippines. The islands had stood under US political control since 1898. Much to the resentment of the white supremacists, Filipinos were legally US nationals due to their colonial status. Even if Filipinos did not enjoy full citizenship, they were exempted from the racist anti-immigration acts targeting other Asians. People like Madison Grant bemoaned the "swarming of the Filipinos into the Pacific States," and stressed the "white ownership of the country." For him and others, Filipino immigration into the United States appeared a particular threat since it was predominantly male and often led to interracial marriages with Caucasian women.[233] Hence, Filipinos became a blatant contradiction of American imperialism, caught between the racially motivated exclusion of Asians and a policy of benevolent assimilation for the island specifically. The 1934 Philippines Independence Act paved the way to freedom, to be achieved after a ten-year transition period. There were many reasons behind the end of colonial rule, but paradoxically the process was also driven by xenophobia and racism. The act reclassified Filipinos as aliens for the purpose of immigration—a step that soon yielded results: thanks to the quota system, a mere seventy-two Filipinos entered the United States in 1936, down from thirty-seven thousand in 1931.[234] In line with this approach, the Filipino Repatriation Act, which Roosevelt signed into law in 1935, granted free passage home for US-based Filipinos—but once they had left America, they were virtually unable to return. Granting self-determination to another nation went hand in hand with insulating the United States for economic and racist reasons. Senator Tydings, one of the main authors of the bill, had not been successful with Puerto Ricans—but he was with Filipinos.[235]

Even more significant, America's traditionally porous southern border hardened. Many Americans hoped that more jobs would become available for them with fewer Mexicans joining the workforce. A series of restrictions kept documented Mexican immigration at two thousand per annum from 1932, and a good portion of the Mexican-born population was pushed out. In the decade after 1929, between four hundred thousand and one million Mexicans and Mexican Americans left the country, either deported as illegals, incentivized to leave, or hoping for a better future in Mexico than in the crisis-ridden United States. Even those who held US citizenship were frequently uninformed about their rights and entitlements.[236] "Repatriation," as Americans chose to call it, not only revealed the racist limits of the American dream. Many of these *pochos* (Americanized Mexicans, or those who were accused of having lost their culture or language) were not welcome south of the border either. A Mexican American child from Los Angeles, for example, reported being harassed in Aguascalientes after relocation: a policeman threatened to put him and his friends in jail unless they spoke Spanish. North of the border, they had been discriminated against as Mexicans; now they suffered as "Americans" whose main language was English.[237]

Enforcing a restrictionist immigration regime also had important domestic consequences. The US farm labor force "whitened" considerably, particularly in the southwestern states. Some Americans found new jobs, but these were typically badly paid. The fate of the Joad family, described in John Steinbeck's novel *Grapes of Wrath*, summarizes this experience, since the hopes of these "Oakies" were by no means fulfilled on their arrival in California. Instead of a promised land, they found a country controlled by big corporate farms with an oversupply of labor. The Joads eventually managed to find work on a peach orchard, although conditions were dire and the workers were forced to strike. In the novel and reality, new federal and statewide programs soon followed, since poverty was less acceptable when endured by white Americans. While also designed to alleviate the hardship of sharecroppers in general, agencies such as the Resettlement Administration (RA) under Rexford Tugwell, or later the Farm Security Administration, sheltered thousands of families like the Joads in their camps. There were many more in need than opportunities available on the new model farms and other settlements, as Steinbeck's heroes soon found out. Still, there was a clear link between the hardening of the United States' southern border and the New Dealers' domestic agenda: insulation through restrictionism and state interventionism at home complemented one another.[238]

The links between the domestic and the international were even more intricate when it came to the treatment of Jews. Since its inception, the New Deal had been criticized as a "Jew Deal." And it was true that minorities and women achieved more senior federal government positions than ever before. Many of the talented Americans who now flocked to Washington were Jewish, including Vienna-born lawyer Felix Frankfurter, Henry Morgenthau, and FDR's speechwriter Samuel I. Rosenman. Jewish voters belonged to the New Deal coalition. While anti-Semites were quick to see a Jewish conspiracy at work, Roosevelt did not let such allegations affect him. In 1938, for instance, Morgenthau and other well-connected Jews urged him not to appoint Frankfurter to the Supreme Court in order to avoid a new wave of anti-Semitism. Roosevelt rejected their advice. While certainly not free of xenophobic ideas, the president was less prejudiced when it came to Jews than most contemporaries of his background.[239] Yet FDR's loyal stead-fastness in the domestic arena had no equivalent in his foreign policy. For the longest time, Nazism's terror against Jews in Germany had little impact on US policies. When, in September 1933, a delegation of American Jewish leaders asked to see State Department officials to lobby for easier immigra-tion, they were told that the person in charge was on vacation. The White House remained silent, refusing to comment on the implications of Nazism for US immigration policy. Secretary of Labor Perkins was slightly more forthcoming, but until 1938 most attempts to help Jewish refugees were checked by restrictionist resistance from the State Department.[240]

The general mood in which the New Dealers made their decisions also has to be considered in this case. The Depression had led to an unprece-dented upsurge of anti-Semitism in the United States, and resistance against Jewish immigration was particularly strong during the 1930s. Its prominent advocates included radio preacher Father Coughlin and Henry Ford. Both reached millions of Americans. Opinion polls reveal that in 1938, for instance, at least 50 percent of all Americans had a low opinion of Jews, 45 percent found them less honest in business than Gentiles, and 77 percent did not want to increase the number of German Jewish refugees in America.[241]

On matters of immigration, therefore, Roosevelt and the New Dealers did little to challenge the dominant nativist view. The Jewish constituency in the United States was small, and the president was especially reluctant to antagonize southern Democrats and organized labor groups, which both strongly opposed more Jewish immigration. In 1935–37, it was still unclear that the Nazi persecution would end in genocide. And the existing system did allow some refugees to immigrate, even if the annual quota for Ger-many was never filled in the prewar years. Roosevelt prioritized domestic concerns, although some New Dealers criticized this policy. In April 1933, for example, Supreme Court justice Louis Brandeis confided to his friend Felix Frankfurter that Roosevelt "has amply shown that he has no antisemi-tism. . . . But this action, or rather determination that there shall be none [that is, on immigration policy], is a disgrace to America and to F.D.'s ad-ministration." America's doors remained shut for most of the "homeless, tempest-tost" (Lazarus).[242]

Generally speaking, questions of immigration remained largely a domes-tic matter, governed by Congress, and driven by electoral politics and the dynamics of economic protectionism along with racist xenophobia. During good parts of the nineteenth century, migration had been more of an inter-national matter, governed through commercial diplomacy. By the 1920s, a restrictionist approach had taken over, and the New Dealers did little to reverse it.[243] Roosevelt's abdication of leadership clearly reflected his political instinct and the constraints on his power.

Attitudes only changed slowly. While nativism was particularly strong during the decade, it was by no means unchallenged. The 1930s saw an intense discussion on ethnicity, and during the second half of the 1930s the antiracist ideas of anthropologists like Franz Boas, Margaret Mead, and Ruth Benedict gained traction while the credibility of eugenics positions declined. Published in 1934, Benedict's *Patterns of Culture* soon became a standard reference, arguing for an analysis of societies based on a notion of culture instead of racial concepts. Reference to Germany—and hence a transnational factor in the American discussion—became a cornerstone of the debate, with Boas in particular fighting Nazi propaganda by falsifying racist theories. The regime of terror in Germany challenged homegrown racist practices, especially when it came to anti-Semitism. The more tolerant view with regard to national origin, race, and ethnicity that emerged post-1945 thus had important roots in the 1930s. In the medium term, the need to contrast American freedom to Nazi terror was a key factor in making the United States move closer to its own ideals.[244]

Despite this unwelcoming stance and the dwindling numbers, some remarkable figures made it to the United States during the New Deal years, either with permanent immigrant status or on temporary visas. The names of distinguished politicians, artists, and academics who fled Europe's fascist dictatorships are well known, including former German Chancellor Heinrich Brüning, Albert Einstein, and Thomas Mann. Their prestige—in Brüning's case, primarily the result of efficient self-fashioning, and in the other two cases fully deserved—eventually also helped to turn the tide against nativism.

Voices of Color

Equally noteworthy, but maybe less known, is the tiny group of Africans that entered New Deal America and forged a new black Atlantic. Many of them belonged to the local elites of British colonies. Unlike their predecessors, they traveled to America rather than to Britain in search of higher education, and the vast majority eventually returned to Africa. A young teacher from Accra in Ghana is a good illustration. In 1935, he first sailed from Takoradi to London. After failing to be admitted at a British university, he secured a visa for the United States, where he enrolled in Pennsylvania's Lincoln University, an elite college with some three hundred African American students and a few young Africans. After obtaining two BA degrees, our traveler continued his education at the University of Pennsylvania, where he earned two MA degrees. This highly educated man was no less than Kwame Nkrumah, a leading advocate of twentieth-century Pan-Africanism and the first president of independent Ghana. Nigeria's Nnamdi Azikiwe studied at Lincoln a few years before Nkrumah and helped pave the way for the Ghanaian. Leaving the United States in 1934, he became another celebrated nationalist leader in West Africa and, in 1963, the first president of independent Nigeria.[245]

Yet these years in the United States did not necessarily turn Africans into diehard fans of America, notwithstanding the inspiration they received from their (black) academic teachers and other American peers. Nkrumah, for instance, dedicated two full chapters of his autobiography to his years in America, but failed to mention Roosevelt or the New Deal once.

Against this backdrop, the effects of this black Atlantic were often greater for America. The admission of African students turned black colleges such as Lincoln into laboratories for the globalization of the United States. Even if the relationship was fraught with tension, African Americans forged new links with Africans. The rewards of this exchange were reaped during the postwar decades, when American desegregation and African decolonization coincided and to some extent coalesced.[246] The generation of Azikiwe and Nkrumah, themselves stepchildren of an earlier Pan-African generation including W.E.B. Du Bois and Marcus Garvey, eventually paved the way for men like Kenyan Barack Obama Sr., whose son would later rise to a position that no black American had ever held before.

Finally, "colored cosmopolitanism" also spanned other parts of the world. African Americans and left-leaning Indians intensified their dialogue during the 1930s, as made evident by a series of articles in the Bombay-based journal the *Aryan Path* in 1936. Writing in March, Du Bois stressed how much both groups could learn from each other in their fight for freedom, and he compared the American system of color lines to the Indian castes. Two months later, N. S. Subba Rao, an intellectual from Mysore in southern India, published a reply. In a piece that generously ignored the racist assumptions underlying the concept of Aryan identity, he argued for closer contacts to African Americans, leading to another public exchange in the journal in October. The discussion exemplified an intensifying global dialogue that challenged ideas of white supremacy both in the United States and other parts of the globe.[247]

In spite of the powerful global links that these migrants and intellectuals created in the medium term, most Americans opted for insulation during the New Deal period. Another factor that reveals the degree to which the United States decoupled from the wider world is the contraction of tourism to international destinations. Taking expenditure as an indicator, overseas travel saw a sharp decrease from $437 million in 1929 to $159 million in 1933. The figures slowly recovered thereafter, but never exceeded $250 million before World War II. Expenditure for travel to Canada and Mexico also plummeted after 1929, but recovered more quickly. At a time when US citizens represented half the world's total tourists, Americans reduced their traveling activities, opting for hemispheric rather than transoceanic adventures. This was, of course, not just the sum of private choices of individuals seeking leisure and amusement; at least by the late 1930s, government support from Washington made tourism an unstated program of public diplomacy. Still, the political choices of Good Neighborism were flanked and reinforced by societal processes.[248]

The decline in foreign travel had consequences in specific localities. In mid-1933, Paris as the true center of America's creative and glamorous during the 1920s had said au revoir to half the twenty-seven thousand expats who had populated the city immediately before the crash. Roosevelt's dollar devaluation in 1933 made living or traveling in gold standard countries like France even more costly, and tourism suffered severely. Only the small American upper class continued to cross the North Atlantic for leisure and amusement during the worst years of the crisis. Whereas transatlantic vacations had always been beyond the means of the lower classes, the affluent American middle and upper-middle classes now tended to motor through the United States, or dreamed of and traveled to Veracruz, or later during the decade to Acapulco. The French connection, in contrast, only reached its pre-1929 level again around 1937.[249]

Seeing America first was not just an economic necessity in times of crisis; it also reflected the more nation-centered view that many Americans were developing. Middle-class people now traveled to the national parks, while working- and lower-middle-class families discovered resorts that were easier to reach by car or train. The Catskill Mountains, for instance, offered leisure landscapes catering specifically to the preferences of Jewish, African, and Italian Americans. Ethnic American identity found its true home in racially differentiated and insulated resorts. Building on the trends of the 1920s, a slightly more pluralist concept of what it meant to be American developed during the 1930s. The New Dealers also propagated this more inclusive ethos. Despite their clear limits, WPA and other programs, for example, acknowledged African American cultural advancement and civil rights issues. The nation-state was still meant to strictly contain identities; diversity came under the banner of patriotism, but it did not foster transnational links.[250]

In this context, the status of Mexican Americans also started to change over the course of the decade. Organizations such as the League of United Latin American Citizens (LULAC) argued for "Mexican Americanism"—a view that embraced assimilation more than adherence to Mexican culture in an attempt to fight discrimination. Here, the status of minorities and international politics were inextricably linked. Specifically, Good Neighborism impacted on domestic affairs when, in 1936, the New Dealers revised a category that had been introduced to the US Census only in 1930. Anti-Mexican and eugenics lobbying had then led to the introduction of a "Mexican race," much to the anger of many Mexican Americans as well as a Mexican middle and upper class that identified as white. Shortly before the president's arrival in Buenos Aires in 1936, LULAC's Frank J. Galvan reminded Roosevelt that these discriminatory census categories undermined his Latin American policy. Mexicans were subsequently reclassified as "white." International relations thus challenged racialized policies at home.[251]

These new views impacted especially on US–Latin American relations, leading to multifaceted forms of transnational cultural interaction that traveled both south and north of the Rio Grande. In Brazil, for instance, the US–Latin American cultural presence competed hard with German culture, be it in relation to products of mass consumption, musical styles, or cultural orientations. Trade, media, and other ties increased cultural affinity over the course of the decade, and Good Neighborism lubricated such cultural contacts.[252]

Commodities and ideas did not just travel south, however. Mexican artist Diego Rivera was highly appreciated in the United States, and the same holds true for Mexican murals more generally. The period saw a real craze for Mexican art, leading to intensive encounters. Not only did Rivera become quite friendly with Henry Ford, he was also commissioned to create a huge mural for the Rockefeller Center in New York in 1933. The same year, mass audiences in the United States were introduced to samba when Fred Astaire and Dolores Del Río danced the carioca in the first US musical comedy set in Brazil, the movie *Flying Down to Rio*. Ten years later, Walt Disney's 1943 production *The Three Caballeros* featured a parrot by the name of Zé Carioca, symbolizing a friendly and elegant Brazil.[253]

Such artifacts and cultural practices did not negate power imbalances and stereotypes. Carioca, for example, was basically invented for the American movie, and audiences in Rio or São Paulo could not help but smile at the hybrid mix of dances presented as typically Brazilian. *The Three Caballeros* presented a highly sanitized picture of Brazil and was part of the propaganda war against the Axis powers. And the fondness for Rivera did not keep the US press from being infuriated when he added a portrait of Lenin to his New York mural. The *Chicago Daily Tribune* described the building as "New York's tower of Babel," and called the decision to commission Rivera a "glorious eccentricity."[254] In light of such protests, the mural was first covered up and then destroyed. Rivera subsequently completed a smaller version in Mexico City.[255] Few episodes give a better illustration of the making, unmaking, and remaking of US–Latin American relations.

In spite of these conflicts, Mexican murals represent a rare case where the New Dealers explicitly emulated cultural and political practices from south of the Rio Grande. In May 1933, the painter George Biddle wrote to his former Groton classmate Franklin, asking him to create a program for visual arts as part of the New Deal's public works. Roosevelt replied politely, stressing that he was "interested in your suggestion in regard to the expression of modern art through mural paintings," and asked Biddle to contact the assistant secretary of the Treasury.[256] In his exchanges with FDR, Eleanor Roosevelt, and various parts of the administration, Biddle referred explicitly to the grand achievements of Mexican muralists. In a letter to Eleanor, Biddle underscored that there were many "younger mural modern artists today who are conscious of the economic and social revolution through which America is going and who would be eager ... to express in permanent art forms the ideals for which the present administration is fighting." Art was clearly meant to serve political ends.[257] And not only did the politicized Mexican muralists themselves serve as an inspiration; so did Mexican politics. Biddle had spent some time during 1928 in Mexico City, where he made the acquaintance of Rivera and was deeply impressed by his work. In Mexico, the government had played an important role in creating the Mexican mural movement just a few years earlier, via publicly commissioned projects by artists such as Rivera and David Alfaro Siqueiros. In his letter to Eleanor, Biddle noted that Rivera had "told me personally that his success in Mexico was due because he went directly to President Obregon" and had found his support.[258] Of course, the United States also had a homegrown tradition of public support for the arts, and Biddle did not get exactly what he wanted. Moreover, he made no mention of the parallel rise of state-supported murals with a political message in Fascist Italy, even if he was acutely aware of this development.[259] Still, his initiative was the main reason why the Treasury Department set up an art program a few months later—a precursor to the famous "Federal One" project of the WPA that supported artists from a variety of fields.[260] The New Deal's visual arts program not only helped muralists such as Lucienne Bloch and Carl Morris but also supported people like Jackson Pollock and Mark Rothko. One of the most lasting achievements of the New Deal was thus deeply inspired by Mexican art and cultural policy.

Taken together, these entanglements led to a slightly greater appreciation of the republics to the south and their peoples. But even Roosevelt liked to ridicule the southern neighbor, at least in private letters. In a note to Rexford Tugwell—since 1933 probably the only man on the planet who dared to write to FDR using an official letterhead yet addressing him as "Dear Skipper"—Roosevelt addressed him as "senor Tugwello" and referred to himself as the "jefe-politico." FDR joked that it was "a pity that the Yankees cannot improve the processes of their civilization by emulating our Mexican culture."[261] Good Neighborism had more facets and effects than one might think at first glance.

Going Global

While the Depression reduced the possibilities for Americans to travel the world, and state policies curbed immigration and for a long time followed an insulationist course, nonstate actors played a critical role in keeping global links alive. In the medium term, they subtly carved out additional space for state action.

Business deserves to be mentioned first, given its role in exporting America's market and mission. It continued to play this part even though the 1930s was an extraordinarily difficult decade, with trade decreasing, foreign investment stagnating, and the international business climate turning negative. "Sam the Banana Man" Zemurray was by no means alone in his attempt to uphold and strengthen business connections despite the Great Slump. Major US corporations, such as in the automobile or office equipment sectors, profited from their huge domestic market, but they also pushed for trade liberalization. Whereas industrial producers in countries with smaller domestic markets such as Great Britain, Germany, or Japan were more likely to favor protectionism, American firms had a much more international strategy.[262] For Gillette, the 1930s was a hard period, even if razor blades were less affected by the crisis than other commodities. The company's advertisements suggested that a good shave reduced the chances of being fired. More important for sales volume and brand recognition was the "Blue Blade," introduced in 1932 to become the most famous double-edge blade ever produced. In 1935, international sales accounted for more than half of Gillette's revenues, and in 1938, the worst Depression year for the firm, almost all its profits came from overseas operations.[263] Oil companies not only expanded their business in the Western Hemisphere but also entered the Dutch East Indies and Middle East. In 1929, Standard Oil of New Jersey produced and refined more oil in the United States than abroad, although a decade later, foreign refining exceeded domestic by 15 percent, producing more than double abroad than at home. This diversification strategy also meant that Mexico's expropriation did not hit the company too hard.[264] Meanwhile, Pan Am—or Pan American, as it was called at the time—fully globalized its business. During the 1930s, it launched its S-42s to fly nonstop to Hawaii, and its founder, Juan Trippe, set his eyes firmly on transatlantic and transpacific connections. On November 22, 1935, a Pan Am M-103 flying boat inaugurated airmail service to China, and in March 1939, transatlantic flights were added.[265] The total number of fare-paying passengers of US airlines increased from 11,000 in 1929 to 111,000 in 1935, and then 476,000 during World War II.[266] Aviation, and a new logic of seeing the world from above in its interconnectedness, ultimately helped to facilitate and legitimize American ascendancy.[267]

Beyond individual companies, business exchange was particularly intense in terms of marketing and advertising strategies. American techniques were emulated in capitalist countries around the world, as much as they were inspired by exposure to non-American markets and competitors. In light of such dynamics, French philosopher Maurice Halbwachs observed in 1934 that "advertising [was] no longer a means subordinated to the ends of enterprise, but an end in itself . . . in search of profits."[268]

Promoting American products and ways of doing business went hand in hand with efforts to win the "hearts and minds" of people around the world. Building on their earlier work, philanthropic foundations like the Carnegie Endowment and Rockefeller Foundation now moved away from the "high politics" of security and peace, where initiatives were increasingly stymied by international tensions. They focused instead on health and social issues, where they often acted in association with the League of Nations. American philanthropists stepped in when many governments reduced their contributions to the League in the wake of the Great Depression, and US dollars thus lubricated global cooperation on issues ranging from the fight against drug trafficking to disease control and education.[269]

The Rockefeller Foundation, for instance, ran programs in no less than forty-two countries across the world in 1938. The China Medical Board and the American University in Beirut received substantial funds, while smaller amounts went to institutions in Stockholm and Toronto. The foundation prided itself on having developed a remedy against yellow fever and vaccinated one million people in South America. For the foundation's president, Raymond B. Fosdick, a different project was the true figurehead, though: the fight against "the threat to the Western Hemisphere." The Rockefeller Foundation, he asserted, was a central player in the struggle against an especially dangerous malaria-transmitting mosquito, which—as an effect of the global transport revolution—had found its way from Africa to South America in the early 1930s. Fosdick ennobled the activities of the foundation's public health workers as "a moral equivalent of war," picking up on a line by American philosopher William James that well described its missionary zeal.[270]

More heartwarming than bananas, blades, and balsam, and in many parts of the world an even more significant business factor, was Hollywood's film industry. By the late 1930s, Hollywood productions were the fourth-ranked export by value. While silent films had already developed a truly global vernacular, American talkies were also able to speak to an international cinema audience. Films such as *King Kong* and Walt Disney's *Three Little Pigs* (both 1933), or Charlie Chaplin's *Modern Times* (1936), addressed the uncertainties and fears of an age that saw radical shifts and ruptures in personal biographies, caused by economic, political, or other shock waves. Whether the *Three Little Pigs* represented Depression-torn America or New Deal optimism has been a matter of debate; anyway, Walt Disney's animated cartoons soon turned into global icons.[271] Mickey Mouse was showing in some forty nations by the mid-1930s. In Great Britain, King George V was one of Mickey Mouse's greatest fans, while in Japan only the emperor was more popular than this fantasy creature.[272] Nazi propaganda minister Joseph Goebbels gave Hitler a collection of twelve Mickey Mouse films as a Christmas present in 1937 and noted that the führer was "truly pleased."[273] Ideological divides mattered little in light of the global allure of these productions.

International sport was another arena of global encounters, dominated by private actors. The 1930s saw a substantial globalization of sports in which the United States was by no means the only, or main point, of reference. Soccer thickened the ties between Europe, Latin America, and North Africa over the course of the decade. The first Soccer World Cup in Uruguay in 1930 gave a foretaste of what the game would become: one of the most globalized phenomena of all, even if the United States remained on the substitutes' bench, so to speak, for a long time.[274] While standing on the touchlines of the global soccer network, America was much more visible in other fields. The 1932 Olympic Games in Los Angeles, for example, was a landmark that transformed the event from a rather marginal and elitist gathering to big entertainment with a global audience. Local businessmen, spearheaded by real estate tycoon William May Garland, took the lead, and Los Angeles was soon identified with new techniques of selling the five rings globally. While local politicians knew how to capitalize on this, President Hoover decided not to hop on the Olympic bandwagon.[275]

Beyond such mega-events, particular American sports forged links between the United States and societies of quite different cultural and political fabric. From the 1890s onward, Japan developed a love of baseball, seeing it as an embodiment of *genki* (vigor). In November 1934, a crowd of one hundred thousand Japanese waving American flags welcomed Babe Ruth and other American League celebrities to Japan. "Babe Ruth, Sultan of Swat, Arrives," wrote the *Osaka Mainichi* triumphantly, while crowds shouted "Banzai Ruth"—as if the country's ultranationalism had never existed. The New Deal state played a relatively small role in these exchanges. The main organizer of Ruth's triumphal procession was a Japanese newspaper, whereas the State Department was largely absent.[276] Roosevelt and the State Department adopted basically the same approach during the 1936 Olympic Games in Berlin. They neither boycotted the event nor strongly supported their own team, but left the initiative in the hands of the American Olympic Committee.[277]

By comparison, Fascist Italy, Nazi Germany, and Japan used sports as a means of gaining international political prestige. While many Americans started to see sports as a key component of their way of life, the New Deal pumped millions of dollars into recreation and sport domestically, especially under the banner of the WPA, and while nonstate actors crusaded internationally for American sports and values such as honesty, fairness, and democracy, the New Dealers did not react strongly to this trend, preferring to leave the limelight to nonstate actors. The US government only began using sports systematically for clearly political means a decade later, and it took until the mid-1930s before the US government started to develop a formal structure of conduct in cultural diplomacy, originally mainly focused on Latin America.[278]

On these cultural and economic levels, therefore, there was no marked contraction of America's global links, and on some issues even an expansion. Although they were powerful actors on the global stage, many Americans were resolutely determined to cocoon themselves mentally. But even these insular and parochial tendencies were fed by global motivations, and they had siblings in many other societies. All in all, the crisis of capitalism and Western, white, male-dominated modernity that America experienced during the 1930s was embedded in global discourses and practices.

New Horizons

Writing in 1943, Vice President and former secretary of agriculture Henry Wallace looked back on the interwar years and reflected,

> The world was waiting for us to take the initiative in leading the way to a people's peace after World War I, but we decided to live apart and work our own way. Hunger and unemployment spawned the criminal free-booters of Fascism.... Ours must be a generation that will distill the stamina and provide the skills to create a warproof world.[279]

Some two years later, in his fourth and final inaugural address, Roosevelt maintained, "We have learned that we cannot live alone, at peace; that our own well-being is dependent on the well-being of other Nations, far away."[280] During good parts of the 1930s, in contrast, the New Dealers' propensity to insulation had global repercussions, and the bombshell message, the passive stance on disarmament, Good Neighborism, and immigration policies supply ample examples of transnational links made and unmade. On some issues, America's inward turn had strong parallels in other countries. Appeasement, regional economic integration, and strict border regimes also characterized the policies of most other sovereign nation-states. As a reaction to the Great Depression, national models started to converge on some issues—even if there was no single global template. Trade is a good case in point: many other countries now joined the United States in concentrating their economies on the domestic market or at most on regional cooperation, with global trade a rather small addendum. For this reason, it would take until the 1960s and even 1970s for the global world economy to be truly re-created.[281]

On other questions, the United States stood out. Despite some forms of multilateralism, mainly in a hemispheric context, it concentrated primarily on domestic concerns. America became a discernible alternative to other nations. The most recent modifications of the Monroe Doctrine stood in marked contrast not only to the imperialist aggression of Japan, Italy, and Germany but also to the old-style imperialism that western European powers continued to practice in the Ivory Coast, India, Indonesia, and other colonies.

Simultaneously, the world had become a different place by the late 1930s in comparison to 1933. In the wake of the Great Depression, transnational economic ties had loosened up. Politically, international tensions grew dramatically, particularly in Europe and East Asia, leading to new debates about international commitments and responsibilities. Some of the new cultural links created during the decade could not compensate for these changes. While the globe was still dominated by white supremacy and capitalism, power balances were shifting. During the early 1930s, it was mainly the economic and political order of societies and states that was at stake, but the imperial appetite of some nations now shifted attention to their territorial integrity and the global ramifications of any such changes.

Although the United States' inward turn reduced its international weight, there were always countertendencies, which added to the inconsistency of New Deal foreign policy. The Good Neighbor policy counterbalanced the torpedoing of the World Economic Conference. Insulation, moreover, was always stronger in security than trade, and neither prevented the United States from assuming a central role in world politics only a few years later. The roots of this process lie in the New Deal years, when both unintentionally and discreetly, the United States paved its path to global leadership.

In fact, many developments during the decade expanded the role of the US government in international relations in subtle and hidden ways. The work of American philanthropic organizations, for one, was neither apolitical nor completely independent of state action. Their programs dovetailed with official US foreign policies. While the New Dealers did not dare to come out in support of the League of Nations, they endorsed the financial support provided by the Rockefeller Foundation and others. The foundation's philosophy, revolving around institutional reform, trade, education, and welfare, was especially close to New Deal values.

A symbolic act sealing the link between official foreign policy actors and philanthropists took place in 1935, when Secretary of State Hull chaired the Carnegie Centenary. He established a subcommittee in charge of examining how the Pan-American Union could participate in the festivities, given that Carnegie had been a lavish donor—most important, through the gift of a splendid building as its headquarters in Washington, DC. In the end, the Pan-American Union held a special session in honor of its greatest benefactor, with Hull delivering an address in which he praised Carnegie as an embodiment of American values and for his interest in "the fostering of closer ties between the American Republics." For the audience, it must have been difficult not to see the connections to Good Neighborism, and for any close observer of the events, it must have been evident that Hull basically invited himself, and that cooperation between the State Department and the Carnegie Endowment hardly could have been closer.[282]

In the highly politicized international atmosphere of the 1930s, sports and entertainment also served political functions. Even if the New Dealers were not particularly proactive on these issues, they closely followed the international reception of US goods and ideas, and valued them as a means of spreading the American way of life. When Babe Ruth toured Japan in 1934, for example, US ambassador Joseph C. Grew generously admitted that during the baseball star's visit, there "were two American Ambassadors to Japan, he and I." In his postwar memoirs, he went even further, "the Bambino ... is a great deal more effective Ambassador than I could ever be."[283] Leaving pride of place to nonstate actors—to business and civil society groups—while staying in the background reflected not just the domestic priorities of the New Dealers but also their view that in cultural matters, heavy-handed state action was less efficient and beneficial than these more subtle, discreet ways of interacting with the wider world.

On other issues, the federal government willingly and visibly assumed a new role and incrementally committed itself to a more multilateral approach. As during the 1920s, US interests abroad were mainly secured through economic influence. The way power was wielded had changed markedly, however. Trade relations with Latin America were increasingly channeled through interventionist agreements struck between Washington and the various governments south of the Rio Grande. In 1935, American and British experts as well as programs helped to clean up the mess created by the Silver Purchase Act in China.[284] Trade with Russia was put on a new footing through recognition. America's international corporations now did business in an international environment shaped by the New Dealers and their search for greater security: the government tolerated cartels and price-setting agreements, which it aided with tariffs. Even more important, the Reciprocal Trade Agreements Act of 1934 gave a new role to the executive in economic diplomacy. Minimizing the risk of international business through legal instruments became the new philosophy, amalgamating the Washington government and corporate headquarters. America's largest, globally oriented companies favored a stronger government role, hoping that it would help stabilize the international economic system and create a propitious environment for doing business.[285] Simultaneously, the federal government was no longer willing to send gunboats to places like Liberia (when it defaulted on its debts to Firestone in 1933) or Mexico (after oil nationalization in 1938). It offered legal advice and put pressure on American business to find compromises.

The New Deal state had a more civilian face than its predecessors; Ivy League lawyers serving on committees became more representative than dashing Marines officers in well-tailored uniforms. Students soon joined these government officials. The Buenos Aires Conference of 1936, for example, saw the creation of the first officially sponsored exchange program for graduate students and teachers between the United States and Latin American countries. Whereas so far Washington had looked benevolently on the work of the philanthropic foundations and educational institutions, it now joined the bandwagon of cultural exchange.[286]

Even if Mickey Mouse was far more popular, Hollywood also did NRA publicity. During the war, hemispheric solidarity was often shown onscreen, and Washington forged close links with Hollywood to make it a tool in the war effort.[287] Back in economics, regulation was the new buzzword in foreign affairs not only vis-à-vis Latin America but also with regard to Europe. The tripartite agreement of 1936 is a good illustration. The Treasury worked out the agreement in cooperation with Great Britain and France to stabilize the three nations' currencies domestically as well as in the international exchange markets. Even if this experiment in international regulation of finance did not achieve its ultimate aim of reviving world trade, it heralded the idea of greater public accountability and an expanded role of the state. The Rough Riders seemed as outdated as the traditional liberal distrust of government, while America moved toward giving greater power over foreign economic policy to the executive branch.[288]

Initiatives by the federal administration were soon picked up elsewhere. The Economic and Financial Organization (EFO) of the League of Nations, for instance, immediately discussed Hullianism. With the support of American government officials and economists, the EFO argued for a similar approach at the international level. While these projects did not achieve many rapid concrete results and the New Dealers would have liked the League to be even more active, such initiatives did yield indirect and long-term effects.[289] Cooperation with the League and particularly the EFO continued during the 1930s, and the organization became a laboratory of ideas that provided the structural scaffolding of internationalism during the 1940s.[290] The same holds true for cooperation with the League over other issues such as illicit drug trafficking. League officials carefully reported America's increased involvement as "a useful enlargement of the relations between the United States and the League."[291]

Beyond trade, where Hullianism was increasingly supported by business circles and philanthropic foundations such as the Carnegie Endowment, America's focus on economic interests, welfare statism, and other questions that are often regarded to be part of "low politics," or technical cooperation, ran parallel with the general trends of international cooperation during the decade, and were even intensified and reinvigorated during the late 1930s.[292] On many of these issues, relations with Latin America were the laboratory in which new and innovative tools and mechanisms were first tried out. They then started to shape the relationship with other parts of the world. In this sense, too, the global acquired a new meaning for Americans during the decade: while the international orientation of mind-sets, at least among the elite, frequently remained Eurocentric, Europe's role was vastly diminished, especially in the years before war preparations kicked in.

These dynamics in the fields of low politics with strong affinity with the New Deal agenda have long been overshadowed by the ultimate failure to secure peace, but should not be underestimated, not least because they help to explain the forms that internationalism adopted post-1945. They reveal global shifts, such as the rising role of actors from the global South, and more crucial to this discussion, the central role reserved for the United States in international affairs—which it sometimes took, and sometimes chose to ignore.[293]

Roosevelt himself was often a chameleon in questions of international relations. He changed his views according to conditions, particularly at the domestic level, and never forgot the constraints on his power. Despite his cosmopolitan upbringing and internationalist credentials, he devoted little attention to foreign policy during most of his first two terms in office. In those cases where he did intervene, the result was frequently ambivalent. Compared to his domestic agenda, for which he did not shy away from conflict, Roosevelt invested much less energy in his international beliefs. FDR remained committed to cooperative internationalism, but for a long time refused to consummate this relationship.

Ultimately, the rise of the United States as the foremost international power was not driven primarily by internal dynamics. Its global role was mainly bestowed on it for international reasons, and in this light, international cooperation only gained in significance in the second half of the 1930s. The United States slowly moved into the cockpit of the international system because most other great powers had been decisively weakened by World War I, the Great Depression, and imperial overstretch. Japan and Germany also rose to new levels of global power, and their attempts to redefine the world order increasingly forced more international commitment on the United States. Especially after 1937, American leaders drew more connections between the rise of Nazism and Fascism in Europe and Japan's expansionist militarism. In summer that year, Roosevelt suggested a meeting with British prime minister Neville Chamberlain to discuss closer cooperation on international issues. Given past frustrations, Chamberlain was not interested, but Roosevelt continued to come up with initiatives. As a result, in 1938–39, Washington accomplished a U-turn from insulation to a definition of national security that prioritized alliances, just war, and global leadership, impacting on fields as diverse as transatlantic relations, immigration policy, and Good Neighborism. And yet the new course remained a "cautious crusade" well into World War II, not least due to a strongly isolationist public at home.[294]

Roosevelt's annual messages to Congress reveal this shift to an assertive foreign policy. While in 1937 and 1938 they were still focused on domestic affairs, the message he delivered on January 4, 1939, was centered wholly on international issues and called for "adequate defense." Specifically, he stressed that "the world has grown so small and weapons of attack so swift that no nation can be safe in its will to peace so long as any other powerful nation refuses to settle its grievances at the council table."[295] While the budget for defense had risen continuously since 1935, the absolute increase from 1939 to 1940 was a staggering $430 million—the largest increase since 1919.[296]

This had clear consequences for the role of the state: at the tail end of the New Deal years, the state turned into the primary legitimate force of progressivism, but this process was by no means preordained. While picking up the thread from Theodore Roosevelt and Woodrow Wilson, the global process this time became far more institutionalized and less reversible. In the medium term, Hull's Reciprocal Trade Agreements would form the basis for the General Agreement on Tariffs and Trade (GATT), concluded thirteen years later.[297] On some issues, it was only during the war or even postwar era that Washington began to embrace an all-encompassing form of New Deal internationalism and one worldliness.

Some ten years after setting out his bold agenda in the *Foreign Affairs* article, Roosevelt was finally moved by global circumstances and pressures to adopt the kind of internationalist agenda that he had outlined long before the New Deal came into being. As the world had become a fundamentally different place, things came full circle for FDR.

Chapter 4

REDEFINING BOUNDARIES

DEEPER INTO THE ALPHABET SOUP

Even if the sense of utter crisis and emergency had receded, the New Deal of the mid-1930s was still awash in ideas and initiatives. Roosevelt and his entourage continued to see government as the remedy for the structural problems of modern industrial capitalism. State action building on domestic intervention and insulation sought to curb the destabilizing effects of the Great Depression as well as create security for American citizens.

Paradoxically, the turn to more statism was the outcome of not only the same flurry of activities that had characterized the first hundred days but also setbacks and failures that had occurred since 1933. In winter and spring 1935, several legislative initiatives were politically deadlocked. Roosevelt was barely able to manage an unruly Congress. The Supreme Court killed the NRA, casting a bad omen on the AAA, which suffered a similar fate the following year. New initiatives were needed to overcome the impasse; if not, the New Deal would be over before it had really begun. Equally paradoxical was the activating effect of domestic opposition. At the beginning of his presidency, Roosevelt had tried to appease conservatives and business leaders, as epitomized by the NRA or early banking legislation. By now, the opposition between "that man in the White House" with his "dictatorial" and "socialist" ideas—as business and conservative circles had it— and those labeled by the New Dealers as "organized money" and "economic royalists" was fully entrenched. A key moment in this respect came in May 1935, when the US Chamber of Commerce publicly broke with Roosevelt and denounced the New Deal, and in response the president denied that the chamber represented the interests of the majority in business.[1] Furthermore, men like Huey Long and Francis E. Townsend challenged the New Deal by advancing even more far-reaching forms of state intervention. Political ambition along with the need to position themselves in this polarized political landscape prompted the New Dealers to launch several large new projects in spring 1935.[2] The contents, timing, and outcome were defined not so much by the crisis as by the need to complement and defend steps already taken, to preempt alternatives, and to live up to the transnational agenda of what a proper state should do. Altogether, this stabilized the redefinition of the relationship between the individual, society, the economy, and the state that had commenced with the Great Depression and then accelerated after 1933. As a result of these dynamics, America's national trajectory was consolidated and reified, or to put it more simply, the New Deal fully became the New Deal.

Tax reform was one of the main points of contention during summer 1935. A debate about "soak-the-rich" tax plans had been ongoing for quite some time, peppered with references to the British tax system and driven by men such as Long, who had launched his "Share Our Wealth" plan in February 1934.[3] As these ideas gained momentum, the administration came out with its own proposal. Now Roosevelt also suggested "very high taxes" for top earners, new taxes on inheritances, and heavier taxation of major corporations, as he declared in a message to Congress in June 1935.[4] While Long trumpeted that the president was finally emulating his ideas, business circles berated Roosevelt for his radicalism, leading to a heated public discussion.[5] Ultimately, the tax reform of 1935 called for redistribution by the federal government. Yet there was a big gap between the symbolic function of radical New Deal rhetoric and the economic effects it entailed. The core tenets of capitalism were left untouched, and the redistributive effects remained low, with reforms targeting only the small group of the most well-heeled Americans.

Despite its limited social and economic results, the reform achieved its most important political aim while exacerbating tensions with the New Deal's opponents. Roosevelt's slashing oratory stymied Long and rallied the New Deal supporters in the fight against the "overprivileged." But it also galvanized bitter enmity in business circles and among adherents of small government, creating a toxic legacy in the medium and long run. Personal and corporate tax exemptions were not pruned until World War II, turning the 1940s into the true watershed in US tax policy. In 1935, Roosevelt would not have found the support for such a drastic measure; it took wartime economic conditions, vigorous public relations by tax administrators, and the American experience with federal state action throughout the 1930s to make the opponents accept this measure in the end.[6]

If the politics of ostracism and polarization were especially visible in the discussion about taxation, they also undergirded the labor debate. The Supreme Court's decision to invalidate the NIRA in May 1935 included scuttling section 7(a) on workers' rights. Calls to resurrect the protection of labor were picked up by a group of congressmen around Senator Robert F. Wagner, a long-standing advocate of greater rights for workers. In late May, Roosevelt jumped on this bandwagon and endorsed Wagner's agenda, after having refused to do so in earlier conversations. With the president's blessing, the National Labor Relations Act was passed in early July. The Wagner Act, as it came to be known, provided much more federal protection for labor than section 7(a) had done. Most important, the newly instituted Na-

tional Labor Relations Board strengthened workers' rights to bargain collectively and unionize. Most corporate leaders were strongly against the act,
further inflaming their anger against the New Deal, even if Roosevelt and
other New Dealers were also somewhat ambivalent.

To this day, the question of why mercurial Roosevelt supported Wagner's
agenda remains controversial. The effects were quite clear, however: the
Wagner Act further solidified the New Deal coalition, and took political
intervention in the economy to a level that Roosevelt had hitherto been
reluctant to accept. Business leaders lost substantial elements of their control of the administration's economic policies. But the Wagner Act also had
clear limits: it concentrated on industrial workers and excluded vast groups
such as agricultural and domestic employees, because many of its supporters feared that this would cost too many votes of representatives in rural
districts. This bias, introduced by southern Democrats, gave the New Deal
welfare state an obvious color dimension, since African Americans and
Mexicans were highly overrepresented among the nonindustrial workforce.
As with tax legislation, capitalism was not challenged, but the state acquired
a new role in defining the rules of the game.[7]

Other initiatives with similar effects included the Banking Act of 1935,
which marked a significant shift toward centralizing the banking system
and expanding federal control; the aforementioned Guffey-Snyder Act,
soon nicknamed the "little NRA" for bituminous coal; and the Public Utility Holding Company Act, which broke up the large utility companies.
That same year also saw the establishment of the WPA as a reorganization
and expansion of public works, which included several projects for artists.
Moreover, the National Youth Administration was set up; it combined
providing work with education for young Americans. A cornucopia of
new agencies emerged, expanding and modulating the New Deal's earlier
agenda.

As during the New Deal's first two years, there was no single philosophy
or political camp that drove developments. An older literature interprets
the "second New Deal" of 1935 as a success of Brandeisian ideas about planning: the economy had to remain capitalistic, but broken down into smaller,
more competitive units. Closer scrutiny reveals that Supreme Court justice
Brandeis and his followers did not have their way in most of the legislation
of 1935, just as planners had not been able to put their stamp on the "first
New Deal."[8] Some of the new interest in "smallness" and community building that gained traction by the mid-1930s also had distinct roots from
Brandeisianism.[9] The years 1933 and 1935 did not stand for different philosophies or economic models. The whole New Deal was characterized by
a maze of divergent tendencies and by intellectual omnivorousness.

More than new policies or programs, it was the domestic and international context that was different two years into the New Deal, and the term "security" in particular took on a new meaning. In the United States, the political debates were much more entrenched in 1935 than in 1933, when the advocates of laissez-faire capitalism had been shell-shocked by the Great Slump. Internationally, things were just as bad, given the triumphs of fascism and communism in various regions of the world. The threat emanating from political and military developments in other parts of the world impacted the domestic agenda much more than before, thus redefining the meaning of the global for American politics. Joseph P. Kennedy summarized these anxieties: "If our democracy is to survive the attacks of dictatorship, whether open or veiled, we must solve the problem of security," which to him meant overcoming the economic crisis through state intervention.[10]

Securing Social Security

The most lasting project on the political agenda of the mid-1930s was Social Security. In Secretary of Labor Perkins's words, the new program was mainly about "fighting for freedom—freedom from insecurity and uncertainty."[11] While Perkins stressed freedom, thereby couching statism in traditional American rhetoric, the New Dealers primarily focused on domestic economic and Social Security (with a capital S), backed by state intervention. Even more than most other initiatives, the program built on transnational exchange and global tendencies, and especially on Atlantic progressive connections—but this does not imply that the eventual outcome was determined by ideas or forces beyond American shores.

Daniel T. Rodgers has demonstrated that the Social Security Act of August 14, 1935, was more than simply a plain response to the challenges of the Great Depression, even if the crisis had exacerbated risks such as unemployment and old-age poverty.[12] Federal social security legislation had been under discussion for several decades, in a debate honeycombed with transatlantic references. Transnational networks had closed ranks before World War I. The core challenges that social security legislation aimed to address—such as unemployment, an aging population, and a thinning of traditional bonds, on the one hand, and growing state and economic capacities for intervention, on the other—had emerged in all industrial societies by that time. Since 1905, the American Association for Labor Legislation (AALL), itself a child of the International Association for Labor Legislation, was one of several organizations pressing for more state action in this field. An AALL-sponsored health insurance scheme launched in 1915 influenced many state legislatures across the country, and in the 1920s the organization argued for state-based pensions for the elderly poor. With social insurance systems for old age, unemployment, health, disability, and other issues growing in Europe during the decade, the AALL and other groups called for similar schemes in America. For instance, Wisconsin economist John R. Commons, the AALL's first executive secretary, proposed a new unemployment policy, peppering his texts with European references. Ideas for action accumulated at the federal level. These and similar plans were of little avail, however, since they fell on deaf ears in business circles, insurance companies, and the Republican administrations of the 1920s.[13]

Internationally, states around the globe introduced various components of social security long before the 1930s. Countries in western Europe were often seen as pioneers, but Uruguay, Canada, and South Africa also implemented such measures. The Great Depression hit many of these programs hard and created an unpropitious moment to launch new proposals. Europe's star fell, and with it the currency of transnationally shared ideas. Some of Europe's flagships, such as the British and German unemployment insurance systems, introduced in 1911–20 and 1927, respectively, quickly sank, taking with them Germany's last fully parliamentary government in 1930 and MacDonald's Labour government in 1931. In times of crisis, unemployment insurance seemed a sure bet for losing power and increasing social tensions. Health and old-age insurance systems were less immediately toxic. While alleviating the crisis, at least for some, many such programs proved too weak to weather the storm. They instead raised false expectations on which they were not fully able to deliver.[14]

While Rodgers has contended that it is for these reasons that few countries instituted social insurance systems post-1929, one should note that quite a few tried. Admittedly, Sweden's 1934 reform of private unemployment societies eschewed strong state involvement. Canada launched a more state-controlled system when Prime Minister Bennett introduced an unemployment insurance bill as the first specific item of his "New Deal" program in early 1935 (shortly after Roosevelt sent his Social Security bill to Congress). In this way, Bennett revoked his earlier conviction that any government copying the New Deal was "recreant in its duty"; rather, he now seemed to out-Roosevelt Roosevelt—even if the substance of his reforms was founded more on British and other European experiences than on policies emanating from Washington. The prime minister's approach, if not recreant, soon proved to be hapless: the Privy Council nullified Bennett's measure in early 1937, highlighting the resistance against such schemes.[15] To the south of the United States, Mexican president Cárdenas tried but ultimately failed to pass social security legislation during the 1930s.[16] Brazil, however, did set up social security during the same period as the United States, and Norway introduced compulsory systems for pension and unemployment insurance in, respectively, 1936 and 1938. New Zealand created an even more comprehensive scheme with its 1938 Social Security Act, and in the Soviet Union social security underwent several important administrative reforms during the 1930s that turned it into an ongoing, comprehensive social institution. Finally, Japan introduced public old-age pensions in 1941, after Greece, Portugal, Peru, Finland, and Austria had taken the same step in the years between 1934 and 1939.[17]

Economically and socially, all these countries were quite different from the United States. This was most obvious in the case of the Soviet Union, yet Brazil, for its part, was much poorer and less industrial, and New Zealand was not only more homogeneous and less crisis damaged but also was merely the size of Colorado and had the population of Nebraska. Still, it would be wrong to argue that the United States was alone in choosing an unfavorable moment to leap into action.[18]

All these schemes epitomized the new social contract between the state and society that had globally gained momentum since World War I, and had been stress tested, as it were, by the Great Depression. The state promised and offered more; in return, it also exerted new forms of control over its population and penetrated aspects of life that had been considered private and remote from the sphere of the political for the longest time. Biopolitics made use of different instruments and reached different degrees, yet it formed part of the global conjuncture of the age.

Additionally, there was a thick layer of transnational cooperation connecting these efforts. The ILO was a hub for discussing issues related to social security and also promoted its own ideas. Chilean president Arturo Alessandri, for instance, worked with ILO suggestions in his social security reforms and proposed the first-ever regional ILO conference in the Americas. Between 1933 and 1936, Brazil ratified eight ILO conventions on social security issues, and important parts of Bennett's program built on ILO ideas. The New Dealers were equally active, seeking to promote their social security ideas globally and through the Geneva organization specifically.[19]

American Social Security, a child of the Great Slump, was anything but a means of immediate economic recovery. The United States eventually opted for an insurance model. Social Security under such terms did not contribute instantly to the economic recovery, since participants first had to pay in for several years. Moreover, an insurance model involved immediate costs for eligible persons, thereby jeopardizing the delicate shoots of a consumer-driven economic revival.

Why, then, did the United States opt for Social Security despite poor international and economic omens? America's global context and links represent one crucial reason. Thanks to several decades of transatlantic progressive exchange, social security had turned into what Rodgers called a "symbolic marker," or a goalpost that sooner or later every modern state had to pass.[20] Behind the scenes, university departments and policy centers promoted ideas with a strong European pedigree. The public was supportive of many social security ideas, such as old-age pensions, and state legislatures had become more and more active.[21] After Social Security had been legislated, Secretary of Labor Perkins saw the act as "deeply significant of the progress which the American people have made in thought in the social field and awareness of methods of using cooperation through government."[22] Roosevelt himself stressed that the act fulfilled "a hope of many years' standing," acknowledging the drawn-out discussion on which the New Deal built both at home as well as internationally.[23]

Transnational references also fundamentally shaped the details of the agenda and mind-set of the actors involved in assembling the bill. When Perkins convened an interdepartmental group of experts in summer 1934 to draft a comprehensive social insurance program, she expected the members of her Committee on Economic Security "to be familiar with every experiment in social insurance in every country."[24] Perkins, an articulate and enormously effective reformer, married to a statistician, and infamous for lengthy and sometimes convoluted lectures in her patrician Boston accent, knew where to look for the experience she needed for this endeavor. Barbara Nachtrieb Armstrong, a law professor at Berkeley, epitomized this ethos: as chief of staff of the committee's old-age section, she exerted a strong influence on the structure of the act. In her 1932 book *Insuring the Essentials*, which served as a source of inspiration, Armstrong deplored the "backwardness of the United States.... Outstanding in its industrial achievements, it has been the laggard of the western world in the field of socio-economic administration." Couching her argument in the usual high modernist language, Armstrong portrayed nations as if they were roosters, hens, and hatchlings on a chicken ladder—all headed in the same direction, with some leading the way, and others trailing behind.[25]

Armstrong, Perkins, and other committee members tried their best to make America "catch up." During the drafting process, they regularly scrutinized the experience of other countries and even shipped over social insurance experts from Great Britain and the ILO in Geneva to ask for advice, not least in light of the ILO's 1933 social security conventions and recommendations, which included specific stipulations on old-age, invalidity, and widow's insurance.[26] Adrien Pierre Tixier, the ILO's assistant director for social security issues, advised the American Social Security Board (SSB) in fall 1935, and the next summer the ILO's social insurance section organized a European tour for American administrators and experts. After a one-week "training course" in Geneva, they visited different agencies in central Europe, Great Britain, and Switzerland. In general, the ILO was an important contact point for the New Dealers.[27]

In contrast to many other New Deal programs, transnational references were cited to add legitimacy to American ideas of Social Security. In a *New York Times* article celebrating the act four days after it passed into law, Perkins prominently referred to Great Britain: its ability to "withstand the effects of the world-wide depression ... in no small part," she contended, resulted from its social insurance benefits. America had now finally made up and offered appropriate security and protection to its citizens, too, she declared.[28] One year later, Armstrong penned an article, "Old-Age Security Abroad," as the "background" of central titles of the Social Security Act. Her piece carefully scrutinized European and global developments since the nineteenth century and used Great Britain to argue for further steps beyond the 1935 act.[29] Catching up, and not pioneering, was the zeitgeist among American experts in the field.

Certainly, not all inspirations for the Social Security Act came from overseas. In America, states such as New York had spearheaded social security provisions. The Empire State's governor set up a special commission in 1930 to study unemployment under his state commissioner of labor.[30] Three years later, the governor was the president of the United States, and his commissioner was the US secretary of labor, or "Madame Secretary," as Perkins liked to be called, priding herself on being the first female Cabinet member. Wisconsin was another hotbed of social welfare ideas, home to the first statewide publicly financed unemployment insurance program as well as people such as economist John R. Commons, his protégé Edwin E. Witte, and Witte's university assistant Wilbur J. Cohen. All three eventually contributed to the Social Security Bill, with Witte and Cohen directly working for the Committee on Economic Security. Born in 1862, 1887, and 1913, respectively, they represented three generations of experts who came to play central roles in American Social Security, especially for unemployment insurance. As such, Wisconsin is often seen as a critical source of inspiration for the New Deal. While that is true, the state was an outward-looking place. Commons was an old hand of transatlantic progressivism from the prewar era, even if he was one of the few prominent social economists who had *not* studied in Germany. The less cosmopolitan Witte had also traveled Europe, and the first job he gave to Cohen was to systematically assess social insurance systems abroad.[31] Perkins sailed to Europe during her time as New York State commissioner, and spent several weeks studying the British and other social security systems. Even if she disliked most of what she saw, she always formed her ideas against this wider context.[32] Social Security, then, is a perfect example of how the distinction between homegrown and foreign does not help to characterize the debates of the time; all ideas were hybrids, and all political solutions adapted to specific local or national needs.

Besides America's global context and the progressive transnational heritage, there was a second reason explaining why the New Deal gave birth to Social Security. In light of the insecurity that the Great Depression had caused, the modernist belief in the necessity of state-run provision translated into concrete political pressure. Old-age pensions are a case in point. From California, physician Townsend lobbied successfully for a plan suggesting that the government pay $200 per month to Americans sixty years or older provided they agreed to spend the money straight away and not work. From its western outpost, support for the Townsend Plan soon swept across the nation "like wildfire," as Townsend himself bragged, with Townsend clubs claiming almost 20 percent of all Americans over sixty as supporters.[33] The plan's impact on the Social Security Act was primarily indirect. As with taxation, the New Dealers hoped to steal the thunder of the social movement by proposing a less radical plan involving lower pension levels and lighter state involvement.[34] Perkins put it quite clearly in August 1935, when she asserted that without the act, it "seemed reasonably likely that . . . this country would be driven to free pensions for all citizens who reach a specific age, regardless of need."[35]

That, obviously, was not in the cards for most New Dealers. In contrast to Townsend's ideas and other noncontributory pension plans, Roosevelt himself insisted on a self-supporting system without a major government contribution to the funding of either old-age or unemployment compensation. Most Americans supported this view. The president made a clear distinction between his vision of social security and the "dole," advocating a mixed federal-state system. Funds for old age were taken out of workers' current earnings through a payroll tax system to which the state did not contribute. Fiscal conservatism was a major reason for this choice. In contrast to temporary public works schemes, for which the president accepted vast federal expenditures through emergency funds, Social Security was perceived as a permanent tool. For political as well as for moral reasons, a self-financed system was seen as the best way of securing fiscal soundness and the program's long-term solvency.[36] Additionally, an insurance model could more easily be kept out of the political battle zone. By making employees work for their own social security rather than having them depend on general revenue financing and the state more broadly, the system was able to steer free of the whims of politicians and future taxpayers.[37]

Secretary of the Treasury Morgenthau was among the staunchest supporters of this approach, and played an important role in excluding farmworkers and domestic servants from Social Security, in contravention of Perkins's original plans. Morgenthau feared that nonindustrial workers would not be paying their way. Southern Democrats also pressed for such this exclusion on racist grounds, since most nonindustrial workers in the South were African Americans. Commons, as a leading thinker in the field, based his welfare ideas on highly racist assumptions.[38] In the end, financial and racist arguments coalesced to discourage universal coverage. Britain again served as a reference, where the inclusion of nonindustrial workers in unemployment insurance had caused major funding problems a few years earlier. During the legislative process, the Committee on Economic Security's bill was changed further by, for instance, excluding small business employees from coverage. Some of this pruning—as well as certain precautions already written into the Committee on Economic Security's draft—also resulted from fears that the Supreme Court might consign a more comprehensive law to the same fate as the AAA and the NIRA. Unlike in 1933, caution ruled the day.[39]

Overall, Social Security in the United States did not simply emulate specific British, German, or other measures. Americans were no prisoners of transnational models. Close scrutiny of programs elsewhere only reaffirmed the idea of avoiding government contributions to pensions or unemployment benefits. For Roosevelt himself, the term "dole" had a negative and particularly English ring.[40] Hopkins's fact-finding mission to Europe in 1934 supported this interpretation.[41] Transnational exchange explains both what Social Security brought and what it did not.[42]

The final result fell a long way short of the universal, citizenship-based program that Roosevelt and many New Dealers had aimed for. By the time it had run the legislative gauntlet, social security had become fragmented, socially stratified, and acquired a racist bias. The vast majority of African Americans and Mexican immigrants found themselves excluded. Explicit racism was less significant than regional and occupational patterns; thanks to the mixed federal-state system that Roosevelt had insisted on, the state context mattered a great deal, and on this level practices varied widely.[43] The effects of the Social Security Act were thus highly diverse; in Rodgers's words, it "wound its way across the socioeconomic map like a gerrymandered congressional district, according to the political strength of the affected groups."[44] Or put more simply, it did little to help the "forgotten man," since those Americans hit hardest by the crisis were not covered.

For all these reasons, many historians have mixed their praise of the Social Security Act with bitter critique. William Leuchtenburg, for instance, called the act "an astonishingly inept and conservative piece of legislation. In no other welfare system in the world did the state shirk all responsibility for old-age indigency and insist that funds be taken out of the current earnings of workers."[45] Such a view, with its Exceptionalist, Eurocentric, and liberal overtones, does not fully reflect reality on the ground, however. A close scrutiny of the history of the global 1930s holds different lessons. The American way of doing social security was not worlds apart from other states. Welfare schemes in Europe also had glaring holes. Pension systems in France, the Netherlands, Italy, and Hungary in 1940 covered only 48, 65, 38, and 16 percent, respectively, of the total economically active population.[46] Between 1933 and 1938, Vargas created a system of *previdência social* in Brazil, building on earlier provisions instituted in 1923. Just as in the United States, the new insurance system principally covered the urban working class while systematically excluding the rural sector, the urban self-employed, and domestic workers. It also instituted a vast apparatus, turning into one of the most significant sources of public employment in Brazil at the time. In addition, it shared with the United States the idea of preserving and reforming capitalism, rather than destroying or fundamentally changing it—as most evident in the ideas of Vargas's foremost adviser on social security, Oliveira Viana. Obviously, there were also differences. Federalism loomed much larger in the *previdência social*, and workers were subdivided into specific national occupational categories. While less individualized than the American model, the Brazilian one was highly stratified as well. Most important, the Brazilian version looked good on paper but was soon undermined by corruption and inefficiency.[47] And while an earlier generation of Brazilian researchers stressed the links to Fascist Italy, more recent work underlines how much Viana's ideas were bound to the New Deal model of state interventionism and heavily influenced by US sociological thinking.[48]

Other countries went into a more statist direction, such as Uruguay with its old-age insurance, which soon ran into serious problems. But that in itself was not fundamentally different from the fate of some European schemes. More significant was the fact that US policy makers did not think that there was anything to learn from Latin America. While expertise on Europe filled whole libraries, an article published in summer 1936 had to concede that "no serious evaluation of the Uruguayan experiment has yet been made."[49] And while Armstrong's *Insuring the Essentials* included a survey of minimum wage provisions in Australia, Asia, and Latin America, she did not find much inspiration for social insurance in those parts of the world.[50]

The Social Security Act of 1935 could not deny its European slant, but it was much more statist than existing accounts would have it. Despite its many references to the British system with its universal, flat-rate benefits, the Social Security Act remained closer to the German model of a mandatory social insurance financed from payroll taxes. American policymakers certainly were not prone to admit this at a time when people associated Germany with swastika flags as opposed to Bismarck, who had launched the whole process in the 1880s. Instead, they evoked the American tradition of individual responsibility and self-reliance. Below the level of general philosophical principles and rhetoric, the effects were rather ironic. In contrast to the British flat-rate principle and the German system of a few broad wage classes, the Social Security Board's approach of employees' "earned rights" implied a calculation of each and every person's benefits on the basis of their individual earnings record. What seemed fair and in line with America's streak of individualism, on the one hand, created a vast bureaucratic apparatus, on the other.

The story of how the SSB began its work with no budget, no staff, and no furniture is part of American political folklore.[51] Its Baltimore Records Office, which commenced operations in November 1936 with eighteen staff members, employed almost one thousand by the year's end, and in the medium term, the Social Security Administration became one of the largest federal agencies and a political actor in its own right.[52] European experts advising the SSB during winter 1935–36, particularly Tixier from the ILO, were appalled by how little attention had been paid to logistical matters and the complexity of the system resulting from its individualist approach.[53] The very word "board," suggesting a light administrative touch, was misleading, and it took until the Truman years for the agency's name to change to the more adequate Social Security Administration. By establishing millions of private contracts between individuals and public agencies at the federal and state levels, individualism acquired a state-guaranteed scaffolding and was based on a vast public bureaucracy.

This statist dimension of the Social Security Act becomes even more apparent in a broader context. Unemployment insurance is a good illustration. Beyond Britain and Germany, a widely copied model that involved the state to a much lesser extent existed throughout Europe. The Ghent system, named after the scenic city in Flanders, was a state-subsidized system organized by trade unions. At the time of the passage of the Social Security Act in the United States, ten countries ran Ghent schemes, including a compulsory variant in Switzerland.[54] Measured against this yardstick, Roosevelt's Social Security Act appears quite statist: while avoiding state subsidies like the plague (at least until 1939, when Social Security became even more statist), the New Deal's unemployment scheme had a broader public dimension at the national and state levels than its counterparts in many European countries. In general, European social security systems often relied on self-governed institutions, and the ILO also heavily promoted this model with the prominent role it gave to labor. The United States instead opted for a more state-run path. Having said this, something else is more important than challenging received opinions; welfare systems are so intricate that a single denominator such as the degree of statism is misleading, since the role of the state can play out at various levels, complicating an overall assessment. This also holds true for the United States: As Jacob S. Hacker has shown, the Social Security Act was an important reason why private pension plans soon flourished in America. Public and private action were often very closely connected.[55]

For America, the New Deal established a new notion of the individual having clear-cut social rights. In the medium run, the elderly were able to leave the job market, and a social safety net secured some of the unemployed in times of economic crisis. Social Security thus profoundly changed the character of American society. From an original focus on "economic security" in the committee chaired by Perkins and "social insurance," the agenda moved on to the fusion of these two terms in the phrase "social security." The New Dealers in this way broadened their concept of security beyond the economic realm and immediate emergency legislation, while carefully avoiding identification with the idea of "welfare" more broadly.[56] Thanks to European and American efforts, the neologism soon turned into

an international trademark, or "watchword," as contemporary expert Oswald Stein contended. Writing in 1941, Stein argued that "a few years ago
social security was little more than a slogan, a bare outline of an idea,"
whereas it now symbolized "the index of industrial civilisation, and indeed
of civilisation itself."[57]

Still, the New Dealers saw the Social Security Act more as a starting point
than a complete edifice. The president himself advanced such an incremental understanding when, on the same day that he signed the Social Security
Act, he interpreted it as a "cornerstone in a structure which is being built
but is by no means complete."[58] And indeed, the Social Security Act left
much unfinished business. It only covered certain groups. And as an "omnibus legislative vehicle," as one of its drafters later called it, the original bill
had aimed to "alleviate the hazard of old age, unemployment, illness, and
dependency."[59] Resistance in the federal administration and by the American Medical Association removed health from the New Deal's agenda early
on during the drafting process, and for decades that was to remain a thorn
in the side of those aiming at a wider form of security.[60]

To summarize, America's social security model was as specific as that of
any other state, but by no means exceptional. Driven by a modernist language and mind-set, from the 1940s onward the United States turned into a
reference point for Latin America and Asia. The survey methods "developed
and perfected in the United States" to identify specific needs found their
way to Chile and Peru by the late 1930s; many other elements were to follow. By then, and thanks to the New Deal, the "laggard" had left its past behind and was setting standards for the "index of industrial civilization."[61]

Slums into (English) Homes

Another concern, complementary to social security, moved up on the New
Dealers' list of priorities during the mid-1930s: public housing. During the
first phase of the New Deal, urban shelter did not figure prominently on
the agenda, even if the housing crisis was one of the most visible effects of
the Great Depression. Homelessness and shantytowns had existed prior to
1929, to be sure, but they expanded massively as the economy plummeted.
So-called Hoovervilles spread from Seattle over Saint Louis to Baltimore;
in New York, families lived on the Great Lawn in Central Park. In the District of Columbia, fifteen thousand persons camped out at Anacostia in
1932, until General MacArthur dispersed them. Their fates represented
only the tip of the iceberg. According to the 1930 census, which did not
yet reflect the full impact of the Great Depression, 20 percent of city dwellers lived in substandard housing. By 1933, action, and action now, was
clearly required.[62]

The Roosevelt administration, though, concentrated first on creating jobs
rather than supplying shelter. Its first measures on housing were geared less

toward the "forgotten man" than the middle class. The 1933 Homeowners Refinancing Act provided mortgage assistance to homeowners and would-be purchasers, while the 1934 National Housing Act expanded these measures by further lubricating private market mechanisms through state support of borrowers and banks.[63]

On the lower end of the social spectrum, the PWA was the foremost New Deal agency to address housing. As one of its many activities, it engaged in slum clearance and rehousing projects. Its Housing Division had funded a handful of projects by 1934, including the Carl Mackley Houses in Philadelphia, where German émigré Oskar G. Stonorov transposed the construction principles and aesthetic maxims elaborated by Le Corbusier and the German Bauhaus School to an American urban site.[64] By 1937, fifty-eight projects had been implemented amounting to some twenty-five thousand dwelling units; roughly one-third of them were for African Americans. All this work added up to less than 1 percent of all the PWA projects and less than 4 percent of its funds. These figures sound small, but it must be remembered that America practically started from zero. Unlike many European and to a lesser degree also Latin American countries, the Housing Division was unable to fall back on existing institutions, procedures, or administrative knowledge. All the European ideas that American experts had familiarized themselves with since the Progressive era could not compensate for this lack. Moreover, the PWA housing program was quite radical in the New Deal context, as Gail Radford has asserted, in that it involved actual government ownership and not just intervention in the economy. Only the TVA went in a similar direction. Nonetheless, the New Deal state remained rather inactive on housing both by transatlantic standards and measured against what was needed. Low-cost federal housing also remained marginal in the United States since it lacked a firm legal or political base.[65]

Roosevelt and many other New Dealers loved their dams and other big infrastructure projects, yet they were quite ambivalent about public housing. In private, the president showed interest in the matter and supported the "public housers," as they were sometimes called, in various ways. Publicly, he displayed much less commitment, even if at a press conference in November 1934 he praised the efforts in "Germany and England and Vienna," where governmental slum clearance projects had "probably done more to prevent communism and rioting and revolution than anything else in the last four or five years." But his bottom line was clear: "we couldn't do anything like that"; this form of "straight socialism" or "so-called socialism" was not for America. Both his arguments—the power of housing to blunt radicalism and the Exceptionalism of the United States—were well established in the American debate at the time.[66] In the New Dealers' inner circle, there was no source of massive support for the issue and the president himself knew that public housing was one of the most divisive domestic debates. Many Americans saw massive, direct, and lasting government action in this area as especially "totalitarian," "socialist," or "red." In contrast, they stressed the Jeffersonian and "virile" qualities of homeownership. They claimed that public housing would promote radicalism, racial integration, and economic dependency. While some viewed public housing as an economic right strengthening the vitality of democracy, the large number of opponents perceived it as detrimental to core American values.[67] In this context, Roosevelt instinctively remained cautious.

Long, Townsend, and their ilk showed little interest in a federal housing program, and it was mainly a comparatively small though highly articulate group of transnationally networked experts who endeavored to use the New Deal window of opportunity to push their ideas through the bottleneck of legislative procedure. Many of them were old hands of transatlantic progressive exchange, including figures such as Catherine Bauer, John Edelman, and Mary Kingsbury Simkhovitch (1867–1951). Simkhovitch, for example, was one of the most prominent social workers of her generation and one of those who implanted concerns from the Progressive era into the New Deal. She received her family name—which sounded quite exotic by New England bourgeois standards—by marrying a Russian student of economics whom she had met while studying in Berlin. Alongside many other activities, she helped to found Greenwich House in New York City in 1902—a settlement house that taught poor urban immigrants middle-class American values, and soon turned into a hub for transatlantic progressives and a hotbed of reform ideas. Furthermore, Simkhovitch in 1931 formed the National Public Housing Conference that called for federal action on housing. In summer 1933, it was Simkhovitch who proposed the idea to Senator Wagner of including a provision on urban housing in the NIRA. This part of the omnibus law then served as the legislative framework for the PWA's Housing Division.[68] Given the role of Simkhovitch and others, Daniel Rodgers has rightly called the New Deal's public housing policy "an eruption of the progressive past into the political possibilities of the Depression"—another feature it shared with social security.[69]

Since the PWA Housing Division's engagement remained limited, Simkhovitch, Bauer, and others soon started to urge more federal support for residential building programs. They had grand ambitions: in a letter to Roosevelt in January 1934, Simkhovitch outlined a public housing program worth $1 billion.[70] Despite disagreements over the content, Secretary of the Interior Ickes shared this agenda as the PWA's director. For most of these activists, European-style cooperative housing associations with limited dividends served as a blueprint. To beef up their credentials and generate public interest, Simkhovitch's National Public Housing Conference organized an international commission on US housing issues in 1934. Headed by Sir Raymond Unwin, the grand old man of British urban planning and a frequent visitor to the United States, a three-person commission traveled the country for seven weeks, advocating publicly assisted, low-cost housing. Unwin, who impressed his high-level audiences not just with his ideas but also with the Windsor knot of his ties and artistic flair of his drooping mustache, maintained that America's housing policy lagged "woefully behind" European countries.[71] The final report, a transatlantic coproduction, emphasized that the "Europeans brought to it years of experience in their own countries, a perspective difficult for an American to attain," and advocated "developing a long-term program to provide better housing for the low-income groups of the community and to remove the slum areas that form serious blots in most cities."[72] Unwin also met with the president on his trip, and they again exchanged views in 1937; he also gave two series of lectures at Columbia University in 1936–37 and again in 1938–39.[73] Transatlantic links were thus instrumental to updating the progressive past and putting it on the New Dealers' radar.

Altogether, the transatlantic network was working at full stretch. In her widely read 1934 book *Modern Housing*, Bauer underscored that the United States was the only nation with no systematic housing policy, and went even further: "'Modern European housing' would be a tautological phrase: there is practically no modern housing outside of Europe."[74] Meanwhile, the State Department instructed its diplomatic officers in Europe to systematically collect information on housing programs.[75] Hopkins used his 1934 tour to the Old World to make his own investigations into the matter.[76] On his trip he met Charles F. Palmer, a successful Atlanta real estate developer, who combined spearheading the PWA's first project, the Techwood project built in his hometown, with yet another tour to study housing projects in Italy, Austria, the Soviet Union, Germany, and Great Britain. Palmer, who corresponded with experts around the world and gathered as much information as he could, found the British experience most relevant for the United States, and after his return, campaigned for slum clearances using a film that he had shot in Europe. One of his most important screenings took place in early 1935, when he drew a Washington audience of some five hundred politicians and experts, including secretaries Ickes, Wallace, and Perkins.[77] Roughly around the same time, political scientist and presidential adviser Louis Brownlow traveled to Great Britain and other parts of Europe, where he, too, became interested in public housing, among many other things.[78] Beyond these specific activities, US philanthropic foundations now became major facilitators of exchange on urban issues, giving American presence in these circles a consistency that it had not had before.[79]

As a next step, both the National Public Housing Conference and Bauer's Labor Housing Conference penned housing bills that were introduced in Congress in 1935. Together with Vienna-born representative Henry C. Ellenbogen, Senator Wagner played a central role in merging the bills. The president remained conspicuously absent until early May 1936, when he came out in support of the combined bill. Simkhovitch, who had encouraged him for many months to voice his support publicly, was so relieved that she sent him a telegram at 1:44 a.m. to thank him.[80]

The reason for Roosevelt's change of opinion was largely economic: news had spread that vast public investments in workers' housing had helped the British economy. Fiscal unorthodoxy was gaining ground incrementally, and proto-Keynesian arguments about public spending as a means of recovery blazed the way for an expansion of public housing. A Senate committee report on the bill, for instance, contended that British government policies had helped to maintain "a fairly level rate of employment and industrial activity, in the stormy period since 1929, by a rapid expansion of building activity."[81] In a letter to Roosevelt, Unwin also stressed that public housing had helped in "priming the pump" in Great Britain.[82]

In 1933, when the PWA's Housing Division commenced its work, business resistance remained weak and mostly local. By 1935, opposition had become vocal and well organized, with the US Chamber of Commerce, the National Association of Real Estate Boards, the U.S. League of Building and Loans, and the National Retail Lumber Dealers Association taking the lead in trying to keep state competition out of the market, or in their own words, argue for Washington to "get out and stay out" of the public housing arena.[83] Significantly, real estate investors dominated this bloc, whereas other parts of the building sector were less critical. Specific reasons explain why the lumber dealers were particularly fierce in their resistance against public housing: in a conventionally built home, wood was the costliest factor, and they feared that a federal program would place its faith in modern construction materials such as steel and concrete.[84] Resistance to public housing was not built on American cedar and cypresses alone, however. Some real estate lobbyists even traveled to Europe to collect evidence on the horrors of public housing, revealing the power of the transnational reference. For them, public housing was "un-American," as shown by the transatlantic links and credentials of the pro camp. The public housers reacted immediately, underscoring that providing shelter simply could not be un-American.[85]

In September 1937, after more than two years of discussions in Congress and a long list of changes, Roosevelt finally signed the United States Housing Act. The result was not quite what its advocates had hoped. Bauer and other social reformers, including their British colleagues with American credentials such as Unwin, stressed that public housing should target the working class, and not begin with the poorest citizens and their slums. Great Britain had had good experience with a working-class-centered approach. From 1933 on, though, the conservative British government slashed these programs, and concentrated solely on slum clearance and rehabilitation. In 1937, this became the model for America. During the legislative process, all more comprehensive ideas were discarded, not least due to business resistance and the allegedly un-American character of such an approach.[86]

By 1941, the United States Housing Authority (USHA), under the unassertive leadership of Nathan Straus, Jr., had built some 130,000 new units at 300 sites across the country—an impressive number, but not especially high in light of the 7.5 to 16 million family units that a Congress report calculated to be the overall housing need. The policy's effects were therefore more indirect than direct, with the New Deal initiating a large-scale reconstruction of American cities that gained further momentum during the Truman administration. In the Roosevelt years, the USHA turned into the New Deal's ugly duckling, excluding all but the lowest-income groups from public housing, and building houses at minimal cost, thereby shaving away the progressive architectural aspects that such agencies often promoted in Europe. Business circles and conservatives who saw public housing as a competitor or immoral prevailed with their arguments. The policy of austerity frequently led to a substandard, alienating architecture. Those pinched by poverty were to live in houses mired in and mirroring low standards.[87]

Paradoxically, transnational adaptation subverted the intentions of experts from both sides of the North Atlantic. As Rodgers has shown, it was exactly the protracted and highly selective transnational borrowing that shuttled Americans off on Exceptionalist tracks. Public housing in Europe did not solely address the poor, but New Deal transatlantic crossings reduced public housing to a specific solution for a small stratum of society. Transatlantic borrowing failed to create a significant noncommercial housing sector in the United States or to produce a new social model for America (to which some of its progressive advocates had aspired). The utopian pretensions of some European projects, like Frankfurt's Römerstadt or the Swedish housing cooperatives, and the progressives' urban agenda connected to them were lost in the mid-Atlantic.[88]

On other levels, the transatlantic connection prevailed. In 1939, for instance, Nathan Straus maintained that the USHA was "modeled upon the most successful public housing experience in the world, that of England."[89] A 1940 USHA pamphlet explaining the US housing program to the average American had a long section on programs in other countries.[90] Some obviously still believed in the rhetoric of transnational links, with Great Britain as a role model.

Transatlantic exchanges proved to be two-way. In 1935, Unwin praised the achievements of the New Deal in a high-profile lecture in London.[91] In a paper presented at the Royal Society of Arts two years later, he stressed how much cheaper American public housing was in comparison to British, and used this assertion to critique the policy of building apartments in his own country.[92] The British in general were by no means uncritical of their own housing policy. Elizabeth Denby, one of the leading British experts at the time, gave "the palm for obtaining the best value for money" to Vienna and praised Sweden's model. Overall, she emphasized that Britain had "much to learn" from other European countries.[93] The 1939 Barlow Report on housing issues contained a twenty-eight-page appendix on international experience; its author, Sir George Pepler, devoted particular attention to the United States, thus representing a transition away from looking to Germany for lessons or simply seeing England as the true pioneer in urban planning. By the 1960s, the United States had become the main external point of reference for British planners, even if feelings remained mixed.[94] Transnational reference, then, continued to be in flux, and as with social security, New Deal housing policies turned into a global reference point after 1945. This holds true for Latin America, for instance, where the 1940s saw a shift from European-oriented *urbanismo* to US-influenced *planificación*. In sum, all this demonstrates the endlessness of these transnational exchanges.[95]

In the United States itself, public housing continued to be a vitriolic issue, stirring up clashes over race, radicalism, foreign influences, and the "right" American way. Repercussions were often local and concrete, such as in summer 1939, when the citizens of Wheeling, West Virginia, held a referendum over the continuation of the USHA.[96] In the medium term, a low level of residential mobility and high level of homeownership came to define the American way thanks to the New Deal. While homeownership frequently is seen as a given in American culture, these elements only became dominant during the interwar years, mainly as an effect of the New Deal's restructuring and stabilization of the mortgage market. In its two-tiered policy, public housing always remained marginal in comparison to support for homeowners through the 1933 Homeowners Refinancing Act and the 1934 National Housing Act. State action remained much more indirect and discreet here, and this approach had the president's unconditional blessing, since Roosevelt associated property with active citizenship, freedom, and democracy. From spaces of transit, "American homes" turned into national, masculine, high-technology devices.[97]

Ironically, Nazi Germany used similar instruments to support homeowners: the regime issued a public guarantee for private mortgages. This massively reduced the cost of borrowing. A subsidy of forty-five million reichsmarks toward the construction of private homes was added, while public housing, so critical during the Weimar Republic, only moved into a higher gear again in 1936.[98] During the Nazis' first years, increasing private ownership was their main goal, using the same toolbox as the New Dealers. More than stabilizing any specific political system, these measures helped to win popular support and—maybe even more important—to overcome the crisis of capitalism. Massive private debts and waves of foreclosures affecting the (lower) middle classes were a bigger threat to the existing economic system than the deplorable housing conditions of the have-nots; priority was given to supporting homeowners in societies as different as Nazi Germany and New Deal America.

In the New Deal, both formats, mortgage and public housing, aimed at making the living conditions of Americans more secure in economic and social terms. The Roosevelt years also saw the final act in the debate about the target group of public housing; from then onward, government action in this area was identified with "projects," a term with negative connotations that came into public use in the mid-1930s.[99] New Deal state action thus gave birth to a federal policy that, in the medium term, undermined the state's authority as a legitimate actor and served as an argument for neoliberals.

Back to the Land

In the mid-1930s, the New Deal not only tackled public housing for the nation's urban centers but also moved in the opposite direction in an attempt to improve living standards in rural and suburban areas. Legislation on social security, tax reform, and public housing was complemented in 1935 by the creation of the Resettlement Administration, a brainchild of Rexford Tugwell.

Although their background, self-understanding, and demeanor smacked of urbanity, modernity, and even cosmopolitanism, a lot of the New Dealers' visionary thinking revolved around agriculture, rural areas, suburbs, and decentralization. One in five Americans still depended on the farm economy, and the sector's crisis had begun long before 1929. Moreover, farming was not just any sector. Roosevelt himself felt deeply and emotionally attached to the land that he had inherited from his forefathers. Insulation, as a general policy line, therefore included a movement back to the land, to more concrete and less complex (as well as less global) contexts. The best antidote to a world in crisis, FDR and many in his circle contended, consisted in building new, more stable, locally rooted communities as part of a reinvigorated nation. This vision was new at the time: interest in the small town and community building at this level only became an important discussion during the 1930s.[100] And it was far from reactionary: the new countryside was to be rationally organized and created with the latest advances in technology, including electricity, the radio, and healthy accommodation. This prorural approach also distinguished the New Deal from most of post-1945 policy making, which regarded agriculture as insignificant and farmers as politically retrograde, and instead focused on urban and industrial issues.

While this general view was widely shared among the New Dealers, Tugwell and other "boys with their hair ablaze," as the AAA's first director famously called them, were political centralizers who believed in a more coercive state than the New Deal had brought thus far.[101] They were far from naive romanticists or solely interested in relief work and saw the crisis as an opportunity to implement far-reaching plans, building on the latest economic and social techniques. The state should not just help those in need but also change the system fundamentally. In a nutshell, Tugwell and others wanted to create what Gunnar Myrdal in Sweden called a "prophylactic" social policy.[102] Having said that, the radical New Dealers' plans also reacted to criticism from the political Left that the administration neglected the country's poorest. It integrated, too, an increasing interest in "thinking small" and implementing communitarian structures at a time when bigness was acquiring totalitarian connotations.[103] In rural as well as in suburban environments, the New Dealers sought to create model islands of modernity, driven by rational science, a cooperative understanding of community, and—of particular note—strong federal action.[104]

The RA, established by executive order in April 1935, was another omnibus agency, pieced together from various smaller projects created since 1933 and infused with new ideas. It built on the efforts of the Department of the Interior's Division of Subsistence Homesteads, which was created during the first months of the New Deal under the NIRA, and made rural homes and part-time farms available to relocate city dwellers. The Resettlement Administration also took over several long-term agricultural planning initiatives from the Department of Agriculture. FERA added its rural rehabilitation division, which gave out small loans to farmers, and other agencies contributed parts of their portfolios as well. Basically, the RA resembled the program that Chardón had proposed for Puerto Rico roughly one year earlier.[105] With an agenda so extensive and patchy that it looked like the New Deal in miniature, the new agency served a double purpose. First, the RA strove to help submarginal farmers with various instruments. Second, it offered city dwellers opportunities to live and work outside congested urban zones. The focus in both cases was on structural measures, in contrast to the price and production controls that the AAA and the NRA stood for. Ultimately, the RA aimed to change not only the economic but also the social fabric of American society.[106]

From 1935 onward, the RA purchased over nine million acres of abandoned and submarginal land, and converted it into parks, preserves, or grazing areas. Tugwell contended that rural rehabilitation had to begin with land retirement: submarginal land—that should never have been farmed in the first place—kept submarginal farmers in a precarious existence as opposed to inducing them to seek their fortune elsewhere. Research by the PWA's National Planning Board and other bodies supported this claim.[107] More than the AAA, the RA concentrated on the poorest producers in agriculture, which the New Deal had failed thus far, combining economic and social goals. Farm economist Lewis C. Gray from the RA reasoned that the purchases were not just motivated by a concern "with the land for its own sake"; instead, the "land problem is essentially a human problem," and the missionary tone of his presentation made it clear that, for him, the state knew best how to sort things out.[108] The federal government therefore sought to relocate the inhabitants of these zones to better land. While such ideas were not completely new and Secretary of Agriculture Wallace also dreamed of "a rational resettlement of America," Tugwell's ideas were quite radical: he calculated that at least five hundred thousand farmers needed to be resettled to make American farming more sustainable and secure.[109]

The other half of this plan involved colonization. Ideas of expert-planned, cooperative farm villages set up by the state had been in the air for some time, promoted most forcefully by the engineer Elwood Mead, who had made a name for himself primarily through his irrigation projects. At the end of World War I, Mead initiated two model farm colonies funded by the state of California that were deeply informed by his eight-year stint in Australia and an extensive study of similar projects in Europe. For Mead, colonization was not just an economic instrument informed by the latest scientific technologies, as Durham and Delhi—the names of his two colonies—were supposed to demonstrate. He also saw it as a means to foster a new community spirit by encouraging (white) farmers to cooperate closely with one another, thereby keeping out "Oriental farmers or other aliens" who—with their "racial aloofness"—had "no interest in rural welfare." Mead's mainstream racism obviously led him to overlook the irony of a place called Delhi protecting the whiteness of American farming. Rather than the widely separated farms characteristic of most of the American countryside, Europe's typical structure of hamlets served as a reference point, but their winding roads and crooked homes were to be replaced by modern, rectangular structures.[110]

Although even Durham, the more successful of Mead's two projects, was soon considered a failure and liquidated in 1935, his ideas served as a blueprint during the mid-1930s. The RA had planned or set up fifty-eight government farm colonies by 1937. As in Durham and Delhi, they were built with prefabricated houses and involved strong cooperative elements—heavy farming machinery, shops, and health care were owned and managed collectively by the farmers.[111] In several RA colonies, such as Lake Dick, Arkansas, the planners from Washington went even further toward collective farming, with shared means of production and distribution. Members of the farm village owned only their "children and chickens," as one of them put it.[112] Even the less radical farm colonies were not particularly popular. Many farmers did not want to relocate, especially those whom the crisis had

hit only recently. Regionally, particularly farmers in the Great Plains resented the RA's interventionist agenda. They, too, wanted government help,
but in order to put them back on their feet, not to resettle them on terms set
by Washington.[113]

Not surprisingly, this branch of the RA was continuously criticized in
public as a "socialistic scheme" reminiscent of the Soviet Union.[114] That, in
fact, would be going too far: even in the most experimental and collective
colonies, members always had the choice to leave, and many in fact did—
displaying their dissatisfaction with the project. The high level of violence
that collective farming entailed in the Soviet Union had no equivalent in
the United States. Still, with the RA, the federal government acquired an
unprecedented role in farming. Arthurdale, West Virginia, for instance,
created overnight in 1933 to rehouse destitute coal miners, consisted of
165 homes around a community center and other facilities. Paraphrasing
a governmental report, the *New York Times* in 1937 called Arthurdale a
"national laboratory out of which might come 'a new American way of
life.'"[115]

Experts did not just plan and build colonies such as Arthurdale. They also
taught housewives how to garden and can food. Success was closely moni-
tored. Each family on an RA project had to prepare complete farm and
home plans for each crop year, to be scrutinized by government men. RA
officials encouraged leisure activities such as weaving, woodworking, and
painting. They kept statistics on social organizations and regarded high
numbers as indicating a lively and active community. Mrs. Franklin D. Roosevelt, as she was called, was very much in favor of these forms of social engineering and visited Arthurdale several times.[116]

Practices elsewhere were similar. One witty Arkansan summarized the
experience as follows:

> Well it's this way. The government spends a million dollars or so to
> buy a forty-acre farm for a down-and-out sharecropper. They give him
> a mule, a bathtub, and an electric shoelacer. They lay a railroad track
> to his house to carry the tons of forms he has to fill in. A bunch of
> experts figure out his milking I.Q.... After we poke fun at their red
> tape for a year or two, they ups and proves their experiment is self-
> liquidatin'—that the feller is makin' his payments and raisin' a family,
> too. And I don't know who's more surprised, me or the 'cropper.[117]

Tugwell's attempt to "make America over" spearheaded a new dimension of
the regulatory welfare state.

The RA's Suburban Resettlement Division had even greater aspirations.
Just as with so many other New Deal programs, it was replete with transatlantic references. Greenbelt, Maryland, Greendale, Wisconsin, and Greenhills, Ohio, the three towns planned and built under RA auspices, all looked

very different at first glance. Greenbelt with its two-story townhouses echoed German Bauhaus modernism, while Greendale replicated a conventional country village. Greenhills was primarily laid out for the automobile, whereas most destinations in Greenbelt were reachable on foot, and its 1930s pedestrian underpasses are still in use today. Yet they all built on the experience of the English garden city movement, developments in Weimar Germany, and the American war workers' villages of 1918, each with its own transatlantic layer. Together, they formed the three largest, most expensive, and most ambitious New Deal communities.[118]

All three planned communities were intended to cater to the needs of low-income rural and industrial families. Situated in the vicinity of large cities, each was an independent unit with its own community center including shops, a post office, meeting rooms, clubs, churches, a library, and a theater. They were surrounded, and symbolically demarcated, by a greenbelt with farms and woodland. For Tugwell and Roosevelt, they marked semiutopian spaces promulgating a new and better American way. Roosevelt himself argued that Greenbelt was "an experiment that ought to be copied in every community in the United States."[119]

Not only organizationally, but also intellectually, the program remained distinct from urban public housing due to its fusion of land, gardens, and industry. Tugwell dreamed of dozens and eventually of thousands of such cities. Construction on the first of the three sites began in October 1935 and the work was completed some three years later. Together, they provided some twenty-three hundred family units at an overall cost of $36 million. As in the farm villages, social engineering loomed large. The applicants were interviewed and screened not only for income, character, health, and occupation but also their willingness to participate in community activities, all guided and scrutinized by well-meaning experts. Shops were run as consumer cooperatives, and only one shop per line of business was permitted. No dogs were allowed in Greenbelt, and no clothes on the lines after 4:00 p.m.[120]

Like the rural colonies, the New Deal's "green" towns fired the imagination of friend and foe alike. Although party divisions formed the main split, some prominent Republicans supported the RA, including Robert La Follette, who argued that parts of the RA in "the end may prove to have been one of the most constructive steps this Government has taken in a great many years."[121] Internationally, the greenbelt towns attracted a lot of interest. Several governments asked the State Department for information; in the international debate about suburban housing, the United States became a central point of reference.[122] Many others were much more critical, and again, allegations that the projects were collectivist, communist, and somehow red ran high. The substantial costs nurtured these condemnations; given that these towns were funded with FERA money and unskilled workers had to build them as a way to ease unemployment, the price per unit was 30 to 45 percent higher than the private industry standard. The model character of the towns stimulated architects' fantasies, and on sites such as Arthurdale, where planners had the First Lady's explicit backing, this also increased costs. According to Paul Conkin, a series of articles by Felix Bruner in the *Washington Post* about Tugwell's agency played a key role in tipping the balance against the RA. Under the heading "Utopia Unlimited," the agency was described as "one of the most far-flung experiments in paternalistic government," using a vast bureaucracy without congressional agreement, support, or control.[123] Ex-president Hoover joined the fray with a speech in Portland, Oregon, coinciding with the publication of Bruner's series. In an article fundamentally critical of the New Deal, he cited the RA as one of its worst sins, creating an enormous bureaucracy with little effect. The *New York Times* immediately published a rebuttal, stressing that Hoover had based his argument against Tugwell's agency on outdated figures. The "mud-slinging" that Hoover accused the New Dealers of went both ways, poisoning the political climate.[124]

In May 1936, the Supreme Court ruled the resettlement program unconstitutional, presaging the demise of the whole enterprise. Fed up with the stiff resistance that he was facing, "Rex the Red"—as his enemies liked to call him—resigned in late 1936, and left the Roosevelt administration some one and a half years after the RA had been set up. At the year's end, the RA was integrated into the USDA, and its community-building program revised and reduced. In fall 1937, Wallace established the Farm Security Administration as a successor. Instead of ambitious social engineering, noncoercive technical demonstration projects now ruled the day.

Was the regulatory impulse of the mid-1930s' RA completely new and foreign to the American tradition? When it came to land management, the US government traditionally played an enormously strong role. The federal government had since the nineteenth century been the largest landowner in the country, possessing roughly one-third of all land. At this level, limited government has always been a myth, and Tugwell's policy of purchasing submarginal land represented no breach with American convention.[125] The RA, in contrast, underscored the differences to most parts of Europe, where many politicians might have envisioned going back to the land, but the state lacked the means to do so, at least without colonial or imperialist adventures.

Morally and culturally, the RA created a new dimension of regulatory welfare state in a short fit of activism that went far beyond economic relief and reform. Social planning and government paternalism played a huge role and went further than in urban public housing, and further, in fact, than in most other parts of the New Deal. This approach had the explicit backing of many New Dealers (well beyond radical outliers such as Rex the

Red), even including Franklin and Eleanor Roosevelt. In FDR's case, love for the land explains why his stance differed as compared to his view on urban housing.

If urban housing was the New Deal's ugly duckling, its suburban and rural counterpart did not turn into a beautiful swan either. For the country as a whole, experiments with suburban and rural settlements were accepted, or at least tolerated, at a reduced level in the first two years of the New Deal. Their expansion in 1935, together with the changed political climate, led to a new discussion. In an atmosphere that was less insecure and intellectually volatile, resistance against freewheeling executive action was now much more pronounced. Paternalism was not new either. Especially vis-à-vis the country's poorest inhabitants, the state had a track record of proactive intervention to elevate mores and social conduct. City reform, eugenics, and Prohibition epitomize these tendencies, but most of these activities—with the notable exception of the "noble experiment" of Prohibition—had taken place chiefly at a local or state level, without much federal action. Building on minor inroads during the early years of the New Deal, the RA now strove to acquire new powers as well as instigate moral improvement and social change in a top-down manner. It took this experience—including its transnational references—to teach Americans what they really wanted. Looking back in 1943, one expert maintained that the whole experience with the RA and its successor organization had been crucial: "The very fact that it has made many mistakes should make us less likely to make the same mistakes again."[126]

Having said all this, the RA's downfall in late 1936 was also caused by the US political system's capacity to correct such "mistakes." The Greenbelt towns were brought down at the hands of the Supreme Court, but the other parts of the RA were downgraded or discontinued by the administration itself. Given that Roosevelt had been reelected in a landslide victory a few months before this decision, a more stubborn and radical policy would have been possible. Yet the New Dealers trimmed their political aspirations; in the end, of the many possible "American ways," they chose one of the traditional brands.

The pendulum of New Deal action thus swung back to programs that were less audacious. The RA, it should be added, had included such less radical provisions since its inception in 1935. Most important, it gave out rehabilitation loans and grants to help farmers overcome the crisis. These measures did not reach the poorest, but focused on "borderline" cases, and were much more popular than rural settlements. While forty-five hundred farmers joined the subsistence homesteads, half a million participated in the loan program. With the Farm Security Administration, this approach of facilitating private ownership ultimately took the lead, revising the strong role attributed to the state in the RA. Saving agrarian republicanism now stood front and center.[127] Hence, the more radical ideas were only implemented during a short period and were limited in scope.

All things considered, few New Deal agencies had a more harried career than the RA, and its history (and legacy) was the cause of bitter infighting. Measured by its bold vision and aspiring program, the agency failed utterly in both its economic and social goals. Construction costs in rural colonies and planned communities were too high. The anticipated synergies between agriculture and industry rarely transpired. Private companies refrained from using the model communities as blueprints. Many residents did not earn enough to pay the expenses. The New Deal's guinea pigs also disliked their lives, and so turnover was high. Careful selection of applicants secured religious diversity, but in terms of race and education, RA communities were extremely homogeneous, in this way reifying existing stratifications. The state raised expectations that it then failed to meet and created a program that alienated many that were exposed to it.

And how do the RA's activities figure in international comparison? Rodgers has argued that the New Deal's rural villages and greenbelt towns were special, since other states were much less active in this area during the decade. Admittedly Britain, as the main transnational reference point for the United States, concentrated on slum clearance during the 1930s, abandoning its bolder plans, while Fascist Italy and Nazi Germany also ventured only a small number of rural and suburban new town projects.[128] What made the RA's activities stand out was their underlying vision rather than their overall size, given how little was achieved. Still, the RA was embedded in an international conversation on rural development and model villages, to which the League of Nations, philanthropic organizations such as the Rockefeller Foundation, and even less industrialized states such as Turkey and Romania contributed.[129] Crucially, a different picture emerges when looking at new settlements on the peripheries of Europe and in the colonies. During the interwar and war years—as the period in which European empires reached their largest expansion during the nineteenth and twentieth centuries—the idea of (white) settlement and colonization in newly created "techno-cities," to borrow a term coined by Robert H. Kargon and Arthur P. Molella, loomed large. Such towns and cities were built using state-of-the-art technology. Their promoters all rallied under the motto "back to the land," and advocated a decentralized vision of civilization to create a simpler and better life. As model cities, these projects aimed at uplifting the nation and—with quite varying implications—building a "better man."[130] Most of these also brought about a higher level of state control, ranging from the technocratic paternalism of the New Dealers to outright violence in some of the world's dictatorships.

There are many examples. In its North African possessions, Fascist Italy built forty new rural towns in the second half of the 1930s, each of them laid out on a grid pattern around a central square with a standard set of public buildings. In a huge state resettlement project launched in 1938, forty thousand colonists migrated to Libya alone.[131] The number of German colonists moving east during World War II was ten times as high, and quite a few were settled in newly built villages or *Musterstädte* (model cities)—among them the so-called Hegewald colony in Ukraine as well as a new settlement at Auschwitz.[132] The Netherlands is another case in point. Here, internal colonization on reclaimed land served as a testing ground for new forms of government intervention in the mid-1930s. In a region called Wieringermeer, new villages were designed and established on state-owned land after rigorous selection and screening processes by social engineers who also ensured the implementation of state-of-the-art agricultural techniques. Administration in these towns and villages became rather technocratic, at odds with the democratic order prevalent in the rest of the country.[133] In 1936, the Japanese government planned to send a million Japanese households to the puppet state of Manchukuo in northeastern China, where they were supposed to live in newly set up *bunson* (branch villages) consisting of two to three hundred households working as cooperatives. While selection criteria for settlers were primarily driven by military considerations, they were also informed by the government's *nōson keizai kōsei undō* (rural rehabilitation program), which aimed at redistributing the land left behind in Japan among the remaining peasants.[134] Beyond this mixture of rural rehabilitation and colonial settlement, there were even more direct parallels and entanglements between Japan and the global trends that also informed the New Deal. In Osaka, for instance, reformers such as Seki Hajime or Kataoka Yasushi pushed for *jūtaku kairyō* (residential reform), and more specifically for working-class garden suburbs based on a survey of European and American developments.[135] Zionist settlements in British Palestine form yet another example, particularly since Mead had served as a consultant there, influencing land purchase and settlement strategies in the Upper Jordan Valley, and praising some of the constructions as "cleverly planned by European experts."[136]

In many of these countries, compulsion and violence played a notable role, in contrast to the New Deal. Administrative and architectural details as well as wider contexts varied across the globe. Still, ideas of state-planned settlement, colonization, and decentralization shaped these projects, which were all conceived as alternatives to urbanization and its ills. There were many cross-references, albeit with a certain hierarchy. The New Dealers were acutely aware of what was going on in Europe, including the Soviet Union, while experiences in Asia and Africa did not figure on their radar; they saw no kinship between their own challenges and solutions and those practices. The yearning for the land thus took many forms, but in all its emanations, it was typical for the efforts of high modern societies to find

the right balance between an agrarian past and an industrial present, between destitute cities and depressed hinterlands, between the plight of their
citizens and the promises of the state.

BROADENING SECURITY

Power to the People

While many parts of the 1935 New Deal legislation only affected small
pockets of society, the Rural Electrification Administration (REA) had a far-
reaching impact across the whole United States. In the mid-1930s, only one
in ten American farms had electricity, sharpening the divide between the
"enlightened" cities with their modern life and the "dark" countryside. Beyond light and lifestyle, the lack of electricity put clear limits on the mechanization and modernization of farms as well as the economic development
of "backward" rural areas. That said, the situation varied greatly across the
country. While California had already achieved no less than 63 percent rural
electrification before the REA began its work, the situation in the Midwest
and South was quite different. In Georgia, for instance, the figure stood at a
meager 3 percent. The New Deal changed all that, in this way helping to
reduce existing imbalances. By 1941, four out of ten American farms had
electricity, and another nine years later, nine out of ten. The New Deal state
yet again demonstrated its intention to change America forever.[137]

The New Dealers did not mount the power poles themselves, however.
Action was primarily indirect, through long-term, self-liquidating loans to
state and local governments, nonprofit organizations, and particularly to
farmers' cooperatives. Unlike the RA, the REA did not give out loans to individuals. Based on the assumption that rural electrification was a public
responsibility, the agency focused on the state's role as facilitator. The main
reason for insufficient rural electrification in the 1930s was that pride of
place had been given to private actors: for investor-owned power utilities, it
was profitable to connect consumers to the grid in densely populated areas,
but not in remote parts of the nation. Thanks to its attractive lending terms
and other mechanisms, the REA helped to plug in "dirt farmers" where
market mechanisms did not work in consumers' favor.[138]

Like so many other New Deal initiatives, rural electrification built on
long-standing national and transnational discussions—in this case, going
back more than twenty-five years. In fact, it drew on "long-range planning
and creative thinking on the part of public and private agencies," as one
REA representative correctly observed.[139] Below the federal level, some
states had been pioneers on this issue: what Wisconsin represented for social security, Pennsylvania was for rural electrification. Already prior to

World War I, the Keystone State had become a hotbed of debate, and when progressive veteran Gifford Pinchot became governor in 1923, the movement acquired a strong advocate in the cockpit of power. Despite such a regional anchor, and as with so many other issues, discussions were full of transnational references. A 1925 article by Philadelphia lawyer Harold Evans, "The World's Experience with Rural Electrification," stressed how much America was lagging behind on "electric farming," especially in comparison to European countries, but also New Zealand and the Canadian province of Ontario. The degree of consensus during the 1920s is revealed by the fact that Evans's text came out in a special issue of the prestigious *Annals of the American Academy of Political and Social Science.* The various contributions—nicely framed with an introduction by Pinchot and a foreword by Morris Llewellyn Cooke, another key advocate on this issue—explored the prospects of electrification.[140]

Over time, Ontario became a critical point of reference. Cooke, Evans, and other US advocates of public electrification, including Senator George W. Norris, regularly referred to the work of the Hydro-Electric Power Commission of Ontario and its founder, Sir Adam Beck, a proponent of a state-driven system of rural electrification.[141] After touring Ontario during summer 1925, Norris noted that there, "a most wonderful demonstration of the possibilities for the generation and distribution of electric current had been given to the civilized world."[142]

Initially, the New Dealers failed to act on electricity. Roosevelt had already promoted rural electrification as governor of New York, and he lit the hearts of men such as Cooke and Norris when he argued in a campaign speech in 1932 that electricity "is not a luxury. It is a definite necessity."[143] After assuming the presidency, as with so many other issues, FDR did not commit himself to any substantial plan, even if particularly Cooke, whom he had chosen as his adviser on conservation and power matters, pressed him to do so. In 1934, Cooke, a trained engineer, proposed a national plan under federal leadership. This report, introduced by a note that it "can be read in 12 minutes" and noticeable for its unconventional zebra-striped cover, was soon read by top figures in the administration, including Ickes, Hopkins, and the president himself. Even if Cooke had made sure that every barn pictured in the report was painted in brilliant red, since Ickes was especially fond of that color, the key players in government were still not persuaded.[144]

During the same months, the TVA made progress on rural electrification. When the authority was set up, public power advocates concentrated their plans on producing electricity, and less on getting it to rural homes. Forced to improvise, TVA officials soon met with local residents to create electricity cooperatives to fill the gap, building on some fifty examples of this kind operating across the country at the time. Such cooperatives typically organized several dozen townspeople. Each person contributed an initial membership fee to meet the construction costs of the power lines and then paid installments in a monthly bill. Citizens thus owned and managed their own system rather than being dependent on private power companies. Most electric cooperatives prior to the TVA had been set up in regions where population density, geography, and other factors facilitated the success of this approach. The TVA now developed this model. Looking back, David E. Lilienthal, the TVA's powerful director, effused about how the whole effort had started "in 1934 in the back of a furniture store in Corinth, a small Mississippi town."[145] While that is not quite true, the TVA's cooperative efforts did demonstrate the feasibility of electricity cooperatives in less advantageous regions—at least if the government offered a helping hand with loans and technical know-how. Experts such as Cooke immediately picked up this thread as an additional argument for a more comprehensive plan, and by and large, there was quite some cross-fertilization from the TVA to the nascent REA.[146]

Advocacy by agricultural pressure groups, such as the American Farm Bureau Federation and the National Grange, and action by states emulating the Ontario model, such as the two Carolinas, finally tipped the balance.[147] Against this backdrop, Roosevelt created the REA in May 1935. As director, he appointed his old hand Cooke, who radiated the high modern belief in progress through science. One year later, the agency's competences were put on a broader footing with a separate act. In spite of some resistance by the power industry and accusations of socialism and subversiveness, the New Dealers proved that their rural electrification policy was able to win parliamentary support—at least when the bill was chaperoned through the hurly-burly of Congress by a politician as savvy and sagacious as Senator Norris.[148]

When the REA was created, the role of business was still undefined. Norris argued for complete exclusion of private companies. He felt that they had had their chance and described the fight between free market advocates and those calling for state action as a conflict in which "from the first gun to the last, there was no armistice, no breathing space, and no truce."[149] Cooke was more forgiving, and he invited business leaders to participate. Only when utility companies failed to propose attractive plans did he opt for the cooperative model. While the New Dealers all agreed that government action was needed, hardly anyone backed a fully state-run system. In the end, a middle course emerged and proved successful. By 1939, the REA had loaned $3.6 million and worked with 417 cooperatives serving 270,000 households.[150]

Electrification, like charismatic leadership and regionalism, was not a new political idea during the 1930s. At the century's dawn, electric power had been bound up with optimism and driven by economic prosperity, epitomizing the belief in a bright future. The New Deal, in contrast, saw electrification as a counterbalance to the industrialization that had been celebrated a few decades earlier. As Wolfgang Schivelbusch has contended, the 1930s saw "a reversal of the previous trend toward industrial concentration in favour of a Rousseauian mixed economy of agriculture and light industry"; electrification was "the technological means of regaining the advantages of premodern society—craftsmanship, communal solidarity, and authenticity—without having to return to a primitive standard of living."[151]

This orientation was quite different from the role of electricity in other parts of the world. Obviously, rural electrification was still off the political agenda in certain regions, including China and Ireland. The same held true for most parts of Africa, where electrification remained firmly urban and white, if it occurred at all.[152] In the Soviet Union, electrification was more central for the political leadership than it was in the United States. It remained closely associated with an industrial, urban future dominated by large-scale technology.[153] In good parts of northern, western, and central Europe, states had adopted rural electrification as a key development program long before the New Deal entered the picture. Some experts and politicians in those states now dreamed of creating peace through a shared European electricity system—an idea that had gained some traction during the late 1920s. In most of these countries, however, defense considerations dominated the agenda in the second half of the 1930s.[154] While the New Dealers hoped to catch up, Europe was moving in a new direction—one that would impact on America, too, only a few years later.

Most rural Americans cared little about these global ramifications and had mundane reasons to like the REA. They saw the advent of electric current as a major improvement. One woman said "that old book that was my life is closed and Book II is begun," while another reflected that "it was the first time I'd seen Pa after dark in thirty years."[155] Beyond seeing Pa, electricity promised to improve the standard of living and generate productivity gains for farmers. Rural inhabitants also acquired new social and political roles. Local leaders advertised the program, negotiated prices with the nearest utilities, enlisted members, applied for REA loans, mapped routes for power lines, and much more.

Indeed, the New Dealers did not impose their agenda on local dynamics, and public control of the power grid remained soft. The approach was markedly less heavy-handed than in the NRA and less paternalistic than the RA. With this comparably light form of intervention and a focus on consumption, the REA became a harbinger of the philosophy that characterized the New Deal from the late 1930s onward.[156]

That said, the REA's effects are best summarized as a series of paradoxes. Politically, it was designed to emphasize local cooperatives and democratic grassroots movements, but it also created a new field of strong federal action and often reaffirmed local power hierarchies. The REA invigorated the rural economy. Indirectly, it helped to strengthen the private sector and hence a return to more market-driven developments. Simultaneously, private enterprises had to acknowledge the role of public power in the hands of the REA.[157] Electrification's economic stimulus aggravated some of the structural problems of American farming as well, such as chronic overproduction, low prices, and environmental degradation.

Despite these paradoxes, the REA broadened the scope and approach of New Deal action. Security meant much more than freedom from want; it aimed at improving and harmonizing living standards across the country and bolstering democracy through cooperatives. Power went to the people, but the New Dealers made sure it was they who called the shots.

Canvassing Consumer Cooperatives

On June 23, 1936, at a White House press conference, a journalist asked Roosevelt about his plans to send a group to Europe to study cooperative enterprises. The president confirmed that a small team had been chosen "to make a report on cooperative enterprises in certain parts of Europe. They are going to the British Isles, Sweden, Denmark and Finland, and, I think, Norway, although it is not down here, Czechoslovakia, Switzerland and France." Their task was to analyze developments "in relation to cooperative stores, housing, credit," and other areas. The president also explained why he wanted this kind of information:

> I became a good deal interested in the cooperative development in countries abroad, especially Sweden. A very interesting book came out a couple of months ago—"The Middle Way." I was tremendously interested in what they had done in Scandinavia along those lines. In Sweden, for example, you have a royal family and a Socialist Government and a capitalistic system, all working happily side by side.[158]

And in fact, only nine days later an official presidential inquiry set off for Europe to study whether European cooperatives held lessons for the United States.[159]

In 1936, Marquis W. Childs published *Sweden: The Middle Way*, the book that Roosevelt referred to as his source of inspiration. The journalist from Iowa had joined the staff of the *Saint Louis Post-Dispatch*, one of the largest midwestern newspapers, in 1926. Ten years later, his book *Sweden: The Middle Way* was an immediate success, selling a thousand copies in its first three days and twenty-five thousand in 1936 alone.[160] This was quite astonishing for such a specialized book, however well written. Childs asserted that Sweden had overcome the economic depression by organizing large parts of society along cooperative lines, through businesses owned and democratically controlled by producers or consumers. Liquor control, low-cost housing, and industrial cooperatives were among Childs's examples illustrating a friendly, democratic, and prosperous society.

Roosevelt read the book in spring 1936 on a fishing trip off the coast of Florida. Between sailfish and tarpon he met with Robert J. Caldwell, a New York industrialist highly interested in European economic affairs. Caldwell put a copy of Childs's book with highlighted passages into the president's hands. Roosevelt was particularly fascinated by Childs's discussion of Swedish consumer cooperatives.[161] Perkins and other activists in the field had informed him about this model as early as the first half of the 1920s, but Roosevelt had shown little prior interest. Childs changed everything.[162]

Roosevelt's shift of attitude occurred at the very moment when the American conversation was gaining momentum. Whereas the national press published only 8 substantial articles on consumer cooperatives in 1934, the number jumped to 85 in 1935 and 235 in the first eight months of 1936.[163] This new interest—and often also enthusiasm—has to be seen against the backdrop of the Great Depression and the search for alternatives to laissez-faire capitalism. Some actors even drew a direct link between consumer cooperatives and the fate of democracy in the United States. Philanthropist Edward A. Filene sent Roosevelt a glowing letter in support of the inquiry, stressing that "the outstanding thing in the cooperative movement" was that "cooperation maintains and nourishes democracy."[164]

More generally, the mid-1930s saw increasing attention paid to building small, local communities as an alternative to large-scale planning. A certain strand in the New Deal—echoing Arthur E. Morgan's plans for the TVA, building on debates in the USDA's Bureau of Agricultural Economics, and profiting from the cooperative dimension of the REA—focused on local participation and communitarian structures to strengthen both democracy and the economy. Consumer cooperatives were an obvious tool in this turn to "thinking small."[165]

On its specific topic, Childs's book broadened public interest in Swedish policies while giving new impetus to the debate about cooperatives. Up to the mid-1930s, experts in social politics had been the main actors to observe Sweden's efforts to fight the Great Depression, analyzing its monetary policy, public works relief programs, and consumer cooperatives. Childs's book brought these expert discussions to a wider audience, connecting the rising US interest in consumer cooperatives to the Swedish trajectory. From there, the debate gained further momentum, expanding its global horizon. In spring 1937, for instance, the *Rotarian*, the official organ of the Rotary International, featured consumer cooperatives as its "debate of the month." The procooperative text started with two pictures, one of a bleak Swedish "konsum" cooperative building, and the other of a leading Japanese cooperative activist surrounded by children, all clad in kimonos and smiling. Consumer cooperatives appeared as a global trend, transcending boundaries of race and time.[166]

Republicans flirting with cooperative ideas could only strengthen the president's determination to act promptly. In April 1936, half a year before the national elections, Colonel Theodore Roosevelt Jr., the eldest son of former president Theodore Roosevelt and hence a remote nephew of FDR, became the most visible supporter of consumer cooperation in the Republican camp. Lobbying the party to adopt a cooperative platform, he explicitly referred to Childs's work. Republican presidential candidate Alf Landon was reported to have a copy of *The Middle Way* in his office, and consumer cooperative members were an intriguing electoral group. In the end, Republicans did not endorse cooperative ideas, but their interest clearly added a sense of urgency to the president's public advocacy and his decision to send an official inquiry to Europe.[167]

Moreover, Childs stood in the right political camp. Weeks before Roosevelt's press conference, he penned an article for *Harper's Magazine* in which he criticized the caustic antipathy for Roosevelt in "the whole upper stratum of American society."[168] At the same time, one good turn deserved another. Days after the president's praise of his book, Childs wrote a grateful letter to the White House and, more important, began to cover Roosevelt's campaign, eulogizing the broad support he won while traveling the country.[169]

After reaching Europe on July 9, 1936, the Inquiry on Cooperative Enterprise in Europe, as it was officially called, amassed a great deal of information, conducted interviews, and visited locations in various parts of Europe, with a particular focus on Sweden and Britain. Given the presidential blessing it enjoyed, the Inquiry's work was reported on at length in the American press.[170]

The insights gathered in Europe did not determine the Inquiry's eventual fate; discussions in the United States were to play that role. On the very day that the Inquiry set sail, Secretary of Agriculture Wallace published another instant best seller, *Whose Constitution: An Inquiry into the General Welfare*.[171] Wallace, as one of the leading figures in Roosevelt's administration, wrote it after the Supreme Court's invalidation of the AAA. He argued for a new interpretation of American institutions and a less conflictual political style. To this end, he maintained that "the cooperative philosophy is the vital ideal of the twentieth century," picking up on reasoning that he had already used long before. The United States should follow the example of other democracies, he wrote, and just like Childs, Wallace highlighted the role of Sweden. At the same time, he described the cooperative idea as a genuinely American concept, buttressing his claim with historical analogies to "the wise young men of 1787." What America needed was "to work out in the spirit of Madison a mechanism which would embody the spirit of the age as successfully as the Constitution of 1787 mirrored the philosophy of the eighteenth century."[172]

Wallace's book triggered heated debate. Analysts did not overlook the irony that Wallace's search for a new American way had led him to Europe. His attempt to "Americanize" the cooperative idea failed. Linking Wallace's considerations to the presidential Inquiry, critical reviewers asserted that consumer cooperation was a harbinger of developments in Roosevelt's expected second term. The statements of other New Dealers added credibility to such charges. NRA veteran Donald Richberg, for instance, also pled for "well-organized cooperation."[173] The American Liberty League therefore saw "Americanism at the crossroads" and concluded a pamphlet with the ringing words, "Delano, Quo Vadis?"[174] By and large, resistance was well organized and vocal, with the small business lobby and the Chamber of Commerce as strongholds of opposition, along with parts of the federal administration.

Wallace's book and the Inquiry alone cannot explain such virulent debate. Since 1933, the New Dealers had experimented with cooperative policies on a reduced scale. The TVA set up rural electrification cooperatives, FERA had a division of self-help cooperatives, and the Rural Electrification Act of 1935 further expanded this approach.[175] Beyond electricity, the New Deal had promoted and facilitated agricultural and urban cooperatives, where small and experimental activities were put on a new footing in the mid-1930s, such as with the RA's creation in 1935.[176] The Inquiry came at a time when the New Dealers seemed ready to embark on a full-fledged, highly contested cooperative course. Particularly because it bore the seal of the president's will, the Inquiry attracted a lot of attention—and exactly this attention was to be its undoing.

The European references cited by the New Dealers made it easy to denounce the cooperative approach as un-American. Driven by the debate about the Inquiry, important sections of the press started to describe the cooperative idea as foreign and undemocratic, with the *Chicago Daily Tribune*, for instance, condemning cooperatives as "a nonprofit communistic system now prevalent in many European countries."[177] While some criticisms were superficial and stereotypical, others drew on more substantive evidence. The adversaries of consumer cooperatives even sent experts to Sweden—returning with the clear message that things were indeed going well in Sweden, albeit not due to consumer cooperatives. As Henry C. Lind, a hardware dealer from San Francisco, contended in *Hardware Age*, Sweden's wealth resulted from the fact that individual ownership and capitalism had basically remained intact, and the consumer cooperative movement was but a sideshow. Thus transnational links were driven not only by the wish to emulate and learn but also by the will to distinguish and delimit.[178]

Against this current, the White House slowly retreated. As a first maneuver, the administration canceled a planned national survey on consumer cooperatives in the United States. In a confidential memo, James V. Fitzgerald, director of information in the Department of Labor, advised that if such a consumer cooperative survey were to be conducted before the election, "the opposition might use it." Together with the Inquiry, it would look as if "the Administration has in mind the fostering of consumer cooperatives"—which as was now underscored, it did not, because this would antagonize "the millions of small business men, who fear ruin through such competition" and because "the effect would be serious at the polls."[179] As a second step, the White House reformulated the mandate of the Inquiry. In his reply to a protesting congressman, Roosevelt stressed that he only wanted to gather information about the situation in Europe.[180] The Inquiry members also were ordered not to make any public statements while still on their trip.[181] Given the heated political climate ahead of the presidential election, Roosevelt announced in September 1936, "I have not sought, I do not seek, I repudiate the support of any advocate of Communism or of any other alien 'ism' which would by fair means or foul change our American democracy."[182] When the Inquiry returned to America, Roosevelt refused to officially receive its members. The president thus not only contributed to the flamboyant start of the endeavor but also took center stage in its final act. At a press conference in February 1937, when a journalist asked about the Inquiry's report, Roosevelt answered laconically that he had not seen it, but "I think it has come in." After thinking about it for a moment, he added, "It did come in and I sent it somewhere; where I do not know."[183]

After this debacle, the public debate slowly ebbed away. Even the publication of the Inquiry's report later that year changed little; the administration made sure that most of it remained purely factual and descriptive. The sections on lessons for America did not offer any single consistent interpretation.[184] Even if Hopkins, Perkins, and Wallace felt "strongly in favor of advancing Cooperatives in the U.S." after having read the report in spring 1937, the president decided not to implement any grand scheme resembling European measures.[185] Within just two to three months, Roosevelt had made a 180-degree turn, demonstrating both his curiosity for transnational links and foreign experiences, and his unwillingness to push for such change against strong domestic resistance.

While the drawn-out saga of the presidential Inquiry put a stop to transnational transfers in the field of consumer cooperatives, it did not end the New Dealers' interest in the matter itself. Electrification cooperatives continued through the second half of the 1930s. The war years also brought a revival of the cooperative idea, albeit under much less benign circumstances. After Pearl Harbor, racist stereotypes describing Japanese Americans as potential collaborators gained great momentum. Roosevelt was reluctant to resist the escalating pressure, and in February 1942, signed an executive order to exclude all people of Japanese ancestry from the Pacific coast and intern them in camps. The War Relocation Authority (WRA) set up to this end was ultimately in charge of some 120,000 Japanese Americans. In debates on the constitutional basis of this program, experts explicitly cited practices in Great Britain and Canada to justify the legality as well as appropriateness of American measures. Obviously, transnationalism could serve many causes.[186] The authority's first director was a brilliant New Deal bureaucrat from the USDA, Milton S. Eisenhower, whose older brother, Dwight, was still an obscure brigadier general profiting from his sibling's excellent contacts in Washington. Milton Eisenhower resented the internment program but accepted the position of director at Roosevelt's personal request. He tried to make the conditions as humane as possible, and originally planned accommodations resembling the subsistence homesteads that the RA had created a few years earlier in the fight against the Great Depression, or CCC-like camps. More extreme voices prevailed, so that men, women, and children alike were placed in detention camps in desolate, forbidding areas of the country. Eisenhower disliked this move, yet he typified the New Dealer who rationalized the given political targets.[187] He thus endeavored to import enlightened New Deal policies into the camps. Experts such as anthropologist Robert Redfield—who had advised a USDA agency and now wrote the blueprint for the community program of the internment camps—stood for intellectual and biographical links to New Deal ideas with a communitarian dimension.[188] Consumer cooperatives were now created as the form "recommended for permanent business enterprises," in the words of the WRA's administrative manual.[189] Overall, some 270 different enterprises or services were organized in the various camps, ranging from a single-employee shoe repair shop to moderate-sized department stores.[190] Some WPA personnel liked their program so much that they planned to advertise it in the regular cooperative movement. For a planned article, one official requested pictures from a colleague, mentioning that she needed "one or two attractive girls who would photograph well." Not even the detainees, whose situation was often dire and depressing, were spared modern public relations activities.[191]

Internment, then, reveals some ironic and unexpected twists in the transatlantic exchanges of the 1930s. After 1933, the New Dealers set up programs with cooperative elements that were informed by transatlantic discussions reaching back to the Progressive era. In 1936–37, they considered expanding this agenda, and Roosevelt sent his presidential Inquiry to Europe to assess foreign experience more systematically. Now, a policy intended to strengthen US democracy and stabilize the economy was discredited as allegedly un-American. The Inquiry, with its transnational dimension, ended in a debacle, while established programs with cooperative dimensions quietly continued. Half a decade later, with nationalist and racist sentiments running high after Pearl Harbor, bureaucrats such as Eisenhower and Redfield resorted to the very same instruments. During a state of emergency and under the auspices of a program that brought one of the worst violations of civil rights in twentieth-century American history, they implemented the same cooperative features that had shaped the fight against the Great Depression a few years earlier.

Inventing Sweden

Transnational links tend to be two-way streets, and the Swedish-American case is no exception. The image of Sweden that Childs propagated was instrumental in raising international interest in the country, and in the medium term helped to forge a perception of the Swedish welfare state as modern and attractive. This view was less the product of Swedish developments alone than of intense transatlantic connections.[192]

In Sweden, Childs's work received a more mixed reception than it did in the United States, basically following party lines. *Sweden: The Middle Way* was a book largely bereft of politics. Neither the political process nor the conflicts over the country's political choices were adequately represented. Many Swedes found Childs's overall interpretation too positive and optimistic. The central concept Swedes used to characterize their sociopolitical model, *folkhemmet*, remained marginal in Childs's book.[193] Instead, his Sweden echoed many elements of American self-image, stressing qualities such as pragmatism, democracy, capitalism, directness, and peacefulness.[194] For this reason, progressive newspapers such as *Dagens Nyheter* sympathized with the book, while conservative ones such as *Svenska Dagbladet* criticized it. Economist Bertil Ohlin, a member and future leader of the social liberal Folkpartiet, in opposition to the ruling Social Democrats, even insisted that it "simply was not true" that Sweden was a "fortunate land." Childs's depiction of Sweden was quite close to the visions and objectives of the Social Democratic Party and some intellectuals, but much less representative of political and social practices on the ground.[195] Childs would even admit this in later years, adding that his "knowledge of the country and the people was very limited," and in fall 1937, US minister to Sweden Fred Morris Dearing conveyed a report by a Swedish informant that "much of the enthusiastic propaganda issuing from Sweden at the present time about the cooperative societies and their successes are misleading foreigners."[196] A Swedish expert touring the United States in 1938 even said that "the American people have been bewitched" by Childs's book, noting that there "could not be a greater misconception" of reality on the ground.[197]

Having said all this, *The Middle Way* was instrumental in putting Sweden on the welfare state mental map from the second half of the 1930s onward, first in the United States and then elsewhere. It popularized Swedish achievements and had a particularly catchy title given that the Great Depression had triggered a general search for "middle" or "third" ways to solve the crises of capitalism and liberal democracy.[198] Moreover, it profited immensely from the international interest in consumer cooperatives that had built up by the mid-1930s. By comparison, earlier publications praising Sweden's social achievements, including earlier texts by Childs or the works of Carl Johann Ratzlaff, had no impact beyond small circles of experts.[199]

International perceptions of Sweden were mixed at the time. In Ethiopia, one of the oldest Christian states in the world and one of the few sovereign states in Africa during this period, Sweden enjoyed a relatively good reputation due to the work of its missionaries and status as a nonimperial power.[200] In Europe, the perceptions were more ambiguous. French intellectuals during the mid-1930s, for instance, still identified Sweden more with "happy mediocrity" than with modern welfare statism.[201] Such positions would soon become marginal. With Childs's book and Roosevelt's press conference, public attention in the United States snowballed and soon turned to other parts of the Swedish welfare state. The number of American visitors to Sweden grew from 9,700 in 1935 to 15,500 in 1936, and doubled by 1937, with many of them coming for political reasons. In January 1937, the *New York Times* reported that cooperative directors and government officials in Europe found it "almost impossible to do any work last Summer due to the influx of Americans to study cooperatives."[202] The impact also rippled beyond American shores, with others, particularly in the English-speaking world, referring to Childs's work and his view of Sweden. Perhaps most importantly, future British Prime Minister Harold Macmillan referred explicitly to Childs's book in his 1938 work entitled *The Middle Way*, describing his future vision of Britain.[203] Sweden now became a reference point in Finland, too—which it had not been before the 1930s.[204]

It is remarkable that US attention transformed Sweden into an internationally recognized social model. Before World War I, particularly after the loss of Norway in 1905, Sweden had been seen as lagging behind, and not as a country bustling with reform ideas. Many of the legal provisions instituted to catch up were inspired by the Danish example; the southern neighbor was frequently seen as a role model.[205] Even *Sweden: The Middle Way* reveals traces of this appreciation, featuring a full chapter on agricultural cooperatives in Denmark simply because Childs believed that the Danes were further advanced in this field.[206] Until the mid-1930s, transnational networks on social policies had been at least as intense between the United States and Denmark as between the United States and Sweden.[207] Furthermore, Denmark had previously served as a transatlantic point of reference on several other issues, including folk high schools, agricultural policies, and old-age pensions (going back to the 1891 law introducing the *alderdomsunderstøttelseslov*).[208]

Still, Denmark did not experience a comparable increase in American and international interest during the 1930s. A lack of contemporary literature cannot serve as explanation. Frederic C. Howe, for example, probably the most prominent American advocate of the relevance of European welfare policy during the Progressive era, organized a commission to visit Denmark in 1935; Josephine C. Goldmark, another key activist of the Progressive era, authored a book on the country in 1936, and Howe came out with another book on Denmark that same year. Even more than Childs, Howe depicted the country as a middle way between capitalism and socialism.[209] Yet Denmark stayed outside the limelight. Howe, a high-placed ex-Progressive turned New Dealer, explicitly bemoaned this situation:

> one cannot help wondering why it is that in a world in which unemployment has been continuous for half a dozen years, in which billions of dollars are being expended annually for relief, that statesmen, scientists and those who search the earth to add human knowledge, do not make a study of a country like Denmark which has done so many things to offer a solution to these problems.[210]

Why, then, Sweden and not Denmark? Sweden's economic performance was a little more spectacular. Whereas it had previously lagged far behind Denmark, this now changed.[211] Another factor was more important, however: the configuration of academic elites and social policies was quite different in the two countries. In response to the country's perceived backwardness, parts of Swedish society had since the late-nineteenth century turned their attention away from Germany and other Scandinavian countries, and toward the United States. Swedish academia in particular had begun to revamp itself early in the twentieth century with a new focus on the American model of research universities engaged in social issues and highlighting policy-oriented research. This process was reinforced by American philanthropic money, especially from the Rockefeller Foundation.[212] From then on, synergies between the academic and political realms were especially intense in Sweden, and it was not only Americans who found this striking. Sir Ernest Simon, a British expert on social policy, for instance, was impressed that five of the eight professors at Uppsala University's law faculty combined academic careers with membership in the Swedish parliament, the Riksdagen.[213] In Denmark, in contrast, academia and politics did not converge nearly as much, and by the second half of the 1930s Danish policies seemed less radical, sticking instead to old-fashioned liberal ways. Sweden, on the other hand, appeared to be a laboratory for social engineering. The rational, state interventionist, and technocratic stance made Sweden so attractive to many American and international observers who found discussion partners on exactly their own wavelength.[214]

Gunnar Myrdal, whose contribution to developing the Swedish welfare state paradigm is widely acknowledged, is a good example. He combined his chair in economics at the Stockholm School of Economics—a hotbed of Swedish-American exchanges—with being a Social Democratic member of the Riksdagen. He was one of the key players of the Social Democratic political elite who sought to build exactly the kind of Sweden that Childs described as reality. Together with his wife, Alva, Gunnar had spent 1929–30 in the United States as a Rockefeller fellow, and America became his main intellectual reference point. This obviously facilitated communication with Americans. Myrdal and his analyses of Sweden turned into a crucial source of information for Childs while also leaving a deep impression on the members of Roosevelt's Inquiry in 1936.[215] International visitors to Sweden met not eccentric eggheads in ivory towers but smart, young technocrats who spoke English, knew American ways, and wanted to transform their country in a controlled manner. When, exactly one year after the Inquiry's trip to Europe, the Carnegie Corporation looked for the "next Tocqueville" to study the situation of African Americans in the United States, they picked Myrdal—a choice that would have been less likely without the intense interest in Sweden and its experts.[216]

On the other side of the Atlantic, a man named Naboth Hedin played a similar role in raising public interest in Sweden. Between 1926 and 1946, he directed the New York office of the American-Swedish News Exchange—an institution established in 1921 by the Sweden-America Foundation to expand US knowledge about Sweden. Not only did he write countless articles on Sweden's successes and coedit a volume celebrating the contribution of Swedes across three hundred years of American history (published in 1938 by Yale University Press, which had also published Childs's book).[217] Hedin also helped Americans like Childs in their work on Sweden. Childs thanked Hedin for his generous assistance in several of his publications, and in the end, both benefited from their cooperation.[218]

Quite generally, Sweden systematically invested in Childs so as to manicure its international image. Childs returned to Sweden in 1943 as a guest of the Swedish Foreign Office, and in 1961 he received the prestigious Nordstjärneorden medal from the Swedish king. The idea of Sweden as a model social welfare state survived World War II, and in the postwar era Childs became a standard point of reference far beyond the Anglo-American literature. Before the war, it was not yet clear that international interest would be more than a flash in the pan. With the benefit of hindsight, though, Childs along with the American-Swedish networks from which he profited and in turn strengthened were the defining moment for Sweden's international image as a model welfare state.[219]

This claim holds especially true if one considers that England had a much longer tradition of consumer cooperatives. Its labor movement in particular had pioneered many ideas in this field, such as with the Rochdale Principles. In the 1930s, Great Britain had the largest consumer cooperative movement in the world.[220] Admittedly, the Inquiry also paid a visit to Britain, but Sweden still received more attention; it became the most

Figure 5. Kagawa Toyohiko (1888–1960),
Japanese Christian reformer. Courtesy of the
Kagawa Archives & Resource Center.

significant new pin on the map. This qualifies Daniel Rodgers's argument that New Deal social planners were primarily thinking backward—in other words, that they were scrutinizing Europe's past in order to learn for America's present and future.[221] In the case of Sweden, it was not the Scandinavian country's past but instead its vibrant present that interested Americans most. It also explains why Roosevelt sent another committee to Sweden in 1938, this time to study industrial relations. The new commission was less widely publicized, and it demonstrated that the New Dealers, including the president himself, had not lost their interest in the Scandinavian country.[222]

Finally, the roads not traveled need to be considered. The presidential Inquiry only visited western Europe. A socialist system of cooperatives existed in the Soviet Union with some 287,000 cooperatives, and in Asia the figure stood at an impressive 168,000—as compared to a mere 51,000 in all of the Americas.[223] The most important foreign advocate of cooperatives in the United States at the time was a Japanese Christian missionary, Kagawa Toyohiko. Some, like John Haynes Holmes, a Unitarian minister and founding member of the National Association for the Advancement of Colored People, went so far as to call Kagawa the "first and noblest Christian in the world since the passing of Tolstoi."[224] During a six-month tour of the United States from December 1935 to July 1936, Kagawa spoke about the cooperative movement in Japan to an estimated audience of 750,000.[225] Not only because of his fight for consumer cooperatives, but also thanks to his theological positions, Kagawa became "a Western hero."[226] While many Americans were eager to listen to him, the New Dealers did not send a study commission to Japan. Persistent racial and cultural antipathies kept Americans from taking any real interest in such developments. The international image of Japan as a formidable and innovative power only emerged during later decades. In that sense, Japan was discovered long after Sweden, and less for political than for economic reasons.

The G-Man's War on Crime

State action and the will to make America more secure also increased in areas that are normally not seen as part of the New Deal. The "war on crime" is a case in point. Roosevelt and the New Dealers argued that through "a broad program of social welfare, we struck at the very roots of crime itself," with research showing that government relief efforts did reduce crimes significantly.[227] In fact, the administration also resorted to more direct means to curb criminality.

The Federal Bureau of Investigation (FBI) is an intriguing example of the New Dealers' approach to security and surveillance. Created in 1908 and renamed several times, the FBI received its present name in 1935. While the Great Depression led to budget cuts for other American intelligence and policing agencies, Director J. Edgar Hoover expanded the FBI from some four hundred agents in the years between 1925 and 1934 to nine hundred in 1940—and that figure jumped to some five thousand by 1945. In tandem with this increase, the New Deal dramatically expanded federal rights over local and state law. Bank robbery became a federal crime. The FBI gained new competences to investigate the interstate transportation of stolen property and, perhaps most famously, pursue kidnappers who crossed state lines. In addition, the FBI professionalized, harnessing science by setting up its own laboratory in 1932 and the National Police Academy in 1935.[228]

Equally important to its new federal role in crime fighting was the change in the FBI's public image during the New Deal years. From an obscure division within the Justice Department, it moved to center stage, and its impact on popular culture was immense. The FBI's public relations office helped to produce radio shows, comic strips, pulp magazines, movies, and television programs. Stationery shops carried bubble gum cards and coloring books, souvenir fingerprint cards, and machine gun targets celebrating the bureau and its successes. Whereas up to the early 1930s gangster films had glorified their criminal protagonists, the FBI under the New Deal developed the new G-man (short for government man) cult. The eponymous 1935 Warner Brothers movie did the most to alter the public image: while James Cagney starred as the vicious gangster in the 1931 film *The Public Enemy*, he now played the impeccable FBI agent.[229]

Other changes were not restricted to celluloid. Like the villains, the federal agents were now equipped with Thompson submachine guns, and working for the federal government became cool. Well-staged successes—the arrest of bank robbers Clyde Barrow and Bonnie Parker in May 1934, bank robber John Dillinger two months later, or the Lindbergh kidnapper Bruno Richard Hauptmann in September that year—helped to establish the bureau's splendid reputation.[230]

The FBI and the new federal role in law enforcement had a dark side, too. The bureau's civil rights balance sheet remained mixed. Long before the 1940s surveillance boom, the FBI started to spy on people who espoused unorthodox political views or seemed to digress from social norms. The bureau's fingerprints collection rose from nine hundred thousand in 1924 to two million in 1930, then to five million in 1935 and thirteen million by 1940 (that is, one-tenth of the overall US population). The FBI created files on many fiction authors, including Ernest Hemmingway and William Faulkner, and it investigated Communist activities. Director Hoover was notorious for keeping files on anyone who mattered, including Eleanor Roosevelt. The FDR administration occasionally made use of these intelligence functions, blurring the line of legality. From 1935 onward, the White House solicited bureau reports on the president's critics, and Roosevelt asked Director Edgar Hoover for information about private meetings of his namesake Herbert. During the war, the administration gave the FBI an ever-larger role.[231]

While the FBI's long-standing director carefully orchestrated his image as the terminator of gangsterism, Attorney General Homer Stille Cummings (who served from 1933 to 1939) was at least as important in reforming the bureau. In late 1933, Cummings declared a "war on crime," and in April 1934, he announced a package of measures leading to the enactment of a long list of laws strengthening the federal role in policing. Back in 1924, when Hoover had been appointed as FBI director, Attorney General Harlan Fiske Stone had planned to remodel the agency along the lines of Britain's Scotland Yard. Stone's successor Cummings was bolder; in a speech at an American Bar Association meeting in August 1933, he explicitly repudiated any reference to Scotland Yard and stressed that the United States had to create its own unique system. In an era in which "the radio, the airplane, the sound-picture have drawn us very close together," more federal powers were needed in crime fighting as in other policy arenas.[232]

The New Deal FBI thus gained many federal powers, and Roosevelt, paradoxically, welcomed the expansion of one of the government's most conservative agencies. Out of respect for local and state sovereignty, his presidential predecessor Herbert Hoover had not been willing to take that step. For Roosevelt, concessions to conservatism seemed a small sacrifice compared to the potential gain of curbing the exclusive prerogative of state and local governments. The New Deal took a big step forward in enhancing the (federal) state's monopoly on the legitimate use of physical force and gathering information about its citizens. Roosevelt's notion of freedom from fear not only pertained to the economy or welfare statism but also included crime control. Considering the antistatist current in American politics, it is quite remarkable that even in its acronym form, G-man could be more than a curse. The success of this kind of FBI pulp is probably the best symbol of how the New Deal changed the United States.

In the final analysis, the securitization of society was a core concern of the decade, with the idea of prevention foremost. Some Americans saw a real "crime wave" swamping the country, created or at least exacerbated by the Depression. Historian Harry Elmer Barnes, for instance, felt that the "volume of crime in the United States, compared to that in other civilized countries, is nothing less than scandalous."[233] But other countries also saw a debate about increasing crime rates, and in this case, the conversation spanned not just industrialized societies but the colonies, too. In Nigeria, a British colony at the time, a March 1931 report identified an "increase in crime caused by the depression in trade and in the tin industry," with highway robbery and theft featuring strongly.[234]

While public fears were globally shared, the actual situation was less clear than it might look at first glance. In Muncie, for instance, the arrest rate was relatively stable prior to the Depression, and then rose sharply in 1930 and 1931. In 1932, however, it fell off abruptly, and then slowly rose again.[235] In New York City, homicide rates also dropped markedly in 1931.[236] More generally, crime rates in industrialized societies remained low during the 1930s in comparison to the nineteenth century, and yet the 1930s were the "peak era" of the death penalty, with an all-time record in American death sentences occurring in 1935–36.[237] The rise of crime control, punishment, and security was not simply a reaction to a greater threat; it was the result of changing attitudes and perceptions. This holds particularly true if one considers that during most of the years from 1933 to 1946, homicide rates and rates of violence more generally in the United States fell continuously.[238] Obviously, leaders like FBI director Hoover or President Roosevelt never wasted a good crisis.

In his 1933 speech before the American Bar Association, Cummings emphasized the need for federal action, not only vis-à-vis state and local levels, but also in place of international cooperation. This was fully in line with the New Deal's overall take on crime control. J. Edgar Hoover resented the Vienna-based International Criminal Police Commission, founded in 1923 and later known as Interpol. The FBI showed little interest in the commission's work during most of the 1930s. City police departments such as the New York Police Department, which had developed an international profile by the 1920s, and had started to exchange knowledge with municipal police forces in the Americas and Europe, now became less active. Attempts to set up a World Organization of Police became bogged down, and American police agencies mainly cooperated among themselves. Only indirectly did US federal police agencies increase their international activities. The United States contributed to the League of Nations' efforts to control opium trafficking.[239] Yet certain unilateral internationalist initiatives were more important than such multilateral commitment. By 1937, the Treasury had more than forty agents stationed in Europe, and as early as 1931, Harry J. Anslinger, director of the Federal Bureau of Narcotics, had set up his own sort of "mini-Interpol," with North American, North African, and European police officials exchanging information on transnational drug traffickers. Anslinger concentrated mainly on formulating new *federal* laws. His fight against cannabis, for instance, culminated in the 1937 Marijuana Tax Act. A few years after the Prohibition debacle, America embarked on another experiment of federal state action and managing mores, although of less epic dimensions than the fight against alcohol. Nationalizing security lay at its core—as a concept that encompassed the economy, domestic affairs, and health matters, to name but a few. In this area, too, insulation dominated American policies.[240]

Other parts of the world took a slightly different course. In Latin America, police cooperation was also discussed, but remained rudimentary. Due to colonial rule, independent cooperation remained impossible for police forces in large parts of Africa or Asia. The League of Nations, in contrast, fostered cooperation in matters of narcotics, the trafficking of women and children, and counterfeiting.[241] Even more important, the International Criminal Police Commission became a real factor in Europe. Building on earlier experience with mutual police assistance, its main tasks were to coordinate investigative cooperation and to serve as a platform of technical know-how sharing. European police experts were mainly concerned with a new class of criminals working transnationally, such as passport, check, and currency forgers as well as hotel and railway thieves. By 1936, the commission had collected information on 3,724 suspects who were considered of international interest, and before World War II, it organized fourteen international meetings in various European cities to share information. Such work continued seamlessly even when an increasing number of European countries installed fascist or authoritarian regimes, as police experts perceived their work as "apolitical."[242]

The lack of US transnational cooperation was not due to the absence of transnational criminality but rather was a political choice, revealing an insulationist mind-set. Indeed, there were criminals with a transatlantic background. The kidnapper of the Lindbergh baby, for example, had a long criminal record in Germany, from where he had migrated to America in 1923. Con artists like Victor Lustig, born in the Habsburg monarchy in 1890, were transatlantic actors. Lustig not only sold the Paris Eiffel Tower twice to gullible scrap-metal dealers. Ocean liners steaming between France and New York were another of his preferred crime scenes, where he scammed clients by selling them machines that allegedly produced $100 bills. In 1934, Lustig together with a gifted photoengraver flooded the US East Coast with near-perfect counterfeit currency.[243]

Despite this lack of international cooperation, the US government followed an international trend of the 1930s in its move toward nationalizing and professionalizing police and intelligence work. Many European states also pushed for more centralization and coordination. In Britain, the government displayed a growing tendency to see police officers as servants of the Crown versus serving local government, while municipal police forces in the Paris region were taken over by the capital in the middle of the decade.[244] Professionalization also figured prominently beyond the United States and even beyond the North Atlantic. In British colonial Africa, new professional technologies such as forensic laboratories, fingerprinting, and radio communication were being introduced.[245] In Europe, both authoritarian and democratic countries used much the same discourse about offenders and carceral solutions, as Clive Emsley has recently demonstrated.[246] Police practices remained quite different, however, and while Nazi Germany and the Soviet Union basically turned into carceral societies, liberal democracies never chose that route, nor did they see the level of expansion of police forces typical of dictatorships.[247]

New ideas of security along with greater surveillance and control were global trends at the time. A more centralized and professionalized police force complemented the relief and welfare components with which societies answered the threats that the Great Depression had exposed. State power was increased in this respect, too, and while the political goals remained radically different, societies of diverse types often employed similar technologies and a shared discourse.

Petering Out

The flurry of activities launched in 1935 moved the New Deal to new sites of political and economic brinkmanship. The election of November 1936 seemed to give enhanced legitimacy to this course of action: in a landslide victory, the Democrats carried all but two states, winning 60.8 percent of the popular vote and gaining clear majorities in both houses. The triumph enhanced the legitimacy of the policies that the New Dealers had pursued since 1933. Understandably, they saw the election result as a broad mandate for future reforms. Roosevelt began his second inaugural address in January 1937, for instance, with a long list of the past four years' achievements. He then pinpointed "the challenge to our democracy" as "one-third of a nation ill-housed, ill-clad, ill-nourished," and left no doubt that the federal administration planned to tackle this central issue and other concerns in the coming term.[248]

Nonetheless, by the end of 1937, the active phase of the New Deal as a reform program of insulation and intervention striving for security and stability had petered out. Several reasons explain the end of reform. While so far, the crisis had served as the glue between political factions, the electoral success of 1936 made the divergent liberal groups more self-confident and reduced their willingness to find compromises. Conservatives likewise became more confrontational. Decimated in Congress, they feared that the president would abuse his vast powers and became less cooperative. Southern voting patterns started to shift away from the New Deal, fearful that new legislation on issues dealing with the labor market, trade unions, and some aspects of welfare statism might undermine Jim Crow and regional autonomy. The recession of 1937–38, which few had predicted and gave the jitters to people in the White House—as Roosevelt told Henry Morgenthau in a phone conversation—also had serious effects. For one, it undermined the recovery as the greatest achievement of the past years, and as such, challenged the credibility of the New Deal in general. For another, it reduced the means and support for new interventionist or insulationist schemes.[249]

A final reason for the impasse lay in the New Dealers' aspirations. Whereas so far, most programs had been designed to address concrete economic problems, the initiatives of 1937 targeted the carefully balanced apparatus of the federal state itself. In February 1937, Roosevelt unveiled plans to "pack" the Supreme Court by adding more justices supportive of the New Deal, and in parallel, the New Dealers launched a discussion about remodeling the executive branch of the federal government. Both projects soon met fierce public resistance and cost the president a lot of support. Many Americans equated the Supreme Court with the Constitution and therefore opposed any form of tinkering. Once again, charges of dictatorship abounded. These were fueled by events in Europe such as Germany's annexation of Austria in March 1938 that seemed to underline the tendency toward totalitarian rule. The *Chicago Daily Tribune*, critical as ever of the New Deal, called Roosevelt's plan of executive reorganization his "dictator bill," and Roosevelt's old hand Hugh Johnson turned into a critic of any kind of "governmental Camorra."[250] As in 1933, a part of this criticism was pure hysteria or empty rhetoric, but it played a role in tipping the balance against the New Dealers. Given their earlier successes and optimism, the humiliation was even deeper.

The end of reform, itself the result of processes quite specific to US history, also concluded a period of intense transnational exposure and entanglement at the level of social policies, with US actors seeing themselves on the receiving end. Informed by a myriad of experts sailing the North Atlantic, the years from 1933 to 1937 pushed America in the direction of European-style social democracy—ironically during the very period in which this political formation in Europe itself was weaker than ever before or after during the twentieth century. Unlike the Progressives a few decades earlier, the New Dealers became increasingly reluctant to admit these European interconnections, particularly after the miscarriage of the presidential Inquiry to Sweden. Given public resistance to learning from abroad, the New Dealers even considered canceling some of their trips to Europe.[251] References to other world regions remained much more rare, with colonial rule and "backwardness" in the various parts of Asia, Africa, and Latin America only partly explaining why. At the economic and social levels, the United States could have learned a lot from Japan, Uruguay, Colombia, New Zealand, and other places, too. Despite Good Neighborism and Japan's military might, the New Dealers denied these countries the attribute of kinship, as the necessary basis for any kind of transfer, or even just for serious scrutiny. In sum, the New Dealers did less to tap the global flows of knowledge and practices, at least in public.

This does not mean that transnational links subsided; quite to the contrary. Informed by this mix of cosmopolitanism and myopia, the New Deal became an international trademark by the mid- to late 1930s. The "laggard of the western world" finally made itself an international rhetorical benchmark and sometimes a source of inspiration as well. When, in January 1935, British liberal politician Lloyd George introduced a radical program of economic reform, he included references to the Roosevelt administration. His ideas were immediately called "Lloyd George's New Deal," although a number of them built on British debates far preceding 1933.[252] Canada's Prime Minister Bennett announced what came to be called his New Deal during that same month of 1935. Bennett was partly inspired by William D. Herridge, his brother-in-law, who held close contacts to top New Dealers, and even more by the symbolic dimension of the state activism that the Roosevelt administration had unleashed. Still, he never called his policies a New Deal. His opponents and the media invented the phrase "Bennett's New Deal," and its association with the United States goes a long way in explaining why the press reacted negatively. The New Deal turned into an international trademark, but most Canadians wanted to be different from their southern neighbors.[253] In Latin America, Raphael Trujillo bragged about his "Dominican New Deal," and Colombian president Alfonso López Pumarejo—who came across to some American observers as a "college professor of the Middle West"—was clearly influenced by the policies of the big northern neighbor. Even today, his first years in government with his Revolución en Marcha program are often referred to as the *Nuevo trato* (New Deal) period.[254] US Americans perceived Cárdenas as *el FDR mexicano* due to his deficit financing and far-ranging reforms on health, labor, and agriculture.[255] In Argentina, too, the New Deal turned into a widely discussed and desired model of democratic revival, with leaders of the several important parties repeatedly declaring themselves to be admirers and Argentinean versions of the US president.[256] Some seven thousand miles to the east, in Ethiopia, Emperor Haile Selassie put together his own "brain trust" in 1934, composed of two European advisers and one American.[257] And another fifty-two hundred miles further east, Gong Xuesui, the mayor of Nanchang, saw his province as a model of reform administration, stating that "Jiangxi has become the center of China's New Deal."[258] In Belgium, meanwhile, the Office de Redressement Economique, founded in 1935, was ironically called the *brain-trust du New-Deal belge*, much to the dismay of French linguistic puritans.[259]

Occasionally, Roosevelt himself contributed to the international hype around the New Deal. During a short stopover in Brazil on the way to the Inter-American Peace Conference in November 1936, he gave an informal address at a banquet hosted by president Vargas. In a rather sentimental mood, Roosevelt reflected,

> I am leaving you tonight with great regret. There is one thing, however, that I shall remember, and that is that it was two people who invented the New Deal—the President of Brazil and the President of the United States.

He ended with a toast "to the health of my good friend President Vargas."[260] Roosevelt's remark was simplistic at best—but it certainly pleased his host.

Simultaneously, foreign observers were frequently struck by the peculiarities of the American political system. The ease with which the Supreme Court killed key elements of the New Deal stunned many observers abroad. While some, particularly in authoritarian states, saw it as proof of the weakness of democracy, others praised it as an example of a properly functioning judiciary.[261] Having said that, the New Dealers never challenged the power of Congress in any fundamental way. This was of special significance at a time when dictatorships around the world strove for the abolition of legislative authority. During the 1930s, though, this did not receive much international attention.[262]

Overall, the New Dealers' agenda had mixed results, specifically on the gender and race fronts. State activism and the goal of making the lives of Americans more secure against all kinds of misfortune demanded classifications and clarifications. Seemingly universalistic public policies divided citizens into different categories of entitlement. More during the legislative process than in the New Dealers' own planning, several biases crept into the

New Deal's edifice of provisions. Work relief was granted primarily to white men, whereas women were more likely to receive cash assistance or be assigned to sewing projects. Celebrating a sexual division of labor, the New Deal treated men and women like members of separate worlds; it carried rather conservative assumptions about innate gender differences. By and large, the New Deal institutionalized a male breadwinner versus female caregiver model that had been challenged by the Great Depression.[263]

On race, the balance was even more ambivalent. Despite new forms of support and greater public recognition, many African Americans were still mired in poverty, and discrimination continued. During the 1930s and 1940s—a period that Ira Katznelson has described as "Jim Crow's last hurrah"—the vast majority of African Americans were excluded or at least treated differently under the new provisions. Segregation and discrimination thus acquired a new federal legitimacy. The new provisions did not inscribe race into law, but their details had highly racial implications. The stronger role that state legislation and administrations had in implementing welfare provisions for women and minorities strengthened this dimension further. Admittedly, the inner circle of the administration was fully aware of this bias and often disliked it. Still, it did little to oppose southern Democrats and others who pushed for such amendments. Pragmatism ruled the day, and as a consequence, security remained selective and frequently overlooked those most in need.[264]

This was nothing new in comparison to the early New Deal. Yet back then, most programs had focused on short-term relief or been ruled unconstitutional. Social Security with its discriminatory burden, in contrast, was here to stay. Resettlement activities also sometimes proved counterproductive. Slum clearance, pursued by the USHA, RA, PWA, and other organizations, did not necessarily entail rehousing. Much more was destroyed than built, and some of the country's poorest people found themselves evicted without being offered an alternative.[265] Forty African American families from the Cahaba community near Birmingham, Alabama, for instance, were forced out of their homes, and watched their slum being burned. "Women folks knew hardly what to do and we just went to cryen and cryen," as one source reported.[266] While the RA built beautiful new homes on the sites, these families had to find new shacks and shanties. Birmingham was not the only such case, and from Great Britain, Unwin warned that British municipalities "are not permitted to clear a slum until they are in a position to offer alternative accommodations for people in the slums.... You cannot just pull down the dwellings and let people filter in anywhere."[267] This time, there was no avid audience for the wise old man from England.

If, as Ira Katznelson has contended, affirmative action was white during the New Deal, it was not fundamentally different from provisions elsewhere. Most European states were ethnically more homogeneous. Class and gender also determined their trajectories of welfare statism from the beginning, however. And where European states encountered racially heterogeneous communities—most obviously in their colonies—support was decidedly hamstrung by racial structures. In the British Empire, for example, attention to "native welfare" (as it was called at the time) increased, but the provision mainly extended to white colonialists, and the overall system remained idiosyncratic and spartan.[268]

In spite of clear racial, class, and gender biases, the New Dealers had accomplished much by 1937–38, even if less than some had hoped. It would be wrong to say that the New Deal was over by then, given that many of the measures instituted since 1933 remained in place. Only its reform boost petered out, and with the escalation of the Sino-Japanese conflict into full-blown war in 1937 and the outbreak of war in Europe two years later, different dynamics kicked in. But before moving on to study the New Deal's legacy, its impact on American society needs closer scrutiny.

ROADS TRAVELED, BUILT, AND UNTRAVELED

New Deal Landscapes

By the mid-1930s, the New Deal had brought about change in another sense, too: the alphabet soup had congealed into a strong federal bureaucracy, at least by US standards, for better or worse. The number of civil servants working for the federal administration rose from 604,000 in 1933 to 867,000 in 1936, and 954,000 in 1939.[269] Federal government spending grew dramatically, from $3.1 billion in 1929 to $4.6 billion in 1933, then $6.6 billion in 1934, $8.4 billion in 1936, and $8.8 billion in 1939—all despite the Great Depression and the need to economize.[270] Compared to its 1929 level, the United States saw a much larger relative increase in government spending than most other nations, including Great Britain, Norway, Brazil, and Argentina as well as most African and Asian colonies, where total central government expenditures rose rather modestly between 1933 and 1939 (with French Equatorial Africa, where it more than tripled, and Nyasaland [present-day Malawi], where it actually fell, as extreme exceptions).[271] Per capita expenditures were roughly as high as in France, but lower than in Great Britain and higher than in Italy.[272] Overall, the United States seemed to move from the rear to the vanguard of state building, as defined by the European standards of the time.

Two caveats to this story about the New Dealers boosting expenditures and taking a lead at the global level must be mentioned. First, the trend had already started under Hoover, as another indication that his approach was less austere than traditional research has it. Growth in government spending relative to the GDP was not especially high during the 1930s; instead, the New Deal continued a general trend that had already begun prior to World War I.[273] Second, the original fiscal impetus was reversed early on during the New Deal. Roosevelt's Economy Act of March 1933, for instance, cut the salaries of federal workers and slashed military bonuses in an effort to bring spending into line with reduced revenues. Emergency relief work programs soon moved in the opposite direction. Government spending and fiscal policy remained volatile, with reversals to a more austere policy in 1933 and 1935.

On a global scale, most other countries resorted to a similarly erratic and variable course of action, with Italy taking the lead in this budgetary roller coaster. Few countries, notably New Zealand, pursued a consistent fiscal policy during the decade, and in general, there was no correlation between the stability or form of the political system and the course of government spending. A globally shared belief in balanced budgets and fiscal austerity set clear limits to the rising Keynesianism. This holds true for Mexico and Great Britain, for instance. Most opinion leaders around the world associated massive state spending with squander. Nonetheless, unconventional fiscal policies were adopted in many countries, with Nazi Germany going the farthest with deficit-led stimulus, while Sweden, the United States, and later France also experimented with such tools. Yet democracies and dictatorships alike remained cautious, and the road to expanded state action remained tortuous.[274]

Besides the new role of government, the federal administration took root in America in another sense, too: the New Deal cast, welded, and sank its foundation deep in the American landscape, thereby materializing in concrete ways. Washington, DC, experienced a building boom during the period. The Federal Triangle, planned to provide work space for 25,000 civil servants, became the most important government construction project in the national capital during the 1930s. Its monumental buildings, inspired by the Louvre in Paris, were meant to express the power, permanence, and grandeur of the federal government. Admittedly, most of these buildings had been planned and initiated long before the New Deal. When it comes to Washington's topography, "big government" had its roots in the Republican 1920s and even the early 1900s. Still, the Federal Triangle was soon staffed with New Dealers identifying with Roosevelt's policies.[275] The number of federal civil servants in DC almost doubled from 70,000 in 1933 to 123,000 barely three years later, doubling again to 265,000 by 1945.[276] When the new Department of Labor edifice on Constitution Avenue was inaugurated in February 1935, Roosevelt stressed the match between the department's "constructive" work, its recently "increased responsibilities," and the "fine building" that had cost $4.5 million.[277] Washington turned into both a vehicle for and product of a new phase of America's nation-building process. With a hint of surprise, *Fortune* magazine argued in 1934 that the city "has paradoxically at last become the capital of the U.S."[278]

Many of its monumental buildings, such as the 1930s' addition to the USDA, the Federal Reserve building of 1937, or the privately established National Gallery of 1941, have been criticized for their resemblance to fascist or Stalinist architecture. And it is true that any of these buildings could easily have been transplanted to Rome, Berlin, or Moscow without raising eyebrows. Some scholars have called the style that characterized fascist capitals as much as Washington and Moscow "stripped classicism" for the way it combined references to ancient Greece and Rome with modernism. This style also shaped the Musée des Colonies in Paris (1931), Helsinki's Diet (1931), the Palace of Nations in Geneva (1936), the three prizewinning entries in the international competition to build the Turkish Grand National Assembly (1937), and other major public buildings in the Western world (and to a lesser extent beyond, including, for example, the 1931 Chinese Ministry of Foreign Affairs in Nanjing).[279] Notwithstanding such similarities, true connoisseurs still saw the difference between beaux arts classicism and other fusions of modernism with the final phase of architectural classicism. The architecture of these buildings had no proclivity to any specific ideology, and in each of these countries, one also finds more traditional architectural designs. At the same time, since the 1920s an ornamentally austere interpretation of classicism had become the international language for public buildings of national significance. All these edifices aimed at affirming internal authority, and by the 1930s they were seen as symbols of national assertion in the international competition between liberal democracy, fascism, and communism. The various political systems, moreover, observed each other closely; in the mid-1930s, Soviet experts documented American architectural developments more intensely than those of any other country, followed by Fascist Italy; admiration and distancing characterized the way that Italian architectural journals covered Soviet urban planning; and the same applied to German reports about Italy and the United States. In their search for the best way to overcome the crises of democracy and capitalism, fundamentally different political systems consciously resorted to the same architectural vernacular. Or, to put it another way, it was quite impossible to infer directly from form to content.[280]

To be sure, architectural activities were not restricted to the urban landscape of the national capital. In America, the New Deal also reshaped vast parts of the country. A PWA grant rescued New York's Triborough Bridge project from insolvency in 1933. Chicago's subway plans, which had laid dormant in drawers for more than two decades, finally began to be implemented thanks to WPA funding in the mid-1930s. The Tennessee valley got its TVA, Los Angeles received new schools after its 1933 earthquake, and

South Carolina initiated seventeen state parks between 1933 and 1939 alone, in this way jump-starting its park system as a major recreation program. Many of the nation's zoos would not have survived without the New Deal; instead, the 1930s saw a substantial increase in their number and quality thanks to federal support. With two-thirds of all federal emergency expenditure going into public works, the WPA alone constructed 480 airports, 78,000 bridges, and 40,000 public buildings across the nation.[281]

The New Deal's infrastructure projects transformed more than the physical landscape. They fundamentally changed the way that Americans saw, moved through, and experienced their country as well. Economically, the new roads and bridges, buildings and dams provided much of the backbone of the postwar economic boom. Culturally, the new highways with their philosophy of unimpeded, frictionless flow led to what one scholar has called a "state-generated spatial deconcentration" that facilitated the rise of the consumer age.[282] Indeed, pioneers of the system such as Thomas H. Mac-Donald, the chief of the Bureau of Public Roads, stressed the "universal utility of the motor vehicle" along with the immense "social values" to which convenient and safe state-built highways contributed.[283] Public works, then, were much more than mere emergency projects; their effects proved to be more lasting than the NRA and many other initiatives that the New Dealers flagged as structural reforms.[284]

In comparison to many parts of the world, the New Deal's infrastructure projects were exemplary. In Australia, for instance, the Commonwealth government expanded its role vis-à-vis the states during the 1930s, but still the main message from Canberra was austerity. Gas taxes went up, car registrations went down, and existing schemes to improve the country's road system were either shelved or slowed down.[285] Some Latin American countries, where a lack of infrastructure had impeded economic growth for decades, increased their transport infrastructure investments during the 1920s and 1930s, concomitant with a shift from railways to highways as the central component of infrastructure expansion. The share of Mexican government investment directed to roads increased from 7 percent in 1925 to more than 30 percent in 1937.[286] In Brazil, Vargas understood road construction as a keystone of national integration, nearly doubling the road network between 1930 and 1938. The road infrastructure, however, remained insufficient, and one contemporary study from 1941 only considered two highways in the whole country to meet US standards.[287] In general, the number of cars in Latin America remained comparatively low, and a grandiose project such as the Inter-American Highway—launched in the 1920s to connect Mexico to Argentina—stagnated during most of the 1930s.[288] From the 1920s on, Chinese road infrastructure improved substantially, and all plans to modernize Washington, DC, paled in comparison to the efforts put into turning Nanjing into a true capital—although ironically planners conceived it as a new Washington, DC, and involved American experts in their efforts.[289] In Persia, officially renamed Iran in 1934, the decade brought five thousand kilometers of gravel roads linking Tehran to most provincial capitals. By the late 1930s, these roads carried as many as twenty-seven thousand vehicles, including some five thousand cars, eight thousand trucks, and seven thousand buses. The nation's showpiece was the Trans-Iranian Railway. A eulogizing biography of the Persian shah emphasized that the country also had "five excellent highroads." Overall, however, the country's transport infrastructure remained underdeveloped, and the "transport revolution" that the decade witnessed was based more on better vehicles than on better roads.[290]

An exact international comparison of the road-building efforts at the time is impossible. The League of Nations worked frantically to coordinate knowledge and collate global statistics, but this goal was only achieved after World War II.[291] But US achievements were less impressive by western European standards. Here, the state had traditionally played a larger role in building national systems, and so American experts continued to sail east in search of inspiration. Thomas MacDonald, who directed national road policy and was responsible for building some 3.5 million miles of highways in the course of his long career, carefully scrutinized Germany's autobahns, not least because American advocates of transcontinental superhighways used them as an argument, and because "no topic in highway engineering was hotter in the mid-1930s," as historian Bruce Seely writes.[292] As late as 1939, Michigan highway commissioner Murray D. Van Wagoner raved that "if Germany can build roads of this type, the United States, home of the world's automobile industry, can do the same."[293] European examples also drove the US debate about toll roads, road surface technology, and other issues, with enthusiastic references particularly to Fascist Italy, just as American parkways had served as a point of orientation for German autobahns a few years earlier.[294] MacDonald even argued that his "opportunity to study traffic conditions in many of the countries of the old world clarified many uncertainties and indicated the very definite directions that federal and state highway policies of the future should take."[295] As so often happens, learning did not lead to direct emulation but rather involved selective borrowing. While shaped by European references, the United States continued its self-fueling system of highways funded by gas taxes, for instance.[296] MacDonald highlighted the differences between conditions in the Old and New Worlds and maintained that America learned best by avoiding the mistakes of Europe. On some issues, such as the need for further functional differentiation of street types, though, he saw Europe as a clear inspiration.

Despite many differences in organization, funding, and technology, highways in dictatorships and democracies alike embodied high modernity's fantasies of national unity, frictionless mobility, and technological progress in times of crisis. In this respect, Brazil and the United States, Italy and Mexico, Germany and France, all shared a lot. And across the Western world and to some degree beyond, infrastructure projects reacted to new structural needs, particularly the rise of automobile transport since World War I.

The New Deal's carved and cast, tarred and typed impact on the United States did not just hail a new age of federal activism. Concomitantly, the political and administrative organs at the state level expanded markedly, ushering in a new phase of "cooperative federalism."[297] Roosevelt himself always remained fond of American localism. The power of Congress, and especially southern Democrats eager to preserve their regional system of racial discrimination and economic exploitation, also acted against excessive centralization. Finally, in spite of its rapid growth, the federal government remained much too small to take care of everything. Using the operational capacity of state and local governments was the only way to create the New Deal state. The Social Security Act, for example, created an arrangement with a federal payroll tax, most of which could be excused by a contribution to a state unemployment insurance system. This triggered a wave of legislation from Alabama to Wyoming: within two years, all states had enacted their own unemployment insurance legislation. Eligibility and benefit levels for unemployed workers were state rather than federal, with standards varying widely. The federal administration *and* the states therefore increased their power as well as their impact on the lives of millions of Americans.[298]

For some projects, subordinate or state bureaucracies even bore the brunt of the work, and some core New Deal agencies in Washington remained surprisingly small. The CCC's Washington headquarters, for instance, employed only about fifty staff members, who were ultimately in charge of some quarter million young men. The bulk of the work was divided between other federal departments, state agencies, and local institutions.[299] This is all the more striking given that the CCC was the only New Deal public works program that was exclusively financed at the federal level. All others required explicit or implicit matching at state and local levels. Quite generally, government spending is again a good indicator of where action took place. While the federal share of government spending rose from 30 percent in 1932 to 46 percent by 1940, the states saw an expansion from 20 to 24 percent (in an ever-expanding overall budget). These figures demonstrate that the states also massively increased their activities, with the local level losing in relative importance in comparison to the other two tiers and basically remaining at the same absolute level as before.[300]

The New Deal also empowered many nonstate actors, who learned to swim in the alphabet soup. The American Red Cross, for example, initially feared that all the New Deal activities would make it redundant. Instead, it reasserted its critical role in disaster relief and cooperated with agencies such as the WPA and the CCC.[301] Or put more simply: not only Washington got a piece of the action.

New Deal landscapes were not spread evenly across the country. The layer was particularly thick in and around Washington, DC, urban districts, and the Tennessee valley. In other rural areas, its effects on American life varied widely. Politically, its impact diminished the further south one went, for instance, and economically, there was a clear color line. In that sense, America's modernity remained fractured—a multifaceted, incoherent landscape, full of promises, former times, asynchronies, and divergences.[302]

Inside the Clockwork

Who were the people populating the New Deal's landscapes? A richly illustrated book published about Washington, DC, in 1939 described the city as America's "nerve center," as the "control point of a whole nation's effort to keep itself running."[303] Thousands of talented young people flooded the city and other New Deal hot spots, with the proportion of federal jobs located in the capital leaping from 30 percent in 1930 to 44 percent ten years later.[304]

Whereas during the 1920s, the brightest among America's young professionals had made their money in business and spent it in speakeasies, Washington now reaped a windfall of talent. The New Deal thus had a vast generational dimension. Even if by the standards of US presidents, Roosevelt himself was not particularly young, the New Deal became a "young man's game."[305] To some extent, this was the result of (old boys') networks with their job brokers. Felix Frankfurter, for instance, marshaled Washington's steady influx of (Harvard) lawyers, while John R. Commons supplied freshly minted economics graduates from the University of Wisconsin. More important, young people really wanted to come. A secure income was only rarely their main motivation; some, like 1932 Harvard law graduate Thomas H. Eliot (born in 1907), scion of a Boston Brahmin family, even accepted a small cut from the $1,800 he had earned with a Buffalo law firm to $1,700 when starting to work for the Department of Labor. He still said to himself, "What a lucky guy you are, Eliot!"[306] Eliot was more interested in the prospect of a vibrant political powerhouse and in joining a noble effort to serve his country. One year into the job, at the age of twenty-seven, he acted as one of the principal draftsmen of the Social Security bill. In the mid-1930s, Eliot shared Georgetown houses with other young New Dealers such as FDR's future administrative assistant James H. Rowe (born in 1909), and Paul M. Herzog (born in 1906), who would later become the chairman of the National Labor Relations Board. Such networks of professionals in their late twenties buttressed the New Deal consensus for the coming decades.

Among the New Dealers, there were also numerous women, but gender conventions of the time explain why most held secretarial, research, or minor administrative posts. Women with a college or university degree were not as common, yet women had more political influence and a bigger role in the administration than ever before. In his memoirs, Eliot remembered several houses filled with bachelors, but also one female counterpart. Irreverently called "the Nunnery," it was inhabited by six graduates from Smith, Bryn Mawr, and Vassar, all of them attractive, and one of them Eliot's future partner. Female New Dealers enjoyed Eleanor Roosevelt's sympathy and sometimes also support, but FDR did not take a proactive stance on gender equality, much less feminism. And yet the expansion of social welfare services, as an area long dominated by women, offered job opportunities. Below the top layer of women such as Secretary of Labor Perkins, Ellen Sullivan Woodward who headed the WPA's Women's and Professional Projects, Josephine A. Roche as assistant secretary of the Treasury, and Ruth Bryan Owen as minister to Denmark, a whole generation of younger women now entered the federal government.[307] Many of them were left-leaning, including Charlotte Tuttle Westwood, who worked on Native American rights at the Interior Department, and Elizabeth Wickenden, who joined FERA together with her husband. Some of these female leftist New Dealers transcended conventional gender and sexual norms, charting their own careers and questioning the sanctity of marriage. Long before the 1960s, Washington turned into a laboratory for challenging dominant social values.[308]

A growing number of the new civil servants also belonged to minority groups and experienced the public sector as less discriminating than private business.[309] James A. Farley, the postmaster general, and Thomas G. Corcoran, one of the president's closest advisers, were both Irish Catholics. A significant proportion were Jewish, among them Leon H. Keyserling (born in 1908), who helped draft major pieces of New Deal legislation including the Wagner Act, and Wilbur Cohen (born in 1913), whom JFK later tagged "Mr. Social Security." In total, some 15 percent of FDR's appointees were Jewish, far exceeding the Jewish proportion of the population.[310] Other minority communities were less well represented, with Robert Clifton Weaver (born in 1907) and William H. Hastie (born in 1904) among the comparatively few African Americans. For this reason, a person such as Mary McLeod Bethume (born in 1875), head of the National Youth Administration's Office of Minority Affairs, was a rare exception in that she was female, African American, and comparatively old.[311]

Never before had such a young, upwardly mobile, and diverse group of people entered national politics. And never again would so many young professionals bear so much governmental responsibility. This was only possible because so much of the New Deal state was newly created. Admittedly, the expansion of state functions also opened new career perspectives for a

slightly older generation. James M. Landis (born in 1899), a professor at
Harvard Law School, was never granted the privilege of an audience by his
university's autocratic president, Abbott Lawrence Lowell. After moving
down to Washington and joining the New Dealers, he started to anticipate
"with pleasure, knowing that there will be an exchange of views," his meetings with a different president, FDR.[312]

The young generation also gained significant political influence in many
other countries. This holds particularly true for those parts of the world
that had lost a whole generation on the battlefields of World War I. Both
Italian Fascism and German Nazism had a strong generational dimension,
as some of the early analysts, like Sigmund Neumann, were already arguing
in the 1930s.[313] Albert Speer in Germany, for instance, was around thirty
when he started to build some of Nazi Germany's most monumental
buildings. Mussolini's son-in-law, Galeazzo Ciano, was thirty-three when he
was appointed foreign minister. Nikolai Alekseevich Voznesensky was
thirty-four when he became head of the mighty Gosplan (Госплáн), the
Soviet Union's State Planning Commission, in January 1938.[314] Democracies offered fewer such options, though America supplied more than most.
Significantly, since the late nineteenth century, youth increasingly had
come to be identified with vitality, virility, dynamism, innovation, modernity, and nationhood.[315] The youth cult was especially strong in dictatorships, which worshipped martyrs such as Pavlik Morozov (Soviet Union)
and Horst Wessel (Germany), or men of only regional or local prominence
such as the twenty-two-year-old worker Silvio Sammarchi in Fascist Italy.
"The World has become conscious of its youth as never before," a National
Youth Administration publication declared in 1937.[316] While America did
not see any comparable hero cult, it did not escape the male-centered
youth zeitgeist of the time. And as with so many other things, Americans
did not see themselves as the avant-garde in this respect. "Hitler, Mussolini,
and Stalin are concentrating their strength on the youth of their countries,"
flamboyant youth activist Viola Ilma argued in 1933, and compared to
them, the United States seemed a laggard to her. From this vantage point,
which soon led to the establishment of the American Youth Congress, the
New Deal was doing nothing but catching up.[317]

With its massive expansion of the state, despite the economic crisis,
America also was not alone on the world. Persia expanded its government
budget about fifteenfold under the authoritarian rule of Reza Shah Pahlavi,
not least due to increasing oil revenues. The country's seven existing ministries expanded, and no less than three were newly created—industry, roads,
and agriculture. Even if at a different level of prosperity and state penetration, the state now assumed much expanded welfare functions and created
a state presence that Iranians had never felt before, violently suppressing the
traditional role of the country's tribes.[318] In a similar vein and yet in a quite
different political environment, Vargas's Brazil in November 1937 publicly

burned the state flags in a pyre on Rio's Russell Beach, symbolizing the
dictator's intention to strengthen the national government's power. Between 1930 and 1945, the number of federal civil servants is estimated to
have grown from 38,000 to 151,000.[319] Vargas launched a substantial civil
service reform, which succeeded in upgrading bureaucratic performance—
while also serving his dictatorial needs. A few years earlier, the government
had been unable to properly quantify its foreign debts because copies of
most loan agreements had not been kept. Vargas changed this. Brazilian
journalist Danton Jobim was right when he stated that the "greater concentration of power in the hands of the Executive" was a clear parallel between
Roosevelt's and Vargas's policies. Having said this, regionalism remained
strong in both countries.[320]

Among the group of more industrialized states, however, there were
many fewer parallels to the New Deal's state expansion. In Europe, World
War I and colonialism both had fostered an increase in state functions long
before the 1930s. In countries such as Britain or Germany, retrenchment
and not expansion of state functions seemed to be the watchword in the
mid-1930s (even if in fact there was actually an increase in personnel and
powers). The British Ministry of Labour, for instance, in charge of many
social policy issues, saw its staff grow by 20 percent during the 1930s.[321]

Quantity and quality sometimes grew together, at least in American eyes.
When Frankfurter, probably the capital's most influential job broker, sent
his "boys" to Washington, his main motive was the "building up of the
equivalent of the British Civil Service in our country."[322] Revealing the kind
of patriotism typical of an immigrant boy thirsting for recognition as a true
American while being accused of being a Jew, Red, or alien, he considered
the emulation of this foreign example as the best way of serving the United
States. It nonetheless does not take a deep analysis of his biography to explain this mind-set. Iowa-born Hopkins displayed the same admiration and
told the British press, "I wish we had something as good as your Civil Service here. Your politicians have little to fear when they have decided on a
policy or programme. They trust the Civil Service to carry it out with efficiency and integrity."[323] British politicians probably raised their eyebrows
and lowered their teacups when reading this, but Frankfurter and Hopkins
provide deep insights into the attitude of the New Dealers.

Shaping (up) America

For all the new bureaucracy it created, the New Deal has been called a
"pencil-sharpener revolution."[324] Indeed, in 1936 alone, "the government
printing office printed over two billion book pages," and no less than
650,000 typewriter ribbons were used annually.[325] The true icon of Washington's administrative tools and form of governance was slightly more sophisticated, though: the tabulating machine. Data processing and book-

keeping with electromechanical devices had already started at the end of the nineteenth century, and the state played a crucial role in facilitating the new technology's success. Herman Hollerith invented one of the first tabulating machines for the 1890 US Census. Whereas it took a full seven years to process the data of the 1880 Census, data processing using punched cards reduced the time required to a few months a mere decade later.[326]

By the 1930s, such unit record equipment became as common in government and business as the computer during later decades. Technological progress now allowed punched cards to be used not only for data processing but also for record management. With the New Deal, the availability of sophisticated statistical techniques intersected with the creation of a modern bureaucracy prepared to put the new tools to full use. Most significant, IBM provided the logistical scaffolding for the Social Security Board; without this advanced technology, the whole logistics of the SSB might have collapsed. While IBM saved the SSB, the SSB helped make IBM a leader in the business machine sector, since its governmental contract was extremely lucrative.[327]

This symbiosis between business and the state was driven by transnational perceptions. Perkins later recalled that it was the experience of seeing the time-consuming British unemployment insurance system in London during a study trip in the early 1930s that convinced her that a technologically more sophisticated solution had to be found, "because the American mind will just not grasp or cope with anything so complicated." Instead of wooden stacks, stepladders, and longhand notes, the secretary of labor wanted a system in which "they punch a few keys on something and the record comes up automatically."[328] It was not to be that easy. During the presidential campaign of 1936, Republican candidate Landon ranted at Social Security, polemically asking if "twenty-six million [workers are] going to be fingerprinted." Other Republicans went even further, insinuating that workers would have to wear metal dog tags.[329] This was sheer polemics, particularly since the colorless Kansan Landon offered no general alternative to Social Security. During the shaping of the programs, however, the New Dealers paid little attention to logistical matters.[330] Luckily for Perkins, the technological means were found soon *after* the SSB had been established, and punched cards became a solution suiting the "American mind."

The SSB system still entailed a lot of bureaucracy and personnel, but it was technologically much more advanced than its British and other counterparts. As of 1937, twenty-one million Americans were entitled to an old-age pension, which was calculated and registered by an agency in Baltimore. This bureaucratic apparatus created a vast register of all wage earners who contributed to an old-age pension. Technologically, Social Security introduced the first national system that did not just process data but also served for bookkeeping. Using machines "that think," as the press put it at the time, the federal government gained direct and individualized access to its citizens' data.[331]

Yet the devil lay in the details. The telephone book of Washington, DC, alone listed more than thirty John Smiths. How to make sure that the one would not be confused with the other? In 1936, the Social Security Administration created the system of Social Security numbers (SSN). The first card issued went to a young man by the name of John D. Sweeney Jr., whom the *New York Times* laconically described as a twenty-three-year-old "Princeton man, shipping clerk, Republican." When interviewed, the young man told the press that he was not particularly enthusiastic about his prospective pension.[332] The system would not only outlive the New Deal but Sweeney, too. Few went so far as Memphis engineer Leon Roffener, who had his SSN tattooed on his left arm.[333] But the SSN, like so many social technologies introduced during the 1930s, was here to stay. Just as radio communication supplied direct access to people's homes and minds, the punched cards offered a revolutionary technology to read and order society. No metal dog tags and not even tattoos were necessary to inscribe the state into the lives of millions of Americans to a degree hitherto unknown in peacetime.

Social Security was only the most visible government user of the new technology. Other ministries and agencies also used punched cards, such as the Department of Justice as an access system for fingerprint files.[334] At the local level, the Chicago police department bragged about its state-of-the-art technology. Thanks to punched cards and telephone calls, robbers could be caught "without moving from desks."[335] State intervention and attempts to make society more secure thus reached a new level.

Other countries had introduced punched card systems long before the 1930s, too. Canada, Austria, Denmark, Russia, and others started counting their populations with Hollerith machines prior to World War I. Against this wider picture, America pioneered putting the new technology to the service of welfare statism during the 1930s. Countries such as Germany, Great Britain, and France had established large state-organized welfare programs long before the Great Depression, relying on written files, key office machines, and decentralized administration for their pensions and other welfare systems.[336] Technologically, the New Deal's Social Security system skipped the stage of written files and jumped directly to punched cards. The United States turned its status as a relative latecomer into a comparative advantage by applying the latest technology.

The latest technological advances fascinated experts throughout the world. In 1936, the director of the Dutch Central Agency of Statistics contended that "population registration ... increasingly commands the attention of all civilized countries," and a "third phase" had begun, integrating records by place of residence and family information, thereby allowing much deeper insights into society.[337] Building on the latest technology, Vichy France introduced a punched card register in 1940, after its defeat by Germany, for military mobilization. The Vichy government hoped to use this tool, which it kept secret from the Germans, in the event of a call to arms, and when Hitler occupied Vichy France in 1942, French officials destroyed it.[338]

Nazi Germany also used the latest generation of tabulating machines, built by IBM's German subsidiary, in the war effort. The main focus was on generating statistics to control industry and raw materials for military production. Already in 1933, the Third Reich's first national census was processed by Hollerith machines, recording—among other things—religious affiliation. The punched cards thus turned into a means of targeting Jews. Alongside the national census, the regime created many other registers cataloging society using questionnaires and bureaucratic procedures. These in turn became a key prerequisite of Nazi terror and the Holocaust.[339] This holds true for Germany itself, but had consequences for other parts of Europe during World War II as well. The Netherlands is a case in point. Historians have argued that the sophistication of Dutch population registration, as compared to states such as France, Belgium, or even more eastern Europe, was a major reason why the proportion of Dutch Jews murdered in the Holocaust was especially high. The tools of "civilized countries" could be used for the vilest purposes.[340]

Also in the United States, population data systems soon revealed their less benign sides. After the attack on Pearl Harbor, it took the Bureau of the Census just a single day to publish its first report on Japanese Americans, followed a few days later by more fine-tuned surveys monitoring this subpopulation for selected counties "by sex and nativity or citizenship."[341] The rapid tabulation of the data depended on the sophistication of the US Census and its underlying technology. Moreover, the Bureau of the Census assisted the military authorities in charge of internment, and even provided microdata with systematic lists of names and addresses—a fact that the bureau denied for decades after the war but that has recently been proved. Such data were particularly useful for "mopping up," as officials called it at the time, of individuals who had eluded internment.[342] Statistics of "Japanese Americans," the majority of whom were US citizens who had never been to Japan, were also created by the newly established War Relocation Authority that handled internment. The agency demanded ever more detailed statistics, including a locator file, a "complete record on repatriation," and other aggregate data, allowing it to order and control internees.[343] The violation of human rights, forced migration, internment, and loss of property that Japanese Americans had to face obviously cannot be compared to the Holocaust. But they demonstrate that it was not only dictatorships that were tempted to abuse the means that the new technology offered.

The punched card story reveals how only a thin line separated security from terror and welfare from warfare. The United States was at the forefront of technological innovation in the field of tabulating machines, and it was here that these machines were put to political use early on. The punched card, as an archetypal high modern instrument of reading and ordering society, was deployed in diverse ways across societies. Nevertheless, identical technological means and similar bureaucratic procedures were instituted to scrutinize as well as organize society on a biopolitical basis. Industrialized states around the world relied on a surprisingly limited range of practices.[344]

Discovering the American Way

In July 1936, Secretary of Agriculture Wallace published an article in *Scribner's Magazine* titled "The Search for an American Way." Against "those who say that the United States is now about ready to follow the same path that has been followed by the Old World," Wallace stressed America's uniqueness. He specifically elaborated on the concept of unity. The "totalitarian or corporative state," he contended, "represents the ultimate in unity but it also represents the loss of democratic privileges." America should strive for "unity amidst diversity," and needed "a concept of the general welfare grounded in both political and economic democracy." This, the farmer-intellectual from Iowa maintained, would define the American way.[345] Wallace's text was part of a burgeoning discussion around the "American way" during the second half of the 1930s, and even the term itself only exploded into popular use at that time. It spoke of the urgency and anxieties with which Americans talked about questions of shared values and national identity along with certain shifts in their self-understanding in the years directly prior to World War II.[346]

Already in his speech accepting the Democratic Party's renomination for the presidential election of 1936, FDR pledged to restore "an American way of life" and continue "the fight for freedom in a modern civilization."[347] He identified the "economic royalists" as the nation's main threat, following up on an old agenda from the Progressive era. In comparison, foreign security threats and global developments remained marginal in his talk. FDR's harsh antibusiness rhetoric was to fade away soon after, whereas the darkening international situation moved into the center of attention. With Fascist Italy triumphant in Ethiopia in 1936, Japan's full-scale invasion of China in 1937, Hitler's annexation of Austria in 1938, and General Franco slowly gaining the upper hand in the Spanish Civil War during that same year, there was constant nourishment for such anxieties. Inroads by fascist and racist groups in America, such as the German American Bund with its ties to Berlin, revealed that democracy also had dangerous enemies at home. In his October 1937 "Quarantine Speech," Roosevelt therefore contrasted "the happiness and security and peace which covers our wide land" with the "very different scenes being enacted in other parts of the world," and emphasized that the "people of the United States under modern conditions must, for the sake of their own future, give thought to the rest of the world."[348] In 1933, fascism, Nazism, and communism were frequently seen as *alternative models* of organizing economy and society—foreign, but fascinating to many. By the late 1930s, these dictatorships had unveiled their full, ugly faces. Now, they were primarily perceived as international and domestic *political threats*, and came to represent the fearsome ideological "other" against which America defined itself.

The debate about the American way has to be seen against this backdrop. The concept strengthened the notion that all Americans belonged to a single national community. More specifically, it celebrated a more pluralist as well as ethnically and religiously diverse definition of national identity, as historian Wendy Wall has convincingly argued. More and more opinion leaders, including cultural anthropologist Margaret Mead and Swedish intellectual Gunnar Myrdal, interpreted diversity as the main feature that made the United States unique. Not long before, America had been defined mainly as a white and Protestant nation. In the face of fascism, communism, and what was now called totalitarianism more generally, a pluralist and diverse notion of national identity gained momentum.[349] The TVA, for instance, refashioned itself at the turn of the 1940s from a symbol of overcoming the Great Depression and catching up with planning efforts elsewhere to a self-assertive, democratic alternative to totalitarian planning efforts and a transnational icon of development. Nobody was more successful in this domestic and international public relations exercise than Lilienthal. In his 1944 book *TVA: Democracy on the March*, the political message was very clear. Where dictatorships used totalitarian instruments, Lilienthal contended, Americans left room for grassroots democracy—gently glossing over the somewhat ambivalent results on the ground.[350]

The New Dealers themselves were by no means the only ones contributing to this conversation—and it is important to stress that the entire discussion refers to self-images and public conversations, whereas social practices on the ground remained much more ambivalent. Business circles also chipped in. In 1938, the National Association of Manufacturers ran a billboard campaign depicting the comforts of American life, with the slogan "There is no way like the American way." This America was a paradise of consumption and family life with high standards of living—free from class conflicts and state interference.[351] The Congress of Industrial Organizations, in contrast, came out with a different vision, promoting "industrial democracy" and defending the rights recently gained under the New Deal, but also espousing the long-standing concerns of American trade unionists. Economically, the Congress of Industrial Organizations' "insurgent Americanism" of the 1930s shared little with the views of the National Association of Manufacturers. Politically, however, both groups hailed America's ethnic, religious, and cultural diversity.[352]

FIGURE 6. "Keeping the Wolf from the Door," caricature in *CIO News*, 1938.

Universities soon joined the chorus. In 1937, the University of Pennsylvania set up its American Civilization Department, focusing on a combination of history, literature, and law, and Harvard established its History of American Civilization graduate program that same year, also with the idea of shoring up Americans' confidence in their own political system and values.[353] Slovenian American journalist Louis Adamic refashioned the United States as a "nation of immigrants" and pointed to the non-WASP elements in the country's history.[354] Trade unions moved in a similar direction. A political cartoon from a Congress of Industrial Organizations' publication in 1938, for instance, displayed a trade unionist with FDR, both heavily armed. Together, they defended a doorway labeled "American Democracy" against a wolf with a swastika brand that had already slain "labor unions" along with "religious and racial minorities" elsewhere.

Attitudes toward domestic minorities were thus strongly influenced by international developments. The need to contrast America with Nazi and

Japanese terror strengthened the tendency toward greater ethnic democracy. Or to put it differently, America's new self-understanding resulted mainly from tectonic changes in the wider world.[355] In this light, it is hardly surprising that Great Britain experienced a comparable development of a more widely shared culture, bridging class and regional divisions while mixing commercial and political traits, during the 1930s.[356] At the other end of the political spectrum, in Japan, the notion of the nation did not become more pluralistic; rather, the focus was on the idea of a genuinely "national" way. Whereas during the early 1930s the country had debated the applicability of European fascism, the decade's second half saw a different development: the emphasis now lay on the "kingly way"—*ōdō*—as a quintessentially Japanese way of doing politics and running one's empire.[357]

That said, there were clear limits to the new, more diverse understanding of American society. Jim Crow remained untouched in the South, and interracial marriage was still forbidden by state laws as miscegenation, despite comparisons in the African American community to Nazism's racial practices. Only after 1945 did such efforts carry real impact.[358]

During the second half of the 1930s, the debate about the American way had two implications for the New Deal. First, it celebrated individual rights, freedom, and opportunities much more than had been the case during the first years of the Roosevelt administration. "Rugged individualism," which the NRA's Hugh Johnson had refuted categorically, was hailed as a quintessential American virtue. Those New Dealers who dreamed of a society characterized by solidarity and a cooperative or even collective approach became marginalized. Both big planning and thinking small (using state action to implement local, communitarian structures) failed to get off the ground. Rather than proposing radical and swift change through government action, the New Dealers now spent their energies on defending programs that they had already instituted. Simultaneously, their momentum for interventionist reform waned. The TVA is a case in point. In 1937, proposals to create several large regional authorities based on the Tennessee experience were killed by Congress—the death knell for any idea of treating public planning as a central component of the American way. And from 1938 onward, the TVA carefully avoided the term planning and incrementally replaced it with democracy as the new buzzword.[359] The fear of totalitarianism thus became a great simplifier and reduced the scope of political options. In general, as Alan Brinkley has brilliantly argued, many American liberals jettisoned earlier far-reaching reform goals by the late 1930s. Instead of economic planning and institutional regulation, their approach to political economy concentrated on creating an economic environment that would allow business to flourish. Industry, they now maintained, only needed light-handed intervention. In contrast to earlier anticapitalist rhetoric, the role of the state was to stimulate consumption through public spending.[360] Plans went so far as to propose a "Department of Welfare," of "which one function should be 'the protection of the consumers.'"[361] Other circles quickly picked up the new agenda of "consumer politics," including trade unionists and activists in groups such as the National Consumer's League, strengthening the Roosevelt administration's new direction of seeing mass consumption as the best American way to democracy and prosperity.[362]

Second, the conversation about the American way revealed a fundamental change in the fabric of the United States' global links. In response to the Great Depression, the New Dealers had sought to learn from experience elsewhere. Their successes in overcoming the crises of capitalism and democracy, the failure of their more interventionist and paternalistic schemes such as the RA, and a more threatening global environment led to a shift of focus: the broad stream of international welfare discussions narrowed to a small, mostly subterranean brook. For all its inclusiveness, the American way set clear limits to the idea of foreign borrowing. It was the extreme exception that proved the rule when, in 1938, Roosevelt personally ordered several reports on Nazi welfare schemes, and when in a highly selective process, the CCC appropriated some elements of vocational training from the German Arbeitsdienst.[363] In contrast to transnational interconnections that even bridged the gulf between democracy and dictatorship, the Dies Committee on Un-American Activities, established by the House of Representatives in 1938, represented only the paranoid tip of the iceberg in a discussion in which charges of being un-American became as ubiquitous as they were toxic.[364]

Against this backdrop, the gear of debates and transnational interconnections shifted to foreign policy and security concerns. Global developments made America seek a more self-asserted and pluralist form of national identity. In the face of perils, the "national" trajectory was stabilized and reified, increasingly building on a notion of America as a civilization with a civilizing mission at home and abroad—and not just as a republic or nation-state. This new form of self-understanding prepared the United States to engage more actively with the world. It culminated in 1941, when *Time* magazine publisher Henry R. Luce described the twentieth century as the "American Century"—displaying a mind-set and perception of the world that was courageous, even impertinent, given that at the time Nazi Germany and Japan seemed much more successful in asserting their "new orders" internationally. Furthermore, it was utterly different from the way that most Americans had perceived their country and its global contexts only a few years earlier.[365]

That said, the American way remained emphatically civilian until the close of the 1930s. Democracy and capitalism, supported by public welfare and a pluralist national identity, were seen as the main defenses against fascist or totalitarian threats. Security had strong political, economic, and cultural elements, whereas the military dimension remained weak. In the mid-1930s, the US military ranked roughly seventeenth in size among the world's armed forces. Military personnel on active duty stood at 334,000 persons in 1939, as compared to 244,000 in 1932—a substantial increase, but still moderate in light of the abyss that the world was about to fall into.[366] Neutrality remained central, and the Atlantic and Pacific seemed wide enough to keep military threats at bay. Roosevelt and some of his advisers, who thought that America needed to strengthen its military capabilities and accept international responsibilities, remained handcuffed by Congress and a war-weary public.[367]

In many other sovereign states, the securitization of society had long since gravitated from job creation to universal conscription, and from building roads to constructing tanks and bombers. This was most obviously the case in fascist countries, the Soviet Union, and states at war, such as Spain, China, and Japan. But the dark shadows of rising international tensions also led to substantial buildups in democracies and authoritarian regimes, including France and Poland, and later in the decade, smaller countries such as Finland and Belgium. Britain started later, but still did more than the United States. In Latin America, Brazil, for instance, stepped up military spending during the 1930s, too. Between 1932 and 1934 alone, spending grew by some 30 percent, less because of international fears than for domestic reasons. Given this general trend to move from welfare to warfare, the United States remained stunningly unprepared to fight and win World War II; its belated militarization stands out in comparison to most other states. The term and the concept of "national security" only rose to prominence at the tail end of the decade. [368]

It was not only military defense that remained limited in the United States. For all the hype around the FBI, what today is called homeland security was also remarkably lax. Nothing demonstrates the civilian nature of the New Deal state better than an incident on December 8, 1941. On the day after the Pearl Harbor attack, the president wanted to address Congress. Given the circumstances, his staff was deeply worried about assassination attempts during the short ride from the White House up to Capitol Hill. The presidential state car had no protective features—despite a long line of presidential assassinations, including Abraham Lincoln, William McKinley, and a failed attempt to kill FDR in February 1933. The only vehicle that could be rustled up in 1941 was a heavily armored 1928 Cadillac limousine that had belonged to Al Capone and been confiscated by the Treasury Department following his arrest. On that cold and clear December day of 1941, a thirteen-year-old gangster's car was needed to transport the president and commander in chief of the United States from the White House to the Capitol.[369]

Chapter 5

THE AMERICAN WORLD ORDER

THE NEW DEAL STATE AT WAR

In the long global perspective, the New Deal had many lives—and died just about as many deaths. It received its first blow in late 1937, when the momentum of domestic reform petered out. The outbreak of World War II less than two years later seemed to announce its death still louder, and overall the global war shifted the terrain of politics and policies in America in many new directions. This epilogue does not seek to give the full picture or do full justice to all such developments since the 1940s but instead aspires to trace the medium- and long-term effects as well as legacy of the New Deal through 1945 and beyond.

Seen from this perspective, discontinuities leap to the eye. With World War II, American society lost the markedly civilian nature that had characterized it during most of the interwar years. The concept of security, so central during the early Roosevelt administration, acquired a fundamentally different meaning, shifting from domestic welfare to international warfare. Even if insulation and isolation remained majority views until Pearl Harbor, and many Americans still believed that their country had no business getting involved in European and Asian wars, by the early 1940s a growing number started to see the global implications of the conflict and began to accept the responsibilities that it implied.

Tectonic changes were not restricted to the realm of ideas. The war gave birth to the military-industrial complex while expanding big business, big labor, big science, and big government far beyond their scope of the 1930s. Military spending not only finally ended the Great Depression but also transformed the nation. Military bases, testing ranges, and airfields were built from scratch overnight. From a state of neglect with woeful mechanized capabilities and no air force to speak of, the US military quickly turned into a global goliath, with some 12 million military personnel on active duty in 1945, as compared to the 330,000 in 1939.[1] The peacetime draft, which marked a sharp break with one of America's most cherished political traditions, was inaugurated in 1940. The federal government changed radically, dramatically increasing national duties and creating a much stronger form of national identification.[2] Besides such political and ideational factors, the buildup's impact on the economy was massive: in 1939, America concentrated less than 2 percent of its national output on war; by 1944, the number stood at 40 percent.[3] The war effort fired an economic boom, doubling the GDP between 1941 and 1945 alone; it was the biggest public works program ever in American history. The federal state played a leading role in these processes: between 1941 and 1946, Washington spent more in six years than it had during the entire period from 1789 to 1941.[4]

The war also reinforced America's global interconnections in ways unknown during the New Deal years. Arms production was not for the US armed forces alone. During the first six months of World War II, American manufacturers delivered four times as many planes to Britain and France as to the United States.[5] From 1941 on, the United States also started supplying the Soviet Union, China, and other Allies under the auspices of the Lend-Lease Program, the largest wartime foreign aid program ever implemented. Altogether, 16 percent of the total US war expenditures were shipped abroad.[6] In comparison to the hemispheric focus during the New Deal years, the United States now fortified some of its transatlantic links and other connections in the global North, too. After Pearl Harbor, America joined the global war; some scholars go as far as to argue that it was the *only* combatant to wage a global war in the literal sense, since it deployed significant forces and resources in all war theaters around the world.[7]

Business contributed greatly to this turn to the world and to the domestic boom that came with it. Under the auspices of thirty-eight-year-old Clay P. Bedford, Kaiser Industries, for example, built a gigantic shipyard in Richmond, California. This project metamorphosed a sleepy town of 24,000 into a bustling industrial city of 150,000 in the span of just three years.[8] Cities like Richmond mushroomed across the United States. The West, in particular, was revamped as during no other period of modern American history. From a colonial economy based on the extraction of raw materials and a "territory of national anxiety" after the economic and environmental crisis of the 1930s, the war catapulted the region to a diversified economy with strong industrial and technological components.[9] Complementarily, the Northeast's economic dominance subsided, underlining the depth of change.[10]

The war years also saw the advent of big labor, with trade union membership almost doubling from 6.6 million in 1939 to 12.6 million in 1945. This, however, did not suffice to match the new role of business, which was often able to press home its advantage.[11] Big science was never far behind: under the auspices of the National Defense Research Committee and other agencies, research and development increasingly filtered into the military-industrial complex. The most famous example of the new forms of cooperation was the Manhattan Project, which eventually produced the atomic bomb. Beginning modestly in 1939, it grew to employ some 130,000 staff members at a dozen sites across the United States and cost some $2 billion.[12] More than any conventional weapon, the fission bomb came to define America's and the world's future during the Cold War and beyond, while the war economy laid the foundation for postwar prosperity and the consumer society. All in all, the war unleashed important new dynamics over and above those that had characterized the New Deal.

The implications for the federal state were massive. The number of civil servants working for the federal administration exploded from 950,000 in 1939 to 2.3 million in 1942, and then 3.8 million in 1945. Federal government spending rocketed from $8.8 billion in 1939 to $34 billion in 1942, and from there to $98.3 billion in 1945. To shoulder these costs, the United States overhauled its taxation system, reaching deeper into its citizens' pockets than any American government had dared before. But not even this sufficed to foot the bill. Between 1941 and 1945, the national debt increased by more than 500 percent, and by 1945, it stood at $258 billion or approximately 120 percent of the GDP. Compared to the roller coaster of alternating fiscal conservatism and big spending that had marked the years after 1933, fiscal prudence became one of the war's first victims. Earlier accusations of the New Deal as gargantuan big government seemed ridiculous in light of this expenditure battle and the accumulated debt.[13]

Administratively, the war effort spawned a whole host of new agencies and organizations. The War Resources Board, the Office of Emergency Management, the National Defense Advisory Commission, the Office of Production Management, and its direct rival, the Office of Price Administration and Civilian Supply, all contributed to war mobilization and economic defense. While some, such as the Council on National Defense, were reactivated relics of World War I, most were new creations. Competences frequently overlapped, leading to factions and frictions, clashes and conflicts. Roosevelt still liked to create competing institutions that ultimately increased his own flexibility and reflected his genius for politics, keeping friends and foes off guard and challenging intellectual convention. In the social Darwinist world of Washington, many agencies proved short lived or were curtailed soon after creation. Efforts became somewhat more centralized in January 1942 with the War Production Board, which possessed broad authorization to exercise general direction over war procurement and production. The board under Donald M. Nelson far exceeded New Deal regulation and the short-lived NRA specifically; it became the main lever for turning the United States into the arsenal of democracy, even if its authority was substantially diluted in May 1943. Leaving all these institutional rivalries and dynamics aside, these agencies together clearly overshadowed and often curtailed the civilian priorities of the original New Deal alphabet soup.[14]

In addition, the war years consolidated the government-business partnership focused on productivity and growth that had gained momentum since the "Roosevelt recession" of 1937: instead of state-led solutions, Keynesian policies regulating demand as well as consolidating war and welfare policies slowly gained in significance. US policies in this way contributed to the international rise of Keynesianism, which was to become yet another global story.[15] In their own society, American policy makers sought to depoliticize conflicts by turning them into problems of output, for lack of a strong economic rights agenda of the social democratic variety. Hence, it was not just the number and focus of organizations that multiplied; their underlying economic theory gravitated in a new direction, too. More than anything else, corporate leverage over national governance and new military priorities distinguished the new conditions from the prewar years.[16]

War production, mobilization, military operations, and the Keynesian elements underlying some of these policies also propelled new faces into leadership, obliviating the headlines that men such as Tugwell, Moley, and NRA's Johnson had made a few years earlier. From the perspective of 1933, ex-general Johnson seemed predestined to play a central role in war mobilization; his military experience, together with his NRA credentials, guts, and hubris, outranked all others, perhaps with the sole exception of Bernard Baruch, the organizer of America's war economy during World War I. But Johnson played no part at all in the call to arms at the decade's end. He endorsed isolationism in 1939, and in 1940 supported Republican candidate Wendell L. Willkie. The Roosevelt administration had no jobs for renegades like him. Instead, a cohort of new leaders moved into the corridors of power, many of them (Republican) corporate figures, high-ranking officers, and labor representatives. They often simply seemed better qualified than Roosevelt's old hands. Before becoming chairman of the mighty War Production Board, Donald Nelson had been in public service for less than two years, and Roosevelt chose him mainly on the basis of his brilliant business career with Sears Roebuck since the 1910s. Edward Stettinius, Jr., administrator of the Lend-Lease Program, then undersecretary, and finally secretary of state, had also spent most of his career in the private sector prior to the war. Danish-born William S. Knudsen was a leading automobile industry executive before Roosevelt appointed him lieutenant general to run the procurement and production program at the War Department. No civilian had ever joined the army at such a high initial rank, even if Knudsen accepted a drop in annual salary from six figures to $8,000.[17] Across the board, the war state brought corporate leaders to the high tables of power to an astonishing extent; Roosevelt's diatribes about "money changers" and "economic royalists" seemed long forgotten. As in any war, high-ranking soldiers rose to prominence, too, with some wielding immense power during the war and postwar years, such as Chief of Staff and future secretary of state

George C. Marshall or generals like Douglas MacArthur, George Patton, and Dwight Eisenhower (the only general in the twentieth century to become US president, as compared to eleven before 1900).

Many old hands from the early New Deal years were deeply worried about the growing prominence of the War Department and other new agencies. The Office of Price Administration and Civilian Supply was an exception, since staunch New Deal planner Leon Henderson headed it. But Henderson, who spent his weekends on his boat off Annapolis fishing, singing, and drinking, soon had to learn that his ideas met strong resistance from the industrialists in the Office of Production Management. Roosevelt mediated by restricting Henderson's competences and taking a proconsumer stance.[18] In light of such defeats, Harold Ickes complained bitterly that the president "gave a clearance to Knudsen and Stettinius and they have already gone far toward creating a supergovernment."[19] Ickes, Ben Cohen, Thomas Corcoran, and others feared that the newcomers, their agencies, and the war dynamics more generally were jeopardizing the peacetime accomplishments. Ironically, it was the New Dealers who now feared supergovernment.

The president's latest metamorphosis seemed to confirm their fears. A man who had never served in uniform himself and had dedicated the bulk of his first years in office to domestic concerns now became the most active commander in chief since Abraham Lincoln. Roosevelt himself summarized this change of persona as Dr. New-Deal yielding to Dr. Win-the-War. Through the Lend-Lease Program, a reorganization of the War Department in 1942, and other steps, Roosevelt gained strong control over the US military. In this respect, administrative setup and workflow organization were hardly less important than formal authority. For instance, Roosevelt stipulated that incoming military dispatches from across the globe should be routed through the War Department, whereas outgoing messages were sent via the Navy Department. This left him as the only person in possession of a complete set of all dispatches. As before, he skillfully created, counterbalanced, and cut back ministries and agencies, but now the war outweighed all domestic concerns.[20]

The shift of priorities did not just manifest itself in new beginnings, but also in the termination of existing programs. Several New Deal agencies were discontinued. Probably the most prominent victim of the wartime economic boom was the Civilian Conservation Corps, Roosevelt's pet agency that even the *Chicago Daily Tribune*'s publisher Robert R. McCormick, a former classmate of Roosevelt's at Groton and one of his most ardent critics, called "relief at its best."[21] The increasing availability of normal jobs meant that fewer and fewer men enrolled in the corps. In mid-1942, Congress therefore decided to dissolve the CCC.[22] The National Youth Administration was wound up in 1943, as was the WPA. The same year, conser-

vatives and Congress killed the National Resources Planning Board under
FDR's uncle Frederic A. Delano.

Finally, programs similar to the original New Deal were also prone to run
into problems for electoral reasons. The 1942 midterm elections were a disaster for the Democrats. Republicans picked up forty-seven seats in the
House and nine in the Senate, and Roosevelt faced the most conservative
Congress of his presidency. Southern Democrats emerged strengthened,
further reducing the prospects of maintaining or expanding social programs. "Normalcy men," as *Fortune* magazine called them, and not New
Dealers called the shots on Capitol Hill.[23] To many reformers, it must have
seemed like the end of an era.

Hidden Continuities

That said, there were significant continuities. Many features of the New
Deal lived on or hibernated during the war. The global conflict even saved
and strengthened many existing programs that peace might have seen canceled or shelved. Most of the central periods in the building of American
statehood coincided with wars—the War of Independence, the Civil War,
World War I—and World War II was no exception. Indeed, the war necessi-
tated deeper state intervention and brought forms of planning that most
New Dealers had never imagined in their wildest dreams just a few years
earlier. This certainly holds true for the economy, but also touched intimate
areas such as gender constructions. State attempts at social control over the
body loomed large. The military, government, and other institutions worked
to overcome the crisis of masculinity of the 1930s and create a hypermasculinized ideal, reflecting the country's rising status as a world power. Mental
tests, medical screenings, fitness programs, and other efforts centered around
a white, able-bodied, and heterosexual ideal that far surpassed the paternalistic schemes of the 1930s, such as in the CCC and the CWA.[24]

Aside from such war-driven developments, the president and his administration had a clear interest in securing their achievements. They were clever
enough not to waste a crisis, cloaking their earlier programs in new, war-
related guise. The Glass-Steagall banking legislation, the REA, the Farm Security Administration, the Federal Housing Administration, and the USHA,
the TVA, the Wagner Act, and the SSB all survived the havoc of war, and
many of them operate to this day, if sometimes under new names and
brands. Roosevelt himself publicly defended this course in the first fireside
chat ever broadcast on a Sunday. In May 1940, he declared that in spite of the
need to mobilize, there should be "no breakdown or cancellation of any of
the great social gains we have made in these past years." The forty-hour week
was to be upheld, the president explained, as were labor standards such as
minimum wages, old-age pensions, and unemployment insurance.[25]

In fact, new layers of welfare statism were added. In 1939, for instance, the SSB created two new categories of benefits: payments to the spouse and minor children of retired workers, and survivor benefits paid for the family in the event of the premature death of a worker. More important, in January 1940 the SSB's payment of monthly retirement benefits commenced; after some five years of existence, the first citizens started to profit from this core pillar of New Deal welfare.[26] Beyond parlaying existing programs, the 1944 GI Bill was awash with the ideas and principles that had informed the creation and work of new agencies since 1933. Among the cornucopia of benefits it provided to World War II veterans were low-cost mortgages, low-interest loans to start a business, unemployment compensation, and cash payments for tuition and living expenses for vocational education or to attend high school and college. The federal state provided security for those who had risked their lives, intervening massively in the economic and educational realms with fundamental effects for postwar American society.

The "Bill of Rights for GI Joe and GI Jane," as the American Legion called it at the time, was even more New Dealish than the New Deal itself. This holds particularly true for its immediate target group, the veterans, as the early Roosevelt years had seen severe cuts in welfare for veterans, followed by narrowly circumscribed expansion. The war context and strong lobbying by the American Legion paved the way for an encompassing program that eventually became central for carrying the New Deal into the postwar era. For veterans—especially for white men, since the 1944 act perpetuated racial and gender discrimination—the New Deal's promises were only fulfilled long after the New Deal's tide had begun to ebb.[27]

The Roosevelt administration adhered to the peacetime institutions largely for practical and ideational reasons. At the most basic level, the military situation never became so dire as to necessitate rolling back the recently introduced quantum of welfare statism and interventionism. No city in continental America was ever strafed by the German Luftwaffe or the Imperial Japanese Navy Air Service. The total number of direct war casualties in the contiguous United States amounted to six—all victims of the same high-altitude balloon bomb carried by the jet stream from Japan's Honchu Island to the Gearhart Mountains in Oregon. The American economy remained much less intensively dedicated to the war effort than the economies of most other major combatants, and the nation's material and physical resources were never stretched to breaking point. In comparison to most other powers, Americans at home had to sacrifice and suffer little during the war years.[28]

There was also another, mundane reason: America needed to massively expand its civilian and military workforce for the war challenge. Because of this, and because of the deep economic intervention that the war effort entailed, labor's voice had to be heard; by the end of the 1930s American trade unions had simply become too strong to ignore. Sidney Hillman, a Lithuanian-born labor leader with a reputation for marshaling support for the New Deal among workers, held positions in several of the new agencies organizing the war economy. Hillman and others would never have achieved such prominent roles without the post-1933 labor legislation: government recognition, coupled with the absence of unemployment, made all the difference. The prewar Roosevelt administration thus played a crucial role in facilitating the rise of big labor during the 1940s.[29] That said, labor's role in the wartime economic system was mostly limited to advisory functions. And many labor representatives despised Hillman for his progovernment stance. In the end, the constant threat of strikes and other labor disputes was even more important in underpinning labor's new role. Severe conflicts flared up now and then, such as the 1943 coal miners' strike where almost half a million walked out. Against this backdrop, the government tried to find compromises between corporate interests and the workforce, putting pressure on employers to recognize unions. In the war effort, security concerns along with labor and business positions were constantly renegotiated. Expanding duties and obligations had to be balanced with rights and entitlements, but all these developments deepened the reciprocal relationship between state and citizens. Given the need for a strong and cooperative workforce, the Wagner Act and related provisions therefore remained basically intact. This state-interventionist course driven by the practical needs of the war economy also explains other developments, such as the work of the Fair Employment Practices Commission. From 1941 onward, it ensured that companies with government contracts did not discriminate on the basis of race or religion. In times of labor shortage, America needed all hands on deck to build its industrial and military muscle, as even the most racist patriot had to concede. This meant that the New Dealers were now confronting divisive race and labor questions more directly than during the prewar years.[30]

A third argument was rooted in economic and social dynamics. The war economy finally allowed the United States to overcome the Great Depression. The boom gave the state new legitimacy, also to expand its welfare functions. This even helped to make the past look rosier. One illustration is found in the sphere of public housing. In Nashville, for instance, no new projects were built during the war for lack of funds, even as the city experienced a growing housing shortage. Projects that had suffered problems during the prewar years were now fully occupied and ran successfully, and public perceptions became more positive. Instead of seeing the projects as expressions of "socialism," more and more Nashvillians viewed public housing "as a legitimate participant in the local political economy," as one scholar contends.[31]

As a consequence of these dynamics, continuities were strong at the level of personnel as well. New faces around Washington maybe attracted more public attention, dressed in green, khaki, blue, or gray, but the number of committed New Deal veterans in top positions remained surprisingly high. From Roosevelt's first Cabinet, Hull served continuously from 1933 until 1944, and Perkins and Ickes remained in their jobs until 1945 and 1946, respectively. Morgenthau worked as secretary of the Treasury from 1934 until the war's end. Wallace, as another veteran of Roosevelt's first Cabinet, stepped down as secretary of agriculture in 1940, only to be elected vice president of the United States. After a career with the WPA and other work relief programs and some two years as secretary of commerce, Hopkins became Roosevelt's closest adviser in 1940. He even moved into the White House and became a key player in the war effort. Altogether, the New Dealers were anything but removed from the hub of power.

Moreover, some of the new agencies and policies were grafted directly onto existing New Deal projects. Oak Ridge, a city established in 1942 as a site for the Manhattan Project, was chosen for its proximity to TVA's Norris Dam, making water and electricity readily available. The existing civilian population, approximately a thousand families, was removed (including some who had been resettled only a few years earlier when the Norris Dam was built, and who now found notices on their doors instructing them to vacate within as little as two weeks). Oak Ridge did not become the location of Project Y, the central site for developing, assembling, and testing the atomic bomb, but it was much larger than the better-known Los Alamos, and grew to seventy-five thousand inhabitants by 1945. The TVA did not just supply the project with power but also supported the US Army Corps of Engineers, which was in charge of Oak Ridge. Social engineering was writ large, leading to endless regulations: occupants of the newly built accommodations were not permitted to have liquor, gamble, or invite visitors of the opposite sex to their rooms. Like the TVA, the Manhattan Project shrank from challenging Jim Crow and established racially segregated communities. Despite the different administrative setup and historical context, Oak Ridge in many ways built on TVA developments.[32] The markedly different environment of the 1940s thus allowed some New Deal programs to put down roots.

Flying New Deal Colors

But pragmatism and the vistas of war do not explain everything. Flying the New Deal colors also made a lot of sense ideologically, and at this level the global dimension was key. During the war even more than before, the New Deal became an icon of the confrontation with fascism, militarism, and authoritarianism. Building on the debates about the American way of the late 1930s, welfare morphed into an ideological weapon: the supremacy of America and democracy would reveal itself not just in military victories but also in an exemplary political and social system. This war-hardened, internationalist consensus was so strong that even Roosevelt's adversary in the 1940 election, Wendell Willkie, refrained from calling for a repeal of the New Deal's main welfare and regulatory programs, instead only claiming he could make them more efficient and effective.[33] Four years later, General MacArthur's presidential ambitions were quickly crushed when Congressman Arthur L. Miller released correspondence showing that MacArthur strongly opposed the New Deal legacy.[34] Such a stance was a nonstarter. Even if many conservatives continued to accuse the Roosevelt administration of being fascist or communist, some previously contested choices were now outside the main battle zone of domestic policy debate.

Minority groups and others who exposed the contradictions between their sacrifices as soldiers and citizens during the war and the discrimination they faced at home contributed to consolidating this critical thread of New Deal reform. In 1942, for example, the African American *Pittsburgh Courier* launched the Double V Campaign for victory over fascism abroad and victory over racial inequality at home.[35] The creation of the Fair Employment Practices Committee was primarily a response to such debates. Admittedly, the commission left Jim Crow in the South untouched, and as during the prewar years, the New Dealers mainly instituted temporary agencies with constrained powers to ease intergroup conflicts, while shying away from radical reform. Yet these temporary tools did reduce some forms of discrimination, and overall the FDR administration did more to correct racial injustice than any other post–Civil War presidency.

While change remained partial, pressure from below made government representatives reflect on the need to satisfy rising expectations. After race riots in Detroit in 1943—which the Japanese war propaganda used as evidence of American racism and insincerity—Vice President Wallace argued that the nation "cannot fight to crush Nazi brutality abroad and condone race riots at home."[36] This was consistent, but such statements also reacted to the decades-old admiration for Japan among African Americans—grounded in the Asian country's role in exposing Western racial hypocrisy.[37] Some liberal intellectuals, such as those organized in the Union for Democratic Action led by theologian Reinhold Niebuhr, advocated liberal policies and the expansion of democratic values at home as well as overseas in ways more radical than many New Dealers deemed realistic.[38] Overall, the Roosevelt administration was pursuing no master plan for the war to help save domestic reforms. The dynamics were much more complex instead. In the end, though, the war fostered the New Deal ideals of welfare and the regulatory state. Some of the core tenets developed a self-binding quality; confronting the lofty ideals that legitimized the war effort with the inner inconsistencies of American society in the end helped to solidify the New Deal reforms.

How, then, to summarize what the war did to the New Deal? In an anti-Vietnam speech in 1967, Martin Luther King Jr. enumerated the victims of the conflict, among them the domestic reform programs of the incumbent president, Lyndon B. Johnson. According to King, "the promises of the Great Society have been shot down on the battlefield of Vietnam."[39] World War II had the opposite effect on the New Deal. It clearly survived the conflict. However war driven the new context was, it continued and reinforced some of the core tenets of the New Deal, such as strong state action along with a focus on welfare, regulation, and security. While all these ideas became filled with new meaning, the war also permeated and preserved many of the characteristics as well as creations of the peacetime years. Basically, the new wartime agencies and dynamics worked like prairie schooners circling around the original New Deal institutions. And like prairie schooners under attack, the war helped to compress the disjointed elements that had been created since 1933 under the heading of the New Deal into a more consistent whole. Put differently, looking back from the 1940s everything began to appear consistent and convincing—at least to some. The war boom, the GI Bill, and other benefits made it easier to overlook the New Deal's inability to fully overcome the Great Depression. In retrospect, its relief and welfare state mechanisms stood out, while its insulationist streak, its moves toward an activist managerial state, and its many contradictions started to fade. It was the war, in this sense, that actually *made* the New Deal.

Recharting the Atlantic

The war also strengthened another tendency that had begun in the second half of the 1930s: a growing multilateral commitment now culminated in ideas of fully internationalizing aspects of the New Deal, applying the lessons of the Great Depression, and avoiding a repetition of the mistakes that Wilson made at the end of World War I, as Elizabeth Borgwardt has convincingly argued.[40]

"Somewhere in the Atlantic," as the British prime minister explained in a BBC broadcast a few days later, Roosevelt and Churchill sealed their wartime alliance at a secret meeting in August 1941.[41] Shuttling between British and American battleships off the Newfoundland coast at Placentia Bay, the two statesmen produced an eight-point joint declaration that soon became known as the Atlantic Charter. The document stressed that the partners aspired not to territorial aggrandizement but rather to the disarmament of aggressor nations and the restoration of self-government. Furthermore, it called for self-determination, free trade, and more global cooperation to improve economic and social conditions.[42]

Several months before Pearl Harbor, Washington highlighted its internationalism. Although the declaration broke with the tradition of international aloofness, it did not start from zero. While neither inevitable nor natural, it was the "culmination of the remarkable mass of published programmes, both by individuals and organizations," as one Australian expert put it at the time.[43] In the American context, for instance, the Atlantic Charter harked back to Roosevelt's January 1941 State of the Union address in which he had proclaimed four essential freedoms—freedom of speech and expression, freedom of worship, freedom from want, and freedom from fear—adding mantralike after each that they ought to apply "everywhere in the world."[44]

Admittedly, neither Roosevelt's speech nor the charter provided a blueprint for the postwar order, and its applicability was disputed from the start. British hopes that Placentia Bay would include a strong line on a new international organization to shape the postwar order remained unfulfilled. Fearing a repetition of Wilson's disaster with the League of Nations and mindful of isolationists at home, Roosevelt preferred a vague formulation, and no concrete organizational arrangements were decided on.

Internationally, the charter also failed to achieve central aims. Neither Berlin nor Rome was particularly impressed or frightened. The charter even became a model for the Joint Declaration of the Greater East Asia Conference, concluded by Japan and its Asian allies in fall 1943, which called for a postwar international order under Japanese leadership and was awash in universalistic claims, just like its Western homologue. Instead of intimidating its enemies, the Atlantic Charter spurred the conflict of ideologies.[45] Disappointment was the dominant mood in Britain, where many had hoped for a clearer sign of American commitment. Sending the prime minister across a submarine-infested Atlantic and getting a few lofty paragraphs in return did not sound like a success. And in the United States itself, the charter did not swing the pendulum of public opinion away from isolationism either.

In the medium term, however, the sparse 312 words of the charter broke free from their original context and became a touchstone for America's war aims.[46] Ideas with a strong New Deal pedigree gained international traction in this way. Clause five, for example, called for cooperation toward "securing, for all, improved labor standards, economic advancement and social security."[47] While the British wanted to go even further, American support for such a line would have been inconceivable without the New Deal experience. The Atlantic Charter had several diverging objectives, but included the idea of translating domestic welfare approaches and institutions, with their focus on economic well-being, to the international level.

Building on the four freedoms speech and Atlantic Charter, Roosevelt soon substantiated his commitment to globalize the New Deal. A much less famous speech made history in the small world of transatlantic internationalism. On November 6, 1941, the president of the United States directly addressed a League of Nations organization for the first time. In remarks concluding an ILO conference at Columbia University, Roosevelt stressed the accomplishments of the ILO, especially during the "long years of de-

FIGURE 7. President Roosevelt looks at a map, 1942.

pression," and briefly mentioned its recent move from Geneva to North America as a safe harbor in light of Europe's turmoil. He emphasized that "there can be no real freedom for the common man without enlightened social policies. In the last analysis, they are the stakes for which democracies are today fighting." Not only did he argue that the ILO should play a key role in postwar planning along these lines; he also committed the United States to such an internationalist undertaking.[48]

Besides their internationalist credo, two things were remarkable about these declarations. For one, the Atlantic Charter and Roosevelt's speeches concentrated not just on the traditional civil and political rights that had driven liberal democracies since the age of revolutions. Instead, they added the layer of economic rights, such as the right to food, shelter, and employment. Not only was this a departure from most internationalist commitments of the 1920s, driven by intense global negotiations in the ILO in the course of the 1930s.[49] It also stands in marked contrast to the Cold War parlance that denounced such concerns as Marxist propaganda from the late 1940s onward. For another, these texts treated the individual as the ultimate object of protection by the international community—as if states and their sovereign rights did not exist. While arguing for a wider governmental role in establishing individual security domestically, the internationalization of the agenda went as far as to challenge conventional multilateralism.

It implied the will to curb national authority in favor of international coop-eration and, if necessary, intervention. The economic rights dimension of this vision was soon to be buried under the Cold War confrontation and the return to a more individualistic notion of capitalism. Its humanitarian elements, on the other hand, formed the backdrop to many post-1945 de-velopments, including intervention in Somalia in the 1990s and Libya in 2011.[50]

Put differently, the new course was everything that democrats around the world had hoped for from America back in 1933. During the fight against the Great Depression, the New Dealers had not lived up to such interna-tional expectations. By the early 1940s, they started to embrace internation-alist ideas more fully. Besides consolidating ties with the United Kingdom, the Atlantic Charter was quickly and widely endorsed by the Allied nations. Its visions soon found their way into three sets of international organiza-tions, too, as Elizabeth Borgwardt has demonstrated: the UN system, the IMF and the World Bank, and the Nuremberg trials. The United States thus played a major role in redefining the international order by trying to pro-ject the principles of the New Deal regulatory state onto the world.[51] In other words, America's domestic agenda from the 1930s was central to giv-ing substance to the United States' postwar role.

A Global Mission

Psychologically, the New Dealers fully overcame the sense of lagging be-hind along with the defensiveness that had colored some of their earlier parlance and programs. Exceptionalism now had its day, and America's mis-sion *in* the world turned into a mission *for* the world: Vice President Wal-lace, the best-known internationalist on the American Left, maintained that it was

> destiny that calls us to world leadership. When we as victors lay down our arms in this struggle against the enslavement of the mind and soul of the human family, we take up arms immediately in the great war against starvation, unemployment and the rigging of the markets of the world.[52]

Along similar lines, Undersecretary of State Welles, as someone deeply committed to long-term postwar planning, believed that World War II was a revolutionary event that would lead to a world reformed under American guidance.[53] Freda Kirchwey, editor of the *Nation*, argued in 1944 that "only a New Deal for the world, more far-reaching and consistent than our own faltering New Deal, can prevent the coming of World War III."[54] Her views went even beyond the concerns of FDR himself, who was more worried about the war than about a possible postwar order. For him, "winning the war" had to come "before we do much general planning for the future."[55]

Civil society actors in general often outpaced government officials in preaching the global New Deal gospel, and experts from abroad joined them in this.[56] In 1943, for instance, Romanian-born British political theorist David Mitrany asserted that the New Deal had "revolutionized the American political system" and that it now had to be applied to international government.[57] All in all, an American view coalesced in the course of the war years; national economic and wartime goals merged entirely. The new mantra held that the United States bore global responsibility and should aim to globalize the New Deal. Antecedents to this missionary-like belief go back to the founding of the republic, but it had never been so self-consciously statist, consistent, or far reaching as its high modernist version of the early 1940s.

Some scholars have contended that the United States transposed its domestic agenda to foreign affairs because it was less experienced in diplomacy than major European powers, where foreign policy had a richer tradition that made it more independent from domestic concerns. In America, in contrast, the boundaries between the two spheres were more permeable.[58] While that is true, one should not overlook the strong transnational pedigree of those concepts and ideas that were now flagged as domestic and American. The United States basically started promoting notions that had been around in global reform debates for quite some time; they were now repackaged and colored in stars and stripes.

Such ideas and policies were partly driven by noble aspirations and largesse but also often took a position of moral superiority and missionary zeal. Soon the New Dealers had to confront their own inconsistencies and hypocrisy. The Atlantic Charter, for instance, was a shot heard around the world, and reached ears for which it was not meant. The hopes of African activists that an Allied victory would end colonialism were quickly dashed. After his safe return to Britain, Churchill clarified that self-government meant Europe. Washington, despite its perfunctory criticism of British imperialism, did not disagree.[59] In response, African activists such as Nigerian Nnamdi Azikiwe scolded the Atlantic powers; in India, Mahatma Gandhi argued that the Allied declaration sounded "hollow, so long as India and, for that matter, Africa are exploited by Great Britain, and America has the Negro problem in her own home."[60] In the United States, W.E.B. Du Bois voiced similar criticism, while the National Association for the Advancement of Colored People tried to use the charter in its fight against racial segregation. White intellectuals such as Kirchwey and novelist Pearl Buck also joined the discussion.[61] Along with many of the aspirations and ideas of the domestic New Deal, its inbuilt tensions and incongruities were also transposed to the international level.

In addition to its strong North Atlantic dimension, US policy had crucial hemispheric components. While the social policy components of the internationalized New Deal agenda only came to full fruition vis-à-vis Europe at the end of the war, efforts were launched much earlier in various parts of Latin America. Given the global situation, a hemispheric approach was the New Dealers' "only available opening" for internationalism, as Irwin Gellman showed long ago.[62] That said, there was never a single new deal for Latin America—simply because a single New Deal had never existed in the first place, because the various agencies in Washington continued to disagree during the 1940s, and because the precise gestalt of interaction and impact also depended on Latin Americans themselves. Latin America policy nonetheless was clearly taken into an untrodden direction. Washington now started to cooperate more with Britain on problems of Latin American commerce and economy, thereby relativizing the hemispheric unilateralism of the interwar years.[63] Even more important, new instruments and ideas shaped Washington's relations with its southern neighbors. In July 1941, Roosevelt established the Office of the Coordinator of Inter-American Affairs (OCIAA) and appointed businessman and philanthropist Nelson A. Rockefeller as its head. The office bought agricultural commodities and mineral products to stabilize Latin American markets as well as protect US military and economic interests. The OCIAA became a channel for propaganda activities, too. In that sense, its policies remained rather conventional and were "dictated by war considerations," as Rockefeller maintained a few years after the war.[64] But the OCIAA also engaged in measures of a different kind: it undertook infrastructure projects, furnishing technical assistance along with contributing part of the costs of new railroads and waterways. There were health and food programs as well that focused particularly on areas or groups of strategic interest to the United States. Despite their circumscribed character, these projects turned into laboratories for applying the New Deal internationally. In contrast to the philanthropic programs implemented prior to the war, the US government now became a major welfare actor, in this way complementing—and by no means supplanting—the nongovernmental organizations and business corporations that had long been active south of the Rio Grande.[65]

Vice President Wallace, whose predecessor had described the second-highest public office in the nation as "not worth a pitcher of warm piss," also chose Latin America as his preferred playground.[66] Roosevelt supported him and made him the first vice president to possess real administrative authority. As chairman of the Board of Economic Warfare (yet another war mobilization and economic defense agency), Wallace intervened even more deeply in domestic Latin American matters than Rockefeller's OCIAA. He introduced "labor clauses" in contracts with Latin American suppliers, compelling producers contracted by the US government to pay fair wages and provide safe working conditions. In return, the United States agreed to pay half the costs of the required improvements. Money and regulations were not the only means. In Bolivia, for example, Wallace's board intervened directly in a work conflict in December 1942, after the "Catavi massacre," where the Bolivian Army shelled a peaceful demonstration of workers, killing several hundred. Since Washington was the main purchaser of the tin mined at Catavi and the resource was deemed to be of vital military significance, Washington insisted on creating the Joint Bolivian-US Labor Commission. Judge Calvert Magruder, a former colleague of Louis Brandeis who now served on the US Court of Appeals for the First Circuit, headed the commission. Moreover, American labor representatives lobbied heavily in favor of their southern counterparts. Since the Bolivian mine owners and government were too weak to withstand this pressure, labor-friendly clauses found their way into the new contract. Instead of red-necked marines, Bolivians and other Latin Americans now had to deal with well-meaning, Harvard-trained liberal reformers such as Magruder, who insisted not only on US economic and military interests but also on welfare and better working conditions for Latin Americans.[67] For some, this was the latest form of imperialism; for others, it characterized the brief moment in which American reformers from both the United States and Latin America agreed on Pan-Americanism with a social democratic bent.[68]

Such measures were complemented by programs that had already been created before the war: the United States reinforced its efforts to thwart Axis purchases of raw materials and other commodities in Latin America and to direct them to the northern half of the hemisphere instead. Intense diplomatic negotiations culminated in an inter-American conference in Rio de Janeiro in January 1942 where most Latin American countries agreed to such a policy. In return, Undersecretary of State Sumner Welles committed the United States to the economic development of Latin America, thus augmenting the approach of Rockefeller, Wallace, and others.[69]

The wartime surge of intervention in Latin America massively deepened the economic, military, and political ties between the United States and Latin America; it also reinforced US hegemony in the Western Hemisphere. Still, many of these bonds remained patchy, paternalistic, and periled. Their most problematic aspects violated human rights standards, antagonized Latin Americans, and challenged the cherished ideals of Good Neighborism by intruding on the sovereignty of other states. For instance, the United States created and enforced a blacklist of German companies and nationals south of the Rio Grande. Like US companies, Latin American firms were asked to boycott all included on the list. This did take some Nazis off the streets. Since US Americans compiled and handled these lists carelessly and unilaterally, however, innocent people and even Jewish refugees were affected as well. Latin Americans greatly resented this infringement of sovereignty. The patronizing dimension of economic warfare therefore led, as Max Paul Friedman has argued, to a demise of Good Neighborism already during the war years and paralleled the state-induced form of discrimination that Japanese American internment brought domestically.[70] The new intensity of hemispheric contacts led Brazilian foreign minister Osvaldo Aranha, cofounder of the pro-US Sociedade Amigos da América, to crack wearily, "One more good-will mission and Brazil will declare war on the U.S.A."[71] Others were not just sardonic but also truly offended and infuriated. Double standards, such as wartime cooperation with dictators like Brazil's Vargas, further discredited the United States and led many Latin Americans to see it as an imperialist power that did not live up to its self-proclaimed ideals.

A GLOBAL LEGACY

The postwar constellation provided yet another opportunity to fundamentally question the nation's political direction. Roosevelt was dead. The Axis powers' hope that his demise would lead to the kind of miracle that had saved Prussia almost two hundred years earlier, after Empress Elizabeth of Russia passed away, remained unfulfilled. Germany and Japan were defeated, along with their allies. The Great Depression had been fully overcome, and an entire decade had elapsed since the heyday of the New Deal. Harry Truman, the new president, was a man of unknown qualities. Conservatives in both parties, many of whom had long cultivated their anger toward the New Deal, now dominated Congress. In sum, the auspices for the New Deal were far from favorable.

Historian Arthur Schlesinger Jr. nevertheless noted in 1949 that he was living in "a New Deal country," and expected "that it will continue to be a New Deal country."[72] Indeed, the Democrats remained the majority party until 1952, and the New Deal coalition continued until the late 1960s. While some scholars see Lyndon B. Johnson's Great Society as the New Deal's "last hurrah," others contend that the wider New Deal order only came to an end in 1981, when Ronald Reagan assumed office, even if culturally many Americans had turned to free market economics already during the decade before.[73] More specifically, quite a bit of the unfinished business of the 1930s was completed during the very years when Schlesinger was writing. In 1949, the federal role in public and private housing was expanded massively. The next year, the most glaring holes that had made the original Social Security Act look like a Swiss cheese were filled. Beyond these specific initiatives, New Deal liberals pushed to systematically expand domestic reform measures, such as introducing guaranteed work and a federal health insurance system. Later presidents, including Kennedy and Johnson, deepened this agenda. Even if at times embracing the social welfare agenda associated with FDR seemed more a question of memory than of priority, Kennedy's Peace Corps has been described as the CCC going

global. Many programs of Johnson's Great Society also qualify as direct de-
scendants of the New Deal, such as in the areas of housing, support for the
arts, and aid to education. While also bearing the imprint of their times and
transcending the New Deal's concerns—for instance, in civil rights—these
programs were powerfully linked to the Roosevelt years and their legacy.

Such continuities at the domestic level have been described many times
and hence deserve no further attention in this short epilogue. Something
else is more important when seen from a global perspective: all this had the
potential to make the United States part of the social democratic experiment that swept through capitalist nation-states across the industrialized
world during the early postwar era. The war's sacrifices had spurred a mood
of change: the rediscovery of democracy in much of Western Europe went
hand in hand with a mixed economy model. Many states now embraced
planning and intervention to an extent unknown during the interwar years.
Former French premier Léon Blum summarized this atmosphere: "A weak
and perverted bourgeois democracy has collapsed, and must be replaced by
a true democracy ... this popular democracy will be, indeed can only be, a
Social Democracy."[74]

In the United States, such radical plans never materialized. Compared to
the ten new federal agencies created between 1933 and 1939, only four
more were established between 1940 and 1960.[75] With the military budget
roughly tripling between 1949 and 1951 alone, Cold War considerations
came to dominate most other issues under the auspices of the national security state. These new priorities also impacted on the legacy of the Roosevelt
era. There was the Taft-Hartley Act of 1947, a conscious effort to retrench the
gains made by trade unions during the New Deal. Truman initially strongly
opposed the legislation, which trade unionists called the "slave-labor" bill—
but subsequently used it several times during his presidency.[76] His Fair Deal
accumulated a mixed domestic legislative record—at least when measured
against expectations and the trajectory of the New Deal.[77]

The postwar political climate witnessed a substantial shift of the American debate in a rapidly changing world of global connections. Isolationists
from the interwar years mostly stuck to their old convictions, with Senator
Vandenberg as one of the rare exceptions. Postwar anticommunism built on
nativist countersubversive ideas dating back to the turn of the century. Various congressional committees, most prominently the Dies Committee, had
been stoking anticommunism long before 1945. Such sentiment not only
became more radical and hysterical with the advent of the Cold War; it also
identified new enemies. Fear of nuclear war and "internal subversion" overshadowed domestic discussions, penalizing undemocratic behavior along
with many positions that were merely unorthodox. Quite a few advocates of
regulatory and redistributive policies were now removed from the political
scene amid accusations of Soviet espionage and infiltration. Compared to

the intellectual openness characteristic of the early 1930s, the second half of the 1940s saw political discussion infested with taboos.[78]

At a more fundamental level, the sense of emergency and insecurity that had promoted unconventional ideas during the Great Depression was now replaced by regained self-confidence. The "laggard nation," as Armstrong had called the United States back in 1932, was now the richest and dominant geoeconomic power. It was unchallenged in world finance, investment, and trade. Its popular culture became a global vernacular. Unlike all other participating nations, America emerged from the global conflict stronger than it had entered. Europe, from which it had drawn so much inspiration since the Progressive era, was devastated and poor, and its political solutions were delegitimized. Some American liberals still tried to relate to reformers elsewhere and, for instance, carefully scrutinized the British Beveridge report. Beyond such small circles, however, a new tone of self-centered superiority drove US debates, insisting that little could be learned from welfare schemes in Europe, Australia, or elsewhere. Transnational inspirations and citations, so important for the New Deal experience, receded to the margins.[79]

Laggard Rebound

This new historical context and mind-set did not entail any reduction of interconnectedness. The end of World War II was the apogee of twentieth-century internationalism. Around the globe, the popularity of international solutions surged.[80] These dynamics also impacted the United States. Visits abroad are but one indicator. In 1957, some 1.5 million Americans traveled internationally, excluding Canada and Mexico, compared to an average of 400,000 per year during the 1930s. Alongside the 1.1 million servicemen stationed overseas, another 100,000 civilians lived abroad during the late 1950s—a third of them on government contracts.[81] Under the surface of such global connections, the postwar era saw a reversal of transnational streams. Instead of tending to sit on the receiving end of transfers, many Americans now saw themselves as pioneers and standard-bearers on issues such as welfare and economic regulation, with a message to spread around the world. US institutions and culture impacted on the world like never before. This had clear consequences for the global legacy of the New Deal, even if Cold War considerations soon dominated many agendas, with security concerns uppermost.

Amid the convoys of ideas and programs that steamed to all four corners of the world, some vessels had an apparent New Deal bent. This holds especially true with regard to the losers of World War II. The American zone of occupation in divided Germany turned into a Puerto Rico writ large. So did Japan. Both defeated societies served as social laboratories, and while parts of the agenda, such as the punishment of war crimes and military concerns, had no particular New Deal pedigree, the economic agenda of American administrators certainly did. "The roots of democracy," President Truman contended in 1946, "will not draw much nourishment in any nation from a soil of poverty and economic distress. It is part of our strategy of peace, therefore, to assist in the rehabilitation and development."[82] In line with this, political radicalism was seen as the direct result of poverty. Some went so far as to reduce Hitler, Hirohito, and their ilk to products of the Great Depression. Liberalism's old belief that capitalism was incompatible with social reform was overturned; instead, democracy seemed to hinge on material improvement and economic rights.[83]

Transposing this experience to the global level and being driven by Cold War considerations, people in postwar Washington believed in the need to create a viable international economy to stabilize friendly governments and keep them from gravitating toward communism and other forms of radicalism. This policy was driven less by philanthropic considerations than by the conviction that America's own freedom ultimately depended on a propitious international environment. In a nutshell, the prosperity of others served American security.[84]

Alternative plans for defeated nations did exist, but they remained marginal. Ironically, the most prominent advocate of the idea of stripping Germany of its industrial capacity, Treasury Secretary Morgenthau, was a New Dealer of sorts. His radical ideas never came true, and only supplied the Nazis with arguments for anti-American propaganda until 1945. The idea of transposing the New Deal approach to defeated and allied countries alike dominated among US policy makers. In Germany, for instance, US government representatives and trade unionists worked to foster the consensus liberalism that had emerged from the New Deal. In Japan, agricultural reforms including cooperatives and land redistribution reflected the most progressive tendencies of the FDR years.[85] Rural sociologist Arthur F. Raper is an example of this nexus: during the 1930s, he worked in the USDA's Bureau of Agricultural Economics— a hotbed of communitarian thinking advocating community building at the local level. In the postwar years, Raper was busy helping to plan land reform in occupied Japan, and tried to transplant some of his earlier ideas into the new context.[86]

Beyond the occupation and reconstruction of the former Axis countries, the United States came to promote its labor and welfare programs globally. Driven by the New Deal experience, American intellectuals felt that they could define modernity—not just as a concept, but also as a template for organizing the world with strong welfare components. Modernization theory soon offered a full rationalization of high modernist ideas: societies could transition from one stage of economic and societal development to the next; even "Third World" countries, as they came to be known at the time, could find their way to prosperity as long as they kept to the path of industrialization and democratization.[87] This approach, which had dominated the New Deal, held the upper hand in America's engagement with the wider world over approaches that focused on communitarianism, enabling village-level democracy, and "thinking small."

Illustrations come from a wide variety of policy areas and agencies. Building on first advances in this direction during the 1930s and cooperation with the ILO, the SSB's Arthur J. Altmeyer traveled the world, and the US program became a model for other countries including Bolivia, Columbia, Mexico, Panama, Japan, and Canada.[88] From an expert on European public housing, Charles "Chuck" Palmer morphed into a consultant in Latin America and elsewhere, and advised the United Nations on housing issues.[89] And rather than taking their cue from Europe, city planners in Brazil and other parts of Latin America increasingly turned to the United States.[90] Simultaneously, the TVA's Lilienthal surpassed all others in promoting his agency as a blueprint for the world. Alongside such state actors, US trade unionists, experts employed by philanthropic organizations, and many others joined the chorus. The AFL, for instance, spearheaded trade union activism in postfascist Italy, supported the labor movement in Algeria, and sought to shape labor unions in Latin America based on the New Deal model. From a country with a relatively weak trade unionist streak—at least by European standards—the United States turned into a standard-bearer of workers' rights.[91]

Apart from these proponents of New Deal ideas, other vessels brought indirect lessons from America's 1930s. Besides the concepts of regulation and redistribution that had loomed comparatively large in the first years after 1933, the Keynesian lessons from the "Roosevelt recession" of 1937 served as inspiration for other programs focused more on productivity and economic growth. This reflected less the axioms of the New Deal, and instead the ambivalences and stalemate it had found itself in during the prewar years along with the ways that the United States had tried to overcome domestic problems. Having sailed alongside programs with a more interventionist streak, consensus capitalism soon became America's flagship—not least because it turned into the dominant approach domestically.[92]

In addition to bilateral advice and intervention, the United States was deeply committed to setting up a new international system of economic governance. As a lesson from the disasters of the interwar years, it finally agreed to assume Britain's traditional role as a lender of last resort. America also played a crucial role in giving birth to an alphabet soup of intergovernmental organizations—particularly the United Nations, the IMF, and the World Bank.[93] Such work was complemented and consolidated with the creation of GATT in 1947 and the North Atlantic Treaty Organization (NATO) two years later, which represented a response to the failures of international economic and security governance during the interwar years. The vulnerable delusion of self-sufficiency, so central in the United States and across the world after World War I, gave way to a fuller understanding of the world's interconnectedness. This reflected a consensus over the lessons of the Great Depression: economic prosperity and political stability were inextricably linked, and the state held a responsibility to ensure at least a minimum level of welfare for its citizens. Such ideas were not only the new creed in the United States but also had parallels in Europe and elsewhere—for instance, with the Briton William Beveridge, Swedish Per Albin Hansson, György Lukács from Hungary, and Ishibashi Tanzan in Japan arguing similarly to the New Dealers.[94]

Still, many postwar programs reflected New Deal *hopes* more than actual New Deal *politics*. The negotiations on free trade that the United States promoted under the auspices of GATT and other organizations represented a continuation of Hullianism—but Hullianism had not dominated the early New Deal years. The IMF, as the solution to international monetary cooperation, combined the international stability of a gold standard with the national flexibility of managed currencies. Roosevelt's unilateral and capricious monetary policy of the 1930s served more as negative foil than a point of inspiration. Reeducation and heavy-handed forms of social engineering were reminiscent of agencies such as the RA, TVA, or Puerto Rico's PRERA, but in those cases, planning of national resources had ultimately overshadowed more radical impulses to remake society. The same holds true of the community-building approach of Kennedy's Peace Corps, which was closer to the hopes of New Deal communitarians such as Arthur E. Morgan and the Bureau of Agricultural Economics than to most New Deal action.

Beyond issues particularly close to the New Deal agenda, US global commitment was sometimes ambivalent. On matters of security, the United States first seemed to return to an inward-looking, insulationist perspective. Many Americans had no desire to maintain substantial military forces overseas, accept strategic commitments, or replace European colonial powers in large parts of the Third World. Only Britain's inability to guarantee Western security in Europe and beyond and increasing tensions with America's former brother in arms, the Soviet Union, dragged the United States back into the world. Massive military engagement in what was then labeled the free world, development aid programs under Truman's so-called Point Four Program, and many other instruments came to drive American foreign policy, especially after 1947.[95] The Marshall Plan, launched in 1947, fused the prosperity and welfare agenda with the new security and Cold War concerns. During the war, the challenge of the Axis powers had saved and started to internationalize the New Deal. The Cold War now came to play that role at a fully global level, while also shifting the multilateral commitment dominant around 1945 toward a superpower position.[96]

As before, the New Deal offered more than one way to carry out reform. Its precise substance remained unclear and contested. Americans felt, for instance, that their system of agriculture was a model for the world, but had different ideas about what exactly made it so special. For some, it was ownership patterns based on small farms, for others it was TVA-style regional planning, and for a third group, it was bottom-up cooperative action. Keynesian concepts fought less interventionist approaches, with both camps citing America's 1930s to back their line of argument. Similar conflicts characterized trade, industrial, and other policies.[97]

On race, the balance was particularly mixed. The war and postwar years expanded opportunities for African Americans and other minorities, thus continuing the trend since 1933 that had seen some first chinks in the armor of racial segregation and discrimination. But the 1940s also perpetuated the tainted aspects of the New Deal, especially state-sanctioned forms of racism. Leaders such as Du Bois criticized the lack of attention to questions of race in the negotiations leading to the creation of the United Nations, and indeed the new global agenda often reflected the racist biases of the domestic policies of the 1930s.[98] Many African American GIs were appalled by the racism they encountered at home, but also, for example, in Great Britain, despite their patriotism and valor. It came as a bitter irony that defeated Germans displayed less explicit racism than their own white superiors and peers. For historian David Brion Davis, who served as a (white) military policeman in early postwar Germany, "the most traumatic and shocking events" were not "pulverized cities" or "escaped SS officers" but instead "American racial conflict."[99] Some black GIs even deserted in the hope of finding a better life in the Soviet Union. Engagement with the world thus exposed the problems of American politics that the New Deal had failed to address effectively. Ironically, this also explains why in occupied Japan, African American soldiers frequently came to share the racialized attitudes toward Asians they knew from their white compatriots.[100] Moreover, such ambiguities explain why the wider world continued to have a strong impact on the United States, such as by fueling the civil rights movement during the postwar era and convincing White House officials that domestic discrimination was a liability for America's image abroad.[101]

As the outcome of a long and winding process, Americans showed a growing willingness and capacity to engage with the world as well as accept and even seek global leadership. After having refused globalism by repudiating the gold standard, the World Court, free trade, and so many other things in favor of national and hemispheric insulation during most of the 1930s, they now drew different lessons from the recent past. America's vulnerability to external and global threats, symbolized by Pearl Harbor and the challenge of radical ideologies in general, was one. For another, the New Deal experience infused Americans with the confidence that strong state action—domestically as well as internationally—could remedy the world's problems. In this sense, the United States was now ready to pursue global power on Exceptionalist terms, and many officials, publicists, experts, and businessmen wanted to refashion the world in America's image. Under the catchword "modernization," a state-based form of Progressivism with its roots in the New Deal and certain Keynesian elements penetrated other countries more deeply than ever before. Economic intervention, reeducation, and other variants of social engineering and planning became central to the projection of American power. The approach remained asymmetrical, expansive, and missionary. While it supported democracy and fostered economic growth in some quarters, the United States also exacerbated political tensions, including the Cold War confrontation with the Eastern Bloc. Initially, economic rights figured prominently on the agenda, but over time the less controversial politics of productivity took center stage.[102] America's global role was partly thrust upon it, and partly it resulted from learning processes during the New Deal and World War II years.

Internationalists by Stroke of Fate

Who were the people engaged in the global New Deal? After the war, quite a few of Roosevelt's closest advisers and allies were either dead or serving as judges or university professors. Hopkins passed away in early 1946; New York's Fiorello La Guardia followed him to the grave a year later. Hugh Johnson and George W. Norris had already perished during the war, and economist John Commons died at eighty-two in May 1945. Tugwell, the man whom the *Chicago Daily Tribune* once advised "to limit himself to words of four syllables and less," taught political science at the University of Chicago.[103] Donald Richberg lectured on law at the University of Virginia, and Milton Eisenhower pursued a particularly bright university career, crowned by the presidencies of Kansas State University, Pennsylvania State University, and finally Johns Hopkins University. Felix Frankfurter, Thurman Arnold, and Robert H. Jackson were prominent judges. Already in 1943, Sumner Welles, intimate friend of the Roosevelts who had often overshadowed Cordell Hull as his boss at the helm of the State Department, had stumbled over allegations of homosexuality—a behavior criminally prosecuted at the time. Welles spent most of the rest of his life out of the public eye, depressed and drinking heavily.

Many others were alive, sober, and ready to answer the call to internationalism. A surprisingly large number of inveterate New Dealers soon staffed the nascent international platforms and gave them an unmistakable bent reminiscent of the post-1933 domestic reforms. Importantly, most of them moved from welfare *state* building during the 1930s to becoming key architects of globalism in the next decade. This process already started during the war. From managing FERA, Hopkins became one of the American fathers of the Lend-Lease Program.[104] Benjamin Cohen, one of Frankfurter's many disciples, whose main credentials to that date had also been domestic, supported Hopkins. This did not keep Cohen from becoming a member of the American delegation to the 1944 Dumbarton Oaks Conference that prepared the ground for the United Nations. Nor did it prevent him from participating in the Potsdam Conference on the establishment of a postwar order in 1945, and from 1948 onward in the UN General Assembly in Paris.[105] Roosevelt appointed his confidant, Herbert H. Lehman, Democratic governor of New York from 1933 to 1942, as director of the State Department's Foreign Relief and Rehabilitation Operations. Soon after, Lehman helped American liberalism to cross the "Rubicon" of becoming "irreversibly internationalist in outlook and perspective," as he himself described it. More precisely, Lehman served as director general of the UN Relief and Rehabilitation Administration (UNRRA) from 1943 to 1946—when New York's La Guardia succeeded him for a few months.[106] Roosevelt's wife, Eleanor, is another example. As First Lady, she had an impact on social policy and, for instance, helped to improve the situation of African Americans. After her husband's death in 1945, President Truman appointed her as a delegate to the UN General Assembly, where she chaired the committee that drafted the Universal Declaration of Human Rights—a document with a genuinely universal claim, but also deep commitments to an American vision of how human rights were to be defined.[107]

Less well-known figures followed similar trajectories. Agriculture expert "Zeke" Ezekiel, one of the AAA's spiritual fathers, helped to organize the Hot Springs Food Conference in 1943. He later worked for the UN Food and Agriculture Organization (FAO) and US Agency for International Development.[108] Kenneth Holland, education director at the CCC, headed the OCIAA's educational division during the war, and after 1945 worked first for the State Department, then for the UN Educational, Scientific, and Cultural Organization, and finally presided over the private nonprofit Institute of International Education.[109] Milton P. Siegel had earned his spurs at the Iowa Emergency Relief Administration, from where he was recruited by the USDA. He joined Lehman at UNRRA in 1943, before moving on to high positions in the World Health Organization.[110] UNRRA also employed Charlotte Tuttle Westwood, a New Deal lawyer with leftist ideas.[111] Norris E. Dodd, the FAO's director from 1949 to 1954, was another former New Deal agricultural administrator who transposed his domestic views to the world. While criticizing American agricultural policies as an impediment to his goal of eradicating global hunger, Dodd wanted to model the FAO administratively on the USDA. Some of his more radical ideas were quickly sunk by the organization's member states, but the FAO's programs for technical assistance and certain of its proposals on disposing of agricultural sur-

FIGURE 8. ILO director general David A. Morse and Indian prime minister Jawaharlal Nehru, 1957. © International Labour Organization.

pluses reflected the American domestic debates of the 1930s.[112] Tugwell's assistant at the USDA, Laurence I. Hewes, helped to implement land reform in postwar Japan, later worked in India for president Kennedy's Agency for International Development, and then returned to the USDA.[113] David A. Morse, a staunch New Dealer with National Labor Relations Board credentials, headed the ILO in the postwar era, and in general the ILO became a hub for advocating New Deal ideas internationally.[114] Finally, Dean Acheson deserves mention. Like other politicians, businessmen, and journalists of the 1940s, he combined a commitment to Wilsonian ideals, the business world, and social reform—as three strands that had only coalesced during the second half of the New Deal. For people like Acheson, economic globalism and domestic reform were no contradiction. A lifelong Democrat and successful businessman, he joined the administration in 1933 when FDR appointed him undersecretary of the Treasury. Acheson was forced out after just six months, after disagreeing with Roosevelt's unorthodox currency management. Reentering the administration as assistant secretary of state in 1941, Acheson joined Hopkins, Cohen, and others at the cradle of the Lend-Lease Program. He then headed the State Department's team at Bretton Woods, where the postwar system of monetary management in the Western world was negotiated, and contributed massively to postwar reconstruction in Europe. Acheson continued in the State Department under Truman, who made him secretary, and in this function oversaw the creation of NATO in 1949.[115]

For sure, there were also other influential voices in the corridors of power. Some of the State Department's conservative "striped-pants boys" whom Roosevelt despised so heartily were catapulted into new positions. Charles "Chip" Bohlen, for instance, who joined the State Department in 1929 and was the scion of an old-stock Yankee family, was the main working-level authority on relations with the Soviet Union and Truman's adviser from 1947 onward. And not all the new internationalism was inspired by the New Deal. Some elements harked back to earlier efforts and programs. On relief matters, for example, an older generation with no proclivity to the New Deal came out of the woodwork during the 1940s. Several of the old hands who had organized international relief under Hoover in the aftermath of World War I now resurfaced. William N. Haskell, Hoover's chief aide in the American Relief Administration, became CARE's executive director in late 1945.[116] Maurice Pate, another veteran of European famine relief under Hoover, together with the Republican ex-president helped found the UN Children's Fund. It was also Pate who served as its first executive director from 1947 to 1965. Like Haskell, Pate had no New Deal credentials; he had been an investment banker and businessman during most of the interwar years.[117] In general, people who had only gravitated to the public sector during the early 1940s were the ones driving the economic approach soon dominating America's Cold War policies. Besides Pate and Haskell, men such as James V. Forrestal, W. Averell Harriman, and John J. McCloy represent this process.[118]

Nonetheless, the number of New Dealers from the 1930s in international circles was remarkably large, particularly on issues related to economic rights and welfare statism. That said, there was not a single, consistent New Deal view or agenda that drove these experts and politicians. Nothing of this kind had united them in the prewar years, and a diversity of views and approaches persisted after 1945. The postwar context, however, clipped off the radical fringes—anticommunism placed taboos on Far Left views, and those flirting with fascism had been marginalized for quite some time. Furthermore, even the staunchest New Dealer had to adapt to the postwar political environment, with many converting to Cold War liberalism. There was a remarkable concentration of expertise and manpower in general, transposed from a domestic American context originally focused on insulation and intervention, to an internationalist agenda revolving around multilateral cooperation and American empire.

Exiles and migrants with social democratic leanings often reinforced the turn to the international. The European exiles staffing US intelligence services as well as colleges and universities around the country during the war helped to bolster both the global and social democratic orientations of the United States. In coordination with the State Department, the Rockefeller Foundation rescued parts of the League of Nations administration, moving them from Geneva to Princeton, New Jersey, in summer 1940, from where its officials connected with like-minded counterparts across the United States and internationally.[119] New York's New School, which turned into a haven for exiled European scholars, is just another illustration of how Progressivism and European left-of-center ideas coalesced as well as contributed to globalizing the New Deal. One concrete example is German academic Ernst Fraenkel, who fled to the United States in 1939. After 1945, he first served as an adviser in liberated Korea and then returned to Germany, where he became a founding father of postwar political science.[120] He would have agreed with Max Kohnstamm, a Dutch exchange student in the United States in 1939 and future architect of Western European integration, that the postwar world had much to learn from the New Deal.[121]

Obviously, the state and intergovernmental organizations were not the only arenas of global interconnection. The Rockefeller Foundation, CARE, and other nongovernmental organizations are reminders that after 1945 as well as before the state was not alone on the international stage. Raymond Fosdick, president of the Rockefeller Foundation from 1936 to 1948, was an important international player regardless of the New Deal state, and the OCIAA built substantially on the work of his foundation and other nonstate actors. A crucial difference from earlier decades was that while private, philanthropic, and other nongovernmental organizations had long prevailed over the scene, Progressivism now acquired a state-dominated form. The 1940s marked a shift in register, too: planning was now more critical than ever before. Agricultural policy in Japan offers a good case in point. Under the auspices of MacArthur's land reform program, state agents now worked to increase agricultural yields with new rice varieties developed by the Rockefeller Foundation. The expertise came from nonstate actors, but it was the federal state that pushed for them internationally.[122]

With their move from the national to the transnational and global levels, Hopkins, Eleanor Roosevelt, Lehman, and legions of others epitomize the mind-set and learning process of a whole generation of prominent Americans. But many ordinary Americans were also exposed to global developments to a much larger extent during the war and postwar years—as newspaper readers, trade unionists, detainees (if they happened to have Japanese roots), and GIs. As always in human history, war made people travel and expand their horizons more than they would have done normally. World War II GIs often received training in several parts of the country before being deployed abroad. One Allen N. Towne, for instance, a combatant medical aidman in the "Big Red One," the First US Infantry Division, was trained in Massachusetts, Colorado, North Carolina, Virginia, Florida, and Georgia before being deployed overseas, where he served in Britain, North Africa, Italy, France, Belgium, and Germany.[123] Admittedly, GIs frequently lived on bases that were little Americas and only saw snippets of the everyday life in the societies in which they fought or were stationed. Yet such experiences underwrote the new global role that the United States came to play in the second part of the century.[124]

Let there be no mistake, though: many of these seasoned experts and politicians entered the international stage because others had taken the interesting national roles. In the machine room of power, New Deal liberals often had to make space for the new networks that Truman and his successors brought to Washington. Going global was not everybody's first choice. The Eisenhower administration ended Dodd's international career in 1954 by denying him the chance to run for a second term at the helm of FAO. The US government thus distanced itself from the New Deal approach to global farming.[125] While the more conservative Chip Bohlen advised President Truman on key security issues, New Deal architect Ben Cohen was just an alternate (rather than full) delegate to the UN General Assembly. There is no evidence to support the publicly conveyed impression that he had been given a really important job in Paris; in fact, he left humiliated and like a "lost lamb."[126] Some elements of high modernist planning associated with the New Deal quickly fell from fashion in Washington. Economist Lauchlin B. Currie, an ardent New Dealer, directed a major World Bank mission to Colombia from 1949 onward. Soon, however, Wall Street people gained influence in the bank, while Currie fell from grace. Ironically, his esteem with the Colombian government rose proportionally.[127] A general onslaught against the New Dealers began in January 1953, when President Truman had the loyalty of all Americans working for international organizations checked. The United Nations and other organizations were purged, and McCarthyism sunk some of the most dynamic cruisers of New Deal thinking.[128]

In his first inaugural address, President Eisenhower opined that "whatever America hopes to bring to pass in the world must first come to pass in the heart of America."[129] At first glance, these words seem to summarize the way that the New Deal internationalized after 1945. The reality on the ground was more complex. While many Americans continued to endorse the New Deal agenda, others did not want any more 1930s-style interventionism at home. Promoting their ideas abroad thus helped old hands from the FDR days to retain their self-image as progressive reformers. For some of them, the world became an ersatz America.

Brave New Worlds

Despite their global promotion, New Deal ideas for the world sometimes crashed and burned after 1945. This was obvious in places dominated by communists, authoritarian regimes, and laissez-faire liberals. Even on less politicized issues where opposition seemed unlikely, there were serious set-backs. Roosevelt himself had to learn this the hard way in February 1945, during a meeting with King Ibn Saud of Saudi Arabia. After Roosevelt had raved about greening the Arabian deserts by setting up TVA-style dams and irrigation systems, Ibn Saud remarked dryly that he was not interested, particularly if "this property would be inherited by the Jews." Anti-Semitism, driven by recent discussions about resettling Jews from Europe, combined with love for the spiritual quality of the desert prompted the king to plead for the status quo. Roosevelt, who had grown up on the fertile lands by the Hudson River and loved trees, had a hard time understanding how someone could think so differently.[130] This did not keep the two nations from forging a multilayered alliance that would survive the president, the king, the Cold War, and the twentieth century. It was also Ibn Saud himself who had asked for American expertise to build up the agricultural sector of his kingdom as early as 1940.[131]

In general, Americans did not seamlessly impose their models on the world, as some accounts have it. Simplistic interpretations of imperialistic domination along with studies centered on US actors and their intentions cannot do justice to the complexity of transnational interconnections. By focusing on the US contribution to wider developments, such authors highlight one set of causes while ignoring the crucial contributions of America's interlocutors from other parts of the globe. Scholars, then, tend to reproduce some of the flawed ideas of US policy makers themselves, who often failed to understand why their noble ambitions and well-meaning schemes to modernize the world met resistance and rejection.

Despite the preponderance of American power and the attractiveness of US models, the role of the Americans on the international scene after 1945 should not be overestimated. The main difference from the interwar years was that Washington now committed itself much more explicitly to contributing to global conversations and sometimes also to lead. Still, non-Americans continued to play some of the star roles. The negotiations around the UN Declaration of Human Rights, for instance, saw Eleanor Roosevelt assume an important position. But debates were also shaped by the conflicting ideas of non-American actors: France's René Cassin, who spoke for a particular rights of man tradition, à la française; Britain's H. G.

FIGURE 9. Israeli postage stamp
featuring Eleanor Roosevelt, 1964.

Wells, a self-declared "Cosmopolitan patriot"; India's feminist, anticolonial-
ist Hansa Mehta; and the Kuomintang's delegate Chang Peng-chun, who
insisted that Enlightenment philosophers were deeply indebted to a Confu-
cian tradition. Early UN documents on human rights were frequently about
defining rights—but also about avoiding serious commitment to enforce
them.[132] There were, for instance, fights over the blueprint for UNRRA, in
which Americans treated the organization as the culmination of their national history of humanitarian aid, while many others wanted to model it
on the multilateral work of the League of Nations. In sum, the New Deal
and other American visions were only one set of ideas negotiated in a global
marketplace, even if they were especially potent.[133]

In the newly established international organizations, Europeans especially made sure that they kept their fingers in the pie, and in general established internationalist elites continued to play a major part. Postwar debates
around food safety, for example, drew heavily on discussions in the League
of Nations, and the same holds true on economic matters.[134] Figures such as
Swedish economists Per Jacobsson, the Myrdals, Polish bacteriologist Lud-
wik Rajchman, and French businessman Jean Monnet played critical roles
in the new international organizations shaping the postwar order and
grafted their views onto them. Alva Myrdal chaired UNESCO's social science section; her husband led the UN's Economic Commission for Europe,
and Jacobsson headed the IMF. Rajchman was the first chairman of UN
Children's Fund and thus a close collaborator of Pate's, while Monnet acted
as the *éminence grise* of postwar Western European integration, which
evolved into the most intense form of regional cooperation in the world. At
the institutional level, finally, the UN system as a whole did not primarily

owe its form to the United States; it was, as Mark Mazower has shown, the result of long debates and involved a much wider set of actors, many of whom came from Britain's global empire.[135]

Also at the bilateral level, Americans were not always at the forefront of transnational connections. The Beveridge report was discussed around the world. Britain continued to play a vital role; the Cold War could not undo connections that had been built up over decades and centuries. Networks of expertise and power between Europe and the global South often survived the advent of decolonization—not least because many former colonial administrators turned to bi- or multilateral development aid.[136]

In addition, people and institutions of Atlantic stock faced stiff challenges at the time. Decolonization soon gave greater influence to actors from the global South, and equally important, the Soviet Union resurged from World War II as a player deeply committed to its own visions of cooperation and high modernity. International economic assistance, development aid, and a discourse centered on global community and the betterment of humanity were not exclusively American or Western marketing tools. Admittedly, the Soviet Union spent much less on international aid than the United States, and in many places it unleashed social revolution implemented with terror, coercion, and show trials. Despite their violent sides, the Eastern models were ideologically and economically appealing to many people around the world. On economic issues, Soviet ideas were frequently more consistent than the hodgepodge of activities represented by the globalized New Deal; with regard to racial equality, the promises of the Soviet Union by far exceeded anything that America had to offer. The New Deal past provided the United States parts of the scaffolding to become a global leader—but a leader involved in a worldwide competition between two superpowers and many other nations.[137]

Besides the multiplicity of actors on a global scale, the world was not a blank slate, even if Americans sometimes treated it as such. Flying over Berlin, Warsaw, Manila, or Hiroshima in 1945, one might have believed in a tabula rasa, but many survivors on the ground felt markedly different. Some perceived the idea of adopting the American model as an imposition. Early on, plans to use the world as a stage to reenact American history received critical comments. While the guns of World War II were still speaking, Polish refugee circles, for example, felt that the US approach was "too pat and homely, too idealistic and oversimple." Instead of a one-size-fits-all template, they argued for locally specific solutions, reflecting individual settings and needs.[138] The success of American reform ideas was therefore much determined by dynamics in the recipient societies, and local elites were remarkably successful in thwarting those US policies that they disliked.

Americans nonetheless time and again found themselves invited to remake the world, often with explicit reference to New Deal accomplishments. US international prestige reached a new climax during and after the "good war"; America was a comparably young global power, and the Vietnam War and other bloody interventions had not yet tainted its international image.

International interest in the TVA is a good example. In 1943, for instance, British biologist Julian Huxley asserted that the TVA was a "symbol of a new possibility for the democratic countries—the possibility of obtaining the efficiency of a co-ordinated plan without totalitarian regimentation."[139] British economists Paul Lamartine Yates and Doreen Warriner jointly called for a "Tennessee Valley Authority for the Danube Basin."[140] Asian experts were just as interested. Indian scientist Meghnad Saha, for instance, argued for a TVA in the Damodar valley, while economist Fang Xianting considered similar plans for China.[141] Writer Lin Yutang was so impressed by a visit to the American South that he sent Lilienthal a classic Chinese poem that for him summarized the TVA experience.[142] Planners, politicians, and engineers from all corners of the world soon joined the chorus, often building on earlier debates during the interwar years. Some New Deal liberals, in turn, readily picked up such calls. In 1947, Ezekiel, for example, referred to the TVA ideas of Yates and Warriner. While stressing that a Danubian TVA was "a long task," he argued that it was not impossible, and that it involved "all the great productive powers of modern science and modern technology."[143] High modernist hopes thus united American and other experts in a transcontinental conversation, and together they repackaged New Deal ideas as global tools to modernize the world.[144]

Finally, it would be wrong to think of these exchanges as a one-way street. Programs projected onto other countries sometimes found their way back home. Daniel Immerwahr has recently shown that community development, designed to alleviate the situation in the global South, had bounced back to the United States by the early 1960s. President Johnson's War on Poverty built on community-building programs in India and elsewhere. Some New Deal ideas in this way embarked on a long global journey before impacting fully on America.[145]

Dreaming Dams

The TVA was frequently singled out as the New Deal's globally most usable achievement. One scholar goes so far as to call it "the granddaddy of all regional development projects," and another describes it as standing at the heart of US postwar development missions.[146] Since there is no way to generalize the global legacy of America's 1930s, the TVA will serve here as an illustration of the complexities of transmission and translation, request and resistance.

Ironically, Americans and others debated an idealized TVA for international consumption at a time when in America itself the precise meaning of the New Deal experience had become blurred. The TVA's domestic results had always remained mixed, and despite ardent lobbying by Roosevelt and others, its model was never replicated in other regions of the United States. Under the auspices of the Manhattan Project, the war transformed the TVA from a symbol of regional planning against the Great Depression into a security site. As a national icon of modernization and wealth creation, it was no longer making domestic headlines by the late 1940s. Regardless of these complications, a community of experts and politicians, with the TVA's exuberant director Lilienthal in the cockpit, projected TVA ideas globally. Lilienthal's 1944 book *TVA: Democracy on the March* sold over two hundred thousand copies and was translated into nineteen languages; it celebrated the TVA as a democratic form of planning and asserted its superiority over fascism and communism.[147] This hype continued under Truman and even Eisenhower, in spite of his fear that the TVA represented a form of socialism.[148]

It did not take long before action on the ground followed. In Afghanistan, for instance, the Helmand Valley Authority was set up in 1952. It represented "a piece of America inserted into the Afghan landscape," as British historian Arnold Toynbee reported after a visit to the US-funded multipurpose dam project in 1960.[149] Hundreds of other dams modeled on the TVA were built between the 1940s and 1960s. The New Deal thus provided the blueprint for rerouting waterways and societies around the globe.

Rarely, though, did things go the way that Toynbee claimed. In reality, not a single dam was an extraterritorial American exclave that fully copied the original TVA, mainly for two reasons. First, the TVA, as propagated internationally, had little to do with the reality on the ground. Planners who cited the TVA presented it as an apolitical and technocratic solution, while glossing over its wartime contribution to the construction of the atomic bomb and its inability to challenge racial segregation. As Daniel Klingensmith has convincingly maintained, postwar planners did not try to copy an originally American design but instead created a simulacrum: they attempted to reproduce something that in actual fact never existed.[150] Second, local dynamics along with the contribution of international organizations such as the IMF and the World Bank also shaped the eventual outcome.[151] All these titanic projects built on a coalition of American, international, and local elite planners and politicians, and frequently had to face the stiff resistance of groups that challenged their claim that the "TVA model" represented a smooth floodgate to modernity.

In India, for instance, a coalition of the colonial government and parts of the Indian elite had already become interested in the TVA prior to independence. Building multipurpose dams on the Mahanadi River in the Damodar valley was intended to demonstrate the late colonial government's vigor and keep the growing independence movement at bay. Such hopes were strong enough to outpace London's fear that emulating an American model would undermine British rule. Roughly a year before Indian independence, the British governor of Orissa, Sir Hawthorne Lewis, laid the project's cornerstone. Some two years later, Indian prime minister Jawaharlal Nehru repeated the ceremony. The Indian TVA thus morphed from a symbol of British rule over India to an emblem of national independence. Fusing modernism and the country's rich religious heritage, Nehru famously called the dams of the Damodar Valley Authority "temples of the New Age."[152] These temples were built with a lot of American know-how, but they carried only some of the TVA's characteristics. They were similar to Lilienthal's ideas centered on science and hydropower, whereas the community-building and social engineering dimensions that Arthur Morgan had insisted on in America were shaved off.[153] In the end, only four of the originally planned eight dams were realized, and the project encountered stiff resistance.[154] So there was quite some distance between the sing-song of the Damodar Valley Authority and the southern drawl of the TVA; the Indian progeny basically became an uncritical, highly selective, and controversial reading of American history.

The dynamics on the Danube were markedly different. Here, New Deal references became a strong current during the early postwar years. By the late 1940s, American experts and the UN's Economic Commission for Europe under Myrdal started planning along TVA lines, but such ideas were soon stifled by the Cold War. The Danube flowed through states of both Cold War blocs as well as formally neutral Austria, and experts were unable to find consensus on cooperation. After 1948, TVA references receded to the margins. On the river's lower (eastern) reaches, Soviet models quickly became influential, and planning commenced under the auspices of the Council for Mutual Economic Assistance. In the end, most of the councils' plans also remained unrealized. Yet the TVA idea was only a short episode in a longer process in which the contending Soviet set of development ideas ultimately impacted more.[155] Generally, the TVA model found a global rival in the Soviet Union, which engaged in strikingly similar projects around the world—along the Danube, but also in China, Vietnam, and Syria.[156] Given the close cooperation of the two powers on multipurpose dams just a few years earlier under the Lend-Lease Program—when the TVA had happily cooperated with Moscow—the gargantuan dams' new role as icons of confrontation belongs to the little-known ironies of the Cold War.[157]

There were further regional variations. The TVA's role as a model for the Mekong in Southeast Asia was also quite mixed and primarily indirect, even if some have argued that it did serve as an important template.[158] In today's Malawi, as another example, plans for the Shire valley failed almost completely: locals resisted the grand schemes that ignored their knowledge; Western experts, in contrast, insisted on the superiority of standardized models, blithely ignoring local agricultural and social environments.[159] And in another completely different case, the TVA exerted influence beyond development projects: its administrative setup inspired organizations with quite different tasks, such as the European Coal and Steel Community's High Authority, a predecessor of today's European Union.[160]

Overall, therefore, TVA's global history was quite mixed. While action in sites like the Damodar valley was a success for Lilienthal, Nehru, Saha, and their ilk, tens of thousands of families fell victim to a violent and arbitrary resettlement process. The tears and traumas—as well as the environmental degradation resulting from these human interventions into complex ecosystems and the idiosyncratic critique of activists such as Kapilprasad Bhattacharjee—cannot be offset by the nationalist dreams and ambitions of a middle class committed to a high modernist project. While promising an apolitical, smooth path to prosperity and modernization, problems and conflicts abounded. High state subsidies turned the Damodar Valley Authority into a white elephant, and the electricity generated in the Damodar valley was and is almost exclusively thermal versus hydroelectric.[161] While the dynamics in the Helmand and Shire valleys, along the Danube, the Mekong, and the Zambezi differed from the Damodar Valley Authority's, the results always remained ambivalent. America did not and could not offer ready-made solutions; instead, large-scale dams opened Pandora's box, unleashing complex conflicts. Many projects ended up as disappointments even for their most ardent supporters, not least because of the unrealistic expectations evoked by the TVA, against which they were measured. Some countries quickly abandoned their projects, most only built torsos, and quite a few were thrown into structural dependency on the United States for the loans, heavy machinery, and know-how needed to build such multi-purpose dams. The global TVA created new, powerful interconnections around the world—but often quite different ones than its original advocates had imagined.[162] The outcomes remained incomplete and hybrid, a kind of default mode for transnational interconnections. Still, debates around the world now focused on an American role model with a specific New Deal pedigree. The global TVA thus symbolized the unprecedented role that New Dealish US institutions and culture had assumed in the world since the 1940s.

There is one last aspect complicating the story of the global TVA as an illustration of the transnational legacy of the New Deal. The TVA's global history also fired the imagination of neoconservatives and neoliberals, for whom it represented the wrong answer to the problems of capitalist modernity. In his 1944 *Road to Serfdom*, Hayek, one of the staunchest defenders of classical economic liberalism, ridiculed the idea of a TVA for the Danube. And having grown up on its beautiful banks in Vienna, he certainly knew more about the diverging interests in its riparian states than most American and international experts. For Hayek the conclusion was clear: anyone with some "knowledge of human nature" and "a little knowledge of the people of Central Europe" knew that such plans could not work.[163]

Beyond Hayek and the example of the TVA, the American Right carefully scrutinized overseas development projects and used their problems as arguments for their antistatist ideology. US-based economists such as Gottfried Haberler, Jacob Viner, and Milton Friedman connected with like-minded thinkers, such as Swiss-based German Wilhelm Röpke, Italian Luigi Einaudi, and Chilean Pedro Ibáñez Ojeda, who also believed in the market and repudiated the global New Deal. The Mont Pèlerin Society, founded in 1947, became a transnational hub for such anti–New Deal thinking. Hotbeds of this approach, including the Chicago school, relied heavily on transatlantic and global networks along with an antitotalitarian rhetoric steeped in Cold War ideology.[164] In the medium and long run, the anti–New Deal Right was at least as successful in globalizing its views as those who clung to the agenda of the FDR era.

A Global Icon

And yet the New Deal remains a potent symbol. Politicians and activists around the world regularly call for some kind of New Deal. While such invocations date back to the 1930s, they have never lost their power. In 2000, for instance, UN secretary-general Kofi Annan called for a "Global New Deal" to remedy the imbalances between the world's rich and poor countries.[165] In a similar vein, British prime minister Gordon Brown argued nine years later for a "global new deal whose impact can stretch from the villages of Africa to reforming the financial institutions of London and New York."[166] In 2013, the European Union demanded a New Deal for Somalia.[167] Meanwhile, the global South's G7+ promoted a New Deal for the Congo and other fragile states.[168] The mayor of London recently declared a New Deal for his city.[169] In Canada, a team of interdisciplinary researchers has made the case for a New Deal for families.[170] Academics use titles such as the "Global New Deal" to market their ideas.[171] More specific programs associated with FDR's prewar administration are often cited in the United States and beyond. The California Conservation Corps, established in the 1970s, took its inspiration from the 1930s' federal CCC and still exists today, while dozens of hydroelectric projects around the globe end on "Valley Authority," emulating the TVA's iconic name.

Symbolic references say little about the concrete parallels to and inspiration of the actual New Deal. The original's complexity already impeded emulation, and changing historical contexts and shifting needs worked to the same effect. On a detailed and specific level, the various programs and projects share little with their model. More broadly, they tend to be associated with strong state action and intervention in times of crisis; politically, such calls often come from the Left of the political spectrum. There are, in this respect, certain similarities to Roosevelt's administration. In contrast, the insulationist streak of the original New Deal is referenced much more rarely. The emphatically internationalist turn of the 1940s in this sense has buried the much more mixed message from the first years after 1933. It is for this reason that the slogans New Deal and Marshall Plan are typically used almost interchangeably to call for policy programs.

Looking back from the early twenty-first century, the New Deal seems to have faded into history. Its global ramifications and repercussions sometimes seem more powerful than its domestic resonance. Today, New Deal references sometimes seem to be more popular with cosmopolitan bureaucrats in international organizations and INGOs (as well as with non-US left-of-center experts and politicians more generally) than in the United States itself. President Obama is a case in point. Experts and the media regularly associate his administration with the reforms under Roosevelt.[172] Yet while he sometimes evokes the spirit of FDR and the New Deal, he only rarely mentions or quotes them explicitly.[173] Obviously, the contested nature of contemporary American politics sets a clear limit to such references.

More important than the New Deal itself, therefore, is the urge to avoid the mistakes of the Great Depression. A case in point is the financial and economic crisis after 2007. Elites in America and beyond were united in a broad internationalist consensus. They felt that their main task was to avoid a crisis as deep as the Great Depression, whatever the price. Cooperation was thus paramount. With some qualifications, the same also holds true for earlier crises in the global economy, even if the concrete recipes have changed. During the turmoil of the 1970s, for instance, cooperation and state action focused more on Keynesian policies, whereas today's reinterpretation is more centered on monetarism.[174] Avoiding a new Great Depression as deep, conflictual, and global as during the 1930s has nonetheless been a key factor in both cases. Significantly, several of the top advisers and decision makers in the Obama administration were leading experts on the history of the Great Depression, and they have used this knowledge to fight economic challenges in our own time. Christina Romer, head of the President's Council of Economic Advisers during a crucial phase of the crisis, and Ben Bernanke, chairman of the Federal Reserve from 2006 to 2014, are only two of the best-known examples. As during the 1930s, the US government created new institutions with a mandate to maintain financial stability, foster international markets, and promote free trade. While such concepts sound familiar, they cannot negate the dramatic differences between the 1930s and today's situation: the deeper level of globalization, the rise of China, the challenge of Islamism, and different domestic dynamics, to name but a few.

Myriad layers thus both connect and distance the New Deal era and to-day's America and globalized world. As a distinctive phase in US history, the New Deal shared more with processes in other parts of the world than is normally recognized. Its contradictory lessons have been repeatedly invoked and repudiated. And as a global icon, it lingers on, increasingly adrift from its historical mooring. This is the fate of the (global) New Deal, forever updated, evermore fading into history.

NOTES

PROLOGUE

1. https://history.state.gov/departmenthistory/travels/president/roosevelt-franklin-d (accessed April 10, 2015).

2. Burton, "Contemporary Presidency."

3. "Acceptance of Renomination, June 27, 1936," in *Public Papers and Addresses of Franklin D. Roosevelt*, 5:236.

4. Rodgers, "Exceptionalism."

5. Kramer, "Power and Connection," 1349.

6. Vandenberg, *Private Papers*, 3–4.

7. Scott, *Seeing Like a State*.

8. Subrahmanyam, "Hearing Voices," 99–100.

9. Schlesinger, *Age of Jackson*.

10. Cohen, *Making a New Deal*.

11. See, for example, Garraty, *Great Depression*; Rodgers, *Atlantic Crossings*; Tyrrell, *Transnational Nation*; Bender, *Nation among Nations*; Nolan, *Transatlantic Century*; Katznelson, *Fear Itself*. Scholars from fields other than history often pioneered multinational comparative work. See, for example, Gourevitch, *Politics in Hard Times*; Weir and Skocpol, "State Structures"; Hall, *Political Power of Economic Ideas*.

12. Maier, "Leviathan 2.0"; Maier, "Consigning the Twentieth Century to History."

13. Foucault, "Governmentality."

14. Burton, "Contemporary Presidency."

15. Sherwood, *Roosevelt and Hopkins*, 671. On the trip, see http://www.fdrlibrary .marist.edu/_resources/images/tully/7_07.pdf (accessed April 12, 2015).

CHAPTER 1
A GLOBAL CRISIS

1. "Inaugural Address, March 4, 1929," in *Public Papers of the Presidents of the United States: Herbert Hoover*, 1929:1.

2. Merz, *Then Came Ford*, 319.

3. *Historical Statistics of the United States: Earliest Times to the Present*, 3:3–25 (GDP growth in real terms).

4. Quoted in Meinig, *Shaping of America*, 7.

5. Ibid., 3–27.

6. See, for example, James C. Young, "Ford's New Car Keeps Motor World Guessing," *New York Times* (hereafter *NYT*), June 26, 1927; Kindleberger, *World in Depression*, 59; Brinkley, *Wheels for the World*, 333–54.

7. Meinig, *Shaping of America*, 24; Schisgall, *Greyhound Story*, 3–42.

8. Tobey, *Technology as Freedom*, esp. 5–7.

9. Hyman, *Debtor Nation*, 10–44.

10. Runte, *National Parks*; Shaffer, *See America First*, 93–129.

11. Fischer, "Movies and the 1920s," 1–22; Jacobs, *Pocketbook Politics*.

12. *Recent Social Trends in the United States*, 1:153.

13. Meinig, *Shaping of America*, 55.

14. Tobey, *Technology as Freedom*, 7.

15. See Cohen, "Encountering Mass Culture." See also Marchand, *Advertising the American Dream*.

16. *Historical Statistics of the United States: Earliest Times to the Present*, 5:5–504; Boyce, *Great Interwar Crisis*, 78–80. For Ford's global spread, see, for example, Wilkins and Hill, *American Business Abroad*; Brinkley, *Wheels for the World*, 369–75.

17. Schultz, "Building the 'Soviet Detroit,'" 202–12; Tzouliadis, *Forsaken*, 30–47; Wilkins and Hill, *American Business Abroad*, 208–27.

18. Goodall, "The Battle of Detroit," 457–80. On illiberal modernism, see Link, "Transnational Fordism," esp. 151–209.

19. Boyce, *Great Interwar Crisis*, 187–88. See also the contemporary public relations film *General Motors around the World, 1927*.

20. Patterson, *America*, 131.

21. Weindling, "Philanthropy and World Health," 269–81. See also Tournès, "La fondation Rockefeller et la naissance," 173–97; Parmar, *Foundations of the American Century*.

22. Mazower, *Governing the World*, 192.

23. Josephson, *James T. Shotwell*, 94; Wegener, "Creating an 'International Mind.'"

24. Herring, *From Colony to Superpower*, 436–83. See, more generally, Cohrs, *Unfinished Peace after World War I*; Gorman, *Emergence of International Society in the 1920s*; Blower, "From Isolationism to Neutrality."

25. Stead, *Americanization of the World*; Russell, *Prospects of Industrial Civilization*, 76.

26. Klautke, *Unbegrenzte Möglichkeiten*; see also Pells, *Not Like Us*; Ellwood, *Shock of America*.

27. de Grazia, *Irresistible Empire*, 3.

28. For various contributions, see Weinbaum et al., *Modern Girl around the World*.

29. Green, "Expatriation, Expatriates, and Expats"; Blower, *Becoming Americans in Paris*.

30. Hoelscher, *Heritage on Stage*.

31. Eckert, "Bringing the 'Black Atlantic' into Global History," 247–50; Gilroy, *Black Atlantic*; Marable, *W.E.B. Du Bois*, 121–43; Vestal, *Lion of Judah in the New World*, 19–27.

32. Manela, *Wilsonian Moment*.

33. Trescott, *Jingji Xue*; Tyrrell, *Reforming the World*, 189–245.

34. McGirr, "Passion of Sacco and Vanzetti"; Boorstin, *America and the Image of Europe*, 25.

35. Addams, *Second Twenty Years at Hull-House*, 7. See also Schüler, *Frauenbewegung und soziale Reform*.

36. Kuehl and Dunn, *Keeping the Covenant*, 58–61.

37. See, for example, Lindert and Williamson, "Does Globalization Make the World More Unequal?"; Boyce, *Great Interwar Crisis*.

38. Iriye, *Global Community*, 18–36; Meinig, *Shaping of America*, 55–61, 87–99.

39. Borah, *Closing Speech of Hon. William E. Borah*, 9.

40. Mazower, *Governing the World*; Nichols, *Promise and Peril*, 273–320.

41. Garis, *Immigration Restriction*, esp. 261; Zolberg, *Nation by Design*, 243–70.

42. Grant, *Passing of the Great Race*, 16, 263. On Grant and his context see, for example, Schrag, *Not Fit for Our Society*, 73–107; Spiro, *Defending the Master Race*, 143–66.

43. Schrag, *Not Fit for Our Society*, 108–38.

44. Zolberg, *Nation by Design*, 248–51 (quotes both on 250).

45. Temin, "Great Depression," 303; Meinig, *Shaping of America*, 117–21.

46. Zolberg, *Nation by Design*, 254–66.

47. Ngai, "The Strange Career of the Illegal Alien," 74, 77. On the limits of enforcement, see Ettinger, *Imaginary Lines*, 145–66.

48. Hoganson, *Consumers' Imperium*; Rhoads, "Long and Unsuccessful Effort," 19. The Country Club District had already been developed since 1906.

49. Gerstle, *American Crucible*.

50. MacLean, *Behind the Mask of Chivalry*; Welskopp, *Amerikas große Ernüchterung*.

51. Lupo, *Quando la mafia trovò l'America*, 5.

52. Handlin, *Uprooted*, 267. On the fault lines of this conflict, see, for example, Dumenil, *Modern Temper*.

53. Zolberg, *Nation by Design*, 244; Ngai, "Strange Career of the Illegal Alien."

54. Boyce, *Great Interwar Crisis*, 84.

55. Torpey, *Invention of the Passport*, 111–21.

56. Tavan, *Long, Slow Death of White Australia*, 7–29; Anderson, *Cultivation of Whiteness*; Lake and Reynolds, *Drawing the Global Colour Line*, 137–65.

57. Conrad and Mühlhahn, "Global Mobility and Nationalism"; Shiraishi, "Anti-Sinicism in Java's New Order."

58. Weitz, *Century of Genocide*, 1–52. On the general trends, see Hoerder, *Cultures in Contact*, 445–507.

59. For the quantitative dimensions, see Levy, "O papel da migração internacional na evolução da população brasileira." For the debates at the time, see Skidmore, *Black into White*, 192–200. See also Dávila, Morgan, and Skidmore, "Since Black into White"; Bletz, *Immigration and Acculturation*.

60. Devoto, *Historia de la inmigración en la Argentina*, 355–61.

61. McKeown, *Melancholy Order*, 320.

62. Slezkine, "USSR as a Communal Apartment"; Martin, *Affirmative Action Empire*.

63. Hess, "'Hindu' in America," 68.

64. Stepan, "*Hour of Eugenics*," 172–95; Kühl, *Die Internationale der Rassisten*; Geulen, "Common Grounds of Conflict."

65. Creel, *War, the World and Wilson*, 163.

66. Tooze, *Deluge*, 14–15.

67. Mauch and Patel, *United States and Germany during the Twentieth Century*.

68. See, for example, Galbraith, *Great Crash*, 88–107.

69. "President's News Conference, October 25, 1929," in *Public Papers of the Presidents of the United States: Herbert Hoover*, 1929:355.

70. Quoted in "Wall Street's 'Prosperity Panic,'" *Literary Digest*, November 9, 1929, 6.

71. Kindleberger, *World in Depression*, 111; James, *Creation and Destruction*, 66–73.

72. Temin, *Did Monetary Forces Cause the Great Depression?* 78–83 (includes similar findings on agency ratings at the time).

73. Quoted in Ahamed, *Lords of Finance*, 343.

74. Kennedy, *Freedom from Fear*, 10. See, similarly, Parker, *Great Crash*.

75. Kent, *Spoils of War*, 17–45; Tooze, *Deluge*, 302; Sauvy, *Histoire économique de la France entre les deux guerres*, 169.

76. Capie, "International Depression and Trade Protection," 126–28.

77. Quoted in Wittek, *Auf ewig Feind?* 224.

78. Winkler, *Weimar*; Winkler, *Geschichte des Westens*.

79. Keynes, *Economic Consequences*. See also, for example, Lutz, "Inter-Allied Debts," 29–61.

80. Turner, *Cost of War*; Pullen, *World War Debts*.

81. Eichengreen, *Golden Fetters*, 222–30; Ritschl, "International Capital Movements."

82. Schedvin, *Australia and the Great Depression*, esp. 96–107.

83. Rothermund, *India in the Great Depression*, 79–134.

84. O'Connell, "Argentina into the Depression"; Rothermund, *Global Impact of the Great Depression*, 98–109; Eichengreen, *Golden Fetters*, 226–27; Limoncic and Martinho, *Grande Depressão*.

85. Gomes, *German Reparations*, 212–17, Self, *Britain, America, and the War Debt Controversy*, 124–32; Eichengreen and Portes, "Interwar Debt Crisis and Its Aftermath."

86. For the two most important rival interpretations, see Kindleberger, *World in Depression*; Eichengreen, *Golden Fetters*. My approach seeks to combine them. See also, for example, Flandreau, "Central Bank Cooperation," 735–63; Drummond, *Gold Standard and the International Monetary System*; Clavin, *Great Depression in Europe*, 40–100.

87. League of Nations (hereafter LoN), *Report of the Gold Delegation of the Financial Committee*. See also Crafts and Fearon, "Depression and Recovery in the 1930s."

88. Hardy, *Is There Enough Gold?* 92–95; Mouré, *Managing the Franc Poincaré*, 45–65; Temin, *Lessons from the Great Depression*, 41–87.

89. Ahamed, *Lords of Finance*, esp. 254–59; Friedman and Schwartz, *Monetary History of the United States*, 407–19.

90. Wandschneider, "Central Bank Reaction Functions during the Inter-War Gold Standard."

91. Cooper, "Fettered to Gold?" 2120–28; Eichengreen, *Golden Fetters*, 249–53.

92. Yonay, *Struggle over the Soul of Economics*.

93. Nakamura and Kaminsky, "Depression, Recovery, and War," 462–67; Large, "Nationalist Extremism in Early Shōwa Japan"; Metzler, *Lever of Empire*.

94. "Letter W. S. Woytinsky to John Maynard Keynes, December 4, 1931," in Wood, *John Maynard Keynes*, 341. See also, for example, Vaïsse, "Le mythe de l'or en France."

95. James, *Creation and Destruction*, 36–97; Temin, "Great Depression," 311–12.

96. Aguado, "Creditanstalt Crisis," 199–221; Bernanke, *Essays on the Great Depression*, esp. 89–105; Friedman and Schwartz, *Monetary History of the United States*, 299–419.

97. Federico, *Feeding the World*, 191.

98. Malenbaum, *World Wheat Economy*, 236–37.

99. White, "Unsung Hero," 21–31. Figure for gasoline tractors; in 1910, there were still some steam traction engines in use. For the structural changes in the US economy at the time, see Bernstein, *Great Depression*.

100. Terkel, *Hard Times*, 109.

101. Kindleberger, *World in Depression*, 86–100; Federico, "Not Guilty?" 949–76 (though with a slightly different argument); Alston, "Farm Foreclosures," 888.

102. LoN, *Economic Stability in the Post-War World*, 85.

103. Whittlesey, "Stevenson Plan," 506–25; Grandin, *Fordlandia*; Boyce, *Great Interwar Crisis*, 183–86; Mitman and Erickson, "Latex and Blood," 45–73.

104. For details, see Federico, "Not Guilty?" 949–76.

105. Kindleberger, *World in Depression*, 85–87; Timoshenko, *World Agriculture and the Depression*.

106. Clavin, *Great Depression in Europe*, 100; Rothermund, *Global Impact of the Great Depression*, 38–47.

107. US Department of State, *Foreign Relations of the United States* (hereafter *FRUS*), 1930, 1:vii–viii. See also Hoover, *Memoirs of Herbert Hoover*, 59–60. Similarly, see, for example, "Radio Address, February 12, 1931," in *Public Papers of the Presidents of the United States: Herbert Hoover*, 1931:74.

108. Feis, *Diplomacy of the Dollar*, 1.

109. Barber, *From New Era to New Deal*, 62–64.

110. "Vauclain Offers Prosperity Slogan," *NYT*, January 24, 1928.

111. Irwin, *Peddling Protectionism*, 11–143; Beaudreau, *Making Sense of Smoot-Hawley*, 86–100.

112. Slichter, "Is the Tariff a Cause of Depression?" 522, 524. See also, for example, Jones, *Tariff Retaliation*, 319.

113. "Veto of a Bill to Amend the Tariff Act of 1930," in *Public Papers of the Presidents of the United States: Herbert Hoover*, 1932–33:207

114. For such an interpretation, see, for example, Parker, *Great Crash*, 131.

115. As an extreme case, see Beaudreau, *Making Sense of Smoot-Hawley*.

116. Soto, *La Revolución de 1933*, 161–98; Pollitt, "Cuban Sugar Economy and the Great Depression," 3–28. Another important reason for Cuba's plight was the Chadbourne agreement of 1930 on sugar, mainly negotiated by New York corporation lawyer Thomas Chadbourne.

117. McDonald, O'Brien, and Callahan, "Trade Wars," 802–26; Hart, *Trading Nation*, 105–8; Kottman, "Herbert Hoover."

118. "El Consejo de Ministros de Ayer," *ABC* (Madrid), June 18, 1930 (own translation).

119. Jones, *Tariff Retaliation*, 34–67.

120. Balachandran, "Interwar Slump in India," 145.

121. Eichengreen, *Golden Fetters*, 279–302; Drummond, *British Economic Policy and the Empire*, 89–120; Teichert, *Autarkie und Großraumwirtschaft*, 7–52.

122. Capie, "International Depression and Trade Protection in the 1930s," 128; Eichengreen and Irwin, "Trade Blocs, Currency Blocs and the Reorientation," 2–3; Nolan, *Transatlantic Century*.

123. Bértola and Williamson, "Globalization in Latin America," 32–38; Capie, "International Depression and Trade Protection," 127.

124. Conybeare, *Trade Wars*, 236.

125. Irwin, *Peddling Protectionism*, 200–203.

126. Dohan, "Economic Origins of Soviet Autarky."

127. Gregory and Sailors, "Soviet Union during the Great Depression"; James, *End of Globalization*, 127, 158–63.

128. Tzouliadis, *Forsaken*, 38–41; Carew, *Blacks, Reds, and Russians*, 67–89. See also Feuer, "American Travelers to the Soviet Union."

129. Manela, "Goodwill and Bad"; Best, *Dollar Decade*, 31.

130. On Pan-Africanism, see, for example, Eckert, "Bringing the 'Black Atlantic' into Global History," 249–50; Bush, *End of White World Supremacy*. On Japan, see Aydin, *Politics of Anti-Westernism in Asia*, 161–190.

131. Bonn, *Prosperity* (for the English translation, see Bonn, *Crisis of Capitalism in America*); Aron and Dandieu, *Le cancer américain*; Kadmi-Cohen, *L'abomination américaine*. See, more generally, Costigliola, *Awkward Domination*.

132. James, *End of Globalization*, 119–33.

133. LoN, *World Economic Conference*, 30.

134. James, "Creation of a World Central Bank?" For other examples, see Clavin and Patel, "Role of International Organizations in Europeanization"; Knab and Forclaz, "Transnational Co-Operation."

135. Réau, *L'idée d'Europe au XXe siècle*, 89–123.

136. Roon, *Kleine Landen in Crisistijd*.

137. Hoover, *Memoirs of Herbert Hoover*, 71.

138. Quoted in Lazarsfeld, Lazarsfeld-Jahoda, and Zeisl, *Die Arbeitslosen von Marienthal*, 30, 46. Zeisl later changed his name to Zeisel.

139. Quoted in Lynd and Lynd, *Middletown*, 111–12.

140. Ibid., 5.

141. Scott, *Seeing Like a State*; Raphael, "Die Verwissenschaftlichung des Sozialen." See also, for example, *Recent Social Trends in the United States*.

142. Reichardt, *Faschistische Kampfbünde*, 310–45.

143. Rodgers, *Atlantic Crossings*.

144. Lazarsfeld, Lazarsfeld-Jahoda, and Zeisl, *Die Arbeitslosen von Marienthal*, 113.

145. Lynd and Lynd, *Middletown in Transition*, 254.

146. Müller, *Marienthal*, 312–330.

147. Caravaca and Plotkin, "Crisis, ciencias sociales y elites estatales."

148. Toynbee, "Annus Terribilis 1931," 1.

149. Maier, "Malaise," 44–45. According to Maier, the other two such situations were the widespread crisis of political representation from 1905 through 1918 and the crisis of industrial society during the 1970s.

150. Rothermund, *Global Impact of the Great Depression*, 126–35.

CHAPTER 2
IN SEARCH OF NEW BEGINNINGS

1. Oakeshott, "Introduction," xi–xii.

2. Wejnert, "Diffusion, Development, and Democracy"; Garraty, "New Deal, National Socialism, and the Great Depression"; Katznelson, *Fear Itself*.

3. Harootunian, *Overcome by Modernity*.

4. See, for example, Eatwell, "Introduction."

5. Barber, *From New Era to New Deal*; Colander and Landreth, *Coming of Keynesianism to America*.

6. Tugwell quoted in Schlesinger, *Politics of Upheaval*, 648; Chase, *New Deal*, 242; Dickinson, *Hold Fast the Middle Way*.

7. Pius XI, *Quadragesimo anno*.

8. Bose, *Indian Struggle*, 351.

9. Rougemont, *Politique de la Personne*, 83. On the wider context, see Sternhell, *Neither Right nor Left* (Rougemont is not even mentioned).

10. And even this claim has been qualified by more recent scholarship. See, for example. Weatherford, "After the Critical Election"; Shafer and Badger, *Contesting Democracy*.

11. See Alpers, *Dictators, Democracy, and American Public Culture*, 30–34.

12. Katznelson, *Fear Itself*, 39.

13. On Austria, see, for example, Bischof, Pelinka, and Lassner, *Dollfuss/Schuschnigg Era in Austria*. On Uruguay, see, for example, Taylor, "Uruguayan Coup d'état of 1933."

14. "Acceptance Address, July 2, 1932," in *Public Papers and Addresses of Franklin D. Roosevelt*, 1:659. See also Leuchtenburg, *Franklin D. Roosevelt and the New Deal*, 8.

15. Lippmann, *Interpretations*, 261.

16. "Address at Oglethorpe University, May 22, 1932," in *Public Papers and Addresses of Franklin D. Roosevelt*, 1:642. See also Kennedy, *Freedom from Fear*, 98–103.

17. Eccles, *Beckoning Frontiers*, 95.

18. Kennedy, *Freedom from Fear*, 54.

19. Winkler, *Weimar*, 408–43; Conway and Romijn, "Belgium and the Netherlands," 97–104; Zanden, *Een klein land in de 20ᵉ eeuw*, 151–63.

20. Alpers, *Dictators, Democracy, and American Public Culture*, 15–16.

21. "Die Bedeutung der amerikanischen Präsidentenwahl," *Neue Zürcher Zeitung*, November 28, 1932.

22. Behrman, *Most Noble Adventure*, 77.

23. Vandenberg, *Private Papers*, 3–4. See also, for example, Gazell, "Arthur H. Vandenberg, Internationalism, and the United Nations"; Meijer, "Arthur Vandenberg and the Fight for Neutrality."

24. Kaplan and Ryley, *Prelude to Trade Wars*.

25. Okrent, *Last Call*; Welskopp, *Amerikas große Ernüchterung*; Post, "Federalism, Positive Law, and the Emergence."

26. See particularly Kennedy, *Freedom from Fear*, 363–80.

27. James, Lindgren, and Teichova, *Role of Banks in the Interwar Economy*; Cassis, *Crises and Opportunities*, 23–30.

28. Nash, "Herbert Hoover and the Origins of the Reconstruction Finance Corporation"; Leuchtenburg, *Herbert Hoover*, 130–35.

29. On the importance of Michigan, see Butkiewicz, "Reconstruction Finance Corporation." See also Wicker, *Banking Panics of the Great Depression*, 63–138; Barber, *From New Era to New Deal*, 125–88; Cassis, *Crises and Opportunities*, 22–31 (with a comparison to 2008).

30. Wigmore, "Was the Bank Holiday?"; Butkiewicz, "Reconstruction Finance Corporation," 285–89.

31. Ahamed, *Lords of Finance*, 451–59.

32. For the text of the act, see Hosen, *Great Depression and the New Deal*, 89–92; Schlesinger, *Coming of the New Deal*, 6–8; Leuchtenburg, *Franklin D. Roosevelt and the New Deal*, 41–45.

33. For the text of the act, see Hosen, *Great Depression and the New Deal*, 153–93. See also Burns, *American Banking Community and New Deal Banking Reforms*, 77–95.

34. See, for example, Badger, *New Deal*, 66–73; Calomiris and Mason, "Fundamentals, Panics, and Bank Distress."

35. Wigmore, "Was the Bank Holiday?"; Friedman and Schwartz, *Monetary History of the United States*, 325–31.

36. "Proclamation No. 2039, March 6, 1933," in *Public Papers and Addresses of Franklin D. Roosevelt*, 2:24.

37. "Inaugural Address, March 4, 1933," in *Public Papers and Addresses of Franklin D. Roosevelt*, 2:12. On the moral-religious tradition that the New Deal was anchored in, see Isetti, "Moneychangers of the Temple."

38. Irmler, "Bankenkrise und Vollbeschäftigungspolitik," 283–308; James, *German Slump*, 283–323.

39. "Im Kampf gegen die Bankenkrise," *Frankfurter Zeitung*, March 11, 1933. Similarly, see "Roosevelt greift ein," *Deutsche Wirtschafts-Zeitung*, March 16, 1933. Neither of these newspapers' reports conformed with Nazi views.

40. "Roland L. Redmond to FDR, March 3, 1933," in McJimsey, *Documentary History of the Franklin D. Roosevelt Presidency* (hereafter *DH-FDRP*), 3:60–61; "Memorandum Alexander Sachs to Allen Lehman, March 15, 1933," in *DH-FDRP*, 3:204–7.

41. On state guarantees, see Bonin, *La Banque nationale de crédit*, 165–77. On preemptive measures, see Hansen, "Banking Crises and Lenders of Last Resort."

42. Beckhart, "German Bank Inquiry," 107. On the overall trend to intervention at the time, see Hanna, "Banking Act of 1935," esp. 764.

43. Federico, *Feeding the World*, 191–96; Rothermund, *Global Impact of the Great Depression*, 38–47. On Britain, see Trentmann, *Free Trade Nation*.

44. See, for example, Zimmermann, *Nahrungsquellen der Welt*, 9–93.

45. Schiller, *Marktregulierung und Marktordnung*, 1 (own translation). See also Tracy, *Agriculture in Western Europe*, 127–53. On Japan, see Sheingate, *Rise of the Agricultural Welfare State*, 81–90.

46. On Laur and Morrison, see Zimmer, "In Search of Natural Identity"; Crowley, "J. J. Morrison and the Transition in Canadian Farm Movements during the Early Twentieth Century."

47. Sanderson, *Land Reform in Mexico*, 38–104. On US property affected by this, see Dwyer, *Agrarian Dispute*.

48. On India, see, for example, Rothermund, *Global Impact of the Great Depression*, 87–97.

49. For the text of the act, see Hosen, *Great Depression and the New Deal*, 61–88; Hamilton, *From New Day to New Deal*, esp. 51–65, 216–36; Paalberg and Paalberg, "Agricultural Policy in the Twentieth Century." On the more radical alternatives to and within the New Deal, see, for example, Gilbert and O'Connor, "Leaving the Land Behind."

50. Saloutos, *American Farmer and the New Deal*.

51. See particularly "Campaign Address, Topeka, September 14, 1932," in *Public Papers and Addresses of Franklin D. Roosevelt*, 1:693–711.

52. As a survey of some of the contemporary ideas, see, for example, Black, "Plans for Raising Prices of Farm Products by Government Action."

53. Hamilton, *From New Day to New Deal*, 195–250; Kirkendall, *Social Scientists and Farm Politics*, 50–69; Finegold and Skocpol, *State and Party in America's New Deal*, 74–84.

54. "New Means to Rescue Agriculture, March 16, 1933," in *Public Papers and Addresses of Franklin D. Roosevelt*, 2:74.

55. Finegold and Skocpol, *State and Party in America's New Deal*, 80–84.

56. Paalberg and Paalberg, "Agricultural Policy in the Twentieth Century."

57. Wallace, "American Agriculture and World Markets," 223.

58. Carter, *New Dealers*, 102.

59. Finegold and Skocpol, *State and Party in America's New Deal*, 104–14.

60. See, for example, US Agricultural Adjustment Administration, *Crop Insurance Features of Agricultural Adjustment Programs*; Warren and Wermel, *Economic Survey of the Baby Chick Hatchery Industry*.

61. Bauman, *Intimations of Postmodernity*, 178–79.

62. Wallace, "American Agriculture and World Markets," 217.

63. Ezekiel, "European Competition in Agricultural Production, with Special Reference to Russia." On the wider context, see Kirkendall, *Social Scientists and Farm Politics*, 11–60.

64. Wallace, "American Agriculture and World Markets," 217. See also, for example, Christy, "Government Aid to Wheat Producers," 497.

65. See Tugwell, "Agricultural Policy of France"; Tugwell, *Diary of Rexford G. Tugwell*, 136–42.

66. Note Tugwell to McInyre, undated (ca. June 27, 1933) with attached report by Ringland, National Archives and Records Administration (hereafter NARA), Hyde Park, Official Files 1, box 1, USDA.

67. Goldstein, "Impact of Ideas on Trade Policy," 43; Leuchtenburg, "'Europeanization' of America."

68. Sagredo Santos, "Franklin D. Roosevelt y la problemática agraria," 407–8.

69. Phillips, "Lessons from the Dust Bowl."

70. See, for example, Tooze, *Wages of Destruction*, 166–99; Segre, *La "battaglia del grano."*

71. Smith, "Scullin Government and the Wheatgrowers."

72. Robbins, *Economic Basis of Class Conflict*, 29–30.

73. Gupta, "International Tea Cartel during the Great Depression"; Palmer, "Nyasaland Tea Industry in the Era of International Tea Restrictions."

74. Graevenitz, "Exogenous Transnationalism."

75. Robbins, *Economic Basis of Class Conflict*, 29.

76. Gordon-Ashworth, "Agricultural Commodity Control."

77. Wallace, "American Agriculture and World Markets," 224; International Historical Statistics (hereafter IHS), *Americas*, 142.

78. *Historical Statistics of the United States: Colonial Times to 1970*, part 1, 488.

79. On the United Kingdom and France, see Tracy, *Agriculture in Western Europe*, 157–91. On Germany, see Patel, "Paradox of Planning." On global wheat, see Zimmermann, *Nahrungsquellen der Welt*, 13–15.

80. See also Gilbert, "Low Modernism and the Agrarian New Deal."

81. Sheingate, *Rise of the Agricultural Welfare State*, 76–126. On corporatism, see, for example, Berger and Compston, *Policy Concertation and Social Partnership in Western Europe*.

82. Agricultural Adjustment Administration, *Agricultural Adjustment*, 217.

83. Quoted in Bedelow, "Depression and the New Deal," 145. On the well-organized resistance, see, for example, Choate, *Disputed Ground*.

84. For the text of the NIRA, see Hosen, *Great Depression and the New Deal*, 194–213. On the National Recovery Administration more broadly, see, as an introduction, Reagan, "Business." See also, for example, Brand, *Corporatism and the Rule of Law*, 33–95.

85. Johnson, *Blue Eagle*, 169. On Roosevelt, see, for example, "Campaign Address, Sioux City, September 29, 1932," in *Public Papers and Addresses of Franklin D. Roosevelt*, 1:762–70.

86. Lyon et al., *National Recovery Administration*; Hawley, *New Deal and the Problem of Monopoly*, 35–71. On Johnson, see, for example, Schlesinger, *Coming of the New Deal*, 105.

87. Shaw, "Fascism and the New Deal," 562. Fess quoted in Wolfskill and Hudson, *All but the People*, 214.

88. Montague, "Is NRA Fascistic?" 159. On Montague, see Wells, "Counterpoint to Reform."

89. Mussolini quoted in Sedda, "Il *New Deal* nella pubblicistica," 250. Selvi quoted in Schivelbusch, *Three New Deals*, 24.

90. Arroyo Vázquez, "Industria y Trabajo en el New Deal de Franklin D. Roosevelt a través de la prensa española," 531.

91. Brockway, *Will Roosevelt Succeed?* esp. 37, 57. See also, for example, Dizikes, *Britain, Roosevelt, and the New Deal*, 95–199.

92. Quoted in Doel, "Tegenover het Amerikanisme," 269.

93. Strauss, "Roosevelt Revolution."

94. Johnson, *Blue Eagle*, 264–65.

95. "Presidential Statement on N.I.R.A., June 16, 1933," in *Public Papers and Addresses of Franklin D. Roosevelt* 2:252.

96. "Change to Close for NRA Parade," *NYT*, September 8, 1933; "Millions Join to Cheer the NRA in New York," *NYT*, September 14, 1933.

97. "Supporting our President," *Riverside Enterprise*, August 4, 1933, reprinted in Tobey, *Technology as Freedom*, 149.

98. Johnson, *Blue Eagle*, 223.

99. Quoted in Vaudagna, "Mussolini and Franklin D. Roosevelt," 158. See also

Vaudagna, "New Deal e corporativismo"; Schlesinger, *Politics of Upheaval*, 648 (on Mussolini and Stalin as "blood brothers").

100. Tugwell, *Diary of Rexford G. Tugwell*, 139.

101. "Accomplishments and Failings of N.R.A., March 5, 1934," in *Public Papers and Addresses of Franklin D. Roosevelt* 3:125. But for the antiparliamentarian overtones of some New Dealers such as Donald Richberg and Hugh Johnson, see Whitman, "Of Corporatism, Fascism, and the First New Deal," 767–69.

102. Letter from Lewis to Roosevelt, May 29, 1933, NARA, College Park, RG 9, 9/530/60/23/4/557, box 318; Memorandum from Thorp to Horner, May 2, 1934, NARA, College Park, RG 9, 9/530/60/25/26/7-1/599, box 433.

103. Schivelbusch, *Three New Deals*, 17–33; Vaudagna, "A Checkered History"; Perfetti, "La discussione sul corporativismo in Italia"; Schmitz, *Thank God They're on Our Side*, 86–97; Engerman, *Modernization from the Other Shore*; Mauch and Patel, *United States and Germany during the Twentieth Century*. This interpretation is markedly different from Goldberg, *Liberal Fascism*, with its extremely broad definition of fascism.

104. Cuff, *War Industries Board*.

105. Moley, *After Seven Years*, 186; Kennedy, *Freedom from Fear*, 149–53.

106. See, for example, Gordon, *New Deals*, 166–203.

107. Schlesinger, *Coming of the New Deal*, 105.

108. Badger, *FDR*, 83–108; Finegold and Skocpol, *State and Party in America's New Deal*, 90–103, esp. 95 (figures of NRA code officials); Reagan, "Business," 193. See also Himmelberg, *Origins of the National Recovery Administration*, 129–66.

109. Bernstein, "New Deal," 264.

110. Address Filene, City Club of Rochester, January 26, 1935, NARA, Hyde Park, President's Private Files, box 2116.

111. Raymond Clapper, "Between You and Me," *Washington Post*, December 4, 1934.

112. Quoted in Philips-Fein, *Invisible Hands*, 5 (see also 1–25); Alpers, *Dictators, Democracy, and American Public Culture*, 35.

113. Rosen, *Republican Party in the Age of Roosevelt*, 45–59.

114. See, for example, Halpern, "Labor"; Schlesinger, *Coming of the New Deal*, 136–51; Richberg, *Rainbow*, 45–64.

115. Lewis, "Labor and the National Recovery Administration," 58. See also, for example, Dubofsky and van Tine, *John L. Lewis*, 181–202.

116. See "NRA, Code of Fair Competition for the Cotton Textile Industry, 1 July 1933," in *DH-FDRP*, 16:297–305. See, more generally, Hodges, *New Deal Labor Policy and the Southern Cotton Textile Industry*, 104–40; Gordon, *New Deals*.

117. Mason, "Labor, the Courts, and Section 7(a)," 1005.

118. Halpern, "Labor," 170–76. For the figures, see *Historical Statistics of the United States: Colonial Times to 1970*, part 1, 178. As a case study, see Faue, *Community of Suffering and Struggle*.

119. *Historical Statistics of the United States: Colonial Times to 1970*, part 1, 179.

120. See, for example, Selvin, "An Exercise in Hysteria."

121. Badger, *FDR*, 104–8.

122. Quoted in Lynd and Lynd, *Middletown in Transition*, 23. See also, for example, *Sunbelt Capitalism*.

123. See, for example, Commission of Inquiry into National Policy in International Economic Relations, *International Economic Relations*.

124. For Japan, albeit with a somewhat different interpretation regarding the United States, see Gao, "The State and the Associational Order of the Economy." On Germany, see, for example, Gosewinkel, *Wirtschaftskontrolle und Recht*; Tooze, *Wages of Destruction*, 99–134. On Brazil, see Hentschke, "The Vargas Era Institutional and Development Model Revisited"; Fonseca, *Vargas*; Levine, *Father of the Poor?* 9. See also Limoncic, "Os inventores do New Deal"; Leopoldi, "O Século do Corporativismo?" On Sweden and Switzerland, see Katzenstein, *Small States in World Markets*. See also Nolan, *Transatlantic Century*. For a different interpretation, see Bertrams, "Planning and the 'Techno-Corporatist Bargain.'"

125. Greaves, *Industrial Reorganization and Government Policy*, esp. 237–43.

126. Temporary National Economic Committee, *Regulation of Economic Activities in Foreign Countries*, 15.

127. Supple, "Political Economy of Demoralization." On the wider context, see Gordon, *New Deals*, 294–305.

128. Madureira, "Cartelization and Corporatism"; Martinho, "Entre o fomento e o condicionamento"; Costa Pinto, "'Corporatist Revolution' of the Portuguese New State."

129. Quote from Piettre, *L'évolution des ententes industrielles*, 10–11. See also, for example, Passmore, "Business, Corporatism, and the Crisis of the French Third Republic"; Kuisel, *Capitalism and the State in Modern France*, 93–119; Dobbin, "Social Construction of the Great Depression."

130. Schaik, "Crisis en Protectie onder Colijn"; Hen, *Actieve en re-actieve industriepolitiek*; Zanden, *Een klein land in de 20ᵉ eeuw*, 148–63.

131. Temporary National Economic Committee, *Regulation of Economic Activities in Foreign Countries*, 103–68; Bulmer-Thomas, "Latin American Economies"; Love, "Economic Ideas and Ideologies in Latin America since 1930"; O'Connell, "Argentina into the Depression"; Jáuregui, "Después de la caída"; Altman, "Cárdenas, Vargas y Perón."

132. Union membership as a percentage of the total number of employees in 1925 and 1938 was as follows: Netherlands, 23 and 31; Belgium, 31 and 37; Great Britain, 32 and 37; France, 8 and 34; Denmark, 36 and 38; Sweden, 31 and 55; Norway, 20 and 57; Australia, 42 and 39; and Canada, 9 and 10. See Zanden, *Een klein land in de 20ᵉ eeuw*, 106. For slightly different figures, see Eichengreen and Hatton, "Interwar Unemployment," 28.

133. Roxborough, "Urban Working Class and Labour Movement," 307–26. On Colombia, see Palacio, "Servicios legales y relaciones capitalistas." On Brazil, see Wolfe, "Faustian Bargain Not Made." See also Limoncic, "Os inventores do New Deal."

134. Leuchtenburg, "Great Depression," 303.

135. On the comparison with Australia, see Archer, *Why Is There No Labor Party?*

136. For a different interpretation, see Hamby, "New Deal."

137. On the idea of a "balanced economy," see Johnson, *Blue Eagle*, 159–71. On the interest of Soviet historians of the 1980s in this turn away from rugged individualism, see Sivachev, "Rise of Statism in 1930s' America."

138. McElvaine, *Great Depression*, 221–23.

139. Smith, *Building New Deal Liberalism*; Kennedy, *Freedom from Fear*, 160–77; Schlesinger, *Coming of the New Deal*, 282–96.

140. "Campaign Address on the Federal Budget, Pittsburgh, PA, October 19, 1932," in *The Public Papers and Addresses of Franklin D. Roosevelt*, 1:795–811.

141. Zelizer, "Forgotten Legacy of the New Deal."

142. John Maynard Keynes, "An Open Letter to President Roosevelt," *NYT*, December 31, 1933. On the New Deal and Keynesianism, see, for example, Salant, "Spread of Keynesian Doctrines."

143. See, for example, Brinkley, *End of Reform*, 65–85.

144. Hopkins, *Spending to Save*, 97–125; Leighninger, *Long-Range Public Investment*, 43–54. See also Singleton, *American Dole*.

145. Smith, *Building New Deal Liberalism*, 2.

146. Carmody and Harrington, *Questions and Answers*; Rose, *Put to Work*, 94–114; Taylor, *American-Made*.

147. Letter from Hickok to Hopkins, November 18, 1933, in Lowitt and Beasley, *One Third of a Nation*, 92. On this trip, see also Golay, *America 1933*, 174–99.

148. Schwartz, *Civil Works Administration*, 186.

149. Leighninger, *Long-Range Public Investment*, 47.

150. "$3,187,000 Relief Is Spent to Teach Jobless to Play," *NYT*, April 4, 1935. See also Garraty, *Great Depression*, 188.

151. Quoted in Leuchtenburg, *Franklin D. Roosevelt and the New Deal*, 339.

152. For a classic study on this issue, see Salmond, "Civilian Conservation Corps and the Negro."

153. Smith, *Building New Deal Liberalism*, 15; Boris and Eifert, "Gender"; Ware, *Holding Their Own*.

154. Wright, "Political Economy of New Deal Spending." For a different view on Hopkins, see Hopkins, *Harry Hopkins*.

155. Klebaner, "Poor Relief and Public Works"; Sautter, "Government and Unemployment."

156. Gayer, *Public Works*, 7.

157. See, for example, LoN, Communications and Transit Organisation, *Records of the Work of the Eighteenth Session*, November 29–December 1, 1933, C.98.M.33.1934. VIII, 18. See also, for example, LoN, Communications and Transit Organisation, *Report on the First Two Sessions of the Committee*, April 15, 1932, C.381.M214.1932. VIII; LoN, Communications and Transit Organisation, *Circular concerning Programmes of Important Public Works*, October 19, 1931, C.736.M341; LoN, Communications and Transit Organisation, *Circular concerning Programmes of Important Public Works*, September 3, 1934, A.16.1934.VIII; LoN, Communications and Transit Organisation, *Documentary Material Collected regarding National Public Works*, June 30, 1936, C.276.M.I66. See especially LoN, Communications and Transit Organisation, *Enquiry on National Public Works*, October 31, 1934, C.482.M.209.1934.VIII. On the committee, albeit with a focus on its European activities, see Schipper, *Driving Europe*, 83–157. For a global contemporary survey, see Lorwin, *International Economic Development*.

158. Clavin, *Failure of Economic Diplomacy*, 153–57; Lorwin, *International Economic Development*, 1–3.

159. Wallis, "Birth of Old Federalism," 146–47.

160. See, for example, Tooze, *Wages of Destruction*, 45.

161. Critchlow, "Political Control of the Economy." See also Gourevitch, "Breaking with Orthodoxy"; LoN, Communications and Transit Organisation, *National Public Works*, C.276.M.166.1936.VIII, R 4260/9A/20961/20961.

162. Middleton, *Towards the Managed Economy*, 167–82; Eichengreen and Hatton, "Interwar Unemployment," 25; Möller, *Swedish Unemployment Policy*.

163. Bulmer-Thomas, "Latin American Economies"; LoN, Communications and Transit Organisation, *Enquiry on National Public Works*, October 31, 1934, C.482. M.209.1934.VIII. On Germany, see Humann, "*Arbeitsschlacht*."

164. Brown, *Civilian Conservation Corps Program*, 6.

165. Salmond, *Civilian Conservation Corps*, 221.

166. Patel, *Soldiers of Labor*, 151–59, 261–85; Salmond, *Civilian Conservation Corps*, 121–34; Maher, *Nature's New Deal*.

167. Patel, *Soldiers of Labor*, 408–9.

168. *Joint Hearings before the Committee on Education and Labor*, 46.

169. Hierl, *Ausgewählte Schriften und Reden*, 380–82.

170. Patel, *Soldiers of Labor*, 41–94.

171. See, for example, "Young Nazis Hail Labor Service Plan," *NYT*, June 17, 1933; "Labor Conscription Less Likely in Reich," *NYT*, November 17, 1933; "Labor Service to Prepare German Youths for Army," *NYT*, March 29, 1935.

172. See, for example, Arnold A. McKay, "The Militaristic C.C.C.," *World Tomorrow*, January 18, 1934; Swing, "Take the Army out of the CCC."

173. Salmond, *Civilian Conservation Corps*, 27–28.

174. Harry H. Woodring, "The American Army Stands Ready," *Liberty Journal*, January 6, 1934, 7–12; Carl Warren, "CCC Generalissimo Bans Guns as Impractible," *Daily News*, December 15, 1934.

175. See, for example, Hagood, "Soldiers of the Shield." On reactions, see Letter from McKinney to Early, March 7, 1934, NARA, Hyde Park, Official Files 268, box 2. For another example, see Letter from Moseley to Early, September 15, 1936, NARA, Hyde Park, Official Files 268, box 4; "General Proposes CCC for All of 18," *NYT*, September 13, 1936; "CCC Assailed by War Foe," *NYT*, September 15, 1936; "Plan for C.C.C. Drill Rejected at White House," *New York Herald Tribune*, September 15, 1936.

176. Götz and Patel, "Facing the Fascist Model," 65–71.

177. Deutsche Studentenschaft, *Der Arbeitsdienst in der Welt und die Studentische Jugend*; Schweizerische Zentralstelle für Freiwilligen Arbeitsdienst, *Arbeitsdienst in 13 Staaten*.

178. This is the overall finding in Patel, *Soldiers of Labor*.

179. Salmond, *Civilian Conservation Corps*, 88–101.

180. Letter from FDR to Wilson, September 3, 1938, NARA, Hyde Park, President's Secretary Files, box 32. See also Patel, *Soldiers of Labor*, 277–85, 399–401.

181. Quoted in Mazower, *Dark Continent*, 136.

182. Iatrides, *Ambassador MacVeagh Reports*, 23.

183. Durbin, "Importance of Planning," 41. See also Brooke, "Problems of 'Socialist Planning.'"

184. Pemberton, "Middle Way," 53–54.

185. Ibid.; Maier, "Between Taylorism and Technocracy."

186. Fitzpatrick, *Russian Revolution*, 151–57; Kotkin, *Magnetic Mountain*.

187. Sanchez-Sibony, "Depression Stalinism."

188. Mauldon, "Doctrine of Rationalisation," 252.

189. Flewers, "Lure of the Plan."

190. Beard, "'Five-Year Plan' for America."

191. Chase, *New Deal*, 252.

192. Clark, "Economic Planning in the Modern State," 531.

193. Fausto, "L'economia del fascismo"; Schivelbusch, *Three New Deals*.

194. Tooze, *Wages of Destruction*, 37–134; Hohmann, *Landvolk unterm Hakenkreuz*.

195. Hofmann, "Fascist Reflection."

196. Gao, "State and the Associational Order of the Economy"; Miwa, *State Competence and Economic Growth in Japan*, 3–121.

197. Olsson, "Planning in the Swedish Welfare State"; Arndt, *Economic Lessons of the Nineteen-Thirties*, 207–20.

198. Brélaz, *Henri de Man*, 687–730; Hansen, "Hendrik de Man and the Theoretical Foundations of Economic Planning"; Horn, *European Socialists Respond to Fascism*, 74–95; Bertrams, "Planning and the 'Techno-Corporatist Bargain.'"

199. Hagemann, Nishizawa, and Ikeda, *Austrian Economics in Transition*; Hansen, "Depression Decade Crisis."

200. "Het antwoord van Minister Colijn," *De Tijd*, June 3, 1933.

201. Lorwin, *National Planning in Selected Countries*, 121–53. On Brazil, see Bielschowsky, *Pensamento econômico brasileiro*, 290–302; Draibe, *Rumos e metamorfoses*, 82–137; Lafer, *Planejamento no Brasil*, 9–27.

202. National Planning Board, *Final Report*, 14. See also National Resources Board, *Report on National Planning and Public Works*.

203. Reagan, *Designing a New America*, 168–95; Clawson, *New Deal Planning*, 7.

204. See particularly his "Proposal for an Economic Council," presented to FDR in spring 1933, in Tugwell, *Brains Trust*, 525–28. See also his controversial Des Moines speech: Yale University, Sterling Memorial Library, Jerome New Frank Papers, box 16.

205. See, for example, Reagan, *Designing a New America*; Graham, *Toward a Planned Society*, 1–68; Brinkley, "National Resources Planning Board."

206. Bertrams, "Une inspiration tout en contrastes."

207. Mazower, *Greece and the Inter-War Economic Crisis*, 278; Greaves, *Industrial Reorganization and Government Policy*, 75–109; Ritschel, *Politics of Planning*; Freeden, *Liberalism Divided*, 351–56.

208. For a different view, see Ciepley, *Liberalism in the Shadow of Totalitarianism*, 88.

209. Wright, "Coping with the World Depression"; Kirby, "Engineering China."

210. Visvesvaraya, *Planned Economy for India*; Zachariah, *Developing India*.

211. Eckert, "We Are All Planners Now."

212. Zimmern, "Reflections on the Crisis," 474.

213. Political and Economic Planning Group, "Planning Begins at Home."

214. Pemberton, "Middle Way."

215. Tennessee Valley Authority, *Development of the Tennessee Valley*.

216. Norris, *Fighting Liberal*, 245–77; Hubbard, *Origins of the TVA*.

217. Phillips, *This Land, This Nation*, 83–87.

218. "Message to Congress, April 10, 1933," in *Public Papers and Addresses of Franklin D. Roosevelt*, 2:122.

219. For the text of the act, see Hosen, *Great Depression and the New Deal*, 93–109. See also, for example, Klingensmith, *"One Valley and a Thousand"*; Hubbard, *Origins of the TVA*; Gray and Johnson, *TVA Regional Planning and Development Program*, 3–35.

220. Ekbladh, *Great American Mission*.

221. Brinkley, "National Resources Planning Board."

222. "One Hundred and Sixtieth Press Conference, November 23, 1934," in *Public Papers and Addresses of Franklin D. Roosevelt*, 3:466; For "social thinker," Schlesinger, *Coming of the New Deal*, 327.

223. Letter from Morgan to McIntyre, May 30, 1933, NARA, Hyde Park, Official Files 42, box 1. See also, for example, Creese, *TVA's Public Planning*; Hargrove, *Prisoners of Myth*, 19–41; Nye, *Electrifying America*, 309–10.

224. Selznick, *TVA and the Grass Roots*; Gray and Johnson, *TVA Regional Planning and Development Program*, 29–50.

225. Lilienthal, "Business and Government in the Tennessee Valley," 47.

226. Hargrove, *Prisoners of Myth*, 42–64.

227. Wescoat, "'Watersheds' in Regional Planning," 155–58.

228. Lilienthal, "Business and Government in the Tennessee Valley," 45.

229. *Congressional Record* 77, April 22, 1933, 2178. On business resistance, see, for example, McCraw, *TVA and the Power Fight*.

230. "Comes the Revolution," *Chicago Daily Tribune*, August 17, 1935.

231. Quoted in Drew Pearson and Leon Pearson, "The Tennessee Valley Experiment," *Harper's Magazine* 5, May 1935, 707.

232. Grant, *TVA and Black Americans*; McDonald and Muldowny, *TVA and the Dispossessed*.

233. Chandler, *Myth of the TVA*; Klingensmith, *"One Valley and a Thousand,"* 41–64; Phillips, *This Land, This Nation*; Scott, "High Modernist Social Engineering."

234. Nye, *American Technological Sublime*.

235. Pritchard, *Confluence*, 45–48; Giandou, *La Compagnie Nationale du Rhône*, 25–96.

236. Swyngedouw, "Not a Drop of Water."

237. Quoted in Shpotov, "Soviet and American Business," 186. See also, for example, Bailes, "American Connection"; Dorn, "Hugh Lincoln Cooper and the First Détente."

238. "Dnieprostroy as Object-Lesson," *NYT*, October 12, 1932.

239. Quoted in Moore, *Constructing East Asia*, 150.

240. Blackbourn, *Conquest of Nature*, 189–249.

241. Phillips, *This Land, This Nation*, 80–88; Hoag, *Developing the Rivers of East and West Africa*, 135–201.

242. Ozden, "Pontifex Minimus." On the imperial context, which is normally highlighted, see, for example, Lambert and Lester, *Colonial Lives across the British Empire*. On Cooper Dorn, see Dorn, "Hugh Lincoln Cooper and the First Détente."

243. Macy, "Architect's Office of the Tennessee Valley Authority"; Gray and Johnson, *TVA Regional Planning and Development Program*, 12–15.

244. Kargon and Molella, *Invented Edens*.

245. Schivelbusch, *Three New Deals*, 153–69.

246. Quoted in "Topics of the Time," *NYT*, March 6, 1934.

247. Quoted in Scott, "High Modernist Social Engineering," 22.

248. Ekbladh, *Great American Mission*.

249. Daughton, "FDR as Family Doctor."

250. Burns, *Roosevelt*, 33. See also Stuckey, *Good Neighbor*.

251. Quoted in Yu, "Great Communicator," 90.

252. Benson, "Introduction," xi; Craig, *Fireside Politics*; Halasz, *Roosevelt through Foreign Eyes*, 21–22.

253. Beasley and Smith-Howell, "No Ordinary Rhetorical President."

254. Winfield, "FDR as Communicator."

255. Badger, *FDR*, xi–xii; Levine and Levine, *Fireside Conversations*.

256. Quoted in Levine and Levine, *Fireside Conversations*, 37. See also Boorstin, *America and the Image of Europe*, 107–11.

257. See, for example, Philips-Fein, *Invisible Hands*.

258. Gallagher, *FDR's Splendid Deception*; Watson, "Physical and Psychological Health."

259. Houck and Kiewe, *FDR's Body Politics*. For a more radical claim, see Lomazow and Fettmann, *FDR's Deadly Secret*, esp. 41–75.

260. Quoted in Schlesinger, *Politics of Upheaval*, 583–84. See also Childs, *Witness to Power*, 22.

261. On Lucy Mercer and others, see, for example, Cook, *Eleanor Roosevelt*. On spinning the press, see, for example, Levin, *Making of FDR*.

262. Judt, *Postwar*, 346.

263. Cohen, *Le siècle des chefs*. See also Tedeschini Lalli and Vaudagna, *Brave New Words*.

264. Jean Edward Smith, "Roosevelt: The Great Divider," *NYT*, September 2, 2009. For a contrasting interpretation, see Stuckey, *Good Neighbor*.

265. See, for example, Kennedy, *Freedom from Fear*, 104–33.

266. "Inaugural Address, March 4, 1933," in *Public Papers and Addresses of Franklin D. Roosevelt*, 2:12. See also Isetti, "Moneychangers of the Temple."

267. Schlesinger, *Politics of Upheaval*, 55.

268. See, for example, Childs, *They Hate Roosevelt!* 14. See, more generally, Brinkley, *Voices of Protest*.

269. Delporte, *La IIIᵉ République*; Nord, *France's New Deal*, 17–87.

270. Courtney, "Prime Ministerial Character."

271. Mazower, *Greece and the Inter-War Economic Crisis*, 20–37, 278.

272. Velde, "Echte mannen"; Jong, "United States and the Netherlands."

273. Quoted in James, *British Revolution*, 443. For a more positive assessment of Baldwin, see Williamson, *Stanley Baldwin*, esp. 78–87; Taylor, "Stanley Baldwin, Heresthetics and the Realignment of British Politics"; Hamby, *For the Survival of Democracy*, 216–55.

274. On oratoria di piazza, see Leso, "Aspetti della lingua del fascismo," 151. See, more generally, Falasca-Zamponi, *Fascist Spectacle*; Passerini, *Mussolini immaginario*; Tedeschini Lalli and Vaudagna, *Brave New Words*.

275. Kershaw, *Hitler, 1889–1936*, 167–219; Kopperschmidt and Pankau, *Hitler der Redner*.

276. See, for example, Rieber, "Stalin, Man of the Borderlands." See, more generally, Plamper, *Stalin Cult*.

277. Eatwell, "Introduction," xxviii; Garraty, *Great Depression*, 182–235; Dahl, *Quisling*.

278. Unabhängige Expertenkommission Schweiz–Zweiter Weltkrieg, *Die Schweiz, der Nationalsozialismus und der Zweite Weltkrieg*, 49–76.

279. León y González, "Cárdenas y la construcción del poder politico"; Hayes, *Radio Nation*, 42–79; Beezley, "Conclusion."

280. Hanioğlu, *Atatürk*, 160–98; Plaggenborg, *Ordnung und Gewalt*, 167–210.

281. Lebra, "Self and Other in Esteemed Status."

282. Pollard, "Electronic Pastors," 182–88; Chiron, *Pie XI*. On Ethiopia, see Marcus, *Haile Sellassie I*, 125–26.

283. Berlin, "Roosevelt through European Eyes," 67.

284. Riddell, "Bennett New Deal," 49–50; Boyko, *Bennett*, 363–85.

285. Hosen, *Great Depression and the New Deal*, 257.

286. "City Greets the New Year in One of Gayest Moods," *NYT*, January 1, 1935.

287. Eckstein, "From the Historical Caesar to the Spectre of Caesarism," 293; Manchester, *American Caesar*, 151–52.

288. Alter, *Defining Moment*, 1–7; Leuchtenburg, "Great Depression."

289. Katznelson, *Fear Itself*, 38.

290. Rosenberg, *Spreading the American Dream*, 172.

291. On Perkins's report, for example, see Columbia University Oral History Collection, part III, no. 182, Interviews Perkins, 171–76, 241–60.

292. On Hopkins's trip, see Roosevelt Study Center (hereafter RSC), Harry Hopkins Papers, roll 6, box 99; Tugwell, *Diary of Rexford G. Tugwell*, 136–42; Hopkins, *Harry Hopkins*, 176–77.

293. Letter from Hull to Roosevelt, July 9, 1934, with enclosed report by R. W. Child, RSC, Office Files, Departmental Correspondence Files, reel 18, box 666.

294. Rodgers, *Atlantic Crossings*; Leuchtenburg, "'Europeanization' of America."

295. Dawley, *Changing the World*, 297–330; Gutzke, "Historians and Progressivism"; Saunier, "Trajectoires, projets et ingéniérie."

296. See, for example, Vanger, *Uruguay's José Batlle y Ordoñez*, 31–76; Bertino et al., *La economía del primer Batllismo y los años veinte*, 343–406; Panizza, "Late Institutionalisation and Early Modernisation."

297. Columbia University Oral History Collection, part I: Reminiscences Ezekiel, 30–37.

298. Higgs, *Crisis and Leviathan*; Purseigle, "First World War and the Transformations of the State."

299. Leuchtenburg, "New Deal and the Analogue of War"; Sherry, *In the Shadow of War*, 1–29; Kotkin, "Modern Times."

300. Ickes, *Secret Diary of Harold L. Ickes*, 1:104.

301. Feuer, "American Travelers to the Soviet Union, 1917–32."

302. Rodgers, *Atlantic Crossings*; Kloppenberg, *Uncertain Victory*.

303. Vaudagna, "Checkered History"; Kotkin, "Modern Times."

304. Kennedy, *Freedom from Fear*, 371.

305. On the debate about a "cultural lag" at the time, see, for example, Susman, *Culture as History*, 156–59.

306. See, for example, Roll-Hansen, "Eugenic Practice and Genetic Science in Scandinavia and Germany"; Tydén, "Scandinavian States." See, more generally, Quine, *Population Politics in Twentieth-Century Europe*.

307. McGirr, "Interwar Years," 134–35.

308. Kline, "Eugenics in the United States"; Currell and Cogdell, *Popular Eugenics*.

309. Ladd-Taylor, "Eugenics and Social Welfare in New Deal Minnesota."

310. On Latin America, see Stepan, *"Hour of Eugenics."* On Romania, see Bucur, *Eugenics and Modernization*. On Italy, see Cassata, *Building the New Man*. On India, see Zachariah, "Rethinking (the Absence of) Fascism in India."

311. Cowie and Salvatore, "Long Exception," 6.

312. Boorstin, *America and the Image of Europe*, 112.

313. As a starting point of the debate, see Schlesinger, *Imperial Presidency*.

314. Loewenstein, "Balance between Legislative and Executive Power," 583. On Ireland's 1937 constitution, see, for example, Kissane, "Éamon de Valéra."

Chapter 3
Into the Vast External Realm

1. "Inaugural Address, March 4, 1933," in *Public Papers and Addresses of Franklin D. Roosevelt*, 2:14.

2. For a different interpretation, see, for example, Hendrickson, *Union, Nation, or Empire*. See also Blower, "From Isolationism to Neutrality."

3. Roosevelt, "Our Foreign Policy."

4. See, for example, Dallek, *Franklin D. Roosevelt and American Foreign Policy*, 3–20; Rhodes, *United States Foreign Policy in the Interwar Period*, 91–111; Harper, *American Visions of Europe*, 7–47.

5. US Department of State, "Press Releases," no. 190, May 20, 1933, 352.

6. Layton, "Tasks of the World Economic Conference," 406.

7. US Department of State, "Press Releases," no. 190, May 20, 1933, 357.

8. Ibid., 347.

9. Clavin, *Securing the World Economy*, 84–123; Clavin, *Failure of Economic Diplomacy*, 80–88.

10. *FRUS*, 1933, General, 673.

11. Ibid., 676–78.

12. Dallek, *Franklin D. Roosevelt and American Foreign Policy*, 54–55; Clavin, *Failure of Economic Diplomacy*, 109–41; Kindleberger, *World in Depression*, 201–21.

13. Clavin, *Failure of Economic Diplomacy*, 134–65.

14. Wells, *Shape of Things to Come*, 135.

15. "Nie mehr Gequassel!" *Völkischer Beobachter*, July 14, 1933. See also Patel, "Amerika als Argument."

16. This is the main argument in Clavin, *Failure of Economic Diplomacy*, esp. 195–201. See also, for example, Eichengreen, *Golden Fetters*, 317–47.

17. Quoted in Schlesinger, *Coming of the New Deal*, 225.

18. McKercher, *Transition of Power*, esp. 1–31, 157–85.

19. For an early use of the term in English in the context of the Paris conference of 1919, see Hayden, *Negotiating in the Press*, 179.

20. Reynolds, "Wheelchair President and His Special Relationships."

21. Clavin, *Failure of Economic Diplomacy*, 3; Eichengreen, *Golden Fetters*, 395–99.

22. Clavin, *Failure of Economic Diplomacy*, 160–61.

23. Quoted in Ahamed, *Lords of Finance*, 468. See also Letter from Stimson to Hoover, July 31, 1933, RSC, Stimson Papers, reel 85.

24. Israel, "Fulfillment of Bryan's Dream"; Brennan, *Silver and the First New Deal*.

25. For the text of the silver agreement, see *FRUS*, 1933, General, 763–66. On Soong, see US Department of State, "Press Releases," no. 190, May 20, 1933, 347; Letter from Phillips to Roosevelt, August 4, 1933, RSC, FDR Office Files, reel 4, 698. On India, see Balachandran, "Gold, Silver, and India in Anglo-American Monetary Relations."

26. Quoted in "Roosevelt at Butte Pledges 'No Evasion on a Silver Parley,'" *NYT*, September 20, 1932.

27. For a detailed account, see Leavens, *Silver Money*, 245–81. For the most relevant documents, see ibid., 372–88; Friedman and Schwartz, *Monetary History of the United States*, 483–89.

28. Friedman, "Franklin D. Roosevelt, Silver, and China."

29. "Business Gets 'Jitters' over Silver Buying," *Chicago Daily Tribune*, October 18, 1934.

30. Rothermund, *Global Impact of the Great Depression*, 110–15; Shiroyama, *China during the Great Depression*, 15–139.

31. Burdekin, "US Pressure on China"; Leavens, *Silver Money*, 293–312.

32. Letter from Fletcher to Johnson, July 3, 1935, NARA, College Park, RG 59, 59/350/3/14/2, box 1893.

33. Dallek, *Franklin D. Roosevelt and American Foreign Policy*, 94–95; Friedman, "Franklin D. Roosevelt, Silver, and China."

34. *Congressional Record* 77, March 10, 1933, 119. See also, for example, "Pittman Explains Plan," *NYT*, July 19, 1933.

35. Sewall, "Key Pittman and the Quest for the China Market," 360, 366.

36. *Congressional Record* 78, January 27, 1934, 1463.

37. Translation of an article in *Asahi Shimbun*, April 18, 1934, Yale University Library, James Harvey Rogers Papers (hereafter JHRP), box 51. On Rogers's trip and his reports, see JHRP, boxes 50–51. Blum, *From the Morgenthau Diaries*, 186. See also *Congressional Record* 78, March 19, 1934, 4814–17.

38. "Rogers Silver Report Submitted," *NYT*, September 21, 1934.

39. Report Leavens, "Silver in India," December 1934, NARA, College Park, RG 56, 56/450/81/3/3, box 15.

40. Letter from Hull to FDR, April 30, 1935, with an attached memorandum of Hull's conversation with Sze, NARA, Hyde Park, PSF, box 26.

41. Letter from Phillips to FDR, December 7, 1934, NARA, Hyde Park, PSF, box 26; Letter from Cunningham to Hull, December 7, 1934, NARA, Hyde Park, PSF, box 26; Cablegram from Kung, December 9, 1934, NARA, Hyde Park, PSF, box 26.

42. Salter, *China and the Depression*, 11; "China and Silver," *NYT*, September 3, 1934.

43. Roosevelt, *Franklin D. Roosevelt and Foreign Affairs*, 585.

44. Jespersen, *American Images of China*, 24–44.

45. See, for example, Dallek, *Franklin D. Roosevelt and American Foreign Policy*, 29.

46. See, for example, Burdekin, "US Pressure on China"; Rogers, "Effects in China of Changes in the Price of Silver," undated, ca. 1934, JHRP, box 50.

47. Rothermund, *Global Impact of the Great Depression*, 110–15; Shiroyama, *China during the Great Depression*, 25–30, 168–99; Best, "Leith-Ross Mission and British Policy."

48. Schell, "Silver Symbiosis."

49. K. Tsuchiya, "On Recent Silver Problem in in [*sic*] China," undated JHRP, box 51.

50. Bullitt, *For the President*, 30.

51. Ibid., 26–28.

52. Moley, *After Seven Years*, 201.

53. McKercher, *Transition of Power*, 159–63; Dallek, *Franklin D. Roosevelt and American Foreign Policy*, 40–48. On France, see *FRUS*, 1933, General, 879–83.

54. Quoted in McKercher, *Transition of Power*, 173. See also Rhodes, *United States Foreign Policy in the Interwar Period*, 95–98.

55. "Fourth 'Fireside Chat,' October 22, 1933," in *Public Papers and Addresses of Franklin D. Roosevelt*, 2:426–27.

56. Dallek, *Franklin D. Roosevelt and American Foreign Policy*, 72–74; Friedman and Schwartz, *Monetary History of the United States*, 462–83.

57. Blum, *From the Morgenthau Diaries*, 69–70. See also Barber, *Designs within Disorder*, 45–52.

58. Dallek, *Franklin D. Roosevelt and American Foreign Policy*, 72–74.

59. Blum, *From the Morgenthau Diaries*, 71.

60. Ibid.; "L'actualité financière," *Journal des débats*, October 24, 1933. See also Vaïsse, "Le mythe de l'or en France"; Mouré, *Managing the Franc Poincaré*, 109–19, 197–217.

61. *FRUS*, 1933, General, 845.

62. Dallek, *Franklin D. Roosevelt and American Foreign Policy*, 73–74. On the December round of debt payments, see the various documents in *FRUS*, 1933, General, 826–920.

63. Roosevelt, *Franklin D. Roosevelt and Foreign Affairs*, 119.

64. Quoted in "Decade of Idiocy Not Enough," *NYT*, November 24, 1932.

65. *FRUS*, 1933, General, 209. See also, albeit with a slightly different interpretation, Dallek, *Franklin D. Roosevelt and American Foreign Policy*, 66–70. On the conference more broadly, see Noel-Baker, *First World Disarmament Conference and Why It Failed*, 114–34. For a different interpretation, see Adams, *FDR, The New Deal and Europe*.

66. *FRUS*, 1933, General, 210.

67. Ibid., 246.

68. On the German withdrawal, see ibid., 265. On Germany's role, see Dengg, *Deutschlands Austritt aus dem Völkerbund und Schachts "Neuer Plan,"* 278–308.

69. *FRUS*, 1933, General, 246. Davis informed Roosevelt about Nadolny's statement directly. On Nadolny, see Wollstein, *Vom Weimarer Revisionismus zu Hitler*, 193–94.

70. *FRUS*, 1933, General, 300. See also, in general, Steiner, *Triumph of the Dark*, 40–45.

71. On the less well-known Japanese fears about the American buildup, see Asada, *Culture Shock and Japanese-American Relations*, 137–73. See, more generally, Asada, *From Mahan to Pearl Habor*, 161–211; Iriye, *Globalizing of America*, 122–27.

72. Dallek, *Franklin D. Roosevelt and American Foreign Policy*, 75–77.

73. Roosevelt, "Our Foreign Policy," 579.

74. *FRUS*, Japan, 1931–41, 1:224–25. There was a long discussion about the correct translation of the statement and how far it represented the official Japanese position; see, for example, *FRUS* 1934, 3:141–42. The Japanese diplomat's correct name is Amou, but most American sources referred to him (and the doctrine) as Amau.

75. Reported in ibid., 3:121.

76. On Hull, see ibid., 3:137. On Hornbeck's view, see, for example, ibid., 3:128–29. See, more generally, Hu, *Stanley K. Hornbeck and the Open Door Policy*, 180–84. For a different interpretation, see, for example, Schmitz, *Triumph of Internationalism*, 32–33. On the Chinese position, see Sun, *China and the Origins of the Pacific War*, 49–53.

77. *FRUS*, 1933, 3:261. On Chinese pressure, see, for example, ibid., 3:262.

78. Ibid., 3:265.

79. Wilson, "Internationalism in Current American Labor Policy," 915, 918. See also article 392 of the Versailles treaty; Hudson, "Membership of the United States"; McKillen, "Beyond Gompers"; Ostrower, "American Ambassador to the League of Nations."

80. Plata, "Le Bureau international du travail"; Jensen, "From Geneva to the Americas."

81. "Address before the Woodrow Wilson Foundation, December 28, 1933," in *Public Papers and Addresses of Franklin D. Roosevelt*, 2:547.

82. Johnson in *Congressional Record* 79, January 16, 1935, 489. Long in *Congressional Record* 79, January 29, 1935, 1131. For Roosevelt's view in 1928, see Roosevelt, "Our Foreign Policy," 581–82.

83. Quoted in Dallek, *Franklin D. Roosevelt and American Foreign Policy*, 71. See also Pomerance, *United States and the World Court*, 120–38.

84. Roosevelt, *Franklin D. Roosevelt and Foreign Affairs*, 581–82. On the wider debate, see Fleming, *United States and the World Court*, 109–16.

85. NARA, Hyde Park, RG 16, box 1837.

86. *FRUS*, 1920, 3:467–68.

87. Glantz, *FDR and the Soviet Union*, 10–13.

88. "J. D. Mooney Urges Soviet Recognition," *NYT*, October 8, 1930. See also Hoff, *Ideology and Economics*, 97–102.

89. Filene, *Americans and the Soviet Experiment*, 202–9; Engerman, *Modernization from the Other Shore*.

90. Witherow, *Foreign Trade of the United States, Calendar Year 1933*, 1:108.

91. Filene, *Americans and the Soviet Experiment*, 236–39.

92. Quoted in Browder, "Soviet Far Eastern Policy and American Recognition," 264n5.

93. US Department of State, "Press Releases," no. 190, May 20, 1933. On the So-

viet reaction, see Browder, "Soviet Far Eastern Policy and American Recognition," 267–69.

94. See, for example, *FRUS*, Soviet Union, 1933–39, 16–17. See also Glantz, *FDR and the Soviet Union*, 19–21.

95. *FRUS*, Soviet Union, 1933–39, 26–27. For a compilation of US losses, see ibid., 8.

96. Ibid., 27.

97. Ibid., 59.

98. See *DH-FDRP*, vol. 27; Dallek, *Franklin D. Roosevelt and American Foreign Policy*, 79–81; Maddux, *Years of Estrangement*, 24–25.

99. Quoted in *FRUS*, Soviet Union, 1933–39, 45.

100. Ibid., 53–62. Litvinov quoted in ibid., 61. See also Bullitt, *For the President*, 70–71.

101. *FRUS*, Soviet Union, 1933–39, 63–67. See also, for example, Bennett, *Franklin D. Roosevelt and the Search for Security*, 33–45.

102. Bullitt, *For the President*, 136. See also Maddux, *Years of Estrangement*, 38–43.

103. Mayers, *Ambassadors and America's Soviet Policy*, 104–7. On the Ukraine, see, for example, Conquest, *Harvest of Sorrow*.

104. Maddux, *Years of Estrangement*, 33–38.

105. *FRUS*, 1934, 3:32–36. On the Soviets, see Browder, "Soviet Far Eastern Policy and American Recognition," 271–73.

106. Tsouras, "Hokushin."

107. Witherow, *Foreign Trade of the United States, Calendar Year 1936*, 160; Bennett, *Franklin D. Roosevelt and the Search for Security*, 70–71.

108. *FRUS*, Soviet Union, 1933–39, 60; Mayers, *Ambassadors and America's Soviet Policy*, 111.

109. Dunn, *Caught between Roosevelt and Stalin*, 13–58; Bennett, *Franklin D. Roosevelt and the Search for Security*, 87–94.

110. *FRUS*, Soviet Union, 1933–39, 557. On the trials, see, for example, ibid., 545–46.

111. Dunn, *Caught between Roosevelt and Stalin*, 61–94; Weisbrode, *Atlantic Century*, 47–48.

112. Margulies, *Pilgrimage to Russia*; Maddux, *Years of Estrangement*, 69–80.

113. See, for example, Schoultz, *Beneath the United States*, 291–303. The role of both the Roosevelt Corollary and Clark Memorandum has been long contested. See, for example, Ricard, "Roosevelt Corollary"; Sessions, "Clark Memorandum Myth." See also LaFeber, *Inevitable Revolutions*, 59–83.

114. Circular White, October 10, 1930, NARA, College Park, RG 59, 59/350/2/11/3, box 352.

115. Schmidt, *United States Occupation of Haiti*, 108–34; Loveman, *No Higher Law*, 250–52.

116. The first two quotes in "Inaugural Address, March 4, 1933," in *Public Papers and Addresses of Franklin D. Roosevelt*, 2:14. The third quote in "Address before Pan-American Union, April 12, 1933," in *Public Papers and Addresses of Franklin D. Roosevelt*, 2:130.

117. Pérez, *Cuba and the United States*, 177–86. Ortiz quoted in ibid., 184. See also Wood, *Making of the Good Neighbor Policy*, 13–47; Schmitz, *Thank God They're on Our Side*, 46–57.

118. Schoultz, *Beneath the United States*, 298–300; Brewer, *Borders and Bridges*, 98–104.

119. *Henry Lewis Stimson Diaries*, November 25, 1930.

120. *FRUS*, 1933, American Republics, 5:362. See also Dur and Gilcrease, "US Diplomacy"; O'Sullivan, *Sumner Welles*, 8–12.

121. *FRUS*, 1933, American Republics, 5:389.

122. Roosevelt, *Franklin D. Roosevelt and Foreign Affairs*, 386.

123. See, for example, Dallek, *Franklin D. Roosevelt and American Foreign Policy*, 60–65; Cronon, "Interpreting the New Good Neighbor Policy"; Wood, *Making of the Good Neighbor Policy*, 48–80.

124. Roosevelt, *Franklin D. Roosevelt and Foreign Affairs*, 390.

125. Roosevelt, "Our Foreign Policy," 583–85.

126. On Wilson, see *FRUS*, 1933, American Republics, 5:392–93. On Daniels, see, for example, ibid., 5:394, 412–13; Daniels, *Shirt-Sleeve Diplomat*, 324–25.

127. *FRUS*, 1933, American Republics, 4:45.

128. Ibid., 4:42.

129. Ibid., 4:168. See also ibid., 4:159–60; Dallek, *Franklin D. Roosevelt and American Foreign Policy*, 81–83; Schoultz, *Beneath the United States*, 303–5.

130. "Hull Pays Respects to President Terra," *NYT*, November 30, 1933.

131. *FRUS*, 1933, American Republics, 4:202. See also, for example, Crawley, *Somoza and Roosevelt*, 39–41.

132. For the Mexican foreign minister's position, see Puig Casauranc, *Remarks*, 96–98.

133. *FRUS*, 1933, American Republics, 4:17. See also ibid., 137–41.

134. On Daniels's role, see Cronon, "Interpreting the New Good Neighbor Policy." On the US reluctance to discuss the Monroe Doctrine at the time, see Haines, "Roosevelt Administration Interprets the Monroe Doctrine."

135. Grandin, "Your Americanism and Mine."

136. "Address before the Woodrow Wilson Foundation, December 28, 1933," in *Public Papers and Addresses of Franklin D. Roosevelt*, 2:545–46.

137. On Welles, see *FRUS*, 1933, American Republics, 5:525–26. Roosevelt quoted in "Presidential Statement on Non-Intervention in Cuba, November 23, 1933," in *Public Papers and Addresses of Franklin D. Roosevelt*, 2:500.

138. Wood, *Making of the Good Neighbor Policy*, 111–12; Schoultz, *Beneath the United States*, 296–305.

139. Towns, "Inter-American Commission of Women and Women's Suffrage"; Jabour, "Relationship and Leadership." On the wider context, see Rupp, *Worlds of Women*.

140. Cox, "Was the Seventh Pan American Conference a Success?" 44.

141. Andrade, *My Missions for Revolutionary Bolivia*, 54; Villaseñor, *Ensayos Interamericanos*, 254. On Latin American perceptions more generally, see Salvatore, *Imágenes de un imperio*, 57–76.

142. Steward, *Trade and Hemisphere*, 23–30.

143. Lusztig, *Risking Free Trade*, 53–70. See Woods, "FDR and the New Economic Order."

144. Letter from Delegation of the United States to President of the Advisory

Committee on Colombia and Peru, League of Nations, May 26, 1933, LoN, R 3621/1/1393/531.

145. Letter from Gilbert to Avenol, December 7, 1934, LoN, R 3641/1/14760/14105. See also LoN, R 3630/1/3045/3044; *Dispute between Bolivia and Paraguay*, May 15, 1934, LoN, C.154.M.64.1934.VII; Mathews, "Roosevelt's Latin-American Policy," 817–18.

146. "Cheering Throngs Welcome Roosevelt to Buenos Aires," *NYT*, December 1, 1936. On this trip, see also Raymont, *Troubled Neighbors*, 25–29; Leonard, "New Pan Americanism."

147. Inter-American Conference for the Maintenance of Peace, *Proceedings*, 793. On the agreement, see ibid., 683.

148. Roosevelt, *F.D.R.: His Personal Letters*, 1:638.

149. Dallek, *Franklin D. Roosevelt and American Foreign Policy*, 133.

150. Andrade, *My Missions for Revolutionary Bolivia*, 54.

151. Pérez, *Cuba and the United States*, 202–5. On the statistics, see also IHS, *Americas*, 189, 461; Dye and Sicotte, "Interwar Shocks to US-Cuban Trade Relations." On the environmental dimension, see Tucker, *Insatiable Appetite*, 14–26.

152. Quoted in Steward, *Trade and Hemisphere*, 113. See also McGillivray, *Blazing Cane*, 226–57.

153. Witherow, *Foreign Trade of the United States, Calendar Year 1933*, 66.

154. Roosevelt, *F.D.R.: His Personal Letters*, 1:638; "Nazis Pick Flaws in Roosevelt Talk," *NYT*, December 3, 1938.

155. *FRUS*, 1937, 5:321.

156. Dodd, *Ambassador Dodd's Diary*, 436.

157. Steward, *Trade and Hemisphere*, 123–51; Lübken, *Bedrohliche Nähe*; Hilton, *Brazil and the Great Powers*.

158. D'Araújo, "Entre a Europa e os Estados Unidos."

159. Hart, *Empire of Ideas*.

160. On Guatemala, see Findling, *Close Neighbors, Distant Friends*, 90–93. On the Dominican Republic, see Roorda, *Dictator Next Door*, esp. 117, 120–21.

161. Eckes and Zeiler, *Globalization and the American Century*, 92.

162. Steward, *Trade and Hemisphere*, 213–14, 240–41; Varg, "Economic Side of the Good Neighbor Policy."

163. Steward, *Trade and Hemisphere*, 243–45.

164. *FRUS*, 1939, 5:321.

165. On this debate, see, for example, Bisson, "Japan's Trade Boom."

166. See, for example, Wood, *Making of the Good Neighbor Policy*; Raymont, *Troubled Neighbors*.

167. On the statistics, see IHS, *Americas*, 222, 531; Findling, *Close Neighbors, Distant Friends*, 92; Bucheli, "Multinational Corporations."

168. O'Brien, *Century of U.S. Capitalism in Latin America*, 73–99.

169. See, particularly, Standard Oil Company, *Mexico Labor Controversy*, 174–99; Gonzalez, *Mexican Revolution*, 232–59.

170. *FRUS*, 1938, 5:665. See also ibid., 674–78; Dwyer, *Agrarian Dispute*; Gilly, *El cardenismo, una utopía mexicana*.

171. *FRUS*, 1938, 5:680; see also Cullather, "Model Nations."

172. Steward, *Trade and Hemisphere*, 198–207.

173. Jayne, *Oil, War, and Anglo-American Relations*.

174. On Nicaragua, see Roorda, "Cult of the Airplane," 270.

175. Crawley, *Somoza and Roosevelt*, 18.

176. Smith, *America's Mission*, 113–24.

177. On Matthews, who ended his career as a brigadier general, see Crawley, *Somoza and Roosevelt*, 18–22.

178. Dosal, *Doing Business with the Dictators*, 183–200.

179. On Cuba, see Benjamin, "New Deal, Cuba, and the Rise."

180. *FRUS*, 1933, General, 925–26, 931–33.

181. Dulles, *Export-Import Bank of Washington*, 1.

182. Ingulstad, "Winning the Hearths and Mines," 32–45.

183. Hyde, "Legal Aspects," 432–33, 443.

184. Eichengreen, *Golden Fetters*, 337–41; Iriye, *Globalizing of America*, 147–48; Teichert, *Autarkie und Großraumwirtschaft*; Fieldhouse, "Metropolitan Economics of Empire"; with a somewhat different argument on Japan: Fujitani, *Race for Empire*.

185. *Henry Lewis Stimson Diaries*, March 7, 1932.

186. Navarro, *Creating Tropical Yankees*.

187. Lewis, *Puerto Rico*, 88. Lewis's interpretation is lopsided and basically praises the New Deal's efforts on Puerto Rico; hence, his account of the period up to 1933 also has to be seen in this light.

188. Johnson, "Anti-Imperialism and the Good Neighbour Policy."

189. Rodríguez, *New Deal for the Tropics*, 21–25; Johnson, "Anti-Imperialism and the Good Neighbour Policy," 95.

190. Letter from Puerto Rican Sugar Producers to Secretary of War Dern, April 20, 1934, NARA, Hyde Park, Official Files, box 23. For the figures, see Appendix to Memo from FDR to Wallace, November 5, 1934, NARA, Hyde Park, Official Files, box 23. See also Mathews, *Puerto Rican Politics and the New Deal*, 117–42.

191. Rodríguez, *New Deal for the Tropics*, 55–59.

192. Tugwell, *Forty-Second Annual Report of the Governor of Puerto Rico*; Rodríguez, *New Deal for the Tropics*, 60–107.

193. Mathews, *Puerto Rican Politics and the New Deal*, 128–31.

194. Puerto Rico Emergency Relief Administration, *Second Report of the PRERA*; Lewis, *Puerto Rico*, 131.

195. Unpublished Diary Tugwell, esp. March 9, 1934 entry, NARA, Hyde Park, Tugwell Papers, box 39. See also "San Juan's Slums Shock First Lady," *NYT*, March 11, 1934. Ickes's impressions in 1936 were similar; see Ickes, *Secret Diary of Harold L. Ickes*, 1:504.

196. "Remarks in San Juan, July 7, 1934," in *Public Papers and Addresses of Franklin D. Roosevelt*, 3:344.

197. Letter from Chardón to Wallace, June 14, 1934, with enclosed "Report of the Puerto Rico Policy Commission," NARA, Hyde Park, Official Files, box 23. See also Mathews, *Puerto Rican Politics and the New Deal*, 173–88.

198. Villaronga, *Toward a Discourse of Consent*, 15–19.

199. Tugwell, "Report on American Tropical Policy," 1934, NARA, Hyde Park, Official Files, box 23. See also Letter from Taussig to FDR, June 28, 1934, NARA, Hyde Park, Official Files, box 23; Mathews, *Puerto Rican Politics and the New Deal*, 143–48.

200. Memo from FDR to Charles West, June 21, 1935, NARA, Hyde Park, Official Files, box 23.

201. Rodríguez, *New Deal for the Tropics*, 125–37.

202. Quoted in Johnson, "Anti-Imperialism and the Good Neighbour Policy," 100.

203. See, for example, Letter from Baldés to FDR, January 11, 1935, NARA, Hyde Park, Official Files, box 23; Villaronga, *Toward a Discourse of Consent*, 25–26.

204. Letter from Tugwell to Roosevelt, November 3, 1941, RSC, reel 29, 494, Office Files, Diplomatic Files. On the "problem," see Statement by Ickes, May 11, 1944, Yale University, Beinecke Library, Felix S. Cohen Papers, box 33.

205. Quoted in Thorne, *Allies of a Kind*, 159.

206. Briggs, *Reproducing Empire*, 101. See also Mass, "Puerto Rico." On the transnational dimension of the discussion around birth control, see Connelly, *Fatal Misconception*, 77–114.

207. Letter from Winship to FDR, May 8, 1935, NARA, Hyde Park, Official Files, box 23. For the figures, see Appendix to Memo from FDR to Wallace, November 5, 1934, NARA, Hyde Park, Official Files, box 23. See also Lewis, *Puerto Rico*, 134.

208. Franqui, "Fighting for the Nation," 182–212.

209. Chatterjee, *Nation and Its Fragments*.

210. Johnson, "Anti-Imperialism and the Good Neighbour Policy"; Gatell, "Independence Rejected."

211. Tugwell, "Report on American Tropical Policy," 1934, NARA, Hyde Park, Official Files, box 23.

212. "The Puerto Rico Problem," *New Republic*, April 14, 1937, 282.

213. Rodríguez, *New Deal for the Tropics*, 13. Rodríguez even calls it a blueprint.

214. May, *Social Engineering in the Philippines*; Stanley, *Nation in the Making*, 226–62.

215. Kim, "Rethinking Colonialism and the Origins of the Developmental State in East Asia."

216. Parker, *Brother's Keeper*, 16–26; Fraser, *Ambivalent Anti-Colonialism*; Thomas, *Empires of Intelligence*.

217. Austen, "Varieties of Trusteeship," 516. See also Shipway, *Decolonization and Its Impact*, 17–60; Fieldhouse, "Metropolitan Economics of Empire."

218. Mazower, *Hitler's Empire*; Young, *Japan's Total Empire*.

219. Seldes, *Iron, Blood and Profits*, 327.

220. Rhodes, *United States Foreign Policy in the Interwar Period*, 131–44; Powaski, *Toward an Entangling Alliance*, 66–75.

221. "Nye and Clark Urge Peace Laws Here," *NYT*, May 28, 1935.

222. Dallek, *Franklin D. Roosevelt and American Foreign Policy*, 101–21, 135–43.

223. On the link to the soft coal bill, see Weiss, "American Foreign Policy and Presidential Power," 695. On the British model, see chapter 2 of this book.

224. "Quarantine Speech, October 5, 1937," in *Public Papers and Addresses of Franklin D. Roosevelt*, 6:408, 410. See also, for example, Doenecke and Stoler, *Debating Franklin D. Roosevelt's Foreign Policies*, 125–26; Dallek, *Franklin D. Roosevelt and American Foreign Policy*, 147–53.

225. *Congressional Record* 85, September 21, 1939, 10.

226. Borchard, "Neutrality," 53.

227. Lettevall, Somsen, and Widmalm, *Neutrality in Twentieth-Century Europe*. On the United States, see Blower, "From Isolationism to Neutrality."

228. "Acceptance of Renomination, June 27, 1936," in *Public Papers and Addresses of Franklin D. Roosevelt*, 5:235–36.

229. Breitman and Kraut, *American Refugee Policy and European Jewry*, 7–10.

230. Dies, "Nationalism Spells Safety," 1–2.

231. On Japan, see Allen, "When Japan Was 'Champion of the Darker Races.'" On Scottsboro, see Miller, Pennybacker, and Rosenhaft, "Mother Ada Wright and the International Campaign to Free the Scottsboro Boys."

232. "Relaxing Quotas for Exiles Fought," *NYT*, May 4, 1934.

233. Grant, *Conquest of a Continent*, 354–55.

234. Tyner, "Geopolitics of Eugenics."

235. Ngai, *Impossible Subjects*, 96–126; Takaki, *Strangers from a Different Shore*, 315–54.

236. St. John, *Line in the Sand*, 187–97; Balderrama and Rodríguez, *Decade of Betrayal*.

237. On the incidence in Aguascalientes, see Guerin-Gonzales, *Mexican Workers and American Dreams*, 97–109. On the experience of Cuban remigrants as another example, see, for example, Pérez, *Cuba and the United States*, 214–18.

238. Grant, *Down and Out on the Family Farm*; Venkataramani, "Norman Thomas, Arkansas Sharecroppers, and the Roosevelt Agricultural Policies"; Guerin-Gonzales, *Mexican Workers and American Dreams*, 111–38; Phillips, *This Land, This Nation*, 107–32.

239. Dinnerstein, *Antisemitism in America*, 105–27.

240. Tichenor, *Dividing Lines*, 156–59. On this issue, see also, for example, Breitman and Lichtman, *FDR and the Jews*; Breitman and Kraut, *American Refugee Policy and European Jewry*; Stewart, *United States Government Policy on Refugees from Nazism*.

241. For opinion poll figures, see Dinnerstein, *Antisemitism in America*, 127.

242. Breitman and Kraut, *American Refugee Policy and European Jewry*. Brandeis quoted in ibid., 8. See also Zolberg, *Nation by Design*, 271–84.

243. On this fundamental shift, see Gabaccia, *Foreign Relations*.

244. Weiss, "Ethnicity and Reform"; Barkan, "Mobilizing Scientists against Nazi Racism"; Grill, "American South and Nazi Racism."

245. Sherwood, *Kwame Nkrumah*, 13–108.

246. On Nkrumah, see Nkrumah, *Ghana*, 24–47. On the impact on black colleges, see Parker, "Made-in-America Revolutions." For a contemporary study analyzing the tensions between US and immigrant black communities, see Reid, "Negro Immigrant."

247. Slate, *Colored Cosmopolitanism*, esp. 78–87. See also Gallicchio, *African American Encounter with Japan and China*. On the role of the United Kingdom for these networks, see Pennybacker, *From Scottsboro to Munich*.

248. LoN, *Balances of Payments, 1931 and 1930*, 38–39; LoN, *Balances of Payments, 1938*, 142. On tourism to Latin America, see Merrill, *Negotiating Paradise*, 65–140; Berger, "Goodwill Ambassadors on Holiday."

249. Levenstein, *We'll Always Have Paris*, 3–26; Wood, "On the Selling of Rey Momo."

250. Miller, "Italian Americans in the 'Bocce Belt'"; Hoelscher, *Heritage on Stage*. See, more generally, Shaffer, *See America First*; Wall, *Inventing the "American Way,"* 15–100; Sklaroff, *Black Culture and the New Deal*.

251. Calderón-Zaks, "Debated Whiteness amid World Events"; Gutiérrez, *Walls and Mirrors*, 74–95.

252. McCann, *Hello, Hello Brazil*, 129–59; Schwoch, *American Radio Industry*.

253. Shaw and Conde, "Brazil through Hollywood's Gaze."

254. "New York's Tower of Babel," *Chicago Daily Tribune*, September 19, 1933.

255. Delpar, *Enormous Vogue of Things Mexican*; Indych-López, "Mural Gambits"; Tota, *Seduction of Brazil*, 81–87.

256. Letter from Roosevelt to Biddle, May 19, 1933, Library of Congress, Washington, DC, Biddle Papers, box 19.

257. Letter from Biddle to Eleanor Roosevelt, June 28, 1933, Library of Congress, Washington, DC, Biddle Papers, box 19.

258. Ibid.

259. Cortesini, *Arte contemporanea italiana e propaganda fascista*.

260. Mathews, "George Biddle's Contribution to Federal Art"; Harrison, "American Art and the New Deal"; McKinzie, *New Deal for Artists*, esp. 3–18.

261. Letter from Tugwell to Roosevelt, March 17, 1933, NARA, Hyde Park, Official Files 1, box 1; Letter from Roosevelt to Tugwell, August 29, 1937, NARA, Hyde Park, President's Private Files, box 564.

262. Chase, "Imperial Protection and Strategic Trade Policy in the Interwar Period."

263. McKibben, *Cutting Edge*, 32–36.

264. Rosenberg, *Spreading the American Dream*, 165.

265. Daley, *An American Saga*, 101–240.

266. Eckes and Zeiler, *Globalization and the American Century*, 100–101.

267. Van Vleck, *Empire of the Air*.

268. de Grazia, *Irresistible Empire*, esp. 130–283. Halbwachs quoted in ibid., 269.

269. Pedersen, "Back to the League of Nations," 1110; Rietzler, "Before the Cultural Cold Wars"; Parmar, *Foundations of the American Century*, 65–96.

270. Rockefeller Foundation, *Annual Report 1938*, 14, 19.

271. Hark, "Movies and the 1930s"; Rubin, "Movies and the New Deal in Entertainment."

272. Eckes and Zeiler, *Globalization and the American Century*, 102.

273. Goebbels, *Die Tagebücher*, December 22, 1937, 64.

274. Taylor, "Global Players?"; Markovits and Hellerman, *Offside*.

275. Keys, *Globalizing Sport*, 90–114.

276. Roden, "Baseball and the Quest for National Dignity in Meiji Japan"; Harootunian, *Overcome by Modernity*, esp. 34–94; Dawidoff, *Catcher Was a Spy*, 76–96. Quote from *Osaka Mainichi* 90, "Banzai" 91, with banzai meaning something like "long life" or "hurrah." On the wider context, see Obojski, *Rise of Japanese Baseball Power*, 3–29.

277. Keys, "Spreading Peace, Democracy and Coca-Cola," 188–96.

278. Department of State, Radio Address, Welles, July 27, 1938, LoN, R 5740/50/22774/15424; Hart, *Empire of Ideas*, 15–40.

279. Wallace, *Democracy Reborn*, 239.

280. "Fourth Inaugural Address, January 20, 1945," in *Public Papers and Addresses of Franklin D. Roosevelt*, 13:524.

281. James, *End of Globalization*, 5.

282. "The Governing Board Pays Homage to Andrew Carnegie," *Bulletin of the Pan American Union* 70, no. 1 (1936): 2. See also "World to Observe Carnegie Birthday," *NYT*, November 24, 1935.

283. Letter from Grew to Landis, December 5, 1934, NARA, College Park, RG 56, 56/350/7/22-2-3, box 786; Grew, *Ten Years in Japan*, 133. See also Dawidoff, *Catcher Was a Spy*, 91. On Grew, see Mayers, *FDR's Ambassadors and the Diplomacy of Crisis*, 14–35.

284. Rogers, "China and the U.S. Silver-Buying Policy," undated, ca. 1934, JHRP, box 50; Leavens, *Silver Money*, 311–43.

285. Rosenberg, *Spreading the American Dream*, 169–90.

286. Iriye, *Globalizing of America*, 155.

287. Clark, *Negotiating Hollywood*, 82–117; Welky, *Moguls and the Dictators*.

288. Rosenberg, *Spreading the American Dream*, 167–90. On this issue, see also, for example, Gardner, *Economic Aspects of New Deal Diplomacy*.

289. Notes by Tyler, July 20, 1939, LoN, R 4605, 10C/33667/9854.

290. Clavin, *Securing the World Economy*, 133–35; Clavin and Patel, "Role of International Organizations in Europeanization"; Ekbladh, "Exile Economics."

291. LoN, Note, April 12, 1937, LoN, R 5740/50/28243/15424.

292. See Wegener, "Creating an 'International Mind'"; Stebenne, "Thomas J. Watson and the Business-Government Relationship."

293. Iriye, *Global Community*, 9–36; Knab and Forclatz, "Transnational Co-Operation."

294. Casey, *Cautious Crusade*.

295. "Annual Message to Congress, January 4, 1939," in *Public Papers and Addresses of Franklin D. Roosevelt*, 8:2–3.

296. *Historical Statistics of the United States: Colonial Times to 1970*, part 2, 1114.

297. Irwin, Mavroidis, and Sykes, *Genesis of the GATT*, 5–22.

CHAPTER 4

REDEFINING BOUNDARIES

1. "Chamber Distorts Voice of Business, Roosevelt Holds," *NYT*, May 4, 1935. See also Gerstle, *American Crucible*, 149–51.

2. On the polarization of the political landscape, see Philips-Fein, *Invisible Hands*; Goldwag, *New Hate*, 247–86.

3. On the British system, see, for example, "Anti-Capital Taxes Assailed by Moley," *NYT*, May 27, 1935; "Douglas Attacks Federal Spending," *NYT*, May 8, 1935; "British Taxes and Ours," *NYT*, May 5, 1935.

4. "A Message to the Congress on Tax Revision, June 19, 1935," in *Public Papers and Addresses of Franklin D. Roosevelt*, 4:274.

5. "Borah Goes to Aid of the President on New Tax Plan," *NYT*, June 24, 1935.

6. See, particularly, Leff, *Limits of Symbolic Reform*; Jones, "Class Tax to Mass Tax."

7. Bernstein, *New Deal Collective Bargaining Policy*; Gross, *Making of the National Labor Relations Board*; Katznelson, *Fear Itself*, 257–60.

8. See, for example, Leuchtenburg, *Franklin D. Roosevelt and the New Deal*, 163–66; Dawson, "Brandeis and the New Deal," 44–56.

9. Immerwahr, *Thinking Small*, 40–65.

10. Kennedy, *I'm for Roosevelt*, 103.

11. Perkins, "The Task That Lies Ahead," *DH-FDRP*, 5:232.

12. In contrast to most other elements of the New Deal, the transatlantic dimension of Social Security is well researched. See, most important, Rodgers, *Atlantic Crossings*, 428–46. For the text of the act, see Hosen, *Great Depression and the New Deal*, 110–36.

13. Commons, "Unemployment Prevention."

14. Toft, "State Action, Trade Unions, and Voluntary Unemployment Insurance"; Rodgers, *Atlantic Crossings*, 433–35.

15. Bennett quoted in Riddell, "Bennett New Deal," 13. See also "Canada's New Deal Stirs Up the Skeptics," *NYT*, February 3, 1935; Scott, "Privy Council and Mr. Bennett's 'New Deal' Legislation."

16. He succeeded in 1943, though. Dion, "Political Origins of Social Security in Mexico."

17. Kasza, *One World of Welfare*, 27.

18. Richards, *Closing the Door to Destitution*, esp. 47–80; Davidson, *Two Models of Welfare*, 131–75; Abramson, "Reorganisation of Social Insurance Institutions in the U.S.S.R."; Madison, *Social Welfare in the Soviet Union*, 57–62.

19. Jensen, "From Geneva to the Americas."

20. Rodgers, *Atlantic Crossings*, 437.

21. Committee on Economic Security, *Social Security in America*, 156–67.

22. Frances Perkins, "Social Security: The Foundation," *NYT*, August 18, 1935.

23. "Presidential Statement upon Signing the Social Security Act, August 14, 1935," in *Public Papers and Addresses of Franklin D. Roosevelt*, 4:324. For another source sprinkled with this language, see Committee on Economic Security, *Social Security in America*. See also Witte, *Development of the Social Security Act*.

24. Perkins, *Roosevelt I Knew*, 286.

25. Armstrong, *Insuring the Essentials*, xiv.

26. International Labour Organization, *Projects des conventions et recommandations*. See also the reports on various countries in NARA, Hyde Park, Winant Papers, box 170.

27. Kott, "Constructing a European Social Model"; Jensen, "From Geneva to the Americas."

28. Frances Perkins, "Social Security: The Foundation," *NYT*, August 18, 1935. Similarly, see, for example, the 1934 "Report of the Unemployment Insurance Committee to the Industrial Advisory Board," in *DH-FDRP*, 5:17–45.

29. Armstrong, "Old-Age Security Abroad." See also Kessler-Harris, *In Pursuit of Equity*, 117–30.

30. Columbia University Oral History Collection, part III, no. 182, Interviews Perkins, 139–47.

31. Rodgers, *Atlantic Crossings*, 442.

32. Columbia University Oral History Collection, part III, no. 182, Interviews Perkins, 171–76, 241–60. See also Martin, *Madam Secretary*, 226–29.

33. Townsend, *New Horizons*, 160.

34. See, among the divergent interpretations, for example, Amenta, *When Movements Matter*; Piven, *Challenging Authority*, 81–108. My interpretation is closer to Amenta's than to Fox's. See also, for example, Altmeyer, *Formative Years of Social Security*; Altman, *Battle for Social Security*, 63–107.

35. Frances Perkins, "Social Security: The Foundation," *NYT*, August 18, 1935.

36. Leff, "Taxing the 'Forgotten Man.'"

37. Cohen, "Development of the Social Security Act of 1935," 385. On public support for the various programs, see Newman and Jacobs, *Who Cares?* 34–39.

38. Roediger and Esch, *Production of Difference*.

39. On Morgenthau, see Zelizer, "Forgotten Legacy of the New Deal." See also Katznelson, *Fear Itself*, 258–60; Lieberman, *Shifting the Color Line*. On the reference to Britain, see Davies and Derthick, "Race and Social Welfare Policy." For a contemporary source along similar lines, see Armstrong, "Old-Age Security Abroad." On preempting a Supreme Court veto, see Eliot, *Recollections of the New Deal*, 95–98.

40. Columbia University Oral History Collection, part III, no. 182, Interviews Perkins, 171–75.

41. Letter Hopkins to Roosevelt, July 25, 1934, RSC, Harry Hopkins Papers, roll 6, box 99.

42. Leff, "Taxing the 'Forgotten Man,'" 361.

43. Fox, *Three Worlds of Relief*, 250–94; Katznelson, *When Affirmative Action Was White*, 42–50.

44. Rodgers, *Atlantic Crossings*, 444.

45. See, for example, Leuchtenburg, *Franklin D. Roosevelt and the New Deal*, 132. See also Kennedy, *Freedom from Fear*, 257–73; Leff, "Taxing the 'Forgotten Man.'"

46. Tomka, *Social History of Twentieth-Century Europe*, 168.

47. Malloy, *Politics of Social Security in Brazil*, 61–71.

48. Limoncic, "Os inventores do New Deal," 251; Gomes, "A práxis corporativa de Oliveira Vianna." Viana is sometimes spelled Vianna.

49. Collado and Hanson, "Old-Age Pensions in Uruguay," 174. See also Bertino et al., *La economía del primer Batllismo y los años veinte*, 343–406.

50. Armstrong, *Insuring the Essentials*. For a similar way of dealing with non-European experience beyond the United States, see Committee on Economic Security, *Social Security in America*.

51. See, for example, http://www.ssa.gov/history/orghist.html (accessed on April 12, 2015).

52. For the figures, see http://www.ssa.gov/history/1930.html (accessed April 12, 2015). See also Barlogh, "Securing Support."

53. McKinley and Frase, *Launching Social Security*, 20–21, 232–38, 311–17.

54. On the Ghent system and its pioneer, see, for example, Van Daele, *Van Gent tot Genève*. On American views, see, for example, Spates and Rabinovitch, *Unemployment Insurance in Switzerland*; Larson and Murray, "Development of Unemployment Insurance in the United States," 182.

55. Hacker, *The Divided Welfare State*, 85–123; Kott, "Constructing a European Social Model."

56. On the change of rhetoric, see Cohen, "Development of the Social Security Act of 1935," 397–98.

57. Stein, "Building Social Security," 247–48.

58. "Presidential Statement upon Signing the Social Security Act, August 14, 1935," in *Public Papers and Addresses of Franklin D. Roosevelt*, 4:324.

59. Cohen, "Development of the Social Security Act of 1935," 383.

60. Hirshfield, *Lost Reform*, 42–134; Gordon, *Dead on Arrival*, 12–16, 46–57.

61. Stein, "Building Social Security," 247–50.

62. Sandeen, "Design of Public Housing in the New Deal." Thanks particularly to the studies of Radford and Rodgers, public housing is another element of the New Deal for which the transatlantic history is already well researched.

63. Fishback, Rose, and Snowden, *Well Worth Saving*; Radford, *Modern Housing for America*, 178–80.

64. Sandeen, "Design of Public Housing in the New Deal"; Pommer, "Architecture of Urban Housing in the United States during the Early 1930s."

65. Radford, *Modern Housing for America*, 89–109; Smith, *Building New Deal Liberalism*, 90.

66. "The One Hundred and Sixty-First Press Conference, November 28, 1934," in *Public Papers and Addresses of Franklin D. Roosevelt*, 3:482. On the debate see, for example, Argersinger, "Contested Visions of American Democracy." See also FDR's enthusiastic letter, which was quite unrepresentative of his correspondence, to Helen Alfred from the National Public Housing Conference: Letter from Roosevelt to Alfred, May 4, 1934, NARA, Hyde Park, Official Files 63, box 1.

67. Argersinger, "Contested Visions of American Democracy."

68. Smith-Rosenberg, "Simkhovitch, Mary Kingsbury," 649–51. See, more generally, Geertse, "Defining the Universal City"; Saunier, "Sketches from the Urban Internationale."

69. Rodgers, *Atlantic Crossings*, 463.

70. Letter from Simkhovitch to Roosevelt, January 27, 1934, NARA, Hyde Park, Official Files 63, box 1.

71. Quoted in Palmer, *Adventures of a Slum Fighter*, 108. The other two members were Alice Samuel from the British Society of Women Housing Estate Managers and Ernst Kahn, the former manager of public housing in Frankfurt, Germany. On their trip, see, for example, Letter from Bohn to Roosevelt, September 8, 1934, NARA, Hyde Park, Official Files 63, box 1. See also McDonnell, *Wagner Housing Act*, 72–76; Miller, *Raymond Unwin*, 223–37.

72. "A Housing Program for the United States," Attachment to Letter from Bohn to Roosevelt, November 13, 1934, NARA, Hyde Park, Official Files 63, box 1. See also, for example, Straus, "Housing Program for the United States."

73. Letter from Bohn to Roosevelt, November 13, 1934, NARA, Hyde Park, Official Files 63, box 1; Letter from Roosevelt to Unwin, June 24, 1937, NARA, Hyde Park, President's Private Files, box 4684.

74. Bauer, *Modern Housing*, 16. For the lectures, see Unwin, *Legacy of Raymond Unwin*, 166–213.

75. State Department to American Diplomatic and Consular Officers, December 29, 1934, NARA, College Park, RG 56, 56/350/7/22/2-3, vol. 787. For the series of

confidential reports by the PWA, see Reed, *European Housing*; Public Works Administration, Housing Division, *British Government in Housing*.

76. See, for example, Letter from US Embassy in Rome to Hopkins, July 27, 1934, RSC, Harry Hopkins Papers, roll 6, box 99.

77. Palmer, *Adventures of a Slum Fighter*, 31–100, 122. On his role in the Atlanta project, see Lapping, "Emergence of Federal Public Housing." On his networks, see Letter from Palmer to Unwin, November 6, 1936, Emory University, Manuscript, Archives, and Rare Book Library of Emory University (hereafter MARBL), Charles F. Palmer Papers, esp. box 63.

78. Brownlow, *Passion for Anonymity*, 302–10, 356–70.

79. Saunier, "Sketches from the Urban Internationale."

80. Telegram from Simkhovitch to Roosevelt, May 5, 1936, NARA, Hyde Park, Official Files 63, box 3.

81. *Congressional Record*, 74th Cong., Senate, Report 2160, June 1, 1936.

82. Letter from Unwin to Roosevelt, June 17, 1937, NARA, Hyde Park, President's Private Files, box 4684.

83. Letter from Lewin, National Retail Lumber Dealers Association, to Roosevelt, February 12, 1936, NARA, Hyde Park, Official Files 63, box 2.

84. Radford, *Modern Housing for America*, 188–89; Clancey, "Vast Clearings."

85. Argersinger, "Contested Visions of American Democracy."

86. Morgan, "Conservative Party and Mass Housing"; Morgan, "Problem of the Epoch."

87. *Congressional Record*, 74th Cong., Senate, Report 2160, June 1, 1936; Radford, *Modern Housing for America*, 191–98.

88. Rodgers, *Atlantic Crossings*, 474–79.

89. Straus, "Housing," 210.

90. US Housing Authority, *Questions and Answers*. For numerous transnational references, see, for example, Straus, *Seven Myths of Housing*.

91. Unwin, "Urban Development."

92. Unwin, "Housing and Planning."

93. Denby, *Europe Re-Housed*, 9, 246.

94. Ward, "Cross-National Learning in the Formation of British Planning Policies," 372–78.

95. See, for example, Benmergui, "Housing Development"; Saunier, "Sketches from the Urban Internationale"; Sánchez Ruiz, *Planificación y urbanismo de la revolución mexicana*; Almandoz, "Urbanization and Urbanism in Latin America."

96. Argersinger, "Contested Visions of American Democracy," 802–3.

97. Tobey, Wetherell, and Brigham, "Moving Out and Settling In"; Clancey, "Vast Clearings."

98. Harlander, *Zwischen Heimstätte und Wohnmaschine*, 39–86; Führer, *Mieter, Hausbesitzer, Staat und Wohnungsmarkt*.

99. See entry "Project" in *Oxford English Dictionary*. See also Goetz, *New Deal Ruins*.

100. Immerwahr, *Thinking Small*, 40–65.

101. Schlesinger, *Coming of the New Deal*, 46.

102. Quoted in Olsson, "Planning in the Swedish Welfare State," 151.

103. Immerwahr, *Thinking Small*; Gilbert, "Low Modernism and the Agrarian New Deal."

104. Gilbert and Howe, "Beyond 'State vs. Society,'" 214–18.

105. Mathews, *Puerto Rican Politics and the New Deal*, 158.

106. Phillips, *This Land, This Nation*, 120–32; Gregg, *Managing the Mountains*, 175–212; Lehman, *Public Values, Private Lands*, 5–41.

107. On the National Planning Board, see Hargreaves, "Land-Use Planning in Response to Drought."

108. Gray, "Social and Economic Implications," 273.

109. Wallace, "American Agriculture and World Markets," 224; Tugwell, "Place of Government in a National Land Program."

110. Mead, *Helping Men Own Farms*, 5. See, more generally, Rodgers, *Atlantic Crossings*, 343–53; Guttenberg, *Language of Planning*, 105–9. On anti-Indian xenophobia, see Hess, "'Hindu' in America."

111. Conkin, *Tomorrow a New World*, esp. 146–85; Rodgers, *Atlantic Crossings*, 448–54.

112. Oren Stephens, "FSA Fights for Its Life," *Harper's Magazine*, April 1, 1943.

113. Philipps, *This Land, This Nation*, 122–32; Worster, *Dust Bowl*, 48–53.

114. See, for example, "Says New Deal Aim Is 'Soviet Industry,'" *NYT*, August 22, 1938.

115. "RA Project Held Model for Future," *NYT*, January 31, 1937. On Arthurdale, see, more generally, Conkin, *Tomorrow a New World*, 237–55; Maloney, *Back to the Land*.

116. Conkin, *Tomorrow a New World*, 189–99.

117. Quoted in Oren Stephens, "FSA Fights for Its Life," *Harper's Magazine*, April 1, 1943.

118. Knepper, *Greenbelt, Maryland*, 13–58; Alanen and Eden, *Main Street Ready-Made*, 12–73. See also Arnold, *New Deal in the Suburbs*; Kargon and Molella, *Invented Edens*, 7–24.

119. "President Views RA Model Town," *NYT*, November 14, 1936.

120. Conkin, *Tomorrow a New World*, 316.

121. *Congressional Record* 80, May 28, 1936, 8183.

122. Conkin, *Tomorrow a New World*, 321.

123. Felix Bruner, "Utopia Unlimited," *Washington Post*, February 10, 1936; his other articles appeared on February 11, 12, and 13, 1936. See also Conkin, *Tomorrow a New World*, 174–79. More precisely, the Supreme Court ruled the ongoing Greenbrook site unconstitutional, and this ended the whole program.

124. "Hoover's Speech," *NYT*, February 13, 1936.

125. Steinberg, *Down to Earth*.

126. Oren Stephens, "FSA Fights for Its Life," *Harper's Magazine*, April 1, 1943.

127. Grant, *Down and Out on the Family Farm*.

128. Rodgers, *Atlantic Crossings*, 456.

129. Murard, "Designs within Disorder."

130. Kargon and Molella, *Invented Edens*, 25–46.

131. Fuller, *Moderns Abroad*, 85–213; Cresti, "Comunità proletarie italiane."

132. Steinbacher, *"Musterstadt" Auschwitz*, esp. 223–52; Lower, *Nazi Empire-Building*, 169–79; Gutschow, *Ordnungswahn*.

133. Grift, "On New Land a New Society."

134. Wilson, "New Paradise"; Duara, *Sovereignty and Authenticity*; Young, *Japan's Total Empire*, 241–59.

135. Hanes, *City as Subject*, 210–68. On the international reception of garden cities, see, for example, Creese, *Search for Environment*, 299–314; Buder, *Visionaries and Planners*, 133–56; Geertse, "Defining the Universal City."

136. Quoted in Rook, "American in Palestine," 78. See also Powell, "Empire Meets the New Deal."

137. Leuchtenburg, *Franklin D. Roosevelt and the New Deal*, 157–58; Brown, *Electricity for Rural America*, ix–xvi, 66.

138. Nye, *Electrifying America*, 292–304; Kline, *Consumers in the Country*, 131–52.

139. Nicholson, "Rural Electrification Act of 1936," 317.

140. Evans, "World's Experience with Rural Electrification," 31.

141. See, for example, Bruère, "What Is Giant Power For?" See, more generally, Cooke, "Early Days of the Rural Electrification Idea"; Tobey, *Technology as Freedom*, 50–52.

142. Quoted in Brown, *Electricity for Rural America*, 17. See also Lowitt, *George W. Norris: The Persistence of a Progressive*, 260–64.

143. "Campaign Address in Portland, September 21, 1932," in *Public Papers and Addresses of Franklin D. Roosevelt*, 1:733.

144. Trombley, *Life and Times of a Happy Liberal*, 112–24.

145. Lilienthal, *TVA*, 20.

146. Phillips, *This Land, This Nation*, 99–100; Brown, *Electricity for Rural America*, 13–40; Selznick, *TVA and the Grass Roots*, 226–46.

147. Brown, *Electricity for Rural America*, 44–45.

148. Lowitt, *George W. Norris: The Triumph of a Progressive*, 126–30.

149. Norris, *Fighting Liberal*, 246.

150. Brown, *Electricity for Rural America*, 75, 122–29; Person, "Rural Electrification Administration in Perspective."

151. Schivelbusch, *Three New Deals*, 165.

152. See, for example, Chikowero, "Subalternating Currents"; Coquery-Vidrovitch, "Electricity Networks in Africa."

153. Josephson, "'Projects of the Century' in Soviet History." For a different interpretation on the Soviet Union, see Schivelbusch, *Three New Deals*, 138–42.

154. Zomers, *Rural Electrification*, 103–40; Lagendijk, *Electrifying Europe*, 104–19.

155. Quoted in Cannon, "Power Relations," 133–34.

156. Cannon, "Power Relations," 139–40. See, more generally, Brinkley, *End of Reform*.

157. Tobey, *Technology as Freedom*, 112–24.

158. *Public Papers and Addresses of Franklin D. Roosevelt*, 5:226–27.

159. Letter from Hopkins to McIntyre, June 22, 1936, and attached press release, NARA, Hyde Park, Official Files 2245.

160. Childs, *Sweden, the Middle Way*; Curti, "Sweden in the American Social Mind," 172.

161. Teeboom, "Searching for the Middle Way," chap. 4, 1 (in this work, every

chapter has its own pagination); Hilson, "Consumer Co-operation and Economic Crisis."

162. Perkins, *Roosevelt I Knew*, 31–32.

163. Bowen, "Report of the General Secretary." See also Panunzio, *Self-Help Coöperatives in Los Angeles*.

164. Letter from Filene to Roosevelt, July 3, 1936, NARA, Hyde Park, Official Files 2245. For Filene's support of consumer cooperatives, see the manuscripts of his talks in NARA, Hyde Park, President's Private Files 2116.

165. Immerwahr, *Thinking Small*; Gilbert, "Low Modernism and the Agrarian New Deal."

166. "Consumer Coöperatives?" *Rotarian*, May 1937, 11–12, 57–58. On US consumer cooperatives at the time, see Deutsch, *Building a Housewife's Paradise*, 105–31.

167. Teeboom, "Searching for the Middle Way," chap. 4, 14–21; Curti, "Sweden in the American Social Mind," 172. On the election in general, see Leuchtenburg, "Election of 1936."

168. Marquis W. Childs, "They Hate Roosevelt!" *Harper's Magazine*, May 1936, 634–42; Childs, *They Hate Roosevelt!* 2.

169. Letter from Childs to Roosevelt, August 4, 1936, NARA, Hyde Park, Official Files 2245. For many quotes from Childs's newspaper articles from this period, see Leuchtenburg, "Election of 1936."

170. Teeboom, "Searching for the Middle Way," chap. 4, 40.

171. Wallace, *Whose Constitution*; "Best Sellers of the Week, Here and Elsewhere," *NYT*, July 20, 1936.

172. Wallace, *Whose Constitution*, 321, 175, 326.

173. Richberg, *Rainbow*, 2. See also, for example, Francis Brown, "In Memory of NRA," *NYT*, March 1, 1936.

174. Desvernine, *Democratic Despotism*, 243.

175. On FERA, see Memorandum from Baker to Hopkins, September 20, 1934, NARA, Hyde Park, Harry Hopkins Papers, box 70. On the TVA, see Letter from Crounse, TVA, to Palmer, June 12, 1935 with attachment, Emory University, MARBL, Charles F. Palmer Papers, box 7; Hawley, *New Deal and the Problem of Monopoly*, 202–3.

176. See, for example, Conkin, *Tomorrow a New World*; Phillips, *This Land, This Nation*.

177. "Roosevelt Will Push Drive for Co-Ops in U.S.," *Chicago Daily Tribune*, August 10, 1936.

178. Teeboom, "Searching for the Middle Way," chap. 4, 63.

179. Confidential Memorandum from Fitzgerald to Early, July 31, 1936, NARA, Hyde Park, Official Files 2246.

180. Letter from Roosevelt to Hennings, August 5, 1936, NARA, Hyde Park, Official Files 2246; Digest of Letter from McIntyre to Glasgow, August 22, 1936, NARA, Hyde Park, President's Secretary Files 3726.

181. Memorandum from Early to Southgate, September 3, 1936, NARA, Hyde Park, Official Files 2245.

182. "Opening of the 1936 Presidential Campaign," in *Public Papers and Addresses of Franklin D. Roosevelt*, 5:384.

183. *Complete Presidential Press Conferences of Franklin D. Roosevelt*, 9:182. FDR did in fact receive the report and had it sent to Wallace. See Confidential Memorandum from McIntyre to Wallace, February 20, 1937, NARA, Hyde Park, Official Files 2246.

184. United States, *Report of the Inquiry on Cooperative Enterprise in Europe*.

185. Digest of Letter from Baker to McIntrye, May 12, 1937, NARA, Hyde Park, Official Files 2246.

186. War Relocation Authority, Memorandum from Glick to Eisenhower, April 15, 1942, NARA, Washington, DC, RG 210, box 225.

187. Daniels, *Prisoners without Trial*, 55–68; Ambrose and Immerman, *Milton S. Eisenhower*, 59–66; Fujitani, *Race for Empire*.

188. Immerwahr, *Thinking Small*, 48–50.

189. War Relocation Authority, *Administrative Manual*, chap. 30.7. See also Hayashi, *Democratizing the Enemy*, 107–47.

190. War Relocation Authority, Memorandum from O'Brien to Ferguson, November 20, 1942, NARA, Washington, DC, RG 210, box 225; Myer, *Uprooted Americans*, 29–58; Drinnon, *Keeper of Concentration Camps*, 29–159.

191. War Relocation Authority, Letter from Macmillan to Smith, July 8, 1943, NARA, Washington, DC, RG 210, box 225.

192. This argument builds on the work of Musiał, *Roots of the Scandinavian Model*; Marklund, "Social Laboratory, the Middle Way, and the Swedish Model"; Hilson, "Consumer Co-operation and Economic Crisis"; Etzemüller, *Die Romantik der Rationalität*.

193. On the use of the term in Swedish during the 1930s and 1940s, see Götz, *Ungleiche Geschwister*, 190–280.

194. Curti, "Sweden in the American Social Mind," 168–72.

195. Quoted in ibid., 170. On Ohlin, see Nycander, "Bertil Ohlin as a Liberal Politician."

196. Letter from Dearing to Roosevelt, September 3, 1937, NARA, Hyde Park, President's Secretary Files, box 51; Childs, *I Write from Washington*, 306–7.

197. Letter from Dearing to Roosevelt, May 9, 1938, NARA, Hyde Park, President's Secretary Files, box 51 (Dearing referred to Eli F. Heckscher).

198. See, for example, Pemberton, "Middle Way."

199. Childs, *Sweden: Where Capitalism is Controlled*; Ratzlaff, "Community Education Movement in Sweden"; Ratzlaff, *Scandinavian Unemployment Relief Program*. On the level of American interest prior to the 1930s, see Curti, "Sweden in the American Social Mind."

200. Spencer, *Ethiopia at Bay*, 5–6.

201. Jackson, *France*, 94.

202. "U.S. Again Eyeing Cooperative Store," *NYT*, January 4, 1937. See also "Tourists to Sweden Rose in 1936," *NYT*, March 21, 1937; Childs, "Sweden Revisited," 33.

203. Macmillan, *Middle Way*, 81.

204. Kettunen, "Transnational Construction of National Challenges."

205. Musiał, *Roots of the Scandinavian Model*, 42–94.

206. Childs, *Sweden*, 133–44. On the British context, see Ellwood, *Shock of America*, 179–83.

207. One good indicator is the amount of Rockefeller Foundation funding. See,

for example, Rockefeller Foundation, *Annual Reports* (New York: Rockefeller Foundation, 1920–35), http://www.rockefellerfoundation.org/about-us/annual-reports/ (accessed April 12, 2015).

208. See, for example, Campbell, *Danish Folk School*; Musiał, *Roots of the Scandinavian Model*, 42–94. See, more generally, Kettunen, "Transnational Construction of National Challenges."

209. Howe, *Denmark: The Coöperative Way*. See also Howe, *Denmark: A Cooperative Commonwealth*, esp. iii–iv; Goldmark, *Democracy in Denmark*; Hollman, *Democracy in Denmark*; Rothery, *Denmark, Kingdom of Reason*.

210. Howe, *Denmark: The Coöperative Way*, 44–45. On Howe, see Miller, *From Progressive to New Dealer*.

211. See, for example, Topp, "Unemployment and Economic Policy in Denmark"; Romer, "Nation in Depression." Danish unemployment figures rose again from 1937 onward—that is, after the period studied here.

212. Craver, "Gösta Bagge"; Lyon, "Education for Modernity."

213. Simon, *Smaller Democracies*, 73.

214. Musiał, *Roots of the Scandinavian Model*, 86–108.

215. Letter from Baker to Roosevelt, August 10, 1936, with attached preliminary report, NARA, Hyde Park, Official Files 2245.

216. Jackson, *Gunnar Myrdal and America's Conscience*; Etzemüller, *Die Romantik der Rationalität*; Barber, *Gunnar Myrdal*, 38–63.

217. Benson and Hedin, *Swedes in America*. See also, for example, NARA, Hyde Park, Official Files 167.

218. See, for example, Naboth Hedin, "New Sweden, Old America," *Forum*, October 1937, 180–84; Hedin, "Sweden's Recovery."

219. Musiał, *Roots of the Scandinavian Model*, 109–64; Marklund, "Social Laboratory, the Middle Way, and the Swedish Model"; Marklund and Petersen, "Return to Sender."

220. Birchall, *International Co-operative Movement*, 1–31, 75–125.

221. Rodgers, *Atlantic Crossings*, 424.

222. Memorandum from Chalmers to Perkins, December 20, 1940, NARA, Hyde Park, Rosenman Papers, box 38.

223. Birchall, *International Co-operative Movement*, 46–54.

224. "New Light from the East," *Consumers' Cooperation* 22, no. 3 (1936): 41. See, more generally, Teeboom, "Searching for the Middle Way," chap. 3, 15–29.

225. "Editorial Epigrams," *Consumers' Cooperation* 22, no. 8 (1936): 114; Letter from Cunningham to Roosevelt, December 13, 1935, NARA, Hyde Park, Official Files 1881, box 1.

226. King, "West Looks East," 302; Birchall, *International Co-operative Movement*, 164–65.

227. "Address at the National Parole Conference, April 17, 1939," in *Public Papers and Addresses of Franklin D. Roosevelt*, 8:219; Fishback, Johnson, and Kantor, "Striking at the Roots of Crime."

228. Jeffreys-Jones, *FBI*, 81–93; Theoharis and Cox, *Boss*, 182; Potter, *War on Crime*.

229. Powers, *G-Men*. See also Weiner, *Enemies*.

230. Jeffreys-Jones, *FBI*, 81–83.

231. O'Reilly, "Roosevelt Administration and Black America"; O'Reilly, "New Deal for the FBI"; Jeffreys-Jones, *FBI*, 120–36; Charles, *J. Edgar Hoover and the Anti-Interventionists*.

232. Cummings, "Modern Tendencies and the Law," 6.

233. Barnes, *Battling the Crime Wave*, i. See also, for example, Vollmer, *Police and Modern Society*.

234. Quoted in Ochonu, "Conjoined to Empire," 135.

235. Lynd and Lynd, *Middletown in Transition*, 345–51. For a more systematic analysis of crime rates during the 1930s, see Fishback, Johnson, and Kantor, "Striking at the Roots of Crime."

236. Lupo, *Quando la mafia trovò l'America*, 116.

237. On the peak era, see Harries and Cheatwood, *Geography of Execution*, 22; Hartung, "Trends in the Use of Capital Punishment." Capital punishment is not a federal but rather a state right; still, it provides insights into the situation at the time.

238. Shelley, "Development of American Crime"; Adler, "Less Crime." On homicide rates, see Hosen, *Great Depression and the New Deal*, 296.

239. Letter from Williamson to Avenol, October 23, 1934, LoN, R 4956, 12/11903/11903.

240. Deflem, *Policing World Society*, 78–96; Nadelmann, "U.S. Police Activities in Europe"; McWilliams, "Unsung Partner against Crime"; Deflem, "Bureaucratization and Social Control," 758–61.

241. Marabuto, *La collaboration policière internationale*, 25–27, 120–51.

242. Deflem, *Policing World Society*, 124–52, 176–98.

243. Melanson, *Secret Service*, 48–49.

244. Emsley, *Crime, Police, and Penal Policy*, 246–74.

245. Killingray, "Maintenance of Law and Order in British Colonial Africa"; Thomas, *Violence and Colonial Order*; Thomas, *Empires of Intelligence*.

246. Emsley, *Crime, Police, and Penal Policy*.

247. Shearer, "Social Disorder, Mass Repression, and the NKVD during the 1930s"; Fijnaut, *Opdat de macht een toevlucht zij?* Police statistics are notoriously vague for the period. But see Flora and Alber, *State, Economy, and Society in Western Europe*, vol. 1.

248. "The Second Inaugural Address, January 20, 1937," in *Public Papers and Addresses of Franklin D. Roosevelt*, 6:4–5.

249. Blum, *From the Morgenthau Diaries*, 386. See, more generally, Brinkley, *End of Reform*, 15–30; Katznelson, *Fear Itself*, 367–402.

250. "Roosevelt Will Press Dictator Bill Next Year," *Chicago Daily Tribune*, July 6, 1938; Johnson, "Totalitarians and the Democracies," 629.

251. Letter from Frank to Tugwell, September 1, 1934, Yale University, Sterling Library, Jerome New Frank Papers, box 16.

252. "A Policy for the Nation," *London Times*, January 18, 1935. See also, for example, Law, "Britain and the New Deal"; Koss, "Lloyd George and Nonconformity." For the wider context, see Dizikes, *Britain, Roosevelt, and the New Deal*, 212–41.

253. Boyko, *Bennett*, 363–97; Waite, *In Search of R. B. Bennett*, 196–228. See also Leuchtenburg, "'Europeanization' of America."

254. See Roorda, *Dictator Next Door*, 117–21. On Colombia, see Bushnell, *Making of Modern Colombia*, 185–92. López quote in Inman, "Emerging America," 171.

255. Cullather, *Hungry World*, 50; Cullather, "Model Nations."

256. Jiménez, "Peronism and Anti-imperialism in the Argentine Press."

257. Marcus, *Haile Sellassie I*, 139–40; Spencer, *Ethiopia at Bay*, 3–26.

258. Quoted in Li, "Reviving China," 115. See also Taylor, *Generalissimo*, 107–14.

259. Vanthemsche, "L'élaboration de l'arrêté royal sur le contrôle bancaire," 403.

260. "Informal Address at Banquet Given by President Vargas, November 27, 1936," in *Public Papers and Addresses of Franklin D. Roosevelt*, 5:603. On this quote, although with a different interpretation, see Limoncic, "Os inventores do New Deal."

261. Gassert, *Amerika im Dritten Reich*; Dizikes, *Britain, Roosevelt, and the New Deal*; Strauss, "Roosevelt Revolution."

262. Katznelson, *Fear Itself*, 20.

263. Mettler, *Dividing Citizens*; Kessler-Harris, *In Pursuit of Equity*; Mink, *Wages of Motherhood*.

264. Katznelson, *When Affirmative Action Was White*, x. See also, for example, Katznelson, *Fear Itself*; King, *Separate and Unequal*; Schulman, *From Cotton Belt to Sunbelt*.

265. Clancey, "Vast Clearings."

266. Quoted in Conkin, *Tomorrow a New World*, 202. For a case study on Baltimore with similar findings, see Williams, *Politics of Public Housing*, 21–53.

267. Quoted in Clancey, "Vast Clearings," 74.

268. Lewis, *Empire State-Building*, 1–81.

269. *Historical Statistics of the United States: Colonial Times to 1970*, part 2, 1102.

270. Ibid., 1104. See also Higgs, *Crisis and Leviathan*, 20–27; Wallis, "Lessons from the Political Economy of the New Deal."

271. Reinhart and Reinhart, "When the North Last Headed South," 266 (includes an index-based, per country calculation). For Asia and Africa, see IHS, *Africa, Asia and Oceania*, 872–83.

272. Studenski, *Taxation and Public Policy*, 17.

273. Wallis, "Birth of the Old Federalism"; Fishback and Wallis, "What Was New about the New Deal."

274. Reinhart and Reinhart, "When the North Last Headed South," 267–68; Zelizer, "Forgotten Legacy of the New Deal"; Weir and Skocpol, "State Structures"; Dickter, "Hacia un análisis 'estado-céntrico' comparativo de las políticas del Cardenismo"; Hall, *Political Power of Economic Ideas*; Gourevitch, *Politics in Hard Times*.

275. Goode, "Introduction," 13.

276. *Historical Statistics of the United States: Colonial Times to 1970*, part 2, 1102.

277. Quoted in "Capital Dedicates New Labor Edifice," *NYT*, February 26, 1935.

278. "Washington, D.C.," *Fortune* 10, December 1934, 55. See also Abbott, "Washington and Berlin."

279. On the Turkish example, see Bozdoğan, *Modernism and Nation Building*, 271–93. On China, see Zhu, *Architecture of Modern China*, 57–58.

280. Schirmer, "State, Volk, and Monumental Architecture"; Bodenschatz, "Diktatorischer Städtebau." See also, for example, Ghirardo, *Building New Communities*; Schivelbusch, *Three New Deals*, 1–9.

281. On South Carolina, see Mielnik, *New Deal, New Landscape*. On New York City and the WPA, see Williams, *City of Ambition*. On zoos, see Donahue and Trump, *American Zoos during the Depression*.

282. Dimendberg, "Will to Motorization," 136.

283. MacDonald, "Tomorrow's Roads," 870.

284. Smith, *Building New Deal Liberalism*; Gregg, *Managing the Mountains*, 175–212.

285. Donovan, *Highways*, 35–68; Broomham, *On the Road*, 47–69.

286. Summerhill, "Development of Infrastructure," 326; Sanz Fernández, "Los Ferrocarriles Iberoamericanos," 15–50.

287. Wolfe, *Autos and Progress*, 91–112. On the study by General Motors, see ibid., 96.

288. IHS, *Americas*, 577–85; Rippy, "Inter-American Highway." The Inter-American was a project with strong roots in the United States.

289. Zhu, *Architecture of Modern China*, 41–74; Kirby, "Engineering China."

290. Farooqi, *Silver Lion*, 112. On the transport revolution, see Clawson, "Knitting Iran Together," 235. See also Abrahamian, *A History of Modern Iran*, 77; Lemańczyk, "Transiranian Railway."

291. On the work of the LoN, see, for example, LoN, Organisation for Communications and Transit, *Coordination of Transport*.

292. Seely, *Building the American Highway System*, 160. See also, for example, Wehner, "Germany Begins Construction of Express Highway System."

293. Quoted in Seely, *Building the American Highway System*, 148. For the wider debate, see ibid., 145–66.

294. See, for example, Crandell, "Touring Engineer's Impressions"; MacDonald, "Tomorrow's Roads." See also Zeller, *Driving Germany*, 2, 48–49, 169–70; Bortolotti, *Fascismo e autostrade*.

295. MacDonald, "Tomorrow's Roads," 868.

296. Wells, "Fueling the Boom."

297. Zimmerman, "National-State Relations."

298. Gordon, *Social Security Policies in Industrial Countries*, 232.

299. Salmond, *Civilian Conservation Corps*, 72.

300. Wallis, "Birth of the Old Federalism"; Fishback and Wallis, "What Was New about the New Deal."

301. Jones, *American Red Cross*, 240–60.

302. See Welskopp, *Fractured Modernity*.

303. Rosskam, *Washington*, 9, 140.

304. Abbott, *Political Terrain*, 101.

305. Fried, "Political Culture," 325.

306. Eliot, *Recollections of the New Deal*, 11. For more examples, see Louchheim, *Making of the New Deal*.

307. Eliot, *Recollections of the New Deal*, 30; Ware, *Holding Their Own*, 87–98. See also, for example, Kessler-Harris, *In Pursuit of Equity*, 64–202.

308. Storrs, *Second Red Scare*, 18–19.

309. Auerbach, *Unequal Justice*, 158–90.

310. Breitman and Lichtman, *FDR and the Jews*, 65.

311. Ware, *Holding Their Own*, 92–93.

312. Quoted in Auerbach, *Unequal Justice*, 174.

313. Neumann, "Conflict of Generations in Contemporary Europe."

314. Harrison, *Soviet Planning in Peace and War*, 13–28.

315. Harvey, "Cult of Youth."

316. Winslow, *Youth*, xi.

317. "Miss Ilma, Back from Europe, Says New Spirit Prevails There," *NYT*, December 10, 1933. See also Nicholson, "In America, the Young Men and Women."

318. Abrahamian, *A History of Modern Iran*, 63–96.

319. Malloy, *Politics of Social Security in Brazil*, 177n10. See also Williams, *Culture Wars in Brazil*; Draibe, *Rumos e metamorfoses*, 82–137.

320. Quote in Jobim, *Two Revolutions*, 146. See also Geddes, "Building 'State' Autonomy in Brazil"; Hentschke, "Vargas Era Institutional and Development Model Revisited."

321. Lowe, *Adjusting to Democracy*, 256.

322. Quoted in Auerbach, *Unequal Justice*, 170.

323. Newspaper Clipping, A. J. Cummings, "Meet America's Harold Lloyd," undated, RSC, Harry Hopkins Papers, roll 6, box 99.

324. Abbott, *Political Terrain*, 119.

325. Rosskam, *Washington*, 15.

326. Heide, *Punched-Card Systems*, 211–21.

327. Stebenne, "Thomas J. Watson and the Business-Government Relationship."

328. Columbia University Oral History Collection, part III, no. 182, Interviews Perkins, 251, 255.

329. Quoted in Cohen, "Development of the Social Security Act of 1935," 404.

330. McKinley and Frase, *Launching Social Security*, 232–38, 311–17.

331. "Machines to Do Tax Cut Figuring Task in 60 Days," *Chicago Daily Tribune*, May 15, 1934.

332. "Republican Gets No. 1 Security Card," *NYT*, December 2, 1936. On the creation of the SSN, see Altmeyer, *Formative Years of Social Security*, 67–68.

333. "Sidelights of the Week," *NYT*, January 17, 1937. For a survey of the role of tattoos in Western culture, see Caplan, "Indelible Memories."

334. "Racketeer File and Statistical Machines Aid Fight on Crime," *Science News Letter*, January 20, 1934.

335. "Nerve Center of the Chicago Police Radio System," *Chicago Daily Tribune*, November 14, 1938.

336. Heide, *Punched-Card Systems*, 211.

337. Methorst, "New System of Population Accounting in the Netherlands," 719. According to Methorst, the other two phases brought about a regular census and civil registers with demographic facts in chronological order.

338. Heide, *Punched-Card Systems*, 222–33.

339. Aly and Roth, *Nazi Census*; Heide, *Punched-Card Systems*, 233–48. Although problematic on this issue, see Black, *IBM and the Holocaust*; moreover, see Milton, "Registering Civilians and Aliens in the Second World War."

340. Moore, *Victims and Survivors*, 194–99; Black, *IBM and the Holocaust*, 292–332. The Dutch system did not use punched cards; while sophisticated in an organizational sense, it was less so technologically.

341. US Department of Commerce, Bureau of the Census, *Japanese Population in Selected Counties and Cities of the United States*. See also US Bureau of the Census, *Catalog of Publications*, 125 (items 1286–88).

342. Seltzer and Anderson, "Census Confidentiality."

343. See, for example, Memorandum from Stauber, War Relocation Authority, November 7, 1942, as well as the box more generally, NARA, Washington, DC, RG 210, entry 16, box 498. See also Seltzer and Anderson, "After Pearl Harbor." For a discussion of the various alternative interpretations in the field, see Tyson and Fleischman, "Accounting for Interned Japanese-American Civilians."

344. Seltzer and Anderson, "Dark Side of Numbers."

345. Henry A. Wallace, "The Search for an American Way," *Scribner's Magazine* 50, July 1936, 22, 26.

346. This argument partly builds on Ciepley, *Liberalism in the Shadow of Totalitarianism*.

347. "Acceptance of Renomination, June 27, 1936," in *Public Papers and Addresses of Franklin D. Roosevelt*, 5:231, 235.

348. "Quarantine Speech, October 5, 1937," in *Public Papers and Addresses of Franklin D. Roosevelt*, 6:406–7.

349. On this neologism, see, for example, Maier, *Concepts for the Comparison of Dictatorships*. On the New Deal more specifically, see Ekbladh, *Great American Mission*, 64–66; Lifka, *Concept "Totalitarianism" and American Foreign Policy*; more generally Wall, *Inventing the "American Way."*

350. Lilienthal, *TVA*. See also Gray and Johnson, *TVA Regional Planning and Development Program*, 32–33. Some historians have therefore placed the totalitarian topic as early as the beginning of the TVA. See, for example, Ekbladh, *Great American Mission*.

351. Wall, *Inventing the "American Way,"* 49–62. See also Cohen, *Making a New Deal*, 333–60.

352. Gerstle, "Politics of Patriotism," 90. See also Wall, *Inventing the "American Way,"* 40–48; Susman, *Culture as History*.

353. Murphey, "American Civilization at Pennsylvania."

354. Adamic, *Plymouth Rock and Ellis Island*; Weiss, "Ethnicity and Reform." See, more generally, Denning, *Cultural Front*.

355. Wall, *Inventing the "American Way,"* 63–100.

356. LeMahieu, *Culture for Democracy*, 225–333.

357. Hofmann, "Fascist Reflection," 140–246. See also Garon, *State and Labor in Modern Japan*, 187–227.

358. Pascoe, *What Comes Naturally*, 200–223.

359. On the use of terms, see Wengert, "TVA," 383. See also Lilienthal, *TVA*.

360. Brinkley, *End of Reform*. See also Ciepley, *Liberalism in the Shadow of Totalitarianism*, esp. 19.

361. Memorandum from James Roosevelt to FDR, July 27, 1937 with attachment, NARA, Hyde Park, Official Files 2245.

362. Jacobs, *Pocketbook Politics*; Cohen, "New Deal State and the Making of Citizen Consumers"; Storrs, *Civilizing Capitalism*.

363. Patel, *Soldiers of Labor*, 277–79.

364. Bentley, *Thirty Years of Treason*.

365. Henry R. Luce, "The American Century," *Time*, February 17, 1941, 61–65. See also Iriye, "Toward Transnationalism."

366. *Historical Statistics of the United States: Colonial Times to 1970*, part 2, 1141.

367. Klein, *Call to Arms*; Dunn, *1940*; Sherry, *In the Shadow of War*, 15–63.

368. See, for example, Harrison, "Resource Mobilization for World War II"; O'Neil, *Interwar U.S. and Japanese National Product and Defense Expenditure*; Eloranta, "Military Competition between Friends?"; Carvalho, "Armed Forces and Politics in Brazil," 211; Preston, "Monsters Everywhere."

369. Siuru and Stewart, *Presidential Cars and Transportation*.

CHAPTER 5
THE AMERICAN WORLD ORDER

1. *Historical Statistics of the United States: Colonial Times to 1970*, part 2, 1141; Collier, "Army and the Great Depression."

2. Sparrow, *Warfare State*.

3. Gropman, "Industrial Mobilization," 56.

4. Frydl, *GI Bill*, 10.

5. Klein, *Call to Arms*, 66.

6. Erlandson, "Lend-Lease."

7. Showalter, "Global Yet Not Total." On World War II as a global war, see Weinberg, *World at Arms*.

8. Heiner, *Henry J. Kaiser, American Empire Builder*, 119–23.

9. Dorman, *Hell of a Vision*, 76.

10. Nash, *American West Transformed*.

11. Troy, *Trade Union Membership*, 1.

12. Hewlett and Anderson, *New World*. On the committee, see Klein, *Call to Arms*, 101–6. One source even maintains that six hundred thousand worked with and directly supported the Manhattan Project. See Groves, *Now It Can Be Told*, 414.

13. *Historical Statistics of the United States: Colonial Times to 1970*, part 2, 1102, 1104; Davidson, "Making Dollars and Sense of the U.S. Government Debt"; Wallis, "Lessons from the Political Economy of the New Deal."

14. Koistinen, *Arsenal of World War II*; Vatter, *U.S. Economy in World War II*; Gropman, "Industrial Mobilization."

15. See, for example, Hall, *Political Power of Economic Ideas*; Weir and Skocpol, "State Structures."

16. Maier, "Politics of Productivity"; Waddell, *War against the New Deal*, 43–118.

17. "Knudsen the Only Civilian to Enter Army at His Rank," *NYT*, January 17, 1942.

18. Klein, *Call to Arms*, 166–72.

19. Ickes, *Secret Diary of Harold L. Ickes*, 3:207.

20. Dickinson, *Bitter Harvest*, 117–203; Stoler, "FDR and the Origins of the National Security Establishment"; Henrikson, "FDR and the 'World-Wide Arena.'"

21. Quoted in Smith, *Colonel*, 320.

22. Patel, *Soldiers of Labor*, 176–77.

23. Kennedy, *Freedom from Fear*, 782.

24. Jarvis, *Male Body at War*.

25. "Fireside Chat on National Defense, May 26, 1940," in *Public Papers and Addresses of Franklin D. Roosevelt*, 9:237. See, in general, Grisinger, *Unwieldy American State*.

26. Altmeyer, *Formative Years of Social Security*, 99–120.

27. Altschuler and Blumin, *GI Bill*, 11–83; Frydl, *GI Bill*, 100–145; Ortiz, *Beyond the Bonus March and GI Bill*.

28. Blum, "World War II." On the bomb, see Mikesh, *Japan's World War II Balloon Bomb Attacks on North America*, 67–68. Japan released some 10,000 balloons, of which some 280 reached North America.

29. Fraser, *Labor Will Rule*, 441–94.

30. Collins, "Race, Roosevelt, and Wartime Production"; Kryder, *Divided Arsenal*.

31. Spinney, *World War Two in Nashville*, 104.

32. Johnson and Jackson, *City behind a Fence*, 39–52, 99–136; Jones, *Manhattan*, 78–79, 432–49.

33. Dunn, *1940*, 157–58.

34. Schonberger, *Aftermath of War*, 44.

35. Wynn, *African American Experience*, 39–41; Kryder, *Divided Arsenal*.

36. Wallace, *Democracy Reborn*, 240.

37. Gallicchio, *African American Encounter with Japan and China*.

38. See, for example, Union for Democratic Action, *Democratic Objectives for World Order*; Warren, *Noble Abstractions*.

39. Quoted in "The Casualties of the Vietnam War (King's Address of February 25, 1967)," *New York Amsterdam News*, June 17, 1967.

40. Borgwardt, *New Deal for the World*.

41. "The Meeting with President Roosevelt, World Broadcast, August 24, 1941," in Eade, *War Speeches of Winston S. Churchill*, 2:59.

42. Wilson, *First Summit*, 173–202; Hoopes and Brinkley, *FDR and the Creation of the U.N.*, 26–42; Kimball, "Atlantic Charter."

43. Stone, "Peace Planning and the Atlantic Charter," 5.

44. "Annual Message to Congress, January 6, 1941," in *Public Papers and Addresses of Franklin D. Roosevelt*, 9:672.

45. Iriye, *Power and Culture*, 118–21.

46. Hughes, "Winston Churchill and the Formation of the United Nations Organization"; Reynolds, "Atlantic 'Flop.'"

47. For the text of the Atlantic Charter, see Brinkley and Facey-Crowther, *Atlantic Charter*, xvii.

48. "Text of President's Address to I.L.O. on Work and Hitler," *NYT*, November 7, 1941. On Perkins, see "Post-War Order Outlined to I.L.O.," *NYT*, October 28, 1941. For Welles's speech in July 1941, see O'Sullivan, *Sumner Welles*, 43–44. For the broader context, see Clavin, *Securing the World Economy*, 271–74.

49. Jensen, "From Geneva to the Americas."

50. Borgwardt, *New Deal for the World*, 14–86. On the Cold War context, see Westad, *Global Cold War*.

51. Borgwardt, *New Deal for the World*.

52. Wallace, *Democracy Reborn*, 239.

53. O'Sullivan, *Sumner Welles*.

54. Freda Kirchwey, "A Program of Action," *Nation*, 158, March 11, 1944, 300. In a similar vein, see, for example, Lorwin, *Economic Consequences of the Second World War*, 486–502.

55. Quoted in Dalfiume, "'Forgotten Years' of the Negro Revolution," 105.

56. On Kirchwey see Warren, *Noble Abstractions*, 7. See also Divine, *Second Chance*.

57. Mitrany, *Working Peace System*, 56.

58. Burley, "Regulating the World."

59. Venkataramani, *Bengal Famine of 1943*, 2–3.

60. *FRUS*, 1942, General, 678.

61. Du Bois, "Realities in Africa." See also Janken, *Rayford W. Logan and the Dilemma of the African-American Intellectual*, 167–69; Pearl Buck, "Make It Freedom's War," *New Republic*, December 21, 1942.

62. Gellman, *Good Neighbor Diplomacy*, 17.

63. Mills, *Post-War Planning on the Periphery*.

64. Quoted in Ingulstad, "Winning the Hearths and Mines," 66. See, more generally, ibid., 62–73.

65. Office of Inter-American Affairs, *History of the Office of the Coordinator of Inter-American Affairs*, 25–40, 115–43; Prutsch, *Creating Good Neighbors?* 33–133.

66. Rosen, "Not Worth a Pitcher of Warm Piss."

67. Stevens, "Organizing for Economic Defense"; Whitehead, "Bolivia," 132; Knudson, "Impact of the Catavi Mine Massacre of 1942."

68. Grandin, "Your Americanism and Mine."

69. Francis, "United States at Rio"; Lübken, *Bedrohliche Nähe*.

70. Friedman, "There Goes the Neighborhood."

71. Quoted in "The Wooing of Brazil," *Fortune* 24, no. 10 (1944): 97. See, more generally, Prutsch, *Creating Good Neighbors?*

72. Schlesinger, *Vital Center*, viii.

73. Milkis and Mileur, "Preface," xv. See also Fraser and Gerstle, *Rise and Fall of the New Deal Order*; Borstelmann, *1970s*.

74. Quoted in Lipgens, *Documents on the History of European Integration*, 278–79. See also Judt, *Postwar*, 63–99.

75. Sunstein, *After the Rights Revolution*, 242–44.

76. "AFL Head and Taft Debate Labor Bills," *NYT*, May 12, 1947.

77. Fordham, *Building the Cold War Consensus*, 1. See, more generally, Hogan, *Cross of Iron*.

78. Storrs, *Second Red Scare*.

79. Bell, "Social Politics in a Transoceanic World." For a slightly different interpretation, see Rodgers, *Atlantic Crossings*, 489–508.

80. Sluga, *Internationalism in the Age of Nationalism*, 79–117.

81. Mangone, "Dungaree and Grey-Flannel Diplomacy."

82. Department of State, *Occupation of Japan*, 47–48.

83. See also, for example, Ezekiel, *Towards World Prosperity*.

84. Leffler, *Preponderance of Power*.

85. On Germany, see, for example, Angster, *Konsenskapitalismus und Sozialdemokratie*. On Japan, see, for example, Schonberger, *Aftermath of War*; Sugita, *Pitfall or Panacea*, 21–28. For a US-centered perspective, see Phillips, *This Land, This Nation*, 242–83.

86. Immerwahr, *Thinking Small*, 54–55.

87. Gilman, *Mandarins of the Future*.

88. Altmeyer, "Progress of Social Security"; Hoskins, "U.S. Social Security at 75 Years"; Jensen, "From Geneva to the Americas."

89. Emory University, MARBL, Charles F. Palmer Papers, boxes 63, 128; Palmer, *Adventures of a Slum Fighter*, 242–62.

90. Mehrtens, "Public and Private, National and International."

91. Van Goethem and Waters, *American Labor's Global Ambassadors*; Romero, *Gli Stati Uniti e il sindacalismo europeo*.

92. Maier, "Politics of Productivity."

93. Borgwardt, *New Deal for the World*; Hoopes and Brinkley, *FDR and the Creation of the U.N.*

94. On Hungary, see Péteri, "Before the Schism." On Japan, see O'Bryan, *Growth Idea*; Hein, *Reasonable Men*.

95. Leffler, *Preponderance of Power*, 16.

96. See, for example, Hogan, *Marshall Plan*; Maier, *Marshall Plan and Germany*.

97. Cullather, *Hungry World*, esp. 6.

98. Du Bois, *Color and Democracy*, 3–16.

99. Davis, "World War II and Memory," 581.

100. Green, *Black Yanks in the Pacific*.

101. Höhn and Klimke, *Breath of Freedom*; Von Eschen, *Race against Empire*; Borstelmann, *Cold War and the Color Line*. On Britain, see Reynolds, "Churchill's Government and the Black GIs."

102. Lichtenstein, "Pluralism, Postwar Intellectuals, and the Demise of the Union Idea."

103. "Roosevelt and Aids Open Big Campaign Soon," *Chicago Daily Tribune*, June 25, 1934.

104. Roll, *Hopkins Touch*.

105. Lasser, *Benjamin V. Cohen*, 270–95.

106. Lehman, *Liberalism*, 15. On Lehman, see Nevins, *Herbert H. Lehman and His Era*, 22–260.

107. Glendon, *World Made New*. See also Shepard, "Becoming Planning Minded"; Reinisch, "We Shall Rebuild Anew a Powerful Nation."

108. NARA, Hyde Park, Ezekiel Papers, box 21.

109. Hoover Institution Archives, Stanford, CA, Kenneth Holland Papers, Inventory, http://pdf.oac.cdlib.org/pdf/hoover/2000C93.pdf (accessed April 12, 2014).

110. Transcript of Interview with Milton P. Siegel, November 15, 1982, World Health Organization, Archives Unit, http://www.who.int/archives/fonds_collections /special/oral_history_siegel/en/ (accessed April 10, 2015).

111. Storrs, *Second Red Scare*, 19.

112. Staples, "Norris E. Dodd and the Connections between Domestic and International Agricultural Policy."

113. "Laurence, Hewes, 86, Land-Use Economist," *NYT*, April 4, 1989.

114. Maul, "Help Them Move the ILO Way"; Jensen, "US New Deal Social Policy Experts and the ILO." On the negotiations over Morse's appointment, see Princeton University, Mudd Library, David Morse Papers, box 3.

115. Frieden, *Global Capitalism*, 264–68.

116. Patenaude, *Big Show in Bololand*; Wieters, "From Post-War Relief to Europe to Global Humanitarian Enterprise," 42. I am grateful to Davide Rodogno for refer-

ring me to this group of actors. CARE originally stood for Cooperative for American Remittances to Europe, but today is short for Cooperative for Assistance and Relief Everywhere.

117. Black, *Children and the Nations*, 15–46.

118. Leffler, *Preponderance of Power*, 19–24.

119. Mazower, *Governing the World*, 192–93.

120. Ladwig-Winters, *Ernst Fraenkel*.

121. Kohnstamm, *Still No War*, 15.

122. Phillips, *This Land, This Nation*, 257

123. Towne, *Doctor Danger Forward*.

124. Reynolds, *America, Empire of Liberty*, 369.

125. Staples, "Norris E. Dodd and the Connections between Domestic and International Agricultural Policy."

126. Quoted in Lasser, *Benjamin V. Cohen*, 297.

127. Sandilands, *Life and Political Economy of Lauchlin Currie*, 159–81.

128. Sluga, *Internationalism in the Age of Nationalism*, 114–17.

129. "Inaugural Address, January 20, 1953," *Public Papers of the Presidents of the United States, Eisenhower, 1953*, 7.

130. Quoted in Ridgon, *White House Sailor*, 172. See also Eddy, *F.D.R. Meets Ibn Saud*. On the wider context, see O'Sullivan, *FDR and the End of Empire*, 89–103.

131. Hinds, "Anglo-American Relations in Saudi Arabia," 63; Sanger, "Ibn Saud's Program for Arabia."

132. Sluga, *Internationalism in the Age of Nationalism*, 81–104; Glendon, *World Made New*; Mazower, *No Enchanted Palace*, 7–9.

133. Reinisch, "Internationalism in Relief."

134. Amrith and Clavin, "Feeding the World."

135. Mazower, *No Enchanted Palace*.

136. Hodge, *Triumph of the Expert*; Rempe, *Entwicklung im Konflikt*.

137. See, for example, Westad, *Global Cold War*; Mazower, *Governing the World*, 290.

138. Quoted in Reinisch, "Internationalism in Relief," 280.

139. Huxley, *TVA*, 7.

140. Yates and Warriner, *Food and Farming in Post-War Europe*, 53.

141. On India, see Klingensmith, "*One Valley and a Thousand*," 109–54. On China, see Zanasi, "Far from the Treaty Ports," 127.

142. Letter from Lin to Lilienthal, April 12, 1945, Princeton University, Mudd Library, David E. Lilienthal Papers, box 111.

143. Ezekiel, *Towards World Prosperity*, 446.

144. Gilman, *Mandarins of the Future*, 30.

145. Immerwahr, *Thinking Small*, 145–55.

146. Scott, *Seeing Like a State*, 6; Ekbladh, *Great American Mission*, 8.

147. Speech by Truman, October 8, 1945, Princeton University, Mudd Library, David E. Lilienthal Papers, box 111; Lilienthal, *TVA*.

148. Cullather, *Hungry World*, 108–13.

149. Toynbee, *Between Oxus and Jumna*, 67.

150. Klingensmith, "*One Valley and a Thousand*," 32. This meaning of the term "simulacrum" was coined by French philosopher Jean Beaudrillard.

151. Grandi, "David Lilienthal, La Banca Mondiale e lo sviluppo."

152. *Jawaharlal Nehru's Speeches*, 1. See also D'Souza, "Damming the Mahanadi River."

153. Klingensmith, *"One Valley and a Thousand,"* 211–75.

154. Nandy, *Romance of the State*, 181–207. On the protests against a similar project in the Narmada valley, see Routledge, "Voices of the Dammed."

155. Lagendijk, "Divided Development." For a different interpretation, see Ekbladh, "Mr. TVA."

156. Shapiro, *Mao's War against Nature*, 21–65; Lopatin, "Technical Assistance of the USSR."

157. Engineering Design Division, Records relating to Lend-Lease Program to Soviet Union, 1942–1945, NARA, Atlanta, RG 142, General Correspondence, boxes 1–9.

158. Lagendijk, "Divided Development." For a different interpretation, see Ekbladh, *Great American Mission*, 190–225.

159. Beinart, "Agricultural Planning and the Late Colonial Technical Imagination."

160. Seidel, *Process of Politics in Europe*, 12.

161. Nandy, *Romance of the State*, 185. For a different interpretation, see Saha, "River-Basin Planning in the Damodar Valley of India."

162. See also, for example, Fernández and Carrillo, *América sumergida*.

163. Hayek, *Road to Serfdom*, 233.

164. Mirowski and Plehwe, *Road from Mont Pèlerin*. On the domestic dimension, see, for example, Friedberg, *In the Shadow of the Garrison State*.

165. "U.N. Chief Blames Rich Nations for Failure of Trade Talks," *NYT*, February 13, 2000.

166. Quoted in http://www.washingtonpost.com/wp-dyn/content/article/2009/03/02/AR2009030202398.html (accessed April 12, 2015).

167. See http://eeas.europa.eu/somalia/new-deal-conference/sites/default/files/somalia_new_deal_conference_communique.pdf (accessed April 12, 2015).

168. See http://buildingpeaceforum.com/2013/04/a-new-deal-for-the-democratic-republic-of-the-congo/ (accessed April 12, 2015).

169. See http://www.london.gov.uk/sites/default/files/archives/uploads-investing-for-recovery.pdf (accessed April 12, 2015).

170. See http://earlylearning.ubc.ca/media/publications/Family%20Policy%20Reports%20and%20Resources/does_canada_work_for_all_generations_fact_sheet.pdf (accessed April 12, 2015).

171. Felice, *Global New Deal*.

172. See, for example, Grunwald, *New New Deal*.

173. See http://www.npr.org/templates/story/story.php?storyId=99618417 (accessed April 12, 2015); Obama, *Audacity of Hope*, esp. 26, 29, 38, 176–78.

174. See, for example, Cassis, *Crises and Opportunities*; various contributions in *Oxford Review of Economic Policy* 26, 3 (2010).

BIBLIOGRAPHY

ARCHIVAL MATERIALS

Columbia University Oral History Collection, Columbia University, New York
  Part III, *Frances Perkins, Interviews from 1951–1955* (Glen Rock, NJ: Microfilm-
    ing Corporation of America, 1976)
  Part I, *Mordecai Ezekiel: The Reminiscences of Mordecai Ezekiel* (New York: Oral
    History Research Office, Columbia University, 1972)
Emory University, Manuscript, Archives, and Rare Book Library, Atlanta, GA
  (MARBL)
  Charles Forrest Palmer Papers
Library of Congress, Washington, DC
  George Biddle Papers
National Archives and Record Administration at Atlanta, Morrow, GA
  RG 142, Tennessee Valley Authority
National Archives and Record Administration, College Park, MD
  RG 9, National Recovery Administration
  RG 16, Office of the Secretary of Agriculture
  RG 56, Department of the Treasury
  RG 59, Department of State
National Archives and Record Administration, Washington, DC
  RG 210, War Relocation Authority
National Archives and Record Administration, Franklin D. Roosevelt Library, Hyde
  Park, NY
  Oscar S. Cox Papers
  Mordecai Ezekiel Papers
  Leon Henderson Papers
  Harry Hopkins Papers
  Hugh Johnson Papers
  Gardiner Means Papers
  Frances Perkins Papers
  Samuel I. Rosenman Papers
  Rexford Tugwell Papers
  Sumner Welles Papers
  John G. Winant Papers
  Official Files of the President
  President's Private Files
  President's Secretary Files
Princeton University, Mudd Library, Princeton, NJ
  David E. Lilienthal Papers
  David Morse Papers
Roosevelt Study Center, Middelburg, Netherlands (RSC)

Eleanor Roosevelt Papers
Henry Lewis Stimson Papers at Yale University Library
Henry A. Wallace Papers at the University of Iowa
United Nations Office, Geneva, Switzerland
    League of Nations Archive
Yale University, Beinecke Rare Books and Manuscript Library, New Haven, CT
    Felix S. Cohen Papers
Yale University, Sterling Memorial Library, New Haven, CT
    Jerome New Frank Papers
    James Harvey Rogers Papers

Printed Primary Sources

Abramson, Alexander, "The Reorganisation of Social Insurance Institutions in the
    U.S.S.R.," *International Labour Review* 31 (1935): 364–82.
Adamic, Louis, *Plymouth Rock and Ellis Island: Summary of a Lecture* (New York:
    Common Council for American Unity, 1940).
Addams, Jane, *The Second Twenty Years at Hull-House: September 1909 to September
    1929* (New York: Macmillan, 1930).
Agricultural Adjustment Administration, *Agricultural Adjustment, 1937–1938* (Wash-
    ington, DC: US Government Printing Office, 1938).
Altmeyer, Arthur J., *The Formative Years of Social Security* (Madison: University of
    Wisconsin Press, 1966).
———, "The Progress of Social Security in the Americas in 1944," *International La-
    bour Review* 51 (1945): 699–721.
Andrade, Victor, *My Missions for Revolutionary Bolivia, 1944–1962* (Pittsburgh: Uni-
    versity of Pittsburgh Press, 1976).
Armstrong, Barbara Nachtrieb, *Insuring the Essentials: Minimal Wage Plus Social Insur-
    ance—a Living Wage Program* (New York: Macmillan, 1932).
———, "Old-Age Security Abroad: The Background of Titles II and VIII of the So-
    cial Security Act," *Law and Contemporary Problems* 3 (1936): 175–85.
Arndt, Heinz Wolfgang, *The Economic Lessons of the Nineteen-Thirties* (Oxford: Oxford
    University Press, 1944).
Aron, Robert, and Arnaud Dandieu, *Le cancer américain* (Paris: Rieder, 1931).
Barnes, Harry Elmer, *Battling the Crime Wave: Applying Sense and Science to the Repres-
    sion of Crime* (Boston: Stratford, 1931).
Bauer, Catherine, *Modern Housing* (Boston: Houghton Mifflin, 1934).
Beard, Charles A., "A 'Five-Year Plan' for America," in *America Faces the Future*, ed.
    Charles A. Beard (1932; repr., Freeport, NY: Books for Libraries Press, 1969),
    117–40.
Beckhart, Benjamin H., "The German Bank Inquiry," *Political Science Quarterly* 52
    (1937): 86–116.
Benson, Adolph B., and Naboth Hedin, eds., *Swedes in America, 1638–1938* (New
    Haven, CT: Yale University Press, 1938).
Bentley, Eric, *Thirty Years of Treason: Excerpts from Hearings before the House Committee
    on Un-American Activities, 1938–1968* (New York: Thunder's Mouth Press, 2002).

Berlin, Isaiah, "Roosevelt through European Eyes," *Atlantic Monthly* 196 (1955): 67–71.

Bisson, T. A., "Japan's Trade Boom—Does It Menace the United States?" *Foreign Policy Reports* 12 (1936): 2–16.

Black, John D., "Plans for Raising Prices of Farm Products by Government Action," *Annals of the American Academy of Political and Social Science* 142 (1929): 380–90.

Blum, John Morton, *From the Morgenthau Diaries: Years of Crisis, 1928–1938* (Boston: Houghton Mifflin, 1959).

Bonn, Moritz Julius, *The Crisis of Capitalism in America* (New York: John Day, 1932).

———, *Prosperity: Wunderglaube und Wirklichkeit im amerikanischen Wirtschaftsleben* (Berlin: Fischer, 1931).

Borah, William E., *Closing Speech of Hon. William E. Borah on the League of Nations in the Senate of the United States, November 19, 1919* (Washington, DC: US Government Printing Office, 1919).

Borchard, Edwin, "Neutrality," *Yale Law Journal* 48 (1938): 37–53.

Bowen, E. R., "Report of the General Secretary," *Consumers' Cooperation* 22 (1936): 168–71.

Brockway, A. Fenner, *Will Roosevelt Succeed? A Study of Fascist Tendencies in America* (London: G. Routledge, 1934).

Brown, Nelson C., *The Civilian Conservation Corps Program in the United States* (Washington, DC: US Government Printing Office, 1934).

Brownlow, Louis, *A Passion for Anonymity: The Autobiography of Louis Brownlow* (Chicago: University of Chicago Press, 1958).

Bruère, Martha Bensley, "What Is Giant Power For?" *Annals of the American Academy of Political and Social Science* 118 (1925): 120–23.

Bullitt, William C., *For the President: Personal and Secret* (London: Andre Deutsch, 1973).

Campbell, Olive Dame, *The Danish Folk School: Its Influence in the Life of Denmark and the North* (New York: Macmillan, 1928).

Carmody, John M., and F. C. Harrington, *Questions and Answers on the W.P.A.* (Washington, DC: Federal Works Agency, 1939).

Carter, John Franklin [published as "Unofficial Observer"], *The New Dealers* (New York: Simon and Schuster, 1934).

Chase, Stuart, *A New Deal* (New York: Macmillan, 1932).

Childs, Marquis W., *I Write from Washington* (New York: Harper, 1942).

———, "Sweden Revisited," *Yale Review* 27 (1937): 30–44.

———, *Sweden, the Middle Way* (New Haven, CT: Yale University Press, 1936).

———, *Sweden: Where Capitalism Is Controlled* (New York: John Day, 1934).

———, *They Hate Roosevelt!* (New York: Harper, 1936).

———, *Witness to Power* (New York: McGraw-Hill, 1975).

Christy, D. F., "Government Aid to Wheat Producers," *Foreign Agriculture* 2 (1938): 489–97.

Clark, Colin, "Economic Planning in the Modern State," *Political Quarterly* 2 (1931): 531–47.

Cohen, Wilbur J., "The Development of the Social Security Act of 1935: Reflections Some Fifty Years Later," *Minnesota Law Review* 68 (1983): 379–408.

Collado, E. G., and Simon G. Hanson, "Old-Age Pensions in Uruguay," *Hispanic American Historical Review* 16 (1936): 173–89.

Commission of Inquiry into National Policy in International Economic Relations, *International Economic Relations* (Minneapolis: University of Minnesota Press, 1934).

Committee on Economic Security, *Social Security in America: The Factual Background of the Social Security Act as Summarized from Staff Reports to the Committee on Economic Security* (Washington, DC: US Government Printing Office, 1937).

Commons, John R., "Unemployment Prevention," *American Labor Legislative Review* 15 (1922): 15–24.

Complete Presidential Press Conferences of Franklin D. Roosevelt, Vol. 9 (New York: Da Capo Press, 1972).

Congressional Record of the United States, various vols. (Washington, DC: US Government Printing Office, various years).

Cooke, Morris Llewellyn, "The Early Days of the Rural Electrification Idea: 1914–1936," *American Political Science Review* 42 (1948): 431–47.

Cox, George Howland, "Was the Seventh Pan American Conference a Success?" *World Affairs* 97 (1934): 38–44.

Crandell, John S., "A Touring Engineer's Impressions of the Roads in Italy," *Engineering News-Record* 115 (1935): 669–74.

Creel, George, *The War, the World and Wilson* (New York: Harper, 1920).

Cummings, Homer S., "Modern Tendencies and the Law" (speech at the American Bar Association meeting, August 31, 1933), http://www.justice.gov/ag/aghistory /cummings/1933/08-31-1933.pdf (accessed April 12, 2015).

Daniels, Josephus, *Shirt-Sleeve Diplomat* (Chapel Hill: University of North Carolina Press, 1947).

Denby, Elizabeth, *Europe Re-Housed* (London: George Allen Unwin, 1938).

Department of State, *Occupation of Japan: Policy and Progress* (Washington, DC: US Government Printing Office, 1946).

Desvernine, Raoul E., *Democratic Despotism* (New York: Dodd, Mead, 1936).

Deutsche Studentenschaft, ed., *Der Arbeitsdienst in der Welt und die Studentische Jugend* (Hamburg: Hanseatische Verlagsanstalt, 1935).

Dickinson, John, *Hold Fast the Middle Way: An Outline of Economic Challenges and Alternatives* (Boston: Little, Brown, 1935).

Dies, Martin, "Nationalism Spells Safety," *National Republic* 21 (1934): 1–2, 32.

Documentary History of the Franklin D. Roosevelt Presidency (*DH-FDRP*), various vols., ed. George McJimsey (Bethesda, MD: University Publications of America, various years).

Dodd, William E., *Ambassador Dodd's Diary, 1933–1938,* ed. William E. Dodd Jr. and Martha Dodd (London: Victor Gollancz, 1941).

Du Bois, W.E.B., *Color and Democracy: Colonies and Peace* (1945; repr., Millwood, NY: Kraus-Thomson, 1975).

———, "The Realities in Africa: European Profit or Negro Development?" *Foreign Affairs* 21 (1943): 721–32.

Dulles, Eleanor Lansing, *The Export-Import Bank of Washington: The First Ten Years* (Washington, DC: US Government Printing Office, 1944).

Durbin, E.F.M., "The Importance of Planning," in *Problems of Economic Planning: Pa-*

pers on Planning and Economics, ed. E.F.M. Durbin (1949; repr., New York: Augustus M. Kelley, 1968), 41–58.

Eade, Charles, ed., *The War Speeches of Winston S. Churchill*, 3 vols. (London: Cassell, 1952).

Eccles, Marriner S., *Beckoning Frontiers: Public and Personal Recollections* (New York: Knopf, 1951).

Eddy, William Alfred, *F.D.R. Meets Ibn Saud* (New York: American Friends of the Middle East, 1954).

Eliot, Thomas H., *Recollections of the New Deal: When the People Mattered* (Boston: Northeastern University Press, 1992).

Evans, Harold, "The World's Experience with Rural Electrification," *Annals of the American Academy of Political and Social Science* 118 (1925): 30–42.

Ezekiel, Mordecai, "European Competition in Agricultural Production, with Special Reference to Russia," *Journal of Farm Economics* 14 (1932): 267–81.

———, *Towards World Prosperity through Industrial and Agricultural Development and Expansion* (New York: Harper, 1947).

Farooqi, Mohammed Ahsan, *The Silver Lion: A Biography of Reza Shah Pahlavi* (Lucknow: Upper India Publishing House, 1939).

Feis, Herbert, *The Diplomacy of the Dollar: First Era, 1919–1932* (New York: W. W. Norton, 1966).

Flora, Peter, and Jens Alber, eds., *State, Economy, and Society in Western Europe, 1815–1975: A Data Handbook*, 2 vols. (Frankfurt am Main: Campus, 1983).

Foreign Relations of the United States (FRUS), various volumes (Washington, DC: US Government Printing Office, various years).

Goebbels, Joseph, *Die Tagebücher von Joseph Goebbels*, Vol. 5, part 1, ed. Elke Fröhlich (Munich: Saur, 2000).

Garis, Roy Lawrence, *Immigration Restriction: A Study of the Opposition to and Regulation of Immigration into the United States* (New York: Macmillan, 1927).

Gayer, Arthur D., *Public Works in Prosperity and Depression* (New York: National Bureau of Economic Research, 1935).

General Motors around the World, 1927 (Detroit: General Motors Corporation, 1927).

Goldmark, Josephine, *Democracy in Denmark, Part I: Democracy in Action* (Washington, DC: National Home Library Foundation, 1936).

Grant, Madison, *The Conquest of a Continent or the Expansion of Races in America* (New York: C. Scribner's Sons, 1933).

———, *The Passing of the Great Race or the Racial Basis of European History*, 4th ed. (1916; repr., New York: Charles Scribner's Sons, 1936).

Gray, Lewis C., "The Social and Economic Implications of the National Land Program," *Journal of Farm Economics* 18 (1936): 257–73.

Grew, Joseph C., *Ten Years in Japan: A Contemporary Record Drawn from Diaries and Private and Official Papers of Joseph C. Grew* (London: Hammond, Hammond, 1944).

Hagood, Johnson, "Soldiers of the Shield," *American Forests* 40 (1934): 103–5.

Hanna, John, "The Banking Act of 1935," *Virginia Law Review* 22 (1936): 757–89.

Hardy, Charles O., *Is There Enough Gold?* (Washington, DC: Brookings Institution, 1936).

Hayek, Friedrich August, *Road to Serfdom* (1944; repr., New York: Routledge, 2005).

Hedin, Naboth, "Sweden's Recovery," *Review of Reviews* 95 (1937): 72.

The Henry Lewis Stimson Diaries in the Yale University Library (New Haven, CT: Yale University, Department of Manuscripts and Archives, 1973).

Hierl, Konstantin, *Ausgewählte Schriften und Reden*, Vol. 2 (Munich: Franz Eher Nachfolger, 1942).

Historical Statistics of the United States: Colonial Times to 1970, bicentennial ed., 2 parts (Cambridge: Cambridge University Press, 1975).

Historical Statistics of the United States: Earliest Times to the Present, millennial ed., 5 vols. (Cambridge: Cambridge University Press, 2006).

Hollman, A. H., *Democracy in Denmark, Part II: The Folk High School* (Washington, DC: National Home Library Foundation, 1936).

Hoover, Herbert, *The Memoirs of Herbert Hoover: The Great Depression, 1929–1941* (New York: Macmillan, 1952).

Hopkins, Harry L., *Spending to Save: The Complete Story of Relief* (New York: W. W. Norton, 1936).

Hosen, Frederick E., ed., *The Great Depression and the New Deal: Legislative Acts in Their Entirety (1932–1933) and Statistical Economic Data (1926–1946)* (Jefferson, NC: McFarland, 1992).

Howe, Frederic C., *Denmark: A Cooperative Commonwealth* (London: George Allen and Unwin, 1922).

———, *Denmark: The Coöperative Way* (New York: Coward-McCann, 1936).

Hudson, Manley O., "The Membership of the United States in the International Labor Organization," *American Journal of International Law* 28 (1934): 669–84.

Huxley, Julian, *TVA: Adventure in Planning* (Cheam: Architectural Press, 1943).

Hyde, Charles Cheney, "Legal Aspects of the Japanese Pronouncement in Relation to China," *American Journal of International Law* 28 (1934): 431–43.

Iatrides, John O., ed., *Ambassador MacVeagh Reports: Greece, 1933–1947* (Princeton, NJ: Princeton University Press, 1980).

Ickes, Harold L., *The Secret Diary of Harold L. Ickes*, 3 vols., 2nd ed. (New York: Simon and Schuster, 1954).

Inman, Samuel Guy, "Emerging America," *World Affairs* 97 (1934): 167–72.

Inter-American Conference for the Maintenance of Peace, *Proceedings (Stenographic Reports)* (Buenos Aires: Imprento del Congreso Nacional, 1937).

International Historical Statistics (IHS), *Africa, Asia and Oceania, 1750–1988*, 2nd ed., ed. B. R. Mitchell (Houndmills: Macmillan, 1995).

———, *The Americas, 1750–1988*, ed. B. R. Mitchell (Houndmills: Macmillan, 1993).

International Labour Organization, *Projects des conventions et recommandations adoptés par la conférence à sa dix–septième session, 8 juin–30 juin, 1933* (London: H. M. Stationery Office, 1933).

Jobim, Danton, *Two Revolutions: F. D. Roosevelt, G. D. Vargas* (New York: Victor Bookstore, 1941).

Johnson, Hugh S., *The Blue Eagle: From Egg to Earth* (Garden City, NY: Doubleday, Doran, 1935).

———, "Totalitarians and the Democracies," *Vital Speeches of the Day* 5, no. 20 (1939): 628–32.

Joint Hearings before the Committee on Education and Labor, U.S. Senate and the Committee of Labor, House of Representatives, Seventy-Third Congress, First Session on S.

598, March 23 and 24, 1933 (Washington, DC: US Government Printing Office, 1933).

Jones, Joseph M., *Tariff Retaliation: Repercussions of the Hawley-Smoot Bill* (Philadelphia: University of Pennsylvania Press, 1934).

Kadmi-Cohen, *L'abomination américaine: Essai politique* (Paris: Flammarion, 1930).

Kennedy, Joseph P., *I'm for Roosevelt* (New York: Reynal and Hitchcock, 1936).

Keynes, John Maynard, *The Economic Consequences of the Peace* (London: Macmillan, 1919).

Kohnstamm, Dolph, ed., *Still No War: A Correspondence between Two Dutchmen—Son Max and Father, Philip Kohnstamm, 1938–1939* (London: Athena Press, 2003).

Kopperschmidt, Josef, and Johannes G. Pankau, eds., *Hitler der Redner* (Munich: Fink, 2003).

Law, Richard, "Britain and the New Deal," *World Affairs* 97 (1934): 149.

Layton, Walter, "The Tasks of the World Economic Conference," *Foreign Affairs* 11 (1933): 406–19.

Lazarsfeld, Paul, Marie Lazarsfeld-Jahoda, and Hans Zeisl, *Die Arbeitslosen von Marienthal: Ein soziographischer Versuch über die Wirkungen langdauernder Arbeitslosigkeit* (Leipzig: S. Hirzel, 1933).

League of Nations, *Balances of Payments, 1930* (Geneva: League of Nations Publications, 1932).

———, *Balances of Payments, 1931 and 1930* (Geneva: League of Nations Publications, 1933).

———, *Balances of Payments, 1938* (Geneva: League of Nations Publications, 1939).

———, *Economic Stability in the Post-War World: The Conditions of Prosperity after the Transition from War to Peace* (Geneva: League of Nations Publications, 1945).

———, *Report of the Gold Delegation of the Financial Committee* (Geneva: League of Nations Publications, 1932).

———, *The World Economic Conference, Geneva, May 1927: Final Report* (Geneva: League of Nations Publications, 1927).

League of Nations, Organisation for Communications and Transit, *Coordination of Transport: Results of an Enquiry Addressed to the Governments* (Geneva: League of Nations Publications, 1938).

Leavens, Dickson H., *Silver Money* (Bloomington, IN: Principia Press, 1939).

Lehman, Herbert H., *Liberalism: A Personal Journey* (New York: Astoria Press, 1958).

Lewis, John L., "Labor and the National Recovery Administration," *Annals of the American Academy of Political and Social Science* 172 (1934): 58–63.

Lilienthal, David E., "Business and Government in the Tennessee Valley," *Annals of the American Academy of Political and Social Science* 172 (1934): 45–49.

———, *TVA: Democracy on the March* (New York: Harper, 1944).

Lipgens, Walter, ed., *Documents on the History of European Integration*, Vol. 1 (Berlin: Walter de Gruyter, 1985).

Lippmann, Walter, *Interpretations, 1931–1932* (New York: Macmillan, 1932).

Loewenstein, Karl, "The Balance between Legislative and Executive Power: A Study in Comparative Constitutional Law," *University of Chicago Law Review* 5 (1938): 566–608.

Lorwin, Lewis L., *Economic Consequences of the Second World War* (New York: Random House, 1941).

Lorwin, Lewis L., *International Economic Development: Public Works and Other Problems* (Washington, DC: US Government Printing Office, 1942).

———, *National Planning in Selected Countries* (Washington, DC: US Government Printing Office, 1941).

Lutz, Harley L., "Inter-Allied Debts, Reparations, and National Policy," *Journal of Political Economy* 38 (1930): 29–61.

Lynd, Robert S., and Helen Merrell Lynd, *Middletown: A Study in Contemporary American Culture* (New York: Harcourt, 1929).

———, *Middletown in Transition: A Study in Cultural Conflicts* (New York: Harcourt, 1937).

Lyon, Leverett S., Paul T. Homan, Lewis L. Lorwin, George Terborgh, Charles L. Dearing, and Leon C. Marshall, *The National Recovery Administration: An Analysis and Appraisal* (Washington, DC: Brookings Institution Press, 1935).

MacDonald, Thomas H., "Tomorrow's Roads," *Engineering News-Record* 117 (1936): 868–70.

Macmillan, Harold, *The Middle Way: A Study of the Problem of Economic and Social Progress in a Free and Democratic Society* (London: Macmillan, 1938).

Marabuto, Paul, *La collaboration policière internationale en vue de la prévention et de la répression de la criminalité* (Nice: École professionelle Don-Bosco, 1935).

Mason, Alpheus T., "Labor, the Courts, and Section 7(a)," *American Political Science Review* 28 (1934): 999–1015.

Mathews, John M., "Roosevelt's Latin-American Policy," *American Political Science Review* 29 (1935): 805–20.

Mauldon, F.R.E., "The Doctrine of Rationalisation," *Economic Record* 7 (1931): 246–61.

Mead, Elwood, *Helping Men Own Farms: A Practical Discussion of Government Aid in Land Settlement* (New York: Macmillan, 1920).

Merz, Charles, *And Then Came Ford* (Garden City, NY: Doubleday, 1929).

Methorst, Henri Willem, "The New System of Population Accounting in the Netherlands," *Journal of the American Statistical Association* 31 (1936): 719–22.

Mitrany, David, *A Working Peace System* (1943; repr., Chicago: Quadrangle Books, 1966).

Moley, Raymond, *After Seven Years* (New York: Harper, 1939).

Möller, Gustav, *Swedish Unemployment Policy* (Stockholm: Royal Swedish Commission, 1939).

Montague, Gilbert H., "Is NRA Fascistic?" *Annals of the American Academy of Political and Social Science* 180 (1935): 149–61.

Myer, Dillon S., *Uprooted Americans: The Japanese Americans and the War Relocation Authority during World War II* (Tucson: University of Arizona Press, 1971).

National Planning Board, *Final Report, 1933–1934* (Washington, DC: US Government Printing Office, 1934).

National Resources Board, *A Report on National Planning and Public Works* (unpublished manuscript, Lamont Library, Harvard University, 1934).

Jawaharlal Nehru's Speeches, Vol. III *(1953–1957)* (New Delhi: Publications Division, 1958).

Neumann, Sigmund, "The Conflict of Generations in Contemporary Europe," *Vital Speeches of the Day* 5, no. 20 (1939): 623–28.

Nicholson, Vincent D., "The Rural Electrification Act of 1936," *Journal of Land and Public Utility Economics* 12 (1936): 317–18.

Nkrumah, Kwame, *Ghana: The Autobiography of Kwame Nkrumah* (Edinburgh: Thomas Nelson and Sons, 1957).

Norris, George W., *Fighting Liberal: The Autobiography of George W. Norris* (New York: Macmillan, 1945).

Oakeshott, Michael, "Introduction," in *The Social and Political Doctrines of Contemporary Europe*, ed. Michael Oakeshott (1939; repr., New York: Cambridge University Press, 1950), xi–xxiii.

Obama, Barack, *The Audacity of Hope: Thoughts on Reclaiming the American Dream* (Edinburgh: Canongate, 2007).

Office of Inter-American Affairs, *History of the Office of the Coordinator of Inter-American Affairs: Historical Reports on War Administration* (Washington, DC: US Government Printing Office, 1947).

Palmer, Charles F., *Adventures of a Slum Fighter* (Atlanta: Tupper and Love, 1955).

Panunzio, Constantine, *Self-Help Coöperatives in Los Angeles* (Berkeley: University of California Press, 1939).

Patterson, Ernest Minor, *America: World Leader or World Led?* (New York: Century, 1932).

Perkins, Frances, *The Roosevelt I Knew* (New York: Viking Press, 1946).

Piettre, André, *L'évolution des ententes industrielles en France depuis la crise* (Paris: Librairie du Recueil Sirey, 1936).

Pius XI, *Quadragesimo anno: After Forty Years: Encyclical Letter of His Holiness Pius XI, in Commemoration of the Fortieth Anniversary of the Encyclical "Rerum novarum"* (New York: Barry Vail, 1931).

Political and Economic Planning Group, "Planning Begins at Home," *Planning* 3 (1933): 1–3.

The Public Papers and Addresses of Franklin D. Roosevelt, 13 vols., ed. Samuel I. Rosenman (New York: Random House, 1938–50).

Public Papers of the Presidents of the United States, Eisenhower, 1953 (Washington, DC: US Government Printing Office, 1960).

Public Papers of the Presidents of the United States: Herbert Hoover, vols. 1929, 1930, 1931, 1932–33 (Washington, DC: US Government Printing Office, 1974–77).

Public Works Administration, Housing Division, *The British Government in Housing, 1851–1935* (Washington, DC: Public Works Administration, 1937).

Puerto Rican Emergency Relief Administration, *Second Report of the Puerto Rican Emergency Relief Administration* (Washington, DC: US Government Printing Office, 1939).

Puig Casauranc, José Manuel, *Remarks on the Position Taken by Mexico at Montevideo* (Mexico City: Press of the Ministry of Foreign Affairs, 1934).

Ratzlaff, Carl Johann, "The Community Education Movement in Sweden," *Journal of Educational Sociology* 9 (1935): 167–78.

———, *The Scandinavian Unemployment Relief Program* (Philadelphia: University of Pennsylvania Press, 1934).

Recent Social Trends in the United States: Report of the President's Research Committee on Social Trends, 2 vols. (New York: McGraw-Hill, 1933).

Reed, William V., *European Housing: A Series of Confidential Reports to the Housing*

Division, PWA (unpublished manuscript, PWA, 1936, retrieved from the Harvard Law School Library).

Reid, Ira De Augustine, "The Negro Immigrant: His Background, Characteristics, and Social Adjustment, 1899–1937" (PhD diss., Columbia University, 1939).

Richberg, Donald R., *The Rainbow* (Garden City, NY: Doubleday, 1936).

Ridgon, William M., *White House Sailor* (Garden City, NY: Doubleday, 1962).

Robbins, Lionel, *The Economic Basis of Class Conflict and Other Essays in Political Economy* (London: Macmillan, 1939).

Rockefeller Foundation, *Annual Report 1938* (New York: Rockefeller Foundation, 1939).

Rockwell, Almon F., "The New Zealand Social Security Act," *Social Security Bulletin*, 2 (1939), 3–9.

Roosevelt, Elliott, ed., *F.D.R.: His Personal Letters*, 2 vols. (New York: Duell, Sloan, and Pearce, 1950).

Roosevelt, Franklin D., *Franklin D. Roosevelt and Foreign Affairs*, Vol. II: *March 1934–August 1935* (Cambridge, MA: Belknap Press, 1969).

———, "Our Foreign Policy: A Democratic View," *Foreign Affairs* 6 (1928): 573–86.

Rosskam, Edwin, *Washington: Nerve Center* (New York: Alliance Book, 1939).

Rothery, Agnes, *Denmark, Kingdom of Reason* (New York: Viking Press, 1937).

Rougemont, Denis de, *Politique de la Personne* (Paris: Éditions "Je sers," 1934).

Russell, Bertrand, *The Prospects of Industrial Civilization* (London: Routledge, 1996).

Salter, Arthur, *China and the Depression: Impressions of a Three Months Visit* (Shanghai: National Economic Council of the National Government of the Republic of China, 1934).

Schiller, Karl, *Marktregulierung und Marktordnung in der Weltagrarwirtschaft* (Jena: Fischer, 1940).

Schweizerische Zentralstelle für Freiwilligen Arbeitsdienst, ed., *Arbeitsdienst in 13 Staaten: Probleme—Lösungen: Berichte und Vorträge der II. Internationalen Arbeitsdiensttagung in Seelisberg, Schweiz vom 5.–10. September 1937* (Zurich: Orell Füssli, 1937).

Scott, F. R., "The Privy Council and Mr. Bennett's 'New Deal' Legislation," *Canadian Journal of Economics and Politial Science* 3 (1937): 234–41.

Seldes, George, *Iron, Blood and Profits: An Exposure of the World-Wide Munitions Racket* (New York: Harper, 1934).

Shaw, Roger, "Fascism and the New Deal," *North American Review* 238 (1934): 559–64.

Simon, Ernest Darwin, *The Smaller Democracies* (London: V. Gollancz, 1939).

Slichter, Sumner H., "Is the Tariff a Cause of Depression?" *Current History* 35 (1932): 519–24.

Spates, T. G., and George S. Rabinovitch, *Unemployment Insurance in Switzerland: The Ghent System Nationalized with Compulsory Features* (New York: Industrial Relations Counselors, 1931).

Spencer, John H., *Ethiopia at Bay: A Personal Account of the Haile Sellassie Years* (Algonac, MI: Reference Publications, 1984).

Standard Oil Company, *Mexico Labor Controversy, 1936–1938: Memoranda on the Controversy Arising out of Mexico's Impositions on Foreign Oil Companies in Mexico Leading up to the Expropriation Decree of March 18, 1938* (New York: Standard Oil Company, 1938).

Stead, William Thomas, *The Americanization of the World, or, the Trend of the Twentieth Century* (New York: H. Markley, 1902).

Stein, Oswald, "Building Social Security," *International Labour Review* 44 (1941): 247–74.

Stone, Julius, "Peace Planning and the Atlantic Charter," *Australian Quarterly* 14 (1942): 5–22.

Straus, Nathan, "Housing: A National Achievement," *Atlantic Monthly* 164 (1939): 204–10.

———, "A Housing Program for the United States" (address delivered at the School of Architecture, Princeton University, April 11, 1935, copy at Loeb Design Library, Harvard University).

———, *The Seven Myths of Housing* (New York: Knopf, 1944).

Studenski, Paul, *Taxation and Public Policy: A Discussion of Current Problems of American and European Public Finance* (New York: R. R. Smith, 1936).

Swing, Raymond G., "Take the Army out of the CCC," *Nation* 141 (1935): 450–60.

Temporary National Economic Committee, *Regulation of Economic Activities in Foreign Countries* (Washington, DC: US Government Printing Office, 1941).

Tennessee Valley Authority, *The Development of the Tennessee Valley* (Washington, DC: US Government Printing Office, 1936).

Timoshenko, Vladimir P., *World Agriculture and the Depression* (Ann Arbor: University of Michigan Press, 1933).

Towne, Allen N., *Doctor Danger Forward: A World War II Memoir of a Combat Medical Aidman, First Infantry Division* (Jefferson, NC: McFarland, 2000).

Townsend, Francis, *New Horizons* (Chicago: J. L. Stewart, 1943).

Toynbee, Arnold, "Annus Terribilis 1931," *Survey of International Affairs, 1931* (1932): 1–160.

———, *Between Oxus and Jumna* (New York: Oxford University Press, 1961).

Tugwell, Rexford G., "The Agricultural Policy of France," *Political Science Quarterly* 45 (1930): 214–30, 405–28, 527–47.

———, *The Brains Trust* (New York: Viking Press, 1968).

———, *The Diary of Rexford G. Tugwell: The New Deal, 1932–1935*, ed. Michael Vincent Namorato (New York: Greenwood Press, 1992).

———, *Forty-Second Annual Report of the Governor of Puerto Rico* (San Juan: Government of Puerto Rico, 1942).

———, "The Place of Government in a National Land Program," *Journal of Farm Economics* 16 (1934): 55–69.

Union for Democratic Action, *Democratic Objectives for World Order* (New York: Union for Democratic Action, 1944).

United States, *Report of the Inquiry on Cooperative Enterprise in Europe, 1937* (Washington, DC: US Government Printing Office, 1937).

US Agricultural Adjustment Administration, *Crop Insurance Features of Agricultural Adjustment Programs* (Washington, DC: US Government Printing Office, 1934).

US Bureau of the Census, *Catalog of Publications, 1790–1972* (Washington, DC: US Government Printing Office, 1974).

US Department of Commerce, Bureau of the Census, *Japanese Population in Selected Counties and Cities of the United States by Sex and Nativity or Citizenship: 1940*, series P-9, no. 5.

US Housing Authority, *Questions and Answers: The Program of the United States Hous-*

ing Authority—Its Record to Date (Washington, DC: US Government Printing Office, 1940).

Unwin, Raymond, "Housing and Planning: English and American Compared," *Journal of the Royal Society of Arts* 85 (1937): 716–28.

———, *The Legacy of Raymond Unwin: A Human Pattern for Planning* (Cambridge, MA: MIT Press, 1967).

———, "Urban Development: The Pattern and the Background," *Journal of the Town Planning Institute* 21 (1935): 261–62.

Vandenberg, Arthur H., *The Private Papers of Senator Vandenberg*, ed. Arthur H. Vandenberg Jr. (Boston: Houghton Mifflin, 1952).

Villaseñor, Eduardo, *Ensayos Interamericanos: Reflexiones de un economista* (Mexico City: Editorial Cultura, 1944).

Visvesvaraya, Mokshagundam, *Planned Economy for India* (Bangalore City: Bangalore Press, 1934).

Vollmer, August, *The Police and Modern Society* (Berkeley: University of California Press, 1936).

Wallace, Henry A., "American Agriculture and World Markets," *Foreign Affairs* 12 (1934): 216–30.

———, *Democracy Reborn* (1944; repr., New York: Da Capo Press, 1973).

———, *Whose Constitution: An Inquiry into the General Welfare* (1936; repr., Westport, CT: Greenwood Press, 1971).

War Relocation Authority, *Administrative Manual* (unpublished manuscript, War Relocation Authority, Washington, DC, ca. 1945, copy in the Library of Congress).

Warren, Edgar L., and Michael T. Wermel, *An Economic Survey of the Baby Chick Hatchery Industry* (Washington, DC: US Government Printing Office, 1935).

Wehner, Bruno, "Germany Begins Construction of Express Highway System," *Engineering News-Record* 113 (1934): 10–12.

Wells, H. G., *The Shape of Things to Come* (New York: Macmillan, 1933).

———, *Foreign Trade of the United States, Calendar Year 1936* (Washington, DC: US Government Printing Office, 1938).

Whittlesey, Charles R., "The Stevenson Plan: Some Conclusions and Observations," *Journal of Political Economy* 39 (1931): 506–25.

Wilson, Francis G., "Internationalism in Current American Labor Policy," *American Political Science Review* 28 (1934): 909–18.

Winslow, Thacher W., *Youth: A World Problem* (Washington, DC: US Government Printing Office, 1937).

Witherow, Grace A., ed., *Foreign Trade of the United States, Calendar Year 1933* (Washington, DC: US Government Printing Office, 1934).

Witte, Edwin E., *The Development of the Social Security Act: A Memorandum on the History of the Committee on Economic Security and Drafting and Legislative History of the Social Security Act* (Madison: University of Wisconsin Press, 1963).

Yates, P. Lamartine, and Doreen Warriner, *Food and Farming in Post-War Europe* (Oxford: Oxford University Press, 1943).

Zimmermann, Werner, *Die Nahrungsquellen der Welt: Handbuch über Erzeugung und Handel der wichtigsten Agrarprodukte* (Berlin: Verlag für Sozialpolitik, Wirtschaft und Statistik, 1941).

Zimmern, Alfred, "Reflections on the Crisis: Thoughts from Geneva," *Political Quarterly* 2 (1931): 472–74.

Secondary Literature

Abbott, Carl, *Political Terrain: Washington, D.C., from Tidewater Town to Global Metropolis* (Chapel Hill: University of North Carolina Press, 1999).

———, "Washington and Berlin: National Capitals in a Networked World," in *Berlin–Washington, 1800–2000: Capital Cities, Cultural Representation, and National Identities*, ed. Andreas W. Daum and Christof Mauch (Cambridge: Cambridge University Press, 2005), 101–24.

Abrahamian, Ervand, *A History of Modern Iran* (Cambridge: Cambridge University Press, 2008).

Adams, D. K., *FDR, the New Deal and Europe* (published inaugural lecture, University of Keele, 1974).

Adler, Jeffrey S., "Less Crime, More Punishment: Violence, Race, and Criminal Justice in Early Twentieth-Century America," *Journal of American History* 102 (2015), 34-46.

Aguado, Iago Gil, "The Creditanstalt Crisis of 1931 and the Failure of the Austro-German Customs Union Project," *Historical Journal* 44 (2001): 199–221.

Ahamed, Liaquat, *Lords of Finance: The Bankers Who Broke the World* (New York: Penguin, 2009).

Alanen, Arnold R., and Joseph A. Eden, *Main Street Ready-Made: The New Deal Community of Greendale, Wisconsin* (Madison: State Historical Society of Wisconsin, 1987).

Allen, Ernest, Jr., "When Japan Was 'Champion of the Darker Races': Satokata Takahashi and the Flowering of Black Messianic Nationalism," *Black Scholar* 24 (1994): 23–46.

Almandoz, Arturo, "Urbanization and Urbanism in Latin America: From Haussmann to CIAM," in *Planning Latin America's Capital Cities, 1850–1950*, ed. Arturo Almandoz (London: Routledge, 2002), 13–44.

Alpers, Benjamin L., *Dictators, Democracy, and American Public Culture: Envisioning the Totalitarian Enemy, 1920s–1950s* (Chapel Hill: University of North Carolina Press, 2003).

Alston, Lee J., "Farm Foreclosures in the United States during the Interwar Period," *Journal of Economic History* 43 (1983): 885–903.

Alter, Jonathan, *The Defining Moment: FDR's Hundred Days and the Triumph of Hope* (New York: Simon and Schuster, 2006).

Altman, Nancy J., *The Battle for Social Security: From FDR's Vision to Bush's Gamble* (Hoboken, NJ: Wiley, 2005).

Altman, Werner "Cárdenas, Vargas y Perón: Una confluencia populista," in *El Populismo en América Latina*, ed. Werner Altman, Mario Miranda Pacheco, Lucia Sala de Tourón, and Marcos Winocur (Mexico City: Universidad Nacional Autónoma de México, 1983), 43–95.

Altschuler, Glenn C., and Stuart M. Blumin, *The GI Bill: A New Deal for Veterans* (Oxford: Oxford University Press, 2009).

Aly, Götz, and Karl Heinz Roth, *The Nazi Census: Identification and Control in the Third Reich* (Philadelphia: Temple University Press, 2004).

Ambrose, Stephen E., and Richard H. Immerman, *Milton S. Eisenhower: Educational Statesman* (Baltimore: Johns Hopkins University Press, 1983).

Amenta, Edwin, *When Movements Matter: The Townsend Plan and the Rise of Social Security* (Princeton, NJ: Princeton University Press, 2006).

Amrith, Sunil, and Patricia Clavin, "Feeding the World: Connecting Europe and Asia, 1930–1945," *Past and Present* 218 (2013): 29–50.

Anderson, Warwick, *The Cultivation of Whiteness: Science, Health and Racial Destiny in Australia* (Carlton: Melbourne University Press, 2005).

Angster, Julia, *Konsenskapitalismus und Sozialdemokratie: Die Westernisierung von SPD und DGB* (Munich: Oldenbourg, 2003).

Archer, Robin, *Why Is There No Labor Party in the United States?* (Princeton, NJ: Princeton University Press, 2007).

Argersinger, Jo Ann E., "Contested Visions of American Democracy: Citizenship, Public Housing, and the International Arena," *Journal of Urban History* 36 (2010): 792–813.

Arnold, Joseph L., *The New Deal in the Suburbs: A History of the Greenbelt Town Program, 1935–1954* (Columbus: Ohio State University Press, 1971).

Arroyo Vázquez, María Luz, "Industria y Trabajo en el New Deal de Franklin D. Roosevelt a través de la prensa española, 1932–1936" (PhD diss., Universidad Complutense de Madrid, 2000).

Asada, Sadao, *Culture Shock and Japanese-American Relations: Historical Essays* (Columbia: University of Missouri Press, 2007).

———, *From Mahan to Pearl Harbor: The Imperial Japanese Navy and the United States* (Annapolis, MD: Naval Institute Press, 2006).

Auerbach, Jerold S., *Unequal Justice: Lawyers and Social Change in Modern America* (Oxford: Oxford University Press, 1976).

Austen, Ralph A., "Varieties of Trusteeship: African Territories under British and French Mandate, 1919–1939," in *France and Britain in Africa: Imperial Rivalry and Colonial Rule*, ed. Prosser Gifford and William Roger Louis (New Haven, CT: Yale University Press, 1971), 515–41.

Aydin, Cemil, *The Politics of Anti-Westernism in Asia: Visions of World Order in Pan-Islamic and Pan-Asian Thought* (New York: Columbia University Press, 2007).

Badger, Anthony J., *FDR: The First Hundred Days* (New York: Hill and Wang, 2008).

———, *The New Deal: The Depression Years, 1933–40* (Basingstoke: Macmillan, 1989).

Bailes, Kendall E., "The American Connection: Ideology and the Transfer of American Technology to the Soviet Union, 1917–1941," *Comparative Studies in History and Society* 23 (1981): 421–48.

Balachandran, Gopalan, "Gold, Silver, and India in Anglo-American Monetary Relations, 1925–1933," *International History Review* 18 (1996): 573–90.

———, "The Interwar Slump in India: The Periphery in a Crisis of Empire," in *The World Economy and National Economies in the Interwar Slump*, ed. Theo Balderston (Basingstoke: Palgrave Macmillan, 2003), 143–71.

Balderrama, Francisco E., and Raymond Rodríguez, *Decade of Betrayal: Mexican Repatriation in the 1930s* (Albuquerque: University of New Mexico Press, 1995).

Barber, William J., *Designs within Disorder: Franklin D. Roosevelt, the Economists, and the Shaping of American Economic Policy, 1933–1945* (Cambridge: Cambridge University Press, 1996).

———, *From New Era to New Deal: Herbert Hoover, the Economists, and American Economic Policy, 1921–1933* (Cambridge: Cambridge University Press, 1985).

———, *Gunnar Myrdal: An Intellectual Biography* (Houndmills: Palgrave Macmillan, 2008).

Barkan, Elazar, "Mobilizing Scientists against Nazi Racism, 1933–1939," in *Bones, Bodies, Behavior: Essays on Biological Anthropology*, ed. George W. Stocking Jr. (Madison: University of Wisconsin Press, 1988), 180–205.

Barlogh, Brian, "Securing Support: The Emergence of the Social Security Board as a Political Actor, 1935–1939," in *Federal Social Security: The Historical Dimension*, ed. Donald T. Critchlow and Ellis W. Hawley (University Park: Pennsylvania State University Press, 1988), 55–78.

Bauman, Zygmunt, *Intimations of Postmodernity* (London: Routledge, 1992).

Beasley, Vanessa B., and Deborah Smith-Howell, "No Ordinary Rhetorical President: FDR's Speechmaking and Leadership, 1933–1945," in *American Rhetoric in the New Deal Era, 1932–1945*, ed. Thomas W. Benson (East Lansing: Michigan State University Press, 2006), 1–32.

Beaudreau, Bernard C., *Making Sense of Smoot-Hawley: Technology and Tariffs* (New York: iUniverse, 2005).

Bedelow, James B., "Depression and the New Deal: Letters from the Plains," *Kansas Historical Quarterly* 43 (1977): 140–53.

Beezley, William H., "Conclusion: Gabardine Suits and Guayabera Shirts," in *Populism in Twentieth Century Mexico: The Presidencies of Lázaro Cárdenas and Luis Echeverría*, ed. Amelia M. Kiddle and María L. O. Muñoz (Tucson: University of Arizona Press, 2010), 190–205.

Behrman, Greg, *The Most Noble Adventure: The Marshall Plan and the Time When America Helped Save Europe* (New York: Free Press, 2007).

Beinart, William, "Agricultural Planning and the Late Colonial Technical Imagination: The Lower Shire Valley in Malawi, 1940–1960," in *Malawi: An Alternative Pattern of Development*, ed. Centre of African Studies, University of Edinburgh (Edinburgh: Centre of African Studies, 1985), 95–148.

Bell, Jonathan, "Social Politics in a Transoceanic World in the Early Cold War Years," *Historical Journal* 53 (2010): 401–21.

Bender, Thomas, *A Nation among Nations: America's Place in World History* (New York: Hill and Wang, 2006).

Benjamin, Jules R., "The New Deal, Cuba, and the Rise of a Global Foreign Economic Policy," *Business History Review* 51 (1977): 157–78.

Benmergui, Leandro Daniel, "Housing Development: Housing Policy, Slums, and Squatter Settlements in Rio de Janeiro, Brazil and Buenos Aires, Argentina, 1948–1973" (PhD diss., University of Maryland, 2012).

Bennett, Edward M., *Franklin D. Roosevelt and the Search for Security: American-Soviet Relations, 1933–1939* (Wilmington, DE: Scholarly Resources, 1985).

Benson, Thomas W., "Introduction: American Rhetoric in the New Deal Era," in *American Rhetoric in the New Deal Era, 1932–1945*, ed. Thomas W. Benson (East Lansing: Michigan State University Press, 2006), ix–xxiii.

Berger, Dina, "Goodwill Ambassadors on Holiday: Tourism, Diplomacy, and Mexico–United States Relations," in *Holiday in Mexico: Critical Reflections on Tourism and Tourist Encounters*, ed. Dina Berger and Andrew Grant Wood (Durham, NC: Duke University Press, 2010), 107–29.

Berger, Stefan, and Hugh Compston, eds., *Policy Concertation and Social Partnership in Western Europe: Lessons for the Twenty-First Century* (New York: Berghahn, 2002).

Bernanke, Ben S., *Essays on the Great Depression* (Princeton, NJ: Princeton University Press, 2000).

Bernstein, Barton J., "The New Deal: The Conservative Achievements of Liberal Reform," in *Towards a New Past: Dissenting Essays in American History*, ed. Barton J. Bernstein (New York: Pantheon Books, 1968), 263–88.

Bernstein, Irving, *The New Deal Collective Bargaining Policy* (Berkeley: University of California Press, 1950).

Bernstein, Michael A., *The Great Depression: Delayed Recovery and Economic Change in America, 1929–1939* (Cambridge: Cambridge University Press, 1987).

Bertino, Magdalena, Reto Bertoni, Héctor Tajam, and Jaime Yaffé, *La economía del primer Batllismo y los años veinte: Auge y crisis del modelo agroexportador (1911–1930)* (Montevideo: Editorial Fin de Siglo, 2005).

Bértola, Luis, and Jeffrey G. Williamson, "Globalization in Latin America before 1940," in *The Cambridge Economic History of Latin America*, Vol. II, ed. Victor Bulmer-Thomas, John H. Coatsworth, and Roberto Cortés-Conde (Cambridge: Cambridge University Press, 2006), 9–56.

Bertrams, Kenneth, "Planning and the 'Techno-Corporatist Bargain' in Western Europe and the United States, 1914–44: Diffusion and Confusion of Economic Models," *Perspectivia* 10 (2013): 43–61.

———, "Une inspiration tout en contrastes: Le New Deal et l'ancrage transnational des experts du planning, 1933–1943," *Genèses* 71 (2008): 64–83.

Best, Antony, "The Leith-Ross Mission and British Policy towards East Asia, 1934–7," *International History Review* 35 (2013): 681–701.

Best, Gary Dean, *The Dollar Decade: Mammon and the Machine in 1920s America* (Westport, CT: Praeger, 2003).

Bielschowsky, Ricardo, *Pensamento econômico brasileiro: O ciclo ideológico do desenvolvimentismo* (Rio de Janeiro: IPEA/INPES, 1988).

Birchall, Johnston, *The International Co-operative Movement* (Manchester: Manchester University Press, 1997).

Bischof, Günter, Anton Pelinka, and Alexander Lassner, eds., *The Dollfuss/Schuschnigg Era in Austria: A Reassessment* (New Brunswick, NJ: Transaction, 2003).

Black, Edwin, *IBM and the Holocaust: The Strategic Alliance between Nazi Germany and America's Most Powerful Corporation* (New York: Crown Publishers, 2001).

Black, Maggie, *The Children and the Nations: The Story of Unicef* (New York: UNICEF, 1986).

Blackbourn, David, *The Conquest of Nature: Water, Landscape, and the Making of Modern Germany* (New York: W. W. Norton, 2006).

Bletz, May E., *Immigration and Acculturation in Brazil and Argentina, 1890–1929* (New York: Palgrave Macmillan, 2010).

Blower, Brooke L., *Becoming Americans in Paris: Transatlantic Politics and Culture between the World Wars* (New York: Oxford University Press, 2011).

————, "From Isolationism to Neutrality: A New Framework for Understanding American Political Culture, 1919–1941," *Diplomatic History* 38 (2014): 345–76.

Blum, John Morton, "World War II," in *The Comparative Approach to American History*, ed. C. Vann Woodward (New York: Basic Books, 1968), 315–27.

Bodenschatz, Harald, "Diktatorischer Städtebau in der Zwischenkriegszeit: Besonderheiten Italiens mit Blick auf das nationalsozialistische Deutschland und die Sowjetunion," in *Für den Faschismus bauen: Architektur und Städtebau im Italien Mussolinis*, ed. Aram Mattioli and Gerald Steinacher (Zurich: Orell Füssli Verlag, 2009), 45–64.

Bogue, Donald J., *The Population of the United States: Historical Trends and Future Projections* (New York: Free Press, 1985).

Bonin, Hubert, *La Banque nationale de crédit: Histoire de la quatrième banque de dépôts française en 1913–1932* (Paris: Plage, 2002).

Boorstin, Daniel J., *America and the Image of Europe: Reflections on American Thought* (New York: Meridian Books, 1960).

Borgwardt, Elizabeth, *A New Deal for the World: America's Vision for Human Rights* (Cambridge, MA: Belknap Press, 2005).

Boris, Eileen, and Christiane Eifert, "Gender: Equality and Differences," in *The United States and Germany during the Twentieth Century: Competition and Convergence*, ed. Christof Mauch and Kiran Klaus Patel (Cambridge: Cambridge University Press, 2010), 161–79.

Borstelmann, Thomas, *The Cold War and the Color Line: American Race Relations in the Global Arena* (Cambridge, MA: Harvard University Press, 2001).

————, *The 1970s: A New Global History from Civil Rights to Economic Inequality* (Princeton, NJ: Princeton University Press, 2012).

Bortolotti, Lando, *Fascismo e autostrade: Un caso di sintesi* (Milan: FrancoAngeli, 1994).

Bose, Subhas Chandra, *The Indian Struggle, 1920–1942* (Delhi: Oxford University Press, 1997).

Boyce, Robert, *The Great Interwar Crisis and the Collapse of Globalization* (Basingstoke: Palgrave Macmillan, 2009).

Boyko, John, *Bennett: The Rebel Who Challenged and Changed a Nation* (Toronto: Key Porter Books, 2010).

Bozdoğan, Sibel, *Modernism and Nation Building: Turkish Architectural Culture in the Early Republic* (Seattle: University of Washington Press, 2001).

Brand, Donald R., *Corporatism and the Rule of Law: A Study of the National Recovery Administration* (Ithaca, NY: Cornell University Press, 1988).

Breitman, Richard, and Alan M. Kraut, *American Refugee Policy and European Jewry, 1933–1945* (Bloomington: Indiana University Press, 1987).

Breitman, Richard, and Allan J. Lichtman, *FDR and the Jews* (Cambridge, MA: Belknap Press, 2013).

Brélaz, Michel, *Henri de Man: Une autre idée du socialisme* (Geneva: Editions des Antipodes, 1985).

Brennan, John A., *Silver and the First New Deal* (Reno: University of Nevada Press, 1969).

Brewer, Stewart, *Borders and Bridges: A History of U.S.-Latin American Relations* (Westport, CT: Praeger, 2006).

Briggs, Laura: *Reproducing Empire: Race, Sex, Science, and U.S. Imperialism in Puerto Rico* (Berkeley: University of California Press, 2002).

Brinkley, Alan, *The End of Reform: New Deal Liberalism in Recession and War* (New York: Knopf, 1995).

————, "The National Resources Planning Board and the Reconstruction of Planning," in *The American Planning Tradition: Culture and Policy*, ed. Robert Fishman (Washington, DC: Woodrow Wilson Center Press, 2000), 173–91.

————, *Voices of Protest: Huey Long, Father Coughlin, and the Great Depression* (New York: Knopf, 1982).

Brinkley, Douglas, *Wheels for the World: Henry Ford, His Company, and a Century of Progress, 1903–2003* (New York: Penguin, 2004).

Brinkley, Douglas, and David R. Facey-Crowther, eds., *The Atlantic Charter* (Houndmills: Macmillan, 1994).

Brooke, Stephen, "Problems of 'Socialist Planning': Evan Durbin and the Labour Government of 1945," *Historical Journal* 34 (1991): 687–702.

Broomham, Rosemary, *On the Road: The NRMA's First Seventy-Five Years* (St Leonards, New South Wales: Allen and Unwin, 1996).

Browder, Robert P., "Soviet Far Eastern Policy and American Recognition, 1932–1934," *Pacific Historical Review* 21 (1952): 263–73.

Brown, D. Clayton, *Electricity for Rural America: The Fight for the REA* (Westport, CT: Greenwood Press, 1980).

Bucheli, Marcelo, "Multinational Corporations, Totalitarian Regimes and Economic Nationalism: United Fruit Company in Central America, 1899–1975," *Business History* 50 (2008): 433–54.

Bucur, Maria, *Eugenics and Modernization in Interwar Romania* (Pittsburgh: University of Pittsburgh Press, 2002).

Buder, Stanley, *Visionaries and Planners: The Garden City Movement and the Modern Community* (New York: Oxford University Press, 1990).

Bulmer-Thomas, Victor, "The Latin American Economies, 1929–1939," in *The Cambridge History of Latin America*, Vol. VI, Part 1, ed. Leslie Bethell (Cambridge: Cambridge University Press, 1994), 65–115.

Burdekin, Richard C. K., "US Pressure on China: Silver Flows, Deflation, and the 1934 Shanghai Credit Crunch," *China Economic Review* 19 (2008): 170–82.

Burley (Slaughter), Anne-Marie, "Regulating the World: Multilateralism, International Law, and the Projection of the New Deal Regulatory State," in *Multilateralism Matters: The Theory and Praxis of an Institutional Form*, ed. John Gerard Ruggie (New York: Columbia University Press, 1993), 125–56.

Burns, Helen M., *The American Banking Community and New Deal Banking Reforms, 1933–1935* (Westport, CT: Greenwood Press, 1974).

Burns, James MacGregor, *Roosevelt: The Lion and the Fox, 1882–1945* (New York: Hartcourt, 1956).

Burton, Michael John, "The Contemporary Presidency: The 'Flying White House': A Travel Establishment within the Presidential Branch," *Presidential Studies Quarterly* 36 (2004): 297–308.

Bush, Roderick D., *The End of White World Supremacy: Black Internationalism and the Problem of the Color Line* (Philadelphia: Temple University Press, 2009).

Bushnell, David, *The Making of Modern Colombia: A Nation in Spite of Itself* (Berkeley: University of California Press, 1993).

Butkiewicz, James L., "The Reconstruction Finance Corporation, the Gold Standard, and the Banking Panic of 1933," *Southern Economic Journal* 66 (1999): 271–93.

Calderón-Zaks, Michael, "Debated Whiteness amid World Events: Mexican and Mexican American Subjectivity and the U.S.' Relationship with the Americas, 1924–1936," *Mexican Studies* 27 (2011): 325–59.

Calomiris, Charles W., and Joseph R. Mason, "Fundamentals, Panics, and Bank Distress during the Depression," *American Economic Review* 93 (2003): 1615–47.

Cannon, Brian Q., "Power Relations: Western Rural Electric Cooperatives and the New Deal," *Western Historical Quarterly* 31 (2000): 133–60.

Capie, Forrest, "The International Depression and Trade Protection in the 1930s," in *The Interwar Depression in an International Context*, ed. Harold James (Munich: Oldenbourg, 2002), 123–37.

Caplan, Jane, "'Indelible Memories': The Tattooed Body as Theatre of Memory," in *Performing the Past: Memory, History, and Identity in Modern Europe*, ed. Karin Tilmans, Frank van Vree, and Jay Winter (Amsterdam: Amsterdam University Press, 2010), 119–46.

Caravaca, Jimena, and Mariano Plotkin, "Crisis, ciencias sociales y elites estatales: La constitucion del campo de los economistas estatales en la Argentina, 1910–1935," *Desarrollo Económico* 47 (2007): 401–28.

Carew, Joy Gleason, *Blacks, Reds, and Russians: Sojourners in Search of the Soviet Promise* (New Brunswick, NJ: Rutgers University Press, 2008).

Carvalho, José Murilo de, "Armed Forces and Politics in Brazil, 1930–45," *Hispanic American Historical Review* 62 (1982): 193–223.

Casey, Steven, *Cautious Crusade: Franklin D. Roosevelt, American Public Opinion, and the War against Nazi Germany* (Oxford: Oxford University Press, 2001).

Cassata, Francesco, *Building the New Man: Eugenics, Racial Science and Genetics in Twentieth-Century Italy* (Budapest: CEU Press, 2011).

Cassis, Youssef, *Crises and Opportunities: The Shaping of Modern Finance* (Oxford: Oxford University Press, 2011).

Chandler, William U., *The Myth of the TVA: Conservation and Development in the Tennessee Valley, 1933–80* (Pensacola, FL: Ballinger, 1984).

Charles, Douglas M., *J. Edgar Hoover and the Anti-Interventionists: FBI Political Surveillance and the Rise of the Domestic Security State, 1939–1945* (Columbus: Ohio State University Press, 2007).

Chase, Kerry A., "Imperial Protection and Strategic Trade Policy in the Interwar Period," *Review of International Political Economy* 11 (2004): 177–203.

Chatterjee, Partha, *The Nation and Its Fragments: Colonial and Postcolonial Histories* (Princeton, NJ: Princeton University Press, 1993).

Chikowero, Moses, "Subalternating Currents: Electrification and Power Politics in Bulawayo, Colonial Zimbabwe, 1894–1939," *Journal of Southern African Studies* 33 (2007): 287–306.

Chiron, Yves, *Pie XI (1857–1939)* (Paris: Perrin, 2004).

Choate, Jean, *Disputed Ground: Farm Groups That Opposed the New Deal Agricultural Program* (Jefferson, NC: McFarland, 2002).

Ciepley, David, *Liberalism in the Shadow of Totalitarianism* (Cambridge, MA: Harvard University Press, 2006).

Clancey, Gregory, "Vast Clearings: Emergency, Technology, and American De-Urbanization, 1930–1945," *Cultural Politics* 2 (2006): 49–76.

Clark, Danae, *Negotiating Hollywood: The Cultural Politics of Actors' Labor* (Minneapolis: University of Minnesota Press, 1995).

Clavin, Patricia, *The Failure of Economic Diplomacy: Britain, Germany, France and the United States, 1931–36* (Basingstoke: Macmillan, 1996).

———, *The Great Depression in Europe, 1929–1939* (New York: St. Martin's Press, 2000).

———, *Securing the World Economy: The Reinvention of the League of Nations, 1920–1946* (Oxford: Oxford University Press, 2013).

Clavin, Patricia, and Kiran Klaus Patel, "The Role of International Organizations in Europeanization: The Case of the League of Nations and the European Economic Community," in *Europeanization in the Twentieth Century: Historical Approaches*, ed. Martin Conway and Kiran Klaus Patel (New York: Palgrave Macmillan, 2010), 110–31.

Clawson, Marion, *New Deal Planning: The National Resources Planning Board* (Baltimore: Johns Hopkins University Press, 1981).

Clawson, Patrick, "Knitting Iran Together: The Land Transport Revolution, 1920–1940," *Iranian Studies* 26 (1993): 235–50.

Cohen, Lizabeth, "Encountering Mass Culture at the Grassroots: The Experience of Chicago Workers in the 1920s," *American Quarterly* 41 (1989): 6–33.

———, *Making a New Deal: Industrial Workers in Chicago, 1919–1939*, 2nd ed. (Cambridge: Cambridge University Press, 2008).

———, "The New Deal State and the Making of Citizen Consumers," in *Getting and Spending: European and American Consumer Societies in the Twentieth Century*, ed. Susan Strasser, Charles McGovern, and Matthias Judt (Cambridge: Cambridge University Press, 1998), 111–25.

Cohen, Yves, *Le siècle des chefs: Une histoire transnationale du commandement et de l'autorité, 1890–1940* (Paris: Editions Amsterdam, 2013).

Cohrs, Patrick O., *The Unfinished Peace after World War I: America, Britain and the Stabilisation of Europe, 1919–1932* (Cambridge: Cambridge University Press, 2006).

Colander, David C., and Harry Landreth, eds., *The Coming of Keynesianism to America: Conversations with the Founders of Keynesian Economics* (Cheltenham: Edward Elgar, 1996).

Collier, Thomas W., "The Army and the Great Depression," *Parameters: The U.S. Army War College Quarterly* 18 (1988): 102–8.

Collins, William J., "Race, Roosevelt, and Wartime Production: Fair Employment in World War II Labor Markets," *American Economic Review* 91 (2001): 272–86.

Conkin, Paul K., *Tomorrow a New World: The New Deal Community Program* (1959; repr., New York: Da Capo Press, 1976).

Connelly, Matthew, *Fatal Misconception: The Struggle to Control World Population* (Cambridge, MA: Belknap Press, 2008).

Conquest, Robert, *The Harvest of Sorrow: Soviet Collectivisation and the Terror-Famine* (London: Pimlico, 2002).

Conrad, Sebastian, and Klaus Mühlhahn, "Global Mobility and Nationalism: Chinese Migration and the Re-Territorialization of Belonging," in *Competing Visions of World Order: Global Moments and Movements, 1880s–1930s*, ed. Sebastian Conrad and Dominic Sachsenmaier (New York: Palgrave Macmillan, 2007), 181–211.

Conway, Martin, and Peter Romijn, "Belgium and the Netherlands," in *Twisted Paths: Europe 1914–1945*, ed. Robert Gerwarth (Oxford: Oxford University Press, 2008), 84–110.

Conybeare, John A. C., *Trade Wars: The Theory and Practice of International Commercial Rivalry* (New York: Columbia University Press, 1987).

Cook, Blanche Wiesen, *Eleanor Roosevelt* (London: Bloomsbury, 1993).

Cooper, Richard N., "Fettered to Gold? Economic Policy in the Interwar Period," *Journal of Economic Literature* 30 (1992): 2120–28.

Coquery-Vidrovitch, Catherine, "Electricity Networks in Africa: A Comparative Study, or How to Write Social History from Economic Sources," in *Sources and Methods in African History: Spoken, Written, Unearthed*, ed. Toyin Falola and Christian Jennings (Rochester, NY: University of Rochester Press, 2003), 346–60.

Cortesini, Sergio, *Arte contemporanea italiana e propaganda fascista negli Stati Uniti di Franklin D. Roosevelt* (Rome: Pioda, 2012).

Costa Pinto, António, "The 'Corporatist Revolution' of the Portuguese New State: An Introduction," in *Les expériences corporatives dans l'aire latine*, ed. Didier Musiedlak (Berne: Lang, 2010), 117–24.

Costigliola, Frank, *Awkward Domination: American Political, Economic, and Cultural Relations with Europe, 1919–1933* (Ithaca, NY: Cornell University Press, 1984).

Courtney, John C., "Prime Ministerial Character: An Examination of Mackenzie King's Political Leadership," *Canadian Journal of Political Science* 9 (1976): 77–100.

Cowie, Jefferson, and Nick Salvatore, "The Long Exception: Rethinking the Place of the New Deal in American History," *International Labor and Working-Class History* 74 (2008): 3–32.

Crafts, Nicholas, and Peter Fearon, "Depression and Recovery in the 1930s," in *The Great Depression of the 1930s: Lessons for Today*, ed. Nicholas Craft and Peter Fearon (Oxford: Oxford University Press, 2013), 1–44.

Craig, Douglas B., *Fireside Politics: Radio and Political Culture in the United States, 1920–1940* (Baltimore: Johns Hopkins University Press, 2000).

Craver, Earlene, "Gösta Bagge, the Rockefeller Foundation, and Empirical Social Science Research in Sweden, 1924–1940," in *The Stockholm School of Economics Revisited*, ed. Lars Jonung (Cambridge: Cambridge University Press, 1991), 79–97.

Crawley, Andrew, *Somoza and Roosevelt: Good Neighbour Diplomacy in Nicaragua, 1933–1945* (Oxford: Oxford University Press, 2007).

Creese, Walter L., *The Search for Environment: The Garden City: Before and After* (Baltimore: Johns Hopkins University Press, 1967).

———, *TVA's Public Planning: The Vision, the Reality* (Knoxville: University of Tennessee Press, 1990).

Cresti, Federico, "Comunità proletarie italiane nell'Africa Mediterranea tra XIX Secolo e periodo fascista," *Mediterranea Ricerche storiche* 12 (2008): 189–214.

Critchlow, Donald T., "The Political Control of the Economy: Deficit Spending as a Political Belief, 1932–1952," *Public Historian* 3 (1981): 5–22.

Cronon, E. David, "Interpreting the New Good Neighbor Policy: The Cuban Crisis of 1933," *Hispanic American Historical Review* 39 (1959): 538–67.

Crowley, Terry, "J. J. Morrison and the Transition in Canadian Farm Movements during the Early Twentieth Century," *Agricultural History* 71 (1997): 330–56.

Cuff, Robert D., *The War Industries Board: Business-Government Relations during World War I* (Baltimore: Johns Hopkins University Press, 1973).

Cullather, Nick, *The Hungry World: America's Cold War Battle against Poverty in Asia* (Cambridge, MA: Harvard University Press, 2010).

———, "Model Nations: US Allies and Partners in the Modernizing Imagination," in *America's "Special Relationships": Foreign and Domestic Aspects of the Politics of Alliance*, ed. John Dumbrell and Axel R. Schäfer (London: Routledge, 2009), 7–23.

Currell, Susan, and Christina Cogdell, eds., *Popular Eugenics: National Efficiency and American Mass Culture in the 1930s* (Athens: Ohio University Press, 2006).

Curti, Merle, "Sweden in the American Social Mind of the 1930s," in *The Immigration of Ideas: Studies in the North Atlantic Community*, ed. J. Iverne Dowie and J. Thomas Tredway (Rock Island: Augustana Historical Society, 1968), 159–84.

Dahl, Hans Fredrik, *Quisling: A Study in Treachery* (Cambridge: Cambridge University Press, 1999).

Daley, Robert, *An American Saga: Juan Trippe and His Pan Am Empire* (New York: Random House, 1980).

Dalfiume, Richard M., "The 'Forgotten Years' of the Negro Revolution," *Journal of American History* 55 (1968): 90–106.

Dallek, Robert, *Franklin D. Roosevelt and American Foreign Policy, 1932–1945* (Oxford: Oxford University Press, 1995).

Daniels, Roger, *Prisoners without Trial: Japanese Americans in World War II* (New York: Hill and Wang, 1993).

D'Araújo, Maria Celina, "Entre a Europa e os Estados Unidos: Diálogos de Vargas com seu diário," *Luso-Brazilian Review* 34 (1997): 17–41.

Daughton, Suzanne M., "FDR as Family Doctor: Medical Metaphors and the Role of Physician in the Fireside Chats," in *American Rhetoric in the New Deal Era, 1932–1945*, ed. Thomas W. Benson (East Lansing: Michigan State University Press, 2006), 33–82.

Davidson, Alexander, *Two Models of Welfare: The Origins and Development of the Welfare State in Sweden and New Zealand, 1888–1988* (Uppsala: Almqvist and Wiksell, 1989).

Davidson, Paul, "Making Dollars and Sense of the U.S. Government Debt," *Journal of Post Keynesian Economics* 32 (2010): 663–69.

Davies, Gareth, and Martha Derthick, "Race and Social Welfare Policy: The Social Security Act of 1935," *Political Science Quarterly* 112 (1997): 217–35.

Dávila, Jerry, Zachary R. Morgan, and Thomas E. Skidmore, "Since Black into White: Thomas Skidmore on Brazilian Race Relations," *Americas* 64 (2008): 409–23.

Davis, David Brion, "World War II and Memory," *Journal of American History* 77 (1990): 580–87.

Dawidoff, Nicholas, *The Catcher Was a Spy: The Mysterious Life of Moe Berg* (New York: Vintage Books, 1994).

Dawley, Alan, *Changing the World: American Progressives in War and Revolution* (Princeton, NJ: Princeton University Press, 2003).

Dawson, Nelson L., "Brandeis and the New Deal," in *Brandeis and America*, ed. Nelson L. Dawson (Lexington: University Press of Kentucky, 1989), 38–64.

de Grazia, Victoria, *Irresistible Empire: America's Advance through Twentieth-Century Europe* (Cambridge, MA: Belknap Press, 2005).

Deflem, Mathieu, "Bureaucratization and Social Control: Historical Foundations of International Police Cooperation," *Law and Society Review* 34 (2000): 739–78.

———, *Policing World Society: Historical Foundations of International Police Cooperation* (Oxford: Oxford University Press, 2002).

Delpar, Helen, *The Enormous Vogue of Things Mexican: Cultural Relations between the United States and Mexico, 1920–1935* (Tuscaloosa: University of Alabama Press, 1992).

Delporte, Christian, *La IIIᵉ République, 1919–1940: De Raymond Poincaré à Paul Reynaud* (Paris: Pygmalion, 1998).

Dengg, Sören, *Deutschlands Austritt aus dem Völkerbund und Schachts "Neuer Plan": Zum Verhältnis von Aussen- und Aussenwirtschaftspolitik in der Übergangsphase von der Weimarer Republik zum Dritten Reich (1329–1934)* (Frankfurt am Main: Lang, 1986).

Denning, Michael, *The Cultural Front: The Laboring of American Culture in the Twentieth Century* (London: Verso, 1997).

Deutsch, Tracey, *Building a Housewife's Paradise: Gender, Politics, and American Grocery Stores in the Twentieth Century* (Chapel Hill: University of North Carolina Press, 2010).

Devoto, Fernando J., *Historia de la inmigración en la Argentina* (Buenos Aires: Editorial Sudamericana, 2003).

Dickinson, Matthew J., *Bitter Harvest: FDR, Presidential Power and the Growth of the Presidential Branch* (Cambridge: Cambridge University Press, 1997).

Dickter, Arturo Grunstein, "Hacia un análisis 'estado-céntrico' comparativo de las políticas del Cardenismo: Las bases político-institucionales del 'keynesianismo social'," *Sociológia* 18 (2003): 147–95.

Dimendberg, Edward, "The Will to Motorization: Cinema, Highways, and Modernity," *October* 73 (1995): 90–137.

Dinnerstein, Leonard, *Antisemitism in America* (Oxford: Oxford University Press, 1994).

Dion, Michelle, "The Political Origins of Social Security in Mexico during the Cárdenas and Ávila Camacho Administrations," *Mexican Studies* 21 (2005): 59–95.

Divine, Robert A., *Second Chance: The Triumph of Internationalism in America during World War II* (New York: Atheneum, 1967).

Dizikes, John, *Britain, Roosevelt, and the New Deal: British Opinion, 1932–1938* (New York: Garland, 1979).

Dobbin, Frank R., "The Social Construction of the Great Depression: Industrial Policy during the 1930s in the United States, Britain, and France," *Theory and Society* 22 (1993): 1–56.

Doel, Hans W. van den, "Tegenover het Amerikanisme moet men een 'Europese moraal' kunnen stellen," in *Nederland en de Nieuwe Wereld*, ed. Hans W. van den Doel, Piet C. Emmer, and Hermann P. Vogel (Utrecht: Aula, 1992), 261–74.

Doenecke, Justus D., and Mark A. Stoler, *Debating Franklin D. Roosevelt's Foreign Policies, 1933–1945* (Lanham, MD: Rowman and Littlefield, 2005).

Dohan, Michael R., "The Economic Origins of Soviet Autarky 1927/28–1934," *Slavic Review* 35 (1976): 603–35.

Donahue, Jesse C., and Erik K. Trump, *American Zoos during the Depression: A New Deal for Animals* (Jefferson, NC: McFarland, 2010).

Donovan, Peter, *Highways: A History of the South Australian Highways Department* (Netley: Griffin Press, 1991).

Dorman, Robert L., *Hell of a Vision: Regionalism and the Modern American West* (Tucson: University of Arizona Press, 2012).

Dorn, Harold, "Hugh Lincoln Cooper and the First Détente," *Technology and Culture* 20 (1979): 322–47.

Dosal, Paul J., *Doing Business with the Dictators: A Political History of United Fruit in Guatemala, 1899–1944* (Lanham, MD: Rowman and Littlefield, 1993).

Draibe, Sônia, *Rumos e metamorfoses: Um estudo sobre a constituição do Estado e as alternativas da industrialização no Brasil, 1930–1960* (Rio de Janeiro: Paz e Terra, 1985).

Drinnon, Richard, *Keeper of Concentration Camps: Dillon S. Myer and American Racism* (Berkeley: University of California Press, 1987).

Drummond, Ian M., *British Economic Policy and the Empire, 1919–1939*, 2nd ed. (Abingdon: Routledge, 2006).

———, *The Gold Standard and the International Monetary System, 1900–1939* (Basingstoke: Macmillan, 1987).

D'Souza, Rohan, "Damming the Mahanadi River: The Emergence of Multi-Purpose River Valley Development in India (1943–46)," *Indian Economic Social History Review* 40 (2003): 81–105.

Duara, Prasenjit, *Sovereignty and Authenticity: Manchukuo and the East Asian Modern* (Lanham, MD: Rowman and Littlefield, 2003).

Dubofsky, Melvyn and Warren van Tine, *John L. Lewis: A Biography* (New York: Quadrangle, 1977).

Dumenil, Lynn, *The Modern Temper: American Culture and Society in the 1920s* (New York: Hill and Wang, 1995).

Dunn, Dennis J., *Caught between Roosevelt and Stalin: America's Ambassadors to Moscow* (Lexington: University Press of Kentucky, 1998).

Dunn, Susan, *1940: FDR, Willkie, Lindbergh, Hitler: The Election amid the Storm* (New Haven, CT: Yale University Press, 2013).

Dur, Philip, and Christopher Gilcrease, "US Diplomacy and the Downfall of a Cuban Dictator: Machado in 1933," *Journal of Latin American Studies* 34 (2002): 255–82.

Dwyer, John J., *The Agrarian Dispute: The Expropriation of American-Owned Rural Land in Postrevolutionary Mexico* (Durham, NC: Duke University Press, 2008).

Dye, Alan, and Richard Sicotte, "The Interwar Shocks to US-Cuban Trade Relations: A View through Sugar Company Stock Price Data," in *The Origins and Development of Financial Markets and Institutions: From the Seventeenth Century to the Present*, ed. Jeremy Atack and Larry Neal (Cambridge: Cambridge University Press, 2009), 345–87.

Eatwell, Roger, "Introduction: New Styles of Dictatorship and Leadership in Interwar Europe," in *Charisma and Fascism in Interwar Europe*, ed. António Costa Pinto, Roger Eatwell, and Stein Ugelvik Larsen (London: Routledge, 2007), xxi–xxxi.

Eckert, Andreas, "Bringing the 'Black Atlantic' into Global History: The Project of Pan-Africanism," in *Competing Visions of World Order: Global Moments and Movements, 1880s–1930s*, ed. Sebastian Conrad and Dominic Sachsenmaier (New York: Palgrave Macmillan, 2007), 237–57.

———, "'We Are All Planners Now': Planung und Dekolonisation in Afrika," *Geschichte und Gesellschaft* 34 (2008): 375–97.

Eckes, Alfred E., and Thomas W. Zeiler, *Globalization and the American Century* (Cambridge: Cambridge University Press, 2003).

Eckstein, Arthur M., "From the Historical Caesar to the Spectre of Caesarism: The Imperial Administrator as Internal Threat," in *Dictatorship in History and Theory: Bonapartism, Caesarism, and Totalitarianism*, ed. Peter Baehr and Melvin Richter (Cambridge: Cambridge University Press, 2004), 279–98.

Eichengreen, Barry, *Golden Fetters: The Gold Standard and the Great Depression, 1919–1939* (New York: Oxford University Press, 1992).

Eichengreen, Barry, and T. J. Hatton, "Interwar Unemployment in International Perspective: An Overview," in *Interwar Unemployment in International Perspective*, ed. Barry Eichengreen and T. J. Hatton (Dordrecht: Kluwer, 1988), 1–59.

Eichengreen, Barry, and Douglas A. Irwin, "Trade Blocs, Currency Blocs and the Reorientation of World Trade in the 1930s," *Journal of International Economics* 38 (1995): 1–24.

Eichengreen, Barry, and Richard Portes, "The Interwar Debt Crisis and Its Aftermath," *World Bank Research Observer* 5 (1990): 69–94.

Ekbladh, David, "Exile Economics: The Transnational Contributions and Limits of the League of Nations' Economic and Financial Section," *New Global Studies* 4 (2010): 1–6.

———, *The Great American Mission: Modernization and the Construction of an American World Order* (Princeton, NJ: Princeton University Press, 2010).

———, "'Mr. TVA': Grass-Roots Development, David Lilienthal, and the Rise and Fall of the Tennessee Valley Authority as a Symbol for U.S. Overseas Development, 1933–1973," *Diplomatic History* 26 (2002): 335–74.

Ellwood, David W., *The Shock of America: Europe and the Challenge of the Century* (Oxford: Oxford University Press, 2012).

Eloranta, Jari, "Military Competition between Friends? Hegemonic Development and Military Spending among Eight Western Democracies, 1920–1938," *Essays in Economic and Business History* 19 (2001): 17–32.

Emsley, Clive, *Crime, Police, and Penal Policy: European Experiences, 1750–1940* (Oxford: Oxford University Press, 2007).

Engerman, David C., *Modernization from the Other Shore: American Intellectuals and the Romance of Russian Development* (Cambridge, MA: Harvard University Press, 2003).

Erlandson, Marcus R., "Lend-Lease: An Assessment of a Government Bureaucracy," in *The Big "L": American Logistics in World War II*, ed. Alan Gropman (Washington, DC: National Defense University Press, 1997), 265–92.

Ettinger, Patrick W., *Imaginary Lines: Border Enforcement and the Origins of Undocumented Immigration, 1882–1930* (Austin: University of Texas Press, 2009).

Etzemüller, Thomas, *Die Romantik der Rationalität: Alva und Gunnar Myrdal—Social Engineering in Schweden* (Bielefeld: Transcript, 2010).

Falasca-Zamponi, Simonetta, *Fascist Spectacle: The Aesthetics of Power in Mussolini's Italy* (Berkeley: University of California Press, 1997).

Faue, Elizabeth, *Community of Suffering and Struggle: Women, Men, and the Labor Movement in Minneapolis, 1915–1945* (Chapel Hill: University of North Carolina Press, 1991).

Fausto, Domenicantonio, "L'economia del fascismo tra Stato e mercato," in *Intervento pubblico e politica economica fascista*, ed. Domenicantonio Fausto (Milan: FrancoAngeli, 2007), 1–47.

Federico, Giovanni, *Feeding the World: An Economic History of Agriculture, 1800–2000* (Princeton, NJ: Princeton University Press, 2005).

———, "Not Guilty? Agriculture in the 1920s and the Great Depression," *Journal of Economic History* 65 (2005): 949–76.

Felice, William F., *The Global New Deal: Economic and Social Human Rights in World Politics*, 2nd ed. (Lanham, MD: Rowman and Littlefield, 2010).

Fernández, Maria, and Miquel Carrillo, eds., *América sumergida: Impactos de los nuevos proyectos hidroeléctricos en Latinoamérica y el Caribe* (Barcelona: Icaria editorial, 2010).

Feuer, Lewis S., "American Travelers to the Soviet Union, 1917–32: The Formation of a Component of New Deal Ideology," *American Quarterly* 14 (1962): 119–49.

Fieldhouse, David K., "The Metropolitan Economics of Empire," in *The Oxford History of the British Empire*, Vol. IV, ed. Judith M. Brown and William Roger Louis (Oxford: Oxford University Press, 1999), 88–113.

Fijnaut, Cyrille, *Opdat de macht een toevlucht zij? Een historische studie van het politieapparaat als een politieke instelling* (Antwerp: Kluwer, 1979).

Filene, Peter G., *Americans and the Soviet Experiment, 1917–1933* (Cambridge, MA: Harvard University Press, 1967).

Findling, John E., *Close Neighbors, Distant Friends: United States–Central American Relations* (New York: Greenwood Press, 1987).

Finegold, Kenneth, and Theda Skocpol, *State and Party in America's New Deal* (Madison: University of Wisconsin Press, 1995).

Fishback, Price V., Ryan S. Johnson, and Shawn Kantor, "Striking at the Roots of Crime: The Impact of Welfare Spending on Crime during the Great Depression," *Journal of Law and Economics* 53 (2010): 715–40.

Fishback, Price V., Jonathan Rose, and Kenneth Snowden, *Well Worth Saving: How the New Deal Safeguarded Home Ownership* (Chicago: University of Chicago Press, 2013).

Fishback, Price V., and John Joseph Wallis, "What Was New about the New Deal?" in *The Great Depression of the 1930s: Lessons for Today*, ed. Nicholas Crafts and Peter Fearon (Oxford: Oxford University Press, 2013), 290–327.

Fischer, Lucy, "Movies and the 1920s: Introduction," in *American Cinema of the 1920s: Themes and Variations*, ed. Lucy Fischer (New Brunswick, NJ: Rutgers University Press, 2009), 1–22.

Fitzpatrick, Sheila, *The Russian Revolution* (Oxford: Oxford University Press, 2008).

Flandreau, Marc, "Central Bank Cooperation in Historical Perspective: A Sceptical View," *Economic History Review* 50 (1997): 735–63.

Fleming, Denna Frank, *The United States and the World Court* (Garden City, NY: Doubleday, 1945).

Flewers, Paul, "The Lure of the Plan: The Impact of the Five-Year Plans in Britain," *Critique* 36 (2008): 343–61.

Fonseca, Pedro Cezar Dutra, *Vargas: O capitalismo em construção, 1906–1954* (São Paulo: Editora brasiliense, 1987).

Fordham, Benjamin O., *Building the Cold War Consensus: The Political Economy of U.S. National Security Policy, 1949–51* (Ann Arbor: University of Michigan Press, 1998).

Foucault, Michel, "Governmentality," in *The Foucault Effect: Studies in Governmentality*, ed. Graham Burchell, Colin Gordon, and Peter Miller (Chicago: University of Chicago Press, 1991), 87–104.

Fox, Cybelle, *Three Worlds of Relief: Race, Immigration, and the American Welfare State from the Progressive Era to the New Deal* (Princeton, NJ: Princeton University Press, 2012).

Francis, Michael J., "The United States at Rio, 1942: The Strains of Pan-Americanism," *Journal of Latin American Studies* 6 (1974): 77–95.

Franqui, Harry, "Fighting for the Nation: Military Service, Popular Political Mobilization and the Creation of Modern Puerto Rican National Identities: 1868–1952" (PhD diss., University of Massachusetts at Amherst, 2010).

Fraser, Cary, *Ambivalent Anti-Colonialism: The United States and the Genesis of West Indian Independence, 1940–1964* (Westport, CT: Greenwood Press, 1994).

Fraser, Steve, *Labor Will Rule: Sidney Hillman and the Rise of American Labor* (New York: Free Press, 1991).

Fraser, Steve, and Gary Gerstle, eds., *The Rise and Fall of the New Deal Order, 1930–1980* (Princeton, NJ: Princeton University Press, 1989).

Freeden, Michael, *Liberalism Divided: A Study in British Political Thought, 1914–1939* (Oxford: Clarendon Press, 1986).

Fried, Richard M., "Political Culture," in *A Companion to Franklin D. Roosevelt*, ed. William D. Pederson (Oxford: Wiley-Blackwell, 2011), 318–39.

Friedberg, Aaron L., *In the Shadow of the Garrison State: America's Anti-Statism and Its Cold War Grand Strategy* (Princeton, NJ: Princeton University Press, 2000).

Frieden, Jeffry A., *Global Capitalism: Its Fall and Rise in the Twentieth Century* (New York: W. W. Norton, 2006).

Friedman, Max Paul, "There Goes the Neighborhood: Blacklisting Germans in Latin America and the Evanescence of the Good Neighbor Policy," *Diplomatic History* 27 (2003): 569–97.

Friedman, Milton, "Franklin D. Roosevelt, Silver, and China," *Journal of Political Economy* 100 (1992): 62–83.

Friedman, Milton, and Anna Jacobson Schwartz, *A Monetary History of the United States, 1867–1960* (Princeton, NJ: Princeton University Press, 1963).

Frydl, Kathleen J., *The GI Bill* (Cambridge: Cambridge University Press, 2009).

Führer, Karl Christian, *Mieter, Hausbesitzer, Staat und Wohnungsmarkt: Wohnungsmangel und Wohnungszwangswirtschaft in Deutschland 1914–1960* (Stuttgart: Steiner, 1995).

Fujitani, Takashi, *Race for Empire: Koreans as Japanese and Japanese as Americans during World War II* (Berkeley: University of California Press, 2011).

Fuller, Mia, *Moderns Abroad: Architecture, Cities and Italian Imperialism* (London: Routledge, 2007).

Gabaccia, Donna R., *Foreign Relations: American Immigration in Global Perspective* (Princeton, NJ: Princeton University Press, 2012).

Galbraith, John Kenneth, *The Great Crash, 1929* (Boston: Houghton Mifflin, 1997).

Gallagher, Hugh Gregory, *FDR's Splendid Deception* (New York: Dodd, 1985).

Gallicchio, Marc, *The African American Encounter with Japan and China: Black Internationalism in Asia, 1895–1945* (Chapel Hill: University of North Carolina Press, 2000).

Gao, Bai, "The State and the Associational Order of the Economy: The Institutionalization of Cartels and Trade Associations in 1931–45 Japan," *Sociological Forum* 16 (2001): 409–43.

Gardner, Lloyd C., *Economic Aspects of New Deal Diplomacy* (Madison: University of Wisconsin Press, 1964).

Garon, Sheldon, *The State and Labor in Modern Japan* (Berkeley: University of California Press, 1987).

Garraty, John A., *The Great Depression: An Inquiry into the Causes, Course, and Consequences of the Worldwide Depression of the Nineteen Thirties, as Seen by Contemporaries and in the Light of History* (Garden City, NY: Anchor Books, 1987).

———, "The New Deal, National Socialism, and the Great Depression," *American Historical Review* 78 (1973): 907–44.

Gassert, Philipp, *Amerika im Dritten Reich: Ideologie, Propaganda und Volksmeinung, 1933–1945* (Stuttgart: Steiner, 1997).

Gatell, Frank Otto, "Independence Rejected: Puerto Rico and the Tydings Bill of 1936," *Hispanic American Historical Review* 38 (1958): 25–44.

Gazell, James A., "Arthur H. Vandenberg, Internationalism, and the United Nations," *Political Science Quarterly* 88 (1973): 375–94.

Geddes, Barbara, "Building 'State' Autonomy in Brazil, 1930–1964," *Comparative Politics* 22 (1990): 217–35.

Geertse, Michael Alexander, "Defining the Universal City: The International Federation for Housing and Town Planning and Transnational Planning Dialogue, 1913–1945" (PhD diss., Free University Amsterdam, 2012).

Gellman, Irwin F., *Good Neighbor Diplomacy: United States Policies in Latin America, 1933–1945* (Baltimore: Johns Hopkins University Press, 1979).

Gerstle, Gary, *American Crucible: Race and Nation in the Twentieth Century* (Princeton, NJ: Princeton University Press, 2001).

———, "The Politics of Patriotism: Americanization and the Formation of the CIO," *Dissent* 33 (1986): 84–92.

Geulen, Christian, "The Common Grounds of Conflict: Racial Visions of World Order, 1880–1940," in *Competing Visions of World Order: Global Moments and Movements, 1880s–1930s*, ed. Sebastian Conrad and Dominic Sachsenmaier (New York: Palgrave Macmillan, 2007), 69–96.

Ghirardo, Diane, *Building New Communities: New Deal America and Fascist Italy* (Princeton, NJ: Princeton University Press, 1989).

Giandou, Alexandre, *La Compagnie Nationale du Rhône (1933–1998): Histoire d'un partenaire régional de l'Etat* (Grenoble: Presses Universitaires de Grenoble, 1999).

Gilbert, Jess, "Low Modernism and the Agrarian New Deal: A Different Kind of State," in *Fighting for the Farm: Rural America Transformed*, ed. Jane Adams (Philadelphia: University of Pennsylvania Press, 2003), 129–46.

Gilbert, Jess, and Carolyn Howe, "Beyond 'State vs. Society': Theories of the State and New Deal Agricultural Policies," *American Sociological Review* 56 (1991): 204–20.

Gilbert, Jess, and Alice O'Connor, "Leaving the Land Behind: Struggles for Land Reform in U.S. Federal Policy, 1933–1965," *Who Owns America? Social Conflict over Property Rights*, ed. Harvey M. Jacobs (Madison: University of Wisconsin Press, 1998), 114–30.

Gilly, Adolfo, *El cardenismo, una utopía mexicana* (Mexico City: León y Cal Editores, 1994).

Gilman, Nils, *Mandarins of the Future: Modernization Theory in Cold War America* (Baltimore: Johns Hopkins University Press, 2003).

Gilroy, Paul, *The Black Atlantic: Modernity and Double Consciousness* (Cambridge, MA: Harvard University Press, 1993).

Glantz, Mary E., *FDR and the Soviet Union: The President's Battles over Foreign Policy* (Lawrence: University Press of Kansas, 2005).

Glendon, Mary Ann, *A World Made New: Eleanor Roosevelt and the Universal Declaration of Human Rights* (New York: Random House, 2001).

Goetz, Edward G., *New Deal Ruins: Race, Economic Justice, and Public Housing Policy* (Ithaca, NY: Cornell University Press, 2013).

Golay, Michael, *America 1933: The Great Depression, Lorena Hickok, Eleanor Roosevelt, and the Shaping of the New Deal* (New York: Free Press, 2013).

Goldberg, Jonah, *Liberal Fascism: The Secret History of the American Left from Mussolini to the Politics of Meaning* (New York: Doubleday, 2007).

Goldstein, Judith, "The Impact of Ideas on Trade Policy: The Origins of U.S. Agricultural and Manufacturing Policies," *International Organization* 43 (1989): 31–71.

Goldwag, Arthur, *The New Hate: A History of Fear and Loathing on the Populist Right* (New York: Pantheon Books, 2012).

Gomes, Angela de Castro, "A práxis corporativa de Oliveira Vianna," in *O Pensamento de Oliveira Vianna*, ed. João Quartim de Moraes and Élide Rugai Bastos (Campinas, Brazil: Editora da Unicamp, 1993), 43–61.

Gomes, Leonard, *German Reparations, 1919–1932: A Historical Survey* (Basingstoke: Palgrave Macmillan, 2010).

Gonzalez, Michael J., *The Mexican Revolution, 1910–1940* (Albuquerque: University of New Mexico Press, 2002).

Goodall, Alex, "The Battle of Detroit and Anti-Communism in the Depression Era," *Historical Journal* 51 (2008): 457–80.

Goode, James, "Introduction," in *Washington by Night*, ed. Judith W. Frank (Washington, DC: Starwood, 1992), 10–17.

Gordon, Colin, *Dead on Arrival: The Politics of Health Care in Twentieth-Century America* (Princeton, NJ: Princeton University Press, 2003).

———, *New Deals: Business, Labor, and Politics in America, 1920–1935* (Cambridge: Cambridge University Press, 1994).

Gordon, Margaret S., *Social Security Policies in Industrial Countries: A Comparative Analysis* (Cambridge: Cambridge University Press, 1988).

Gordon-Ashworth, Fiona, "Agricultural Commodity Control under Vargas in Brazil, 1930–1945," *Journal of Latin American Studies* 12 (1980): 87–105.

Gorman, Daniel, *The Emergence of International Society in the 1920s* (Cambridge: Cambridge University Press, 2012).

Gosewinkel, Dieter, ed., *Wirtschaftskontrolle und Recht in der nationalsozialistischen Diktatur* (Frankfurt am Main: Klostermann, 2005).

Götz, Norbert, *Ungleiche Geschwister: Die Konstruktion von nationalsozialistischer Volksgemeinschaft und schwedischem Volksheim* (Baden-Baden: Nomos, 2001).

Götz, Norbert, and Kiran Klaus Patel, "Facing the Fascist Model: Discourse and the Construction of Labour Services in the USA and Sweden in the 1930s and 1940s," *Journal of Contemporary History* 41 (2006): 57–73.

Gourevitch, Peter Alexis, "Breaking with Orthodoxy: The Politics of Economic Policy Responses to the Depression of the 1930s," *International Organization* 38 (1984): 95–129.

———, *Politics in Hard Times: Comparative Responses to International Economic Crises* (Ithaca, NY: Cornell University Press, 1986).

Graevenitz, Fritz Georg von, "Exogenous Transnationalism: Java and 'Europe' in an Organised World Sugar Market (1927–1937)," *Contemporary European History* 20 (2011): 257–80.

Graham, Otis L., *Toward a Planned Society: From Roosevelt to Nixon* (New York: Oxford University Press, 1976).

Grandi, Elisa, "David Lilienthal, La Banca Mondiale e lo sviluppo di una rete transnazionale di economic advising (1950–1957)," *Diacronie: Studi di Storia Contemporanea* 6 (2011): 1–13.

Grandin, Greg, *Fordlandia: The Rise and Fall of Henry Ford's Forgotten Jungle City* (New York: Metropolitan Books, 2009).

———, "Your Americanism and Mine: Americanism and Anti-Americanism in the Americas," *American Historical Review* 111 (2006): 1042–66.

Grant, Michael Johnston, *Down and Out on the Family Farm: Rural Rehabilitation in the Great Plains, 1929–1945* (Lincoln: University of Nebraska Press, 2002).

Grant, Nancy, *TVA and Black Americans: Planning for the Status Quo* (Philadelphia: Temple University Press, 1990).

Gray, Aelred J., and David A. Johnson, *The TVA Regional Planning and Development Program: The Transformation of an Institution and Its Mission* (Aldershot: Ashgate, 2005).

Greaves, Julian, *Industrial Reorganization and Government Policy in Interwar Britain* (Aldershot: Ashgate, 2005).

Green, Michael Cullen, *Black Yanks in the Pacific: Race in the Making of American Military Empire after World War II* (Ithaca, NY: Cornell University Press, 2010).

Green, Nancy L., "Expatriation, Expatriates, and Expats: The American Transformation of a Concept," *American Historical Review* 114 (2009): 307–28.

Gregg, Sara M., *Managing the Mountains: Land Use Planning, the New Deal, and the Creation of a Federal Landscape in Appalachia* (New Haven, CT: Yale University Press, 2010).

Gregory, Paul R., and Joel Sailors, "The Soviet Union during the Great Depression: The Autarky Model," in *The World Economy and National Economies in the Interwar Slump*, ed. Theo Balderston (Basingstoke: Palgrave Macmillan, 2003), 191–221.

Grift, Liesbeth van de, "On New Land a New Society: Internal Colonisation in the Netherlands, 1918–1940," *Contemporary European History* 22 (2013): 609–26.

Grill, Johnpeter Horst, "The American South and Nazi Racism," in *The Impact of*

Nazism: New Perspectives on the Third Reich and Its Legacy, ed. Alan E. Steinweis and Daniel E. Rogers (Lincoln: University of Nebraska Press, 2003), 19–38.

Grisinger, Joanna, *The Unwieldy American State: Administrative Politics since the New Deal* (Cambridge: Cambridge University Press, 2012).

Gropman, Alan, "Industrial Mobilization," in *The Big "L": American Logistics in World War II*, ed. Alan Gropman (Washington, DC: National Defense University Press, 1997), 1–95.

Gross, James A., *The Making of the National Labor Relations Board: A Study in Economics, Politics, and the Law* (Albany: State University of New York Press, 1974).

Groves, Leslie R., *Now It Can Be Told: The Story of the Manhattan Project* (New York: Da Capo Press, 1975).

Grunwald, Michael, *The New New Deal: The Hidden Story of Change in the Obama Era* (New York: Simon and Schuster, 2012).

Guerin-Gonzales, Camille, *Mexican Workers and American Dreams: Immigration, Repatriation, and California Farm Labor, 1900–1939* (New Brunswick, NJ: Rutgers University Press, 1994).

Gupta, Bishnupriya, "The International Tea Cartel during the Great Depression, 1929–1933," *Journal of Economic History* 61 (2001): 144–59.

Gutiérrez, David, *Walls and Mirrors: Mexican Americans, Mexican Immigrants, and the Politics of Ethnicity* (Berkeley: University of California Press, 1995).

Gutschow, Niels, *Ordnungswahn: Architekten planen im "eingedeutschten Osten," 1939–1945* (Basel: Birkhäuser, 2001).

Guttenberg, Albert Z., *The Language of Planning: Essays on the Origins and Ends of American Planning Thought* (Urbana: University of Illinois Press, 1993).

Gutzke, David W., "Historians and Progressivism," in *Britain and Transnational Progressivism*, ed. David W. Gutzke (New York: Palgrave Macmillan, 2008), 11–22.

Hacker, Jacob S., *The Divided Welfare State: The Battle over Public and Private Social Benefits in the United States* (Cambridge: Cambridge University Press, 2002).

Hagemann, Harald, Tamotsu Nishizawa, and Yukihiro Ikeda, eds., *Austrian Economics in Transition: From Carl Menger to Friedrich Hayek* (New York: Palgrave Macmillan, 2010).

Haines, Gerald K., "The Roosevelt Administration Interprets the Monroe Doctrine," *Australian Journal of Politics and History* 24 (1978): 332–45.

Halasz, Nicholas, *Roosevelt through Foreign Eyes* (Princeton, NJ: Van Nostrand, 1961).

Hall, Peter A., ed., *The Political Power of Economic Ideas: Keynesianism across Nations* (Princeton, NJ: Princeton University Press, 1989).

Halpern, Martin, "Labor," in *A Companion to Franklin D. Roosevelt*, ed. William D. Pederson (Oxford: Wiley-Blackwell, 2011), 155–85.

Hamby, Alonzo L., *For the Survival of Democracy: Franklin Roosevelt and the World Crisis of the 1930s* (New York: Free Press, 2004).

———, "The New Deal: Avenues for Reconsideration," *Polity* 31 (1999): 665–81.

Hamilton, David E., *From New Day to New Deal: American Farm Policy from Hoover to Roosevelt, 1928–1933* (Chapel Hill: University of North Carolina Press, 1991).

Handlin, Oscar, *The Uprooted: The Epic Story of the Great Migrations That Made the American People*, 2nd ed. (Philadelphia: University of Pennsylvania Press, 2002).

Hanes, Jeffrey E., *The City as Subject: Seki Hajime and the Reinvention of Modern Osaka* (Berkeley: University of California Press, 2002).

Hanioğlu, M. Şükrü, *Atatürk: An Intellectual Biography* (Princeton, NJ: Princeton University Press, 2011).

Hansen, Erik, "Depression Decade Crisis: Social Democracy and Planisme in Belgium and the Netherlands, 1929–1939," *Journal of Contemporary History* 16 (1981): 293–322.

——, "Hendrik de Man and the Theoretical Foundations of Economic Planning: The Belgian Experience, 1933–40," *European History Quarterly* 8 (1978): 235–57.

Hansen, Per H., "Banking Crises and Lenders of Last Resort: Denmark in the 1920s and the 1990s," in *The Evolution of Financial Institutions and Markets in Twentieth-Century Europe*, ed. Youssef Cassis, Gerald D. Feldman, and Ulf Olsson (Aldershot: Scolar Press, 1995), 20–46.

Hargreaves, Mary W. M., "Land-Use Planning in Response to Drought: The Experience of the Thirties," *Agricultural History* 50 (1976): 561–82.

Hargrove, Erwin C., *Prisoners of Myth: The Leadership of the Tennessee Valley Authority, 1933–1990* (Princeton, NJ: Princeton University Press, 1994).

Hark, Ina Rae, "Movies and the 1930s," in *American Cinema of the 1930s: Themes and Variations*, ed. Ina Rae Hark (New Brunswick, NJ: Rutgers University Press, 2007), 1–24.

Harlander, Tilman, *Zwischen Heimstätte und Wohnmaschine: Wohnungsbau und Wohnungspolitik in der Zeit des Nationalsozialismus* (Basel: Birkhäuser, 1995).

Harootunian, Harry, *Overcome by Modernity: History, Culture, and Community in Interwar Japan* (Princeton, NJ: Princeton University Press, 2000).

Harper, John Lamberton, *American Visions of Europe: Franklin D. Roosevelt, George F. Kennan, and Dean G. Acheson* (Cambridge: Cambridge University Press, 1996).

Harries, Keith, and Derral Cheatwood, *The Geography of Execution: The Capital Punishment Quagmire in America* (Lanham, MD: Rowman and Littlefield, 1997).

Harrison, Helen A., "American Art and the New Deal," *Journal of American Studies* 6 (1972): 289–96.

Harrison, Mark, "Resource Mobilization for World War II: The U.S.A., U.K., U.S.S.R., and Germany, 1938–1945," *Economic History Review* 41 (1988): 171–92.

——, *Soviet Planning in Peace and War, 1938–1945* (Cambridge: Cambridge University Press, 1985).

Hart, Justin, *Empire of Ideas: The Origins of Public Diplomacy and the Transformation of U.S. Foreign Policy* (Oxford: Oxford University Press, 2013).

Hart, Michael, *A Trading Nation: Canadian Trade Policy from Colonialism to Globalization* (Vancouver: University of British Columbia Press, 2002).

Hartung, Frank E., "Trends in the Use of Capital Punishment," *Annals of the American Academy of Political and Social Science* 284 (1952): 8–19.

Harvey, Elizabeth R., "The Cult of Youth," in *A Companion to Europe, 1900–1945*, ed. Gordon Martel (Oxford: Blackwell, 2006), 66–81.

Hawley, Ellis W., *The New Deal and the Problem of Monopoly: A Study in Economic Ambivalence* (Princeton, NJ: Princeton University Press, 1966).

Hayashi, Brian Masaru, *Democratizing the Enemy: The Japanese American Internment* (Princeton, NJ: Princeton University Press, 2004).

Hayden, Joseph, *Negotiating in the Press: American Journalism and Diplomacy, 1918–1919* (Baton Rouge: Louisiana State University Press, 2010).

Hayes, Joy Elizabeth, *Radio Nation: Communication, Popular Culture, and Nationalism in Mexico, 1920–1950* (Tucson: University of Arizona Press, 2000).

Heide, Lars, *Punched-Card Systems and the Early Information Explosion, 1880–1945* (Baltimore: Johns Hopkins University Press, 2009).

Hein, Laura, *Reasonable Men: Political Culture and Expertise in Twentieth-Century Japan* (Washington, DC: Woodrow Wilson Center Press, 2004).

Heiner, Albert P., *Henry J. Kaiser, American Empire Builder: An Insider's View* (New York: Lang, 1989).

Hen, Paul Erik de, *Actieve en re-actieve industriepolitiek in Nederland: De overheid en de ontwikkeling van de Nederlandse industrie in de jaren dertig en tussen 1945 en 1950* (Amsterdam: De Arbeiderspers, 1980).

Hendrickson, David C., *Union, Nation, or Empire: The American Debate over International Relations, 1789–1941* (Lawrence: University Press of Kansas, 2009).

Henrikson, Alan K., "FDR and the 'World-Wide Arena,'" in *FDR's World: War, Peace, and Legacies*, ed. David B. Woolner, Warren F. Kimball, and David Reynolds (New York: Palgrave Macmillan, 2008), 35–61.

Hentschke, Jens R., "The Vargas Era Institutional and Development Model Revisited: Themes, Debates, and Lacunas," in *Vargas and Brazil: New Perspectives*, ed. Jens R. Hentschke (New York: Palgrave Macmillan, 2006), 1–29.

Herring, George C., *From Colony to Superpower: U.S. Foreign Relations since 1776* (Oxford: Oxford University Press, 2008).

Hess, Gary R., "The 'Hindu' in America: Immigration and Naturalization Policies and India, 1917–1946," *Pacific Historical Review* 38 (1969): 59–79.

Hewlett, Richard G., and Oscar E. Anderson, *The New World, 1939–1946: A History of the United States Atomic Energy Commission*, Vol. 1 (University Park: Pennsylvania State University Press, 1962).

Higgs, Robert, *Crisis and Leviathan: Critical Episodes in the Growth of American Government* (New York: Oxford University Press, 1987).

Hilson, Mary, "Consumer Co-operation and Economic Crisis: The 1936 Roosevelt Inquiry on Co-operative Enterprise and the Emergence of the Nordic 'Middle Way,'" *Contemporary European History* 22 (2013): 181–98.

Hilton, Stanley E., *Brazil and the Great Powers, 1930–1939: The Politics of Trade Rivalry* (Austin: University of Texas Press, 1975).

Himmelberg, Robert F., *The Origins of the National Recovery Administration: Business, Government, and the Trade Association Issue, 1921–1933* (New York: Fordham University Press, 1976).

Hinds, Matthew, "Anglo-American Relations in Saudi Arabia, 1941–1945: A Study of a Trying Relationship" (PhD diss., London School of Economics and Political Science, 2012).

Hirshfield, Daniel S., *The Lost Reform: The Campaign for Compulsory Health Insurance in the United States from 1932–1943* (Cambridge, MA: Harvard University Press, 1970).

Hoag, Heather J., *Developing the Rivers of East and West Africa: An Environmental History* (London: Bloomsbury Academic, 2013).

Hodge, Joseph M., *Triumph of the Expert: Agrarian Doctrines of Development and the Legacies of British Colonialism* (Athens: Ohio University Press, 2007).

Hodges, James A., *New Deal Labor Policy and the Southern Cotton Textile Industry, 1933–1941* (Knoxville: University of Tennessee Press, 1986).

Hoelscher, Steven D., *Heritage on Stage: The Invention of Ethnic Place in America's Little Switzerland* (Madison: University of Wisconsin Press, 1998).

Hoerder, Dirk, *Cultures in Contact: World Migrations in the Second Millennium* (Durham, NC: Duke University Press, 2002).

Hoff, Joan Wilson, *Ideology and Economics: U.S. Relations with the Soviet Union, 1918–1933* (Columbia: University of Missouri Press, 1974).

Hofmann, Reto, "The Fascist Reflection: Japan and Italy, 1919–1950" (PhD diss., Columbia University, 2010).

Hogan, Michael J., *A Cross of Iron: Harry S. Truman and the Origins of the National Security State, 1945–1954* (Cambridge: Cambridge University Press, 1998).

———, *The Marshall Plan: America, Britain, and the Reconstruction of Western Europe, 1947–1952* (Cambridge: Cambridge University Press, 1987).

Hoganson, Kristin L., *Consumers' Imperium: The Global Production of American Domesticity, 1865–1920* (Chapel Hill: University of North Carolina Press, 2007).

Hohmann, Joachim Stephan, *Landvolk unterm Hakenkreuz: Agrar- und Rassenpolitik in der Rhön* (Frankfurt am Main: Lang, 1992).

Höhn, Maria and Martin Klimke, *A Breath of Freedom: The Civil Rights Struggle, African American GIs, and Germany* (New York: Palgrave Macmillan, 2010).

Hoopes, Townsend, and Douglas Brinkley, *FDR and the Creation of the U.N.* (New Haven, CT: Yale University Press, 1997).

Hopkins, June, *Harry Hopkins: Sudden Hero, Brash Reformer* (New York: St. Martin's Press, 1999).

Horn, Gerd-Rainer, *European Socialists Respond to Fascism: Ideology, Activism, and Contingency in the 1930s* (New York: Oxford University Press, 1996).

Hoskins, Dalmer D., "U.S. Social Security at 75 Years: An International Perspective," *Social Security Bulletin* 70 (2010): 79–87.

Houck, Davis W., and Amos Kiewe, *FDR's Body Politics: The Rhetoric of Disability* (College Station: Texas A&M University Press, 2003).

Hu, Shizhang, *Stanley K. Hornbeck and the Open Door Policy, 1919–1937* (Westport, CT: Greenwood Press, 1995).

Hubbard, Preston John, *Origins of the TVA: The Muscle Shoals Controversy, 1920–1932* (Nashville: Vanderbilt University Press, 1961).

Hughes, E. J., "Winston Churchill and the Formation of the United Nations Organization," *Journal of Contemporary History* 9 (1974): 177–94.

Humann, Detlev, *"Arbeitsschlacht": Arbeitsbeschaffung und Propaganda in der NS-Zeit, 1933–1939* (Göttingen: Wallstein, 2011).

Hyman, Louis, *Debtor Nation: The History of America in Red Ink* (Princeton, NJ: Princeton University Press, 2011).

Immerwahr, Daniel, *Thinking Small: The United States and the Lure of Community Development* (Cambridge, MA: Harvard University Press, 2015).

Indych-López, Anna, "Mural Gambits: Mexican Muralism in the United States and the 'Portable' Fresco," *Art Bulletin* 89 (2007): 287–305.

Ingulstad, Mats, "Winning the Hearths and Mines: Strategic Materials and American Foreign Policy, 1939–1953" (PhD diss., European University Institute, Florence, 2011).

Iriye, Akira, *Global Community: The Role of International Organizations in the Making of the Contemporary World* (Berkeley: University of California Press, 2002).

———, *The Globalizing of America, 1913–1945: The Cambridge History of American Foreign Relations*, Vol. III (Cambridge: Cambridge University Press, 1993).

———, *Power and Culture: The Japanese-American War 1941–1945* (Cambridge, MA: Harvard University Press, 1981).

———, "Toward Transnationalism," in *The Short American Century: A Postmortem*, ed. Andrew J. Bacevich (Cambridge, MA: Harvard University Press, 2012), 121–41.

Irmler, Heinrich, "Bankenkrise und Vollbeschäftigungspolitik (1931–1936)," in *Währung und Wirtschaft in Deutschland 1876–1975*, ed. Deutsche Bundesbank (Frankfurt am Main: Fritz Knapp, 1976), 283–329.

Irwin, Douglas A., *Peddling Protectionism: Smoot-Hawley and the Great Depression* (Princeton, NJ: Princeton University Press, 2011).

Irwin, Douglas A., Petros C. Mavroidis, and Alan O. Sykes, *The Genesis of the GATT* (Cambridge: Cambridge University Press, 2008).

Isetti, Ronald, "The Moneychangers of the Temple: FDR, American Civil Religion, and the New Deal," *Presidential Studies Quarterly* 26 (1996): 678–93.

Israel, Fred L., "The Fulfillment of Bryan's Dream: Key Pittman and Silver Politics, 1918–1933," *Pacific Historical Review* 30 (1961): 359–80.

Jabour, Anya, "Relationship and Leadership: Sophonisba Breckinridge and Women in Social Work," *Affilia: Journal of Women and Social Work* 27 (2012): 22–37.

Jackson, Julian, *France: The Dark Years, 1940–1944* (Oxford: Oxford University Press, 2001).

Jackson, Walter A., *Gunnar Myrdal and America's Conscience: Social Engineering and Racial Liberalism, 1938–1987* (Chapel Hill: University of North Carolina Press, 1990).

Jacobs, Meg, "'Democracy's Third Estate': New Deal Politics and the Construction of a 'Consuming Public,'" *International Labor and Working-Class History*, 55 (1999), 27–51.

———, *Pocketbook Politics: Economic Citizenship in Twentieth-Century America* (Princeton, NJ: Princeton University Press, 2005).

James, Harold, *The Creation and Destruction of Value: The Globalization Cycle* (Cambridge, MA: Harvard University Press, 2009).

———, "The Creation of a World Central Bank? The Early Years of the Bank for International Settlements," in *The Interwar Depression in an International Context*, ed. Harold James (Munich: Oldenbourg, 2002), 159–70.

———, *The End of Globalization: Lessons from the Great Depression* (Cambridge, MA: Harvard University Press, 2001).

———, *The German Slump: Politics and Economics, 1924–1936* (Oxford: Oxford University Press, 1986).

James, Harold, Håkan Lindgren, and Alice Teichova, eds., *The Role of Banks in the Interwar Economy* (Cambridge: Cambridge University Press, 1991).

James, Robert Rhodes, *The British Revolution: British Politics, 1880–1939* (London: Methuen, 1978).

Janken, Kenneth Robert, *Rayford W. Logan and the Dilemma of the African-American Intellectual* (Amherst: University of Massachusetts Press, 1993).

Jarvis, Christina S., *The Male Body at War: American Masculinity during World War II* (DeKalb: Northern Illinois University Press, 2004).

Jáuregui, Aníbal Pablo, "Después de la caída: La regulación económica y la representación corporativa en la Argentina y Brasil," in *Industrialismo y nacionalidad en Argentina y el Brasil (1890–1950)*, ed. Teodoro Blanco, Angel Cerra, Aníbal Jáuregui, Cristina Lucchini, and Renato M. Perissinotto (Buenos Aires: Ediciones del Signo, 2000), 81–108.

Jayne, Catherine E., *Oil, War, and Anglo-American Relations: American and British Reactions to Mexico's Expropriation of Foreign Oil Properties, 1937–1941* (Westport, CT: Greenwood Press, 2001).

Jeffreys-Jones, Rhodri, *The FBI: A History* (New Haven, NJ: Yale University Press, 2007).

Jensen, Jill, "From Geneva to the Americas: The International Labor Organization and Inter-American Social Security Standards, 1936–1948," *International Labor and Working-Class History* 80 (2011): 215–40.

———, "US New Deal Social Policy Experts and the ILO, 1948–1954," in *Globalizing Social Rights: The International Labour Organization and Beyond*, ed. Sandrine Kott and Joëlle Droux (New York: Palgrave Macmillan, 2013), 172–89.

Jespersen, T. Christopher, *American Images of China, 1931–1949* (Stanford, CA: Stanford University Press, 1996).

Jiménez, Laura Ruiz, "Peronism and Anti-imperialism in the Argentine Press: 'Braden or Perón' Was Also 'Perón Is Roosevelt,'" *Journal of Latin American Studies* 30 (1998): 551–71.

Johnson, Charles W., and Charles O. Jackson, *City behind a Fence: Oak Ridge, Tennessee, 1942–1946* (Knoxville: University of Tennessee Press, 1981).

Johnson, Robert David, "Anti-Imperialism and the Good Neighbour Policy: Ernest Gruening and Puerto Rican Affairs, 1934–1939," *Journal of Latin American Studies* 29 (1997): 89–110.

Jones, Carolyn C., "Class Tax to Mass Tax: The Role of Propaganda in the Expansion of the Income Tax during World War II," *Buffalo Law Review* 37 (1988): 685–737.

Jones, Marian Moser, *The American Red Cross: From Clara Barton to the New Deal* (Baltimore: Johns Hopkins University Press, 2013).

Jones, Vincent C., *Manhattan: The Army and the Atomic Bomb* (Washington, DC: Center of Military History, US Army, 1985).

Jong, Janny de, "The United States and the Netherlands during the Great Depression," in *Four Centuries of Dutch-American Relations, 1609–2009*, ed. Hans Krabbendamm, Cornelis A. van Minnen, and Giles Scott-Smith (Amsterdam: Boom, 2009), 509–19.

Josephson, Harold, *James T. Shotwell and the Rise of Internationalism in America* (Rutherford, NJ: Fairleigh Dickinson University Press, 1975).

Josephson, Paul R., "'Projects of the Century' in Soviet History: Large-Scale Technologies from Lenin to Gorbachev," *Technology and Culture* 36 (1995): 519–59.

Judt, Tony, *Postwar: A History of Europe since 1945* (New York: Penguin, 2005).

Kaplan, Edward S., and Thomas W. Ryley, *Prelude to Trade Wars: American Tariff Policy, 1890–1922* (Westport, CT: Greenwood Press, 1994).

Kargon, Robert H., and Arthur P. Molella, *Invented Edens: Techno-Cities of the Twentieth Century* (Cambridge, MA: MIT Press, 2008).

Kasza, Gregory J., *One World of Welfare: Japan in Comparative Perspective* (Ithaca, NY: Cornell University Press, 2006).

Katznelson, Ira, *Fear Itself: The New Deal and the Origins of Our Time* (New York: Liveright, 2013).

———, *When Affirmative Action Was White: An Untold History of Racial Inequality in Twentieth-Century America* (New York: W. W. Norton, 2005).

Katzenstein, Peter J., *Small States in World Markets: Industrial Policy in Europe* (Ithaca, NY: Cornell University Press, 1985).

Kelley, Ninette and Trebilcock, Michael, *The Making of the Mosaic: A History of Canadian Immigration Policy*, 2nd ed. (Toronto: University of Toronto Press, 2010).

Kennedy, David M., *Freedom from Fear: The American People in Depression and War, 1929–1945* (Oxford: Oxford University Press, 1999).

Kent, Bruce, *The Spoils of War: The Politics, Economics, and Diplomacy of Reparations, 1918–1932* (Oxford: Clarendon Press, 1989).

Kershaw, Ian, *Hitler, 1889–1936: Hubris* (London: Allen Lane, 1998).

Kessler-Harris, Alice, *In Pursuit of Equity: Women, Men, and the Quest for Economic Citizenship in 20th-Century America* (Oxford: Oxford University Press, 2001).

Kettunen, Pauli, "The Transnational Construction of National Challenges: The Ambiguous Nordic Model of Welfare and Competitiveness," in *Beyond Welfare State Models: Transnational Historical Perspectives on Social Policy*, ed. Pauli Kettunen and Klaus Petersen (Cheltenham: Edward Elgar, 2011), 16–40.

Keys, Barbara J., *Globalizing Sport: National Rivalry and International Community in the 1930s* (Cambridge, MA: Harvard University Press, 2006).

———, "Spreading Peace, Democracy, and Coca-Cola: Sport and American Cultural Expansion in the 1930s," *Diplomatic History* 28, no. 2 (2004): 165–96.

Killingray, David, "The Maintenance of Law and Order in British Colonial Africa," *African Affairs* 85 (1986): 411–37.

Kim, Wonik, "Rethinking Colonialism and the Origins of the Developmental State in East Asia," *Journal of Contemporary Asia* 39 (2009): 382–99.

Kimball, Warren F., "The Atlantic Charter: 'With All Deliberate Speed,'" in *The Atlantic Charter*, ed. Douglas Brinkley and David R. Facey-Crowther (Houndmills: Macmillan, 1994), 83–114.

Kindleberger, Charles P., *The World in Depression 1929–1939* (London: Allen Lane, 1973).

King, David P., "The West Looks East: The Influence of Toyohiko Kagawa on American Mainline Protestantism," *Church History* 80 (2011): 302–20.

King, Desmond S., *Separate and Unequal: Black Americans and the US Federal Government* (Oxford: Clarendon Press, 1995).

Kirby, William C., "Engineering China: Birth of the Developmental State, 1928–1937," in *Becoming Chinese: Passages to Modernity and Beyond*, ed. Wen-hsin Yeh (Berkeley: University of California Press, 2000), 137–60.

Kirkendall, Richard S., *Social Scientists and Farm Politics in the Age of Roosevelt* (Columbia: University of Missouri Press, 1966).

Kissane, Bill, "Éamon de Valéra and the Survival of Democracy in Inter-War Ireland," *Journal of Contemporary History* 42 (2007): 213–26.

Klautke, Egbert, *Unbegrenzte Möglichkeiten: "Amerikanisierung" in Deutschland und Frankreich, 1900–1933* (Stuttgart: Steiner, 2003).

Klebaner, Benjamin J., "Poor Relief and Public Works during the Depression of 1857," *Historian* 22 (1960): 264–79.

Klein, Maury, *A Call to Arms: Mobilizing America for World War II* (New York: Bloomsbury, 2013).

Kline, Ronald R., *Consumers in the Country: Technology and Social Change in Rural America* (Baltimore: Johns Hopkins University Press, 2000).

Kline, Wendy, "Eugenics in the United States," in *The Oxford Handbook of the History of Eugenics*, ed. Alison Bashford and Philippa Levine (Oxford: Oxford University Press, 2010), 511–22.

Klingensmith, Daniel, *"One Valley and a Thousand": Dams, Nationalism, and Development* (Oxford: Oxford University Press, 2007).

Kloppenberg, James T., *Uncertain Victory: Social Democracy and Progressivism in European and American Thought, 1870–1920* (New York: Oxford University Press, 1986).

Knab, Cornelia, and Amalia Ribi Forclaz, "Transnational Co-Operation in Food, Agriculture, Environment and Health in Historical Perspective," *Contemporary European History* 20 (2011): 247–55.

Knepper, Cathy D., *Greenbelt, Maryland: A Living Legacy of the New Deal* (Baltimore: Johns Hopkins University Press, 2001).

Knudson, Jerry W., "The Impact of the Catavi Mine Massacre of 1942 on Bolivian Politics and Public Opinion," *Americas* 26 (1970): 254–76.

Koistinen, Paul A. C., *Arsenal of World War II: The Political Economy of American Warfare, 1940–1945* (Lawrence: University Press of Kansas, 2004).

Koss, Stephen, "Lloyd George and Nonconformity: The Last Rally," *English Historical Review* 89 (1974): 77–108.

Kotkin, Stephen, *Magnetic Mountain: Stalinism as a Civilization* (Berkeley: University of California Press, 1995).

———, "Modern Times: The Soviet Union and the Interwar Conjuncture," *Kritika: Explorations in Russian and Eurasian History* 2 (2001): 111–64.

Kott, Sandrine, "Constructing a European Social Model: The Fight for Social Insurance in the Interwar Period," in *ILO Histories: Essays on the International Labour Organization and Its Impact on the World during the Twentieth Century*, ed. Jasmien Van Daele, Magaly Rodríguez-García, Geert van Goethem, and Marcel van der Linden (Berne: Lang, 2010), 173–95.

Kottman, Richard N., "Herbert Hoover and the Smoot-Hawley Tariff: Canada, a Case Study," *Journal of American History* 62 (1975): 609–35.

Kramer, Paul A., "Power and Connection: Imperial Histories of the United States in the World," *American Historical Review* 116 (2011): 1348–91.

Kryder, Daniel, *Divided Arsenal: Race and the American State during World War II* (Cambridge: Cambridge University Press, 2000).

Kuehl, Warren F., and Lynne K. Dunn, *Keeping the Covenant: American Internationalists and the League of Nations, 1920–1939* (Kent, OH: Kent State University Press, 1997).

Kühl, Stefan, *Die Internationale der Rassisten: Aufstieg und Niedergang der internationalen Bewegung für Eugenik und Rassenhygiene im 20. Jahrhundert* (Frankfurt am Main: Campus, 1997).

Kuisel, Richard F., *Capitalism and the State in Modern France: Renovation and Economic Management in the Twentieth Century* (Cambridge: Cambridge University Press, 1981).

Ladd-Taylor, Molly, "Eugenics and Social Welfare in New Deal Minnesota," in *A Century of Eugenics in America: From the Indiana Experiment to the Human Genome Era*, ed. Paul A. Lombardo (Bloomington: Indiana University Press, 2011), 117–40.

Ladwig-Winters, Simone, *Ernst Fraenkel: Ein politisches Leben* (Frankfurt am Main: Campus, 2009).

LaFeber, Walter, *Inevitable Revolutions: The United States in Central America* (New York: W. W. Norton, 1984).

Lafer, Betty Mindlin, *Planejamento no Brasil* (São Paulo: Editôra Perspectiva, 1970).

Lagendijk, Vincent, "Divided Development: Post-War Ideas on River Utilisation and Their Influence on the Development of the Danube," *International History Review* 37 (2015): 80–98.

———, *Electrifying Europe: The Power of Europe in the Construction of Electricity Networks* (Amsterdam: Aksant, 2008).

Lake, Marilyn, and Henry Reynolds, *Drawing the Global Colour Line: White Men's Countries and the International Challenge of Racial Equality* (Cambridge: Cambridge University Press, 2008).

Lambert, David, and Alan Lester, eds., *Colonial Lives across the British Empire: Imperial Careering in the Long Nineteenth Century* (Cambridge: Cambridge University Press, 2006).

Lapping, Mark B., "The Emergence of Federal Public Housing: Atlanta's Techwood Project," *American Journal of Economics and Sociology* 32 (1973): 379–85.

Large, Stephen S., "Nationalist Extremism in Early Shōwa Japan: Inoue Nisshō and the 'Blood-Pledge Corps Incident,' 1932," in *Imperial Japan and the World, 1931–1945: Critical Concepts in Asian Studies*, Vol. I, ed. Antony Best (London: Routledge, 2011), 280–306.

Larson, Arthur, and Merrill G. Murray, "The Development of Unemployment Insurance in the United States," *Vanderbilt Law Review* 181 (1954): 181–217.

Lasser, William, *Benjamin V. Cohen: Architect of the New Deal* (New Haven, CT: Yale University Press, 2002).

Lebra, Takie Sugiyama, "Self and Other in Esteemed Status: The Changing Culture of the Japanese Royalty from Showa to Heisei," *Journal of Japanese Studies* 23 (1997): 257–89.

Leff, Mark H., *The Limits of Symbolic Reform: The New Deal and Taxation, 1933–1939* (New York: Cambridge University Press, 1984).

———, "Taxing the 'Forgotten Man': The Politics of Social Security Finance in the New Deal," *Journal of American History* 70 (1983): 359–81.

Leffler, Melvyn P., *A Preponderance of Power: National Security, the Truman Administration, and the Cold War* (Stanford, CA: Stanford University Press, 1992).

Lehman, Tim, *Public Values, Private Lands: Farmland Preservation Policy, 1933–1985* (Chapel Hill: University of North Carolina Press, 1995).

Leighninger, Robert D., Jr., *Long-Range Public Investment: The Forgotten Legacy of the New Deal* (Colombia: University of South Carolina Press, 2007).

LeMahieu, D. L., *A Culture for Democracy: Mass Communication and the Cultivated Mind in Britain between the Wars* (Oxford: Clarendon Press, 1988).

Lemańczyk, Szczepan, "The Transiranian Railway: History, Context and Consequences," *Middle Eastern Studies* 49 (2013): 237–45.

León y González, Samuel, "Cárdenas y la construcción del poder politico," in *El*

cardenismo, 1932–1940, ed. Samuel León y González (Mexico City: Centro de In-
vestigación y Docencia Económica, 2010), 11–55.

Leonard, Thomas M., "The New Pan Americanism in U.S.–Central American Relations, 1933–1954," in *Beyond the Ideal: Pan Americanism in Inter-American Affairs*,
ed. David Sheinin (Westport, CT: Praeger, 2000), 95–113.

Leopoldi, Maria Antonieta P., "O Século do Corporativismo? O empresariado industrial brasileiro e suas associações de classe," in *Les expériences corporatives dans l'aire
latine*, ed. Didier Musiedlak (Berne: Lang, 2010), 391–440.

Leso, Erasmo, "Aspetti della lingua del fascismo: Prime linee di una ricerca," in *Storia
linguistica dell'Italia del Novecento*, ed. Maurizio Gnerre, Mario Medici, and Raffa-
ele Simone (Rome: Bulzoni, 1973), 139–58.

Lettevall, Rebecka, Geert J. Somsen, and Sven Widmalm, eds., *Neutrality in Twentieth-
Century Europe: Intersections of Science, Culture, and Politics after the First World War*
(New York: Routledge, 2012).

Leuchtenburg, William E., "The Election of 1936," in *The FDR Years: On Roosevelt and
His Legacy*, ed. William E. Leuchtenburg (New York: Columbia University Press,
1995), 101–58.

———, "The 'Europeanization' of America, 1929–1950," in *The FDR Years: On Roosevelt and His Legacy*, ed. William E. Leuchtenburg (New York: Columbia University
Press, 1995), 283–305.

———, *Franklin D. Roosevelt and the New Deal, 1932–1940* (New York: Harper, 1963).

———, "The Great Depression," in *The Comparative Approach to American History*, ed.
C. Vann Woodward (New York: Basic Books, 1968), 296–314.

———, *Herbert Hoover* (New York: Henry Holt, 2009).

———, "The New Deal and the Analogue of War," in *Change and Continuity in
Twentieth-Century America*, ed. John Braeman, Robert H. Bremner, and Everett
Walters (Columbus: Ohio State University Press, 1964), 81–143.

Levenstein, Harvey, *We'll Always Have Paris: American Tourists in France since 1930*
(Chicago: University of Chicago Press, 2004).

Levin, Linda Lotridge, *The Making of FDR: The Story of Stephen T. Early, America's First
Modern Press Secretary* (Amherst, MA: Prometheus Books, 2008).

Levine, Lawrence W., and Cornelia R. Levine, *The Fireside Conversations: America
Responds to FDR during the Great Depression* (Berkeley: University of California
Press, 2010).

Levine, Robert M., *Father of the Poor? Vargas and His Era* (Cambridge: Cambridge
University Press, 1998).

Levy, Maria Stella Ferreira, "O papel da migração internacional na evolução da população brasileira (1872 a 1972)," *Revista de Saúde Pública* 8 (1974): 49–90.

Lewis, Gordon K., *Puerto Rico: Freedom and Power in the Caribbean*, intro. Anthony
Maingot, rev. ed. (Kingston, Jamaica: Ian Randle, 2004).

Lewis, Joanna, *Empire State-Building: War and Welfare in Kenya, 1925–52* (Athens:
Ohio University Press, 2000).

Li, Guannan, "Reviving China: Urban Reconstruction in Nanching and the
Guomindang National Revival Movement, 1932–37," *Frontiers of History in China*
7 (2012): 106–35.

Lichtenstein, Nelson, "Pluralism, Postwar Intellectuals, and the Demise of the
Union Idea," in *The Great Society and the High Tide of Liberalism*, ed. Sidney M.

Milkis and Jerome M. Mileur (Amherst: University of Massachusetts Press, 2005), 83–114.

Lieberman, Robert C., *Shifting the Color Line: Race and the American Welfare State* (Cambridge, MA: Harvard University Press, 1998).

Lifka, Thomas E., *The Concept "Totalitarianism" and American Foreign Policy, 1933–1949* (New York: Garland, 1988).

Limoncic, Flávio, "O 'New Deal,' by Vargas," *Revista de História* 47 (2009), http://www .revistadehistoria.com.br/secao/artigos-revista/o-new-deal-by-vargas (accessed April 10, 2015).

———, "Os inventores do New Deal: Estado e sindicato nos Estados Unidos dos anos 1930" (PhD diss., Universidade Federal do Rio de Janeiro, 2003).

Limoncic, Flávio, and Francisco Carlos Palomanes Martinho, eds., *A Grande Depressão: Política e Economia na Década de 1930: Europa, Américas, África e Ásia* (Rio de Janeiro: Civilização Brasileira, 2009).

Lindert, Peter H., and Jeffrey G. Williamson, "Does Globalization Make the World More Unequal?" in *Globalization in Historical Perspective*, ed. Michael D. Bordo, Alan M. Taylor, and Jeffrey G. Williamson (Chicago: University of Chicago Press, 2003), 227–71.

Link, Stefan, "Transnational Fordism: Ford Motor Company, Nazi Germany, and the Soviet Union in the Interwar Years" (PhD diss., Harvard University, 2012).

Lomazow, Steven, and Eric Fettmann, *FDR's Deadly Secret* (New York: Public Affairs, 2009).

Lopatin, N. A., "Technical Assistance of the USSR in the Construction of Hydroelectric Stations Abroad," *Hydrotechnical Construction* 17 (1983): 481–87.

Louchheim, Katie, *The Making of the New Deal: The Insiders Speak* (Cambridge, MA: Harvard University Press, 1983).

Love, Joseph L., "Economic Ideas and Ideologies in Latin America since 1930," in *The Cambridge History of Latin America*, Vol. VI, Part 1, ed. Leslie Bethell (Cambridge: Cambridge University Press, 1994), 393–460.

Loveman, Brian, *No Higher Law: American Foreign Policy and the Western Hemisphere since 1776* (Chapel Hill: University of North Carolina Press, 2010).

Lowe, Rodney, *Adjusting to Democracy: The Role of the Ministry of Labour in British Politics, 1916–1939* (Oxford: Clarendon Press, 1986).

Lower, Wendy, *Nazi Empire-Building and the Holocaust in Ukraine* (Chapel Hill: University of North Carolina Press, 2005).

Lowitt, Richard, *George W. Norris: The Persistence of a Progressive, 1913–1933* (Urbana: University of Illinois Press, 1971).

———, *George W. Norris: The Triumph of a Progressive, 1933–1944* (Urbana: University of Illinois Press, 1978).

Lowitt, Richard, and Maurine Beasley, *One Third of a Nation: Lorena Hickok Reports on the Great Depression* (Urbana: University of Illinois Press, 1981).

Lübken, Uwe, *Bedrohliche Nähe: Die USA und die nationalsozialistische Herausforderung in Lateinamerika, 1937–1945* (Stuttgart: Steiner, 2004).

Lupo, Salvatore, *Quando la mafia trovò l'America: Storia di un intreccio intercontinentale, 1888–2008* (Turin: Einaudi, 2008).

Lusztig, Michael, *Risking Free Trade: The Politics of Trade in Britain, Canada, Mexico, and the United States* (Pittsburgh: University of Pittsburgh Press, 1996).

Lyon, E. Stina, "Education for Modernity: The Impact of American Social Science on Alva and Gunnar Myrdal and the 'Swedish Model' of School Reform," *International Journal of Politics, Culture, and Society* 14 (2001): 513–37.

MacLean, Nancy, *Behind the Mask of Chivalry: The Making of the Second Ku Klux Klan* (Oxford: Oxford University Press, 1994).

Macy, Christine, "The Architect's Office of the Tennessee Valley Authority," in *The Tennessee Valley Authority: Design and Persuasion*, ed. Tim Culvahouse (New York: Princeton Architectural Press, 2007), 26–51.

Maddux, Thomas R., *Years of Estrangement: American Relations with the Soviet Union, 1933–1941* (Tallahassee: University Presses of Florida, 1980).

Madison, Bernice Q., *Social Welfare in the Soviet Union* (Stanford, CA: Stanford University Press, 1968).

Madureira, Nuno Luís, "Cartelization and Corporatism: Bureaucratic Rule in Authoritarian Portugal, 1926–45," *Journal of Contemporary History* 42 (2007): 79–96.

Maher, Neil M., *Nature's New Deal: The Civilian Conservation Corps and the Roots of the American Environmental Movement* (Oxford: Oxford University Press, 2008).

Maier, Charles S., "Between Taylorism and Technocracy: European Ideologies and the Vision of Industrial Productivity in the 1920s," *Journal of Contemporary History* 5 (1970): 27–61.

———, "Consigning the Twentieth Century to History: Alternative Narratives for the Modern Era," *American Historical Review* 105 (2000): 807–31.

———, "Leviathan 2.0: Inventing Modern Statehood," in *A World Connecting, 1870–1945*, ed. Emily S. Rosenberg (Cambridge, MA: Belknap Press, 2012), 29–282.

———, "'Malaise': The Crisis of Capitalism in the 1970s," in *The Shock of the Global: The 1970s in Perspective*, ed. Niall Ferguson, Charles S. Maier, Erez Manela, and Daniel J. Sargent (Cambridge, MA: Belknap Press, 2010), 25–48.

———, *The Marshall Plan and Germany: West German Development within the Framework of the European Recovery Program* (New York: Berg, 1991).

———, "The Politics of Productivity: Foundations of American International Economic Policy after World War II," *International Organization* 31 (1977): 607–33.

Maier, Hans, *Concepts for the Comparison of Dictatorships: Theory and History of Interpretation: Totalitarianism and Political Religions*, Vol. 3 (London: Routledge, 2004).

Malenbaum, Wilfred, *The World Wheat Economy, 1885–1939* (Cambridge, MA: Harvard University Press, 1953).

Malloy, James M., *The Politics of Social Security in Brazil* (Pittsburgh: University of Pittsburgh Press, 1979).

Maloney, C. J., *Back to the Land: Arthurdale, FDR's New Deal, and the Costs of Economic Planning* (Hoboken, NJ: Wiley, 2011).

Manchester, William, *American Caesar: Douglas MacArthur, 1880–1964* (Boston: Little, Brown, 1978).

Manela, Erez, "Goodwill and Bad: Rethinking US-Egyptian Contacts in the Interwar Years," *Middle Eastern Studies* 38 (2002): 71–88.

———, *The Wilsonian Moment: Self-Determination and the International Origins of Anticolonial Nationalism* (Oxford: Oxford University Press, 2007).

Mangone, Gerard J., "Dungaree and Grey-Flannel Diplomacy," in *The Art of Overseasmanship*, ed. Harlan Cleveland and Gerard J. Mangone (Syracuse, NY: Syracuse University Press, 1957), 11–29.

Marable, Manning, *W.E.B. Du Bois: Black Radical Democrat* (Boulder, CO: Paradigm, 1986).

Marchand, Roland, *Advertising the American Dream: Making Way for Modernity, 1920–1940* (Berkeley: University of California Press, 1985).

Marcus, Harold G., *Haile Sellassie I: The Formative Years, 1892–1936* (Berkeley: University of California Press, 1987).

Margulies, Sylvia R., *The Pilgrimage to Russia: The Soviet Union and the Treatment of Foreigners, 1924–1937* (Madison: University of Wisconsin Press, 1968).

Marklund, Carl, "The Social Laboratory, the Middle Way and the Swedish Model: Three Frames for the Image of Sweden," *Scandinavian Journal of History* 34 (2009): 264–85.

Marklund, Carl, and Klaus Petersen, "Return to Sender: American Images of the Nordic Welfare States and Nordic Welfare State Branding," *European Journal of Scandinavian Studies* 43 (2013): 245–57.

Markovits, Andrei S., and Steven L. Hellerman, *Offside: Soccer and American Exceptionalism* (Princeton, NJ: Princeton University Press, 2001).

Martin, George, *Madam Secretary: Frances Perkins* (Boston: Houghton Mifflin, 1976).

Martin, Terry, *The Affirmative Action Empire: Nations and Nationalism in the Soviet Union, 1923–1939* (Ithaca, NY: Cornell University Press, 2001).

Martinho, Francisco Carlos Palomanes, "Entre o fomento e o condicionamento: A economia portuguesa em tempos de crise (1928–1945)," in *A Grande Depressão: Política e Economia na Década de 1930: Europa, Américas, África e Ásia*, ed. Flávio Limoncic and Francisco Carlos Palomanes Martinho (Rio de Janeiro: Civilização Brasileira, 2009), 305–30.

Mass, Bonnie, "Puerto Rico: A Case Study of Population Control," *Latin American Perspectives* 4 (1977): 66–81.

Mathews, Marcia M., "George Biddle's Contribution to Federal Art," *Records of the Columbia Historical Society* 49 (1973–74): 493–520.

Mathews, Thomas, *Puerto Rican Politics and the New Deal* (Gainesville: University of Florida Press, 1960).

Mauch, Christof, and Kiran Klaus Patel, eds., *The United States and Germany during the Twentieth Century: Competition and Convergence* (New York: Cambridge University Press, 2010).

Maul, Daniel, "'Help Them Move the ILO Way': The International Labor Organization and the Modernization Discourse in the Era of Decolonization and the Cold War," *Diplomatic History* 33 (2009): 387–404.

May, Glenn Anthony, *Social Engineering in the Philippines: The Aims, Execution, and Impact of American Colonial Policy, 1900–1913* (Westport, CT: Greenwood Press, 1980).

Mayers, David, *The Ambassadors and America's Soviet Policy* (Oxford: Oxford University Press, 1995).

———, *FDR's Ambassadors and the Diplomacy of Crisis: From the Rise of Hitler to the End of World War II* (Cambridge: Cambridge University Press, 2013).

Mazower, Mark, *Dark Continent: Europe's Twentieth Century* (London: Penguin, 1998).

———, *Governing the World: The History of an Idea* (New York: Penguin, 2012).

———, *Greece and the Inter-War Economic Crisis* (Oxford: Clarendon Press, 1991).

Mazower, Mark, *Hitler's Empire: How the Nazis Ruled Europe* (New York: Penguin, 2009).

———, *No Enchanted Palace: The End of Empire and the Ideological Origins of the United Nations* (Princeton, NJ: Princeton University Press, 2009).

McCann, Bryan, *Hello, Hello Brazil: Popular Music in the Making of Modern Brazil* (Durham, NC: Duke University Press, 2004).

McCraw, Thomas K., *TVA and the Power Fight, 1933–1939* (Philadelphia: J. B. Lippincott, 1971).

McDonald, Judith A., Anthony Patrick O'Brien, and Colleen M. Callahan, "Trade Wars: Canada's Reaction to the Smoot-Hawley Tariff," *Journal of Economic History* 57 (1997): 802–26.

McDonald, Michael J., and John Muldowny, *The TVA and the Dispossessed: The Resettlement of Population in the Norris Dam Area* (Knoxville: University of Tennessee Press, 1982).

McDonnell, Timothy L., *The Wagner Housing Act: A Case Study of the Legislative Process* (Chicago: Loyola University Press, 1957).

McElvaine, Robert S., *The Great Depression: America, 1929–1941*, 2nd ed. (New York: Times Books, 1993).

McGillivray, Gillian, *Blazing Cane: Sugar Communities, Class, and State Formation in Cuba, 1868–1959* (Durham, NC: Duke University Press, 2009).

McGirr, Lisa, "The Interwar Years," in *American History Now*, ed. Eric Foner and Lisa McGirr (Philadelphia: Temple University Press, 2011), 125–50.

———, "The Passion of Sacco and Vanzetti: A Global History," *Journal of American History* 93 (2007): 1085–115.

McKeown, Adam M., *Melancholy Order: Asian Migration and the Globalization of Borders* (New York: Columbia University Press, 2008).

McKercher, Brian J. C., *Transition of Power: Britain's Loss of Global Pre-eminence to the United States, 1930–1945* (New York: Cambridge University Press, 1999).

McKibben, Gordon, *Cutting Edge: Gillette's Journey to Global Leadership* (Boston: Harvard Business School Press, 1998).

McKillen, Elizabeth, "Beyond Gompers: The American Federation of Labor, the Creation of the ILO, and US Labor Dissent," in *ILO Histories: Essays on the International Labour Organization and Its Impact on the World during the Twentieth Century*, ed. Jasmien Van Daele, Magaly Rodríguez García, Geert Van Goethem, and Marcel van der Linden (Berne: Lang, 2010), 41–66.

McKinley, Charles, and Robert W. Frase, *Launching Social Security: A Capture-and-Record Account, 1935–1937* (Madison: University of Wisconsin Press, 1970).

McKinzie, Richard D., *The New Deal for Artists* (Princeton, NJ: Princeton University Press, 1973).

McWilliams, John C., "Unsung Partner against Crime: Harry J. Anslinger and the Federal Bureau of Narcotics, 1930–1962," *Pennsylvania Magazine of History and Biography* 113 (1989): 207–36.

Mehrtens, Cristina, "Public and Private, National and International: Crossed Paths in São Paulo's Process of Urban Consolidation, 1900–1940," *Yearbook of European Administrative History* 15 (2003): 243–66.

Meijer, Hank, "Arthur Vandenberg and the Fight for Neutrality, 1939," *Michigan Historical Review* 16 (1990): 1–21.

Meinig, D. W., *The Shaping of America: A Geographical Perspective on 500 Years of History, Volume 4: Global America, 1915–2000* (New Haven, CT: Yale University Press, 2004).

Melanson, Philip H., *The Secret Service: The Hidden History of an Enigmatic Agency* (New York: Carroll and Graf, 2002).

Merrill, Dennis, *Negotiating Paradise: U.S. Tourism and Empire in Twentieth-Century Latin America* (Chapel Hill: University of North Carolina Press, 2009).

Mettler, Suzanne, *Dividing Citizens: Gender and Federalism in New Deal Public Policy* (Ithaca, NY: Cornell University Press, 1998).

Metzler, Mark, *Lever of Empire: The International Gold Standard and the Crisis of Liberalism in Prewar Japan* (Berkeley: University of California Press, 2006).

Middleton, Roger, *Towards the Managed Economy: Keynes, the Treasury, and the Fiscal Policy Debate of the 1930s* (London: Methuen, 1985).

Mielnik, Tara Mitchell, *New Deal, New Landscape: The Civilian Conservation Corps and South Carolina's State Parks* (Columbia: University of South Carolina Press, 2011).

Mikesh, Robert C., *Japan's World War II Balloon Bomb Attacks on North America* (Washington, DC: Smithsonian Institution Press, 1973).

Milkis, Sidney M., and Jerome M. Mileur, "Preface," in *The Great Society and the High Tide of Liberalism*, ed. Sidney M. Milkis and Jerome M. Mileur (Amherst: University of Massachusetts Press, 2005), xi–xxi.

Miller, James A., Susan D. Pennybacker, and Eve Rosenhaft, "Mother Ada Wright and the International Campaign to Free the Scottsboro Boys, 1931–1934," *American Historical Review* 106 (2001): 387–430.

Miller, Kenneth E., *From Progressive to New Dealer: Frederic C. Howe and American Liberalism* (University Park: Pennsylvania State University Press, 2010).

Miller, Laura A., "Italian Americans in the 'Bocce Belt': 'Old World' Memories and 'New World' Identities," *National Identities* 15 (2013): 33–49.

Miller, Mervyn, *Raymond Unwin: Garden Cities and Town Planning* (Leicester: Leicester University Press, 1992).

Mills, Thomas C., *Post-War Planning on the Periphery: Anglo-American Economic Diplomacy in South America, 1939–1945* (Edinburgh: Edinburgh University Press, 2012).

Milton, Sybil, "Registering Civilians and Aliens in the Second World War," *Jewish History* 11 (1997): 79–87.

Mink, Gwendolyn, *The Wages of Motherhood: Inequality in the Welfare State, 1917–1942* (Ithaca, NY: Cornell University Press, 1995).

Mirowski, Philip, and Dieter Plehwe, eds., *The Road from Mont Pèlerin: The Making of the Neoliberal Thought Collective* (Cambridge, MA: Harvard University Press, 2009).

Mitman, Gregg, and Paul Erickson, "Latex and Blood: Science, Markets, and American Empire," *Radical History Review* 107 (2010): 45–73.

Miwa, Yoshiro, *State Competence and Economic Growth in Japan* (London: Routledge, 2004).

Moore, Aaron Stephen, *Constructing East Asia: Technology, Ideology, and Empire in Japan's Wartime Era, 1931–1945* (Stanford, CA: Stanford University Press, 2013).

Moore, Bob, *Victims and Survivors: The Nazi Persecution of the Jews in the Netherlands, 1940–1945* (London: Arnold, 1997).

Morgan, Kevin, "The Conservative Party and Mass Housing, 1918–39," in *Mass Con-*

servatism: The Conservatives and the Public since the 1880s, ed. Stuart Ball and Ian Holliday (London: Frank Class, 2002), 58–77.

————, "The Problem of the Epoch? Labour and Housing, 1918–51," *Twentieth Century British History* 16 (2005): 227–55.

Mouré, Kenneth, *Managing the Franc Poincaré: Economic Understanding and Political Constraint in French Monetary Policy, 1928–1936* (Cambridge: Cambridge University Press, 1991).

Müller, Reinhard, *Marienthal: Das Dorf—Die Arbeitslosen—Die Studie* (Innsbruck: StudienVerlag, 2008).

Murard, Lion, "Designs within Disorder: International Conferences on Rural Health Care and the Art of the Local, 1931–39," in *Shifting Boundaries of Public Health: Europe in the Twentieth Century,* ed. Susan Gross Solomon, Lion Murard, and Patrick Zylberman (Rochester: University of Rochester Press, 2008), 141–74.

Murphey, Murray G., "American Civilization at Pennsylvania," *American Quarterly* 22 (1970): 489–502.

Muşat, Raluca, "'Lessons for Modern Living': Planned Rural Communities in Interwar Romania, Turkey and Italy," *Journal of Modern European History,* 14 (2016): forthcoming.

Musiał, Kazimierz, *Roots of the Scandinavian Model: Images of Progress in the Era of Modernisation* (Baden-Baden: Nomos, 2002).

Nadelmann, Ethan, "U.S. Police Activities in Europe," in *The Internationalization of Police Cooperation in Western Europe,* ed. Cyrille Fijnaut (Deventer: Kluwer Law and Taxation, 1993), 135–54.

Nakamura, Takafusa, and Jacqueline Kaminsky, "Depression, Recovery, and War, 1920–1945," in *The Cambridge History of Japan,* Vol. 6, ed. Peter Duus (Cambridge: Cambridge University Press, 1988), 451–93.

Nandy, Ashis, *The Romance of the State and the Fate of Dissent in the Tropics* (New Delhi: Oxford University Press, 2003).

Nash, Gerald D., *The American West Transformed: The Impact of the Second World War* (Bloomington: Indiana University Press, 1985).

————, "Herbert Hoover and the Origins of the Reconstruction Finance Corporation," *Mississippi Valley Historical Review* 46 (1959): 455–68.

Navarro, José-Manuel, *Creating Tropical Yankees: Social Science Textbooks and U.S. Ideological Control in Puerto Rico, 1898–1908* (London: Routledge, 2002).

Nevins, Allan, *Herbert H. Lehman and His Era* (New York: C. Scribner's Sons, 1963).

Newman, Katherine S., and Elisabeth S. Jacobs, *Who Cares? Public Ambivalence and Government Activism from the New Deal to the Second Gilded Age* (Princeton, NJ: Princeton University Press, 2010).

Ngai, Mae M., *Impossible Subjects: Illegal Aliens and the Making of Modern America* (Princeton, NJ: Princeton University Press, 2004).

————, "The Strange Career of the Illegal Alien: Immigration Restriction and Deportation Policy in the United States, 1921–1965," *Law and History Review* 21 (2003): 69–107.

Nichols, Christopher McKnight, *Promise and Peril: America at the Dawn of a Global Age* (Cambridge, MA: Harvard University Press, 2011).

Nicholson, Bryan W., "'In America, the Young Men and Women Would Be Told

HOW, Not WHAT, to Think': Transnational Exchanges That Shaped U.S. Youth Politics, 1932–43," *New Global Studies* 4 (2010): 1–29.

Ninkovich, Frank A., *The Diplomacy of Ideas: U.S. Foreign Policy and Cultural Relations, 1938–1950* (Cambridge: Cambridge University Press, 1981).

Noel-Baker, Philip, *The First World Disarmament Conference and Why It Failed* (Oxford: Pergamon Press, 1979).

Nolan, Mary, *The Transatlantic Century: Europe and America, 1890–2010* (Cambridge: Cambridge University Press, 2012).

Nord, Philip G., *France's New Deal: From the Thirties to the Postwar Era* (Princeton, NJ: Princeton University Press, 2010).

Nycander, Svante, "Bertil Ohlin as a Liberal Politician," in *Bertil Ohlin: A Centennial Celebration, 1899–1999*, ed. Ronald Findlay, Lars Jonung, and Mats Lundahl (Cambridge, MA: MIT Press, 2002), 71–114.

Nye, David E., *American Technological Sublime* (Cambridge, MA: MIT Press, 1994).

———, *Electrifying America: Social Meanings of a New Technology, 1880–1940* (Cambridge, MA: MIT Press, 1990).

O'Brien, Thomas, *The Century of U.S. Capitalism in Latin America* (Albuquerque: University of New Mexico Press, 1999).

O'Bryan, Scott, *The Growth Idea: Purpose and Prosperity in Postwar Japan* (Honolulu: University of Hawaii Press, 2009).

Obojski, Robert, *The Rise of Japanese Baseball Power* (Radnor, PA: Chilton Book, 1975).

Ochonu, Moses, "Conjoined to Empire: The Great Depression and Nigeria," *African Economic History* 34 (2006): 103–45.

O'Connell, Arturo, "Argentina into the Depression: Problems of an Open Economy," in *Latin America in the 1930s: The Role of the Periphery in World Crisis*, ed. Rosemary Thorp (Oxford: Macmillan, 1984), 188–221.

Okrent, Daniel, *Last Call: The Rise and Fall of Prohibition* (New York: Scribner, 2010).

Olsson, Ulf, "Planning in the Swedish Welfare State," *Studies in Political Economy* 34 (1991): 147–71.

O'Neil, William D., *Interwar U.S. and Japanese National Product and Defense Expenditure* (Alexandria, VA: CNA, 2003).

O'Reilly, Kenneth, "A New Deal for the FBI: The Roosevelt Administration, Crime Control, and National Security," *Journal of American History* 69 (1982): 638–58.

———, "The Roosevelt Administration and Black America: Federal Surveillance Policy and Civil Rights during the New Deal and World War II Years," *Phylon* 48 (1987): 12–25.

Ortiz, Stephen R., *Beyond the Bonus March and GI Bill: How Veteran Politics Shaped the New Deal Era* (New York: New York University Press, 2010).

Ostrower, Gary B., "American Ambassador to the League of Nations—1933: A Proposal Postponed," *International Organization* 25 (1971): 46–58.

O'Sullivan, Christopher D., *FDR and the End of Empire: The Origins of American Power in the Middle East* (New York: Palgrave Macmillan, 2012).

———, *Sumner Welles, Postwar Planning, and the Quest for a New World Order, 1937–1943* (New York: Columbia University Press, 2008).

Ozden, Canay, "The Pontifex Minimus: William Willcocks and Engineering British Colonialism," *Annals of Science* 71 (2014): 183–205.

Paalberg, Robert, and Don Paalberg, "Agricultural Policy in the Twentieth Century," *Agricultural History* 74 (2000): 136–61.

Palacio, Germán, "Servicios legales y relaciones capitalistas: Un ensayo sobre los servicios jurídicos populares y la práctica legal crítica," *El Otro Derecho* 3 (1989): 51–70.

Palmer, Robin, "The Nyasaland Tea Industry in the Era of International Tea Restrictions, 1933–1950," *Journal of African History* 26 (1985): 215–39.

Panizza, Francisco, "Late Institutionalisation and Early Modernisation: The Emergence of Uruguay's Liberal Democratic Political Order," *Journal of Latin American Studies* 29 (1997): 667–91.

Parker, Jason C., *Brother's Keeper: The United States, Race, and Empire in the British Caribbean, 1937–1962* (Oxford: Oxford University Press, 2008).

——, "'Made-in-America Revolutions'? The 'Black University' and the American Role in the Decolonization of the Black Atlantic," *Journal of American History* 96 (2009): 727–50.

Parker, Selwyn, *The Great Crash: How the Stock Market Crash of 1929 Plunged the World into Depression* (London: Piatkus Books, 2008).

Parmar, Inderjeet, *Foundations of the American Century: The Ford, Carnegie, and Rockefeller Foundations in the Rise of American Power* (New York: Columbia University Press, 2012).

Pascoe, Peggy, *What Comes Naturally: Miscegenation Law and the Making of Race in America* (Oxford: Oxford University Press, 2009).

Passerini, Luisa, *Mussolini immaginario: Storia di una biografia, 1915–1939* (Rome: Editori Laterza, 1991).

Passmore, Kevin, "Business, Corporatism and the Crisis of the French Third Republic: The Example of the Silk Industry in Lyon, 1928–1935," *Historical Journal* 38 (1995): 959–87.

Patel, Kiran Klaus, "Amerika als Argument. Die Wahrnehmungen des New Deal am Anfang des 'Dritten Reichs,'" *American Studies* 45 (2000): 349–72.

——, "The Paradox of Planning: German Agricultural Policy in a European Perspective, 1920s to 1970s," *Past and Present* 212 (2011): 239–69.

——, *Soldiers of Labor: Labor Service in Nazi Germany and New Deal America, 1933–1945* (New York: Cambridge University Press, 2005).

Patel, Kiran Klaus, and Sven Reichardt, "The Dark Side of Transnationalism: Social Engineering and Nazism, 1930s–1940s," *Journal of Contemporary History* 51 (2016): forthcoming.

Patenaude, Bertrand M., *The Big Show in Bololand: The American Relief Expedition to Soviet Russia in the Famine of 1921* (Stanford, CA: Stanford University Press, 2002).

Pedersen, Susan, "Back to the League of Nations," *American Historical Review* 112 (2007): 1091–117.

Pells, Richard, *Not Like Us: How Europeans Have Loved, Hated, and Transformed American Culture since World War II* (New York: Basic Books, 1997).

Pemberton, Joanne, "The Middle Way: The Discourse of Planning in Britain, Australia and at the League in the Interwar Years," *Australian Journal of Politics and History* 52 (2006): 48–63.

Pennybacker, Susan D., *From Scottsboro to Munich: Race and Political Culture in 1930s Britain* (Princeton, NJ: Princeton University Press, 2009).

Pérez, Louis A., Jr., *Cuba and the United States: Ties of Singular Intimacy* (Athens: University of Georgia Press, 1990).

Perfetti, Francesco, "La discussione sul corporativismo in Italia," in *Les expériences corporatives dans l'aire latine*, ed. Didier Musiedlak (Berne: Lang, 2010), 103–15.

Person, H. S., "The Rural Electrification Administration in Perspective," *Agricultural History* 24 (1950): 70–89.

Péteri, György, "Before the Schism: Revisiting György Lukács's 'Plebeian Democracy' in a Global Perspective," in *Samtidshistoria och politik: Vänbok till Karl Molin*, ed. Ragnar Björk and Alf W. Johnsson (Stockholm: Hjalmarson and Högberg, 2004), 357–90.

Philips-Fein, Kim, *Invisible Hands: The Making of the Conservative Movement from the New Deal to Reagan* (New York: W. W. Norton, 2009).

Phillips, Sarah T., "Lessons from the Dust Bowl: Dryland Agriculture and Soil Erosion in the United States and South Africa, 1900–1950," *Environmental History* 4 (1999): 245–66.

———, *This Land, This Nation: Conservation, Rural America, and the New Deal* (Cambridge: Cambridge University Press, 2007).

Piven, Frances Fox, *Challenging Authority: How Ordinary People Change America* (Lanham, MD: Rowman and Littlefield, 2006).

Plaggenborg, Stefan, *Ordnung und Gewalt: Kemalismus—Faschismus—Sozialismus* (Munich: Oldenbourg, 2012).

Plamper, Jan, *The Stalin Cult: A Study in the Alchemy of Power* (New Haven, CT: Yale University Press, 2012).

Plata, Véronique, "Le Bureau international du travail et la coopération technique dans l'entre-deux-guerres," *Relations internationales* 157 (2014): 55–69.

Pollard, John F., "Electronic Pastors: Radio, Cinema, and Television, from Pius XI to John XXIII," in *The Papacy since 1500: From Italian Prince to Universal Pastor*, ed. James Corkery and Thomas Worcester (Cambridge: Cambridge University Press, 2010), 182–203.

Pollitt, Brian H., "The Cuban Sugar Economy and the Great Depression," *Bulletin of Latin American Research* 3 (1984): 3–28.

Pomerance, Michla, *The United States and the World Court as a "Supreme Court of the Nations": Dreams, Illusions and Disillusion* (The Hague: Martinus Nijhoff, 1996).

Pommer, Richard, "The Architecture of Urban Housing in the United States during the Early 1930s," *Journal of the Society of Architectural Historians* 37 (1978): 235–64.

Post, Robert, "Federalism, Positive Law, and the Emergence of the American Administrative State: Prohibition in the Taft Court Era," *William and Mary Law Review* 48 (2006): 1–183.

Potter, Claire Bond, *War on Crime: Bandits, G-Men, and the Politics of Mass Culture* (New Brunswick, NJ: Rutgers University Press, 1998).

Powaski, Ronald E., *Toward an Entangling Alliance: American Isolationism, Internationalism, and Europe, 1901–1950* (New York: Greenwood Press, 1991).

Powell, J. M., "The Empire Meets the New Deal: Interwar Encounters in Conservation and Regional Planning," *Geographical Research* 43 (2005): 337–60.

Powers, Richard Gid, *G-Men: Hoover's FBI in American Popular Culture* (Carbondale: Southern Illinois University Press, 1983).

Preston, Andrew, "Monsters Everywhere: A Genealogy of National Security," *Diplomatic History* 38 (2014): 477–500.

Pritchard, Sara B., *Confluence: The Nature of Technology and the Remaking of the Rhône* (Cambridge, MA: Harvard University Press, 2011).

Prutsch, Ursula, *Creating Good Neighbors? Die Kultur- und Wirtschaftspolitik der USA in Lateinamerika, 1940–1946* (Stuttgart: Steiner, 2008).

Pullen, William George, *World War Debts and United States Foreign Policy, 1919–1929* (New York: Garland, 1987).

Purseigle, Pierre, "The First World War and the Transformations of the State," *International Affairs* 90 (2014): 249–64.

Quine, Maria Sophia, *Population Politics in Twentieth-Century Europe: Fascist Dictatorships and Liberal Democracies* (London: Routledge, 1996).

Radford, Gail, *Modern Housing for America: Policy Struggles in the New Deal Era* (Chicago: University of Chicago Press, 1996).

Raphael, Lutz, "Die Verwissenschaftlichung des Sozialen als methodische und konzeptionelle Herausforderung für eine Sozialgeschichte des 20. Jahrhunderts," *Geschichte und Gesellschaft* 22 (1996): 165–93.

Raymont, Henry, *Troubled Neighbors: The Story of U.S.–Latin American Relations from FDR to the Present* (Cambridge, MA: Westview Press, 2005).

Reagan, Patrick D., "Business," in *A Companion to Franklin D. Roosevelt*, ed. William D. Pederson (Oxford: Wiley-Blackwell, 2011), 186–205.

———, *Designing a New America: The Origins of New Deal Planning, 1890–1943* (Amherst: University of Massachusetts Press, 1999).

Réau, Élisabeth du, *L'idée d'Europe au XXe siècle: Des mythes aux réalités* (Brussels: Editions Complexe, 1996).

Reichardt, Sven, *Faschistische Kampfbünde: Gewalt und Gemeinschaft im italienischen Squadrismus und in der deutschen SA* (Cologne: Böhlau, 2002).

Reinhart, Carmen M., and Vincent R. Reinhart, "When the North Last Headed South: Revisiting the 1930s," *Brookings Papers on Economic Activity* 2009 (2009): 251–72.

Reinisch, Jessica, "Internationalism in Relief: The Birth (and Death) of UNRRA," *Post-War Reconstruction in Europe: International Perspectives, 1945–1949*, ed. Mark Mazower, Jessica Reinisch, and David Feldman (Oxford: Oxford University Press, 2011), 258–89.

———, "'We Shall Rebuild Anew a Powerful Nation': UNRRA, Internationalism and National Reconstruction in Poland," *Journal of Contemporary History* 43 (2008): 451–76.

Rempe, Martin, *Entwicklung im Konflikt: Die EWG und der Senegal, 1957–1975* (Cologne: Böhlau, 2012).

Reynolds, David, *America, Empire of Liberty: A New History* (New York: Allen Lane, 2009).

———, "The Atlantic 'Flop': British Foreign Policy and the Churchill-Roosevelt Meeting of August 1941," in *The Atlantic Charter*, ed. Douglas Brinkley and David R. Facey-Crowther (Houndmills: Palgrave Macmillan, 1994), 129–50.

———, "Churchill's Government and the Black GIs, 1942–1943," in *From World War to Cold War: Churchill, Roosevelt and the International History of the 1940s*, ed. David Reynolds (Oxford: Oxford University Press, 2006), 199–216.

————, "The Wheelchair President and His Special Relationships," in *From World War to Cold War: Churchill, Roosevelt, and the International History of the 1940s*, ed. David Reynolds (Oxford: Oxford University Press, 2006), 165–76.

Rhoads, William B., "The Long and Unsuccessful Effort to Kill Off Colonial Revival," in *Re-creating the American Past: Essays on the Colonial Revival*, ed. Richard Guy Wilson, Shaun Eyring, and Kenny Marotta (Charlottesville: University of Virginia Press, 2006), 13–28.

Rhodes, Benjamin D., *United States Foreign Policy in the Interwar Period, 1918–1941: The Golden Age of American Diplomatic and Military Complacency* (Westport, CT: Praeger, 2001).

Ricard, Serge, "The Roosevelt Corollary," *Presidential Studies Quarterly* 36 (2006): 17–26.

Richards, Raymond, *Closing the Door to Destitution: The Shaping of the Social Security Acts of the United States and New Zealand* (University Park: Pennsylvania State University Press, 1994).

Riddell, Norman H., "The Bennett New Deal: An Essay" (MA thesis, University of Saskatchewan, 1967).

Rieber, Alfred J., "Stalin, Man of the Borderlands," *American Historical Review* 106 (2001): 1651–91.

Rietzler, Katharina, "Before the Cultural Cold Wars: American Philanthropy and Cultural Diplomacy in the Inter-war Years," *Historical Research* 84 (2011): 148–64.

Rippy, J. Fred, "The Inter-American Highway," *Pacific Historical Review* 24 (1955): 287–98.

Ritschel, Daniel, *The Politics of Planning: The Debate on Economic Planning in Britain in the 1930s* (Oxford: Clarendon Press, 1997).

Ritschl, Albrecht, "International Capital Movements and the Onset of the Great Depression: Some International Evidence," in *The Interwar Depression in an International Context*, ed. Harold James (Munich: Oldenbourg, 2002), 1–14.

Roden, Donald, "Baseball and the Quest for National Dignity in Meiji Japan," *American Historical Review* 85 (1980): 511–34.

Rodgers, Daniel T., *Atlantic Crossings: Social Politics in a Progressive Age* (Cambridge, MA: Belknap Press, 1998).

————, "Exceptionalism," in *Imagined Histories: American Historians Interpret the Past*, ed. Anthony Molho and Gordon S. Wood (Princeton, NJ: Princeton University Press, 1998), 21–40.

Rodríguez, Manuel R., *A New Deal for the Tropics: Puerto Rico during the Depression Era, 1932–1935* (Princeton, NJ: Markus Wiener, 2010).

Roediger, David R., and Elizabeth D. Esch, *The Production of Difference: Race and the Management of Labor in U.S. History* (Oxford: Oxford University Press, 2012).

Roll, David L., *The Hopkins Touch: Harry Hopkins and the Forging of the Alliance to Defeat Hitler* (Oxford: Oxford University Press, 2013).

Roll-Hansen, Nils, "Eugenic Practice and Genetic Science in Scandinavia and Germany," *Scandinavian Journal of History* 26 (2001): 75–82.

Romer, Christina D., "The Nation in Depression," *Journal of Economic Perspectives* 7 (1993): 19–39.

Romero, Federico, *Gli Stati Uniti e il sindacalismo europeo, 1944–1951* (Rome: Edizioni lavoro, 1989).

Rook, Robert E., "An American in Palestine: Elwood Mead and Zionist Water Re-source Planning, 1923–1936," *Arab Studies Quarterly* 22 (2000): 71–89.

Roon, Ger van, *Kleine Landen in Crisistijd: Van Oslostaten tot Benelux, 1930–1940* (Amsterdam: Elsevier, 1985).

Roorda, Eric Paul, "The Cult of the Airplane among U.S. Military Men and Domini-cans during the U.S. Occupation and the Trujillo Regime," in *Close Encounters of Empire: Writing the Cultural History of U.S.–Latin American Relations*, ed. Gilbert M. Joseph, Catherine C. Legrand, and Ricardo D. Salvatore (Durham, NC: Duke University Press, 1998), 269–310.

———, *The Dictator Next Door: The Good Neighbor Policy and the Trujillo Regime in the Dominican Republic, 1930–1945* (Durham, NC: Duke University Press, 1998).

Rose, Nancy E., *Put to Work: Relief Programs in the Great Depression* (New York: Monthly Review Press, 1994).

Rosen, Elliot A., "'Not Worth a Pitcher of Warm Piss': John Nance Garner as Vice President," in *At the President's Side: The Vice Presidency in the Twentieth Century*, ed. Timothy Walch (Columbia: University of Missouri Press, 1997), 45–53.

———, *The Republican Party in the Age of Roosevelt: Sources of Anti-Government Con-servatism in the United States* (Charlottesville: University of Virginia Press, 2014).

Rosenberg, Emily S., *Spreading the American Dream: American Economic and Cultural Expansion, 1890–1945* (New York: Hill and Wang, 1982).

Rothermund, Dietmar, *The Global Impact of the Great Depression, 1929–1939* (Lon-don: Routledge, 1996).

———, *India in the Great Depression, 1929–1939* (New Delhi: Manohar, 1992).

Routledge, Paul, "Voices of the Dammed: Discursive Resistance amidst Erasure in the Narmada Valley, India," *Political Geography* 22 (2003): 243–70.

Roxborough, Ian, "The Urban Working Class and Labour Movement in Latin Amer-ica since 1930," in *The Cambridge History of Latin America*, Vol. VI, Part 2, ed. Leslie Bethell (Cambridge, Cambridge University Press, 1994), 305–78.

Rubin, Martin, "Movies and the New Deal in Entertainment," in *American Cinema of the 1930s: Themes and Variations*, ed. Ina Rae Hark (New Brunswick, NJ: Rutgers University Press, 2007), 92–116.

Runte, Alfred, *National Parks: The American Experience*, 4th ed. (Lanham, MD: Taylor, 2010).

Rupp, Leila J., *Worlds of Women: The Making of the International Women's Movement* (Princeton, NJ: Princeton University Press, 1997).

Sagredo Santos, Antonia, "Franklin D. Roosevelt y la problemática agraria: Su eco en la prensa española, 1932–1936" (PhD diss., Universidad Complutense de Madrid, 2004).

Saha, Suranjit Kumar, "River-Basin Planning in the Damodar Valley of India," *Geo-graphical Review* 69 (1979): 273–87.

Salant, Walter S., "The Spread of Keynesian Doctrines and Practices in the United States," in *The Political Power of Economic Ideas: Keynesianism across Nations*, ed. Peter A. Hall (Princeton, NJ: Princeton University Press, 1989), 27–51.

Salmond, John A., "The Civilian Conservation Corps and the Negro," *Journal of American History* 52 (1965): 75–88.

———, *The Civilian Conservation Corps, 1933–1942: A New Deal Case Study* (Dur-ham, NC: Duke University Press, 1967).

Saloutos, Theodore, *The American Farmer and the New Deal* (Ames: Iowa State University Press, 1982).

Salvatore, Ricardo D., *Imágenes de un imperio: Estados Unidos y las formas de representación de América Latina* (Buenos Aires: Editorial Sudamericana, 2006).

Sánchez Ruiz, Gerardo G., *Planificación y urbanismo de la revolución mexicana: Los sustentos de una nueva modernidad en la Ciudad de México* (Mexico City: Universidad Autónoma Metropolitana, 2002).

Sanchez-Sibony, Oscar, "Depression Stalinism: The Great Break Reconsidered," *Kritika: Explorations in Russian and Eurasian History* 15 (2014): 23–49.

Sandeen, Eric J., "The Design of Public Housing in the New Deal: Oskar Stonorov and the Carl Mackley Houses," *American Quarterly* 37 (1985): 645–67.

Sanderson, Susan R. Walsh, *Land Reform in Mexico: 1910–1980* (Orlando, FL: Academic Press, 1984).

Sandilands, Roger J., *The Life and Political Economy of Lauchlin Currie: New Dealer, Presidential Adviser, and Development Economist* (Durham, NC: Duke University Press, 1990).

Sanger, Richard H., "Ibn Saud's Program for Arabia," *Middle East Journal* 1 (1947): 180–90.

Sanz Fernández, Jesús, "Los Ferrocarriles Iberoamericanos en perspectiva histórica," in *Historia de los ferrocarriles de Iberoamérica (1837–1995)*, ed. Jesús Sanz Fernández (Madrid: Unión Fenosa, 1998), 15–50.

Saunier, Pierre-Yves, "Sketches from the Urban Internationale, 1910–50: Voluntary Associations, International Institutions and US Philanthropic Foundations," *International Journal of Urban and Regional Research* 25 (2001): 380–403.

———, "Trajectoires, projets et ingéniérie de la convergence et de la différence: Les régimes circulatoires du domaine social, 1800–1940," *Genèses* 71 (2008): 4–25.

Sautter, Udo, "Government and Unemployment: The Use of Public Works before the New Deal," *Journal of American History* 73 (1986): 59–86.

Sauvy, Alfred, *Histoire économique de la France entre les deux guerres*, Vol. 1 (Paris: Fayard, 1965).

Schaik, Alexander van, "Crisis en Protectie onder Colijn: Over economische doelmatigheid en maatschappelijke aanvaardbaarheid van de Nederlandse handelspolitiek in de jaren dertig" (PhD diss., Vrije Universiteit te Amsterdam, 1986).

Schedvin, C. B., *Australia and the Great Depression: A Study of Economic Development and Policy in the 1920s and 1930s* (Melbourne: Sydney University Press, 1970).

Schell, William, Jr., "Silver Symbiosis: Re-Orienting Mexican Economic History," *Hispanic American Historical Review* 81 (2001): 89–133.

Schipper, Frank, *Driving Europe: Building Europe on Roads in the 20th Century* (Amsterdam: Aksant, 2008).

Schirmer, Dietmar, "State, Volk, and Monumental Architecture in Nazi-Era Berlin," in *Berlin–Washington, 1800–2000: Capital Cities, Cultural Representation, and National Identities*, ed.. Andreas W. Daum and Christof Mauch (Cambridge: Cambridge University Press, 2005), 127–53.

Schisgall, Oscar, *The Greyhound Story: From Hibbing to Everywhere* (Chicago: J. G. Ferguson, 1985).

Schivelbusch, Wolfgang, *Three New Deals: Reflections on Roosevelt's America, Mussolini's Italy, and Hitler's Germany, 1933–1939* (New York: Picador, 2006).

Schlesinger, Arthur M., Jr., *The Age of Jackson* (New York: Book Find Club, 1945).

———, *The Coming of the New Deal: The Age of Roosevelt*, Vol. II (Boston: Houghton Mifflin, 1959).

———, *The Imperial Presidency* (Boston: Houghton Mifflin, 1973).

———, *The Politics of Upheaval: The Age of Roosevelt*, Vol. III (Boston: Houghton Mifflin, 1960).

———, *The Vital Center: The Politics of Freedom* (Boston: Houghton Mifflin, 1949).

Schmidt, Hans, *The United States Occupation of Haiti, 1915–1934* (New Brunswick, NJ: Rutgers University Press, 1971).

Schmitz, David F., *Thank God They're on Our Side: The United States and Right-Wing Dictatorships, 1921–1965* (Chapel Hill: University of North Carolina Press, 1999).

———, *The Triumph of Internationalism: Franklin D. Roosevelt and a World in Crisis, 1933–1941* (Washington, DC: Potomac Books, 2007).

Schonberger, Howard B., *Aftermath of War: Americans and the Remaking of Japan, 1945–1952* (Kent, OH: Kent State University Press, 1989).

Schoultz, Lars, *Beneath the United States: A History of U.S. Policy toward Latin America* (Cambridge, MA: Harvard University Press, 1998).

Schrag, Peter, *Not Fit for Our Society: Nativism and Immigration* (Berkeley: University of California Press, 2010).

Schrag, Philip G., *A Well-Founded Fear: The Congressional Debate to Save Political Asylum in America* (New York: Routledge, 2000).

Schüler, Anja, *Frauenbewegung und soziale Reform. Jane Addams und Alice Salomon im transatlantischen Dialog, 1889–1933* (Stuttgart: Steiner Verlag, 2004).

Schulman, Bruce J., *From Cotton Belt to Sunbelt: Federal Policy, Economic Development, and the Transformation of the South, 1938–1980* (Oxford: Oxford University Press, 1991).

Schultz, Kurt S., "Building the 'Soviet Detroit': The Construction of the Nizhnii-Novgorod Automobile Factory, 1927–1932," *Slavic Review* 49 (1990): 200–212.

Schwartz, Bonnie Fox, *The Civil Works Administration, 1933–1934: The Business of Emergency Employment in the New Deal* (Princeton, NJ: Princeton University Press, 1984).

Schwoch, James, *The American Radio Industry and Its Latin American Activities, 1900–1939* (Urbana: University of Illinois Press, 1990).

Scott, James C., "High Modernist Social Engineering: The Case of the Tennessee Valley Authority," in *Experiencing the State*, ed. Lloyd I. Rudolph and John Kurt Jacobsen (Oxford: Oxford University Press, 2006), 3–52.

———, *Seeing Like a State: How Certain Schemes to Improve the Human Condition Have Failed* (New Haven, CT: Yale University Press, 1998).

Sedda, Marco, "Il *New Deal* nella pubblicistica politica italiana dal 1933 al 1938," *Il Politico* 64 (1999): 241–75.

Seely, Bruce E., *Building the American Highway System: Engineers as Policy Makers* (Philadelphia: Temple University Press, 1987).

Segre, Luciano, *La "battaglia del grano": Depressione economica e politica cerealicola fascista* (Milan: Clesav, 1982).

Seidel, Katja, *The Process of Politics in Europe: The Rise of European Elites and Supranational Institutions* (London: Tauris, 2010).

Self, Richard, *Britain, America and the War Debt Controversy: The Economic Diplomacy of an Unspecial Relationship, 1917–1941* (London: Routledge, 2006).

Seltzer, William, and Margo Anderson, "After Pearl Harbor: The Proper Role of Population Data Systems in Time of War" (unpublished paper, 2000), http://www.amstat.org/about/statisticiansinhistory/index.cfm?fuseaction=PaperInfo&PaperID=1 (accessed April 12, 2015).

———, "Census Confidentiality under the Second War Powers Act (1942–1947)" (paper prepared for the Population Association of America annual meeting, March 30, 2007), https://pantherfile.uwm.edu/margo/www/govstat/integrity.htm (accessed April 12, 2015).

———, "The Dark Side of Numbers: The Role of Population Data Systems in Human Rights Abuses," *Social Research* 68 (2001): 481–513.

Selvin, David F., "An Exercise in Hysteria: San Francisco's Red Raids of 1934," *Pacific Historical Review* 58 (1989): 361–74.

Selznick, Philip, *TVA and the Grass Roots: A Study in the Sociology of Formal Organization* (New York: Harper, 1966).

Sessions, Gene A., "The Clark Memorandum Myth," *Americas* 34 (1977): 40–58.

Sewall, Arthur F., "Key Pittman and the Quest for the China Market, 1933–1940," *Pacific Historical Review* 44 (1975): 351–71.

Shafer, Byron E., and Anthony J. Badger, eds., *Contesting Democracy: Substance and Structure in American Political History, 1775–2000* (Lawrence: University Press of Kansas, 2001).

Shaffer, Marguerite S., *See America First: Tourism and National Identity, 1880–1940* (Washington, DC: Smithsonian Institution Press, 2001).

Shapiro, Judith, *Mao's War against Nature: Politics and the Environment in Revolutionary China* (Cambridge: Cambridge University Press, 2001).

Shaw, Lisa, and Maite Conde, "Brazil through Hollywood's Gaze: From the Silent Screen to the Good Neighbor Policy Era," in *Latin American Cinema: Essays on Modernity, Gender and National Identity*, ed. Lisa Shaw and Stephanie Dennison (Jefferson, NC: McFarland, 2005), 180–208.

Shearer, David R., "Social Disorder, Mass Repression, and the NKVD during the 1930s," *Cahiers du Monde russe* 42 (2001): 505–34.

Sheingate, Adam D., *The Rise of the Agricultural Welfare State: Institutions and Interest Group Power in the United States, France, and Japan* (Princeton, NJ: Princeton University Press, 2001).

Shelley, Louise I., "The Development of American Crime: A Comparative Perspective," in *Crime and Control in Comparative Perspectives*, ed. Hans-Günther Heiland, Louise I. Shelley, and Hisao Katoh (Berlin: W. de Gruyter, 1991), 83–105.

Shepard, Ben, "'Becoming Planning Minded': The Theory and Practice of Relief, 1940–1945," *Journal of Contemporary History* 43 (2008): 405–19.

Shermer, Elizabeth Tandy, *Sunbelt Capitalism: Phoenix and the Transformation of American Politics* (Philadelphia: University of Pennsylvania Press, 2013).

Sherry, Michael S., *In the Shadow of War: The United States since the 1930s* (New Haven, CT: Yale University Press, 1995).

Sherwood, Marika, *Kwame Nkrumah: The Years Abroad, 1935–1947* (Legon: Freedom Publications, 1996).

Sherwood, Robert E., *Roosevelt and Hopkins: An Intimate History*, rev. ed. (New York: Harper, 1950).

Shipway, Martin, *Decolonization and Its Impact: A Comparative Approach to the End of the Colonial Empires* (Malden, MA: Blackwell, 2008).

Shiraishi, Takashi, "Anti-Sinicism in Java's New Order," in *Essential Outsiders: Chinese and Jews in the Modern Transformation of Southeast Asia and Central Europe*, ed. Daniel Chirot and Anthony Reid (Seattle: University of Washington Press, 1997), 187–207.

Shiroyama, Tomoko, *China during the Great Depression: Market, State, and the World Economy, 1929–1937* (Cambridge, MA: Harvard University Press, 2008).

Showalter, Dennis, "Global Yet Not Total: The U.S. War Effort and its Consequences," in *A World at Total War: Global Conflict and the Politics of Destruction*, ed. Roger Chickering, Stig Förster, and Bernd Greiner (Cambridge: Cambridge University Press, 2005), 109–33.

Shpotov, Boris M., "The Soviet and American Business: Unique Examples of Economic Collaboration, 1920s–1930s," *History Research* 2 (2012): 178–94.

Singleton, Jeff, *The American Dole: Unemployment Relief and the Welfare State in the Great Depression* (Westport, CT: Greenwood Press, 2000).

Siuru, William D., and Andrea Stewart, *Presidential Cars and Transportation* (Iola, WI: Krause Publications, 1995).

Sivachev, Nikolai, "The Rise of Statism in 1930s' America: A Soviet View of the Social and Political Effects of the New Deal," *Labor History* 24 (1983): 500–525.

Skidmore, Thomas E., *Black into White: Race and Nationality in Brazilian Thought* (Durham, NC: Duke University Press, 1993).

Sklaroff, Lauren Rebecca, *Black Culture and the New Deal: The Quest for Civil Rights in the Roosevelt Era* (Chapel Hill: University of North Carolina Press, 2009).

Slate, Nico, *Colored Cosmopolitanism: The Shared Struggle for Freedom in the United States and India* (Cambridge, MA: Harvard University Press, 2012).

Slezkine, Yuri, "The USSR as a Communal Apartment, or How a Socialist State Promoted Ethnic Particularism," *Slavic Review* 53 (1994): 414–52.

Sluga, Glenda, *Internationalism in the Age of Nationalism* (Philadelphia: University of Pennsylvania Press, 2013).

Smith, Jason Scott, *Building New Deal Liberalism: The Political Economy of Public Works, 1933–1956* (New York: Cambridge University Press, 2006).

Smith, R.F.I., "The Scullin Government and the Wheatgrowers," *Labour History* 26 (1974): 49–64.

Smith, Richard Norton, *The Colonel: The Life and Legend of Robert R. McCormick, 1880–1955* (Boston: Houghton Mifflin, 1997).

Smith, Tony, *America's Mission: The United States and the Worldwide Struggle for Democracy in the Twentieth Century* (Princeton, NJ: Princeton University Press, 1994).

Smith-Rosenberg, Carroll, "Simkhovitch, Mary Kingsbury," in *Notable American Women: The Modern Period*, ed. Barbara Sicherman and Carol Hurd Green (Cambridge, MA: Harvard University Press, 1980), 649–51.

Soto, Lionel, *La Revolución de 1933: Historia de Cuba* (Havana: Editorial Si-Mar, 2003).

Sparrow, James T., *Warfare State: World War II Americans and the Age of Big Government* (Oxford: Oxford University Press, 2011).

Spinney, Robert G., *World War II in Nashville: Transformation of the Homefront* (Knoxville: University of Tennessee Press, 1998).

Spiro, Jonathan Peter, *Defending the Master Race: Conservation, Eugenics, and the Legacy of Madison Grant* (Burlington: University of Vermont Press, 2009).

St. John, Rachel, *Line in the Sand: A History of the Western U.S.-Mexico Border* (Princeton, NJ: Princeton University Press, 2011).

Stanley, Peter W., *A Nation in the Making: The Philippines and the United States, 1899–1921* (Cambridge, MA: Harvard University Press, 1974).

Staples, Amy L. S., "Norris E. Dodd and the Connections between Domestic and International Agricultural Policy," *Agricultural History* 74 (2000): 393–403.

Stebenne, David, "Thomas J. Watson and the Business-Government Relationship, 1933–1956," *Enterprise and Society* 6 (2005): 45–75.

Steinbacher, Sybille, *"Musterstadt" Auschwitz. Germanisierungspolitik und Judenmord in Ostoberschlesien* (Munich: Saur, 2000).

Steinberg, Ted, *Down to Earth: Nature's Role in American History* (New York: Oxford University Press, 2013).

Steiner, Zara, *The Triumph of the Dark: European International History 1933–1939* (Oxford: Oxford University Press, 2011).

Stepan, Nancy Leys, *"The Hour of Eugenics": Race, Gender, and Nation in Latin America* (Ithaca, NY: Cornell University Press, 1991).

Sternhell, Zeev, *Neither Right nor Left: Fascist Ideology in France* (Berkeley: University of California Press, 1986).

Stevens, Donald G., "Organizing for Economic Defense: Henry Wallace and the Board of Economic Warfare's Foreign Policy Initiatives, 1942," *Presidential Studies Quarterly* 26 (1996): 1126–39.

Steward, Dick, *Trade and Hemisphere: The Good Neighbor Policy and Reciprocal Trade* (Columbia: University of Missouri Press, 1975).

Stewart, Barbara McDonald, *United States Government Policy on Refugees from Nazism, 1933–1940* (New York: Garland, 1982).

Stoler, Mark A., "FDR and the Origins of the National Security Establishment," in *FDR's World: War, Peace, and Legacies*, ed. David B. Woolner, Warren F. Kimball, and David Reynolds (New York: Palgrave Macmillan, 2008).

Storrs, Landon R. Y., *Civilizing Capitalism: The National Consumers' League, Women's Activism, and Labor Standards in the New Deal Era* (Chapel Hill: University of North Carolina Press, 2000).

———, *The Second Red Scare and the Unmaking of the New Deal Left* (Princeton, NJ: Princeton University Press, 2013).

Strauss, David, "The Roosevelt Revolution: French Observers and the New Deal," *American Studies* 14 (1973): 25–42.

Stuckey, Mary E., *The Good Neighbor: Franklin D. Roosevelt and the Rhetoric of American Power* (East Lansing: Michigan State University Press, 2013).

Subrahmanyam, Sanjay, "Hearing Voices: Vignettes of Early Modernity in South Asia, 1400–1750," *Daedalus* 127 (1998): 75–104.

Sugita, Yoneyuki, *Pitfall or Panacea: The Irony of US Power in Occupied Japan, 1945–1952* (New York: Routledge, 2003).

Summerhill, William R., "The Development of Infrastructure," in *The Cambridge Economic History of Latin America*, ed. Victor Bulmer-Thomas, John Coatsworth, and

Roberto Cortes-Conde (Cambridge: Cambridge University Press, 2008), 293–326.

Sun, You-Li, *China and the Origins of the Pacific War, 1931–41* (New York: St. Martin's Press, 1993).

Sunstein, Cass R., *After the Rights Revolution: Reconceiving the Regulatory State* (Cambridge, MA: Harvard University Press, 1990).

Supple, Barry, "The Political Economy of Demoralization: The State and the Coalmining Industry in America and Britain between the Wars," *Economic History Review* 41 (1988): 566–91.

Susman, Warren I., *Culture as History: The Transformation of American Society in the Twentieth Century* (New York: Pantheon Books, 1984).

Swyngedouw, Erik, "'Not a Drop of Water . . .': State, Modernity and the Production of Nature in Spain, 1898–2010," *Environment and History* 20 (2014): 67–92.

Takaki, Ronald, *Strangers from a Different Shore: A History of Asian Americans,* rev. ed. (New York: Little, Brown, 1998).

Tavan, Gwenda, *The Long, Slow Death of White Australia* (Melbourne: Scribe Publications, 2005).

Taylor, Andrew J., "Stanley Baldwin, Heresthetics and the Realignment of British Politics," *British Journal of Political Science* 35 (2005): 429–63.

Taylor, Jay, *The Generalissimo: Chiang Kai-shek and the Struggle for Modern China* (Cambridge, MA: Belknap Press, 2009).

Taylor, Matthew, "Global Players? Football, Migration and Globalization, c. 1930–2000," *Historical Social Research* 31 (2006): 7–30.

Taylor, Nick, *American-Made: The Enduring Legacy of the WPA: When FDR Put the Nation to Work* (New York: Bantam Books, 2008).

Taylor, Philip B., "The Uruguayan Coup d'état of 1933," *Hispanic American Historical Review* 32 (1952): 301–20.

Tedeschini Lalli, Biancamaria, and Maurizio Vaudagna, eds., *Brave New Words* (Amsterdam: VU University Press, 1999).

Teeboom, Piebe B., "Searching for the Middle Way: Consumer Cooperation and the Cooperative Moment in New Deal America" (PhD diss., University of Amsterdam, 2009).

Teichert, Eckart, *Autarkie und Großraumwirtschaft in Deutschland 1930–1939. Außenwirtschaftliche Konzeptionen zwischen Wirtschaftskrise und Zweitem Weltkrieg* (Munich: Oldenbourg: 1984).

Temin, Peter, *Did Monetary Forces Cause the Great Depression?* (New York: W. W. Norton, 1976).

———, "The Great Depression," in *The Cambridge Economic History of the United States,* Vol. III, ed. Stanley L. Engerman and Robert E. Gallman (Cambridge: Cambridge University Press, 2000), 301–28.

———, *Lessons from the Great Depression* (Cambridge, MA: MIT Press, 1989).

Terkel, Studs, *Hard Times: An Oral History of the Great Depression* (New York: Pantheon Books, 1970).

Theoharis, Athan G., and John Stuart Cox, *The Boss: J. Edgar Hoover and the Great American Inquisition* (Philadelphia: Temple University Press, 1988).

Thomas, Martin, *Empires of Intelligence: Security Services and Colonial Disorder after 1914* (Berkeley: University of California Press, 2008).

—, *Violence and Colonial Order: Police, Workers and Protest in the European Colonial Empires, 1918–1940* (Cambridge: Cambridge University Press, 2012).

Thorne, Christopher, *Allies of a Kind: The United States, Britain and the War against Japan, 1941–1945* (Oxford: Oxford University Press, 1978).

Tichenor, Daniel J., *Dividing Lines: The Politics of Immigration Control in America* (Princeton, NJ: Princeton University Press, 2002).

Tobey, Ronald C., *Technology as Freedom: The New Deal and the Electrical Modernization of the American Home* (Berkeley: University of California Press, 1996).

Tobey, Ronald C., Charles Wetherell, and Jay Brigham, "Moving Out and Settling In: Residential Mobility, Home Owning, and the Public Enframing of Citizenship, 1921–1950," *American Historical Review* 95 (1990): 1395–422.

Toft, Christian, "State Action, Trade Unions and Voluntary Unemployment Insurance in Great Britain, Germany, and Scandinavia, 1900–1934," *European Economic Review* 39 (1995): 565–74.

Tomka, Béla, *A Social History of Twentieth-Century Europe* (London: Routledge, 2013).

Tooze, Adam, *The Deluge: The Great War and the Remaking of Global Order, 1916–1931* (London: Allen Lane, 2014).

—, *The Wages of Destruction: The Making and Breaking of the Nazi Economy* (London: Allen Lane, 2006).

Topp, Niels-Henrik, "Unemployment and Economic Policy in Denmark in the 1930s," *Scandinavian Economic History Review* 56 (2008): 71–90.

Torpey, John, *The Invention of the Passport: Surveillance, Citizenship and the State* (Cambridge: Cambridge University Press, 2000).

Tota, Antonio Pedro, *The Seduction of Brazil: The Americanization of Brazil during World War II* (Austin: University of Texas Press, 2009).

Tournès, Ludovic, "La fondation Rockefeller et la naissance de l'universalisme philanthropique américain," *Critique Internationale* 35 (2007): 173–97.

Towns, Ann, "The Inter-American Commission of Women and Women's Suffrage, 1920–1945," *Journal of Latin American Studies* 42 (2010): 779–807.

Tracy, Michael, *Agriculture in Western Europe: Challenge and Response, 1880–1980* (London: Granada, 1982).

Trentmann, Frank, *Free Trade Nation: Commerce, Consumption, and Civil Society in Modern Britain* (Oxford: Oxford University Press, 2008).

Trescott, Paul B., *Jingji Xue: The History of the Introduction of Western Economic Ideas into China, 1850–1950* (Hong Kong: Chinese University Press, 2007).

Trombley, Kenneth E., *The Life and Times of a Happy Liberal: A Biography of Morris Llewellyn Cooke* (New York: Harper, 1954).

Troy, Leo, *Trade Union Membership, 1897–1962* (New York: National Bureau of Economic Research, 1965).

Tsouras, Peter G., "Hokushin: The Second Russo-Japanese War," in *Rising Sun Victorious: The Alternate History of How the Japanese Won the Pacific War*, ed. Peter G. Tsouras (London: Greenhill Books, 2001), 17–38.

Tucker, Richard P., *Insatiable Appetite: The United States and the Ecological Degradation of the Tropical World* (Lanham, MD: Rowman and Littlefield, 2007).

Turner, Arthur, *The Cost of War: British Policy on French War Debts, 1918–1932* (Brighton: Sussex Academic Press, 1998).

Tydén, Mattias, "The Scandinavian States: Reformed Eugenics Applied," in *The Oxford Handbook of the History of Eugenics*, ed. Alison Bashford and Philippa Levine (Oxford: Oxford University Press, 2010), 363–76.

Tyner, James A., "The Geopolitics of Eugenics and the Exclusion of Philippine Immigrants from the United States," *Geographical Review* 89 (1999): 54–73.

Tyrrell, Ian, *Reforming the World: The Creation of America's Moral Empire* (Princeton, NJ: Princeton University Press, 2010).

———, *Transnational Nation: United States History in Global Perspective since 1789* (Basingstoke: Palgrave Macmillan, 2007).

Tyson, Thomas N., and Richard K. Fleischman, "Accounting for Interned Japanese-American Civilians during World War II: Creating Incentives and Establishing Controls for Captive Workers," *Accounting Historians Journal* 33 (2006): 167–202.

Tzouliadis, Tim, *The Forsaken: From the Great Depression to the Gulags: Hope and Betrayal in Stalin's Russia* (London: Little, Brown, 2008).

Unabhängige Expertenkommission Schweiz–Zweiter Weltkrieg, *Die Schweiz, der Nationalsozialismus und der Zweite Weltkrieg* (Zurich: Pendo, 2002).

Vaïsse, Maurice, "Le mythe de l'or en France: les aspects monétaires du New Deal vus par les Français," *Revue d'Histoire Moderne et Contemporaine* 16 (1969): 462–79.

Van Daele, Jasmien, *Van Gent tot Genève: Louis Varlez, een biografie* (Gent: Academia Press, 2002).

Van Goethem, Geert, and Robert A. Waters Jr., eds., *American Labor's Global Ambassadors: The International History of the AFL-CIO during the Cold War* (New York: Palgrave Macmillan, 2013).

Van Vleck, Jenifer, *Empire of the Air: Aviation and the American Ascendancy* (Cambridge, MA: Harvard University Press, 2013).

Vanger, Milton I., *Uruguay's José Batlle y Ordoñez: The Determined Visionary, 1915–1917* (Boulder, CO: Lynne Rienner, 2010).

Vanthemsche, Guy, "L'élaboration de l'arrêté royal sur le contrôle bancaire (1935)," *Belgisch Tijdschrift voor Nieuwste Geschiedenis* 11 (1980): 389–437.

Varg, Paul A., "The Economic Side of the Good Neighbor Policy: The Reciprocal Trade Program and South America," *Pacific Historical Review* 45 (1976): 47–71.

Vatter, Harold G., *The U.S. Economy in World War II* (New York: Columbia University Press, 1985).

Vaudagna, Maurizio, "A Checkered History: The New Deal, Democracy, and Totalitarianism in Transatlantic Welfare States," in *The American Century in Europe*, ed. R. Laurence Moore and Maurizio Vaudagna (Ithaca, NY: Cornell University Press, 2003), 219–42.

———, "Mussolini and Franklin D. Roosevelt," in *FDR and His Contemporaries: Foreign Perceptions of an American President*, ed. Cornelis A. van Minnen and John F. Sears (New York: St. Martin's Press, 1992), 157–70.

———, "New Deal e corporativismo nelle riviste politiche ed economiche italiane," in *Italia e America dalla Grande Guerra a Oggi*, ed. Giorgio Spini, Gian Giacomo Migone, and Massimo Teodori (Venice: Marsilio Editori, 1976), 101–40.

Velde, Henk te, "Echte mannen: De tijd van Colijn," in *Stijlen van leiderschap: Persoon en politiek van Thorbecke tot Den Uyl*, ed. Henk te Velde (Amsterdam: Wereldbibliotheek, 2002), 107–52.

Venkataramani, M. S., *Bengal Famine of 1943: The American Response* (Delhi: Vikas, 1973).

———, "Norman Thomas, Arkansas Sharecroppers, and the Roosevelt Agricultural Policies, 1933–1937," *Arkansas Historical Quarterly* 24 (1965): 3–28.

Vestal, Theodore M., *The Lion of Judah in the New World: Emperor Haile Selassie of Ethiopia* (Santa Barbara, CA: Praeger, 2011).

Villaronga, Gabriel, *Toward a Discourse of Consent: Mass Mobilization and Colonial Politics in Puerto Rico, 1932–1948* (Westport, CT: Praeger, 2004).

Von Eschen, Penny M., *Race against Empire: Black Americans and Anticolonialism, 1937–1957* (Ithaca, NY: Cornell University Press, 1997).

Waddell, Brian, *The War against the New Deal: World War II and American Democracy* (DeKalb: Northern Illinois University Press, 2001).

Waite, Peter B., *In Search of R. B. Bennett* (Montreal: McGill-Queen's University Press, 2012).

Wall, Wendy L., *Inventing the "American Way": The Politics of Consensus from the New Deal to the Civil Rights Movement* (Oxford: Oxford University Press, 2009).

Wallis, John Joseph, "The Birth of the Old Federalism: Financing the New Deal, 1932–1940," *Journal of Economic History* 44 (1984): 139–59.

———, "Lessons from the Political Economy of the New Deal," *Oxford Review of Economic Policy* 26 (2010): 442–62.

Wandschneider, Kirsten, "Central Bank Reaction Functions during the Inter-War Gold Standard: A View from the Periphery," in *The Origins and Development of Financial Markets and Institutions: From the Seventeenth Century to the Present*, ed. Jeremy Atack and Larry Neal (Cambridge: Cambridge University Press, 2009), 388–415.

Ward, Stephen V., "Cross-National Learning in the Formation of British Planning Policies 1940–99: A Comparison of the Barlow, Buchanan and Rogers Reports," *Town Planning Review* 78 (2007): 369–400.

Ware, Susan, *Holding Their Own: American Women in the 1930s* (Boston: Twayne, 1982).

Warren, Frank A., *Noble Abstractions: American Liberal Intellectuals and World War II* (Columbus: Ohio State University Press, 1999).

Watson, Robert P., "Physical and Psychological Health," in *A Companion to Franklin D. Roosevelt*, ed. William D. Pederson (Oxford: Wiley-Blackwell, 2011), 59–76.

Weatherford, M. Stephen, "After the Critical Election: Presidential Leadership, Competition and the Consolidation of the New Deal Realignment," *British Journal of Political Science* 32 (2002): 221–57.

Wegener, Jens, "Creating an 'International Mind'? The Carnegie Endowment for International Peace in Europe, 1911–1940" (PhD diss., European University Institute, 2015).

Weinbaum, Alys Eve, Lynn M. Thomas, Priti Ramamurthy, Uta G. Poiger, and Madeleine Yue Dong, eds., *The Modern Girl around the World: Consumption, Modernity, and Globalization* (Durham, NC: Duke University Press, 2008).

Weinberg, Gerhard L., *A World at Arms: A Global History of World War II* (Cambridge: Cambridge University Press, 1994).

Weindling, Paul, "Philanthropy and World Health: The Rockefeller Foundation and the League of Nations Health Organisation," *Minerva* 35 (1997): 269–81.

Weiner, Tim, *Enemies: A History of the FBI* (New York: Random House, 2012).

Weir, Margaret, and Theda Skocpol, "State Structures and the Possibilities for 'Keynesian' Responses to the Great Depression in Sweden, Britain, and the United States," in *Bringing the State Back In*, ed. Peter Evans, Dietrich Ruschemeyer, and Theda Skocpol (Cambridge: Cambridge University Press, 1985), 107–63.

Weisbrode, Kenneth, *The Atlantic Century: Four Generations of Extraordinary Diplomats Who Forged America's Vital Alliance with Europe* (Cambridge, MA: Da Capo Press, 2009).

Weiss, Richard, "Ethnicity and Reform: Minorities and the Ambience of the Depression Years," *Journal of American History* 66 (1979): 566–85.

Weiss, Stuart L., "American Foreign Policy and Presidential Power: The Neutrality Act of 1935," *Journal of Politics* 30 (1968): 672–95.

Weitz, Eric D., *A Century of Genocide: Utopias of Race and Nation* (Princeton, NJ: Princeton University Press, 2003).

Wejnert, Barbara, "Diffusion, Development, and Democracy, 1800–1999," *American Sociological Review* 70 (2005): 53–81.

Welky, David, *The Moguls and the Dictators: Hollywood and the Coming of World War II* (Baltimore: Johns Hopkins University Press, 2008).

Wells, Christopher W., "Fueling the Boom: Gasoline Taxes, Invisibility, and the Growth of the American Highway Infrastructure, 1919–1956," *Journal of American History* 99 (2012): 72–81.

Wells, Wyatt, "Counterpoint to Reform: Gilbert H. Montague and the Business of Regulation," *Business History Review* 78 (2004): 423–50.

Welskopp, Thomas, *Amerikas große Ernüchterung. Eine Kulturgeschichte der Prohibition* (Paderborn: Ferdinand Schöningh, 2010).

————, ed., *Fractured Modernity: America Confronts Modern Times, 1890s to 1940s* (Munich: Oldenbourg, 2012).

Wengert, Norman, "TVA—Symbol and Reality," *Journal of Politics* 13 (1951): 369–92.

Wescoat, James L., Jr., "'Watersheds' in Regional Planning," in *The American Planning Tradition: Culture and Policy*, ed. Robert Fishman (Washington, DC: Woodrow Wilson Center Press, 2000), 147–71.

Westad, Odd Arne, *The Global Cold War: Third World Interventions and the Making of Our Times* (Cambridge: Cambridge University Press, 2005).

White, William J., "An Unsung Hero: The Farm Tractor's Contribution to Twentieth-Century United States Economic Growth" (PhD diss., Ohio State University, 2000).

Whitehead, Laurence, "Bolivia," in *Latin America between the Second World War and the Cold War, 1944–1948*, ed. Leslie Bethell and Ian Roxborough (Cambridge: Cambridge University Press, 1992), 120–46.

Whitman, James Q., "Of Corporatism, Fascism, and the First New Deal," *American Journal of Comparative Law* 39 (1991): 747–78.

Wicker, Elmus, *The Banking Panics of the Great Depression* (Cambridge: Cambridge University Press, 1996).

Wieters, Heike, "From Post-War Relief to Europe to Global Humanitarian Enterprise: Care, Inc. (1945–1980)" (PhD diss., European University Viadrina, 2013).

Wigmore, Barrie A., "Was the Bank Holiday of 1933 Caused by a Run on the Dollar?" *Journal of Economic History* 47 (1987): 739–55.

Wilkins, Mira, and Frank Ernest Hill, *American Business Abroad: Ford on Six Continents* (Detroit: Wayne State University Press, 1964).

Williams, Daryle, *Culture Wars in Brazil: The First Vargas Regime, 1930–1945* (Durham, NC: Duke University Press, 2001).

Williams, Mason B., *City of Ambition: FDR, La Guardia, and the Making of Modern New York* (New York: W. W. Norton, 2013).

Williams, Rhonda Y., *The Politics of Public Housing: Black Women's Struggles against Urban Inequality* (Oxford: Oxford University Press, 2004).

Williamson, Philip, *Stanley Baldwin: Conservative Leadership and National Values* (Cambridge: Cambridge University Press, 1999).

Wilson, Sandra, "The 'New Paradise': Japanese Emigration to Manchuria in the 1930s and 1940s," *International History Review* 17 (1995): 249–86.

Wilson, Theodore A., *The First Summit: Roosevelt and Churchill at Placentia Bay 1941* (Boston: Houghton Mifflin, 1969).

Winfield, Betty Houchin, "FDR as Communicator," in *A Companion to Franklin D. Roosevelt*, ed. William D. Pederson (Oxford: Wiley-Blackwell, 2011), 222–37.

Winkler, Heinrich August, *Geschichte des Westens. Die Zeit der Weltkriege, 1914–1945* (Munich: Beck, 2011).

———, *Weimar, 1918–1933. Die Geschichte der ersten deutschen Demokratie* (Munich: Beck, 1994).

Wittek, Thomas, *Auf ewig Feind? Das Deutschlandbild in den britischen Massenmedien nach dem Ersten Weltkrieg* (Munich: Oldenbourg, 2005).

Wolfe, Joel, *Autos and Progress: The Brazilian Search for Modernity* (Oxford: Oxford University Press, 2010).

———, "The Faustian Bargain Not Made: Getúlio Vargas and Brazil's Industrial Workers, 1930-1945," *Luso-Brazilian Review* 31 (1994): 77–95.

Wolfskill, George, and John A. Hudson, *All But the People: Franklin D. Roosevelt and His Critics, 1933–39* (New York: Macmillan, 1969).

Wollstein, Günter, *Vom Weimarer Revisionismus zu Hitler. Das Deutsche Reich und die Großmächte in der Anfangsphase der nationalsozialistischen Herrschaft in Deutschland* (Bonn: Edition Ludwig Voggenreiter, 1973).

Wood, Andrew Grant, "On the Selling of Rey Momo: Early Tourism and Marketing of Carnival in Veracruz," in *Holiday in Mexico: Critical Reflections on Tourism and Tourist Encounters*, ed. Dina Berger and Andrew Grant Wood (Durham, NC: Duke University Press, 2010), 77–106.

Wood, Bryce, *The Making of the Good Neighbor Policy* (New York: Columbia University Press, 1961).

Wood, John Cunningham, ed., *John Maynard Keynes: Critical Assessments* (London: Croom Helm, 1983).

Woods, Randall B., "FDR and the New Economic Order," in *FDR's World: War, Peace, and Legacies*, ed. David B. Woolner, Warren F. Kimball, and David Reynolds (New York: Palgrave Macmillan, 2008), 175–91.

Worster, Donald, *Dust Bowl: The Southern Plains in the 1930s* (New York: Oxford University Press, 1979).

Wright, Gavin, "The Political Economy of New Deal Spending: An Econometric Analysis," *Review of Economics and Statistics* 56 (1974): 30–38.

Wright, Tim, "Coping with the World Depression: The Nationalist Government's Relations with Chinese Industry and Commerce, 1932–1936," *Modern Asian Studies* 25 (1991): 649–74.

Wynn, Neil A., *The African American Experience during World War II* (Lanham, MD: Rowman and Littlefield, 2010).

Yonay, Yuval P., *The Struggle over the Soul of Economics: Institutionalist and Neoclassical Economists in America between the Wars* (Princeton, NJ: Princeton University Press, 1998).

Young, Louise, *Japan's Total Empire: Manchuria and the Culture of Wartime Imperialism* (Berkeley: University of California Press, 1998).

Yu, Lumeng, "The Great Communicator: How FDR's Radio Speeches Shaped American History," *History Teacher* 39 (2005): 89–106.

Zachariah, Benjamin, *Developing India: An Intellectual and Social History, c. 1930–50* (New Delhi: Oxford University Press, 2005).

———, "Rethinking (the Absence of) Fascism in India, c. 1922–45," in *Cosmopolitan Thought Zones: South Asia and the Global Circulation of Ideas*, ed. Sugata Bose and Kris Manjapra (New York: Palgrave Macmillan, 2010), 178–209.

Zanasi, Margherita, "Far from the Treaty Ports: Fang Xianting and the Idea of Rural Modernity in 1930s China," *Modern China* 30 (2004): 113–46.

Zanden, Jan Luiten van, *Een klein land in de 20ᵉ eeuw: Economische geschiedenis van Nederland 1914–1995* (Utrecht: Het Spectrum, 1997).

Zeidel, Robert F., *Immigrants, Progressives, and Exclusion Politics: The Dillingham Commission, 1900–1927* (DeKalb: Northern Illinois University Press, 2004).

Zelizer, Julian E., "The Forgotten Legacy of the New Deal: Fiscal Conservatism and the Roosevelt Administration, 1933–1938," *Presidential Studies Quarterly* 30 (2000): 331–58.

Zeller, Thomas, *Driving Germany: The Landscape of the German Autobahn, 1930–1970* (New York: Berghahn Books, 2007).

Zhu, Jianfei, *Architecture of Modern China: A Historical Critique* (London: Routledge, 2009).

Zimmer, Oliver, "In Search of Natural Identity: Alpine Landscape and the Reconstruction of the Swiss Nation," *Comparative Studies in Society and History* 40 (1998): 637–65.

Zimmerman, Joseph F., "National-State Relations: Cooperative Federalism in the Twentieth Century," *Publius* 31 (2001): 15–30.

Zolberg, Aristide R., *A Nation by Design: Immigration Policy in the Fashioning of America* (Cambridge, MA: Harvard University Press, 2006).

Zomers, Adriaan N., *Rural Electrification* (Twente: University of Twente Press, 2001).

INDEX

NOTE: Page numbers followed by *f* indicate a figure; those followed by *t* indicate a table.

fascism (*cont.*)

167–69, 185, 217, 238; racial policies of, 168–69, 175–76, 255; sports promotion of, 183–84; US debates on the CCC and, 85–90; US industrial reform debates and, 72–73, 78, 311n103; US NRA debates and, 66–70; youth cult of, 250. *See also* Germany; Italy; Japan

Faulkner, William, 234

Fechner, Robert, 88

Federal Bureau of Investigation (FBI), 233–36

Federal Deposit Insurance Corporation (FDIC), 53–54

Federal Emergency Relief Administration (FERA), 81–85, 161; rural rehabilitation division of, 210; self-help cooperatives of, 225

Federal Farm Board, 58–59, 61

Federal Housing Administration, 266

Federal Reserve, 29–31, 53, 124, 132, 244, 299

Feis, Herbert, 34

Fengman Dam, 101

Fess, Simon, 67

Filene, Edward A., 72, 223

Filipino immigration, 173

film industry, 182–83

Finland, 39; consumer cooperatives in, 222, 229; executive powers in, 120; government buildings of, 244; military spending in, 260; social security program of, 195; World War I debt of, 131, 133

fireside chats, 53, 104–12, 132, 266

Fitzgerald, James V., 226

Flying Down to Rio, 179

Ford, Henry, 11, 14, 139, 175, 179

Fordism, 3, 16, 139–40

Ford Motor Company, 11–12, 14, 33, 169

Fordney-McCumber Act of 1922, 26, 34

foreign relations, 121–89, 255; black Atlantic and, 176–80; defense policies and, 188–89; disarmament negotiations and, 134–35; economic nationalism in, 121–34, 185; executive powers in, 122, 127; global business and cultural links and, 180–89; immigration restrictions and, 112; with Japan, 135–37, 142; with Latin America, 145–57, 179, 185–86; the Ludlow Amendment and, 169; militarization of, 135–37; neutrality debates in, 121, 167–71, 260; prospect of World War II and, 157, 159,

167–69, 188–89, 260; public opinion on, 141–42, 144–45; with Puerto Rico, 160–67; with the Soviet Union, 139–45; US gold policies and, 132–33; US silver policies and, 5, 8, 126–31; on World War I debt and reparations, 131, 133–34. *See also* immigration policy; insulationism; League of Nations; trade protectionism; World War I; World War II

Forrestal, James V., 288

Fort Peck Dam, 99

Fosdick, Raymond B., 182, 289

Foucault, Michel, 6–7

Fraenkel, Ernst, 289

France: agricultural reforms in, 61, 63; American expatriates in, 17, 178; banking reforms in, 51, 55; colonial reformism of, 167; consumer cooperatives in, 222; dam and power projects in, 101–2; gold reserves of, 29; gold standard of, 36, 132; government spending by, 242, 243; human rights tradition in, 291–92; impact of World War I on, 116; industrial reforms in, 65, 77; infrastructure programs in, 102, 247; military spending in, 260; pension programs of, 199; political change in, 46; political leadership in, 108, 109; on the Swedish welfare state, 229; tabulation technology in, 253–54; tourism from the US to, 178; trade and currency bloc of, 36, 160; union membership in, 77, 312n132; US Lend-Lease Program in, 262; World War I debt of, 26–28, 131–33

Franco, Francisco, 64, 101, 110, 255

Frankfurter, Felix, 174–75, 248, 251, 285–86

free market economics, 93, 278, 282–83, 298. *See also* capitalism

Freiwilliger Arbeitsdienst, 87–90

Friedman, Max Paul, 277–78

Friedman, Milton, 128, 298

Gabriel over the White House, 47

Galvan, Frank J., 179

Gandhi, Mahatma, 58, 111, 275

Garibaldi, Giuseppe, 109

Garland, William May, 183

Garraty, John A., 5

Garvey, Marcus, 17, 177

Gayer, Arthur D., 83

gender discrimination, 85, 240–42, 249, 266–67

Woodring, Harry H., 88
Woodward, Ellen Sullivan, 249
work creation programs, 79–90; debates on fascism and, 86–90; dismantling of, 85; financing of, 84; infrastructure improvement projects of, 81–82, 244–48; for women, 89
Works Progress Administration (WPA), 81–85, 180, 248; dismantling of, 265; infrastructure improvement projects of, 244–45; reorganization and expansion of, 192
World Bank, 274, 282, 290, 295
World Court, 14, 137–39, 284
World Disarmament Conference, 134–35
World Economic Conference of 1927, 32, 39, 56
World Economic Conference of 1933, 122–26, 185
World Health Organization (WHO), 15, 286
"The World's Experience with Rural Electrification" (Evans), 219
World War I, 2, 10, 69, 167–68, 170, 250; agricultural crisis of, 31–32, 56; Bonus March veterans of, 113; debt and reparations from, 25–28, 131–34; emergence of the state in, 2, 73, 116–17, 251; global cooperation of, 115; government spending of, 243; industrial policies of, 70–71, 76; National Defense Act of 1916 and, 97; Versailles Peace Treaty of, 26, 137, 168; War Finance Corporation of, 52; war profiteers of, 167–68; workers' villages of, 213
World War II, 156, 242, 261–78; Atlantic

Charter of, 271–75; big science and, 262–63; dismantling of the New Deal during, 261, 265–66; early warning signs of, 157, 159, 167–69, 188–89; economic expansion of, 262, 267–69; expanded military of, 260–62; expansion of labor during, 261–63, 267–68; export of New Deal principles during, 274–78; and GI Bill of 1944, 267; global connections created by, 262, 269–71; government spending during, 263; Holocaust and, 254; hypermasculinized ideal of, 266; internationalism of, 271–74, 289–90; Japanese-American internments of, 226–28, 254; Lend-Lease Program of, 262, 286, 288; military-industrial complex of, 261–65; New Deal programs continued during, 266–69; Nuremburg trials following, 274; organized labor and, 267–68; Pearl Harbor attack of, 170, 260, 262, 284; racial policies of, 268, 270–71; social engineering of, 266; tabulation technology in, 254; tax policies of, 191
Woytinsky, Wladimir, 31

Yates, Paul Lamartine, 294
Young Men's Christian Association (YMCA), 17
youth cult, 248–51

Zeisel, Hans, 41–43
Zemurray, Samuel, 159, 181
Zimmern, Alfred E., 96
Zionism, 217